Thesis Watch
— Common law & Civil law
— Language & translation barriers
— Recent Brexit with pull UK work
at a state of confusion / instability.
→ Access to german material.

DUTFIELD AND SUTHERSANEN ON GLOBAL INTELLECTUAL PROPERTY LAW

For our dads – Henry (1929–2014) and Sutha

DUTFIELD AND SUTHERSANEN ON GLOBAL INTELLECTUAL PROPERTY LAW

SECOND EDITION

GRAHAM DUTFIELD

*Professor of International Governance, School of Law,
University of Leeds, UK*

UMA SUTHERSANEN

*Professor in International Intellectual Property Law,
Centre for Commercial Law Studies, Queen Mary University of London, UK*

With

GAETANO DIMITA

*Senior Lecturer in International Intellectual Property Law, Centre for
Commercial Law Studies, Queen Mary University of London, UK*

MARC D. MIMLER

Senior Lecturer in Law, Bournemouth University, UK

 **EE** Edward Elgar
PUBLISHING

Cheltenham, UK · Northampton, MA, USA

Cover image:
THE ANALYSIS OF BEAUTY Plate 1 – 1753 engraving
by William Hogarth.
Pictorial Press Ltd / Alamy Stock Photo.

Published by
Edward Elgar Publishing Limited
The Lypiatts
15 Lansdown Road
Cheltenham
Glos GL50 2JA
UK

Edward Elgar Publishing, Inc.
William Pratt House
9 Dewey Court
Northampton
Massachusetts 01060
USA

A catalogue record for this book
is available from the British Library

Library of Congress Control Number: 2019951852

ISBN 978 1 78254 882 9 (cased)
ISBN 978 1 78254 884 3 (paperback)
ISBN 978 1 78254 883 6 (eBook)

Printed and bound in Great Britain by TJ International Ltd, Padstow, Cornwall

CONTENTS

FULL CONTENTS

PART II CREATING AND BRANDING

PART III SHIFTING CONTOURS

PREFACE TO THE SECOND EDITION

The mainstreaming of intellectual property has been accompanied by issues, concerns and un-resolved questions that are relevant to the lives of people everywhere, and that go well beyond international trade. Is there a conflict between copyright and freedom of expression? Is copying tantamount to theft, or is it often legitimate, or even necessary to perpetuate human creativity into the future? Are IPRs human rights, or alternatively do they impinge on human rights? Are there situations in which the public has the overriding right to access and use protected intellectual pro-ductions that are owned by companies? If so, how should the law respond? And are the powerful countries using intellectual property to keep poor countries poor? These are a few questions that seem pertinent in this young twenty-first century of ours. In our view, the complex, interactive and conflict-ridden nature of the globalisation process must inevitably force us to rethink how we learn intellectual property law. We hope this book provides a few responses to these questions and to many others that may form in the minds of curious readers who should of course come to their own conclusions.

The present volume is the culmination of teaching in and research for Queen Mary's LLM pro-gramme on Global Intellectual Property Law, which has been running successfully for 20 years, and also the LLM in Intellectual Property Law at the University of Leeds which is now well estab-lished. As with these programmes, the book sets out to trace and explain the evolving remits of intellectual property, which are rapidly expanding to embrace new subject matter and (usually) increase the extent of protection. It does this by analysing intellectual property rules in various jurisdictions and in key international instruments like the TRIPS Agreement. We also look into the relationships between intellectual property law and science, education and culture, as well as more philosophical issues such as the commodification of persona, the commons, and of life itself. Most significantly of all, perhaps, the book examines the impact of intellectual property on the in-ternational stage, especially in respect of trade, development, economics, law, technology, human rights, and biological and cultural diversity.

Accordingly, the book offers international and comparative perspectives on intellectual proper-ty law and policy. It presents all of the main IPRs, identifying their basic features and tracing their evolution up to the present day by reference to statutes, cases and international treaties viewed through the lenses of the authors' own perspectives and experiences of law in different countries. The book also examines the evolving activities in the international arena, especially debates and new intellectual property rules concerning or impinging on creativity and innovation, consumer choice, trade, economics, social welfare and culture. We also look at how these activities interact with what is happening at regional and domestic levels. A focal point for us is the analysis of the philosophical, political and socio-economic parameters within which intellectual property pro-ducers and consumers operate whether or not those involved consider these consciously. Instead of the conventional formalistic learning method in which we must choose whether to focus on national (typically United States), regional (such as the European Union) or international law (for example, the WTO–TRIPS Agreement or the treaties governed by the World Intellectual Property Organization), in this book we cover all three.

Our volume is not an ordered array of facts as to what the law is, accompanied by interpretations of court rulings. We make no apologies for the multi-faceted and rather renaissance approach to intellectual property that we employ. We have a passion for literature, music, art, science, and human creativity in all their manifold manifestations where these enrich human lives. We believe philosophy, economics, geography, history of science, and environmental studies have much to contribute to the study of intellectual property law. This book is our attempt, then, to make the study of global law and policy of intellectual property transcend territorially-based case studies or statutes, but without excluding them either; and also transcend academic disciplinary boundaries. In our view, no single jurisdiction, however important or influential it may be, can possibly be treated as representing any other. While there is much similarity in intellectual property law, and the forces favouring harmonisation are very strong, divergent forces operate too as countries seek to translate (or mistranslate) international obligations in ways that further domestic economic interests. It is not a foregone conclusion that the harmonisers will win.

We were prepared to substantially update and revise the first edition; what we had not prepared for was the complete re-writing of all the chapters in this edition due to the seismic shift of beliefs and focuses in this area. We bear joint responsibility for Chapters 1 and 3. Uma Suthersanen wrote Chapters 2, 4, 7, 10–12, while Graham Dutfield wrote Chapters 5, 8–9, 13–15. We have invited two further contributors on board: Uma Suthersanen and Marc Mimler revised and updated Chapter 6; Uma Suthersanen and Gaetano Dimita revised and updated Chapter 16. And we must thankfully acknowledge the substantial contribution of Pinar Oruç to the writing of the 'communication to the public right' section in Chapter 4.

We are grateful to all who have supported us throughout this endeavour. We were inspired and buoyed by the conversations and goodwill of so many of our colleagues and students from all over the world including Adrian and Caroline Sterling, Maria Mercedes Frabboni, Paula Westenberger, César Ramírez-Montes, Guido Westkamp, Subhajit Basu, Stathis Arapostathis, Berris Charnley, Amrita Mukkherjee, Alison Firth, Gillian Davies, Florian Koempel, Spyros Maniatis, Kelvin Sum, Shubha Ghosh, Ruth Okediji, Joshua Sarnoff, Jerome Reichman, Pedro Roffe, Malcolm Langley and those eminent scholars who graciously endorsed this and the first edition. We remain thankful that there are still 'real' publishers like Luke Adams in existence – those who believe in their authors' vision and have the undaunted patience to wait from the inception of an idea to its materialisation. Our hats off to the Edward Elgar Publishing editorial team who had to deal with two (slightly) stubborn authors in relation to Pantone colour schemes, baroque writing styles and what constitutes 'fair dealing' – thank you Fiona Briden, Stephanie Tytherleigh, Saffron Watts and Christine Gowen for your insights, suggestions and diligence in getting this second edition through. Thanks also to Sally Philip for your editing assistance. And (as dictated by him), boldly and bravely did Oliver give his unwavering support to his mother, constantly nudging her away from Netflix towards finishing 'that book'.

All weblinks to cited references were effective at the time of final editing October 2019.

Graham Dutfield and Uma Suthersanen

October 2019

ABBREVIATIONS AND ACRONYMS

National and regional laws

Australian Copyright Law
Copyright Act, No 63 of 1968, as amended

Canadian Copyright Law
Copyright Act, R.S.C., 1985

Canadian Patent Law
Patent Act, R.S.C., 1985

Dutch Copyright Law
Author's Right Law of September 23, 1912, as amended

French Intellectual Property Code
Intellectual Property Code, Law No 95-597 of July 1, 1992, as amended[1]

German Copyright Law
Authors' Rights and Related Rights Law of September 9, 1965, as amended[2]

Italian Copyright Law
Law No 633 of April 22, 1941, as amended

UK Copyright Law
Copyright, Designs and Patents Act, c. 48, 1988, as amended

US Copyright Law
Copyright Act 1976, codified 17 U.S.C. ss 101 *et seq.*, as amended

US Patent Act
Patent Act 1952, codified 35 U.S.C. ss 100 *et seq.*, as amended

EC Rental Directive 2006/115/EC
Directive 2006/115/EC of the European Parliament and of the Council of 12 December 2006 on rental right and lending right and on certain rights related to copyright in the field of intellectual property (codified version), OJ L 376, 27.12.2006, p. 28–35

---

[1] Official version available at www.legifrance.gouv.fr/content/download/1959/13723/.../Code_35.pdf.

[2] Official version available at www.gesetze-im-internet.de/englisch_urhg/englisch_urhg.html.

EC Software Directive
Directive 2009/24/EC of the European Parliament and of the Council of 23 April 2009 on the legal protection of computer programs (codified version), OJ L 111, 5.5.2009, p. 16–22

EU Copyright in the Information Society Directive (or InfoSoc Directive)
Directive 2001/29/EC of the European Parliament and of the Council of 22 May 2001 on the harmonisation of certain aspects of copyright and related rights in the information society, OJ L 167, 22.6.2001, p. 10–19

EU Copyright in the Digital Single Market Directive
Directive (EU) 2019/790 of the European Parliament and of the Council of 17 April 2019 on copyright and related rights in the Digital Single Market and amending Directives 96/9/EC and 2001/29/EC, OJ L 130, 17.5.2019, p. 92–125

EU Database Directive
Directive 96/9/EC of the European Parliament and of the Council of 11 March 1996 on the legal protection of databases, OJ L 77, 27.3.1996, p. 20–28

EU Orphan Works Directive
Directive 2012/28/EU of the European Parliament and of the Council of 25 October 2012 on certain permitted uses of orphan works, OJ L 299, 27.10.2012, p. 5–12

EU Term Directive
Directive 2006/116/EC of the European Parliament and of the Council of 12 December 2006 on the term of protection of copyright and certain related rights (codified version), OJ L 372, 27.12.2006, p. 12–18; as amended by Directive 2011/77/EU of the European Parliament and of the Council of 27 September 2011 amending Directive 2006/116/EC on the term of protection of copyright and certain related rights, OJ L 265, 11.10.2011, p. 1–5

EU E-Commerce Directive
Directive 2000/31/EC of the European Parliament and of the Council of 8 June 2000 on certain legal aspects of information society services, in particular electronic commerce, in the Internal Market, OJ L 178, 17.7.2000, p. 1–16

EU Trade Marks Directive
Directive of the European Parliament and of the Council of 16 December 2015 to Approximate the Laws of the Member States Relating to Trade Marks (2015/2436/EU)

EU Trade Mark Regulation (or EUTMR)
Council Regulation (EC) No 207/2009 of 26 February 2009 on the European Union Trade Mark (as amended)

International laws

Beijing Audiovisual Treaty	Beijing Treaty on Audiovisual Performances 2012
Berne Convention	Berne Convention for the Protection of Literary and Artistic Works of September 9, 1886 (1979 Paris version)
CBD	Convention on Biological Diversity 1993
EPC	European Patent Convention 1973, as amended in 1991, and 2000
GATT	General Agreement on Tariffs and Trade
ICCPR	International Covenant on Civil and Political Rights 1966
ICESCR	International Covenant on Economic, Social and Cultural Rights 1966
Lisbon Agreement 1958	Lisbon Agreement for the Protection of Appellations of Origin and their International Registration 1958
Marrakesh Treaty	Marrakesh Treaty to Facilitate Access to Published Works for Persons Who are Blind, Visually Impaired or Otherwise Print Disabled 2013
Nagoya Protocol	Nagoya Protocol on Access to Genetic Resources and the Fair and Equitable Sharing of Benefits Arising from their Utilization (ABS) to the Convention on Biological Diversity 2010
Paris Convention	Paris Convention for the Protection of Industrial Property of March 20, 1883 (1967, Stockholm revision)
PLT	Patent Law Treaty
PCT	Patent Cooperation Treaty 1970
Rome Convention	International Convention for the Protection of Performers, Producers of Phonograms and Broadcasting Organisations, Rome, 1961
TRIPS	Agreement on Trade-Related Aspects of Intellectual Property Rights, including Trade in Counterfeit Goods, Annex 1C to the Agreement Establishing the World Trade Organization, Marrakesh, 1994
UCC	Universal Copyright Convention 1952

UDHR   Universal Declaration of Human Rights 1948

UPOV   Union Internationale pour la Protection des Obtentions Végétales
                        (International Union for the Protection of New Varieties of Plants),
                        1961

WCT   WIPO Copyright Treaty 1996

WPPT   WIPO Performances and Phonograms Treaty 1996

Acronyms

ABS   access and benefit sharing
AIPPI   Association Internationale pour la Protection de la Propriété Industrielle (International
           Association for the Protection of Industrial Property)
ALAI   Association Littéraire et Artistique Internationale
AOC   Appellations d'Origine Contrôlée
BIRPI   Bureaux Internationaux Réunis de la Protection de la Propriété Intellectuelle (Interna-
           tional Bureaux)
CJEU   Court of Justice of the European Union
CMO   Collective management organisation
DNA   Deoxyribonucleic acid
DSM   Digital Single Market
EBA   Enlarged Board of Appeal
ECJ   European Court of Justice (now CJEU)
EPO   European Patent Office
EUIPO   European Union Intellectual Property Office
FAO   Food and Agriculture Organization of the United Nations
FDA   Food and Drug Administration
FTA   Free trade agreement
GIs   Geographical indications
ICTSD   International Centre for Trade and Sustainable Development
IFPI   International Federation of the Phonographic Industry
IGC   Intergovernmental Committee on Intellectual Property and Genetic Resources, Tradi-
           tional Knowledge and Folklore (of WIPO)
ILO   International Labour Organisation
INAO   Institut National de l'Origine et de la Qualité
IP   Intellectual property
IPRs   Intellectual property rights
LDCs   Least-developed countries
MFN   Most- favoured nation

NGO	Non-governmental organization
OECD	Organisation of Economic Co-operation and Development
OHIM	Office for Harmonisation in the Internal Market (now EUIPO)
PDO	Protected designation of origin
PGI	Protected geographical indication
pma	*post mortem auctoris* (after the death of the author)
PVP	Plant variety protection
SME	small- and medium-sized enterprises
SPC	supplementary protection certificates
SPLT	Substantive Patent Law Treaty
TBA	Technical Board of Appeal (of the European Patent Office)
TCE	traditional cultural expressions
TBT	WTO Agreement on Technical Barriers to Trade
TK	Traditional knowledge
TPMs	Technological protection measures
TSGs	Traditional specialities guaranteed
UNCTAD	United Nations Conference on Trade and Development
UNDP	United Nations Development Programme
UNESCO	United Nations Educational, Scientific and Cultural Organization
USDA	United States Department of Agriculture
USPTO	United States Patent and Trademark Office
WHO	World Health Organization
WIPO	World Intellectual Property Organization
WTO	World Trade Organization

TABLE OF CASES

TABLE OF LEGISLATION

European Union

United Nations

Treaties, Conventions and Other Instruments

International Treaties and Conventions

International Legislation

Australia

Canada

Egypt

Regional Instruments

ACCLAIM FOR THE FIRST EDITION

'The writing is very clear and lucid and avoids some of the almost evangelical rhetoric that informs some overview works of this type. The book is balanced, and the pros and cons of various rights are explored. It is a thought-provoking work, and the clarity of argument rises above the swirl of often intemperate special pleading by one group or another. In short, this is a book that repays reading before a student plunges into the detail of a specific regime and – as can be the case with some IP teaching – it is taken for granted that IP is a good thing.'
Howard Johnson, Communication Law

'[…] the book is enlightening for practitioners who are often required to take into account global considerations when advising clients […] It would be of particular interest to policy-makers in the intellectual property field.'
Australian Intellectual Property Law Bulletin

'Dutfield and Suthersanen have skillfully captured in one concise work all the important things you need to know about international intellectual property law. The materials are accessible, timely, methodically presented and at times critical. The book's detailed, in-depth and comparative analyses provide helpful insights into the increasingly complex international intellectual property system. Global Intellectual Property Law *is not only an effective textbook for students interested in the subject, but a desktop companion for policy-makers and professionals who need a quick and up-to-date overview of global intellectual property issues.'*
Peter K. Yu, Drake University, USA and Zhongnan University of Economics and Law, China

'Today global intellectual property rules affect everything from poor peoples' access to essential medicines to farmers' rights in seeds to access to knowledge on the Internet. But at the same time that pundits declare that intellectual property has come of age, this body of law is more contested than ever, with critics asking whether intellectual property is even necessary to stimulate innovation, and whether and how intellectual property ought to be tailored to address the health and developmental needs of the global South. Dutfield and Suthersanen's Global Intellectual Property Law *is a timely and lucid contribution to the field. This tome covers every hot button area of international intellectual property law and policy, from debates over the affect of intellectual property on development, to controversy over biotechnology and property rights in life, to claims by indigenous people and developing countries for new property rights in traditional knowledge. Dutfield and Suthersanen describe the current terrain, comparing North American, European, and developing world approaches; much to their credit, they do not shy away from describing points of tension among global actors.* Global Intellectual Property Law *is a must have for scholars and practitioners in the field for whom, I anticipate, the book will become a trusted and oft-used reference on their bookshelf. The book is clearly written and engaging enough to be perfect for students or laypersons interested in acquiring a comprehensive and critical appraisal of the field.'*
Madhavi Sunder, University of California, Davis, USA

'Dutfield and Suthersanen have succeeded in writing an engaging treatise that offers a truly modern perspective on intellectual property today. With examples from every continent, from every level of jurisdiction (national, regional, international), their study covers all the traditional fundamentals of intellectual property law as well as the current critical interrogations that their development raises. It is a book with character.'

Ysolde Gendreau, Université de Montréal, Canada

'Global Intellectual Property Law by Dutfield and Suthersanen provides a broad overview of the issues at stake concerning fair and effective ways to organise the information resources upon which the well-being of us all depends. The book highlights international and comparative perspectives on IP law and policy. Although primarily targeted at postgraduate level students, the book is enlightening also for practitioners, and a must-read for all policy-makers and opinion leaders in the IP field.'

Thomas Dreier, University of Karlsruhe, Germany

ACCLAIM FOR THE SECOND EDITION

'Dutfield and Suthersanen on Global Intellectual Property Law, now in its second edition, has established itself as a reference work for all those who are interested in international and comparative perspectives on intellectual property law and its policy aspects. Written by two leading scholars in intellectual property law, it offers a comprehensive view on all main intellectual property rights at international level and in various jurisdictions, whilst making sure that the technical legal analysis is always embedded in a broader socio-economic perspective. A very useful and inspiring read for all those who want to dig deeper into this fascinating field of growing importance.'

Christophe Geiger, CEIPI, University of Strasbourg, France

'This second edition considers the globalisation of intellectual property across a comparative range of local jurisdictions. As well as accounting for the various species of intellectual property, the book looks at larger over-arching themes of intellectual property and human rights; copyright law, cultural heritage, and education; plant breeders' rights, farmers' privileges, and geographical indications; gene patents and access to medicines; and Indigenous intellectual property. The work lights the way to implementing intellectual property reforms to promote the United Nations Sustainable Development Goals.'

Matthew Rimmer, Queensland University of Technology, Australia

'Professors Dutfield and Suthersanen reinvent the world of intellectual property law in a way that is doctrinally neat, yet breathtaking. Veteran scholars of Global Intellectual Property Law will be further tantalised; tyros will desire to seek further expertise. The world, intellectual property, and your political convictions will not be the same after you work through this invaluable contribution to the field.'

Shubha Ghosh, Syracuse University, USA

PART I

INTELLECTUAL PROPERTY AS GLOBALISED
LOCALISM

1

Globalisation, law and development

Intellectual property has become one of the major issues of our global society. Globalization is one of the most important issues of the day, and intellectual property is one of the most important aspects of globalization, especially as the world moves toward a knowledge economy. How we regulate and manage the production of knowledge and the right of access to knowledge is at the center of how well this new economy, the knowledge economy, works and of who benefits. At stake are matters of both distribution and efficiency.[1]

Joseph Stiglitz, *winner of the Nobel Memorial Prize in Economic Sciences, 2001*

1.1   LEGAL GLOBAL NORMS

Globalisation is a process, or a series of processes, which creates and consolidates a unified world economy, and a complex and dynamic network of communications that covers the world.[2] This process is not at all irreversible. Nationalistic and anti-globalisation movements are challenging globalisation as they re-assert the autonomy of states and oppose what they see as the homogenisation of cultures, lifestyles and consumer choices, excessive deference to corporate and financial interests, and the erosion of national sovereignty and local autonomy. Undoubtedly, political boundaries persist and the nation state is still very much with us.

In understanding globalisation processes, an important distinction to bear in mind is that between localised globalism and globalised localism, which shows that globalisation occurs in

---

[1] J.E. Stiglitz, 'Economic Foundations of Intellectual Property Rights' (2008) 57 *Duke Law Journal* 1693, 1695.

[2] W. Twining, *Globalisation and Legal Theory* (Butterworths, 2000), 4–10.

opposing directions often with great tensions between the two.[3] Localised globalism focuses on the recipients, who may be victims or beneficiaries depending on your standpoint. Globalised localism concentrates on the standard-setters, often situated in a small number of places. These are the ones who set the rules the rest of the world ends up following. Let us look at these terms in more detail before proceeding.

Globalised localism occurs when a local phenomenon is successfully globalised, for example, the widespread adoption of English as the language of social and business discourse, the ubiquitous Coca Cola logo and the drink's now universal consumption, or the adoption of EU or American copyright laws by other countries. Much usage of the concept of 'globalisation' concentrates on this phenomenon. Often, the entire process of international policy-making, negotiation, dialogue, rule-making, implementation and enforcement, and commercialisation practices, is driven by globalised localism whereby a small group of powerful countries, or even a single country, gets its way.

Localised globalism refers to the situation where international and transnational influences are localised sometimes through creative adaptations. The World Trade Organization's Agreement on Trade-Related Aspects of Intellectual Property Rights (TRIPS) is an example of globalised localism, whereby general principles recognised initially in a few countries force the remaining nations to adopt broadly similar intellectual property laws. This may have the consequence that better adapted local laws are set aside with the local context being completely disregarded. But the opposite can happen too: localised globalism may arise, in which TRIPS is creatively adapted to local conditions and in ways intended to benefit the public in those countries. Potentially these adaptations could themselves become globalised if a sufficient number of countries decides to apply them too.[4]

Notwithstanding this more nuanced interpretation of globalisation, which suggests there is still space for tailor-made as opposed to off-the-peg rule-making, developing countries implementing new multilateral or bilateral intellectual property agreements continue to complain that their interpretative scope concerning rights, exceptions and limitations is curtailed or limited to how the EU or the US interprets the treaties. We would argue that instead of automatically adopting the EU or US interpretations of certain international intellectual property provisions, it would be far better for countries to craft their rights, exceptions and limitations as they see fit, assuming their interpretations of these are consistent with their international obligations. And if these obligations run counter to their economic interests they are justified in proposing reforms or advocating for new treaties. The trouble is that the EU and US sometimes intervene and discourage them in various ways from doing so.

The complex way that intellectual property law is made, is subsequently 'traded' in the form, for example, of 'you "buy" our patent law and we'll buy more of your wine' types of transaction, and the contested nature of the rights granted requires us to look at the law from all perspectives – local, regional, global, and also holistically. One consequence of such a multi-faceted approach is that we are bound to encounter clashes between national, transnational, international,

---

[3] Ibid.

[4] This appears to be the case for disclosure of origin. This is a requirement that patent applications on inventions claiming, based or derived from biological matter sourced from living natural resources disclose the relevant geographical origin and, in some cases, the origin of associated traditional knowledge.

customary and socio-economic rules as they relate to specific objects, works and ideas. We may also find tensions between the rules, and even within them. Twining's approach to jurisprudence within a globalised world is concerned with a holistic approach to laws and entitlements. Twining's (and our) approach is more aptly summarised by Tamanaha:

> A general jurisprudence with genuinely global reach, Twining argues, must recognise the multiplicity of forms and manifestations of law that actually exist around the world today. Twining thus brings within his purview not just state law – heretofore the almost exclusive focus of analytical jurisprudents – but also global law, international law, transnational law, regional law, communal and inter-communal law, sub-state law, and non-state law. Going beyond the law of the US […] and the UK, Twining raises the law of the EU, lex mercatoria, Gypsy law, the unofficial law in favelas (urban slums), Islamic law, various forms of customary law, and much more.[5]

To make the situation even more tricky, current studies of the law tend to overlook the tensions inherent in the very basis of the legal entitlements provided under a given intellectual property right (IPR). An IPR may be granted to a corporation in a symbol, but such legal protection may also interfere with claims on the same symbol by a local or indigenous community, based on chthonic laws. In the wider world, tensions between private property and commercial interest and non-economic issues like human rights and cultural and spiritual values, continually create sparks, some of which turn into conflagrations. This is particularly noticeable when we explore the relationship between the different IPRs on the one hand, and traditional knowledge and traditional cultural expressions, on the other. On the one hand, IPRs are viewed as national innovation and economic tools, while local and indigenous groups orientate moral entitlements, customary norms, and in some cases property rights, largely around the group or community. But in no country are IPRs purely economic or purely moral in nature. Frequently the result is confusing and internally inconsistent law.

1.2 KNOWLEDGE-BASED ECONOMIES

In 1852, Lyon Playfair, a politician and public intellectual of his day, warned that Britain needed to realise, as he thought its foreign competitors already did, that 'the competition of industry has become a competition of intellect'.[6] Later in life he noted that 'all countries of the world have been brought into a common market to compete for the margins of profit'.[7] Reading the two together,

---

[5] B. Tamanaha, 'What is "General" Jurisprudence? A Critique of Universalistic Claims by Philosophical Concepts of Law' (2011) 2(3) *Transnational Legal Theory* 287, 293; and Twining, *supra* note 2, Chapter 3.

[6] Dr Lyon Playfair, CB, FRS, *Industrial Instruction on the Continent* (London: George E. Eyre & William Spottiswoode, 1852), 3.

[7] The Right Honourable Sir Lyon Playfair, KCB, MP, 'On Industrial Competition and Commercial Freedom. Being an Address Delivered at the National Liberal Club. April 24th, 1888', London: The Liberal and Radical Publishing Co, 6.

it is 'intellect' that provides the competitive advantage. What may have been a radical notion in his day is the current orthodoxy.

Intellectual property has moved into the mainstream of national economic and developmental planning, and has emerged as a central element of multilateral, regional and bilateral trade relations. The current conventional wisdom is that the world's most successful nations are those best at producing, acquiring, deploying and controlling valuable knowledge. Knowledge, especially new knowledge unavailable to one's rivals, is key to international competitiveness and therefore to national prosperity. However clichéd such a view may be, the fact is that many policy-makers believe it to be true and are acting accordingly.

Can intellectual property ever outpace tangible property as a fundamental base of modern economies? According to governments and organisations, it can and perhaps already has. The United Kingdom government has asserted, for example, that the economic competitiveness of the UK as of its competitors 'is increasingly driven by knowledge-based industries, especially in manufacturing, science-based sectors and the creative industries'.[8] The increasing prominence of services in modern economies does not change this situation, and arguably reinforces it. In 2004, ex-Chairman Greenspan of the US Federal Reserve commented that the fraction of the US GDP 'that is essentially conceptual rather than physical has been rising. This trend has, of necessity, shifted the emphasis in asset valuation from physical property to intellectual property and to the legal rights inherent in intellectual property'.[9]

The 2016 US Department of Commerce report values 81 IP-intensive industries as generating 38 per cent of total US GDP, i.e. almost four in every ten dollars generated in the US economy relates to IP intensive industries.[10] Those who concur with such views, whether or not they accept the all too frequent hyperbole, tend to assume that knowledge-based economies are nowadays wealthier, almost by definition, than traditional or natural resource-based ones.

Nonetheless, reality defies lazy platitudes. While Singapore is a prosperous and increasingly creative economy, the similarly sized Qatar and Brunei are just plain rich. India, with Bollywood, its impressive and rapidly expanding software industry, and its sizeable and growing biotechnological capacity in relation to its GNP, is mired in poverty, which will probably take generations to eliminate. Of course, India cannot become a rich oil-based economy when there is no oil on which to base its economy. But most Indians still work on the land, and the diffusion of state-of-the-art knowledge and technologies is only one part of the whole solution to the problem of how to eke out a decent income from agriculture.

This kind of thinking is not as new as people might think. Policy-making inspired by such ideas goes back centuries. In the Middle Ages, Venetian glass-makers, whose techniques were

---

[8] A. Gowers, *Review of Intellectual Property: A Call for Evidence* (HM Treasury, 2006).

[9] A. Greenspan, 'Remarks on Intellectual property rights', the Stanford Institute for Economic Policy Research Economic Summit, Stanford, California February 27, 2004.

[10] *Intellectual Property and the US Economy: 2016 Update*, a joint project led by US Patent and Trademark Office (Michelle K. Lee) and Economics & Statistics Administration (Justin Antonipillai). IP intensive industries include: software and music publishing, pharmaceuticals, and the creative industries such as sound recording, audio and video equipment manufacturing, cable and other subscription programming, performing arts companies, and radio and television broadcasting.

acquired partly from Germany and Syria, were forbidden from plying their trade outside the city state or giving away their secrets. Transgressors could lose their lives. At the same time, foreign glass makers were banned from operating there. It may not be entirely coincidental that Venice was the first place to pass legislation providing patents for inventions. Venetian-style 'knowledge mercantilism'[11] has not been historically uncommon. But since the Industrial Revolution, knowledge economy rhetoric is often expressed in ways favouring more open trade. In this respect, some nineteenth-century voices manage to sound very twenty-first century.

Unsurprisingly, the 'importance' of IP within national economies has historically accompanied the expansion of the remits of intellectual property to include new types of knowledge and creations, and new manners of exploitation. This is partly understandable given the constant changes in socio-economic conditions, including shifting and previously unforeseen market opportunities, and technological transformations that nobody could have anticipated. Even the way IP is conceived changes over time. Patents and copyright originated out of monopoly privileges granted by monarchs to traders, book printers, manufacturers and artisans. In time, they became forms of personal property granted to inventors and authors. While to some extent they still are, it is probably more accurate to portray IPRs as a class of intangible business asset that is usually held by companies performing the manifold roles in the modern economy of investor, innovator, employer, distributor and marketer. Individual creators are less and less frequently the ones owning and controlling the rights. This trend, rooted in the second industrial revolution of the late nineteenth century and early twentieth centuries which professionalised and corporatised science, engineering and creative production, brings to the fore the issue of whether and to what extent IPRs interact with current norms relating to human rights, national economic governance, fairness, efficiency and development.

However, even if one accepts the economic and strategic importance of knowledge, it is not necessarily to be concluded that the more intellectual property you have and the stronger the rights are the better, or even that intellectual property is necessary at all. One may more safely conclude that intellectual property policy-making is an inherently political activity where different stakeholders, irrespective of their allegiances, compete to influence and control the intellectual property rules.

Increasingly, intellectual property finds itself at the centre of local, national, regional and global debates on how human society and the resources upon which our well-being depends should best be developed, utilised and organised to achieve just and effective outcomes that are good for us, and also for our planet.[12] Thus, we see demands from indigenous peoples for proprietary protection of their knowledge and cultural productions, protests about the perceived approval of controversial fields of research through the aegis of patent laws from genetically modified food to human embryonic stem cells, campaigns to improve access to educational materials and life-saving drugs, the development and use of technologies that can mitigate climate change and biodiversity loss, demands to restrict the branding of unhealthy products, criticisms of the alleged anti-development

---

[11] Stuart Macdonald coined the phrase 'information mercantilism'. See S. Macdonald, *Information for Innovation: Managing Change from an Information Perspective* (Oxford: Oxford University Press, 1998).

[12] S.F. Halabi, *Intellectual Property and the New International Economic Order: Oligopoly, Regulation, and Wealth Distribution in the Global Knowledge Economy* (Cambridge: Cambridge University Press, 2018).

biases of current intellectual property rule-making, calls for protecting one's dignity and persona through copyright and trade mark law, and so on.

1.3   LOCAL INNOVATION AND KNOWLEDGE

It is generally assumed that wealth-creating knowledge of the kind that turns economies into knowledge-based ones, comes almost exclusively out of universities, corporate laboratories and film, music, art and design studios, and not out of such unlikely places as peasant farmers' fields and indigenous communities. Furthermore, that kind of economic transformation requires the availability of high US- or European-style standards of intellectual property protection and enforcement. Basically, rich countries have such standards, poor countries do not. Therefore, to be like rich countries, poor countries must adopt these standards; the 'magic of the marketplace' will presumably conjure up the rest.

Are such assumptions validated by reality? Statistics produced by international organizations like the UN Development Programme (UNDP), WIPO and the World Bank suggest that most developing countries are not only failing to be innovative but actually have to improve their innovation climate dramatically before they can be competitive in high-technology fields, except perhaps as assemblers and exporters of technology-intensive goods invented elsewhere. Admittedly, our usual indicators of innovation, such as R&D spending, education statistics and patent counts do not tell the whole story and may in fact be misleading. But there appears clearly to be a massive innovation gap between the rich and poor worlds that is not going to be bridged for a long time except by a few countries. China is, of course, catching up fast, but few others are.

Is such a negative and pessimistic view about developing countries entirely accurate? Is there really a massive knowledge and innovation gap between the rich and poor worlds? Confusingly, the best answer to both questions is 'yes and no'. The 'yes' part is obvious. North America, Western Europe and East Asia have a massive lead over the rest of the world in virtually all of the usual social and economic indicators. But why is there a 'no' in the answer at all? Because there is a cultural bias in how we use terms like 'knowledge economy', 'information society', 'intelligent community' and 'creative industry'. The effect of this bias is to underestimate the presence and vital role of applied knowledge in all societies including those appearing to be the most backward and traditional.

Creativity and innovation are not the sole preserve of suited knowledge workers in glassy offices, unsuited bohemians in garrets, professional artists and musicians, or of laboratory scientists. If necessity really is the mother of invention, you would surely expect to see most innovation where the needs are greatest. And no needs are greater than those of desperately poor people getting themselves and their families through each day alive and well. Whether we look at health or agriculture, we find that peasant communities are often able to draw upon a huge body of knowledge passed down through many generations.[13] The same applies to hunters and gatherers. Local knowledge, technologies, products and fashions can be highly evolutionary, adaptive and even novel.

---

[13] G. Dutfield, *Africa and the Economy of Tradition* (Fondation pour l'Innovation Politique, 2005); D.A. Posey, (ed.), Cultural and Spiritual Values of Biodiversity (Nairobi and London: UNDP & IT Publications, 1999).

In short, knowledge held within 'traditional' societies can be new as well as old. We should not be surprised by this. Traditional knowledge and culture has always had adaptive elements because the ability to adapt is one of the keys to survival in precarious environments.

So can we just assume, as we tend to do, that the world's knowledge and innovation 'hotspots' are urban areas located almost exclusively in Europe, North America and East Asia? In fact, there are many other innovation hotspots, some in the most remote and isolated regions of the world. The problem is that few people recognise them as such, and few of those are in positions of real power or authority. Consequently, innumerable opportunities to harness local knowledge and innovation for trade and development are missed, especially where the innovative knowledge emanates from the female population. Another susceptible field of innovation is the highly lucrative area of fashion and textile design where African designs (such as Basotho-inspired and Maasai-inspired blankets) consistently 'inspire' haute couture houses such as Louis Vuitton. Today's more positive view seriously challenges the idea that knowledge wealth necessarily goes hand in hand with material wealth, and that innovation cannot be common where there is mass poverty.[14] What they point out also is that knowledge and creative people may be far less scarce than are the institutions to help convert knowledge into wealth for local people and for the benefit of the wider economy. Consequently, traditional knowledge, local innovations and traditional culture are being under-utilised.[15]

There is very little evidence that strong intellectual property protection and enforcement à la American or European standards achieves national prosperity and international competitiveness. Naturally, transnational corporations like governments to believe this. To this end, corporate lobbying has largely been responsible for the barely accountable extension of patents, copyright and trade marks to completely new kinds of subject matter in recent decades. Intellectual property law now encompasses such 'stuff' from a celebrity's image to the smell of fresh cut grass on treated tennis balls,[16] to television show formats (such as Who Wants to Be a Millionaire) and to newly discovered medical uses for aspirin. We can patent microbes, plants and animals, even genes that have just been discovered and found to have some link to a disease. The binary code behind software programs is classed as a copyrightable work of literature. We can trademark the

---

[14] A.K. Gupta, 'Why Does Poverty Persist in Regions of High Biodiversity? A Case for Indigenous Property Right System', (unpublished manuscript), http://anilg.sristi.org/why-doespoverty-persist-in-regions-of-high-biodiversity/ [https://perma.cc/XRK9-2VNA].

[15] B. Boateng, *The Copyright Thing Doesn't Work Here: Adinkra and Kente Cloth and Intellectual Property in Ghana* (Univ. of Minnesota Press, 2011); A.K. Gupta, 'From Sink to Source: The Honey Bee Network Documents Indigenous Knowledge and Innovations in India' (2006) 1(3) *Innovations: Technology, Governance, Globalization*, 49–66; BBC News, 'When does cultural borrowing turn into cultural appropriation?', 28 September 2017. https://www.bbc.co.uk/news/world-africa-41430748; see *A Tree and Traditional Knowledge: A Recipe for Development*, WIPO Case Study on the Eudafano Women's Cooperative, https://www.wipo.int/ipadvantage/en/details.jsp?id=2651.

[16] *Vennootschap onder Firma Senta Aromatic Marketing*, CTM Application No. 428870, filed December 11, 1996, registered October 11, 2000, the mark has not been renewed); and 'the scent or smell of raspberries' for engine fuels – *Myles Limited's Application*, Appeal No. R0711/1999-3 (OHIM Third Board of Appeal, Dec. 5, 2001), the application was rejected on the ground that the mark was not distinctive in relation to the goods.

Metro Goldwyn Mayer's (MGM) lion's roar. Protection terms have been extended. The copyright term for authored works in Europe, the US and many of their trade partners now continues for 70 years after the author's death. Does every country in the world need to adopt such standards, as they increasingly have to do, if not because of TRIPS, then as a result of new commitments arising from bilateral trade agreements? Arguably not. In fact, such standards may make them worse off.

The historical record strongly suggests that many of today's economic leader countries were themselves 'knowledge pirates' in the past, and benefited from being so.[17] As for the present, a case could be made for arguing that we in the developed world are not becoming knowledge-based economies as quickly as we are becoming knowledge-protected economies, or even – and this is a bit more worrying – knowledge-overprotected economies, in which dominant industries maintain their market power by tying up their knowledge in complex bundles of legal rights and instruments such as patents, copyrights, trade marks and restrictive contracts and licensing agreements. Such bundles of rights often cover just one product; a drug for example may be protected by a trade mark, multiple patents, trade secrets, safety and efficacy test data exclusivity, and copyright on the instructions. Smartphones are likely to be covered by even more rights which may well be owned by several firms.

It is far from clear that the creativity and innovation coming out of laboratories and studios is increasing at a rate anywhere near as fast as the rapidly growing size of corporate intellectual property portfolios. This heightened level of protection may not only be bad for consumers in terms of higher prices, but may stifle far more innovation than it promotes. And things may be getting worse. Every major company is expected to have an intellectual property management strategy, which frequently entails the aggressive acquisition and enforcement of rights, because everybody else has one. Among the harmful consequences are increased prices, and a reduced access to knowledge that the generation of new knowledge encouraged by IPRs is insufficient to compensate for.

Ironically, overly zealous enforcement of rights may be bad for business too. Most large corporations rely on strong IP protection, whether in software, fashion, pharmaceuticals or music sectors. But they also appropriate constantly from other cultures and enterprises. Ironically, mass-scale usage of an illegally reproduced product can sometimes make the lawful product a *de facto* standard in the marketplace as has been the case with Microsoft's Windows operating system.

Of course, some would argue that copying is bad and that is the end of it. But others plausibly argue that a certain amount of copying and free-riding is necessary, if not beneficial, for competition in any economy, and even for innovation.[18] As for developing countries, imitation there as elsewhere is an essential stage in learning to innovate. Paradoxical as it might sound, imitation

---

[17] D.S. Ben-Atar, *Trade Secrets: Intellectual Piracy and the Origins of American Industrial Power* (New Haven and London: Yale University Press, 2004); H.-J. Chang, *Kicking away the Ladder: Development Strategy in Historical Perspective* (London: Anthem, 2002); G. Dutfield and U. Suthersanen, 'Harmonisation or Differentiation in Intellectual Property Protection? The Lessons of History' (2005) 23(2) *Prometheus* 131–47.

[18] K.W. Dam, 'Some Economic Considerations in the Intellectual Property Protection of Software' (1995) 24 *Journal of Legal Studies* 321.

can be creative in itself. According to Kim and Nelson, 'imitation ranges from illegal duplicates of popular products to truly creative new products that are merely inspired by a pioneering brand'.[19] Distinct imitations may include 'knockoffs or clones, design copies, creative adaptations, techno-logical leapfrogging, and adaptation to another industry'.[20] One should not take this argument too far, though. Wholesale copying and distribution of films or the misappropriation of another's trade mark does not necessarily provide scope for learning at all. Moreover, if it is too easy to profit from uncreative imitation, there is unlikely to be much incentive to innovate.

1.4   DISRUPTIVE LAWS FROM DEVELOPING COUNTRIES

Until recently, for developing and emerging economies, intellectual property policy taking was the norm rather than policy-making. What we mean is that the developed countries, in reality just a few of them, set the standards for other countries to follow. Public interest and pro-com-petitive provisions were being questioned, and narrowed. That is a serious concern for developing countries seeking to acquire expensive life-saving drugs. Other likely negative effects include un-due constraints on the reproduction and distribution of educational materials in countries where such materials are scarce, expensive and desperately needed. This may still be the general trend but developing nations are starting to devise bespoke policy approaches, which other countries are imitating.

There are several examples of this starting with the fact that since the 1990s many developing countries have adopted disclosure of origin provisions in their patent laws to counter biopiracy. A few European countries have similar measures but developing countries have taken the lead. Another example is Canada, which has introduced the concept of 'user rights' into the discourse, thereby displacing the traditional onus of proof when construing limitations and exceptions (see Chapter 12). A third example is India's patent law measure to restrict secondary pharmaceutical patenting (see Chapter 13).[21] This has attracted much interest from other developing countries. In the ever-controversial area of patents and the pricing of life-saving drugs, there have been fresh inroads, the most recent being the 2018 South African Intellectual Property Policy. That document clearly intends to actively ensure that patent protection does not stop the expansion of access to medicines or the promotion of food security and farmers' rights or environmental concerns.[22] The

---

[19] L. Kim and R.R. Nelson, 'Introduction', in L. Kim and R.R. Nelson (eds), *Technology, Learning, and Innovation: Experiences of Newly Industrializing Economies* (Cambridge: Cambridge University Press, 2000).

[20] Ibid., citing S. Schnaar, *Managing Imitation Strategy: How Later Entrants Seize Markets from Pioneers* (New York: Free Press, 1994).

[21] C. Arup, 'The Transfer of Pharmaceutical Patent Laws: The Case of India's Paragraph 3(d)', in J. Gillespie and P. Nicholson (eds), *Law and Development and the Global Discourses of Legal Transfers* (Cambridge: Cambridge University Press, 2012), 121–42.

[22] *Intellectual Property Policy of the Republic of South Africa Phase I*, Department of Trade & Industry, South Africa, May 2018.

trend in focusing on limits to protection now underpin the current W̲
especially in relation to educational activities, libraries and archives, an̲
While all developing countries have good reason to defend their righ̲
property rules and policies to suit their specific needs and conditions, th̲
interests identical. Lall's research found ample evidence that the need for IPRs varies wi̲
of development. Based in part on the work of Maskus, he went on to say that:

> Many rich countries used weak IPR protection in their early stages of industrialisation to develop local technological bases, increasing protection as they approached the leaders. Econometric cross-section evidence suggests that there is an inverted-U shaped relationship between the strength of IPRs and income levels. The intensity of IPRs first falls with rising incomes, as countries move to slack IPRs to build local capabilities by copying, then rises as they engage in more innovative effort. The turning point is $7,750 per capita in 1985 prices [...], a fairly high level of income for the developing world.[24]

A more recent economic survey accepts that the rationale behind the current pushback from developing countries such as India, South Africa and Brazil lies in the over-reliance on market-failure based rationales for IP protection (see Chapter 2). The authors are clear that the current IP regime, based on this particular view of knowledge-based economies (namely that IP is the only means to inventivise and finance research and knowledge) is wrong. Instead, the study points to the development histories of Japan, Korea and China which show that weak enforcement of IPRs and an extensive use of 'creative imitation' are: 'necessary for the inflow of foreign investment, domestic technological development and the transfer of technology'.[25]

It is one thing to say that relatively advanced developing countries prefer to weaken their IPRs to advance their capacities to innovate through imitation-derived technological learning, and then strengthen them later when they are more innovative. It is quite another thing to assume that such a policy works just because many governments have favoured it. Nonetheless, intuitively it makes much sense and there is a wealth of historical experience to back it up.

1.5 LEX MERCATORIA FOR CORPORATIONS

Globalisation of trade means that goods, services and intangible property having material, informational, scientific, entertainment or cultural value are now produced, exchanged and consumed

---

[23] WIPO Standing Committee on Copyright and Related Rights: Thirty-Seventh Session, November 2018.

[24] S. Lall (with the collaboration of M. Albaladejo), 'Indicators of the Relative Importance of IPRs in Developing Countries', Issues Paper no. 3, UNCTAD-ICTSD Project on Intellectual Property Rights and Sustainable Development, Geneva, 2003 (citing K.E. Maskus, *Intellectual Property Rights in the Global Economy* (Washington, DC: Institute for International Economics, 2000), 95–6).

[25] D. Baker, A. Jayadev and J. Stiglitz, *Innovation, Intellectual Property, and Development: A Better Set of Approaches for the 21st Century* (Centre for Economic and Policy Research, July 2017), 30.

anywhere and everywhere. International trading provokes tensions with – but of course does not eliminate – territoriality and the jurisdictional powers of national governments. In recent decades international cooperation has led to an increasing focus not just on reducing tariffs and quotas imposed on goods entering countries at borders but on reducing barriers to trade in services, and on internal regulations covering such issues as human safety, animal welfare, consumer rights, and fair competition. Intellectual property comprises a set of legal trade-affecting regulatory norms, albeit of a special nature being private property rights vested in legal and natural persons.

Internal regulations can facilitate legitimate trade for the public benefit, but from a liberal trade perspective they can also constitute non-tariff barriers to trade in goods and services. There is nothing inherently wrong with non-tariff barriers. Indeed, they may be necessary. However, they can also be flagrantly protectionist, arbitrary, unnecessary, discriminatory, unreasonable, or needlessly complicated. Hence the need for such barriers to comply with the disciplines provided in the various World Trade Organization (WTO) agreements. Even with the WTO, such norms continue to diverge widely. This is not just a matter of different national interests but also relates to divergent ideologies and social and cultural norms, and perceptions of, for example, risk. Harmonisation processes as encouraged by the WTO and agreed through regional trade arrangements are ongoing, though.

For some people, the mobilisation efforts of corporate bodies, such as IBM in the arena of copyright protection of computer programs, and Novartis in the arena of patent protection of pharmaceuticals, epitomise how global, ambitious intellectual property-intensive companies seek to dictate intellectual property law and policy to the world. As may be inferred from Chapter 3, when we realise how much corporate lobbying was behind the TRIPS Agreement and some other recent international intellectual property agreements, those concerned about the undue influence of large corporations have a point. From a historical perspective, when these corporations impose their preferred intellectual property rules on the world, they echo the *lex mercatoria* spirit of the ancient guilds. The original 12 members of the Intellectual Property Committee that lobbied for what became TRIPS in the 1980s, for instance, were Pfizer, IBM, Merck, General Electric, Du Pont, Warner Communications, Hewlett-Packard, Bristol Myers, General Motors, Johnson & Johnson, Rockwell International and Monsanto. In her political analysis of TRIPS, Sell argues that:

> TRIPS closely mirrors the expressed wishes of the twelve chief executive officers of US-based multinational corporations who spear-headed the effort. The stated rationale for this IP agreement – that it will promote economic development worldwide – has virtually no empirical support.[26]

Perhaps one can reconceptualise modern-day corporations with their tremendous market and political power as a globalised guild system representing a curious throwback to the early-capitalist era of mercantilism. Historically, the mercantilist regarded the state as the appropriate instrument

---

[26] S.K. Sell, *Private Power, Public Law: The Globalization of Intellectual Property Rights* (Cambridge, UK: Cambridge University Press, 2003), 13; see also 1, 96. See also P. Drahos, 'Global Property Rights in Information: The Story of TRIPS at the GATT' (1995) 13(1) *Prometheus* 6–19.

for promoting the well-being of his country and pursued national interests at all costs. Moreover, in his view the country was regarded as a unit; there were national interests to promote, quite irrespective of the interests of particular commercial sectors or individuals. In accordance with such an approach, the state harnessed and controlled resources, skills and products for the purposes and profit of the state. The late historian Lisa Jardine noted that financial investment by way of patronage was often conferred on artists and craftsmen as a means of attaining social and political advantage. 'The valuable artefacts which they created (or obtained) for their patron were at the same time intrinsically costly commodities and potentially exploitable as the basis for a significant power-broking transaction.'[27]

Other forms of state support included the encouragement of commercial enterprises by the issue of patents, charters, licences and regulatory monopolies in respect of the introduction of new technologies, the creation of privileged trading companies, the foundation of colonies and plantations in order to secure supplies of material as well as a market for the finished commodities, and the establishment of manufactories financed and controlled by the state. The mercantilist world was a dog-eat-dog one in which protectionism was the norm and trade advantages for a country were seen as trade disadvantages for its neighbours. The rise of the shopkeeper or merchant class also brought new social distinctions as the cream of the trade fraternity sought to set itself above the rest by forming guilds.[28]

Realisation that intellectual property has wide-ranging repercussions is evidenced by the way intellectual property controversies more and more frequently find their way on to the front pages of newspapers. Trade negotiators were largely unaware of these repercussions when the issue of IPRs was linked with global trade during the Uruguay Round trade negotiations that culminated in the 1994 Agreement Establishing the World Trade Organization, annexed to which was the TRIPS Agreement. Far more attention was paid to the need to satisfy the pharmaceutical and entertainment industries than to ensure an intellectual property regime that was good for public health, education, food security and the interests of developing countries. Returning to Stiglitz who opened this chapter:

> To critics of globalization, the fight over intellectual property is a fight over values. TRIPS reflected the triumph of corporate interests in the United States and Europe over the broader interests of billions of people in the developing world. It was another instance in which more weight was given to profits than to other basic values – like the environment, or life itself [...] Intellectual property does not really belong in a trade agreement.[29]

---

[27] L. Jardine, *Wordly Goods – A New History of the Renaissance* (London: Macmillan, 1996), 238–9. For further exploratory reading on mercantilism, see F. Braudel, *The Wheels of Commerce* (London: Collins, 1982), 542; J.S. Mill, *Principles of Political Economy*, Book V, Chapters VI (ss 1–2) and X (s 1), 1848 (reference is made to the 7th edition of Mill, as prepared by W.J. Ashley in 1909), available online.

[28] Braudel, ibid., 68, 81; C. May, 'The Venetian Moment: New Technologies, Legal Innovation and the Institutional Origins of Intellectual Property' (2002) 20(2) *Prometheus* 159; F. Machlup and E. Penrose, 'The Patent Controversy in the 19th Century' (1950) 1 *Journal of Economic History* 2.

[29] J.E. Stiglitz, *Making Globalization Work* (New York/London: WW Norton, 2006), pp. 105, 117.

13

...ssible we are now turning full circle. Nowadays, calls are being made to legislate ...clopment-orientated bases (see below). Moreover, some countries are legislating, making policies and taking legal decisions they consider to best further their priorities as developing nations albeit in the face of external pressures not to do so.

1.6   DEFINING INTELLECTUAL PROPERTY LAW

In its purest sense, it is the only absolute possession in the world. As Chaffe stated, 'The man who brings out of nothingness some child of his thought has rights therein which cannot belong to any other sort of property.'[30] Cornish in an early edition of his textbook defines IP as the 'branch of the law which protects some of the finer manifestations of human achievement'; the authors add that 'it also shields much that is trivial and ephemeral.'[31] Bently and Sherman state that intellectual property law 'regulates the creation, use and exploitation of mental or creative labour'.[32] Vaver suggests a more honest account arguing that the phrase 'intellectual property' starts 'from the premise that ideas are free as the air – a common resource for all to use as they can and wish. It then proceeds systematically to undermine that principle'.[33] Harris, from the perspective of a property purist, views IP slightly differently:

> The law takes an intangible thing and builds around it a property structure modelled on the structure which social and legal systems have always applied to some tangible things. By instituting trespassory rules whose content restricts uses of the ideational entity, intellectual property law preserves to an individual or group of individuals an open-ended set of use-privileges and powers of control and transmission characteristic of ownership interests over tangible items.[34]

In our view, intellectual property is a type of property regime whereby creators and entrepreneurs are granted a right, the nature of which is entirely dependent on the nature of the creation on the one hand, and the legal classification of the creation on the other. To a certain extent, we agree with Merges's stark observation that IP is 'a perfectly plausible, and even desirable, system for administering intangible assets'.[35] To be placed within one or other of the different classifications of 'intellectual property', one must fulfil the relevant criteria (for example, novelty, originality, distinctiveness or individual

---

[30] Z. Chaffe, 'Reflections on the Law of Copyright: I and II' (1945) 45(4/5) *Columbia Law Review* in R.C. Berrings (ed.), *Great American Law Reviews* (Birmingham: Legal Classics Library, 1984).

[31] W. Cornish and D. Llewelyn, *Intellectual Property: Patents, Copyright, Trade Marks and Allied Marks* (5th ed., London: Sweet & Maxwell, 2003), 3.

[32] In an earlier edition, L. Bently and B. Sherman, *Intellectual Property Law* (2nd ed., Oxford: Oxford University Press, 2004), 1.

[33] D. Vaver, *Intellectual Property Law* (Toronto: Irwin Law, 2011), 1.

[34] J.W. Harris, *Property and Justice* (Oxford: Oxford University Press, 1996), 44.

[35] R.P. Merges, *Justifying Intellectual Property* (Cambridge, MA: Harvard University Press, 2011), 5. For an intriguing perspective, see M. Koktvedgaard, 'The Universe of Intellectual Property' (1996) *GRUR Int.* 296.

character) and comply with certain formalities – although not for copyright. Depending on these legal (and often artificial) classifications, the creation is accorded a bundle of rights, which vary considerably across the intellectual property spectrum in terms of number, scope and duration (see Figure 1.1). Patent, copyright, and trade mark are the accepted bastions of the intellectual property world, with their respective legal satellites that include utility model and design laws (see Table 1.1 below).

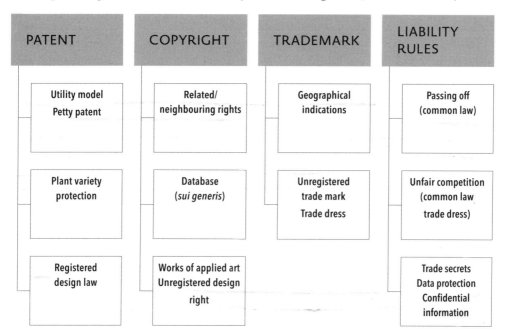

PATENT	COPYRIGHT	TRADEMARK	LIABILITY RULES
Utility model Petty patent	Related/ neighbouring rights	Geographical indications	Passing off (common law)
Plant variety protection	Database (*sui generis*)	Unregistered trade mark Trade dress	Unfair competition (common law trade dress)
Registered design law	Works of applied art Unregistered design right		Trade secrets Data protection Confidential information

Figure 1.1 Typology of intellectual property protection

Table 1.1 Summary of the three main IP rights based on the WIPO Convention classification*

Patent law: Exclusive protection of a limited duration for inventions in all fields of technology as long as they are new, inventive and industrially applicable/useful. Related to this species of law is the second-tier patent regime (known as petty patents or utility models).

Copyright law: Protection against copying for a duration, which ranges from 20 years (for broadcasts) to 70 years after the death of the author (authored works). Protected works range from sound recordings to performances to computer programs to artistic designs to printed works.

Trade mark law: Protection granted to distinctive marks which function as signs in the marketplace. Related to this area are the common law tort of passing off, unfair competition, and geographical indications.

Note: *WIPO Convention (1967), Art 2, para viii.

ration is that there is considerable overlap between the different rights causing ~~it~~ ~~y~~ to evolve continuously into a complex array of overlapping rights. One should ~~...~~ ~~il~~ as a discipline often intersects with liability rules on deceit, inequitable behaviour and secrecy. Thus, unpublished data can be protected (within certain jurisdictions) under copyright law, or under the common law of confidentiality, or trade secrets law. Similarly, in several EU countries, slavish copying of a product can be protected under unfair competition law, even where traditional intellectual property rights are inapplicable.[36]

Intellectual property is hardly a static conception, but is rather in a state of constant evolution and reconsideration. The first English and Venetian patent laws, for instance, were arguably public in nature as measures to harness and import foreign technologies; early copyright laws were employed largely to regulate and censor the indigenous printing trade. By the nineteenth century, intellectual property had become re-cast as a private economic right. By the end of the twentieth century, one finds environmental, health, library and educational sectors lobbying for a re-purposing of IP law as a legal system with increasing influence in the public sphere than before. Along with this evolution, one sees old rights changing and new rights being created. Essentially, when it comes to extending intellectual property to new types of creations, the options available to policy-makers are to fit such products into existing intellectual property categories or to create new intellectual property rights. In the words of Cornish:[37]

> Intellectual property may be extended to new subject matter either by accretion or by emulation. Accretion involves re-defining an existing right so as to encompass the novel material; emulation requires the creation of a new and distinct right by analogy drawn more or less eclectically from the types already known.

The accretion option was taken, for example, for photographs, films and computer software, where copyright law was stretched in ways that these burgeoning industries found to be satisfactory, albeit with some disagreement about how far and at what speed the stretching should be done. The accretion principle is frankly untenable in the case of sound recordings and television broadcasts. In such instances, the preferred option is Cornish's emulation option and we see further on in the book how new international norms are forged to embrace new entitlements (see Chapter 4). Utility models are another example of emulation although, as we will see, emulation is an inherently

---

[36] For the distinction between property and liability rules, see Guido Calabresi and A. Douglas Melamed, 'Property Rules, Liability Rules, and Inalienability: One View of the Cathedral' (1972) 85 *Harvard Law Review* 1089, 1092:

> An entitlement is protected by a property rule to the extent that someone who wishes to remove the entitlement from its holder must buy it from him in a voluntary transaction in which the value of the entitlement is agreed upon by the seller [...] Whenever someone may destroy the initial entitlement if he is willing to pay an objectively determined value for it, an entitlement is protected by a liability rule.

For a discussion on the considerable overlap between different IP rights, see U. Suthersanen, 'Breaking down the Intellectual Property Barriers' (1998) *IPQ* 267; and E. Derclaye, 'Overlapping Rights', in R. Dreyfuss and J. Pila (eds), *Handbook on Intellectual Property Rights* (Oxford: Oxford University Press, 2017).

[37] W.R. Cornish, 'The International Relations of Intellectual Property' (1993) 52(1) *Cambridge Law Journal* 46, 54–5.

risky approach in the case of inventions since the new rights are essenti
Chapter 10).

The emulation option also leads us to the *sui generis* ('of its own kind') option. .
sometimes chosen to enable innovators in certain fields of science, technology, culture o.
ness to appropriate the outputs of their research in a more effective and balanced manner that
policy-makers believe, would have been difficult to achieve under existing regimes. Examples include plant variety protection, the European database right, and the myriad *sui generis* design laws
including silicon chip topography design protection, vessel hull design protection, and the EU
Community design protection (see Chapter 7).

In conclusion, we should return to our earlier definition of IP and assert that in this book we
interpret the act of creativity as being any material realisation of an idea. From this premise, IP law
is the legal expression of people's recognised interests in valuable ideas, such interests being either
economic or moral in nature, or both. The rights holders are not necessarily creators themselves;
however, determining what is creative and protectable at the policy level is subject to constant revision and debate, and is an inherently political and commercial matter. It is rarely decided on the
basis of genuine objectivity. With this dynamic perspective, it seems inevitable that the intellectual
property regime would outgrow its eighteenth and nineteenth century boundaries to encompass
all sorts of new, esoteric subject matter such as plant varieties and semiconductor topographies,
often as it happens with relatively low thresholds of creativity. As ever, but more than ever before,
market trends and international business interests drive the political, legislative and judicial definitions of existing and potential intellectual property subject matter.

2

Justifying intellectual property

Historically, the first English and Venetian patent and copyright laws were driven by state and mercantilist interests. The laws were primarily tools for harnessing and regulating foreign technologies or censoring domestic printing.[1] The eighteenth century saw the rise of Renaissance and enlightenment doctrines, challenging spiritual authority and divinity, questioning the bases of laws and customs, and promulgating new rights and constitutions.[2] By the nineteenth century, IP had become intertwined with natural law and was increasingly viewed as private property, dealing with intangible rights residing in material objects.[3]

[1] C. May and S. Sell, *Intellectual Property: A Critical History* (Boulder: Lynne Rienner Publishers, 2005). For brief histories of specific IP rights, see Part II of this book.

[2] For a discussion on the Enlightenment debate in France in relation to copyright protection, see H. van den Belt, 'Robert Merton, Intellectual Property and Open Science: A Sociological history for our Times', in H. Radder (ed.), *The Commodification of Academic Research: Science and the Modern University* (Pittsburgh: University of Pittsburgh Press, 2010).

[3] F. Machlup and E. Penrose, 'The Patent Controversy in the Nineteenth Century' (1950) 10 *Journal of Economic History*, 5 *et seq.*

Significant new challenges were mounted against IP law towards the end of the twentieth century from pressure groups in relation to environmental, health and educational concerns. There is the growing view that IP law today has considerable influence in the global public sphere – a view that has undoubtedly been reinforced by the TRIPS Agreement. Conversely, more than ever before, market trends and international business interests rewrite the political and legislative boundaries of protectable subject matter; inevitably, the modern IP regime has outgrown its nineteenth-century boundaries, currently encompassing semiconductor topography rights, trade secrets, plant variety protection, database rights, and geographical indications.[4] This expansion is further manifested in the lumping together of rather disparate works under the same IP category, and the splitting of justifications in relation to other IP categories. The result is that the IP system embraces not only property principles, but also liability-based rules and criminal sanctions.

2.1 A PLURALISTIC FRAMEWORK

In our view, the main objectives of critically analysing IP justifications, which is what we do here, are twofold. The first accepts the likelihood that conventional justifications have shaped the contours of IP law. Accordingly, such an analysis provides a critical lens to view how the boundaries and extent of a specific IPR are pitched for the benefit of current creators and entrepreneurs and how doing so impacts on the interests and needs of today's public and tomorrow's burgeoning group of creative and entrepreneurial stakeholders. The second objective, and this is something we largely leave up to the reader, is to apply such analysis to help us to imagine what an optimal and contextually sensitive IPRs framework might look like; one that gives creators and entrepreneurs their due but achieves positive outcomes for follow-on creators and entrepreneurs and the general public that in the absence of IP would be precluded.[5]

Justifications thus claim to serve as theoretical and empirical tools of logic aimed at determining the optimal and fair boundaries for IP rights; and, of course, why we have these rights in the first place. As such they are all contestable. Some of the rationales are complementary, and others are contradictory, and nearly all *ex post facto*, based on existing regimes and histories. They do not necessarily lead to any grand claims. As Machlup sceptically observed:

> If we did not have a patent system, it would be irresponsible on the basis of our present knowledge of its economic consequences to recommend instituting one. But since we have

---

[4] R. Dreyfuss, D.L. Zimmerman and H. First (eds), *Expanding the Boundaries of Intellectual Property: Innovation Policy for the Knowledge Society* (Oxford: Oxford University Press, 2001).

[5] There is a tendency to assume that underlying and alternative norms that might achieve some of the same goals as IP protection do not exist and did not when patents and copyright came into existence. In fact, they may do, and have done. For example, in the clamour to create alternative positive legal rights for traditional knowledge, it tends to be overlooked that many indigenous groups have customary legal rules, regulations and norms, often articulated in spiritual discourse, that control knowledge in ways that are acceptable and functional from their perspectives. The problem is that these custom-based approaches are unknown or unrecognised, not that they do not exist. See Chapter 15.

a patent system for a long time, it would be irresponsible on the basis of our present knowledge to recommend abolishing it.[6]

As monopoly privileges, which is what IPRs started off as being, it is hardly surprising that they have always countered opposition. Indeed, the famous Statute of Monopolies, which brought patents for inventions into English law, largely sought to ban trading monopolies granted by the Crown; *inventor's* monopolies were the exception to the prohibition. There was a balance to be struck: not all monopolies were bad. The question was where to strike it. Early decisions on royal printing privileges simultaneously decried such monopolies while allowing exceptions where the technology or trade was disclosed publicly and disseminated. Philosopher J.S. Mill viewed 'free enterprise' based arguments against IP as an attempt to 'enthrone free stealing under the prostituted name of free trade, and make the men of brains, still more than at present the needy retainers and dependants of the men of money-bags'.[7]

Conversely, the present-day jurist Waldron cautions us against justifying IP rights merely on the basis that they are fair and necessary 'rewards or incentives' for the purpose of encouraging authors.

> It sounds a lot less pleasant if, instead of saying we are rewarding authors, we turn the matter around and say we are imposing duties, restricting freedom, and inflicting burdens on certain individuals for the sake of the greater social good [...] To say that rights are a means to an end is one thing; but the correlative proposition that some should be forced to bear sacrifices for the greater social good smacks dangerously of throwing Christians to the lions for the delectation of Roman society.[8]

Is this a matter for philosophers to decide alone, or do we need economists? Should economists in fact be the ones to lead the conversation? On whether arguments based on economic efficiency are more valid than those based on natural law or morality, the free market economist Friedman notes the 'curious and convenient coincidence: in most cases, the rules I conclude to be efficient are also the rules I believe to be just'.[9] This suggests, perhaps rather arrogantly, that philosophers are not required: leave it to the economists to determine what is just – on the basis of what is efficient. To the present authors such claims are highly questionable.

Thus, when we examine the justificatory framework for IP regimes, there are several levels of consideration. Since ancient times and within different civilisations, justifications have

---

[6] Subcomm. on Patents, Trademarks, & Copyrights, Senate Comm. on the Judiciary, 85th Cong., *An Economic Review of the Patent System*, 45–46 (Comm. Print 1958) (Study No. 15, prepared by Fritz Machlup).

[7] R. Godbolt, *Clothworkers of Ipswich* (1615), 252; J.S. Mill, *Principles of Political Economy* (1848) (London: Penguin, 1985), Book V, Chap X, ss 4–5, 296.

[8] J. Waldron, 'From Authors to Copies: Individual Rights and Social Values in Intellectual Property' (1993) 68 *Chi-Kent L.R.* 842, 842–4, 862.

[9] D. Friedman, 'A Positive Account of Property Rights', in E.F. Paul, F.D. Miller and J. Paul (eds), *Property Rights* (Cambridge: Cambridge University Press, 1994), 13.

incorporated a wide variety of metaphors and terms from other disciplines inclu
bour, desert and reward, natural rights, social justice and public interest, devel
human rights, protectionism and free trade, and free-riding ('reaping without
philosophical, social, economic and even religious arguments have been employe
protection of creations, investments and business assets, on behalf of authors, inventors, producers
and traders. While it is not entirely clear to us that all these disparate justificatory tools fit neatly
with each other, they do highlight how the successful deployment of contrasting justifications have
ensured a tremendous expansion in the nature and scope of IP law, albeit in contradictory and
quite confusing ways.[10]

2.1.1   Rawls and societal justice

Far from being a static concept, IP law has been in a state of constant evolution and reconsideration. On the subjective level, a work is the result of the creator's deep and inherent need or impulse
to imprint her thought and personality into the material and tangible world. From the objective
perspective, we can understand the impact of extrinsic driving forces. These include to earn an
independent living, fulfil employment or other contractual obligations, or to pursue market power
for one's business, to name just a few motivations that one could think of. In addition, creativity
may have an entirely altruistic motivation, namely, to maximise social welfare, or wishing to 'make
the world a better place' in more everyday language. Surely IP law should do more than just enable
creators to pursue their personal goals but also to help build a more just society that serves all of
its members.

In John Rawls's celebrated book, *A Theory of Justice*, we are offered a thought experiment that
helps us to imagine what a just society should look like and how we might go about creating one.[11]
According to Rawls's 'original position', we start from lacking the most fundamental information
about ourselves or our society. We may be geniuses or morons, young or old, male or female, eth-
nically in the majority or in the minority. We may be able-bodied or handicapped, rich people or
paupers, talented or not. We do not even know what our conception of the good life is to be, or
anything of our psychological make-up. Neither do we know a thing about the kind of society in
which we live. Behind this 'veil of ignorance', Rawls then invites us to consider what a just and fair
society would look like. His belief is that in pursuing our own interests we would not be utilitarian. Neither, evidently, does he think we would strive for economic bliss as defined by Pareto or
Kaldor–Hicks optimality (discussed below). Rather, we would opt for a set of principles – a hypothetical social contract – that would promote a society that was fair to everyone – just in case. One
can compare this conception of the 'social contract' to that of Hobbes, whose original position was

---

[10] For a similar approach to economic justifications, see T.-J. Chiang, 'The Paradox of IP' (2017) 30 *Harvard Journal of
Law & Technology*, Special Symposium 9. American scholars tend to adopt Fisher's four justifications for intellectual
property law: (i) utilitarian/economic; (ii) Lockean/labour desert; (iii) personhood/personality; (iv) promotion of cultural
development, see W. Fisher, 'Theories of Intellectual property', in S. Munzer (ed.), *New Essays in the Legal and Political
Theory of Property* (Cambridge University Press, 2000), 168–99.

[11] J. Rawls, *A Theory of Justice* (Cambridge, MA: Harvard University Press, 1971), 1–3.

the terrifying anarchy of the 'state of nature', and that of Locke whose state of nature was far more benign, and who sought to show that the individual society member's consent to be governed could be withdrawn if that government became despotic.[12]

Rawls's thought experiment cannot help us when it comes to the nitty-gritty of IP law and policy-making. But perhaps it can help us to come up with the right principles especially as Rawls's theoretical exercise of working out the abstract principles adopts a similar pattern to pluralist approaches, such as multi-stakeholder analysis. For example, several analyses adopt the rhetoric of the Romantic creator who apparently advocates property as the natural and just result of either the author's persona or the inventor's labour.[13] Nineteenth-century debates shifted towards a more societal approach with lobbyists arguing that creators' rights benefited the common weal by promoting and preserving indigenous literature, sciences and arts. Early philosophies relying on Locke, Kant, Mill, or Hegel offer a bifurcated rationale for IP: property rights are granted either on the principle of rewarding or incentivising labour, or on the more deontological and humanist principle of a person's right to autonomy, personality and dignity. In the mid-twentieth century, economic and institutional theories abounded, as IP was viewed as a regulatory and institutional tool, wielded by powerful corporate interests. The 1948 Universal Declaration of Human Rights codified the sentiment by recognising the creator's moral and material interests resulting from any scientific, literary or artistic production.[14] Moreover, the human development impacts, both good and bad, of IP rules – *contra* Friedman – make it irresponsible if not callous to treat economic efficiency as the sole and primary criterion for 'good' IP rules. As this book shows time and again, while IP is increasingly conceived as being little more than a certain class of business assets held by companies, this is not all they are. Oddly, some critics of IP hold to this view even as they decry the damage to social and cultural life wrought by IP 'extremism'.[15]

2.1.2 Stakeholder theory

A stakeholder is classically defined as 'any group or individual who can affect or is affected by the achievement of an organization's objectives'.[16] The theory holds that stakeholders can be natural persons, groups or legal entities; nor are they limited to 'insiders' within the organisation. Modern

---

[12] Ibid., 285–303; *Thomas Hobbes: Leviathan*, C.B. Macpherson (ed.) (Penguin Books, 1968); J. Locke, *Two Treatises of Government*, Peter Laslett (ed.) (Cambridge University Press, 1991).

[13] E. Young, *Conjectures on Original Composition* (1759), expounded in M. Woodmansee and P. Jaszi (eds), *The Construction of Authorship: Textual Appropriation in Law and Literature* (Duke University Press, 1994), Chapters 1 and 2. Also see A. Rahmatian, *Copyright and Creativity: The Making of Property Rights in Creative Works* (Cheltenham: Edward Elgar Publishing, 2011), Chapter 4.

[14] Universal Declaration of Human Rights, 1948, Art 27(1).

[15] For a quick review of these arguments, see C. McManis, 'A Rhetorical Response to Boldrin and Levine: Against Intellectual (Property) Extremism' (2009) 5(3) *Review of Law and Economics* 1081.

[16] R.E. Freeman, *Strategic Management: A Stakeholder Approach* (Boston: Pitman, 1984), 46. The earliest definition of stakeholder analysis stems from an early internal memo produced in 1963 by the Stanford Research Institute which defines stakeholders as: 'Those groups without whose support the organisation would *cease to exist*', in Freeman, 31.

stakeholder theories include any 'group or individual that can be influenced by, or can itself influence, the activities of the organisation'. One can push the definition further to include anyone who has a stake or a vested interest in the organisation, including all living entities, as well as non-living entities such as the biosphere and water.[17] If one applies a basic premise that the competing interests of the main stakeholders in the IP game should be balanced using all possible principles, one will have three main categories of actors: the presumptive initial creator; the underpinning industry/entrepreneur/investor; and the consumer/user/derivative innovator. There may be other stakeholders but this initial taxonomy lies at the heart of the different justifications for patent, copyright, and trade mark laws.

Given that stakeholders range from the rich and powerful to the poor and underprivileged, Rawls's challenge can perhaps help us construct a balanced and equitable framework. A framework that allows the maximisation of fairness for all, and an equal distribution of societal resources, unless an unfair distribution would make at least someone better off without harming others. One academic goes further and suggests that Rawls' contractarian theory should be incorporated in all future stakeholder analyses with a primary rule being: 'Rights holders are entitled to a degree of equality which results in maximum fairness to all right holders.'[18] After all patents are considered to be contracts between inventors and the state, while Kant's discourse on the author's right involves an inherent acceptance of an agency contract between author and publisher. Why not take this contract idea further along the lines of Rawls? And if we do so, what principles would we base our IP regimes upon to ensure equality and fairness for all?[19]

Those opposing such a suggestion might argue that utilitarianism and economic efficiency provide perfectly sound and practical starting points for designing IP rules and defending them from critics. Why should IP rights have to give priority to fairness for all members of society when this may be at the expense of the creators and may also compromise economic efficiency? Nowadays, patents (and other industrial property such as utility models and designs) are said to be an institutional means for investors and research corporations to be rewarded, or alternatively, incentivised, for investing in research and development, for deterring the misappropriation of their inventions by competitors, and for harnessing a nation's inventive or creative spirit.[20] Table 2.1 extrapolates the typical rationales of different stakeholders which underpin the IP regulatory framework.

---

[17] A. Friedman and S. Miles, *Stakeholders: Theory and Practice* (Oxford: Oxford University Press, 2006), 8–10; M. Starik, 'Should Trees have Managerial Standing? Toward Stakeholder Status for Non-human Nature' (1995) 14 *Journal of Business Ethics* 207–17.

[18] K. Gibson, 'The Moral Basis of Stakeholder Theory' (2000) 26 *Journal of Business Ethics* 245, 249.

[19] For a similar approach, see A. Chander and M. Sunder, 'Is Nozick Kicking Rawls's Ass? Intellectual Property and Social Justice' (2007) 40(3) *UC Davis Law Review* 563–80.

[20] See, for example, *Gorham Mfg. Co. v. White* 81 US (14 Wall) 511 (S Ct), 524-5, justifying design protection in terms encouraging the decorative arts, which in turn is 'a meritorious service to the public' and the European Commission Report, *Legal review on industrial design protection in Europe*, 2016, para 2.1, the EU design law is similarly premised on encouraging marketing tools (such as designs) which is essential in regional competitiveness.

Table 2.1 A stakeholder map

Stakeholders	Needs and Interests	Justification rhetoric	Jurisprudential and equitable rules
Creator, author, inventor, performers	Recognition, honour, respect, remuneration.	Reward, equity, dignitarian and ethical bases.	Natural property rights, right to be named author or inventor, moral right to integrity, right to equitable remuneration, compensation to employee-inventors.
Educational and scientific users, consumers, future and derivative creators and innovators	Access to and affordability of scientific and cultural data and technology, need for market substitutes (for example, generic products).	Public domain needs, social contract, human rights to health and education.	Data mining exceptions, limitations pertaining to educational uses, experimental use defences, public interest rules, freedom of expression, compulsory licensing.
Industries, single and corporate producers, entrepreneurs and broadcasters	Barriers to protect investment and deter competitors, incentives to encourage investment and capital.	Market regulation, fair competition, reward doctrines, demarcation between competitors.	Property rights, tort actions including misappropriation, trade dress, unfair competition rules, contractual boundaries, presumptive transfers of rights to producers, use of trade marks and signs to distinguish competitors.
Institutions, governmental offices, non-state actors, NGOs, collecting societies	Public choice and public interest theories, power and involvement in policy and law-making arenas, access to creators and consumer, observer status.	Democratic participation, efficient administration or reduction of transaction costs, public interest (or conversely, regulatory capture).	IP law, international IP agreements and treaties, medical data exclusivity rules, copyright collective management laws, private copying levies, access and benefit sharing (especially in relation to plant genetic resources).

Many individual inventors continue to claim their rights, at least implicitly, in terms of natural and dignitary rights. Romantic authorship rhetoric within copyright law allows authors to claim their natural and dignitary rights to their creative attainments. Ironically, we find corporations employing similar justifications based on dignitary rights and natural laws whenever it suits them – a recent example being the recording industry which persuades legislators to extend the sound-recording protection term by referring to impoverished elderly musicians subsisting on inadequate pensions;[21] or the recent spate of French litigation whereby companies repeatedly claim moral rights (see Chapter 5). On the other hand, IP industries routinely refuse to assist creators in pursuing stronger economic and moral rights, in practice and via contracts. Trade marks are trickier but nevertheless attempts are still made to place trade mark justifications within property and more recently human rights frameworks.[22]

2.1.3 Institutionalism

Institutionalism has its origins in the work of certain US economists of the late nineteenth and early twentieth centuries, such as Thorstein Veblen and Robert Hale. Economic institutions were central to their analyses of the economic system, and one of the most important of these institutions was property rights. The state plays an active role in defining, allocating and enforcing these rights, or providing the legal and administrative infrastructure to allow owners to enforce them. So for those who wonder 'what is the government doing when it "protects a property right"', Hale's response is 'passively, it is abstaining from interference with the owner when he deals with the thing owned; actively, it is forcing the non-owner to desist from handling it, unless the owner consents'.[23] Any changes to rights structures may well have distributional repercussions throughout the economy. Existing beneficiaries may have their rights strengthened, weakened or eliminated. New beneficiaries may appear. And those who are excluded may find their duties, responsibilities and liabilities increased further. Economic efficiency is unlikely to be considered a key objective for those interest groups most involved in designing rights structures. One approach is to accept that public servants in democracies strive to regulate in the public interest independent of the influence of special interests and are successful in doing so. It is further argued therefore that:

> The state acts in the public interest to tackle market imperfections. Public officials thus translate public preferences into legal regulatory institutions and elected legislatures direct

---

[21] D. Standeford, *EU Extends Copyright Protection From 50 To 70 Years, IP-WATCH*, 12/09/2011, available at http://www.ip-watch.org/2011/09/12/eu-extends-copyright-protection-from-50-to-70-years/.

[22] M. Lemley, 'The Modern Lanham Act and the Death of Common Sense' (1999) 108 *Yale Law Journal* 1687; A. Rahmatian, 'Trade Marks and Human Rights', in P. Torremans (ed.), *Intellectual Property and Human Rights* (Cheltenham: Edward Elgar Publishing, 2008), 335, 337.

[23] R.J. Hale, 'Coercion and Distribution in a Supposedly Non-Coercive State' (1923) 38(3) *Political Science Quarterly* 470, 471. See also T. Veblen, *Absentee Ownership and Business Enterprise in Recent Times* (New York: Huebsch, 1923); J.R. Commons, *Institutional Economics* (New York: Macmillan, 1934).

ırsuit of the public good. Those pressing for regulation, on such a view, act ʼblic interest.[24]

...ay be sceptical that this really happens, at least in the case of IP. On the one hand, it is arguable that IP systems are public policy regulatory institutions and as such may reasonably be judged according to how far they further the public interest (while admitting that 'the public interest' is hard to define). On the other hand, this perspective is challenged by other approaches that seek to explain how and why governments, legislatures and bureaucracies come to act as if the public interest is identical to that of powerful commercial interests whether or not this is really the case.[25]

New institutionalism is a further analytical approach for investigating the evolution of rights over time at national and international levels, for explaining how their present structures were arrived at and what the implications may be for the general public. Applying institutionalism also encourages us to expect that private interest stakeholders will play important roles in driving changes in IP as in other areas of regulation where the economic stakes are high. Where the new institutionalism perspective is helpful is in the way it treats property rights not as a priori rights but as state-granted rights. The state enjoys the formal powers to grant these rights, restructure them, supplement them, and take them away. But the state may not be in the best position to design the rights to achieve the most desirable outcomes. At the same time, it becomes very clear that, however rights are defined and allocated, the opportunity sets of everybody else are potentially, and for many people actually, affected.[26]

To what extent may such perspectives be relevant to IP rights? On the face of it, treating inventive knowledge as analytically comparable to scarce finite 'things' such as land and non-renewable resources is wrong. New knowledge is constantly being generated and is theoretically inexhaustible. Therefore, one might argue, granting property rights over newly created valuable intangibles can harm nobody; nor are others affected when the legal incidents of these rights are changed by statute or a new juridical interpretation, whether or not influenced by self-interested interpretative custodians. Doremus gives support to the view that IP rights are regulatory institutions that clearly affect the opportunity sets and freedoms of right and non-right holders, and are thus bound to be the focus of interest group competition when reforms are being considered:

> IPR reform potentially affects not only the interests of prospective rights holders and related users, but also the interests of long-standing right holders, whether or not they are in economically related arenas. Accordingly, one would expect the politics of IPR reform to be shaped considerably by the classic organizational characteristics of affected groups – their

---

[24] L. Hancher and M. Moran, 'Organizing Regulatory Space', and T. Makkai and J. Braithwaite, 'In and Out of the Revolving Door: Making Sense of Regulatory Capture', both in R. Baldwin et al. (eds), *A Reader on Regulation* (Oxford: Oxford University Press, 1998), 148–72 and 195–215.

[25] For an intriguing exploration on how culture, history, politics and ideology shape the way the public interest is framed and is translated into national or regional intellectual property policies, rules and institutions, see S. Parthasarathy, *Patent Politics: Life Forms, Markets and the Public Interest in the United States and Europe* (Chicago: Chicago University Press, 2017).

[26] G. Dutfield, 'Patent Systems as Regulatory Institutions' (2006) 54(1) *Journal of the Indian Economic Association* 62.

structure (concentrated or dispersed), their cohesiveness (cooperative or conflictual), and the general nature of the policy cleavage (within an industry or between industries).[27]

Merges agrees on the usefulness of the new institutional economics approach:

> Property rights, firms, institutions, governments: all of these are the subject of extensive study by social scientists operating within the NIE framework. It is time to integrate the study of IP rights into this framework [...] For here, finally, is an economics literature that makes thorough sense for our field.[28]

2.1.4 Traditional theories applied to intellectual property

The two traditional theories justifying IP have either consequentialist or deontological bases. The first approach argues that producing intellectual goods brings about valuable and correct societal consequences such as providing incentives or encouraging learning or incubating economic development or generally causing societal happiness. Thus, IP protection, irrespective of the legal classification (i.e., property, tort, civil or criminal rules), is a necessary institutional strategy aimed at protecting and advancing the manifold interests of influential stakeholders, and at maximising the production of IP goods. This justificatory approach is simple but powerful as it can accommodate rationales for IP regulation based on positive rights, social contract, utilitarianism, public choice, innovation and economics. Consequentialist thinking typically formed the basis of pre-modern IP privileges as well as modern statutory or constitutional rights. Thus, for example, US patent and copyright laws are premised on the fact that the rights are conferred on authors and inventors to 'promote the progress of science and useful arts'.[29] As the Supreme Court succinctly noted in *Sony Corp. v. Universal Studios, Inc.*, there are two different justifications for copyright protection under the Constitution: reward for the authorial labour and creativity, and stimulation of general creative activity and access to products of such activity. The Court then held that the reward aspect of copyright law was a secondary consideration. Instead, the ultimate aim of copyright law is the achievement of a *public purpose*: to stimulate creative activity for the general public good and to ensure public access to the products of such activity.[30]

Similarly, EU IP laws are justified on several consequentialist platforms including, inter alia, the need for the copyright system to 'protect and stimulate the development and marketing of new products and services', the desirability for trade mark law to promote 'the development of economic activities' and to prevent the distortion of competition, and the need for the patent system to 'respect the fundamental principles safeguarding the dignity and integrity of the person' and to encourage 'research into and production of biotechnological medicines which are

---

[27] P.N. Doremus, 'The Externalization of Domestic Regulation: Intellectual Property Rights Reform in a Global Era' (1996) 3(2) *Indiana Journal of Global Legal Studies* 361.

[28] R. Merges, 'Intellectual Property Rights and the New Institutional Economics' (2000) 53 *Vanderbilt Law Review* 1857, 1877.

[29] US Constitution, Art 1, § 8, cl. 8.

[30] 464 US 417 (S Ct, 1984), 429–432.

needed to combat rare or "orphan' diseases"'.[31] More holistically, the harmonisation of national IP law within the EU is justified on the grounds of fundamental freedoms of property, trade and the public interest.[32]

The second traditional justification for IP rights emphasises creators having a just and fair reward based on natural rights, and dignitary rights namely a right to control one's image, reputation, and personality.[33] By focusing on the inventor and author as individuals, this approach shifts the act of creativity from the divine or from the natural to the private personae. Immanuel Kant and Johann Gottlieb Fichte, for example, insisted that authors did not imitate nature, but rather 'spoke' original works derived from their inner personalities. The French intellectual Denis Diderot argued for the inviolability of ideas as natural and eternal property.[34] The reward doctrine, in particular, is ubiquitous in many cultures and histories: the idea of patent protection, for example, can be traced back to the fourth century where Hippodamus of Miletus, a Greek architect, proposed a system of rewards to those who discovered new and useful things to the state.[35]

Deontological justifications for IP emphasise that rights are enforced with respect to persons who are entitled to IP as a matter of natural rights or as a matter of classical liberal or human rights or as a matter of duty. Kant's essay on author's rights, discussed below, is a prime example of this theoretical axiom, which focuses on natural rights and duties rather than on the consequences of an action. To take another example, there are rules within IP laws, which recognise the moral rights of attribution and integrity of individual authors and inventors. These rules are based on the view that such rights are manifestations of the duty of others to respect a creator's dignity and name, and also arise from the natural principle of the inviolability of persons.[36]

We now focus on writings of foundational thinkers on intellectual property, starting with John Locke.

---

[31] Recital (2), EC Directive 2001/29/EC on copyright in the information society; Recitals (3) and (5), Regulation (EU) 2017/1001 on the European Union trade mark; Recitals (16)–(18), EC Directive 98/44/EC on the legal protection of biotechnological inventions.

[32] TFEU, Art 114 (intellectual property law justified for functioning of the market); Protocol 1 of the European Convention on Human Rights, Art 1; Charter of the Fundamental Rights of the EU, 2000, Art 17(2) (intellectual property clarified as a human right); and Treaty of European Union, Art 6(1), (3) (fundamental rights are EU rights).

[33] S. Breyer, 'The Uneasy Case for Copyright' (1970) 84 Harv L. Rev 281, 289–91.

[34] M. Woodmansee, The Author, Art & the Market: Rereading the History of Aesthetics (New York: Columbia University Press, 1994), 53–4; Henk van den Belt, 'Robert Merton, Intellectual Property and Open Science: A Sociological History for our Times', in H. Radder (ed.), The Commodification of Academic Research: Science and the Modern University (Pittsburgh: University of Pittsburgh Press, 2010).

[35] R.P. Merges and J.F. Duffy, Patent Law and Policy (Lexis, 2002), 1–2.

[36] C.R. Beitz, 'The Moral Rights of Creators of Artistic and Literary Works' (2005) 13(3) Journal of Political Philosophy 330, 337.

2.2 LOCKE ON LABOUR AND REWARD

Irrespective of whether Locke's theory of property is classified as deontological or utilitarian, employing Locke to rationalise IP rights invites controversy.[37] It is suggested that Locke starts his justificatory journey for private property within natural law but increasingly progresses towards a consequentialist argument. He tempers his initial approach with his provisos to argue for a more societal-based property regime that has limits, especially where it conflicts with fundamental human entitlements. This, he argues, is necessary to build a civil society. Nevertheless, the notion of an inalienable or natural right to the works of the mind corresponds with the Lockean concepts of property and 'commons'; moreover, it converges somewhat with other schools of thought, including economic reasoning.

2.2.1 Labour

The right to property exists naturally since one has a right to the fruits of one's labour. Consequently, it is a government's duty to protect such natural rights, especially 'as property rights are one of the bastions that are supposed to protect the individual from the overreaching power of the state'.[38] This is the starting analytical strand in Locke's view namely that all resources given by God are part of the 'commons' other than one's own body; and the use of such resources involving the expenditure of labour results in the extension of property from the labourer's body to the resources:

---

[37] A.P. Brogan, 'John Locke and Utilitarianism' (Jan., 1959) 69(2) *Ethics* 79–93, arguing that Locke's basic tenets are the basis of utilitarian philosophy; Viktor Mayer-Schonberger, 'In Search of the Story: Narratives of Intellectual Property' (2005) 10 *Va. J.L. & Tech.* 1, 4–5, categorising Locke as the basis of the utilitarian basis of intellectual property law; Robert Merges, *Justifying Intellectual Property* (Harvard University Press, 2011), 38, note 24, disagreeing vehemently that Locke's views are utilitarian; Barbara Friedman, Note, 'From Deontology to Dialogue: The Cultural Consequences of Copyright' (1994) 13 *Cardozo Arts & Ent. LJ* 157, 162 *et seq.*, suggesting that Locke begins his theory by employing a libertarian and deontological argument, but shifts away towards a more collectivist and social approach once he gets to civil society concerns. The following authors have, to some degree, referred to Locke's concept in relation to intellectual property: Waldron, *supra* note 8, 871, 879–84, using the concept of corrodible and non-crowdable objects in a convincing argument against the application of Locke *in toto* to intellectual property; J. Litman, 'The Public Domain' (1990) 39 *Emory L.J.* 965, 999; J. Hughes, 'The Philosophy of Intellectual Property' (1988) 77 *Geo. L.J.* 287, 311–15, applying Lockean concepts to the idea-expression dichotomy; P.J. Proudhon, in D. Kelly and B. Smith (eds), *What is Property* (Cambridge: Cambridge University Press, 1994), 84–5, disagreeing with Lockean justification of property as the latter is created only by prescription; A. Strowel, *Droit d'auteur et copyright – Divergences et convergences – Etude de droit comparé* (Paris: LGDJ, 1993), 185–6, 188–90, the ramifications of Locke's concept of property within the context of the French Revolution, resulting in the rationale for *droit d'auteur*; W.J. Gordon, 'A Property Right in Self-Expression: Equality and Individualism in the Natural Law of Intellectual Property' (1993) 102 *Yale L.J.* 1533, arguing for a more natural law appreciation of Locke, especially in relation to justifying exclusions and limitations; and L. Zemer, 'The Making of a New Copyright' (2006) 29(3) *Harvard Journal of Law & Public Policy* 891, arguing that Locke's writings are applicable to intellectual property, based on a reading of Chapter V in the *Two Treatises*, as well as his *Essay Concerning Human Understanding* and his letter *Liberty of the Press*.

[38] J.L. Schroeder, 'Unnatural Rights: Hegel and Intellectual Property' (2006) 60 *U. Miami L. Rev.* 453, 462.

[E]very man has a property in his own person [...] The labour of his body, and the work of his hands [...] are properly his. Whatsoever then he removes out of the state that nature hath provided, and left it in, he hath mixed his labour with, and joined to it something that is his own, and thereby makes it his property. It being by him removed from the common state nature hath placed it in, it hath by this labour something annexed to it, that excludes the common right of other men: for this labour being the unquestionable property of the labourer, no man but he can have a right to what that is once joined to, at least where there is enough, and as good, left in common for others.[39]

The attraction of Locke's labour lies in extending the individual's inalienable ownership of his body and his labour to ownership rights over the original commons. As long as one has mixed one's labour (be it physical or mental labour) with resources found in the commons, one can appropriate this resource and own it as personal property. As Merges explains:

The creator of a new work claims property not by virtue of contributing some new thing to a preexisting thing, but to the transformation of the preexisting thing by the expenditure of labour. Inventors, authors, composers, and the like do not add physical items like juice to the prior art or to culture; they add effort and on that basis, claim property rights.[40]

The notion of transforming the original commons was applied in the early nineteenth century by English courts to justify property rights in derivative works or follow-on innovations, as well as to have expansive notions of fair dealing since 'everyone has an inalienable right to his labour'.[41] Locke's reliance on labour and effort further serves to justify property rights in works which evince little creativity, but are the product of intensive investment or organisational effort (whether it be in the form of capital or labour), including databases and compilations, non-original publications, sound recordings, sub-patentable innovations, and broadcast productions. The labour theory can be extrapolated into further consequential reasoning: not only can the natural author claim a right but so can legal entities – including pharmaceutical and entertainment corporations, producers, performers, etc.

---

[39] John Locke, *The Second Treatise of Government*, in *Two Treatises of Government* (London: J.M. Dent, 1993), Chapter V, para 27.

[40] R. Merges, *Justifying Intellectual Property* (Harvard University Press, 2011), 15.

[41] An early English decision indicates the attraction of the labour theory – thus, it was held in *Hogg v. Scott* (1874) 18 LR Eq 444, 445:

[...] the true principle in all these cases is, that the Defendant is not at liberty to use or avail himself of the labour which the Plaintiff has been at for the purpose of producing his work – that is, in fact, merely to take away the result of another man's labour, or, in other words, his property.

Indeed, historically, courts tended not to find infringement if copying an existing work produced a 'new work' – *Longman v. Winchester* (1809) 16 Ves Jr 269, 272, holding that there is nothing to 'prevent any person from giving a work of this kind; if it is the fair fruit of original labour: the subject being open to all the world'.

Lockean theory has been criticised as applying implausible seventeenth-century notions on tangible property to modern intangible rights.[42] One primary objection is that Locke's theory works in the tangible world, where the appropriation of physical matter from the commons does diminish the opportunities for others to gain from the commons. This does not work in relation to intangible creations where the labourer, in the absence of prescriptive laws, does not diminish anything by using incorporeal elements from the commons. A correlated proposition is that Locke's doctrine is only applicable to subject matter of finite capacity, as in crops or land, but not in instances of non-finite resources such as informational goods. There is some ambiguity here as Locke himself has a more generalised concept of property, which is not confined to 'physical' objects but also includes property in person, life and liberty.[43]

As we see from other justifications, intangible things defy the presumptions within property rights as they are characteristically non-rivalrous and only capable of arising out of the scarcity of objects. Locke's contemporary David Hume would not have recognised IP as a form of property. As noted by twentieth-century economist Arnold Plant:

> The significance of private property in the economic system was enunciated long ago with great clarity by David Hume in his *Enquiry Concerning the Principles of Morals*. Property, he argued, *has no purpose where there is abundance*; it arises, and derives its significance, out of the *scarcity* of the objects which become appropriated, in a world in which people desire to benefit from their own work and sacrifice.[44]

It is instructive that Locke himself acknowledges this non-rivalrous aspect of information in that basic concepts such as numbers and the alphabet are part of an inexhaustible and infinite stock.[45] The counter-argument to this is that there is far too much focus on labour as expended on the commons, which allows for excessive capture of what we might refer to as the information ecosystem. Plant hinted at this in the 1950s when he noted with wonderment at how technological developments in photography, sound recording, film and broadcasting spheres had captured, isolated, and transformed transient information such as images, sound and performances into permanent records:

> No human voice, no musical performance by human agency, intended to be recorded and overheard, no sound, even those outside the range of the unassisted ear, need now be missed

[42] Merges, *supra* note 40, 36–9; Waldron, *supra* note 8, 842, 871, 879–80; W. Kingston, *Innovation, Creativity and Law* (Deventer: Kluwer Academic Publishers, 1990), 83.

[43] Locke, *supra* note 39, paras 123, 173.

[44] Original emphasis. Sir Arnold Plant, 'Economic Theory Concerning Patents for Inventions' (1934) 1 *Economica* 30; also see H.L. MacQueen, 'Law and Economics, David Hume and Intellectual Property', in N. Kuenssberg (ed.), *Argument Amongst Friends: Twenty-Five Years of Sceptical Enquiry* (Edinburgh: David Hume Institute, 2010), 9–14.

[45] John Locke, *An Essay Concerning Human Understanding* (1690), Alexander Campbell Fraser (ed.) (Oxford: Clarendon Press, 1894), Book II, Chapter VII, para 10.

by anybody, anywhere and at any time that he might wish to pay his share of the cost of recording it and reproducing it.[46]

In this instance, a Lockean perspective would advocate that organisations which enable such transformations, by virtue of mixing their capital/labour with preexisting creations, are entitled to property rights in the resultant sound recordings, broadcasts and films. Turning to Merges once again:

> The relationship between labor, appropriation, and human flourishing lies at the heart of Locke's thinking. His property theory is not a theory about noninterference with tangible goods that have been labored over. It is a theory why individual appropriation helps people to survive and thrive. Locke's theory does not concern itself with the difference between tangible and intangible assets; that is large irrelevant. It is centrally concentred with the conditions under which an individual claim to property may be justified in light of the overarching goal of human flourishing.[47]

This sort of reasoning does nevertheless lead us to another concern with the labour theory, which is that almost anything can constitute private property if labour is expended on it. Moreover, the property right can vest in any body, collective or organisation. Consider the following example in relation to ethnobotanical and traditional knowledge. Pharmaceutical companies which rely on ethnobotanical knowledge and traditional knowledge will argue that much of the informational resources residing within plant genetic resources have little utility to humankind unless the active pharmaceutical ingredient is identified, synthesised or distilled, and finally manufactured in an industrially efficient manner. The Lockean approach readily provides an equitable basis for conferring property rights on the pharmaceutical company since R&D (labour) is expended to transform the raw biological or genetic resources and/or traditional knowledge into a useful, mass-produced product. Conversely, the local or indigenous group can argue that they have property or remuneration claims, based on the 'firstness' argument: namely, that they are the first to formulate the relevant link between existing genetic or plant resources and the location and medicinal utility of such resources. This 'firstness' claim, especially as embedded in some of Locke's passages, is discussed by Munzer and Raustiala:

> Assigning a property right to the party who was 'first' promotes order because often priority can be determined even when other things cannot. Thus, property rights to a wild animal might be given to the first person who captures it, and property rights to land might be granted to the first person who occupies the land and makes productive use of it. Lurking in this thinking may be some form of a desert claim, for granting ownership to those who are second might equally promote order [...].[48]

---

[46] Sir Arnold Plant, *The New Commerce in Ideas and Intellectual Property* (London: Athlone Press, 1953), 7–9.

[47] Merges, *supra* note 40, 40–41.

[48] S. Munzer and K. Raustiala, 'The Uneasy Case for Intellectual Property Rights in Traditional Knowledge' (2009) 27 *Cardozo Arts & Ent. L.J.* 37, 62–5.

A further dilemma develops should one go further and apply Lockean logic to all labour-derived claims such as self-replicating products like genetically modified seeds. The company that is responsible for the invention, development and distribution of genetically modified seeds is of course entitled to a property claim in the form of a patent (assuming patents are allowed on plants). However, what of the farmer who buys such patented seeds, and toils away to harvest the product of those seeds: is he entitled to claim ownership rights as to the full use or sale of the harvested seeds? Can he plant these seeds to produce a second generation and repeat the process of harvesting and replanting *ad infinitum*? Patent law answers these questions, but Locke's labour theory of property seems not to offer much help.[49]

2.2.2   Locke's commons

The main counter-argument against the sceptics is to point out that under Locke, property is not absolute. His provisos are set thus:

> [...] there is enough, and as good left in common for others'; and 'as much as any one can make use of to any advantage of life before it spoils; so much he may by his labour fix a Property in. Whatever is beyond this, is more than his share, and belongs to others. Nothing was made by God for Man to spoil or destroy.

Therefore, the initial common resources or their equivalent should be used and appropriated by means of labour but only according to the labourer's share. Any excess to the legitimate share would be invalid and contrary to the claims of others to the common resources. The importance of maintaining the commons is underpinned by the spoilage provision, which suggests that the use and propertisation of the commons must be non-wasteful and non-destructive.[50]

Locke's demarcation between the commons and private property is arguably equivalent to the parallel demarcation within IP law of the public domain from protectable intellectual subject matter. Locke's initial resources are the raw materials and basic building blocks of creation (let's call them Lockean blocks). The Lockean block theory, as advocated by us, advances that the public domain, which comprises a vast repository of basic building blocks of creation per se, as well as combinations or permutations of such building blocks, is a natural exclusion zone in respect of any property right. So much is acknowledged, for example, by the recent US Supreme Court's jurisprudence on software patenting, forbidding protection of 'building blocks of human ingenuity'.[51] Merges offers a similar approach to the public domain:

> [...] the addition of individual labor is what transforms public domain starting materials

---

[49] See *Bowman v. Monsanto Co*, 133 S Ct 1761, 1768 (S Ct, 2013), 1764–6, where the US Supreme Court had to determine the extent of a farmer's rights over lawfully obtained genetically modified seeds. See the discussion below in Chapter 14.

[50] Locke, *supra* note 39, paras 27, 31, 39, 41.

[51] *Alice Corp. v. CLS Bank International*, 134 S Ct 2347 (2014); also see *Gottschalk v. Benson* 409 US 63 (1972), 'Phenomena of nature, though just discovered, mental processes, and abstract intellectual concepts are not patentable, as they are the basic tools of scientific and technological work.'

nique creative product. So for IP the public domain serves the same function as the *i* nature in Locke's property theory. It supplies the raw material, the thick scattering of unowned resources, that surrounds the individual creator.[52]

From his view, we should turn to the spoliation proviso in order to see why Locke remains relevant within IP theory – it is a legal device to enable law-makers to check the instances of overextending IP rights.[53] This would probably be relevant in cases where copyright is eagerly extended to pure data compilations or commonplace themes, or when patent law is pushed through reach-through or ever-greening clauses to protect known products and/or known uses, or when trade mark law is cleverly utilised to extend the protection of subject matter of expired patent or design rights. The criticism that can be levelled is that Locke's notion of property does not offer guidelines, which would enable us to construct a rule of law to determine protectable subject matter, as opposed to common resources. Indeed, it can be, and has been, argued that all works of intellect are 'emanations of the current state of civilisation' and the prior state of art, which should remain as common property.[54] A dogmatic adherence to the Lockean block theory would thus suggest that informational resources should always remain in the commons (such as ideas or discoveries or even traditional knowledge), or should be returned to the commons after a short exclusive duration (such as inventions or in relation to things which have become *de facto* standards), or should be understood as allowing non-exclusive, shared consumption with others (as envisaged under compulsory licensing rules or competition law).

2.3   ECONOMIC RATIONALES

Economic justifications focus on explaining why IP rules are necessary to encourage innovation and development within competitive market environments. These justifications should be viewed cautiously as much of the analyses rely on instinctive guesses as opposed to unbiased and objective empirical data. Moreover, do economic rationales help us control overly-strong IPRs? The latter can lead to the growth of rapid short-term monopolies which, once established, are hard to dislodge (as Microsoft, Google and GlaxoSmithKline have demonstrated). Moreover, the power of IP owners is not limited to one primary market but extends to secondary, downstream markets. Thus, scholars of law and economics, while accepting the incentive function of the patent system, doubt whether the system is necessary for inducing the optimal or even an adequate amount of innovation.[55]

---

[52] Merges, *supra* note 40, 36.

[53] Ibid., 56.

[54] Jessica Litman notes that architects and sculptors 'all engage in the process of adapting, transforming, and recombining what is already out there in some other form', J. Litman, 'The Public Domain' (1990) 39 *Emory L.J.* 965, 966. This reasoning was also used to argue why inventions could never be protected – see Machlup and Penrose, *supra* note 3, 13–14.

[55] Machlup and Penrose, ibid., 1, notes 78–84 and text attached; Adam B. Jaffe and Josh Lerner, *Innovation and its Discontents: How our Broken Patent System is Endangering Innovation and Progress, and What to do About it* (Princeton, NJ: Princeton University Press, 2004); U. Suthersanen, G. Dutfield and K.B. Chow, *Innovation without Patents: Harnessing the Creative Spirit in a Diverse World* (Cheltenham: Edward Elgar Publishing, 2007), 57–61.

2.3.1   Basic tenets

The conventional view is that economic well-being depends on achieving a workable competitive market economy. A competitive market is achieved when the number of firms selling a homogenous commodity is so large, and each individual firm's share is so small, that no individual firm finds itself able to influence appreciably the commodity's price by varying the quantity of output it sells.[56] In setting out such conditions for an ideal economy, traditional and contemporary concerns lie with: (i) how can a firm or nation generate an effective allocation of resources so as to satisfy economic needs, and (ii) whether such an allocation can simultaneously generate the highest possible level of social well-being (and even happiness[57]) throughout the community as a whole. The difficulties arising from Locke's property theory as applied to IP correspond to those arising when applying economic arguments as to why an efficient allocation of informational resources requires property rights.

IP is categorised as an unusual economic resource. As it comprises intangible creations and informational goods, it is treated as a public good due to two unique characteristics. First, unlike tangible land, intangible creations are non-rivalrous. The consumption of the good by one does not limit or leave less for the other to use. Second, intangible things are non-excludable in that it is practically difficult to exclude others from consuming the good.[58] Therefore, once an idea is disclosed and in the public domain, it loses its scarcity. Once information is disclosed to all, it can be used, enjoyed, consumed, transformed simultaneously by all. As Harris emphasises, the abstract entity is 'incapable of being exclusively occupied by anyone, and it will never wear out or be destroyed through use'.[59] In such instances and where the information/idea entity falls within the IP typology, the law creates an artificial scarcity.

Otherwise, if we only rely on the exigencies of market forces to efficiently allocate such intangible and informational things, the result is free-riding.[60] The assumption here is that free-riders who misappropriate the creative efforts of others will offer these goods (or services) at a lower cost, thus undermining the original creator or producer of such goods. Is this necessarily harmful within a competitive market economy? Traditional schools dictate that free-riding is symptomatic of a privately supplied public good, and this can lead to non-appropriability: due to the unavoidable presence of free-riders, the production and dissemination of public goods is predicted to be lower

---

[56] F.M. Scherer and D. Ross, *Industrial Market Structure and Economic Performance* (3rd ed., Houghton Mifflin, 1990), 16.

[57] E. Derclaye and T. Taylor, 'Happy IP: Aligning Intellectual Property Rights with Well Being' (2015) *IPQ* 1.

[58] W.M. Landes and R.A. Posner, *The Economic Structure of Intellectual Property Law* (Cambridge, MA and London: Belknap Press/Harvard University Press, 2003), 13–16; *cf* K. Arrow, 'Welfare Economics and Inventive Activity', in *The Rate and Direction of Inventive Activity* (Princeton: National Bureau of Economic Research, 1962), 617–18. For a discussion on public goods, see P. Drahos, 'The Regulation of Public Goods' (2004) 7(2) *The Journal of International Economic Law* 321.

[59] J.W. Harris, *Property and Justice* (Oxford: Oxford University Press, 1996), 44.

[60] H. Demsetz, 'Towards a Theory of Property Rights', (1967) 57 *American Economic Review* 347, 347–8, 'A primary function of property rights is that of guiding incentives to achieve a greater internalization of externalities.' For a criticism of Demsetz, who views intellectual property, like real property, as existing to internalise negative externalities like free-riding, see M. Lemley, 'Property, Intellectual Property, and Free Riding' (2005) 83 *Texas Law Review* 2031.

_ ഗe optimally efficient. This leads to two further assumptions. First, with unchecked appropriation of goods, there will be an oversupply of goods leading to a drop in trading value as there will be no scarcity of goods. Secondly, the creator or manufacturer will have difficulty in appropriating the value of the goods through its sale and dissemination, which will lead to a drop in the supply of such goods; thus there is a looming market failure scenario as consumer demand will be inadequately met.[61] To counteract this market failure and to create an artificial scarcity, state intervention in the form of property rights may be the most efficient means by which to secure beneficial progress at a minimum public cost.

Patents are especially susceptible to the economic argument that industrial innovation requires incentivisation. Technical innovation has been institutionalised to the extent that most justifications for patent law are premised on the corporate persona, with its teams of inventors backed up by a fully funded research and development laboratory. Thus, the 20-year patent term is not so much a reward as an encouragement to firms to invest in important industries. The rationale is that all investments in inventions and their subsequent commercial development are 'sunk' costs: once spent, such costs are irretrievable. Thus, corporations need some degree of protection from competition – and ideally, to be in the market holding a monopolistic power, with the ability to control pricing.[62] Patents ideally confer a property right allowing the corporate investor to not only protect the investment but to commercialise the patented subject matter in various ways such as assigning or licensing the patented product or process. The trade-off within patent law is easy to perceive and understand: the 20-year anti-competitive monopoly which ensures new products and processes is set off by the short duration, and the fact that the patent system serves as an accessible information source.[63] It is even argued that stronger IPRs will ensure that a country's resources will be allocated to the most valuable uses, thus promoting the country's economic growth.[64]

Such a view is consistent with J.S. Mill's view who, though being vehement as to the crippling effects of state monopolies, nevertheless accepted the need for monopolistic patent rights, and the compensation to intellectual labourers:

> That he ought to be both compensated and rewarded for it, will not be denied, and also that if all were at once allowed to avail themselves of his ingenuity, without having shared the labours or the expenses which he had to incur in bringing his idea into a practical shape, either such expenses and labours would be undergone by nobody except very opulent and very public-spirited persons or the state must put a value on the service rendered by an inventor, and make him a pecuniary grant.[65]

---

[61] Landes and Posner, *supra* note 58, 22–3.

[62] Scherer and Ross, *supra* note 56, 615–22.

[63] For an extensive economic modelling discussion on optimal patent life and the trade off to maximise consumer welfare, see W.D. Nordhaus, *Invention, Growth and Welfare: A Theoretical Treatment of Technological Change* (Cambridge, MA: MIT Press, 1969), Chapter 5.

[64] G.S. Jr. Lunney, 'Patents and Growth: Empirical Evidence from the States' (2009) 87 *N.C.L. Rev.* 1467.

[65] Mill, *supra* note 6, Book V, Chapter X, ss 4–5, 295–6. For other supporters of the reward doctrine, see Machlup and Penrose, *supra* note 3, 17–21.

Similarly, Adam Smith, who was a firm supporter of granting a temporary monopoly to inventors, viewed patents as a justifiable exception to free trade principles. The utilitarian perspective also applies the Benthamite idea of 'the greatest good for the greatest number'.[66] Cloaked in more current concepts such as 'maximisation of social welfare' or 'wealth-maximisation', the focus is to measure the consequences of allocating rights, and to eventually achieve a balanced costs-benefits framework in the protection of intangible things. Whether the allocation is efficient or good is dependent on a theoretical evaluation of the consequences that can or do arise, and whether the beneficial effect of the right outweighs the negative consequence. This theory, which utilises various elegant propositions (such as the Pareto or Kaldor–Hicks efficiency criteria) can also be devilishly difficult to implement in practice – especially as a means to achieve balances between strong property rights, public domains, and sustainable outputs.[67]

2.3.2 Alternative schemes and new technologies

Should intellectual 'property' in fact be treated at all as property? According to Landes and Posner:

> 'Depropertizing' intellectual property rights may sometimes be the soundest policy economically. Even the strongest defenders of property rights acknowledge the economic value of preserving public domains – that is, of areas in which property is available for common use rather than owned – even in regard to physical property and a fortiori in regard to intellectual property.[68]

The criticism against employing the property metaphor for informational goods is not new. MacQueen points to Scottish philosophers such as Hume, Smith and Kame who rejected the reliance on the property metaphor to explain copyright and patent:

---

[66] A. Smith, *Wealth of Nations* (London: Henry Growde, 1904), Book V, chap. 1, Part III, 388; J. Bentham, 'A Manual of Political Economy', in *The Works of Jeremy Bentham* [1843], Vol. 3, published under the Superintendence of his Executor, John Bowring (Edinburgh: William Tait, 1838–1843) (available online at oll.libertyfund.org).

[67] The theoretical underpinnings and language of traditional economic rationales can also add to the confusion. Take for example the notion of 'optimal efficiency'. Optimal allocative efficiency (or 'Pareto efficient allocation of resources' named after the economist Vilfredo Pareto), is reached when there can be no possible reallocations or changes so as to make one individual better off without making someone else worse off. Market failure (where the market outcomes are not Pareto-efficient) is said to be caused by a variety of factors, including the public goods phenomenon, the existence of market power to the extent of absence of perfect competition, and situations where externalities exist. Scholars all acknowledge that in reality, it is impossible to generate a Pareto-optimal market for any goods since it is contingent on there being a purely competitive market, including the absence of externalities or public goods, the presence of private rights, and the perfect enforcement of such rights. Thus, the alternative Kaldor–Hicks efficiency or the wealth maximisation criterion (named again after its inventors – Nicholas Kaldor and John Hicks). According to this, any change within an economy that favours *some individuals* at the expense of others will constitute an improvement, if the gains to the winners exceed the losses to the losers. For a concise introduction, see N. Mercuro and S. Medema, *Economics and the Law: From Posner to Post-Modernism* (2nd ed., Princeton, NJ: Princeton University Press, 2006), Chapter 1.

[68] Landes and Posner, *supra* note 58, 14–15.

They preferred to see copyright (and patents) as grants of particular (or 'exclusive') privileges by the state to individual subjects which created markets that otherwise would not exist, because it was in the public interest that they should. But the grants were carefully limited – for example, to specific periods of time – to avoid or minimise the possible ill-effects of the private monopolies to which they gave rise.[69]

The aforementioned Arnold Plant was another critic of the property regime in relation to intellectual labour.[70] In his works on patent and copyright, he argues that the literary industry progressed remarkably well without copyright institutions, with authors receiving remuneration by other institutional means. Plant concluded that it is possible to envisage book production without copyright laws with authors or scholars willing to pay for publication of research. An obvious counter-argument to this is that without adequate IP protection, publishers and other entrepreneurs would be reluctant to make the necessary investment, especially in less popular and more subsidised works, for example, academic works or documentaries. What Plant and others show is that the property-based economic model does not accommodate nor explain all market and societal behaviours. For instance, authors who embrace the Creative Commons movement do not necessarily appreciate that the phenomenon is based on copyright; such property rules are necessary for authors to assert their moral rights of attribution and integrity (especially in countries with weak moral rights such as the US).

Plant's questioning as to the need for formal rules, and especially for entrepreneurial rights is valid if one accepts that contemporary creative and innovative industries are increasingly engaging in digital production and dissemination, coupled with enhanced technological protection tools. Such industries can now use different contractual business models coupled with accepted e-commerce norms, to attract readership and viewing consumption and payment without reliance on property rights. Investors in academic publishing may not need property rights since they can rely on a framework fusing contract and patronage from learned societies, universities and industries. Digitisation and open access schemes, underpinned by soft law options (such as the Creative Commons licensing scheme), advertising revenues, and even private self-funding, allows for a more flexible author model, within the learned and academic scholarly world. The open access movement in the UK, for instance, has cleverly twinned the public pressure on universities to make publicly funded research accessible and free of charge with the private interests of the oligopolistic publishing industry to safeguard their control on academic publishing. This sounds all to the good. In practice, however, universities (and their faculty) assume all academic journal articles are owned by the publishers (although much is actually dependent on individual contractual terms) and offer untenable sums of money to them for the release of journal articles into the public domain (see Chapter 12). In other words, the publishing world as envisaged by Plant in the 1930s can survive without IP laws and without imposing 'locks' on the

---

[69] MacQueen, *supra* note 44, 12.

[70] Plant, *supra* note 44, 42 *et seq.*; Plant, *supra* note 46, 7–9.

goods as long as someone else underwrites the costs. Whether this particular approach, which seems tantamount to corporate welfare, is fair is another question.[71]

Much of the criticisms levelled against the property-based model are in relation to the unacceptable cost-benefit trade-offs, namely that the economic efficiencies, rewards and incentives dolled out by IP rules are often outweighed by the costs imposed on society. The latter comprise transaction and rent-seeking costs. Transaction costs within any IP framework would comprise: search costs (discovering someone who wants to buy what you want to sell/licence or vice versa); bargaining or negotiation costs; and enforcement costs. The difficulty arises inevitably from the intangible nature of IP. Due to the protectable core being conceptual and non-material, there can be an over-allocation of rights, and the wrong subject matter is treated as being protected. This, in turn, results in very high search and enforcement costs. Hence, the accepted exclusion of ideas from copyright laws or the exclusion of discoveries and theories from patent laws.[72]

Related to this is the second major cost of the property rights system, where low thresholds of protection coupled with a wide scope of protection can lead to rent-seeking behaviour. An excessive investment of resources can be caused by those firms indulging in patent races or encouraging imitative creativity, merely in order to secure monopolistic positions. Wasteful rent-seeking behaviour has further consequences such as the use of such resources to persuade governments or legislatures to impose regulations, which assist in the creation of monopolies or pursuing litigation exercises under various rights in order to secure a monopoly position.[73]

One suggestion is to employ the classical 'access versus incentives' balancing approach.[74] This approach allows us to appreciate why IP laws can behave differently from rights in physical property. The following are examples of how courts and law-makers restrain rights by way of creativity thresholds, limiting extent or duration of rights, and by excluding subject matters that could otherwise be protectable:

---

[71] In relation to digitisation and open access schemes, see U. Suthersanen, 'Creative Commons — the Other Way?' (2007) 20 *Learned Publishing* 59–68; G. Frosio, 'Open Access Publishing: A Literature Review', 2014, CREATe Working Paper 2014/1, available at http://www.create.ac.uk/publications/000011. In relation to publishers' rights, see the proposed press publishers' right – European Commission's Synopsis Report on the Results of the Public Consultation on the Role of Publishers in the Copyright Value Chain, available at http://ec.europa.eu/information_society/newsroom/image/document/2016-37/synopsis_report_-_publishers_-_final_17048.pdf; R. Xalabarder, 'Press Publisher Rights in the New Copyright in the Digital Single Market Draft Directive', CREATe Working Paper 2016/15 (December 2016), available at https://zenodo.org/record/183788/files/CREATe-Working-Paper-2016-15.pdf.

[72] TRIPS Agreement, Art 9(2); WCT, Art 2; EPC, Art 52(3); *Diamond v. Diehr* 450 US 175 (S Ct, 1981), 185: 'Laws of nature and natural phenomena are in essence manifestations of nature and are not new, free to all men and reserved exclusively to none.'

[73] For a general discussion on rent seeking behaviour, see Mercuro and Medema, *supra* note 67, 9–67; and Landes and Posner, *supra* note 58, 17–18. *Cf* K. Dam, 'The Economic Underpinnings of Patent Law' (1994) 23 *J. Leg. Stud.* 247, 252–63, not viewing all rent-seeking behaviour as being a problem as it may lead to new products and lower prices, as well as allowing for cross-licensing opportunities.

[74] Landes and Posner, ibid., 20–21.

(i)   IPRs are granted on fulfilling specific criteria such as novelty and inventive step for patents, originality for copyright, and distinctiveness for trade marks;

(ii)   IPRs contain limitations and public policy measures to promote follow-on creativity and ensure public access where its denial is causing harm;

(iii) IPRs are limited in duration from 20 years (patents) to 70 years *post mortem auctoris* (copyright/authors' rights) – though trade marks are potentially infinite subject to renewals;

(iv)   IPRs are *ab initio* excluded from certain types of creative innovation: on technical, public policy or morality grounds, including discoveries, scientific theories, ideas, commonplace phrases and designs, and dangerous or immoral inventions.

At the other end of the spectrum, we see a push towards non-IP, alternative compensatory models which arguably accommodate societal well-being including the following:

- public ownership or public subsidies, which would incentivise and reward creative and entrepreneurial efforts, allow access to IP goods such as education and health, and/or stimulate more relevant and targeted research in areas of national concern such as climate change or public health;[75]

- governmental economic intervention including targeted taxation concessions, procurement policy, research funding and grants, and venture capital;[76]

- commercial sales taxes or private commercial levies on copying equipment or broadband or internet services (such as current schemes in various EU member states);[77]

- tort law or a liability-rules regime such as a confidentiality, trade secret, trade dress or unfair competition laws;[78]

---

[75] D.G. Lichtman, 'Pricing Prozac: Why the Government Should Subsidize the Purchase of Patented Pharmaceuticals' (1997) 11 *Harvard Journal of Law & Technology* 123.

[76] Mill, *supra* note 6, approving of patent and copyright laws, arguing that in their absence, the result would be 'a small temporary tax, imposed for the inventor's benefit, on all persons making use of the invention', s 4. Also see T. Pogge and A. Hollis, 'The Health Impact Fund: Making New Medicines Accessible to All', Report for Incentives for Global Health, 2008; S. Shavell and T. van Ypersele, 'Rewards versus Intellectual Property Rights', (2001) 44(2) *Journal of Law and Economics* 525; J. Stiglitz, 'Give Prizes Not Patents', *New Scientist*, 16 September 2006, 21; S. Sidney, 'On the Effect of Prizes on Manufacturers' (1862) 10 *J. Soc'y Arts* 374.

[77] A.L.D. Pereira, 'Levies in EU Copyright Law: an Overview of the CJEU's Judgments on the Fair Compensation of Private Copying and Reprography' (2017) 12(7) *Journal of Intellectual Property Law & Practice* 591–600.

[78] Gordon, for example, uses the externality notion to conclude that intellectual property is 'tort law turned upside down'. W. Gordon, 'Intellectual Property', in P. Cane and M. Tushnet (eds), *The Oxford Handbook of Legal Studies* (Oxford: Oxford University Press, 2003), 622–3. See also the extensive writings of J.H. Reichman in relation to hybrid intellectual property rights such as designs or plant variety in order to argue for a more liability-based intellectual property regime including 'Using Liability Rules to Stimulate Local Innovation in Developing Countries: Application to Traditional Knowledge', in K.E. Maskus and J.H. Reichman (eds), *International Public Goods and Transfer of Technology Under a Globalized Intellectual Property Regime* (Cambridge University Press, 2005), 337–66; and 'Of Green Tulips and Legal Kudzu: Repackaging Rights in Subpatentable Innovation' (2000) 53 *Vanderbilt Law Review* 1743.

- contract-based solutions including digital rights management and technology-based access mechanisms;
- royalty-free licensing or voluntary commons, such as under the Creative Commons, Science Commons and Eco-Patent Commons schemes;[79]
- compulsory licensing of all IPRs;
- inducement or innovation prizes.[80]

As economists Boldrin and Levine boldly assert: 'There is also much evidence that ideas flourish in competitive markets without government intervention in the form of patents and copyright.'[81] Their argument is that a sole focus on IPRs as a means of ameliorating free-riding effects or boosting innovation can deliberately lead to inefficient monopolistic markets leading to fewer and lower-quality goods at greater costs. A better course of action would be to increasingly tighten IPRs and to instead provide for alternative incentivisation and funding mechanisms such as those listed above, including government monopolies regulated through compulsory licensing.[82] After all, the first mover would normally enjoy *de facto* advantages. Scherer and Ross opine that bringing a new product onto the market in technological and pharmaceutical industries, irrespective of the patent protection, confers:

> A substantial reputational advantage over imitators, permitting the innovation to maintain elevated prices while defending a sizable market share. Also […] the first mover has a head start in the race down learning curves, gaining cost advantages which, if exploited sufficiently aggressively, can be used to deter entry and enjoy supra-normal profits until the relevant technology matures.[83]

---

[79] J.H. Reichman, A.K. Rai, R.G. Newell and J.B. Wiener, 'Intellectual Property and Alternatives: Strategies for Green Innovation', Chatham House Energy, Environment and Development Programme Paper No. 08/03, December, 2008 available at http://scholarship.law.duke.edu/cgi/viewcontent.cgi?article=2915&context=faculty_scholarship.

[80] J. Love and T. Hubbard, 'The Big Idea: Prizes to Stimulate R&D for New Medicines' (2007) 82(3) *Chicago-Kent Law Review* 1519; F. Abbott and J.H. Reichman, 'The Doha Round's Public Health Legacy: Strategies for the Production and Diffusion of Patented Medicines Under the Amended TRIPS Provisions' (2007) 10(4) *Journal of International Economic Law* 983; *cf* for an empirical historical account of why innovation prizes do not necessarily work, see Z. Khan, 'A Page of History: Patents, Prizes and Technological Innovation' (2013) 5 *WIPO Journal* 17.

[81] M. Boldrin and D. Levine, 'The Economics of Ideas and Intellectual Property' (2005) 102(4) *PNAS* 1252, 1254, 1256:
Although many economists would not recommend eliminating patents and copyrights altogether, all recognize a strong need for reform. We suggest that insofar as it is desirable for the government to provide extra incentives for invention and creation, this is not best done through grants of monopoly, but rather through proven mechanisms such as subsidies, prizes, or monopoly regulated through mandatory licensing.

[82] Tun-Jen Chiang, 'The Paradox of IP' (2017) 30 *Harvard Journal of Law & Technology* Special Symposium 9; and also M. Boldrin and D. Levine, *Against Intellectual Monopoly* (Cambridge University Press, 2010).

[83] Scherer and Ross, *supra* note 56, 627.

2.3.3   Innovation and development[84]

As the economist Ricardo stated more than a century ago, 'nearly all useful inventions depend less on any individual than on the progress of society'.[85] This accords with the Schumpeterian view that innovation does not occur purely within a natural or legal individual but tends to arise from social interaction, which involves both creators and other actors.[86] This utopian vision materialises within certain political, economic and social environments, where IPRs are allowed to act as competitive boosts to national innovation and growth. From this standpoint, the argument for patents is that they promote innovation by conferring market power on the individual or firm, enabling either of them to introduce new technologies by placing a protective buffer of protection against other competitors; this guaranteed term of patent protection will act as a stimulus for further innovation. Societal welfare is assured as the innovation, in exchange for patent protection, will be divulged in the form of detailed patent specifications thus ensuring a public knowledge base upon which future technological progress will be built.[87, 88] Since monopoly privileges and exclusivity arising from patents affect other public spheres, the rigorous eligibility standards are essential to prevent excessive patenting.

A more nuanced argument is that IP rights are 'a drain on learning and a source of market power that is inimical to development'.[89] While patent protection can certainly contribute to innovation and economic growth in developed countries, this is not necessarily true in developing countries. This is ascribed to the fact that patent protection tends to be useful within industrial activities only after countries have achieved a threshold level of indigenous innovative capacity, accompanied by an extensive science and technology infrastructure.[90] The corollary argument is that patent registration figures are also not indicators of national innovation.[91]

---

[84] This discussion is also linked to Chapter 10, section 10.2.

[85] Cited by Machlup and Penrose, *supra* note 3, 17–18.

[86] J.A. Schumpeter, *The Theory of Economic Development: An Inquiry into Profits, Capital, Credit, Interest, and the Business Cycle* (Transaction Publishers, 1983 [1934]), 66.

[87] The extensive historical and current literature on the link between intellectual property, public interest, and national innovation includes J. Harrison, *Encouraging Innovation in the Eighteenth and Nineteenth Centuries: The Society of Arts and Patents, 1754–1904* (Gunnislake, Cornwall, High View, 2006); Commission on Intellectual Property Rights (2002); K. Maskus and J. Reichman (eds), *International Public Goods and Transfer of Technology Under a Globalised Intellectual Property Regime* (Cambridge University Press, 2005); K. Maskus, *Private Rights and Public Problems: The Global Economics of Intellectual Property in the 21st Century* (PIEE, 2012). For a sceptical view of the role played by the intellectual property system in industrial progress, see, D. Vaver, 'Some Agnostic Thoughts on Intellectual Property' (1991) 6 *Intellectual Property Journal* 125, 126–7.

[88] E. Kitch, 'The Nature and Function of the Patent System' (1977) 20 *Journal of Law & Economics* 265, 281.

[89] Maskus, *supra* note 87, 234.

[90] Y.K. Kim, K. Lee, W.G. Park, K. Choo, 'Appropriate Intellectual Property Protection and Economic Growth in Countries at Different Levels of Development' (March 2012) 41(2) *Research Policy* 358, 359, citing L. Kim, *Imitation to Innovation: The Dynamics of Korea's Technological Learning* (Harvard Business School Press, 1997).

[91] Adam B. Jaffe and Josh Lerner, *Innovation and Its Discontents: How Our Broken Patent System is Endangering Innovation and Progress, and What to do About It* (Princeton University Press, 2004), 11 *et seq.*

This argument is often utilised to argue for *sui generis* patent-type rights such as the utility model law. The utility model right is perceived as being beneficial for developing countries seeking to advance their technological capacities through local innovation by small- and medium-sized enterprises (SMEs). For example, Juma put forward five reasons why hybrid patent-type rights are appropriate for many developing countries. The first is that they enable artisans to secure protection for innovations that do not meet the stricter novelty and inventive step requirements of patent law. Developing economies, with their cottage and fledgling industries, may produce more incremental innovations. Second, they make it possible to increase the role of small-scale innovators and artisans in economic development and help them stay in business in the face of new technologies that might threaten their livelihoods. Third, they act as a spur to enhanced levels of innovation. Fourth, they are cheaper to acquire than patents. And finally, they may become a source of data on innovative activity and experience in technological management.[92]

A well-cited study by Kumar found that in East Asian countries (namely, Japan, South Korea and Taiwan), a combination of relatively weak IP protection and the availability of second-tier rights like utility models and design patents encouraged technological learning in their developmental years.[93] The weak IPRs helped by allowing for local absorption of foreign innovations and R&D spillovers. Second-tier systems encouraged minor adaptations and inventions by local firms. Consequently, such economies became stronger partly because local technological capacity was sufficiently advanced to generate a significant amount of innovation, and also as a result of international pressure. The report situates India's experience as being somewhat similar, except that in her case, no second-tier protection was provided. While this apparently did not hurt the growth of the Indian chemical or pharmaceutical industries, it may have hindered the development of innovative engineering industries.[94] Similarly, the study by Kim et al. in relation to Korean firms and indigenous technological developmental noted that:

> Utility model innovations contribute to firm performance when firms are technologically lagging and that those minor innovations can be a learning device and thus a stepping stone for developing more patentable inventions later on. Upon reaching higher levels of technological capabilities, firms become more reliant upon patents and less on utility models. Thus the lesson here is that patent protection enhances innovation and economic growth in countries where the capacity to conduct innovative research exists. Where this capacity is weaker, a system that provides incentives to conduct minor, incremental inventions is more conducive to growth.[95]

---

[92] C. Juma, *The Gene Hunters: Biotechnology and the Scramble for Seeds* (Princeton University Press, 1989), 231–2.

[93] N. Kumar, 'Intellectual Property Rights, Technology and Economic Development: Experiences of Asian Countries' (2003) 38(3) *Economic and Political Weekly* 209, 211–12; D. Prud'homme, 'Utility Model Patent Regime "Strength" and Technological Development: Experiences of China and other East Asian Latecomers' (2017) 42 *China Economic Review* 50, 59 *et seq.*

[94] Kumar, ibid.

[95] Kim et al., *supra* note 90, 358–75.

The Korean case study concludes that strong IP rights do not necessarily lead to development, but that countries have to tailor their regimes to pick the appropriate cocktail of rights, which will suit the national innovative and economic environment.

A more recent 2013 Australian economic review confirmed that the economic effect of utility models decreases with the rise of technological capacity in industries; the report concluded however that the continued use of utility models in Japan, Germany, France and Italy suggests that these low-threshold and low-cost property rights may have a role in innovation and economic growth even in developed economies.[96]

Other studies similarly note that countries do tailor their patent and utility model regimes as part of national innovation policies. The studies also indicate that developing economies can have mixed results due to changing national policies: on the one hand, utility model and patent laws are transplanted from other more mature legal regimes, and then countries are faced with the task of transforming such laws to meet evolving local needs of the recipient country. Thus, patent regimes have been weakened in certain countries in order to shift low-income economies into the middle-income stages.[97] Conversely, technologically strong and developed economies begin to distrust an 'easy' system and switch to more rigorous patent and utility model regimes, as their concerns shift to competitiveness, the need to attract foreign direct investment, and the use of the utility model system by foreign companies. We discuss these issues in Chapter 10.

2.4 NATURAL RIGHTS, PROPERTY AND AUTHORSHIP

There is a surge of interest from creators, industries and law-makers as to the argument that IPRs are necessary for the recognition of personal or expressive autonomy of creators (and producers). Machlup and Penrose's classic discussion on the history of patent law in the nineteenth century clearly shows that the discourse between economists and philosophers grappled with a similar juridical dilemma. Do property rights emanate from natural law? Are they a natural mechanism whereby the worker-inventor's inalienable right to her labour is recognised? Was perpetual patent protection for inventions necessary for industrial progress?[98] German philosophers, including Fichte, Kant, and Hegel, reflect a similar dilemma in their writings as to whether authorial, printing and publishing rights should emanate from labour (akin to Locke's theory on property), natural rights or on dignitary grounds.

---

[96] J. Zeitsch, *The Economic Value of the Australian Innovation Patent: The Australian Innovation Patent Survey*, Verve Economics, March 2013, available at http://www.acip.gov.au/reviews/all-reviews/review-innovation-patent-system/.

[97] Prud'homme, *supra* note 93, citing many empirical studies but of note is that by K. Maskus and M. Penubarti, 'How Trade-related are Intellectual Property Rights?' (1995) 39(3–4) *Journal of International Economics* 227.

[98] Machlup and Penrose, *supra* note 3, 9 *et seq.*

2.4.1   Kant on authors' entitlements

Consider the famous seventeenth and eighteenth-century books fairs in Europe, esp. German-speaking towns of Frankfurt, Leipzig and Nuremberg. These were the main ￼ ￼ for the barter trade in books. The prevailing institutional ethos was that the property in books vested in whoever held the physical manuscript, once sold or assigned to the publishers. The author as a legal object as such was an unstable concept, whereas the physical pirated book was more accessible, affordable, and not immediately against the public interest. Any solution would still remain precarious in the then political and legal environment, which comprised hundreds of small German-speaking independent states, most of which having no compensation schemes or cross-border/extraterritorial treaties in place.

It was within this pre-unified German-speaking region that Kant's 1785 essay on the unlawfulness of reprinting books was written. It clearly sets out the growing dissatisfaction of authors under the traditional patronage system; it has also resulted in very diverse interpretations as to what Kant really meant vis-à-vis authors' rights.[99]

One view is that the Romantic movement generated authors such as Goethe and Kant who began to conceive of themselves as individuals. For them, authors 'spoke' original works which were derived from their inner personalities.[100] Some of this is derived from Kant's essay on counterfeit works where he argues for the right of an author to prevent unauthorised book publishing. First, he internalises the source of inspiration within the author (thereby implicitly rejecting the notion that man's creation emanates from an extrinsic muse or divine beings). Secondly, the internalised author-centred inspiration is subsequently equated with 'original genius'. The book is no longer merely a physical commodity to be traded but is the manifestation of the authorial personality and speech. Kant explains:

> For the author's ownership to his thoughts (assuming in the first place that such ownership applies according to external rights) remains his in spite of any reprinting […] A book is the instrument for delivering a speech to the public – not just thoughts, as paintings for example do, or the symbolical representation of some idea or event. From this follows the essential point that it is not a thing which is thereby delivered, but an act [opera], namely a speech, and, what is more, literally. By calling it a mute instrument I distinguish it from those means there are for communicating a speech through sound – like a speaking-trumpet, for example, or even the mouths of other persons.[101]

---

[99] Immanuel Kant, 'On the Wrongfulness of the Unauthorised Publication of Books', 1785, reprinted in Mary J. Gregor (ed.), *Cambridge Edition of the Works of Immanuel Kant: Practical Philosophy* (Cambridge University Press, 1996). For other views and versions of the essay, see F. Kawohl, 'Commentary on Kant's essay *On the Injustice of Reprinting Books* (1785)', in L. Bently and M. Kretschmer (eds), *Primary Sources on Copyright (1450–1900)*, www.copyrighthistory.org (2008) (henceforth referred to as *Primary Sources on Copyright*), and Merges, *supra* note 40, 77 *et seq.*

[100] M. Woodmansee, *The Author, Art and the Market: Rereading the History of Aesthetic* (Columbia University Press, 1994), 51–4, Chapter 2; R.R. Bowker, *Copyright: Its History and Its Law* (Houghton Mifflin, 1912), 12.

[101] Kawohl, *supra* note 99.

Hence, where the book manifests itself as speech, the book is no longer an inert thing or opus; instead it transforms into the author's ownership. If we explore this argument visually – see Figure 2.1 below – one also appreciates this nascent understanding of the conceptual distinction between the *corpus mechanicum* (the tangible object) and the *corpus mysticum* (the intangible creation), the latter being the repository of property retained by the author.

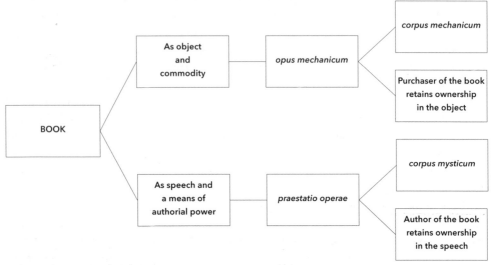

Figure 2.1 Splitting the 'book'

Kawohl's Commentary on Kant's essay can be a rewarding read though we are not entirely convinced with several aspects of it. His view is that Kant eschewed the property construct entirely by equating books to actions (as opposed to goods). Kawohl claims that this theoretical didactic made Kant's approach deeply unpopular for generations, although he adds that Kant's analogy is perhaps very relevant in understanding contemporary issues on non-proprietary regulation of information.[102] In any event, it should be remembered that Kant resolutely avoids the Lockean labour construct to underpin the authors' property but instead employs the speech metaphor as the basis for realising two types of entitlements within a single book, i.e., the printed paper and the author's ideas. A similar trend towards splitting the written work was drawn 40 years earlier in the English decision of *Pope v. Curll* where Lord Chancellor Hardwicke forged a ground-breaking judicial rule as to what copyright (as recognised within the Statute of Anne 1710) meant:

> I am of opinion that it is only a special property in the receiver, possibly the property of the paper may belong to him; but this does not give a licence to any person whatsoever to publish them to the world, for at most the receiver has only a joint property with the writer.[103]

---

[102] Kawohl, ibid.; and also see Woodmansee, *supra* note 100, 37.

[103] *Pope v. Curll* [1741] 26 ER 608; for a detailed discussion of why the decision is pivotal in Anglo-American law, see M. Rose, *Authors and Owners: The Invention of Copyright* (Harvard University Press, 1993), Chapter 4.

Part of Kant's essay relies on agency principles to underpin the unlawfulness of the co.. action. For Kant, authorial power is not economically feasible without the author part up his right to control printing and distribution of the work to an authorised publish.. ..oth the authorised publisher and the counterfeiter engage in publishing the author's book to the same public, then 'the labour of the one must render that of the other useless and be ruinous to both of them'. Indeed, much of the essay's focus is on the economic effects of two competing substitute products within the same consuming market, and the eventual conclusion that book piracy results in more harm to the publisher than to the author. Nevertheless, Kant's concern for the economic ramifications of piracy are, obviously based on his belief that authors should be vested initially with property rights. The publisher may have the 'right to appropriate th[e] profit to himself', but this right arises from the publisher being the authorial agent, and with the author's property vesting as a natural right.[104]

2.4.2   Hegel on property and autonomy

Another normative framework, often considered as the alternative to Locke's theory on property, centres on the dynamic relationship between personal autonomy, individuality and property. Hegel's theory centres on the notion of the 'will' as being the core of an individual's existence. Unless one actualises or concretises the 'will', the autonomous individual will not gain the capacity to self-determine, or to actualise freedom. Thus, in order to achieve fulfilment as a person, one must have control over one's resources within the environment and this can be effectively achieved by property rights.[105] Failure to obtain property is akin to a failure to attain self-conscious knowledge of oneself as a free person.[106]

Unlike Locke and Kant, Hegel directly addresses the issue of property rights in 'intellectual objects', albeit in a slightly convoluted manner. Hegel admits, as Kant before him, that products of the mind can become 'things' which may then be produced by other people.

> The result is that by taking possession of a thing of this kind, its new owner may make his own the thoughts communicated in it or the mechanical invention which it contains, and it is ability to do this which sometimes (i.e., in the case of books) constitutes the value of these things and the only purpose of possessing them. But besides this, the new owner at the same

---

[104] For the different translations, editions and controversies, see Merges, *supra* note 40, notes 39 and 40, 340–41; disagreeing that Kant was responsible for the personhood theory, see M. Spence, *Intellectual Property* (Oxford: Oxford University Press, 2007), 50.

[105] G.W.F. Hegel, *Philosophy of Right* T.M. Knox (trans. and ed.) (Oxford: Clarendon Press, 1967), First Part: Abstract Right, Sub-section 1 on Property.

[106] D. Knowles, *Hegel and the Philosophy of Right* (London: Routledge, 2002), 112; J. Waldron, *The Right to Property* (Oxford: Clarendon Press, 1990), 351 *et seq.*; C.J. Berry, 'Property and Possession: Two Replies to Locke: Hume and Hegel', in J.R. Pennock and J.W. Chapman (eds), *Property* (New York: New York University Press, 1980), 89–100, 97.

time comes into possession of the universal methods of so expressing himself and producing numerous other things of the same sort.[107]

Justifying IP, Hegel categorically states:

> Since the owner of such a product, in owning a copy of it, is in possession of the entire use and value of that copy qua a single thing, he has complete and free ownership of that copy qua a single thing, even if the author of the book or the inventor of the machine *remains the owner of the universal ways and means of multiplying such books and machines*, etc. Qua universal ways and means of expression, he has not necessarily alienated them, but may reserve them to himself as means of expression which belong to him.[108] (Emphasis added)

Thus, an author or inventor reserves the right of manufacture or reproduction, although his right to control individual products of his mental property may be exhausted since Hegel is clear that the owner of such a 'product' can use that particular copy. Hegel does challenge one's categorisation of his philosophy as being purely based on personhood since he consequently states that the author's or inventor's right and power to reproduce 'has a special character, viz. it is that in virtue of which the thing is not merely a possession but a capital asset [...]'. Indeed, some parts of his writings on this issue adopt consequentialist and social welfare terms. He classifies IP as a purely negative right for instance, and states that the primary:

> [...] means of advancing the sciences and arts is to guarantee scientists and artists against theft and to enable them to benefit from the protection of their property, just as it was the primary and most important means of advancing trade and industry to guarantee it against highway robbery.[109]

As matter of natural right, one of Hegel's basic tenet is that property can be occupied, can be alienable and is capable of abandonment. Indeed, it has been argued that alienation of property through contract is the key to the recognition of a persona, and that Hegel is vital for understanding why contracts of/for service for labour are justified (though perhaps not abandonment of property):

> The reason I can alienate my property is that it is mine only in so far as I put my will into it. Hence I may abandon (derelinquere) as a res nullius anything that I have or yield it to the will of another and so into his possession, provided always that the thing in question is a thing external by nature.[110]

---

[107] Hegel, *supra* note 105, para 68.

[108] Ibid., para 69.

[109] Ibid.

[110] Ibid., para 68. See also J.L. Schroeder, 'Unnatural Rights: Hegel and Intellectual Property' (2006) 60 *U. Miami L. Rev.* 453, 476–8.

There are, nevertheless, limits to the type of properties that one can alienate. Goods which constitute an individual's 'own private personality' and the 'universal essence of [his] self-consciousness' are inalienable and imprescriptible. Thus, slavery is not permissible under his theory as this would be tantamount to alienating one's whole universal essence and personality. This aspect can be helpful in understanding why some aspects of IP rights are inalienable such as the right to be named as inventor, or the moral right of integrity and attribution.

It is further arguable that his philosophy accommodates the need for excluding and limiting certain types of intellectual work, so as to allow others to access and use IP works and produce derivative works:

> Thus copyright legislation attains its end of securing the property rights of author and publisher only to a very restricted extent, though it does attain it within limits. The ease with which we may deliberately change something in the form of what we are expounding or *invent a trifling modification in a large body of knowledge or a comprehensive theory which is another's work*, and even the impossibility of sticking to the author's words in expounding something we have learnt, all lead of themselves […] to an endless multiplicity of alterations which more or less superficially stamp someone else's property as our own. For instance, the hundreds and hundreds of compendia, selections, anthologies, &c., arithmetics, geometries, religious tracts, &c., show how every new idea in a review or annual or encyclopaedia, &c., can be forthwith repeated over and over again under the same or a different title, and yet may be claimed as something peculiarly the writer's own. *The result of this may easily be that the profit promised to the author, or the projector of the original undertaking, by his work or his original idea becomes negligible or reduced for both parties or lost to all concerned.*[111]

It is well worth noting Hegel's take on some specific issues: exceptions for teachers, including law professors (good), plagiarism (bad but to be solved as a matter of honour, rather than legislation), transformative use (good, but worryingly reduces profits to author and producer), and minor modifications on inventions (allowable). These concepts have in time distilled into legal norms such as the educational exceptions or the three-step tests found in international instruments.[112] Hegel is rather prescient in predicting that the line between misappropriation and inspiration is thin, and difficult to draw. What is food for thought is whether future international law and policy should be based, as he suggests, more on autonomy, dignity and honour rather than on positivist or economic rationales.

---

[111] Hegel, ibid., paras 66 and 69 (emphasis added).

[112] Ibid., para 69; for example, Berne Convention Art 10(2), teaching exceptions; TRIPS, Arts 13 and 30, three-step test for limitations and exceptions.

3
International governance of intellectual property

The commercial importance of IP rights has grown considerably since the nineteenth century but has really accelerated since the 1970s. The background to this growth is the incessant and increasing pressure on businesses and national economies to be competitive in goods other than non-primary products and basic commodities, and the tremendous expansion of global trade in manufactures and services. This puts a premium on creativity in terms of bringing new products and services to market, and of marketing existing products and services more effectively. It also encourages both market leaders and aspiring new entrants to use IP rights as business assets, and as a means of restraining imitation and derivative innovations by competitors for limited times.

IP rule-making has become ever more responsive to this increased pressure. National governments, for instance, are keen to enhance the industrial landscape and competitiveness of their economies to effectively give transnational corporations what they want, at least most of the time. Consequently, since the 1960s and 1970s and up to the present, developed-country intellectual property regimes have undergone some quite profound changes. These changes are of three kinds.[1]

The first of these is the widening of protectable subject matter, including a tendency to reduce or eliminate exceptions. Examples of such accretion include the extension of copyright protection to computer programs as if they are literary works, the application of patent protection to cover computer programs (or at least 'computer-implemented inventions'), life forms, cells and genes, and the removal of exclusions on product patents for drugs. This has been achieved in various ways including legal reforms, rule changes, court decisions, and through the assumption (propounded by legal practitioners who may have a vested interest) that the inclusion of such newly valuable products is fully consistent with existing practices and legal doctrines. The second change is the creation of new rights. Examples of new systems created during the twentieth century included plant variety protection (or plant breeders' rights) and semiconductor topography rights. *Sui generis* traditional knowledge protection can be regarded as an emerging right, although we do not yet know when or if it will be provided in an international treaty. Both changes have given rise to concerns about overlap where products, techniques, and other intangible assets may be protected directly or otherwise by two or more types of IP right.[2] The third change was the progressive standardisation of the basic features of IP rights. For instance, patent regulations increasingly provide 20-year protection terms, require prior art searches for novelty and examinations for inventive step (or non-obviousness), assign rights to the first applicant rather than the first inventor, and provide protection for inventions in a widening range of industries and technological fields.

These developments in IP law, all of which began in Europe or North America, are spreading to the rest of the world at an accelerating pace through the World Trade Organization-administered TRIPS Agreement, bilateral, multilateral and regional free trade agreements (FTAs). Consequently, national IP regimes throughout the world are being increasingly held to standards of protection based on those of the most economically and politically influential countries. Admittedly there are reversals and counter-trends towards differentiation. In addition, some developing countries are developing norms of their own that differ from those of Europe and North America and these have the potential themselves to become adopted widely. You will find some examples in this book. It is hardly a foregone conclusion that the role of developed countries as IP policy-makers and developing countries as policy takers will continue indefinitely. Where did this internationalisation process start? Or to put it another way, what are the origins of international IP rule-making? To answer, we go back to the late nineteenth century.

---

[1] G. Dutfield, *Intellectual Property Rights and the Life Science Industries: A Twentieth Century History* (Aldershot: Ashgate, 2003).

[2] N. Wilkof and S. Basheer (eds), *Overlapping Intellectual Property Rights* (Oxford: Oxford University Press, 2012); E. Derclaye and M. Leistner, *Intellectual Property Overlaps: A European Perspective* (Oxford: Hart, 2011).

3.1   THE PILLARS OF INTERNATIONAL IP LAW

In the nineteenth century, countries chose to further their economic interests by having quite distinct IP laws, or even no laws. With no multilateral IP agreements to establish common legal standards, this divergence was quite extreme compared to the present day. If this was the case, why would so many countries have come together to adopt international IP treaties and create unions of participating countries, as they did from the 1880s? In reality, there were common interests in what hitherto was an unprecedented era of international cooperation in commercial law, which saw the creation of unions. These included the International Telecommunication Union in 1865 and the Universal Postal Union in 1874. There was much interest among businesses, authors, artists, designers and traders in acquiring patents, copyright, industrial designs and trade marks in those foreign countries where they sought to do business. And as international trade expanded, this interest increased resulting in the foundation of the Paris and Berne Unions for the protection of certain forms of IP.

3.1.1   The Paris Convention

The Paris Convention for the Protection of Industrial Property was the first major international IP treaty concluded in 1883. It has been revised several times, with the last revision being the Stockholm revision of 1967. The Convention lays down several constructs by which an international industrial property regime can be laid down and recognised, including the following: rules for establishing industrial property offices, and other administrative rules; minimum terms of protection for industrial property. This should be contrasted to the very different situation in the mid-1880s where there were no universal norms. Especially frustrating to cross-border trade in goods were the five key areas of variation among national patent systems:

1.   *Interpretations of novelty*: these varied widely in nineteenth-century patent laws. In some countries, inventions could not be patented if there were prior knowledge, use or publication anywhere in the world. In most other countries, only unpublished foreign use or knowledge did not destroy novelty.[3] In Britain, on the other hand, only 'public manufacture, use or sale in England' invalidated patent applications for lack of novelty.[4]

2.   *Length of protection terms*: there were no standard protection terms. The longest period of protection was provided by the USA, where patents were for 17 years from the date the patent was granted. France and Germany awarded patents for 15 years.

3.   *Treatment of foreign applicants*: British patents had a duration of 14 years from the filing date, but the protection term of foreign inventions previously patented abroad automatically ended upon the expiry of the foreign patent even if this was less than 14 years.

---

[3] As with the US until this decade.

[4] S.P. Ladas, *Patents, Trademarks, and Related Rights: National and International Protection. Volume 1* (Cambridge, MA: Harvard University Press, 1975), 26–7.

4.   *The issue of whether or not patents needed to be 'worked' domestically*: there were
     tions concerning regulation of local manufacture or use (the 'working') of patented products
     or processes. In some countries (such as the USA),[5] patent holders were under no obligation
     to work the invention or even to commercialise it. In others, rival manufacturers could ap-
     ply for a compulsory licence if the patent holder refused to work the invention or license it
     willingly. In some others (such as France), merely importing a patented product would lead
     to revocation of the patent. The original text of the Paris Convention made no reference to
     compulsory licensing and stated that patents could not be revoked solely on the grounds of
     importation from a member state to the country where the patent was granted. However,
     members were otherwise free to require patents to be worked. This provision was a compro-
     mise that allowed importing as long as there was also local working.
5.   *Exceptions to patentability*: in the US and Great Britain no classes of inventions were explicit-
     ly excepted. Elsewhere exceptions were usually indicated in the statutes. The most common
     of these were medicines and foods (as in France and Germany).

Because the differences between national laws were so great, there was little expectation that har-
monising national laws through a single convention was achievable. But there was broad understanding that certain common principles and administrative procedures should be agreed upon.
An agreed text of the Paris Convention was opened for signature at a conference in Paris in 1883,
and the Convention entered force in 1884.[6] The Convention established the Paris Union for the
Protection of Industrial Property, to consist of all member states, and whose International Bureau
would be located in Switzerland. The founder members were Belgium, Brazil, France, Guatemala,
Italy, the Netherlands, Portugal, El Salvador, Serbia, Spain and Switzerland. Great Britain, Tunisia
and Ecuador joined within a year. Ironically, while the US and Germany were notable absentees,
two founder members (the Netherlands and Switzerland) were without a patent system. The US
did not join the Paris Union until 1887, and Germany not until 1903. According to Article 1 of the
Convention, the following definition of 'industrial property' was adopted:

> Industrial property shall be understood in the broadest sense and shall apply not only to
> industry and commerce proper, but likewise to agricultural and extractive industries and to
> all manufactured or natural products, for example, wines, grain, tobacco leaf, fruit, cattle,
> minerals, mineral waters, beer, flowers, and flour.

---

[5] Interestingly, the patent regime currently in force in the US *does* have certain provisions relating to local working. See
Chapter 18 ('Patent rights in inventions made with federal assistance') of the US Patent Code.

[6] For history and background to the Paris Convention, see S. Ricketson, *The Paris Convention for the Protection of Industrial
Property: A Commentary* (Oxford: Oxford University Press, 2016); U. Anderfelt, *International Patent Legislation and
Developing Countries* (The Hague: Martinus Nijhoff, 1971); M. Blakeney, 'Commentary', in A. Ilardi and M. Blakeney (eds),
International Encyclopaedia of Intellectual Property Treaties (Oxford: Oxford University Press, 2004), 1–183; E.T. Penrose,
The Economics of the International Patent System (Baltimore: Johns Hopkins University Press, 1951); G.H.C. Bodenhausen,
Guide to the Application of the Paris Convention for the Protection of Industrial Property (Geneva: BIRPI, 1968).

Initially, the Paris Convention covered 'patents, industrial designs or models, trade-marks and trade names'. Since then the scope of industrial protection has been expanded in the Convention to embrace 'patents, utility models, industrial designs, trademarks, service marks, trade names, indications of source or appellations of origin, and the repression of unfair competition'. Nonetheless, it is probably best known for its provisions dealing with patents.

The most important patent-related matters dealt with in the Convention concerned national treatment, the right of priority, and rules relating to local manufacture. The right of priority had been particularly troublesome – an applicant for a patent in one member state was permitted a six-month period from the date of the first application (the priority date) to file for patents in other countries. During this period the applicant could prevent third parties from applying for a patent on the same invention. Moreover, subsequent applications during this period could not be invalidated on the grounds of prior registration, publication, or working by a third party. The USA and Germany, both of which granted patents only after examination, were unhappy with this provision. According to US practice, priority began from the date of publication of the patent, not of its filing. The German government felt that the priority period should be 12 months, since it often took at least that length of time for patents to be granted.[7] While such technical matters affected the decisions of these countries to delay joining the Union, strategic considerations are likely also to have been involved.

On the other hand, the Convention made, and continues to make, no reference to three important areas of variation among national patent laws, indicating a lack of consensus. These were, first, the matter of whether national patent institutions had to examine patent applications or could serve merely as registration offices; second, the term of a patent; and third, exceptions from patentability on the basis of industrial or technological fields, or of morality concerns.

Since 1883, the Paris Convention has been revised six times, most recently in 1967, and its membership has expanded tremendously, including many developing countries which joined in large numbers during the 1960s and 1970s. Apart from the extension of the priority date for patents to 12 months, the main substantive differences between the 1883 version and subsequent ones have been to do with working and compulsory licensing. Under Article 19, members of the Paris Union are permitted 'to make separately between themselves special agreements for the protection of industrial property, in so far as these agreements do not contravene the provisions of this Convention'. Over the years, several such special agreements have been adopted, including: the Madrid Agreement for the Repression of False or Deceptive Indications of Source on Goods; the Madrid Agreement Concerning the International Registration of Marks; and the Lisbon Agreement for the Protection of Appellations of Origin and their International Registration (Lisbon Agreement 1958). Most of the Convention's substantive provisions have been incorporated by reference into WTO law by virtue of TRIPS Article 2.

3.1.2   The Berne Convention

By the middle of the nineteenth century, after decades of combating cross-border importation and piracy of books in Europe, major European publishers' and authors' societies began to search

---

[7] UK Board of Trade, *Report of the Committee Appointed by the Board of Trade to Inquire into the Working of the Patents Acts on Certain Specified Questions ('The Fry Committee')* (London: HMSO, 1901).

for an international solution, with a set of coherent and codified copyright norms. Although bilateral agreements between England, France, Belgium and the Netherlands, had partly worked in limiting piratical acts, the web of bilateral trade agreements with reciprocity clauses to protect works across borders had been difficult to negotiate, and complex to maintain. However, the nineteenth-century improvements in transport and communications made it easier than ever for individuals in different countries to exchange ideas, organise themselves into societies and promote common demands across national boundaries. It should therefore not be surprising that, like the Paris Convention, the initiative to produce a multilateral treaty was taken by those who stood to benefit directly from enhanced international protection of literary and artistic works, in this case authors, publishers, lawyers and representatives of literary and publishers' societies.[8]

In 1878, *the Société des Gens de Lettres de France* held an international congress, under the presidency of Victor Hugo. It achieved two things. First, it formulated an international basis for universal protection of authors' rights. Second, it created the International Literary Association (later, ALAI), whose purpose was to promote rights of authors by seeking an international treaty to this end. After much deliberation, lobbying and inter-governmental conferences, a draft convention was drawn up in 1883. The text of this document provided the basis for the Berne Convention for the Protection of Literary and Artistic Works, which was adopted at a diplomatic conference in 1886 attended by representatives of the following governments: Germany, Belgium, Spain, France, Haiti, Italy, Liberia, Switzerland, the UK and Tunisia. The USA and Japan were represented by observers.

The main tenets of the Berne Convention are national treatment, minimum levels of protection for the author, and the removal of any dependence on registration or other formalities in order to enjoy and exercise the rights provided. Over the years, the provisions of the Berne Convention have become more substantial and detailed than the Paris Convention with respect to subject matter and the definition of the rights, including the limitations and exceptions. Since 1886, the Berne Convention has been amended six times to keep pace with the emergence of new technologies: the Berlin revision (1908) incorporated photography, film, and sound recording; the Rome amendments (1928) added broadcasting; whilst the Brussels conference (1948) added television.

Often breakaway countries from the Berne Union joined the Universal Copyright Convention (UCC), including the US, India, and many South American nations. The UCC, governed under the UNESCO mandate for education and scientific advancement, was an understandable haven for developing countries as it had the same provisions as the Berne Convention but with far fewer requirements, while recognising compulsory licences of translations. Several further reasons can be proffered as to why the US did not become a party to the Convention until 1989. Apparently, the continental authors' rights orientation of the Convention, which appeared to prioritise the moral and material interests of authors over the economic interests of publishers and printers, was more than the US felt it could accept, despite the fact that the Convention was acceptable to other common law countries such

---

[8] For the history and development of international copyright law, see S. Ricketson and J.C. Ginsburg, *International Copyright and Neighbouring Rights: The Berne Convention and Beyond* (Oxford: Oxford University Press, 2005), Chapters 1–2; C. Seville, *The Internationalisation of Copyright Law: Books, Buccaneers and the Black Flag in the Nineteenth Century* (Cambridge University Press, 2009), 23; S. Ricketson, 'The Birth of the Berne Union' (1986) 11 *Colum.-VLA J.L. & Arts* 9 at 15–16.

as the UK, Canada and Australia who were (and remain) similarly hostile to civil law concepts such as moral rights and authorial priorities.[9] A more probable reason for not joining the Berne Convention was the desire to protect the US publishing industry and its 'manufacturing clause'.[10]

A major weakness of the Berne Convention was the limited nature of its application to natural authors as opposed to legal owners of related rights such as performers, phonogram and film producers and broadcasters. These parties finally obtained an international rights regime under the 1961 Rome Convention for the Protection of Performers, Producers of Phonograms and Broadcasting Organisations (see discussion in Chapter 4). As with the Paris Union, Berne Union members are permitted to make special agreements. The WIPO Copyright Treaty (WCT) is one such agreement (see below).

Debates over the translation right saga was responsible, at least in part, for agreement between the developed and developing nations to adopt an extensive special compulsory licensing regime. This was to be implemented through an Appendix which provided faculties for developing countries to apply special terms for reproduction and translation. The Appendix to the 1971 Paris Act of the Convention provides – subject to just compensation to the right owner – 'for the possibility of granting non-exclusive and non-transferable compulsory licensing in respect of (i) translation for the purpose of teaching, scholarship or research, and (ii) reproduction for use in connection with systematic instructional activities, of works protected under the Convention'.[11] However, the Appendix's provisions are complicated, laden with restrictions and qualifications, and therefore difficult to put into practice – only nine developing countries are currently availing themselves of the Appendix options (see Chapter 12).

It is clear that prior to the 1948 Brussels revision, there had been no serious impediments to seeking to expand authors' rights from the initial translation right to include public performance, cinematographic adaptation and moral rights. However decolonisation and the increased membership within the Berne Union between 1948 and 1967 led to objections by the new members (many of whom were also former colonial territories) against the introduction of further new 'Eurocentric' or 'old order' rights.[12] This was especially true of the attempt to introduce for the first time into international copyright law the fundamental right of reproduction in the 1967 Stockholm Convention. The counter-proposal, led by a bloc of developing countries, was for provisions in the Berne Convention which would allow access to materials for educational purposes.

---

[9] The US publishing industry did manage to avail itself of the Berne Union protection and its qualification requirements by publishing in Canada; this attempt to take advantage of the first publication rules under the Convention was effectively stymied by Berne Convention, Art 6(1).

[10] From 1891 until 1986, US copyright law discriminated against foreign works in the notorious 'manufacturing clause', a protectionist measure intended to benefit American printers. Originally, this required all copyrighted literary works to be printed in the country. The fact that the US had by this time become by far the world's biggest exporter of copyrighted works suggests that its creative industries were not exactly held back by a copyright system that appears initially to have been inspired by infant-industry protectionism.

[11] World Intellectual Property Organization, *Intellectual Property Reading Material* (WIPO, 1998), 260–61.

[12] C. Masouyé, 'Décolonisation, Indépendence et Droit d'Auteur' (1962) 36 *Revue International de Droit D'auteur* 85; I.A. Olian, 'International Copyright and the Needs of Developing Countries: the Awakening at Stockholm and Paris', (1974) 81 *Cornell International Law Journal* 7.

The developing nations' argument of access to knowledge is not new. In the nineteenth century, for example, countries like Sweden, Japan, Ireland and the Netherlands fought hard to limit the new international translation right, arguing that the right to make free translation was of considerable value to less developed countries. Moreover the mechanism of compulsory licensing was not unknown, and the final version of the translation right allowed an author to enforce this right only if he had already licensed and authorised a translation of the work in that particular country.[13] The history of the first international right of translation is salutary in that the growing needs of developing countries politicised the Berne Union conferences in a manner not previously witnessed.

As with Paris, most of the Convention's substantive provisions have been incorporated by reference into WTO law by virtue of TRIPS Article 9, excepting those concerning moral rights.

3.1.3   National treatment

National treatment was first forged in Article 2, Paris Convention and Article 5(1), Berne Convention. National treatment is the right of foreign citizens to be treated in the same way as nationals with respect to legal rights, benefits and remedies.

In respect of the Paris Convention, discrimination between foreigners and nationals is prohibited and all persons, in respect of industrial property which has been created in one Union state, must be given the same protection in each of the other Union states as the latter grants to the works of its own nationals. In most countries, the owner of the industrial property will qualify for protection if he has a personal relationship (national or habitual domicile) with a Paris Union member state.

Under the Berne Convention, the same principle applies, namely works of a protected author which originate in one of the Union countries must be given the same protection in each of the other Union countries, as the latter grants to the works of its own nationals. Nevertheless, the Berne Convention introduces several exceptions to the principle of national treatment:

(i)   works of applied art or designs are entitled to protection in other countries of the Union only to the extent of the nature of protection they are granted in the country of origin; if no special protection is granted, then such works should be protected as artistic copyright works;

(ii)   works of nationals from non-Union countries can be discriminated against on the grounds that the latter country does not adequately protect the works of authors of a Union country. Thus prior to the entry of the US to the Berne Union, the provision allowed Canada to exclude Berne Convention protection to US works first published in Canada;

(iii) Berne Union countries do not need to offer a term of protection which exceeds the term fixed in the country of origin of the work;

(iv)   the *droit de suite* right (resale royalty right) may be claimed in a Union country only to the extent that the author's own country offers the right.[14]

---

[13] Ricketson and Ginsburg, *supra* note 8, 2.29; M. Freegard, 'The Berne Convention, Compulsory Licensing and Collecting Societies' (1986) 11(1) *Colum.-VLA J.L. & Arts* 137.

[14] The respective articles are: Berne Convention, Arts 2(7), 6(1), 7(8), *14ter*(2).

2 THE WORLD INTELLECTUAL PROPERTY ORGANIZATION

3.2.1 History

Lying at the heart of the international IP regime is the World Intellectual Property Organization (WIPO). The organisation was established by the 1967 Convention Establishing the World Intellectual Property Organisation, and came into existence in 1970 when the Convention entered into force. In 1974, WIPO became a United Nations specialised agency. WIPO's two objectives as stated in Article 3 of the Convention are: (i) to promote the protection of IP throughout the world through cooperation among states and, where appropriate, in collaboration with any other international organisation; and (ii) to ensure administrative cooperation among the Unions. WIPO currently administers 26 multilateral agreements, including the WIPO Convention.

The organisation was not created *de novo*. Its origins lie in the 1893 merger of the secretariats (or 'international bureaux') of the Paris and Berne Unions. The merged organisation was known as the *Bureaux Internationaux Réunis de la Protection de la Propriété Intellectuelle* (BIRPI). The idea of transforming BIRPI into an international IP organisation arose at a 1962 meeting of the Permanent Bureau of the Paris Union and the Berne Union. The meeting recommended the setting up of a Committee of Governmental Experts in order to consider administrative and structural reforms to the Paris and Berne Union systems and prepare for a diplomatic conference. It is important to note that during this time, the decolonisation process, which had begun after the Second World War, was gathering pace and many new developing countries were becoming independent and seeking to join the United Nations and other international organisations. The UN itself was undergoing a period of transformation as it sought to accommodate a rapidly increasing membership with a wide range of interests and concerns. Which parts of the UN system should have jurisdiction over complex and politically contentious matters such as IP was some way from being determined. In consequence, BIRPI could no longer remain as a developed country 'club' and needed to have a more multilateral character that could attract developing countries including the newly independent ones.

However, some developing nations had their own ideas about international IP norm-setting and were becoming assertive in expressing them. This was cause for concern in some quarters. Indeed, the proposal to establish a new organisation based on BIRPI was intended in part to ensure that politicised organisations, including those known for accommodating the specific concerns of the developing countries, would not be chosen as the forum for negotiating IP norms. According to Ladas, the intent was 'to head off any attempt by outsiders, such as the United Nations Economic and Social Council or the United Nations Conference on Trade and Development, to deal with the subject of IP and eventually to form a Specialized Agency of the United Nations in this field'.[15]

A second meeting of the Committee took place in 1966 and was attended by representatives from 39 nations of which nine were developing countries, the rest being developed or European

---

[15] S. Ladas, *Patents, Trademarks, and Related Rights: National and International Protection* (Harvard University Press, 1975) 92.

communist countries. The draft Convention prepared by BIRPI on the basis of the views e.
by the Committee at these two meeting was presented to a diplomatic conference in 1967 at Stockholm, where a final text was approved. The WIPO secretariat, located in Geneva, Switzerland, is
still known as the International Bureau.[16]

3.2.2   WIPO's intellectual property treaties

The international law of IP in its present form consists of three types of agreement.[17] These are
multilateral treaties, regional treaties or instruments, and bilateral treaties. Of these, the agreements that affect the greatest number of countries are the TRIPS Agreement, and some of the
multilateral treaties administered by WIPO, especially the Paris and Berne Conventions. We will
deal here with WIPO's own treaties.

The WIPO International Bureau administers 26 treaties.[18] There are other multilateral treaties
which either deal exclusively with intellectual property or concern other areas of law or policy but
that contain provisions on, or relating to, IP. WIPO divides its treaties into three categories, into
which we can also place some of these non-WIPO agreements.

1.   The *standard-setting treaties*, which define agreed basic standards of protection for the differ-
     ent IP rights, and also typically require national treatment. These include the Paris Conven-
     tion, the Berne Convention, the Rome Convention,[19] the WCT and WPPT, the 2006 Singa-
     pore Treaty on the Law of Trademarks, and the 2013 Marrakesh Treaty to Facilitate Access to
     Published Works for Persons Who Are Blind, Visually Impaired, or Otherwise Print Disabled.

2.   The *global protection system treaties*, which facilitate filing or registering of rights in more
     than one country. These include the 1891 Madrid Agreement Concerning the International
     Registration of Marks, the Lisbon Agreement 1958, and the 1970 Patent Cooperation Treaty
     (PCT).

3.   The *classification treaties*, which organise information concerning inventions, trade marks
     and industrial designs into indexed, manageable structures for easy retrieval. All these instru-
     ments are WIPO-administered including the 1957 Nice Agreement Concerning the Interna-
     tional Classification of Goods and Services for the Purposes of the Registration of Marks, the

---

[16] For detailed discussion on WIPO, including how it operates and its legal and political role in the world, see C. Deere
Birkbeck, *The Governance of WIPO: A Reference Guide* (Cheltenham: Edward Elgar Publishing, 2016); C. May, *The World
Intellectual Property Organization: Resurgence and the Development Agenda* (Routledge, 2007); F.S. Musungu and G.
Dutfield, 'Multilateral Agreement and a TRIPS Plus World: The World Intellectual Property Organization', TRIPS Issues
Paper no. 3, QUNO & QIAP, 2003.

[17] UNCTAD-ICTSD, *Intellectual Property Rights: Implications for Development*, Geneva, 2003.

[18] See https://www.wipo.int/edocs/pubdocs/en/intproperty/442/wipo_pub_442.pdf; and http://www.wipo.int/treaties/
index.html.

[19] The Rome Convention is jointly administered by WIPO with the International Labour Organization and UNESCO.

1968 Locarno Agreement Establishing an International Classification for Industrial Designs, and the 1971 Strasbourg Agreement Concerning the International Patent Classification.

3.3 RELEVANT NON-WIPO MULTILATERAL TREATIES AND INSTRUMENTS

Important non-WIPO standard-setting treaties include UNESCO's 1952 Universal Copyright Convention, the 1961 International Convention for the Protection of New Varieties of Plants (UPOV Convention), and the World Trade Organization-administered TRIPS Agreement. Other multilateral agreements dealing with important global issues that do not primarily concern intellectual property rights but that contain provisions on, or relating to, IP, include the following:

- The Convention on Biological Diversity, 1992 including the Nagoya Protocol of 2010 (see Chapter 15).
- The FAO International Treaty on Plant Genetic Resources for Food and Agriculture, 2001.
- Pandemic Influenza Preparedness Framework for the sharing of influenza viruses and access to vaccines and other benefits ('PIP Framework'), 2011.

Some of these agreements plus the Marrakesh Treaty operate in some respects to counter the tendency to increase and strengthen IP rights to the advantage of transnational corporations. Some of these reflect concerns from developing countries about IP being treated as an end as opposed to being a means to pursue a range of aspirations such as food security, sustainable development, conservation of genetic resources, public health and technology transfer.[20]

3.4 THE TRIPS AGREEMENT

3.4.1 Background

The 1994 Agreement on Trade-Related Aspects of Intellectual Property Rights ('TRIPS' or 'the TRIPS Agreement'), one of the main outcomes of the Uruguay Round of the General Agreement on Tariffs and Trade (GATT), which is administered by the Geneva-based World Trade Organization (WTO), is of special importance in that it establishes enforceable global minimum (and high) standards of protection and enforcement for virtually all the most important IP rights such as patents, copyrights, designs, and trade marks in one single agreement.

The first attempt to frame IP as an issue to be discussed in wider trade negotiations was made

---

[20] S.F. Halabi, *Intellectual Property and the New International Economic Order: Oligopoly, Regulation, and Wealth Distribution in the Global Knowledge Economy* (Cambridge: Cambridge University Press, 2018) 227, refers to such agreements as 'international intellectual property shelters'.

by a group of trademark-holding firms organised as the Anti-Counterfeiting Coalition, ,
successfully lobbied for the inclusion of an anti-counterfeiting code in the 1973–79 GATT ɪ↺
Round. Following the lead set by the US trade mark industries, the copyright, patent and semiconductor industries also decided during the early 1980s to frame the relative (and sometimes absolute) lack of effective IP protection in overseas markets as a trade-related issue and as a problem
for the US economy that the government ought to respond to. By the time the contracting parties
of the GATT met in Punta del Este, Uruguay, in September 1986 to launch another trade round,
US corporations had forged a broad cross-sectoral alliance and developed a coordinated strategy.

For those seeking high standards of IP protection and enforcement throughout the world by
way of the GATT, the strategy had three advantages. First, if successful the strategy would glo-
balise these standards much more rapidly than could be achieved through the WIPO-administered
conventions. This is because it allowed for the possibility of including all the main IP rights in a
single agreement (which could also incorporate by reference provisions of the major WIPO Conventions); and because once it was agreed that the Uruguay Round agreements had to be accepted
as a package (that is, a 'single undertaking'), countries could not opt out of any one of them and
be a member of the new World Trade Organization. Second, the GATT already had a dispute settlement mechanism, albeit a flawed one. WIPO has no enforcement or dispute settlement mechanisms except through the treaties that it administers, and these treaties do not provide much
recourse for countries concerned about the non-compliance of other parties. Third, the broad
agenda of the Uruguay Round provided opportunities for linkage-bargain diplomacy that WIPO,
with its exclusive focus on IP rights, did not allow. Hard bargaining by the US, Europe and Japan
on IP could thus be linked to concessions in such areas as textiles and agriculture, where exporting
countries in the developing world were eager to achieve favourable settlements.[21]

In the event, the Punta del Este Declaration included 'trade-related aspects of IP rights, including trade in counterfeit goods' as a subject for negotiations in the forthcoming trade round, which
became known as 'the Uruguay Round'. In full, the Declaration's provisions on IP are as follows:

> In order to reduce the distortions and impediments to international trade, and taking into
> account the need to promote effective and adequate protection of IP rights, and to ensure
> that measu res and procedures to enforce IP rights do not themselves become barriers to
> legitimate trade, the negotiations shall aim to clarify GATT provisions and elaborate as ap-
> propriate new rules and disciplines.
> Negotiations shall aim to develop a multilateral framework of principles, rules and disci-
> plines dealing with international trade in counterfeit goods, taking into account work al-
> ready underway in GATT.
> These negotiations shall be without prejudice to other complementary initiatives that may
> be taken in the World Intellectual Property Organization and elsewhere to deal with these
> matters.

---

[21] M.P. Ryan, *Knowledge Diplomacy: Global Competition and the Politics of Intellectual Property* (Washington, DC: Brookings
Institution Press, 1998); S.K. Sell, *Power and Ideas: North-South Politics of Intellectual Property and Antitrust* (Suny Series in
Global Politics, Albany: State University of New York Press, 1998).

Eight years later, the outcome of these negotiations was the Agreement on Trade-Related Aspects of Intellectual Property Rights (TRIPS). While the original purpose of an agreement on IP rights at the Uruguay Round was to prevent the trade in 'counterfeit goods', the resulting agreement turned out to be much more ambitious than this.[22] The insertion of 'trade-related' IP rights into the Uruguay Round agenda and the subsequent adoption of an agreed text for an IP agreement could not have been achieved without the effective lobbying activities in the US of legal and policy activists and corporations, and a government and political establishment that, during the 1980s, was especially receptive to the diagnoses and prescriptions propounded by these individuals, firms and business associations.

According to Sell, TRIPS is a case of 12 US corporations making public law for the world.[23] Nonetheless, representatives of the US, Europe and Japan did not just sit down together and write the TRIPS Agreement themselves. Not only did divisions emerge between Europe and the US that required compromises, but developing countries were much more involved in the drafting than they are often given credit for. As Watal explains, they achieved favourable language in ten of the 73 articles albeit with the necessary support of a few developed countries.[24] The ten include those dealing with the objectives and principles of TRIPS, limitations and exceptions to copyright, exceptions to patents and compulsory licensing, and control of anti-competitive practices in contractual licensing.

3.4.2 Objectives, principles, non-discrimination and exhaustion of rights

The preamble affirms the desire of member states 'to take into account the need to promote effective and adequate protection of IP rights', while 'recognizing the underlying public policy objectives of national systems for the protection of IP, including developmental and technological objectives'. Dealing with counterfeiting is clearly considered as important. Its main importance lies in the fact that the trade in counterfeit goods is what makes IP most clearly trade-related. The preamble indicates that members recognise 'the need for a multilateral framework of principles, rules and disciplines dealing with international trade in counterfeit goods'.

And yet, the objectives as stated in Article 7 make no reference to the eradication of counterfeiting. Rather, TRIPS is explicitly aimed at promoting public policy objectives, the nature of such objectives presumably being left to national governments, although technological development is given priority. In a similar vein, Article 8(1) allows member states implementing their IP regulations to 'adopt measures necessary to protect human health and nutrition, and to promote the public interest in sectors of vital importance to their socio-economic and technological development'. These measures are not obligatory but, again, they highlight the socio-economic welfare implications of IP rights. On the other hand, the proviso that such measures be consistent with the provisions of TRIPS appears to narrow their possible scope quite considerably. These provisions are discussed in greater detail in Chapter 11.

---

[22] In fact, it was agreed to delete the reference to counterfeit goods from the title of the agreement.

[23] S.K. Sell, *Private Power, Public Law: The Globalization of Intellectual Property Rights* (Cambridge: Cambridge University Press, 2003), 1, 96.

[24] J. Watal, *Intellectual Property Rights in the WTO and Developing Countries* (New Delhi: Oxford University Press, 2001), 43.

By virtue of Article 3, TRIPS Agreement, members accept the principle of national treatment, that is, each country must treat nationals of other members at least as well as it treats its own nationals. In other words, IP protection and enforcement must be non-discriminatory as to the nationality of rights holders. This does not prevent countries, however, from 'differentiating' between foreign traders and domestic ones as long as such grounds are legitimate.

Article 4 upholds the most-favoured nation (MFN) principle. In essence, while national treatment prohibits discrimination *against* foreigners, MFN prohibits discrimination *between* foreigners. Accordingly, any concession granted by one member to another must be accorded to all other members 'immediately and unconditionally'. So, if country X agrees to take special measures to prevent the copying of the products of a company from country Y, but turns a blind eye when the company is from country Z, such inconsistency of treatment will violate this principle. That TRIPS is part of international trade law explains why it represents the first time that international IPRs have been associated with MFN.

It is worthwhile mentioning Article 6, which states that 'for the purposes of dispute settlement under this Agreement [...] nothing in this Agreement shall be used to address the issue of the exhaustion of IP rights'. This is very significant in that it allows countries to adopt a regime of international exhaustion of rights. Accordingly, they cannot be challenged at the WTO if their laws permit the importation of IP-protected goods legally placed on the market in a foreign country. Consider the example of a patented medicine. For a developing country where the drug is too expensive to be widely available to patients, the possibility exists for it to be purchased in a country where it is sold more cheaply and then imported, thereby undercutting the price of the same patented drug already on the domestic market. International exhaustion is unpopular with many international businesses since it makes it harder for them to divide the international market into national and regional zones with targeted pricing. The WTO has nevertheless confirmed this position, namely that TRIPS permits member countries to choose international, regional or national exhaustion.[25]

Despite (or perhaps in spite of) this international exhortation to ignore national exhaustion rules in dispute settlement situations, there is growing consternation as to the recent rulings by the US Supreme Court in *Kirtsaeng* and the EU Court of Justice in *Oracle*, both of which embrace a more liberal exhaustion doctrine (see 4.6.3 below; also 12.3.3). This domestic US and EU policy may arise from a growing view that international exhaustion is essential for promoting competition and incentivising new markets, especially within the digital goods markets.[26]

---

[25] Para 5(d), WTO Doha Declaration on the TRIPS Agreement and Public Health, 2001 (discussed in detail below).

[26] See Chapter 12 discussing *Kirtsaeng v. John Wiley & Sons, Inc.*, US Supreme Court, 133 S Ct 1351 (2013) and Case C-128/11 *UsedSoft GmbH v. Oracle Int'l Corp.* EU Court of Justice ECLI:EU:C:2012:407. See also F.M. Abbott, 'First Report to the International Trade Law Committee of the International Law Association on the Subject of Parallel Importation' (1998) 1 J. *Int'l Econ. L.* 607; K. Maskus, *Parallel Imports in Pharmaceuticals: Implications for Competition and Prices in Developing Countries, Final Report to World Intellectual Property Organisation*, April 2001; A. Wiebe, 'The Economic Perspective: Exhaustion in the Digital Age', in L. Bently, U. Suthersanen and P. Torremans (eds), *Global Copyright: Three Hundred Years Since the Statute of Anne, From 1709 to Cyberspace* (Cheltenham: Edward Elgar Publishing, 2010), 321 et seq.; W. Kerber, 'Exhaustion of Digital Goods: An Economic Perspective' (2016) 8(2) *Zeitschrift fuer Geistiges Eigentum/ Intellectual Property Journal* 149.

d enforcement

... out a very comprehensive *de minimis* definition of the nature of international
... property (namely, protected subject, the rights and limitations thereof). The list com-
...es the following IPRs:

1. Copyright and related rights.
2. Trade marks.
3. Geographical indications.
4. Industrial designs.
5. Patents.
6. Layout designs (Topographies) of integrated circuits.
7. Protection of undisclosed information.
8. Control of anti-competitive practices in contractual licences.

While the copyright provisions are substantially based on all the existing provisions of the Berne
Convention (barring moral rights), the other provisions on IP law are substantially new, due to
the failure of the Paris Convention to address substantive aspects of patent, trade mark and design
laws. This has two implications. All WTO members are required to implement substantial parts
of the Paris and Berne Conventions whether or not they are signatories to them. Secondly, most
developing countries will need to reform their laws drastically, as opposed to the more developed
nations. The latter is unsurprising since many of the IP standards provided in TRIPS were invariably modelled on the laws of the US, Japan, Europe or are a hybrid mix of the rules of these
jurisdictions.

TRIPS places much emphasis on enforcement. With respect to the general enforcement obligations, procedures must be available that 'permit effective action against any act of infringement
of IP rights'.[27] They must be fair, equitable and not unnecessarily complicated, costly or time-consuming.[28] The judicial authorities must be granted the power to require infringers to pay damages adequate to compensate the right holder for the injury suffered due to the infringement.[29]
Members are required to provide for criminal procedures and penalties 'at least in cases of wilful
trademark counterfeiting or copyright piracy on a commercial scale'.[30] Remedies may include im-
prisonment and/or monetary fines. Such remedies may also be applied in other cases of IP right
infringement if done 'wilfully and on a commercial scale'. Members are not required to put in
place a judicial system for enforcing rights separate from that for the enforcement of law in general.[31] Moreover, TRIPS creates no obligation to shift resources away from the enforcement of law
in general towards the enforcement of rights. Nonetheless, poor countries may face a difficult

---

[27] TRIPS Agreement, Art 41.1.

[28] Ibid., Art 41.2.

[29] Ibid., Art 45.1.

[30] Ibid., Art 61.

[31] Ibid., Art 41.5.

dilemma when determining how to allocate the scarce resources they have. The dynamic efficiencies of stronger and more effective IPR systems may more than make up for the administrative and enforcement costs. Whether or not this turns out to be true, the costs must be borne before the benefits accrue and, for least-developed countries especially, these are likely to be particularly onerous. In addition, regulators and courts are likely to lack experience in dealing with intellectual property-related matters.

3.4.4   Transitional and institutional arrangements

All countries had to apply Articles 3–5 on national treatment, most-favoured nation, and concerning multilateral agreements on acquisition or maintenance of protection within one year of the entry into force of the WTO Agreement. But the developing countries and the former centrally planned socialist states were allowed a period of five years from the date of entry into force of the WTO Agreement to apply the full provisions of TRIPS, that is, 1 January 2000. The least-developed countries (LDCs), who are recognised as the poorest of the poor countries, were allowed until 1 January 2006 to apply TRIPS in full. This period has since been extended (see below).

Article 68 (Council for Trade-Related Aspects of Intellectual Property Rights) sets out the role of the WTO Council for TRIPS. The Council is responsible for:

* monitoring the operation of TRIPS, and in particular members' compliance;
* affording members the opportunity to consult on matters relating to trade-related IPRs;
* assisting members in the context of dispute settlement procedures; and
* carrying out other duties assigned to it by the members.

The Council is supposed to review the implementation of TRIPS at two-year intervals from January 2000. Article 71.1 states in addition that 'the Council may also undertake reviews in the light of any relevant new developments which might warrant modification or amendment of this Agreement'.

3.4.5   TRIPS-related developments at the WTO

Developing country representatives continue to express concerns that TRIPS raises prices of drugs and educational materials in poor countries, legitimises the 'biopiracy' of genetic resources and traditional knowledge (see Chapter 15), and blocks transfers of much-needed technologies. They have successfully resisted the further tightening of TRIPS rules and have put forward substantial counter-proposals relating to such matters as public health, the specific needs of least-developed countries, traditional knowledge and the compatibility between TRIPS and the provisions of the Convention on Biological Diversity (CBD) concerning benefit-sharing, protection of traditional knowledge and biotechnology transfer. And outside the WTO their improved negotiating strategies have delayed moves to harmonise international patent law and moderated some recent copyright treaties.

As for the developed countries and international businesses, who are constantly seeking ever higher levels of intellectual property protection and enforcement, TRIPS has to some extent been a disappointment. For one thing, the WTO system of trade governance currently does not make it easy to achieve radical revision of existing agreements or, for that matter, consensus on the need for new ones. For another, developing countries have tended not to implement TRIPS with much enthusiasm, and enforcement measures continue to be inadequate from the view of the intellectual property owners. Moreover, other forms of trade diplomacy seem to further their interests more effectively.

At the November 2001 Doha Ministerial Conference of the WTO, members agreed on the texts of three statements, all of which have provisions concerning intellectual property: (i) the Ministerial Declaration, (ii) the Decision on Implementation-related Issues and Concerns, and (iii) the Declaration on the TRIPS Agreement on Public Health (see Chapter 14).

The Ministerial Declaration covered a number of TRIPS-related matters including geographical indications (see Chapter 8), the relationship between TRIPS and the CBD and the protection of traditional knowledge and folklore (see Chapter 15), and technology transfer.

Concerning the latter, the Declaration expressed agreement on the establishment of a Working Group to examine 'the relationship between trade and transfer of technology, and of any possible recommendations on steps that might be taken within the mandate of the WTO to increase flows of technology to developing countries'.

As to the specific needs of the LDCs, the Decision on Implementation-related Issues and Concerns reaffirmed the mandatory nature of Article 66.2 ('Developed country Members shall provide incentives to enterprises and institutions in their territories for the purpose of promoting and encouraging technology transfer to least-developed country Members in order to enable them to create a sound and viable technological base'). The TRIPS Council was directed to establish 'a mechanism for ensuring the monitoring and full implementation of the obligations in question'.

Pursuant to this, in February 2003, the Council for TRIPS adopted a decision requiring the developed country WTO members to 'submit annually reports on actions taken or planned in pursuance of their commitments under Article 66.2'.[32] Such reports must provide the following information: (a) an overview of the incentives regime put in place to fulfil the obligations of Article 66.2, including any specific legislative, policy and regulatory framework; (b) identification of the type of incentive and the government agency or other entity making it available; (c) eligible enterprises and other institutions in the territory of the Member providing the incentives; and (d) any information available on the functioning in practice of these incentives.

It is hard to see such pressure on developed countries to comply with Article 66.2 going very far. The real difficulty is that technologies tend to be privately owned and governments are limited in terms of how far they are able and willing to intervene so as to ensure they are transferred to the LDCs.

In addition, the Doha Declaration on the TRIPS Agreement and Public Health allowed LDCs to delay implementation of patent protection for pharmaceutical products and legal protection of undisclosed test data submitted as a condition of approving the marketing of pharmaceuticals until 1 January 2016. This has now been extended to 1 January 2033.

In November 2005, the TRIPS Council extended the deadline for fully implementing the rest

---

[32] World Trade Organization, 'Implementation of Article 66.2 of the TRIPS Agreement: Decision of the Council for TRIPS of 19 February 2003' [WTO document IP/C/28].

of TRIPS by a further seven and a half years to 1 July 2013. Since then it has been extended for a further eight years to 1 July 2021. Undoubtedly these are achievements for LDCs, even if some of them have already implemented some or all of TRIPS.

3.5 THE REVIVAL OF IP SCEPTICISM

3.5.1 Increasing IP awareness

Unquestionably, globally IP awareness has increased and this has led to enthusiasm about the potential for IP to stimulate economic growth. However, awareness has led to much criticism and a sense that IP has 'gone too far' and ought to be re-balanced in favour of consumers, small businesses and developing countries.

Notwithstanding the fact that TRIPS was a 'price' developing countries agreed – quite grudgingly in some quarters it must be said – to 'pay' for WTO membership with all its potential gains from trade liberalisation, it gave rise also to much discontent. Studies from international organisations and NGOs gave much legitimacy to their dissatisfaction. Several reports were published by respectable institutions that either claimed that TRIPS and current trends in international intellectual property rule-making are harmful for development, or suggested that some aspects of them may be. Among these were the UNDP *Human Development Reports* of 1999,[33] 2000,[34] 2001,[35] the UNDP publication, *Making Global Trade Work for People*[36] – which was especially critical – and the World Bank's *Global Economic Prospects and the Developing Countries 2002*,[37] which was more cautious, and the report of the Commission on Intellectual Property Rights (CIPR), a UK government-sponsored body convened to investigate concerns such as those expressed in the above reports. It was headed by the late Professor John Barton of Stanford University, and comprised widely respected authorities on intellectual property from developed and developing countries with varied backgrounds and expertise. It was mandated to look at how IPRs might work better for poor people and developing countries by providing balanced, evidence-based policy recommendations. Published in 2002, the document contained some quite far-reaching recommendations directed at the global intellectual property system including the institutions within it (such as the WTO and WIPO), national intellectual property policy-making, and covering the following six areas: intellectual property and development; health; agriculture and genetic resources; traditional knowledge, access and benefit-sharing and geographical indications; copyright, software and the internet; and patent reform.[38]

---

[33] UNDP, *Human Development Report 1999* (New York and Oxford: UNDP and Oxford University Press), 67–76.

[34] UNDP, *Human Development Report 2000*, 84.

[35] UNDP, *Human Development Report 2001*, 97–109.

[36] UNDP, *Making Global Trade Work for People* (London: Earthscan, 2003), 203–34.

[37] The World Bank, *Global Economic Prospects and the Developing Countries 2002: Making Trade Work for the World's Poor* (Washington, DC: The World Bank, 2001), 129–50.

[38] The report is available at http://www.iprcommission.org/.

ngly, developing countries are much better able to acquire alternative sources of tech-
rtise and documentation. It is partly for this reason that they have enhanced their capacity to put forward substantial and technically sound counter-proposals at the WTO and WIPO
relating to such matters as public health, technology transfer, development, traditional knowledge
and the compatibility between TRIPS and the provisions of the CBD concerning benefit-sharing
and protection of traditional knowledge. And through improved negotiating strategies they have
upheld their freedom to provide generic versions of patented essential medicines to the poor, delayed moves to harmonise international patent law, as we will see below, and moderated some
recent copyright treaties. The alternative expertise has come from certain NGOs and in some
cases private individuals including academics acting as consultants. Very useful and high-quality
documentation has been produced by some of these NGOs and individuals. Organisations publishing rigorous technical materials include the Quaker United Nations Office,[39] the South Centre
and the (now disbanded) International Centre for Trade and Sustainable Development (ICTSD),
the latter working in collaboration with UNCTAD.[40] It is this more sceptical stance, informed in
part by such works, that resulted in firm opposition to patent law harmonisation, as we see below.

3.5.2   The failure of substantive patent law harmonisation

During the 1990s TRIPS seemed to be the most important element of the effort to pull up developing countries' intellectual property standards of protection and enforcement to the level of
the developed countries and to modernise intellectual property protection so as to accommodate
rapid advances in emerging fields like biotechnology and the digital technologies. It also attracted
most of the criticism from those who took the position that intellectual property laws should be
designed according to countries' levels of development.

For those countries seeking to raise the standards of IP protection globally, the WTO system
of trade governance turned out to be something of an obstacle. It has proven difficult politically
and diplomatically to revise or update existing WTO agreements. Second, a number of leading
developing countries have taken advantage of the flexibilities of TRIPS to further their national
interests by introducing measures that diverge from IP laws in the developed countries.

What do the major corporations, especially those whose products are knowledge intensive, actually want? In the area of patents, the priority is global harmonisation pitched at a level such that
TRIPS is the floor; the absolute minimum that is acceptable. Harmonisation at the level of principles, rules and institutional structures is a highly ambitious goal. Its practical intent is twofold:
(i) facilitating secure patent coverage on a global scale and for the longest period possible, and (ii)
accelerating and cheapening the process of attaining it. Seen this way, the stakes are self-evidently

---

[39] Musungu and Dutfield, *supra* note 16; G. Dutfield, 'Food, Biological Diversity and Intellectual Property: The Role of
the International Union for the Protection of New Varieties of Plants (UPOV)' Intellectual Property Issues Paper no. 9
(Quaker United Nations Office, 2011).

[40] UNCTAD-ICTSD, *Intellectual Property Rights: Implications for Development.* 2003 (available at www.iprsonline.org);
UNCTAD-ICTSD, *Resource Book on TRIPS and Development* (Cambridge University Press, 2005 (available at www.
iprsonline.org)).

very high. Unsurprisingly, advocacy from some stakeholders has been very determined. These are obviously those who stand to benefit the most. It is hardly controversial to say that the primary beneficiaries of the standardisation of patent law and practice are the transnational corporations, who are best placed to generate vast numbers of patent families covering the same inventions throughout the world. This is as intended.[41] Presumably those national economies where the head-quarters of such firms reside stand to benefit too, hence the supportiveness of certain governments.

Taken to its extreme, full harmonisation would entail the following:

- Textually identical legislation.
- Identical interpretation of claims by granting offices made possible by sharing of search and examination reports.
- National courts that reliably come to the same decisions on any given patent concerning validity, scope, infringement, limitations and defences.

Substantive patent law harmonisation is not a new idea, going back to the mid-1960s, but little happened to further it for two more decades. A Diplomatic Conference took place in 1991 at which WIPO presented a draft Patent Law Treaty. The Conference resulted in deadlock, largely because of differences between the US and Europe.[42] WIPO was requested to lower its ambitions, and in consequence the Patent Law Treaty adopted in 2000 dealt only with procedural matters.

Nonetheless, as the century came to an end, with the completion of the Uruguay Round and the establishment of the World Trade Organization to administer its resultant agreements including TRIPS, interest in patent law harmonisation enjoyed a revival. In response to interest from certain corporate associations, professional and expert groups like the *Association Internationale pour le Protection de la Propriété Industrielle* (AIPPI), and developed countries governments, WIPO accept-ed a mandate to revive the Substantive Patent Law Treaty (SPLT) process and the organisation's Standing Committee on the Law of Patents began in 2001 to debate the text of a draft treaty along with accompanying patent office regulations and practice guidelines.

Since 1995, and especially after 2000, developing country diplomats based in Geneva improved their capacity to negotiate in pursuit of the collective interests of the countries they represent. As mentioned already, NGOs and so-called 'counter-experts' also played a crucial role in offering alternative critical perspectives. In 2006, shortly after an event held by WIPO called the Open Forum on the Draft Substantive Patent Law Treaty, at which several speakers nominated by WIPO member states presented papers strongly critical of the idea that patent law harmonisation is ben-eficial for economic development,[43] the SPLT process was effectively halted.

However, harmonisation in terms of patent office practice is being actively pursued through co-operation between developed and developing country patent-granting offices including technical

---

[41] Sell, *supra* note 23.

[42] H. Bardehle, 'A New Approach to Worldwide Harmonization of Patent Law' (1999) 81 *J. Pat. & Trademark Off. Soc'y* 303, 304–5.

[43] The programme is available at https://www.wipo.int/meetings/en/details.jsp?meeting_id=9763.

assistance programmes,[44] training courses for practitioners and judges, and the drafting of intellectual property laws and implementing regulations by developed country experts, often funded from overseas aid budgets.

Harmonisation is equally important in relation to copyright, especially in such areas as term of protection and subject matter. For example, Europe and the US have been encouraging a *de facto* global policy of life plus 70 years for authors – which is beyond that required by TRIPS. However, harmonisation within copyright law is especially difficult due to the number of stakeholder groups having divergent interests, and the fact that copyright law is becoming increasingly complicated.

3.5.3   The WIPO Development Agenda

WIPO's Development Agenda is an initiative first mooted by the governments of Brazil and Argentina. It is another result of developing countries organising together to question what is sometimes referred to as 'IP maximalism'. These countries submitted a document to WIPO which was circulated and discussed at its General Assembly which took place in 2004.[45] The initiative of these countries was so well received by several other developing countries that they united to form a 14-country-strong grouping called the Friends of Development,[46] which produced a follow-up submission to WIPO. This latter document elaborated on the first one and responded to some developed countries, especially the US, that were opposed to any comprehensive initiative to explicitly incorporate development concerns into the mandate and activities of WIPO.[47] The four issues covered in the second submission were: (i) WIPO's mandate and governance; (ii) norm-setting; (iii) technical cooperation; and (iv) transfer of technology.

With regard to WIPO's mandate, the Friends of Development noted that as a UN agency, WIPO should be guided by the UN's development goals including the Millennium Development Goals (that have since been replaced by the Sustainable Development Goals). Moreover, development concerns should be incorporated into all of WIPO's work. Indeed, the Development Agenda is partially premised along the UN mandate to WIPO to be responsible:

> For promoting creative intellectual activity and for facilitating the transfer of technology related to industrial property to the developing countries in order to accelerate economic, social and cultural development, subject to the competence and responsibilities of the United Nations and its organs, particularly the United Nations Conference on Trade and

---

[44] P. Drahos, *The Global Governance of Knowledge: Patent Offices and their Clients* (Cambridge: Cambridge University Press, 2010).

[45] WIPO, 'Proposal by Argentina and Brazil for the Establishment of a Development Agenda for WIPO. Note prepared by the Secretariat', 2004 [Document WO/GA/31/11].

[46] The Friends of Development comprised Argentina, Bolivia, Brazil, Cuba, Dominican Republic, Ecuador, Egypt, Iran, Kenya, Peru, Sierra Leone, South Africa, Tanzania and Venezuela.

[47] WIPO, 'Proposal to Establish a Development Agenda for the World Intellectual Property Organization (WIPO): An Elaboration of Issues Raised in Document WO/GA/31/11. Submission by the Group of Friends of Development', 2005 [Document IIM/1/4].

Development, the United Nations Development Programme and the United Nations Industrial Development Organization, as well as of the United Nations Educational, Scientific and Cultural Organization and of other agencies within the United Nations system.[48]

As to pro-development intellectual property norm-setting, the document offered some principles and guidelines to make negotiations more inclusive and pro-development. These include:

(a) undertaking independent, evidence-based 'Development Impact Assessment' (DIA) to consider the possible implications of each norm-setting initiative for core sustainable development indicators;

(b) incorporating provisions recognising the difference between developed and developing WIPO member states in all norm-setting initiatives;

(c) holding public hearings prior to the initiation of any discussion towards norm-setting in WIPO, with the broad participation of different stakeholders, including other intergovernmental organisations, academia, consumer groups, and other civil society organisations.

The idea that international intellectual property norm-creation proposals should be subjected to a development impact assessment was initially suggested by, among others, one of the authors of the present volume who subsequently elaborated a tentative framework for conducting such an evaluation.[49] The use of human development indices, as provided by the annual United Nations Development Programme's Human Development Reports, as a metric might be one way to take this further.[50]

After considerable debate, the submission of a vast range of proposals and counter-proposals by numerous governments, and a certain amount of resistance, even from WIPO, members of the organisation agreed in September 2007 to formally adopt the Development Agenda by establishing a new Committee on Development and Intellectual Property. The Committee, which continues to meet on a regular basis, is charged with overseeing the implementation of 45 proposals about which consensus was reached.[51]

---

[48] Art 1, Agreement between the United Nations and the World Intellectual Property Organization, 1974. This was, interestingly, never part of WIPO's own constitutional mandate. See Arts 3 and 4, Convention Establishing the World Intellectual Property Organization (as amended in 1979), which states two objectives and its function. One of the objectives is to promote the protection 'of intellectual property throughout the world through cooperation', and the preamble to the Convention notes that one rationale for setting up the WIPO is to 'to encourage creative activity' by the promotion of the protection of intellectual property throughout the world'. There is, however, no mention within the Convention of 'transfer of technology' or encouragement of social, economic or cultural development.

[49] G. Dutfield, 'Assessing the Development Impacts of Intellectual Property Negotiations, Proposals, Reforms and Agreements. *Quaker United Nations Office*, Occasional paper 19, Geneva: QUNO, 2006; G. Dutfield, 'Making TRIPS Work for Developing Countries, in G.P. Sampson and W.B. Chambers (eds), *Developing Countries and the WTO: Policy Approaches* (Tokyo: United Nations University Press, 2008), 141–68.

[50] J.J. Osei-Tutu, 'Human Development as an Intellectual Property Metric' (2017) 90(3) *St. John's Law Review* 711.

[51] WIPO, 'Report of the Provisional Committee on Proposals Related to a WIPO Development Agenda', 2007 [WIPO document A/43/13 Rev.].

3.6   TRIPS PLUS – FREE TRADE AGREEMENTS WITH IP CHAPTERS

There are two kinds of non-multilateral agreement on IP. First, there are regional treaties or instruments that solely concern the granting or protection of IP rights in more than one country. Examples of these kinds of agreement include the 1973 European Patent Convention (EPC), the 1994 Eurasian Patent Convention, the 1998 European Community Directive on the Legal Protection of Biotechnological Inventions, the 1982 Harare Protocol on Patents and Industrial Designs within the Framework of the African Regional Industrial Property Organization (ARIPO), and the 2000 Andean Community Common Regime on Industrial Property. Regional agreements may appear to be far less important parts of the international IP architecture than the multilateral agreements (and bilateral agreements less so still). Yet such instruments are extremely important. First, their membership may be quite large, covering 20 or more countries. Second, it is possible that novel provisions in such agreements could subsequently be globalised through their incorporation into new multilateral agreements.[52] Third, countries may be required to introduce provisions that go beyond what TRIPS requires such as extending patents to new kinds of subject matter and eliminating certain exceptions. Fourth, regional agreements might stipulate that contracting parties should accede to certain international conventions. The third and fourth points also apply to the second kind of non-multilateral agreements, which is what the rest of this subsection of the book will cover.

Since TRIPS came into being developed countries and international corporations, have actively and aggressively pursued the strategy of conditioning market access for developing country exports on adherence to standards of IP protection that go beyond what the TRIPS Agreement obliges WTO member states to put in place. In consequence, perhaps the most significant new development in the field of international intellectual property is the proliferation of bilateral and regional negotiations on trade and investment of which either the US or the EU are a party – and a very dominant one. The resulting agreements have proved to be a useful way to get individual, or sometimes groups of, developing countries to introduce so-called 'TRIPS plus' provisions that go beyond what TRIPS requires, such as:

(i)   extending patents and copyright to new kinds of subject matter;
(ii)   extending protection terms;
(iii)   introducing new pharmaceutical and agrochemical test data protection rules with extended terms of protection; and
(iv)   ratifying new WIPO treaties containing TRIPS plus measures.

One of the first of such bilateral trade agreements containing IP provisions was the 2000 Agreement

---

[52] For example, some of the language of the European Patent Convention and of Chapter 17 of the North American Free Trade Agreement was incorporated into TRIPS. Having made this point, the national laws of some influential countries may also be used as sources of text to be incorporated into multilateral agreements, although such countries are likely to be few in number (perhaps only the US).

between the United States of America and the Hashemite Kingdom of Jordan on the Establishment of a Free Trade Area. The agreement required patents to be available for any invention in all fields of technology without including the exceptions allowable from Article 27.3(b) of TRIPS. Jordan was also required to join UPOV. In addition, a supplementary memorandum of understanding required Jordan to allow the patenting of business methods and computer-related inventions, neither of which is expressly required by TRIPS.

There is now a very large number of such agreements, which are generally referred to as Free Trade Agreements (FTAs), or Economic Partnership Agreements when they involve the EU. The intellectual property chapters of these agreement tend to be based upon measures insisted upon by the USA and EU and in many cases go well beyond what TRIPS requires. However, attempts to deliver plurilateral agreements on IP, or having IP chapters that bring together countries from different parts of the world have turned out to be highly complex and politically difficult. For example, the Anti-Counterfeiting Agreement (ACTA), negotiations for which were announced in 2007, 'two weeks after WIPO adopted its recommendations for the Development Agenda', Yu pointedly mentions, involved up to 39 countries before being adopted in 2011.[53] However, Switzerland and five EU member states refused to sign it and it was rejected by the European Parliament. Its future is uncertain to say the least.

---

[53] P.K. Yu, 'The Non-multilateral Approach to International Intellectual Property Normsetting', in D.J. Gervais (ed.), *International Intellectual Property: A Handbook of Contemporary Research* (Cheltenham: Edward Elgar Publishing, 2015), 83–120.

PART II
CREATING AND BRANDING

4
Copyright

4.1 ORIGINS

A jurist once remarked that copyright law only arose when media technology and market conditions made piracy profitable.[1] It is true that successive innovative technologies have revolutionised the socio-legal infrastructure of the creative industries, from the advent of the printed book to mass-produced engravings, prints and art works, to films and sound recordings, and finally to digitised works. The radical legal transformation continues today as copyright law embraces rights management rules and extends the communication right and making available right (see 4.6 below) to control the effects of streaming and networking technologies.

---

[1] P.E. Geller, 'Copyright History and the Future: What's Culture got to do with it?' (2000) 47 J. Copyright Soc'y U.S.A. 209, 210.

Nevertheless, technology alone does not create the need or market for authored
evolution of copyright, since its modern inception in the eighteenth century to the
copyright norms, has been also driven by the interests of a chain of actors including sovereign
states, authors, producers, the consuming public, and more recently, information Samaritans.

4.1.1   Ancient and post-classical practices[2]

Although there is no clear indication that literary or artistic property rights existed in ancient
times, there was a distinct concept of the 'author' and a discernible demand for authored manuscripts in the ancient Egyptian world of recorded texts and images. However, while literacy
and writing were regarded as elite status symbols, the actual task of writing itself was delegated
to scribes.[3] A similar recognition of the status of the author is seen within Greek literature.
Writers such as Aristotle and Plato were part of an authorial/personality cult, largely derived
from medieval text compilations, which crystallised the unique identity of a writer.[4] Personality cults may also have been the only means by which Roman authors such as Tacitus and Cicero
gained protection. These were men with private wealth, devoting their lives to civic duties
and wealth-generating pursuits such as advocacy, politics, public service or land management.
They were also well-known authors, and personally embraced the epithets of 'poet' or 'orator'.
If a writer wished copies of his work circulated, he paid for this; if a third party wished to have
a copy made, that person paid for the materials and the copying. The genre of the work, the
type of audience it was intended for, its purpose and its symbolic value and authority were all
attributable to the name inscribed on the work. And no compensation was due – such men
were perceived to eschew remuneration in preference to political or pedagogical fame and
recognition.[5]

---

[2] The following account of the origin of copyright law focuses on historical norms within a literate culture, as opposed to
oral, and indigenous cultures.

[3] J. Baines, 'Literacy and Ancient Egyptian Society' (Sept 1983) 18(3) *Man, New Series* 580. Dating from the invention of
the script, followed by the invention of an artificial platform to record such writings namely the papyrus, early 'books'
comprised baked clay tablets, which held Ancient Egyptian, Babylonian and Assyrian writings. The 'Book of the Dead',
for instance, was one of the first important (and surviving) authored works, which depicts, through text and images,
the deceased's voyage through the next life. Early versions of the text were inscribed on monuments or tombs, whereas
latter and existing versions were recorded on papyrus rolls. See generally Baines, ibid., 575; A. Champdor, *The Book of the
Dead from the Ani, Hunefer and Anhai Papyri in the British Museum* (New York: Garrett Publications, 1966), 36–8; also F.A.
Mumby, *Publishing and Bookselling: A History from the Earliest Times to the Present Day* (4th ed., London: Jonathan Cape,
1956), 15.

[4] R. Chartier, *The Order of Books: Readers, Authors and Libraries in Europe between the Fourteenth and Eighteenth Centuries*
(Stanford University Press, 1994).

[5] E. Fantham, *Roman Literary Culture: From Cicero to Apuleius* (Baltimore and London: Johns Hopkins University Press,
1996), 193; R. Starr, 'The Circulation of Literary Texts in the Roman World' (1987) 37(1) *The Classical Quarterly* 215,
223, financial gain would derive from patronage; S.M. Stewart, *International Copyright and Neighbouring Rights* (2nd ed.,
London: Butterworths Law, 1989), 13.

Arguably, such considerations of fame and personality still affect current dimensions of authorship; the criterion of originality is often viewed as demanding evidence of the author's 'personality', while the moral right of attribution and integrity focus on name and reputation. Of course, Roman authors did despair as to their economic status, complaining that their patrons were stingy and did not value poetry and other higher forms of authorship, with one author going so far as to claim that poets could only make ends meet by selling pantomime scripts.[6]

By the first century, one can fathom the beginnings of the European publishing industry in the Roman commercial book trade, which was producing books that were a fraction of the expense of copying done by a scribe, and was fuelled by the rapid growth of the market and the great increase in the number of manuscripts written.[7] The publishers collectively formed an association in order to protect their entrepreneurial investments, and to prevent their cohorts from misappropriating texts.[8] There were no clear authors' or publishers' property rights, and the patrician ethics of honesty, modesty and candour, rather than legal principles, regulated the literary and publishing practices.[9] Nevertheless, the misappropriation of authorship or of the work was a common basis for complaints. The Roman author Martial famously employed the term *plagiarus* (a Roman label for the theft of slaves or children) in relation to the misappropriation of works, while his compatriot, Vitruvius, likened unauthorised copying to violent robbery:

> Our predecessors, wisely and with advantage, proceeded by written records, to hand down their ideas to after times, so that they should not perish [...] While, then, these men deserve our gratitude, on the other hand, we must censure those who plunder their works and appropriate them to themselves; writers who do not depend upon their own ideas, but in their envy boast of other men's goods whom they have robbed with violence, should not only receive censure but punishment for their impious manner of life.[10]

---

[6] Fantham, ibid., 196.

[7] Mumby, *supra* note 3, 17; J. Feather, *A History of British Publishing* (London and New York: Routledge, 1988), 1; F. Reichmann, 'The Book Trade at the Time of the Roman Empire' (Jan, 1938) 8(1) *The Library Quarterly* 42, 43; *cf* Starr, *supra* note 5, note 54, and p. 222, noting that pricing policy, trade and distribution volume were meaningless concepts prior to the first century A.D. since motivations such as economies of scale and market demand by an affluent and well-read public were absent.

[8] Mumby, *supra* note 3, 22, citing G.H. Putnam, *Authors and their Public in Ancient Times: A Sketch of Literary Conditions and of the Relations with the Public of Literary Producers, From the Earliest Times to the Fall of the Roman Empire* (New York: G.P. Putnam's Sons, 1894).

[9] J. Loewenstein, *supra* note 10, at 78–82; K. de la Durantaye, 'The Origins of the Protection of Literary Authorship in Ancient Rome' (2007) 25 *Boston Univ. International Law Journal* 37.

[10] M.C. Dock, 'Genèse et Évolution de la Notion de Propriété Littéraire', [1974] *Revue Internationale Droit D'auteur* 127 at 135, citing Martial, *Epigrams Book I*, 52–3; J. Loewenstein, *Ben Jonson and Possessive Authorship* (Cambridge: Cambridge University Press, 2002), 74 citing Vitruvius, VII, Preface, 1, 3 – De Architectura.

Between the fall of the Roman Empire and the twelfth century, the monopoly of storing, copying and producing books was extended to and enjoyed by the monasteries and other ecclesiastical establishments. It is often alleged that the 'Monastic Age' gave rise to the first copyright decision in *Finnian v. Columba* (c. 550 AD). The alleged facts of this decision involved an Irish abbot Finnian who accused another monk Columba from a rival monastery of surreptitiously making a copy of a Book of Psalms, which the former had acquired previously in Rome. The dispute was resolved with King Diarmid's oft-quoted words: 'To every cow her calf, to every book its copy.' As modern notions of copyright were still virtually unknown in the medieval era, it is likely that the fable echoes an early ecclesiastical norm whereby ownership of the physical vellum manuscript underpinned an ownership of the knowledge, and an affiliated possessory right to access and copy the work – rather akin to how some contemporary cultural heritage institutions view their own collections. The only way to control unauthorised copying and dissemination was to control access to the manuscript itself, which the monasteries did by charging a fee to access works within their collections.[11]

As the book markets shifted within the subsequent decades to the main European university cities (such as Paris, London, Bologna and Oxford), the chain of interested parties extended to comprise not only authors, publishers and libraries, but also stationers or booksellers. The latter established themselves as the primary publishers and intermediaries between the author and his public, being responsible for the coordination of manuscript production, which included the illuminators, bookbinders and paper/vellum suppliers, book lending, and sale of paper/vellum, and other bookmaking accessories. Mass copying was a phenomenon from Greek times, albeit not to the extent encountered with the introduction of the printing press. In order to control the market, the booksellers created a divided market by producing purely textual materials, which were cheaper and faster to produce, and the more luxuriously illuminated manuscripts for higher end consumption. The establishment of universities further led to a growing demand by scholars for new works reflecting the growing number of new disciplines.[12]

Once divulged, it was impossible, of course, for authors or booksellers to retain any possessory rights in the manuscript itself, which led to a heavy reliance on a system of patronage. As noted by a historian:

> From the economic viewpoint, the author's rights may be considered to be vested in that first edition, even if it only consisted of a single copy, since thereafter he had no rights in his

---

[11] Scholarship shows the Battle of the Psalter tale of warring saints to be apocryphal as there are no contemporary records of this judgment – the earliest account of the story is 1532. For accounts of the dispute and origins of the tale, see R.R. Bowker, *Copyright: Its History and Its Law* (1912), 9; M. Rose, *Authors and Owners: The Invention of Copyright* (Harvard University Press, 1993), 7; E. Armstrong, *Before Copyright: The French Book-Privilege 1498–1526* (Cambridge University Press, 1990), 1; G.H. Putnam, *Books and their Makers in the Middle Ages*, 46; S.G. Breyer, 'The Uneasy Case for Copyright: A Look Back Across Four Decades' (2010–2011) 79 *Geo. Wash. L. Rev.* 1635, 1641; E. Rogers, 'Some Historical Matter Concerning Literary Property' (1908/1909) 101(7) *Mich. L. Rev.* 101, 104.

[12] M. Thomas, 'Manuscripts', in L. Febvre and H.-J. Martin, *The Coming of the Book: The Impact of Printing 1450–1800* (Verso, 1976), 19 *et seq.*

work. Hence to some extent the patronage system allowed literary men to live by the pen; the price paid by the author was his obligation not to say anything displeasing to his patron, while at the same time trying to write to please a growing public.[13]

4.1.2   Printing privileges

The invention and spread of printing in major European cities in the fifteenth and sixteenth centuries supplanted the medieval arrangements between the key players within the book trade. One encounters the creation of legal fictions to accommodate diverse state and commercial interests ranging from the encouragement of innovative activities, to the protection of investments in the new technologies, to the protectionism of booksellers and printers, and to the censorship of printed output. The primary legal devices that arose included booksellers' regulations, as well as printing and licensing privileges which, in turn, offered a legal basis for the concept of literary property.[14]

The printing revolution in Europe was buoyed by several socio-economic and industrial factors. First, an emerging merchant class produced significant stakeholders including a reading public, interested investors, and a more varied group of innovators. Secondly, the existing medieval book trade infrastructure was able to absorb the changes wrought by the printing press through the existing booksellers and stationers. Thirdly, the printing and paper developments led to the marriage of the book trade with the artisan workshops which produced illustrations and engravings, to subsequently give rise to novel trades and activities including playing cards, bill posters and advertising. This symbiotic trade link also led to standardisation of 'repeatable pictorial statements' such as maps, charts, diagrams, and other visual aids, which was to result in more standardised products. Indeed, the spurt in book production in Europe led to the introduction of new genres of reading materials, including vernacular Bibles as well as uncensored religious tracts and indulgences.[15]

These printing privileges, being commercial monopolies, were usually accorded to the inventor or initiator or importer of a new process, a new product or a new source of supply, which was capable of exploitation, either permanently or for a fixed period of time.[16] It is tempting to analogise them with some contemporary intellectual property practices and justifications in that: (i) the entitlements vested in the entrepreneurial and investment actors within the trade, namely, printers, publishers, booksellers, or guilds; and (ii) the privilege mechanism acted as a legal measure to

---

[13] Ibid., 25; also Bowker, *supra* note 11, 9–10.

[14] E. Eisenstein, 'Some Conjectures about the Impact of Printing on Western Society and Thought: A Preliminary Report' (Mar, 1968) 40(1) *Journal of Modern History* 12, 21, 31, 34; and E. Armstrong, *Before Copyright: The French Book-Privilege 1498–1526* (Cambridge: Cambridge University Press, 1990), 1 *et seq.*

[15] The printing 'revolution' is characterised not so much by the singular event of the invention of the press itself, but is rather the equivalent to the establishment of printing presses throughout Europe – E. Eisenstein, *The Printing Press as an Agent of Change* (Cambridge: Cambridge University Press, 1980); E. Eisenstein, *The Printing Revolution in Early Modern Europe* (Cambridge: Cambridge University Press, 1979).

[16] Rogers, *supra* note 11, 102–3.

protect investments by quashing competition in relation to certain works or genres. Indeed, historical intellectual property landmarks were reached in the Venetian State with the enactment of the 1469 privilege granted to Johannes of Speyer, and the 1486 privilege granted to Marcus Antonius Sabellicus. The former was akin to a modern patent and granted Speyer an exclusive right over the entire 'art of printing' in Venice for five years. This included the right to stop the operation of competing printing presses with fines and with the confiscation of tools and books. Speyer's privilege records that the possible rationale for this privilege was that such an innovation, 'unique and particular to our age and entirely unknown to the ancients, must be supported and nourished with all our goodwill and resources'.[17] This over-arching measure was short-lived as Speyer died in 1470. The Venetian printing and book industries continued, however, to flourish, with the establishment of 134 separate presses by 1473.

While it has been argued that the 1486 privilege to Sabellicus is the earliest recordation of an author's literary property, it is rather a recognition of the 'author's right to choose a printer', and to bestow protection against reprinting of the work in Venice.[18] Despite this early prescription of property as a reward for creative labour, the Venetian privileges system was doomed through its own success. The framework had become so complicated and huge that by 1517, the Venetian Senate revoked all printing privileges, and decreed that privileges would be granted henceforth for a new work (*opus novum*) never published before.[19]

The grant of book privileges was soon prevalent in a number of other European countries, the rationale being increasingly based on both moral and economic grounds namely, to preserve the fame and honour of the author, and to prevent free-riding of his efforts. The Milanese author Donatus Bossius was granted, for example, a ten-year territorial printing and importation privilege in 1492, on the basis that the author was entitled to the 'fruits of his exertion, in addition to the honour and glory which the publication would bring him'.[20] A similar socio-economic basis is evident in other privileges granted within other Italian states namely privileges are necessary to protect the 'fruits of the author's labour'.[21]

There are further noteworthy traces of literary property in some of the privileges awarded in the German states, including the early sixteenth century Nuremberg decisions recognising

---

[17] J. Kostylo (2008), 'Commentary on Johannes of Speyer's Venetian monopoly (1469)', in Bently and Kretschmer, *Primary Sources on Copyright*. For a fine overview of the Venetian privileges, see G. Mandich, 'Venetian Patents (1450–1550)', (1948) 30 *Journal of the Patent Office Society* 166.

[18] J. Loewenstein, *The Author's Due: Printing and the Prehistory of Copyright* (Chicago: University of Chicago Press, 2002), 71; J. Kostylo (2008), 'Commentary on Marcantonio Sabellico's privilege (1486)', in *Primary Sources on Copyright*, ibid.; R. Chavasse, 'The First Known Author's Copyright, September 1486, in the Context of a Humanist Career' (1986–7) 69 *Bulletin of the John Rylands Univ. Library of Manchester 26*.

[19] Bowker, *supra* note 11, 15; Armstrong, *supra* note 14, 6–7.

[20] Armstrong, ibid., 4; Z. Khan, 'An Economic History of Copyright in Europe and the United States', EH.Net Encyclopedia (R. Whaples (ed.)); at http://eh.net/encyclopedia/an-economic-history-of-copyright-in-europe-and-the-united-states/.

[21] Armstrong, ibid., 5–6.

attribution right in relation to forged engravings.[22] For the most part, however, rights were tangential, without any specific mentions of the author. Instead lo- booksellers by prohibiting the publication of competing editions of the same example, the 1479 Episcopal privilege granted by the Bishop of Würzburg for the printing of the breviary book. Not only was the book made a mandatory purchase for all the clergy within that diocese, the protection ensuing from the privilege buffered it from effective competition from other booksellers in the region, and ensured a return 'for the outlay involved in printing these large and handsome books'.[24]

4.1.3 Proto-property and licensing regimes

Statutory copyright was forged, first in England, and then in France, from the twin axis of state-sanctioned printing privileges and guild-controlled licensing regimes.

Institutionally linked to the privileges system was the licensing regime usually administered by guilds or trades through their private internal regulations, as well as being sanctioned and authorised by the sovereign power. Surprisingly, the Venetian print industry did not organise itself into a guild until 1548–49 which may explain the ad hoc basis of the Venetian printing privileges as well as the failure of effective intellectual property rules to emerge from Venice.[25] Instead, the origins of the current global copyright systems derive from European proto-legal regimes.

In England, a growing copyright regime comprised royal printing privileges derived from the Crown and state, the private legal regime of the Stationers' Company which excluded non-stationers and non-Londoners from printing, the licensing system, and the registration of stationers' copyright. The stationers' guild, which had been in place since the fifteenth century, had controlled the book trade via a private legal regime based on two fundamental principles: (i) a mutual trust and respect of guild members' claims; and (ii) a registration scheme for the manuscript or 'copy'. In order to extend its private monopoly regulations to the entire book trade in the country, the guild sought and obtained, after much lobbying, a royal charter in 1557. This Crown-sanctioned environment worked well for over 150 years, with the newly incorporated Stationers' Company being empowered not only to legally limit all printing to its members but also to pursue non-guild stationers from engaging in unlicensed copying. By the end of the seventeenth century, a further statutory layer was introduced, namely the Licensing Acts, which was to sustain the company's grip on the book trade until the lapse of the Licensing Act of 1695.[26]

---

[22] Bowker, *supra* note 11, 11, arguing that the cause in action was probably fraud, rather than authorial property; 'Imperial Privilege for Albrecht Dürer, Nuremberg (1511)', *Primary Sources on Copyright, supra* note 17.

[23] Rogers, *supra* note 11, 103, ascribing the lack of authors' rights to the fact that most works printed during this era in Germany (and France) comprised compilations of earlier works, which involved editorship, rather than the authorship.

[24] Armstrong, *supra* note 14, 3.

[25] See Bowker, *supra* note 11, 16; and J. Kostylo, 'From Gunpowder to Print: The Common Origins of Copyright and Patent', in R. Deazley, M. Kretschmer and L. Bently (eds), *Privilege and Property: Essays on the History of Copyright* (Cambridge: Open Book Publishers, 2010), 25, 37, with reference to the 1474 Venetian Statute.

[26] Loewenstein, *supra* note 18, generally Chapter 4; Rose, *supra* note 11, 12–16; Lowenstein, *supra* note 10, 3–9, 29–32.

While there was an implicit acceptance of some sort of property rights in the copies of books, a conceptual recognition of innate authors' rights is absent in the period preceding the enactment of the Statute of Anne 1710. Authors had no need for printing rights, as they derived their remuneration in the form of sinecures or gratifications;[27] moreover, as a group, authors wielded minuscule power as shown in Milton's denouncement of the licensing system which forces an author to 'appear in print like a puny with his guardian, and his censor's hand on the back of his title to be his bail and surety that he is no idiot or seducer'. This Milton condemns as 'a dishonour and derogation to the author, to the book, to the privilege and dignity of learning'.[28] Despite the absence of the author's interests, the English era comprising printing privileges, guild monopolies, licensing regulations, and booksellers' disputes has been accepted as the leading bases for the origin of copyright norms, culminating in the first modern copyright law – the Statute of Anne 1710.[29]

A similar situation can be seen in France where the early publishing privileges were both royal rewards and exceptions, the exception being to the 'liberté publique de l'imprimerie', where the presses were allowed to freely produce and disseminate published works. The development of regulatory measures began earnestly when the de facto monopoly enjoyed by the Parisian guild, by virtue of royal favours, metamorphosed into a legally enforceable system. It was henceforth unlawful to publish or distribute any literary work unless accompanied by a licence and a privilege from the royal chancellery.[30]

The subsequent Parisian booksellers' conflict arose from the fossilisation of the guild system, and the growing imbalance of privilege ownership vesting in the Paris guild members, as opposed to all other national traders. The privilege covered one work and benefited one publisher and forbade all other publishers to print or copy the work. The provincial traders argued for a wider publication policy, with fewer privileges, as this was essential to the maintenance of the public

---

[27] Although the records of the Stationers' Company show that authors were occasionally recorded as having retained printing rights in their own works, the circumstances reveal that this may merely indicate the financial unattractiveness of the work, and that the author was underwriting the cost and risk of publication. R. Chartier, 'Figures of the Author', in B. Sherman and A. Strowel, *Of Authors and Origins* (Oxford: Clarendon Press, 1994), 16–17; L.R. Patterson, *Copyright in Historical Perspective* (Nashville: Vanderbilt University Press, 1968), 66–7.

[28] J. Milton, *Areopagitica: A Speech For The Liberty Of Unlicensed Printing To The Parliament Of England*, 1644, available on Project Gutenberg at http://www.gutenberg.org/files/608/608-h/608-h.htm. For a fluent critique, see M. Rose, 'The Public Sphere and the Emergence of Copyright: Areopagitica, the Stationers' Company, and the Statute of Anne', in *Privilege and Property: Essays on the History of Copyright*, supra note 25, 67–88.

[29] For a detailed history of the charter, and the Star Chamber decrees, Interregnum Ordinances and Licensing Acts which followed, see R. Deazley, *On the Origin of the Right to Copy: Charting the Movement of Copyright Law in 18th Century Britain (1695–1775)* (Oxford: Hart Publishing, 2004); and Patterson, *supra* note 27.

[30] F. Rideau (2008), 'Commentary on Simon Marion's plea before the Parlement of Paris (1586)', in *Primary Sources on Copyright supra* note 17; for the early book-privilege system in France and the rest of Europe, see Armstrong, *supra* note 11; J-D. Mellot, 'Counterfeiting Principle as an Agent of Diffusion and Change – The French Book-Privilege System and Its Contradictions (1498–1790)', in S.A. Baron, E.N. Lindquist, E.F. Shevlin (eds), *Agent of Change: Print Culture Studies After Elizabeth L. Eisenstein* (University of Massachusetts Press, 2007).

the spread of learning especially among the poorer sectors, and in the public interest for ~~ tion. The Paris guild, on the other hand, argued that the work was a creation of the author, and that the author had transferred property in the work to the publisher who had to absorb all the commercial risk; thus the argument that individual Parisian booksellers had acquired authors' rights in perpetuity inadvertently laid the groundwork for the revolutionary decree recognising authors' rights.[31]

4.1.4   From the Statute of Anne to 'copyright'

The Statute of Anne 1710 did not confer a bundle of rights under the heading of 'copyright' but rather the right to print and reprint books. As some historians have argued, the statute was a trade regulatory device that 'restored' order to the book trade after the lapse of the proto-copyright regime. Others have argued against this reductionist view, stating that the Statute of Anne 1710 was an 'originating text' in some parts, while other provisions were a 'reversion to what had gone on before'. In retrospect, the Act set out fundamental principles which still remain global copyright norms: authors' property for a limited duration for justified purposes.[32]

First, the preamble to the statute clearly expresses valid justifications for copyright law. The Act was for 'the encouragement of learned men to compose and write useful books'; and the Act was to protect 'authors or proprietors of books and writings' from unauthorised printing and publishing, which were to 'their very great detriment and too often to the ruin of them and their families'.

Secondly, the Act expressly granted the right, in the first instance, to the 'author' of a 'book', or to any person who had 'purchased or acquired' the copy of the book. This was in contrast to the prevailing system of vesting printing privileges in members of the Stationers' Company. Although property rights of some sort were being granted, it would take a further 50 years or so before the justifications and parameters of the right were reified. There has been contemporary debate as to whether the author was truly recognised under the Statute of Anne. Mark Rose, in defence of authorial status, asserts that the Act redefined copyright:

---

[31] Mellot, ibid., 51 *et seq.*, stating that competition principles (such as more employment) were often invoked to remedy the perceived iniquity of privilege monopolies; Armstrong, *supra* note 11, 191–2, arguing that privileges served as objects of formal transfer of ownership whereby the Letters Patents would be sold in return for payment and/or copies of published books. Moreover, licensing agreements were made under the aegis of a privilege allowing a publisher who held a privilege to licence another seller to publish or reprint.

[32] Preamble, Copyright Act 1709 8 Anne (c.19), enacted in 1709, with effect from 10 April 1710. For detailed discussions on the passage and influence of the Act, see Rose, *supra* note 11, suggesting the Statute of Anne not only stimulated the emergence of the 'modern proprietary author', but also the progression of copyright history from one of trade regulation and marketplace economics to the liberal culture of possessive individualism, 142. *Cf* Deazley, *supra* note 24, xxii; B. Kaplan, *An Unhurried View of Copyright* (New York: Columbia University Press, 1967); W.R. Cornish, 'The Statute of Anne 1709–10: Its Historical Setting', in L. Bently, U. Suthersanen and P. Torremans (eds), *Global Copyright: Three Hundred Years since the Statute of Anne, From 1709 to Cyberspace* (Cheltenham: Edward Elgar Publishing, 2010), the Statute of Anne gave practical effect to an ideal of literary property that had an independent existence, 17–19.

No mention of ⁊ʳ the type of [handwritten marginal note]

[...] as a matter of right rather than privilege, an automatic grant to the author b
his literary endeavour. Thus the statute gives legal reality to the public sphere, proviumg ..
regime in which individual authors [...] are encouraged to bring the fruits of their efforts
into the public forum on no other authority but that of their reason, their learning, and their
deliberation.[33]

Thirdly, there was a temporal limit, and the right of printing and reprinting unpublished books
lasted for a maximum duration of 28 years, accompanied by a right of forfeiture and penalties.[34]
As Cornish notes, the durational limit for each separate book 'set a legal pattern which would
be imitated in a great many countries as they introduced copyright systems'.[35] The absence of an
express civil right of action under the statute, was followed by decades of debate as to the residual
common law copyright within the English legal system, buttressed by a natural rights theory, initially supported by the courts in *Millar v. Taylor*.[36] A contrary interpretation in *Donaldson v. Becket*
acknowledged the instrumentalist function of the Statute of Anne: the common law property right
had been merged into and subsumed by the Statute of Anne, while authors' rights in books had
been re-born as a positive right, governed primarily by statutory policy.[37] Authors of other genres
of creative work had to wait patiently as the legislature passed statutes in a piecemeal fashion for
engravings, sculptures, fine arts, dramatic and musical works.[38]

The first American state copyright law, modelled after the UK Statute of Anne, was passed
in Connecticut in 1783. Entitled 'An Act for the Encouragement of Literature and Genius', the
statute granted US authors and their heirs and assigns 'the sole liberty of printing, publishing
and vending' in relation to new books, pamphlets, maps, or charts within the State of Connecticut for two renewable terms of 14 years. Another 12 states followed suit until the enactment
of the first US federal copyright statute – the Act of 1790.[39] This first federal copyright law was

---

[33] M. Rose, 'The Public Sphere and the Emergence of Copyright: Areopagitica, the Stationers' Company, and the Statute
of Anne', *supra* note 28, 83–4; *cf* R. Deazley, 'Re-reading Donaldson (1774) in the Twenty-First Century and Why it
Matters' (2003) 25(6) *EIPR* 270–79, rebutting this and instead arguing that author's rights originated with the subsequent
1735 Engravings (or Hogarth's) Act.

[34] Copyright Act 1710 (8 Anne c.19), ss 1, 11.

[35] Cornish, *supra* note 32, 22.

[36] *Millar v. Taylor* (1769) 4 Burr 2303; 98 Eng Rep 201 (KB).

[37] *Donaldson v. Beckett* (1774) 2 Bro PC 129; (1994) 17 Hansard Parl. Hist. 953. For varying views, see Cornish, *supra* note
32, 19–20; R. Deazley, 'The Myth of Copyright at Common Law' (2003) 62 *Cambridge Law Journal* 106, 126; R. Deazley,
On the Origin of the Right to Copy: Charting the Movement of Copyright Law in Eighteenth-Century Britain (1695–1775)
(Oxford: Hart Publishing, 2004), 191–220.

[38] The most influential in current UK copyright law being: the Engraving Copyright Act was passed in 1734, after pressure
from artists such as Hogarth; the Sculpture Copyright Act in 1798; and the Dramatic Copyright Act in 1833. For other
statutes passed in from 1710–1911, see *Primary Sources on Copyright (1450–1900)*, United Kingdom, *supra* note 17.

[39] Act of May 31, 1790 ch. 15, 1 Stat. 124; prior to the 1790 federal statute, the following states passed copyright statutes:
Massachusetts, Maryland, New Jersey, New Hampshire, Rhode Island, Pennsylvania, South Carolina, Virginia, North
Carolina, Georgia and New York.

based on the original states' statutes which reflected, in varying degrees, the basic tenets of the Statute of Anne. Nevertheless, the 1790 Act was of a different character, enacted and justified under a more social constitutional charter which also linked copyright and patent laws. It would take a further 40 odd years to determine whether there was any residual common law copyright when the US Supreme Court in *Wheaton v. Peters* concluded that the 1790 law had not sanctioned an existing right, but had instead created a new right, underpinned by the Constitutional Clause.[40]

4.1.5   From revolutionary decrees to '*droit d'auteur*'

It is enlightening to note that on the eve of the French Revolution, Louis XVI issued a noteworthy edict whereby the author was granted a privilege in perpetuity, which if assigned to a bookseller or printer, would then last only for the lifetime of the author.[41] The printing privileges nevertheless were abolished by the National Assembly in 1789, although the right to property per se was preserved in the Declaration of the Rights of Man and Citizen. The 1789 Declaration upheld the preservation of the natural and imprescriptible rights of man, which included the rights of liberty and property. A fresh basis thus arose for the author's right, which was emphasised by the first two post-Revolutionary decrees passed by the National Assembly for authors. The 1791 Decree granted the author of a dramatic work the right to control the public staging of their works, while the subsequent 1793 Decree extended the right of reproduction, distribution and sale to authors of 'any production of the mind or genius belonging to the fine arts'.[42] These two decrees were remarkably long-lived, and governed French copyright law for the next 150 years, until the 1957 Law on Literary and Artistic Property, which codified the preexisting law.

The French notion of the author has been linked often to the conceptually romantic author, which in turn is based on the revolutionary insistence on the supremacy of the literary property of an author. This derives in part from the speech of one of the key draftsmen of the 1793 Act, Le Chapelier, who describes the author's property right as follows: 'The most sacred, the most legitimate, the most unassailable, and if I may say, the most personal of all properties is the work, fruit of the thought of a writer [...].' As others have pointed out, these words are often quoted out of context, since Le Chapelier continues further on to note that once a work is published and disclosed to the public:

---

[40] *Wheaton v. Peters* 33 US (8 Pet.) 591 (1834), 661. The IP clause is Art I § 8, cl. 8 of the US Constitution. For further interpretation of the Clause, see E.C. Walterscheid, 'Understanding the Copyright Act of 1790: The Issue of Common Law Copyright in America and the Modern Interpretation of the Copyright Power' (2005–06) 53 J. Copyright Soc'y U.S.A. 313; C.E. Walterscheid, *The Nature of the Intellectual Property Clause: A Study in Historical Perspective* (Buffalo and New York: William S. Hein, 2002); B. Beebe, '*Bleistein*, The Problem of Aesthetic Progress, and the Making of American Copyright Law' (2017) 117 Colum. L. Rev. 319.

[41] J. Lowndes, *An Historical Sketch of the Law of Copyright* (London: Saunders & Benning, 1840), Appendix 1, 116.

[42] French law of 13 January 1791, concerning the works of living playwrights, and French Literary and Artistic Property Act, Paris (1793), *Primary Sources on Copyright, supra* note 17.

When the work is in the hands of everyone, when all educated men know it and have imbued it with happy memories, it seems that since then, the writer has affiliated the public with his property, or rather has fully transmitted his property to the public.[43]

Indeed, Article 2 of the 1791 Decree declared that the works of authors who had been dead for five years become 'public property'. Thus, Le Chapelier highlights that the French law on authorial rights are temporary property rights which are based on and around the more fundamental claims of the public interest, and on the crucial need for these works to fall into the public domain for the enjoyment of all. The notion that French law offers a more balanced view of the rights of the author on the one hand, and the concept of the public's need for a healthy public domain on the other hand, is similarly expressed nearly a century later by Victor Hugo, one of the proponents of the Berne Convention on Literary and Artistic Property:

The book, as a book, belongs to the author, but as thought, it represents – and the word is not too large – the human race. All minds are entitled. If one of the two rights, namely, the right of the author and the right of humanity, had to be sacrificed, it would certainly be the right of the author, because the public interest is our sole concern [...].[44]

The thrust of modern discourse is that the traditional view is incorrect in labelling the first French laws as being auteur-centric and based on natural rights rather than economic considerations. Kerever, for example, has argued that the revolutionary decrees were propelled by economic considerations such as opening up the book industry to provincial booksellers, and promoting the press industries.[45] Hesse similarly argues that the revolutionary laws were 'explicitly intended to dethrone the absolute author, a creature of privilege, and recast him, not as a private individual (the absolute bourgeois), but rather as a public servant, as the model citizen'.[46] Hesse further asserts that:

If the Old Regime first accorded Voltaire and Rousseau the possibility of legal status as privileged authors with perpetual private lineages for their texts, the Revolution relocated these figures in

---

[43] C. Hesse, *Publishing and Cultural Politics in Revolutionary Paris, 1789–1810* (Berkeley: University of California Press, 1991), Chapters 3 and 4; and C. Colombet (ed.), *Propriété littéraire et artistique et droits voisins* (3rd ed., Paris: Dalloz, 1990), 8 *et seq.*; C. Geiger, 'The Influence (Past and Present) of the Statute of Anne in France' in Bently, Suthersanen and Torremans, *supra* note 32, 128; J.C. Ginsburg, '"Une chose publique?" The Author's Domain and the Public Domain in Early British, French and US Copyright Law', in P. Torremans, *Copyright Law: A Handbook of Contemporary Research* (Cheltenham: Edward Elgar Publishing, 2007), 145–6; J.C. Ginsburg, 'A Tale of Two Copyrights: Literary Property in Revolutionary France and America', in Sherman and Strowel, *supra* note 27, 131–58, 144.

[44] Victor Hugo, *Discours d'ouverture du Congrès littéraire international de 1878*, 1878 (available over the internet in French; the above translation attributable to U. Suthersanen and T. Straub).

[45] A. Kerever, 'The French Revolution and Authors' Rights' (1989) 141 RIDA 3.

[46] C. Hesse, 'Enlightenment Epistemology and the Laws of Authorship in Revolutionary France, 1777–1793' (1990) 30 *Representations* 130.

the public domain, the legal parallel to the civic rituals that reposed their bodily remains in the public temple of the Pantheon. By inventing the 'public domain' the French revolutionary laws on authorship shifted the problem of determining the meaning of the text away from its source, the author, and toward its destination, its re-presentation and reception by the editor and reader.[47]

In contrast to the French codification of copyright law, early regulatory history in Germany was piece-meal and dispersed in the conglomerate of different states and principalities, all with their individual privileges. That the situation was untenable is clear in the writings of Luther, Kant and Fichte who collectively complained of the rampant book piracy that was the norm within the competing Leipzig and Frankfurt book markets.[48] The first unified statutes only began to emerge after the formation of the Prussian Zollverein. The Prussian Civil Code 1794, for instance, went some way towards assisting the author, albeit using a contrived legal path based on publishing rights and contractual means. The law asserted that the bookseller acquired 'the right to publish only through a written contract with the author', the assumption being there is an underlying proprietary right of the author.[49] Similar pieces of laws conferring some rights on authors existed in other states, one of the most famous being the Baden Civil Code 1810 which had incorporated provisions on literary property, and was the first German copyright law to calculate the term of copyright in relation to the life of the author.[50]

In contrast to the English and French laws, which were narrow in their coverage with little or no guidance on transfer of rights or limitations on the scope of protection, the next fully-fledged copyright law to emerge in Europe was the Prussian Copyright Act 1837 which can, perhaps, lay claim to the status of the 'first modern copyright law'. It sets out specific provisions on the nature of works, the beneficiaries of protection, the conditions for licences, duration of rights, and the scope of protection.[51] As Kawohl claims:

> Though provisions in Baden had acknowledged the author's rather than the publishers' property in his works as early as 1806 and 1809, it was the Prussian Statute that for the first time comprised the core concepts of what has been termed a 'modern' copyright: the author rather than the publisher was at the centre of the protection, and the protected subject matter consisted of abstract works, rather than specific physical goods.[52]

---

[47] Ibid., 131.

[48] Bowker, *supra* note 11, 12; M. Woodmansee, *The Author, Art and the Market* (New York: Columbia University Press, 1994), 35 *et seq.*, 51–2.

[49] Art 998, Prussian Law 1794 available in F. Kawohl (2008), 'Commentary on the reprinting provisions in the Prussian Statute Book (1794)', in *Primary Sources on Copyright, supra* note 17; also see Woodmansee, ibid., 52–4.

[50] F. Kawohl (2008), 'Commentary on the copyright provisions in the Baden Statute Book (1809)', in *Primary Sources on Copyright, supra* note 17; Woodmansee, ibid.

[51] Law for the Protection of Property in Works of Scholarship and the Arts against Reprinting and Reproduction, available in F. Kawohl (2008), 'Commentary on the Prussian Copyright Act (1837)', in *Primary Sources on Copyright, supra* note 17.

[52] Ibid.

4.2   TECHNOLOGY AND GLOBAL EXPANSIC

4.2.1   The modern author

It was accepted by the nineteenth and twentieth centuries that the author deserved some sort of protection to prevent the misappropriation of creative outputs. There were, nevertheless, major challenges that had to be resolved in the genesis of copyright law during this era. Who were the beneficiaries of the law? What was the extent and scope of protection? What type of rights should be accorded to the author, and other beneficiaries? What was the territorial extent of copyright law?

What had changed significantly by the end of the nineteenth century was the influence and importance of authors as they actively deployed the rhetoric of 'authorship', 'labour' and 'genius' to advance their causes. We can see this nascent authorial influence when William Hogarth assembled other creators in Britain to press for and obtain copyright protection for the artist-engraver. The preamble to the British Engravers' Act 1735 clearly acknowledges that a 14-year term of protection was necessary in order for artists to reap 'the sole Benefit of their Labours' for prints and engravings created by their 'Genius, Industry, Pains and Expense'.[53] The authorship rhetoric solved the paradox of the creative professions in that previously, imitation and borrowing had been accepted as being part of the creative act whereas now, such acts were characterised as plagiaristic and wrongful misappropriation. No longer were they mere writers or craftsmen labouring under a patronage or master-servant system. They were now engaged in the noble profession of creating, with commensurate rights of remuneration and enforcement in relation to their outputs.[54] The rhetoric of authorship helped convince the legislatures and the public that far from the law being a corporate interest, copyright was for the individual labouring author. Established nineteenth-century British authors such as William Wordsworth and Charles Dickens drew national attention to their need to obtain a sustainable remuneration to support themselves and their families from their writings through the copyright system.[55] Wordsworth wrote in his personal Petition to Parliament:

---

[53] An Act for the Encouragement of the Arts of Designing, Engraving and Etching Historical and other Prints, by Vesting the Properties thereof in the Inventors and Engravers, during the Time therein Mentioned, 1735 (UK), 8 Geo 2, c 13. For the passage of this Act and the role played by artists such as William Hogarth, see R. Paulson, *Hogarth: High Art and Low, 1732–1750, Volume II* (Cambridge: The Lutterworth Press, 1991), Chapters 1–2.

[54] The dismantling of the patronage system and the recognition of the importance of the public had already been noted in the eighteenth century by authors, such as Oliver Goldsmith who stated that authors no longer depended on the 'Great for subsistence, they have no other patrons but the public, and the public, collectively considered, is a good and generous master.' O. Goldsmith, *The Citizen of the World and the Bee*, 233 (Austin Dobson, ed., Everyman's Library, 1934) (1762).

[55] P.L. Shillingsburg, *Pegasus in Harness: Victorian Publishing and W.M. Thackeray* (University Press of Virginia, 1992), 68; S. Eilenberg, *Strange Power of Speech: Wordsworth, Coleridge and Literary Possession* (Oxford University Press, 1992), 204.

The [Copyright] Bill has for its main object, to relieve men of letters from the thraldom of being forced to court the living generation, to aid them in rising above degraded taste and slavish prejudice, and to encourage them to rely upon their own impulses, or to leave them with less excuse if they should fail to do so.[56]

Crucially, the 'author' banner has been employed tenaciously since the nineteenth century in order to rationalise a variety of policies and concepts including personality/personhood, the extension of protection to different genres of works, burgeoning economic rights, and longer terms of protection (see Chapter 2 on justifications). As the remaining discourse in this section indicates, the prominence and power of the author is in sharp decline as global copyright law and policy is being increasingly shaped by copyright industries, intellectual property-intensive countries, and technological challenges.

4.2.2   From pirate to sentry[57]

Domestic protection is to no avail without international protection and enforcement. The advent of industrialisation and the ensuing technological advances in the reproduction, dissemination and commercialisation of works led to a paradoxical situation. On the one hand, such improvements meant increased print runs, improved sales of works, and the availability of new markets for new writers. This would lead to higher and more sustainable returns for the authors and also those involved in the entrepreneurial industries, especially publishing and communications. On the other hand, faster and cheaper reproduction and distribution technologies meant an increase in counterfeit and unauthorised copies of works.

In the case of the US, for example, the first 1790 federal copyright failed to extend copyright protection to foreign authors.[58] The justification was the need for a new, developing nation to protect its fledgling culture and industries against the established trade in England. Unsurprisingly, between 1800 and 1860, almost half of the bestsellers in the US were reprinted without authorisation from English novels, at approximately one-tenth of the total cost. The government policy of imposing tariffs on imported books that ranged as high as 25 per cent also encouraged local reprinting of foreign works.

---

[56] 1839 Petition; for this and other petitions in support of an extension of copyright term, see T.N. Talfourd, *Three Speeches delivered (18th May, 1837, 25th April, 1838, and 28th February, 1839) in the House of Commons in favour of a measure for an extension of Copyright, etc.* (London: Edward Moxon, 1840 (available on Google books)).

[57] This section is a summary of the following writings: U. Suthersanen, 'The First Global Copyright Act', in U. Suthersanen and Y. Gendreau (eds), *A Shifting Empire: 100 Years Of The Copyright Act 1911* (Cheltenham: Edward Elgar Publishing, 2012); Patterson, *supra* note 27, 199; B.Z. Khan, 'Copyright Piracy and Development: United States Evidence in the Nineteenth Century' (2008) 10(8) *Rev. Econ. Inst.* 21; B.Z. Khan, 'Does Copyright Piracy Pay? The Effects of U.S. International Copyright Laws on the Market for Bs, 1790–1920', National Bureau of Economic Research Working Paper 10271, 2004; H.G. Henn, 'The Quest for International Copyright Protection' (1953) 39 *Cornell L.Q.* 43; S. Vaidhyanathan, *Copyrights and Copywrongs: The Rise of Intellectual Property and how it Threatens Creativity* (Cheltenham: New York University Press, 2001).

[58] 1790 Copyright Act, s 5.

The campaign to bring the US into the nascent global copyright system is well docum. and indeed there was an awareness of the need for reciprocal copyright recognition by Ame. authors including H.W. Longfellow and Louisa May Alcott. Eventually, a bilateral agreement was signed between the UK and the US, although this did not come into effect until 1891, five years after the Berne Convention.[59]

Indeed, a similar situation arose in Europe as cheaper reprints of French and English language books were increasingly being published without authorisation in Belgium, the Netherlands, and Ireland, infiltrating bookshops and circulating libraries. By the middle of the nineteenth century, after decades of combating cross-border importation and piracy of books in Europe, major European publishers and authors' societies began to search for an international solution, with a set of coherent and codified copyright norms. As discussed previously, this search led to the Berne Convention 1886.[60]

Although the US was not to join the Berne Convention until 1989,[61] it has transformed itself in the last 150 years from a pirate nation to a global sentry, as its economy expanded to include IP-intensive industries contributing more than US$5 trillion to the US gross domestic product.[62] The same is true of other newer entrants on the copyright scene such as India, Canada and Australia which have taken leadership in developing newer and stronger international norms of protection, especially in relation to moral rights (rare for common law countries) and educational exceptions.

4.2.3   Performers and producers

A key copyright axiom is that the advent of technology invariably increases the scope of rights and the revenue stream of authors and owners. Industry cries of panic and revulsion which greeted many technological revolutions during the nineteenth and twentieth centuries soon turned into demands for a broader and more robust international copyright regime which would negate the effects of the cinematographic, broadcasting, reprographic, digital and compression technologies. Just note, for example, the evolution of rights and subject matter within the Berne Convention from 1886 to 1971:

- the 1908 Berlin Revision recognised photographic works as a protectable category, and mechanical reproduction right for musical works, and rights in relation to cinematographic adaptations, as well as the recognition of cinematographic works as a literary or artistic work in their own right;

---

[59] International Copyright Act of 1891, 26 Stat. 1106. For a discussion, see B.Z. Khan, *The Democratization of Invention: Patents and Copyrights in American Economic Development, 1790–1920* (New York: Cambridge University Press, 2005), 260; Geller, *supra* note 1, 229.

[60] J.J. Barnes, *Authors, Publishers and Politicians: The Quest for an Anglo-American Copyright Agreement 1815–1854* (London: Routledge, 1974), 95.

[61] Berne Convention Implementation Act of 1988, Pub L. No. 100-568, 102 Stat.2853 s.2(3) (1988).

[62] Equivalent to 34.8 per cent of the US GDP – see *Intellectual Property and the U.S. Economy: Industries in Focus*, prepared by Economics and Statistics Administration and the United States Patent and Trademark Office, US Department of Commerce, 2012.

- the 1928 Rome Revision introduced broadcasting and other communication to the public rights;
- the 1948 Brussels Revision extended broadcasting and communication rights to include television broadcasts, retransmissions, public communication of transmissions, and the fixation of works after transmissions, of works, while clarifying rights in cinematographic works;
- the 1967 Stockholm Revision introduced the right to reproduction.[63]

Subsequent international instruments confirm this general approach of expanding global copyright law. The TRIPS Agreement, for instance, extends copyright protection for computer programs and electronic databases; while the 1996 WIPO Copyright Treaty (WCT) and WIPO Performances and Phonograms Treaty (WPPT) (the 'Internet Treaties') introduce three new copyright concepts in order to assist rights owners' control over access to and reproduction of digital works, as well as the subsequent distribution of such works over the internet (see discussion below and Chapter 16).

Despite this expansion of rights, entrepreneurial producers of recognised Berne works, including film producers, sound recording producers and performers, began lobbying for control and a share of revenues in the early twentieth century, especially with the advent of public radio broadcasting of both live and recorded music. Although the sound recording industry's interests were discussed at the 1908 Berne Convention Revision, it was impossible to accommodate them within the author-centric Berne Convention as mechanical recordings were arguably not 'authored' works. The recording industry held its own congress in 1933, which culminated not only in the founding of the International Federation of the Phonographic Industry (IFPI), but also facilitated the discussion on a new convention for protection of recording producers, advocating *sui generis* or remuneration rights. The Austrian 1936 law was the first regulation which solved the problem by introducing 'related rights' (*Verwandte Schutzrechte*) to cover this new group of rights holders. Similarly, in Italy, a 1937 law gave Italian record companies a remuneration right for secondary uses of their records, on the radio, in restaurants and other entertainment venues.[64]

Performances were, and still are, difficult to categorise. The principal bar to treating performers as authors is that they do not create works, they merely execute or interpret preexisting works. The counterargument is just as convincing: many performers do not mechanically execute the works but rather re-cast such works in their own individualistic manner. For example, performers routinely impose their own personality in cadenzas or jazz improvisations. The usual justifications for granting rights to authors (natural justice, economic incentives, and public interest arguments) seem to apply equally to performers. Early nineteenth-century laws allowed an individual performer some copyright claims to a recording as long as the interpretation constituted an original adaptation of the

---

[63] S. Ricketson and J. Ginsburg, *International Copyright and Neighbouring Rights: The Berne Convention and Beyond* (Oxford: Oxford University Press, 2005), Chapter 3 (for a detailed discussion on these revisions).

[64] S. Frith, 'The Industrialization of Music', in A. Bennet, B. Shank and J. Toynbee (eds), *The Popular Music Studies Reader* (Routledge, 2006); G. Davies, 'The 50th Anniversary Of The Rome Convention For The Protection Of Performers, Producers Of Phonograms And Broadcasting Organisations: Reflections on the Background and Importance of the Convention' (2012) *Queen Mary Journal of Intellectual Property* 206; R. Fleischer, 'Protecting the Musicians and/or the Record Industry? On the History of "neighbouring rights" and the role of Fascist Italy' (2015) 5 *Queen Mary Journal of Intellectual Property* 327, 336.

musical work.[65] Performers' rights were first considered by the International Labour Organization (ILO) in 1926, due to the problem of 'technological unemployment', which could be solved by the introduction of a performer's right. Within the Berne Convention context, performers' rights were first considered at the Berne Revision Conference in 1928 but failed to join as authors.

The phonogram producers, performers and even the broadcasters finally got international recognition under the 1961 Rome Convention.[66] More recent international laws, such as the WPPT and the Beijing Audiovisual Treaty, confer moral rights on performers, thus taking these stakeholders a step closer towards the 'authorhood' status. Moreover, the Beijing Audiovisual Treaty extends the global umbrella of protection to a hitherto unprotected group of performers, i.e., those whose performances are incorporated in audiovisual works (for example, actors, musicians and dancers).[67]

Historically, US law has been reluctant to recognise performers and phonogram producers. In the absence of federal copyright protection of sound recordings, unfair competition or common law copyright was often the basis of protection for the economic and moral rights of the artistes concerned and production companies. Today, performances, phonograms and broadcasts receive some sort of protection under US federal copyright law, although protection for such related works remains idiosyncratic,[68] and the situation in relation to pre-1972 recordings remains incredibly complex. For instance, in *Capitol Records, Inc v. Naxos of America, Inc*, a court held that pre-1972 published sound recordings are protected under New York common law copyrights until 15 February 2067. In 2015, the US appellate court caused an uproar in *Garcia v. Google Inc* when the 9th Circuit first held that an actress had a possible copyright interest in her creative, individual performance in a film; only for the same court en banc to reverse the decision.[69]

An identical tension arose in relation to protecting films as productions as opposed to 'authored films'. Original films were easily recognised within the Berne Convention as cinematographic adaptations or cinematographic works; moreover, films were also recognised as authorial works

[65] Fleischer, ibid., 330.

[66] Rome Convention, Arts 10, 12.

[67] WPPT, Arts 3, 5; Beijing Audiovisual Treaty, Arts 3, 5.

[68] US Copyright Law 1976, ss 106(6), 114. Moreover, performers only have performance rights in relation to digital rather than analogue recordings – Digital Performance Right in Sound Recordings Act of 1995 grants a public performance right in sound recordings applicable to digital transmissions.

[69] *Capitol Records, Inc v. Naxos of Am, Inc*, 830 NE 2d 250, 263-64 (NY, 2005); *Garcia v. Google, Inc*, 766 F 3d 929 (9th Cir, 2014), rev'd en banc, 786 F 3d 733 (9th Cir, 2015). Early cases extending unfair competition law to phonograms and performers include *Victor Talking Machine Co. v. Armstrong*, 132 F 711 (SDNY, 1904); *Fonotipia Ltd v. Bradley*, 171 F 951 (EDNY, 1909); *Metropolitan Opera Ass'n v. Wagner-Nichols Recorder Corp*, 101 NYS 2d 483 (S Ct, 1950). For state common law copyright/unfair competition in sound recordings, see *Capitol Records, Inc v. Mercury Records Corp*, 221 F 2d 657 (2d Cir, 1955). In addition to unfair competition and common law copyright, protection is also provided for pre-1972 recordings through 'a patchwork of criminal laws, civil statutes and common law' – US Copyright Office Report, *Federal Copyright Protection for Pre-1972 Sound Recordings*, 2011, 20 *et seq.* For the historical account, see B.A. Ringer, *Copyright Law Revision Study no 26: The Unauthorised Duplication of Sound Recordings*, 1957, 21–37, available at www.copyright.gov/ history/studies/study26.pdf; J.E. Mason, 'Performers Rights and Copyright: The Protection of Sound Recordings from Modern Pirates' (1971) 59 *Cal. L. Rev.* 548.

in civil law countries, and to some extent in common law ones too.[70] Notwithstanding this recognition, a parallel set of rights were adopted which vested ownership in film producers. Thus, within authors' rights countries, the film director was, and still is, considered the 'creative author', whereas the film producer is treated as a subaltern rights owner with protection for his financial investment in making and distributing the derivative product. A different approach was adopted in common law systems, where the film director was essentially ignored as a beneficiary of rights, in contrast to the film producer. Depending on the legal mechanisms, it is often the case that production companies will end up as the sole or joint owner of economic rights for the full copyright term. Within the EU, this disparity of rights and beneficiaries under a double regulatory tier was eventually resolved by formally recognising two sets of beneficiaries: (i) the principal 'author' of a film must include the director of the film (and member states are free to designate other 'authors'); (ii) the film producer is recognised as a related rights owner.[71]

Turning to the US, 'motion pictures and audiovisual works' are categorised as 'original works of authorship', though the reality is that film producers can acquire rights under the federal law both as 'authors' or under the 'work made for hire' doctrine.[72] Similarly, there are no broadcasting 'rights' as such under US copyright law but copyright protection can be gained through recording the broadcast work, and hence claiming a performance right which will cover the act of broadcasting, and under the Communications Act.[73]

4.2.4   EU copyright *acquis*

A brief conceptual note on 'EU copyright law' is necessary at the outset. When the founding EU treaties were first drafted in 1957, copyright, along with other IPRs, were clearly not priorities. The importance of IP rights was only realised when it was used by owners to divide the different markets, thus disrupting the internal market rules within the EU. Various economic studies on IP-related industries mushroomed, which gave estimates as to the industries' growing contribution to the GDP in the EU, ranging from 3.3 per cent in 2006 to almost 39 per cent in 2012 (worth €4.7 trillion).[74]

Copyright law has transformed and grown in this period. In the first stage covering roughly a period between 1957 and 1987, the focus was on the relationship between copyright and the

---

[70] Berne Convention, Arts 14, 14*bis*; the first countries to recognise such related rights for film producers included Italy (1925), UK (1956) and Germany (1965).

[71] For current laws reflecting this position, see Directive 2006/115/EC of the European Parliament and of the Council of 12 December 2006 on rental right and lending right and on certain rights related to copyright in the field of intellectual property (codified version); and P. Kamina, *Film Copyright in the European Union* (Cambridge University Press, 2016).

[72] US Copyright Law, 1978, s 101. See also 16 *Casa Duse, LLC v. Merkin*, 791 F 3d 247 (2d Cir, 2015), confirming that where multiple individuals lay claim to the copyright in a single work, the copyright will belong to the 'dominant author' of the work, in this case the film producer, and not the director.

[73] US Copyright Law, ss 112(e), 123, 119, 501.

[74] European Patent Office/Office for Harmonization in the Internal Market, 'Intellectual Property Rights Intensive Industries: Contribution to Economic Performance and Employment in the European Union Industry-Level Analysis Report', September 2013.

basic tenets of the European Community rules. In the second stage, there was an intense period of harmonisation, starting with the ground-breaking Green Paper on Copyright and the Challenge of Technology whereby the European Commission attempted to solve the urgent problems at the pan-EU level. Since 2015, we have been in the third stage where the EU legislators have been particularly active in the area of the digital market. The most current legislative attempts are outlined in the Commission's Digital Single Market (DSM) Strategy identifying the need for more modernised copyright rules which focuses on four general themes: (i) offering better choice and access to content online and across borders; (ii) improving copyright rules on research, education and cultural heritage; (iii) achieving a well-functioning marketplace for copyright; (iv) facilitating access to more content for the visually impaired or people with print disabilities.[75]

The position for trade marks and designs, and more increasingly patents, is more harmonised. There are Community trade mark and design laws whereby a unitary EU right is applicable throughout the EU region, and which exist in parallel to harmonised national laws.[76] This is not true for copyright law whereby the 'EU copyright law' is regulated by eleven directives, which broadly govern and harmonise the following areas:

(i)   subject matter and criterion: computer programs; databases; photographs;
(ii)   economic rights and limitations in relation to authors, performers, broadcasters, phonogram and film producers;
(iii)   licensing framework for the copyright in satellite broadcasting and cable re-transmission services;
(iv)   resale royalty rights in original manuscripts and artworks;
(v)   regulation of orphan works and use of works for visually impaired persons;
(vi)   duration of protection for authored and neighbouring works;
(vii)   collective management of music; and
(viii) enforcement of rights.[77]

In addition to the laws, several new and proposed laws have been published in order to regulate the following areas: cross-border portability of online content services;[78] cross-border exchange of

---

[75] *EC Green Paper on Copyright and Challenges of the New Technology 1988*; Communication From The Commission To The European Parliament, The Council, The European Economic Social Committee and The Committee Of The Regions, *Towards a Modern, More European Copyright Framework, COM(2015) 626 final; Promoting a Fair, Efficient and Competitive European Copyright-based Economy in the Digital Single Market*, COM(2016)592.

[76] Regulation (EU) No 2015/2424 of the European Parliament and the Council amending the Community trade mark; Directive 2008/95/EC on trade marks; Council Regulation No 6/2002 on Community designs; Directive 98/71/EC on designs.

[77] For the full and current list, see: http://ec.europa.eu/internal_market/copyright/acquis/index_en.htm.

[78] Regulation (EU) 2017/1128 on cross-border portability of online content services in the internal market, OJ L168, 30.6.17; see European Commission, *Staff Working Document/Impact Assessment*, COM(2015) 627 final/SWD(2015) 271 final, Brussels, 9/12/2015, available at http://ec.europa.eu/smart-regulation/impact/ia_carried_out/docs/ia_2015/swd_2015_0270_en.pdf#page=18.

works for the benefit of persons who are blind, visually impaired or otherwise print-disabled;[79] on-line broadcast transmissions and retransmissions;[80] and finally an overhaul of copyright law within the promised Digital Single Market.[81] This final proposed legislation had been highly controversial especially in relation to:

- text and data mining exceptions for the purposes of research and access;
- the 'hyperlink tax' provision (referred to alternatively as the 'press publishers' rights') which vests a new neighbouring right over use of online contents (including news snippets which are not necessarily protected under copyright law), especially by online news aggregators (such as Google News), thus requiring licences before links to news websites;
- the 'meme ban' and 'value gap' provisions, namely two complex provisions which require us-er-content platforms to take effective and proportionate measures to prevent unauthorised postings of copyrighted content, and to also provide fair remuneration for authors and artists.[82]

All the above have been now incorporated, to varying extents, within the 2019 Directive on copy-right and related rights in the Digital Single Market.[83] These various laws have effectively provided a TRIPS-plus level of copyright protection in the EU. Moreover, the absence of a unitary copyright code within the region has resulted in the Court of Justice of the EU (CJEU) adopting an active role in constructing the copyright *acquis*. In contrast to the early days of the copyright harmonisation programme at the turn of the twentieth century, the CJEU has rendered at least 20 important decisions since 2012. It has also adopted a distinctly teleological approach in interpreting the rules within the directives. Thus, in addition to the above, the CJEU has furthered the codification of national laws by offering EU-wide interpretations of, inter alia, originality, subject matter of pro-tection, the right of communication to the public, exhaustion doctrine, private copying levies, and parody. In addition to the internal copyright measures adopted, EU copyright law also reflects its separate obligations under various international treaties, including the TRIPS Agreement, the WIPO Internet Treaties, the Beijing Audiovisual Treaty, and the Marrakesh Treaty.[84] On a final

---

[79] Regulation (EU) 2017/1563 OJ L 242/1, 20.9.2017; Directive (EU) 2017/1564 OJ L 242/6, 20.9.2017.

[80] Proposal for a Regulation laying down rules on the exercise of copyright and related rights applicable to certain online transmissions of broadcasting organisations and retransmissions of television and radio programmes, COM/2016/0594 final, 14.9.2016.

[81] Proposal for a Directive on Copyright in the Digital Single Market, COM(2016) 593 final – 2016/0280 (COD).

[82] M. Reynolds, 'What is Article 13? The EU's divisive new copyright plan explained' *Wired*, January 2019, https://www.wired.co.uk/article/what-is-article-13-article-11-european-directive-on-copyright-explained-meme-ban.

[83] Directive (EU) 2019/790 of 17 April 2019 on copyright and related rights in the Digital Single Market, OJ L130/92, 17.05.2019.

[84] For an up-to-date discussion on EU copyright law, see *Copinger and Skone James on Copyright*, G. Davies, G. Harbottle and N. Caddick (eds) (2nd sup, 17th ed., Sweet & Maxwell, 2019), Chapter 24. See also M. Favale, M. Kretschmer and P. Torremans, 'Is There a EU Copyright Jurisprudence? An Empirical Analysis of the Workings of the European Court of Justice' (2016) 79(1) *Modern Law Review* 31–75; T. Dreier, 'The Wittem Project of a European Copyright Code', in C. Geiger (ed.), *Constructing European Intellectual Property* (Cheltenham: Edward Elgar Publishing, 2013), 292–313.

point, it should be noted that EU intellectual property laws have been incorporated trade agreements with third parties (see Chapter 3).

4.2.5 Comparative copyright law

Within the EU, the harmonisation exercise has resulted in the convergence of several legal norms, although some areas remain controversial, and in such cases one must defer to national copyright norms. To drive further harmonisation, should we look to specific approaches adopted in French, British or other European national laws? Or should we cast our net even further afield and consider, say, Australian, Japanese or Canadian jurisprudence, or that of other countries not generally assumed to have come up with innovative measures in their laws thus far? It is true that the traditional taxonomy of the copyright order reflects the manner by which the legal history of copyright has evolved within a Euro-American classification.[85] And this chapter reflects this, depicting the global copyright taxonomy as being divided between the following two traditions:

(i)   Anglo-American common law 'copyright' tradition, as represented mainly by the UK, the US, Australia, Canada, Ireland, Singapore, New Zealand, India, Commonwealth Caribbean, and Anglophone African nations (such as Nigeria and Kenya);

(ii) European-based civil law 'droit d'auteur' tradition, as represented by a vast majority of EU member states, Latin America, Indonesia, Japan, the French West Indies, and Francophone African nations (such as Cameroon and Mali).

In a very general sense, the common law copyright approach centres on the economic labour and power that the copyright industries harness. Hence, protection extends to works displaying, in the UK 'skill, labour and judgement', and in some instances even to computer-generated works. Initial authorship and ownership can vest in both natural or legal persons who have either authored the work or who have economically supported the production of the work (such as phonogram or audiovisual producers), or who have been in charge of the creation of the work (for example, employers).

This utilitarian approach is in contrast with the European *droit d'auteur* tradition, with its multi-justificatory bases of natural justice, personality, and human rights. The author-emphasis is reflected in the terminology and concepts employed within such traditions. For example, rather than 'copyright', the rights are referred to in the original language as author's right (*droit d'auteur* – French, *diritto d'autore* – Italian, *Urheberrecht* – German). The criterion of protection requires the author's personality or imprint, or at least some evidence of creative input. There are also extensive provisions within such copyright laws in relation to employment or licensing contracts which strongly resist any attempts by third parties to dilute an author's economic rights or to alienate or to interfere with the absolute nature of moral rights (see below on moral rights).

---

[85] See ss 4.1.4 and 4.1.5 above. On the common/civil law traditions, see S. von Lewinski, *International Copyright Law and Policy* (Oxford University Press, 2008), Chapter 3; A. Dietz, 'Transformation of Authors Rights: Change of Paradigm' (1988) 138 *RIDA* 22; A. Strowel, 'Droit d'auteur and Copyright: Between History and Nature', in Sherman and Strowel, *supra* note 27; A. Strowel, *Droit d'auteur et copyright – divergences et convergences* (Bruylant-LGDJ, 1993).

This divergence produces practical and academic disparities in relation to basic issues such as types of works protected (for example, derivative works, labour-intensive works, and neighbouring works), ownership of works (for example, employee-authors, commissioned authors and contractual arrangements), moral rights (and the need, for example, to assert them in certain common law countries), the validity of some types of assignments, and the extent of defences. Furthermore, there are more nuanced differences within similar classifications. In relation to civil law, for example, rules on assignments and moral rights differ greatly between the French-influenced and German-influenced doctrines. Within common law traditions, the US fair use doctrine is markedly different from the UK fair dealing defence (adopted in many common law countries), although there is now a trend to incorporate the fair use elements into national laws. Of course, in many respects these jurisdictions despite their different traditions share more in common now than ever before, partly as a consequence of trade regulatory harmonisation generally, but in large part to the increasingly internationalised legal framework under the various international legal instruments. However, one should not disregard hybrid systems such as Canada and China which due to their mixed legal heritage and their perceived national interests offer different perspectives on some copyright norms, and may have something to offer Europe and elsewhere too.

4.3 PROTECTABLE SUBJECT MATTER

Copyright is a bundle of discrete property rights, which arise automatically upon the creation of a particular class of works. The property right authorises the copyright creator or owner to prevent third parties from committing certain acts for a limited duration. The ambiguous nature of national copyright law derives in part from the flexibility within international copyright law – besides setting out minimum standards of protection, countries are free to adopt higher and different national standards. Pragmatically, and irrespective of jurisdiction, a person concerned with copyright protection of a work will need to focus on the following areas of diversity: criteria of copyright and excluded subject matter; ownership of copyright, including authorship, joint creations and assignments; duration of copyright in different categories of works; economic and moral rights conferred, including the scope of protection and limitations.

4.3.1 Authors' works

The Berne Convention enumerates two categories of works. The first category refers to works whose coverage is either optional or excluded from the Convention – in such cases, Union countries retain ultimate copyright sovereignty as to whether a production or work is eligible for protection. Thus it is a matter for Union countries to decide whether to protect official texts and their translations, or political speeches; in respect of works of applied art, the Convention leaves it to countries to offer copyright or design protection.[86]

---

[86] Berne Convention, Art 2(4), (7), 2*bis* – for example, there are special rules to offer further flexibility for works of applied art and designs. See Chapter 7.

The second list refers to subject matter to be protected, albeit the open and inclusive of the Convention leaves it to Union countries to extend protection to non-Berne subject matter. The Berne Convention refers to protecting 'literary and artistic works' which is defined as including 'every production in the literary, scientific and artistic domain, whatever may be the mode or form of its expression'.[87] The provision further sets out an extensive and open list including books, and other writings, lectures and other works of the same nature, dramatic works, choreographic works, musical compositions, cinematographic works, works of drawing, painting, etc., photographic works, works of applied art, illustrations, translations and adaptations.[88] Collections of such works (and presumably electronic databases) will also be protectable if 'by reason of the selection and arrangement of their contents, constitute intellectual creations'.[89] The more recent TRIPS Agreement and the WCT expressly extend the definition of 'literary works' to include computer programs and certain types of databases.[90]

This open-ended approach has allowed national courts to experiment with the parameters of protected expressions over the last two centuries, from oral, visual and textual works, grounded in the physical and analogue world (such as photographs, films), to digital manifestations of works (such as computer programs, electronic databases, and computer-generated works).[91] In recent years, the nature of a copyright work within national laws has extended to literary fictional characters,[92] perfume compositions[93] re-constructed/re-created eighteenth-century gardens and

---

[87] Berne Convention for the Protection of Literary and Artistic Works 1886 (Paris Act, 1971), Arts 1, 2(1); all references are to the Paris text unless otherwise stated. For a detailed discussion, see Ricketson and Ginsburg, *supra* note 63, Chapter 8.

[88] Berne Convention, Art 2(1).

[89] Ibid., Art 2(5).

[90] The historical debate as to the classification of computer programs (either as patentable or copyright works) is well recounted in P. Samuelson, R. Davis, M.D. Kapor and J.H. Reichman, 'A Manifesto Concerning the Legal Protection of Computer Programs' (1994) 94 *Columbia Law Review* 2308; and P. Samuelson, 'The Strange Odyssey of Software Interfaces as Intellectual property', in M. Biagioli, P. Jaszi, M. Woodmansee (eds), *Making and Unmaking Intellectual Property: Creative Production In Legal And Cultural Perspective* (University of Chicago Press, 2011).

[91] Directive 96/9/EC of the European Parliament and of the Council of 11 March 1996 on the Legal Protection of Databases, 1996 OJ (L77) 20; UK Copyright Law, s 9, in relation to computer-generated works.

[92] *Wolf v. Hergé* (Tintin Character protected), TGI Paris, May 11, 1988, (1989) 142 RIDA 344; CA Paris, 4 Ch, Dec 20, 1990, (1992) 151 RIDA 295; 'Alcolix', German Supreme Court, BGH, March 11, 1993, (1994) 25 IIC 605 (cartoon characters Asterix and Obelisk protected); *Roy Export Co v. National Lottery*, Israeli Supreme Court, February 17, 2000, [2000] EIPR N–68 (Charlie Chaplin's 'Little Tramp' character protected).

[93] *Société Bellure v. Société L'Oréal et al*, Cour d'Appel Paris, 4 Ch. January 25, 2006, (2006) 28 RIDA 286, [2006] ECDR 16; and *Lancôme Parfums v. Kecofa B.V.*, Dutch Supreme Court, Case 04/327HR, 16 June 2006, (2006) IIC 997, (2006) ECDR 26; *cf, Bsiri-Babir v. Haarmann et Remier*, French Supreme Court, Cass. 1 civ., June 13, 2006 [2006] ECDR 380, holding that perfume fragrance was ineligible for protection under French author's right as it was simply a result of know how (*savoir faire*). For a further discussion, see C. Cronin, 'Genius in a Bottle: Perfume, Copyright, and Human Perception' (2009) 56 J. Copyright Soc'y. U.S.A 427.

music,[94] urban light creations,[95] the layout of stores,[96] and traditional cultural expressions.[97]

Both US and British copyright laws adopt a category approach, with copyright subsisting in works which are carefully classified and enunciated in the statutes. There is a difference between the two laws. Section 1 of the British copyright law states that copyright subsists in the following 'descriptions of work': (a) original literary, dramatic, musical or artistic works; (b) sound recordings, films or broadcasts; and (c) the typographical arrangement of published editions.[98] Thus, works must clear two hurdles in order to be protected under the law – they must fall within the strict, closed classificatory system in relation to subject matter; and certain types of works must fulfil the criterion of originality. A similar approach can be seen under US copyright law, which protects 'original works of authorship fixed in any tangible medium of expression, now known or later developed, from which they can be perceived, reproduced, or otherwise communicated, either directly or with the aid of a machine or device'. The term 'works of authorship' is further defined into categories except that the latter remains an open list.[99]

As many civil law countries adopt the French or German approaches – where the law offers an open list of protected subject matter – the only real criterion for determining the protectability of a creation is with reference to the criteria of protection and exclusions, discussed below. Article L.111-1 of the French copyright law states: 'The author of a work of the mind shall enjoy in that work, by the mere fact of its creation, an exclusive incorporeal property right which shall be enforceable against all persons.' Further on, Article L112-1 emphasises: 'The provisions of this Code shall protect the rights of authors in all works of the mind, whatever their kind, form of expression, merit or purpose.'[100] The current approach under French copyright law is clearly to embrace all sorts of works, and to this end, French copyright law has unhesitatingly protected laser light shows,[101] articles of fashion, as well as fashion shows[102] as copyright works. Article 1 of the German copyright law states: 'The authors of works in the literary, scientific and artistic domain enjoy

---

[94] *Société Valterre v. Roubakineh and others*, Cour d'Appel Paris, February 11, 2004, (2004) 201 RIDA 303, the re-created gardens of eighteenth-century architect Le Nôtre were held to constitute an original work); *Sawkins v. Hyperion Records Ltd* [2004] EWHC 1530, [2005] EWCA Civ 565 (CA), [2005] ECDR 10 (Ch.D); *Sawkins v. Harmonia Mundi, TGI Nanterre, 1ch, January 19, 2005*, (2006) 207 RIDA 391, the re-created edition of the music of an eighteenth-century composer Lalande was held to be protectable.

[95] *L'Atelier Lumière and M. Nègre v. Les Eclaireurs and M. Goy*, TGI de Lyon, Ch. 3 cab 3 C, 16 May 2017.

[96] *KIKO v. Folies Douces*, Court of Appeal Douai, Chambre 2 section 2, n° 15/03286, 16 March 2017.

[97] For example, Kenya Copyright Act No. 12 of 2001; and Papua New Guinea Copyrights and Neighbouring Rights Act 2000.

[98] UK Copyright Law.

[99] US Copyright Law, ss 101, 102(a).

[100] French Intellectual Property Code.

[101] *Eiffel Tower*, Cass. civ, I, March 3, 1992, DS 1993, 358.

[102] *Vanessa Bruno v. Zara France*, CA Paris, Oct. 17, 2012; *Céline v. Zara France*, CA Paris, Feb. 27, 2013 – in both decisions, fashion wear was granted protection against Zara, a well-known pan-European high street store; *Roberts A. D. et al. v. Chanel et al.*, Cass Civ Crim, 5 February 2008, fashion shows per se are copyright works.

protection for their works in accordance with this Act.'[103] In Germany, the *de jure* position h... .ong been that copyright law will not discriminate against all manner of subject matter, as long as the object under consideration passes the singular threshold of creativity (discussed below).

The CJEU indicates that all subject matter will be protectable within EU copyright law subject to two cumulative conditions. First, the subject matter must be original in the sense that it is the author's own intellectual creation (discussed below). Secondly, it should be classified as a 'work' under international and EU copyright laws. Thus in the *BSA* decision, the CJEU accepted that graphic user interfaces (a subject matter which is not regulated under the EU Directives) could constitute a work if it is its author's own intellectual creation.[104] This may change the current closed-category approach in the UK.[105] The CJEU has further attempted a definition of 'work' as used within both international and EU copyright laws. Thus, in *Levola*, faced with the question of whether the taste of a food could be a copyright work, the court defined a work as subject matter, which 'must be expressed in a manner which makes it identifiable with sufficient precision and objectivity, even though that expression is not necessarily in permanent form'.[106] The CJEU went further to emphasise the economic importance of this issue in that not every creation can constitute a copyright work for two reasons: (i) users must be able to 'identify, clearly and precisely' what is the subject matter of protection; (ii) the law must ensure that there is no element of subjectivity in the process of identifying the protected subject matter. In this case, it was not possible in the current state of scientific development to achieve by technical means a precise and objective identification of the taste of a food product, which enables it to be distinguished from the taste of other products of the same kind.

4.3.2 Entrepreneurial and neighbouring works

Performances, phonograms or sound recordings, and broadcasts are protectable works under the Rome Convention, with the scope of rights for performers and phonogram producers being successively improved under TRIPS, WPPT, and more recently under the Beijing Audiovisual Treaty.[107] Once again, it is up to individual nations and regions to expand the list of protected works, and the beneficiaries for such neighbouring rights. Thus German law recognises non-creative

---

[103] German Copyright Law.

[104] Case C393/09 *Bezpečnostní softwarová asociace – Svaz softwarové ochrany (BSA) v. Ministerstvo kultury*, 22 December 2010, ECLI:EU:C:2010:816, paras 45–46.

[105] *SAS Institute Inc v. World Programming Ltd*, [2013] EWHC 69 (Ch), para 27:

    In the light of a number of recent judgments of the CJEU, it may be arguable that it is not a fatal objection to
    a claim that copyright subsists in a particular work that the work is not one of the kinds of work listed in [UK
    copyright law] [...] it remains clear that the putative copyright work must be a literary or artistic work within the
    meaning of Article 2(1) of the Berne Convention.

[106] Case C310/17 *Levola Hengelo BV v. Smilde Foods BV* ECLI:EU:C:2018:899, 13 November 2018, paras 39–44, holding that the taste of a food product cannot be a copyright work.

[107] The focus shifts from subject matter protected to the persons protected ie performer, phonogram producer and the broadcaster – Rome Convention 1961, Arts 2–3; WPPT 1996, Art 2; Beijing Audiovisual Treaty, Art 2.

photographs, published editions of previously unpublished works, new critical editions of public domain works or technical writings, as well as databases as related rights works, whilst the 2019 EU Directive on the Digital Single Market has extraordinarily conferred the authorial rights of reproduction and communication on press publishers – albeit only for a two year period, and only in relation to online use of press publications by information society service providers.[108]

4.4 CRITERIA FOR PROTECTION

There are three accepted universal rules in relation to the availability of copyright protection. First, a work has to be original. Second, a work must qualify for protection under national law based on the nationality of the author/corporation or the place of first publication, as governed under international rules. There may also be other national rules such as fixation. Finally, the work must not be excluded for stated legal or public policy reasons. Unlike patent, design or trade mark laws, with their strict subject matter delineation and exclusion, the global corpus of copyright, as represented by the various conventions, agreements, and treaties, has no definitive or exhaustive list of protectable subject matter, whether in respect of authors' or neighbouring works. As the law can expand indefinitely to cover any work irrespective of manner or form of expression, national courts have developed various doctrinal tools to prevent the protection of some objects and creations. Thus, the varying concept of 'originality' is employed to shape national policies on excluded subject matter. The national doctrines on the idea-expression principle (which prevents the protection of basic ideas and concepts) has also been transformed into an international copyright norm under the TRIPS Agreement.[109]

4.4.1 Excluded and limited subject matter

Berne Convention

Article 2(8) of the Berne Convention contains a mandatory exclusion, which is applicable, via the TRIPS Agreement, to all WTO members. Copyright protection 'shall not apply to news of the day or to miscellaneous facts having the character of mere items of press information'. It is not at all clear what the scope of this mandatory exclusion is considering the enormous battle that is being fought now between publishers and news aggregators such as Google in relation to copyright in news reports. It may be that the Berne exclusion only applies to individual words and facts per se

---

[108] German Copyright Law, ss 70 *et seq.*; Art 15, Directive (EU) 2019/790 on copyright and related rights in the Digital Single Market (the latter having been referred during the debates as the Google Tax).

[109] TRIPS Agreement, Arts 9–10; WCT, Arts 4–5.

while copyright protection can attach to newspaper articles, which represent 'thro
sequence and combination of those words' the author's creativity.[110]

Other than this provision, the Berne Convention leaves it entirely in the hands ᴏꜰ ꜱᴀᴛɪᴏɴᴀʟ ʟᴇɢ-
islation to exclude the following from copyright protection: political speeches and other speeches
delivered in legal proceedings; and official legal, legislative and administrative texts (and their
translations thereof). National laws vary considerably in this matter. German and US copyright
laws, for instance, do not protect statutes, government reports and court decisions. In contrast,
British Crown copyright subsists in a bewildering range of works including legislation, government reports and statutory codes of practice, the Book of Common Prayer and the Authorised
Version of the King James Bible.[111]

The idea-expression principle

Related to the criterion of originality is the important distinction between ideas, principles, abstract subject matter, commonplace elements and facts on the one hand, and their expression on
the other hand. The idea-expression principle is stated in various ways in various jurisdictions, and
has since the late 1990s become a universally acknowledged principle, enshrined in the TRIPS
Agreement and the WCT.[112] The TRIPS formulation is as follows: 'Copyright protection shall extend to expressions and not to ideas, procedures, methods of operation or mathematical concepts
as such.'

The parameters of the principle are elusive and difficult to apply. An attempt was made in the
early UK decision of *University of London Press v. University Tutorial Press* to explain that the law
was 'not concerned with the originality of ideas', but 'with the expression of thought in print or
writing'.[113] Further attempts to define this principle within UK law have resulted in a range of
vague propositions. Take, for example, the House of Lords attempt in *Designers Guild Ltd v. Russell
Williams* to define the idea-expression rule as referring to two separate propositions: (i) copyright
works which 'express certain ideas' are not protected because they have no connection with the
literary, dramatic, musical or artistic nature of the work, examples including a literary or artistic
work which describes an invention or inventive concept; (ii) certain ideas expressed by a copyright

---

[110] Case C-5/08 *Infopaq International A/S v. Danske Dagblades Forening* 16 July 2009, EU:C:2009:465, paras 44–48:
'newspaper articles can be copyright works'; 'It is only through the choice, sequence and combination of those words that
the author may express his creativity in an original manner and achieve a result which is an intellectual creation':

> The reproduction of an extract of a protected work which, like those at issue in the main proceedings, comprises
> 11 consecutive words thereof, is such as to constitute reproduction in part within the meaning of Article 2 of
> Directive 2001/29, if that extract contains an element of the work which, as such, expresses the author's own
> intellectual creation; it is for the national court to make this determination.

[111] Berne Convention Arts 2*bis*, 2(4), and respectively; German Copyright Law, Art 5; US Copyright Law, s 105; UK
Copyright Law, s 163. The copyright status in relation to British judgments remains unclear – *Crown Copyright in the
Digital Age – Green Paper on Crown Copyright*, 1998, available at http://www.opsi.gov.uk/advice/crown-copyright/crown-
copyright-in-the-information-age.pdf.

[112] TRIPS, Art 9(2) and WCT, Art 2.

[113] *University of London Press v. University Tutorial Press* (1916) 2 Ch 601.

work are not protected because they are not original, or so commonplace as not to form a substantial part of the work.[114]

In France, it is an accepted tenet within statute and jurisprudence that mere ideas, methods, procedures or techniques are not protectable under copyright law, the rationale being that such subject matter belongs to the common heritage of mankind, a type of 'cultural fund, a space and memory which are open to everyone'.[115] The principle is also applied in tandem with limits on the scope of protection where the idea and expression merges closely. In the *Christo* decision, for example, one French court recognised copyright subsisting in the artist's work which comprised an elaborate wrapping technique of the Pont Neuf bridge in Paris using canvas and ropes; nevertheless the scope of protection was limited in that the author could not oppose other types of works using the same style of wrapping. On the other hand, the artist could object to the photography of the wrapped bridge.[116]

Under US law, the idea-expression principle is codified so as to exclude 'any idea, procedure, process, system, method of operation, concept, principle, or discovery, regardless of the form in which it is described, explained, illustrated, or embodied in such work'.[117] The test is applied so as to also exclude standard or commonplace features, 'necessary expression', and '*scenes à faire*'; the latter doctrine refers to 'incidents, characters or settings, which are as a practical matter indispensable, or at least standard, in the treatment of a given topic'.[118] All these variations are often (and according to Samuelson perhaps wrongly) referred to as the merger doctrine – where a work is not protected when there are only a limited number of alternative ways to express certain ideas, functions or facts. The doctrine is not only prevalent in US copyright law but can be seen emerging in other jurisdictions.[119]

---

[114] [2001] ECDR 10; also note *L.B. Plastics Ltd v. Swish Products Ltd* (1979) RPC 551 (HL), 'There can be no copyright in a mere idea.'

[115] B. Edelman, 'The Law's Eye: Nature and Copyright', in Sherman and Strowel, *supra* note 27, 82–3; French Intellectual Property Code, Art L112-1, 'The provisions of this Code shall protect the rights of authors in all works of the mind, whatever their kind, form *of expression*, merit or purpose' (emphasis added).

[116] TGI Paris, 26 May 1987, *cf* Paris, 13 March 1986; for an account Sabine Lipovetsky and Emmanuèle de Dampierre, 'The Protection of the Image of a Building under French Law: Where Judges Create Law' (2012) 7(8) *Journal of Intellectual Property Law & Practice* 580–89.

[117] US Copyright Law, s 102(b); see *Baker v. Selden*, 101 US 99 (1879), copyright in book-keeping book does not extend to the book-keeping system; *Herbert Rosenthal Jewelry Corp. v. Kalpakian*, 466 F 2d 738 (9th Cir, 1971), no copyright for the idea of creating jewel-encrusted, bee-shaped pins.

[118] *Alexander v. Haley*, 200 USPQ 239 (SDNY, 1978); see L.A. Kurtz, 'Copyright: The Scenes a Faire Doctrine' (1989) 41(1) *Fla L Rev* 79.

[119] See P. Samuelson, 'Reconceptualizing Copyright's Merger Doctrine' (2016) 63 *J. Copyright Soc'y U.S.A.* 417, claiming that the doctrine emerged in *Apple Computer, Inc. v. Franklin Computer Corp.*, 545 F Supp. 812, 823 (ED Pa, 1982), *rev'd*, 714 F 2d 1240, 1253 (3d Cir, 1983). Also see: *Satava v. Lowry*, 323 F 3d 805 (9th Cir, 2003), idea and expression in glass jellyfish sculpture had not merged; *Ets-Hokin v. Skyy Spirits, Inc.*, 323 F 3d 763 (9th Cir, 2003), photograph of vodka bottle showed no evidence of merger; *Computer Associates International v. Altai*, 23 USPQ 2d 1241 (2nd Cir, 1992), noting the inevitable similarities in a representation of German beer halls; *Ideal Toy Corp v. Fab-Lu Ltd*, 149 USPQ 800 (2nd Cir,

Public interest

Copyright protection can be denied to works that are found to be illegal, blasphemous, ᵘᵉᵉ immoral or fraudulent. These are generally based on ancient manifestations of the public interest rule, and there is an internationally accepted policy in general IP laws of not according protection where public morality is offended or if the protection is against public policy. One can argue that some of the older decisions reflect the prurient tastes of the nineteenth century and cannot seriously be considered today as being the basis for allowing courts to act as moralists in preventing copyright enforcement. Furthermore, the inclusion of a clause excluding immoral or obscene works may be in conflict with national constitutions of many countries in according freedom of speech.[120]

4.4.2 Originality

Under British copyright law, copyright is accorded to 'original literary, dramatic, musical or artistic works', which has been classically defined as meaning that 'the work must not be copied from another work – that it should originate from the author'.[121] Under US copyright law, protection is only extended to 'original works of authorship'. Most common law systems adopt a similar pattern of conferring copyright protection on original authored works.[122] European civil law countries may not explicitly employ the term original within the statutes, opting for a variety of phrases including 'personal intellectual creations' (Germany), 'works of the mind' (France), or 'intellectual works of a creative character' (Italy).[123]

Although there is no universally definition or standard with which we can define originality, this is the enduring criterion of protection for authored works. At the lowest level, one merely has to show that a work has not been copied, and has 'originated' from the author. All national laws have at various times historically employed a low threshold of originality in order to extend the umbrella of copyright protection to works of cumulative creativity and low authorship values.[124]

1966), children's stories only capable of expression in a stereotypical form and thus would be necessarily similar. For France, see *N. Box v. F. Sagan*, TGI Paris, 4 June 1997, (1997) 174 RIDA 196, authors of two novels illustrating the same theme of conduct of a man of 40, who learns that he has an incurable illness; the court rejected *droit d'auteur* action despite similarities between composition, scenes, dialogues and characters, since they stemmed from similar situations, rather than copying; *Ravenscroft v. Herbert* (1980) RPC 193 (UK), 'Therefore, it seems reasonable to suppose that the law of copyright will allow a wider use to be made of a historical work than of a novel so that knowledge can be built upon knowledge'.

[120] For a historical precedent, see *Murray v. Benbow* (1822) 1 Jac 474, where Lord Eldon refused to condemn and restrain pirated editions of *Cain* written by the famous poet Byron on the ground that the poem was 'intended to vilify and bring into discredit that portion of Scripture history to which it relates'. For the uneasy relationship between religion and copyright, see I. Azmi, 'Authorship and Islam in Malaysia: Issues in Perspective' (1997) 28 *IIC* 671.

[121] UK Copyright Law, s 1(1)(a); *University of London Press v. University Tutorial Press*, [1916] 2 Ch 601.

[122] US Copyright Law, s 102(a).

[123] German Copyright Law, Art 2(2) (*persönliche gestige Schöpfungen*); French Intellectual Property Code, Art L111-1 (*l'oeuvres d'esprit*); and Italian Copyright Law, Art 1 (*le opere dell'ingegno di carattere creativo*).

[124] G. Dutfield and U. Suthersanen, 'The Innovation Dilemma: Intellectual Property and The Historical Legacy of

Nevertheless, the current trend globally is that some sort of minuscule creative input or authorial personality should be manifested in the work.

Labour and low-creative works

Originality has been interpreted, especially within British and common law traditions, to require that a work has to show some level of labour. This standard of originality arose historically as courts attempted to recast the concept of property to absorb incorporeal property, particularly in respect of books. Objections to incorporeal property ranged from the incapacity of literary property to be subsumed within definitional limits (the concept was considered too chimerical) to the difficulty of claiming that intellectual ideas were capable of occupancy, a fundamental requirement in traditional property law. The British system finally latched onto the notion of 'labour' as being a quantifiable basis for literary property and to the criterion of registration or fixation of works as being the identifier of this incorporeal right. Later eighteenth and nineteenth-century Chancery rulings readily acquiesced with this rationale of copyright protection as protecting 'labour and investment'. In the early English case of *Lamb v. Evans*[125] for instance, elaborate multilingual title headings within a trade directory were granted copyright on the basis that they were the result of 'literary labour, both as regards the composition of the headings themselves and their collocation or concatenation in the book'.[126] This has been interpreted leniently enough to extend copyright protection to works which evince very little creativity as compared to the pre-existing corpus of works, including informational works comprising compilations of data or their arrangements thereof.[127] A low level of originality is often adopted in order to allow copyright law to act as a substitute for the tort of misappropriation or unfair competition, or for the law to extend protection to works of little or low creativity which would be otherwise unprotected.

For instance, under German and Dutch laws, factual literary works, which show a very modest degree of originality are protected under the German *kleine Muenze* principle or the Dutch 'catalogue rule' (discussed below).[128] In the US, a low threshold of originality was applied through

---

Cumulative Creativity' (2004) 4 *IPQ* 379, 391–4.

[125] [1893] 1 Ch 218 (Court of Appeal, UK).

[126] B. Sherman and L. Bently, *The Making of Modern Intellectual Property Law: The British Experience, 1760–1911* (Cambridge University Press, 1999), 37–8, 73, 142–57, 180; A. Birrell, *Seven Lectures on the Law and History of Copyright in Books* (Cassell & Co, 1899), 170–71; Simon Stern, 'Copyright, Originality, and the Public Domain in Eighteenth-Century England', in R. McGinnis (ed.), *Originality and. Intellectual Property in the French and English Enlightenment* (Routledge, 2008), 69–101.

[127] *Ladbroke (Football) Ltd v. William Hill (Football) Ltd* [1964] 1 All ER 465, HL; *Express Newspaper plc v. News (UK) Ltd.* [1990] FSR 359 (Ch D); *Walter v. Lane* [1900] AC 539.

[128] *Headnotes* (1993) 24 IIC. 668 (German Supreme Court); *Attorney's Brief* (1988) 19 IIC. 854 (German Supreme Court). For Dutch law prior to the implementation of the EU database law, see Dutch Copyright Law, Art. 10(1)(I); *Nederlandse Omroep Stichting v. NV Holdingmaatschappij de Telegraaf*, [2000] ECDR 129, discussing the *geschriftenbescherming* rule. A similar position can be seen under Swedish law, which provided a limited term of protection to producers of non-original compilations under a 'catalogue' rule. Swedish Author's Right Law 1960, Art 49; *EMAP Business Communications Ltd. v. Planit Media AB*, [2000] ECDR 93.

the 'sweat of the brow' doctrine to protect factual compilations until the *Feist* decision (discussed below). British courts have hinted at the unfair behaviour of competing defendants as an indicator of copyright infringement.[129] Under French law, mundane or one word book titles are protected not only for the duration of the literary copyright but beyond the expiry of copyright if subsequent use is liable to create confusion.[130]

However, labour as the sole criterion of protection has been displaced in recent times in both common and civil law jurisdictions, with the criterion of 'skill' or 'creativity' increasingly becoming the global standard.

Intellectual effort, skill and judgement

In the context of common law systems, originality as a criterion of protection was never completely anchored to the notion of labour per se as early English courts adopted a more fluid and complex legal formula. In the 1881 decision in *Dick v. Yates*, for example, the court held, in relation to a title of a book, that for protection, a work must be 'the product of something which if it were applied to patent rights would be called invention'. The Court refused protection on the grounds that the title was not original in that there was 'nothing in it that indicates *any intellectual effort*'.[131] The view that copyright could not be awarded merely on the basis of labour is clear in later twentieth-century decisions. In *Macmillan & Co Ltd v. Cooper*,[132] the Court observed that it is vital that 'labour, skill and capital should be expended sufficiently to impart to the product some quality or character which the raw material did not possess, and which differentiates the product from the raw material'. In applying this distinction between the existing corpus of works, and the derivative work for which copyright is claimed, the Court was adamant that this did not mean that a work had to be 'novel nor ingenious'. A similar emphasis can be read in the British decision of *Cramp v. Smythson*. In denying copyright to factual compilations, the House of Lords noted that there was no feature in the works, which 'could be pointed out as novel or specially meritorious or ingenious from the point of view of the judgement or skill of the compiler'.[133]

In *Feist Publications v. Rural Telephone Service Co*[134] the US Supreme Court held that factual compilations were not protected under copyright law for several interrelated reasons: the labour exerted in compiling the facts was an irrelevant consideration; diligent and laborious effort expanded in creating the compilation did not meet the minimal constitutional standard of creativity; the 'sweat of the brow' standard was no longer feasible; and finally originality consisted of an independent creation plus 'a modicum' of creativity. Canadian decisions reflect a more nuanced approach: mere industry or 'sweat of the brow' works is not sufficient; however, creativity is not required either.

---

[129] *Weatherby v. International Horse Agency* [1910] 2 Ch 297 (UK); note especially the notorious and heavily criticised *Red Bus* case – *Temple Island Collections Ltd v. New English Teas Ltd and another* [2012] EWPCC 1 (UK).

[130] French Intellectual Property Code, Art L112-4.

[131] *Dicks v. Yates*, 24 May 1881, Court of Appeal, (1880) 18 Ch D 76 (emphasis added).

[132] (1923) 40 TLR 186 (Privy Council appeal from High Court of Bombay).

[133] *Cramp (GA) & Sons Ltd v. Smythson (Frank) Ltd* (1944) AC 329 (HL).

[134] *Feist Publications, Inc v. Rural Telephone Service Co* 499 US 340 (1991), 348–50, 362–4.

.he Canadian Supreme Court has devised another common law variant namely 'non-me-
.l and non-trivial exercise of skill and judgement'.[135]

Creativity, individuality and personality

French copyright law declares that all 'works of the mind, whatever their kind, form of expression, merit or purpose' will be protected.[136] Notwithstanding the absence of the word 'original', French jurisprudence decrees that a work must be original before copyright protection can be granted.[137] The fact that a work has not been copied can go towards establishing the author's individuality or personality within a work; the underlying concern being that a work should reflect the 'stamp of the author's personality' (*l'empreinte de la personnalité d'auteur*), taking into account the level of freedom the author has to exercise his creative choices.[138] The Court of Cassation has also held that artistic value or the aesthetic merit of creations should not be taken into account when gauging the originality of an artistic work.[139]

Under German copyright law, one has to show that the work is creative, and that there is evidence of authorial individuality or personality. The *de jure* position has long been that copyright law will not discriminate against all manner of subject matter, as long as the work constitutes an author's 'personal intellectual creation'. A related determining factor is the notion of '*Spielraum*', whereby the work is judged by measuring the margin or degree of freedom the author possesses within which to create the work, and whether the author of the work has a wealth of choices available to him. The presence of individual character in a work presupposes that the work is a result of a creative act within the '*Spielraum*' and that the author's personality has thus been incorporated within the work.[140] Historically, the high threshold of creativity has never been applied with equal vigour to all categories of works and objects, but varies according to the nature of the subject matter under review.

German copyright law does appear to bend and extend protection to works that are economically significant despite the philosophical and statutory barriers which call for 'creativity'. Past decisions have

---

[135] *CCH Canadian Ltd v. Law Society of Upper Canada*, (2004) 1 SCR 339; for a further discussion on Canadian law, see D. Vaver, *Intellectual Property* (Toronto: Irwin Law, 2011), 100–107.

[136] French Intellectual Property Code, Arts L.112-1, L.112-2 and L.112-3.

[137] Early decisions and jurists rarely referred to the criterion of originality, and the concept appears to have been introduced into French copyright law under the influence of Henri Desbois in, *Le droit d'auteur en France* (Paris: Dalloz, 1950). See also Vivant and Bruguière, *Droit d'auteur et droits voisins* (Paris: Dalloz, 2013); J.C. Ginsburg, 'The Concept of Authorship in Comparative Copyright Law' (2003) 52 *DePaul L. Rev.* 1063.

[138] CA Paris, 21 November 1994, (1995) RIDA 381, economic textbooks can be original if the authors structure the contents according to their personality; Cour de Cass., 29 May 1996, (1996) 170 RIDA 17; Dutfield and Suthersanen, *supra* note 124, 392.

[139] Cass. civ. 1ère, 11 February 1997, *Sté Zip Zag*, JCP G 1997, II, 22973, note X. Daverat, copyright protection given to a clothing button in the shape of a marine node; *Cts Lemaître v. Guerlain*, CA Paris, Cass. 4e ch., June 11. 1987. D. 1988. Somm. 192. obs. Colombet.

[140] German Copyright Law, Arts 2(2) and 11; G. Schricker, 'Farewell to the 'Level of Creativity' (Schopfungshohe) in German Copyright Law' (1995) 26 *IIC* 41; F. Grosheide, 'Paradigms in Copyright Law', in Sherman and Strowel, *supra* note 27, 224.

upheld copyright protection in law report headnotes and technical handbooks, which are
by technical specifications. Accordingly, the creativity level can be low for literary, musical and fine art
works; indeed, copyright protection is often justified under the 'kleine münze' ('small change') doctrine
for mundane works such as catalogues and technical documents, with little evidence of high creative
input.[141] And while this particular doctrine was not traditionally extended to works of applied art, the
German Supreme Court in *Birthday Train* overturned its own jurisprudence to hold that the level of
creativity required for works of applied art will be no higher than that required for works of fine art.[142]

EU law

The EU concept of originality is defined as the 'author's own intellectual creation' and it is strictly
speaking a standard that is applicable to four types of subject matter: computer programs; photographs; databases, and reproductions of works of visual art in the public domain.[143] In relation to
photographs, the position is further elaborated in the Term Directive:

> A photographic work within the meaning of the Berne Convention is to be considered orig-
> inal if it is the author's own intellectual creation reflecting his personality, no other criteria
> such as merit or purpose being taken into account.[144]

The criterion was first introduced under the Computer Program Directive in order to counter the
growing disparity of protection of software between the different EU member states, especially in
France, Germany and the UK. German copyright law was criticised for demanding 'a significant
amount of creativity with respect to selection, accumulation, arrangement and organisation' within programs before protection was accorded.[145] Conversely, the French Supreme Court was of the
view that the technical character of the software did not preclude copyright protection; rather
it depended on the amount of 'intellectual contribution' (*l'apport intellectuel*) put into the work.

---

[141] *Bedienungsanweisung (Operating Instructions)* decision, BGH, (1992) 23 IIC 846, copyright granted to an operating
manual for a technical device which consisted of drawings, photographs and text; *Re Copyright in Road Construction
Materials Handbooks*, BGH 11 April 2002, Case I ZR 231/99, [2005] ECC 13, copyright cannot be precluded in technical
books since a person who writes a complex technical handbook, the substance of which is predetermined, retains a not
insignificant creative scope for the conception and execution of the linguistic presentation; *Headnotes*, BGH 21 November
1991, Case No. I ZR 190/89, (1993) 24 IIC 668.

[142] *Silberdistel*, BGH, June 22, 1995, GRUR 1995, p. 581; (1997) 28 IIC 140; *Birthday Train*, BGH, 24 November 2013, I ZR
143/12, (2014) 45 IIC 831 – see a further discussion in Chapter 7.

[143] Directive 2009/24/EC on the legal protection of computer programs, Art 1(3); Directive 2006/116/EC on the term of
protection, Art 6; Directive 96/9/EC on the legal protection of databases, Art 3(1); Art 14, Directive (EU) 2019/790 on
copyright and related rights in the Digital Single Market.

[144] Directive 2006/116/EC, Recital (16).

[145] *Inkassoprogramm* , BGH May 9, 1985, I ZR 52/83, (1986) 17 IIC 681; *Operating system – Betriebssystem*, BGH 4 October
1990, I ZR 139/89, (1991) 22 IIC 723, upholding previous decision. For a historical overview, see M.-C. Janssens, 'The
Software Directive', in I. Stamatoudi and P. Torremans (eds), *EU Copyright Law: A Commentary* (Cheltenham: Edward
Elgar Publishing, 2014).

Protection would only be refused if 'an automated or a constraining logic' dictated how much 'intellectual contribution' was put into the work.[146] Thus, the rationale for the concept of 'author's own intellectual creation' was an attempt to reconcile the continental European notion of creativity with the Anglo-Irish notion of originality namely the work must not be copied.[147]

Since 2009, the CJEU has handed down several landmark decisions which have relentlessly employed the criterion of the 'author's own intellectual creation' as a 'uniform notion for all copyright works in the EU'.[148] The standard of this test appears to veer between the European civil law notion of personality, and the Anglo-Saxon test of comprising skill and judgement.[149] The following rules have been accepted by successive national courts: (i) the notion of originality is the ability of an author to express his creative ability in an original manner by making free and creative choices, and thus stamps his 'personal touch'; (ii) 'technical considerations, rules or constraints leave no room for creative freedom';[150] (iii) live football matches cannot constitute 'intellectual creations' because they were 'subject to the rules of the game, leaving no room for the creative freedom for the purposes of copyright'.[151] A further possible area of overlap arises due to the CJEU's 2011 decision in *Flos v. Semeraro* in the field of artistic copyright and designs (discussed further in Chapter 12).

4.4.3 Registration and fixation

Copyright protection results automatically from the point of creation, and no formalities (such as recordation, deposit, or copyright notice) are required to trigger protection under international copyright law.[152] The Berne Convention leaves it to Union countries to determine whether or not fixation in 'some material form' should be a pre-requisite before protection is conferred. British copyright law demands that certain works must be fixed – for instance, 'literary works' must be fixed in that they must be 'recorded, in writing or otherwise'; most common law countries such as Canada adopt this stance.[153] A similar provision exists in US copyright law where copyright

---

[146] *Babolat Maillot Witt v. Jean Pachot*, Cass., March 7, 1986, (1986) 129 RIDA 130.

[147] European Commission, *Green Paper on Copyright and the Challenge of Technology: Copyright Issues Requiring Immediate Action*, 1988, para 5.6.3; M. Walter and S. von Lewinski, *European Copyright Law: A Commentary* (Oxford University Press, 2010), 5.1.9–5.1.16.

[148] Case C-5/08 *Infopaq International A/S v. Danske Dagblades Forening* EU:C:2009:465; Case C-393/09 *Bezpečnostní softwarová asociace (BSA) v. Ministerstvo kultury* EU:C:2010:816; Case C-604/10 *Football Dataco Ltd and Others v. Yahoo! UK Ltd and Other* EU:C:2012:115; Case C-429/08 *Football Association Premier League and Others (FAPL) v. QC Leisure and Others* with *Karen Murphy v. Media Protection Services* [2011] ECR I-09083; Case C-145/10 *Eva-Maria Painer v. Standard VerlagsGmbH and Others* [2011] ECR I-12533.

[149] I. Stamatoudi, 'Originality under EU copyright law', in P. Torremans (ed.), *Research Handbook on Copyright Law* (Cheltenham: Edward Elgar Publishing, 2017), 57–84.

[150] *Football Dataco*, para 38; also see *Painer*, para 88, *BSA*, para 50.

[151] *FAPL v. QC Leisure; Karen Murphy*, para 98.

[152] Berne Convention, Art 5(2) (and now part of TRIPS Agreement). Also see S. van Gompel, *Formalities in Copyright Law. An Analysis of Their History, Rationales and Possible Future* (Wolters Kluwer, 2011).

[153] Berne Convention Art 5(2), UK Copyright Law, s 3, Canadian Copyright Law, s 3.

protection is accorded to 'original works of authorship fixed in any tangible medium of expres. now known or later developed, from which they can be perceived, reproduced, or otherwise communicated, either directly or with the aid of a machine or device'.[154] In contrast, civil law countries contain no similar provision regarding fixation; thus in the past, copyright protection has been granted to ethereal and truly intangible subject matter such as laser light displays which were considered a 'visual creation' intended to reveal and highlight the lines and forms of the Eiffel Tower.[155]

4.5 BENEFICIARIES OF PROTECTION

4.5.1 Initial authorship and ownership

The usual rule is that ownership of copyright in a work vests initially in the author of the work, that is, the person who creates the work. Slightly different rules exist in respect of employee works and films, and related rights, as discussed below. International law offers little assistance in respect of rules on authorship and ownership of copyright. The preamble to the Berne Convention refers to the 'rights of authors in their literary and artistic works', while elsewhere the Convention states that protection is for the benefit of the 'author and his successors in title'; there is a presumption that the author of a work will be regarded as the person whose name appears on the work. It is ambiguous as to whether the Convention limits authorship to natural persons or whether authorship can vest in a legal entity. In light of the ambiguity, most common law countries vest authorship *ab initio* in corporate entities or employers, whereas civil law countries usually vest authorship in natural persons (of course, with exceptions especially in relation to collective works).[156]

Where two or more authors contribute to create a work, both authors will be entitled to an undivided share of the copyright in the work, namely, joint ownership of the copyright. Authorship in such circumstances is determined with reference to the person who expends skill or creativity in making the work, as opposed to the person who merely supplies suggestions or ideas. UK copyright law also provides for an anomalous situation where, in the case of a literary, dramatic, musical or artistic work, such works are computer-generated (and not created by a natural person), the author shall be taken to be the person by whom the arrangements necessary for the creation of the work are undertaken.[157]

---

[154] US Copyright Law, ss 101, 102(a).

[155] *Eiffel Tower*, Cass. civ, I, March 3, 1992, DS 1993, 358; see Y. Gendreau, 'The Criterion of Fixation in Copyright Law' (1994) 159 *Revue Internationale du Droit d'Auteur* 110.

[156] Berne Convention, Arts 2(6), 15(1); *cf* Art 14*bis* (on films). See Ricketson and Ginsburg, *supra* note 63, paras 7.02–7.21; S. Ricketson, 'People or Machines: The Berne Convention and the Changing Concept of Authorship' (1991) 16 *Colum VLA J L & the Arts* 1; P. Baldwin, *The Copyright Wars: Three Centuries of Trans-Atlantic Battle* (Princeton University Press, 2014), Chapter 6; and J. Seignette, *Challenges to the Creator Doctrine* (Kluwer Law, 1994).

[157] UK Copyright Law, s 178. See *Julia Kogan v Nicholas Martin et al*, [2019] EWCA Civ 1645 (suggesting that ideas can sometimes constitute creative authorship).

4.5.2   Employee authors

Despite the lack of attention under international law, this area of law is well governed under nation-al laws.[158] Common law countries adopt important exemptions in relation to the 'creator is the first author/owner' rule. If the work is made by an employee in the course of employment, his or her em-ployer is the owner of any copyright in the work, unless an agreement exists between them which specifies otherwise. The main juridical criterion that determines whether the creator is an em-ployee or an independent contractor is whether the other party exercises control over the creator's work. Factors which the courts look at include whether the author has responsibility for investing and managing the work, for purchasing his own equipment, and for hiring and firing assistants.[159]

Under US copyright law, the 'work made for hire' doctrine applies if a work is 'prepared by an employee within the scope of his or her employment', and if so the employer will be the author. When determining whether an author is in fact an employee, the court takes into account, in-ter alia, the following factors: the skill required to create the work; the source of the necessary instrumentalities and tools; the duration of the relationship between the parties; the method of payment, and provision of employee benefits and the tax treatment of the hired party.[160]

The position in civil law countries is less harmonised. The concept of authorship denotes that property rights should vest in natural persons as creators. Nevertheless, one finds exceptions in national laws whereby both corporate entities and employers can claim authorship and ownership rights. For instance, under French law, ownership usually vests in the natural person who creates the work, irrespective of his status; thus, an employee who creates a work during employment retains copyright in his work. The employer may have the economic rights in the work transferred to him, but the contract of transfer should be in writing and should explicitly list the rights to be assigned to the employer. Another exception to be noted is when a work qualifies as a collective work. This arises where contributions of several authors are merged into a single work in such a manner that it is impossible to identify the discrete contributions. In such instances then, the work is legally presumed to have been created on the initiative of a single principal, and authorship vests *ab initio* in that principal, which can be a natural person or a legal entity.[161] Other exceptions

---

[158] For example, UK Copyright Law, ss 9, 11; US Copyright Law, s 201; French Intellectual Property Code, Arts L.111-1, L.113-1; German Copyright Law, Arts 7, 8, 43.

[159] UK Copyright Law, s 11; *Market Investigations Ltd v. Minister of Social Security* [1968] 2 QB 173; *Stevenson Jordan v. Macdonald & Evans* (1951) 69 RPC 10; Canadian Copyright Law, s 13(3). Also see K. Puri, 'Copyright and Employment in Australia' (1996) 27 IIC 53; Vaver, *supra* note 135, 125–33. An intriguing decision can be found in *King v. South African Weather Service* [2009] FSR 6 (Supreme Court of Appeal, South Africa).

[160] US Copyright Law, ss 101(b)(1), 201(b); *Community for Creative Non-Violence v. Reid* 490 US 730; 109 S. C. 2166 (1989); *Carter v. Helmsley-Spear Inc* 71 F 3d. 77; (2nd Cir, 1995), cert denied, 116 S Ct 1824 (1996); for collective works, see *New York Times Co Inc v. Tasini* 533 US 121 (2001).

[161] French Intellectual Property Code, Arts L.111-1, L.113-1, 113.5; *Robert v. Dictionnaires Le Robert*, Cass 1 civ, November 16, 2004 (2005) 204 RIDA 236, note by Kéréver, 166, a dictionary can be a collective work and therefore ownership can vest in the publishers; *House of Chanel Case*, Cass. civ. I, 4 May 1994, (1995) 163 RIDA 201, a presumption of authorship can be held in favour of the corporate entity, which exploits the collective work commercially.

rules can be found in the following countries: the Netherlands, where employers are ues.g as authors where works are created within the course of employment; Spain, where there is a presumption of a transfer of economic rights to an employer in cases 'for the exercise of the customary activity of the [employer] at the time of the delivery of the work'.[162]

At the other end of the spectrum, we can appreciate the purist approach within German copyright law, which only allows for natural persons to be recognised as authors. Save for the EU rule on computer programs, discussed below, the author of a work is always the creator of a work irrespective of whether she is self-employed, employed or engaged on a particular commission. Authorial rights cannot vest in legal persons though the latter may acquire derivative exploitation rights. Nevertheless where an author has created a work in execution of his duties under a contract of employment, the employer may have an implied exclusive licence to use the work.[163]

Finally, the EU Software Copyright Directive governs the status of employee-authors but only in relation to economic rights. Where a computer program is created by an employee in the execution of his duties, the employer is 'entitled to exercise all economic rights in the program so created', unless otherwise provided by contract.[164] The position on moral rights is still governed by individual national laws although some states such as France limit the moral rights of such employee-authors.[165]

4.5.3   Commissioned works

Where a work is commissioned or made for hire, the author of the work is the owner of copyright. As usual, there are rare exceptions. In France and Italy, for example, the copyright in commissioned advertisements or photographs can vest in the commissioners under implied licences.[166] Similarly under British law, the ownership of copyright in commissioned works will usually belong to the creator of the work, but in certain circumstances the court may find that the commissioner has an implied licence to exploit the work in a limited manner, or that the commissioner of the work has an equitable title to the copyright in the work.[167] Under US copyright law, the 'works made for hire' category comprises not only employee works, but nine categories of specially commissioned works. Should a work fall within one of these categories, and if the parties have expressly agreed in writing that the work is to be considered a work made for hire, then copyright will vest in the commissioner of the work. Economically important genres of creative works in this nine-category commissioned work list include collective works, motion pictures or other audiovisual works, and compilations.[168]

---

[162] Dutch Copyright Law, Art 7; Spanish Copyright Law, Art 51.

[163] German Copyright Law, Arts 7, 43; *Hummelrechte* decision, cited in Adolf Dietz, *Letter from the Federal Republic of Germany*, (1980) 3 *Copyright* 129, 132.

[164] EC Software Directive, Art 2(1), 2(3).

[165] For example, French Intellectual Property Code, Arts L.121-7, L.122-6.

[166] French Intellectual Property Code, Arts L.132-31–132-33, implied assignment of exploitation rights to the commissioner of a work used for advertising; Italian Copyright Law, Art 88.

[167] *Ray v. Classic FM* (1998) FSR 622; *Pasterfield v. Denham* (1999) FSR 168; *Griggs Group Ltd v. Evans* [2005] FSR 14 (CA).

[168] US Copyright Law, s 201(b). For the full list, see s 101(b)(2); *Community for Creative Non-Violence v. Reid* 490 US 730 (S Ct, 1989); *Carter v. Helmsley-Spear Inc* 71 F 3d 77; (2nd Cir, 1995), cert denied, 116 S Ct 1824 (1996).

4.5.4   Performances, sound recordings, broadcasts and films

The global norm is that performers, sound recording companies and broadcasters own the copyright (or the related/neighbouring right) in performances, phonograms, and broadcasts respectively. There can be national divergences in the scope of protection, outside the minimum eligibility requirements set down in the Rome Convention (1961) and the WPPT. Performers' rights will also extend to audiovisual performances once the Beijing Audiovisual Treaty is in force.[169]

The minimum threshold is that: (i) performers have the right to prevent first fixation, broadcasting and communication to the public of their live performances, and the right to prevent reproductions of such fixations of their performances; (ii) sound recording producers have the right to prohibit reproduction, importation, rental and distribution of their sound recordings and copies thereof, and the right to equitable remuneration for the broadcasting and communication to the public of their sound recordings; (iii) broadcasting organisations have the right to authorise or prohibit rebroadcasting, fixation and reproduction of their broadcasts. Of course, further rights are granted under some laws including the rental right and the cable re-transmission right. Under some laws, additional rights are granted.

The position in relation to films is trickier. The Berne Convention states that 'ownership of copyright' in cinematographic works is a matter for the legislation in the country where protection is claimed.[170] Civil law *droit d'auteur* systems tend to view films as authorial works created, first and foremost, by the director, and this norm has been strengthened by EU copyright law.[171] Such systems tend to also recognise other persons who have made creative contributions to the work. French copyright law, for example, considers the following as authors of the film: the author of the scenario, the author of the adaptation, the author of the dialogue, the author of musical compositions, and the director.[172] Under German copyright law courts have recognised the director, cameraman and the film cutter as authors of a film. Moreover, France, Germany, Italy and Austria provide that economic rights are presumed to have been transferred to the producer who has, upon contractual exploitation, a related entrepreneurial right.[173] The common law approach is that the film producer is the initial owner of the film. British law recognises the principal director as a joint owner of the copyright in the film, with the producer unless the director is an employee of the producer, in which case the latter takes it all.

An analogous situation is apparent under US law: the producer is the initial owner of the copyright in the film if the film falls within the 'work made for hire' category. More recent decisions

---

[169] Rome Convention, Art 3. For a full discussion, see S. Lewinski, *International Copyright* (Oxford University Press, 2008), paras 6.14 *et seq.*

[170] Berne Convention, Art 14*bis*; Ricketson and Ginsburg, *supra* note 63, paras 7.24–7.41.

[171] EU Term Directive, Art 2(1).

[172] F. Pollaud-Dulian, 'Les auteurs de l'oeuvre audiovisuelle' (The authors of the audiovisual work), (1996) 169 *RIDA* 51.

[173] EU Directive 2006/115/EC, film producers are granted a 50-year term of related rights protection; German Copyright Law, Arts 88, 89, 90, 91; French Intellectual Property Code, Arts L.113-7, L.132-24 *et seq.*, L.121-5, L.121-6. Also see R. Xalabarder, 'International Protection of Audiovisual Works: Authorship and Initial Ownership Issues' (2002) 193 *RIDA* 3; for a more extensive discussion see Kamina, *supra* note 71, Chapters 4–5.

have confirmed the stark difference between the European and US approaches. In *Garcia v. Goog*, the US Ninth Circuit court held that an actor's performance in a film could not constitute a copyrightable work, and therefore an actress (who had, in this case, appeared for five seconds in the film), had no copyright interest within the film. Following the *Garcia* analysis, the Second Circuit court held that a director could not claim copyright for his directorial input separate and apart from the film itself.[174]

4.6   ECONOMIC RIGHTS AND SCOPE OF PROTECTION

Economic rights protect the author's financial well-being by allowing him to prohibit various types of unauthorised use of his work in the marketplace, and by guaranteeing the author's participation in any income derived from any exploitation of the work. Historically, authors have had the right of reproduction and the right of communication vested in them. International copyright law has seen the gradual inflation of economic rights including, inter alia: reproduction; adaptation; communication; making available to the public; performing; displaying; distribution; renting and lending.[175] We focus our discussion here on the main economic rights (also see Chapter 16). The WIPO Treaties confirm that the main reproduction, distribution and communication rights are available not only to all authors, but also to performers and phonogram producers; broadcasters, on the other hand, are granted limited economic rights under the Rome Convention and the TRIPS Agreement. Regional and national laws extend these economic rights to a further group of beneficiaries including film producers, database producers, and publishers.[176]

The scope of copyright protection is dependent on the nature of the work. Lesser protection is available for historical or factual works as compared to fictional works due to the fact that such works must necessarily rely upon and copy factual sources to a certain extent. Thus, the law will allow a wider use to be made of a historical work than of a novel; having said this, it should be emphasised that this does not offer a carte blanche to subsequent users to copy substantial amounts and there is some responsibility on the later author to inject some creativity when using a previous factual work.[177]

---

[174] *Garcia v. Google, Inc*, 766 F 3d 929 (9th Cir), rev'd en banc; 786 F 3d 733 (9th Cir, 2015), the dissenting opinion by Judge Kozinski is noteworthy as he analogises performances and each scene in a film to chapters within a book, and relies on the Beijing Audiovisual Treaty; 16 *Casa Duse LLC v. Merkin*, 791 F 3d 247 (2nd Cir, 2015).

[175] For example, TRIPS Agreement, Art 11; WCT, Art 8; WPPT, Arts 10, 14.

[176] EC Rental Directive 2006/115/EC and EU Copyright in Information Society Directive 2001/29/EC, according economic rights to film producers; EU Database Directive 96/9/EC, and EU Term Directive 2006/116/EC, granting rights to publishers of hitherto unpublished works; EU Copyright in the Digital Single Market Directive EU/2019/790 granting rights to press publishers for online usage.

[177] U. Suthersanen, 'Copyright in the Courts: The Da Vinci Code' (2006) 3 *WIPO Magazine; Baigent and Leigh v. The Random House Group Ltd (CA)* [2007] EWCA Civ 247.

4.6.1 Reproduction rights, including adaptation and translation rights

Despite the early acceptance of the reproduction right within national regimes, this right was only imported into the Berne Convention's package of minimum rights at the 1967 Stockholm Revision.[178] In fact, the earliest internationally recognised economic right was that of translation, which was claimed to be the codifying factor in international copyright negotiations:

> It was 'la question internationale par excellence', as translation was really the only international means of reproduction in the case of books. It was clearly conceived of as a form of reproduction, but was recognised only in a limited form in the Berne Act.[179]

Article 9(1) of the Berne Convention confers on authors of literary and artistic works 'the exclusive right of authorizing the reproduction of these works in any manner or form'. The wide language of the reproduction right encompasses not only direct, substantial copying of the work within the same medium, but also extends to acts of alteration and adaptation which, directly or indirectly, transform the work's context or medium such as sound or visual recordings of a literary or artistic work.[180] Therefore, there is no need to prove that the whole work has been reproduced, as long as there has been reproduction of a substantial part of it, both in qualitative and quantitative terms. With the advent of more technological means of reproducing a work, legal concepts have been stretched to accommodate digital uses such as display, storage, temporary or transient copying, and non-literal copying. In respect of storage and temporary copying, the matter may have been resolved by the 1996 WIPO Diplomatic Conference, which adopted the following Agreed Statement:

> The reproduction right, as set out in Art.9 of the Berne Convention, and the exceptions permitted thereunder, fully apply in the digital environment, in particular to the use of works in digital form. It is understood that the storage of a protected work in digital form in an electronic medium constitutes a reproduction within the meaning of Art.9 of the Berne Convention.

In the case of written or printed literary works, infringement is assessed by comparison of two works, and judging whether there is a similarity of expression between the two. However, the concept of non-literal copying had to be invented by courts in order to deal with instances where there had been no direct copying of text but the final visual or entertainment effect had been reproduced. This is useful, for example, in the case of computer programs where the exact program code is not copied but the end-result is that the allegedly offending program creates the same overall organisation, structure, user interface and screen display as the protected program. The second program will have same 'look and feel' or 'structure, sequence and organisation' of the

---

[178] Berne Convention, Art 9(1); for a detailed discussion, see Ricketson and Ginsburg, *supra* note 63, Chapter 11.

[179] Ricketson and Ginsburg, ibid., para. 11–15.

[180] Berne Convention, Art 9(3).

protected program.[181] One also finds further subaltern versions of the reproduction right within the Berne Convention including rights to authorise adaptation (including arrangements and other alterations) of all works, and cinematic adaptations and reproductions.[182]

The German Copyright Act defines reproduction as the 'right to produce copies of the work, whether on a temporary or on a lasting basis and regardless of by which means of procedure or in which quantity they are made'.[183] The British copyright law deviates slightly by reversing the definition – the author is conferred a right to 'copy' which means 'reproducing the work in any material form', which in turn includes: storing the work in any medium by electronic means; making a three-dimensional copy of a two-dimensional work, and vice versa; making a photograph of the whole or any substantial part of any image forming part of the film or broadcast; and making of copies which are transient or are incidental to some other use of the work.[184] The French copyright law, on the other hand, adopts a more simple and bifurcated approach by conferring on the author the 'right of exploitation', which comprises the rights of performance and reproduction. Reproduction is confined to a 'physical fixation' of the work, by various processes, only insofar as the work can be communicated to the public.[185]

EU copyright law firmly defines the reproduction right as including: 'direct or indirect, temporary or permanent reproduction by any means and in any form, in whole or in part'. Insofar as usage of a computer program necessitates copying, the right of reproduction will include: loading; displaying; running; transmission or storage of the computer program.[186] There is no pan-EU adaptation or translation right although all EU member states offer protection either under the reproduction right or as a separate economic right.

4.6.2   Distribution rights, including rental and resale royalty rights

International and national laws grant rights holders some sort of right to control the distribution and commercial exploitation of the physical copy of the intangible creation. It is arguable that this bundle of rights (including the distribution, importation, rental and resale royalty rights/*droit de suite*) is far too broad. The rental right, for example, purports to give authors the ability to control and charge for the hiring out of copyright goods – the right remains with the copyright owner even after the first sale of the product. Furthermore, 'technological' rights such as anti-circumvention measures and digital rights management techniques, plus the abandonment of the exhaustion

---

[181] N. Shemtov, *Beyond the Code: Protection of Non-Textual Features of Software* (Oxford University Press, 2017), Chapters 4 and 7.

[182] Berne Convention, Arts 12, 14(1), 8(1); see Ricketson and Ginsburg, *supra* note 63, paras 11.23 *et seq.*; von Lewinski, *supra* note 84, paras 5.120 *et seq.*

[183] German Copyright Law, Art 16(1).

[184] UK Copyright Law, s 17.

[185] French Intellectual Property Code, Arts L.111-1, L.122-1, L.122-3, L.122-4.

[186] Copyright in the Information Society Directive 2001/29/EC, Art 2; Computer Program Directive 2009/24/EC, Art 4(1).

doctrine in relation to digital goods have to a certain extent prevented the emergence of truly global markets, as well as second-hand digital goods markets.[187]

It is not suggested that these rights of distribution, importation, rental and *droit de suite* are wrong per se but rather that there has to be a clearer balance between the rights of the author of the intangible work to control his physical manifestation of the product, and those of the owner of the physical goods themselves. The former rights appear, at times, to overwhelm and interfere with the latter rights especially with the reluctance to apply the exhaustion principle to digital goods.

The right of distribution has theoretically been outside the scope of the author's right to control physical copies of his work once such works have been placed on the market. The Berne Convention does not confer a general right of distribution on authors although it does recognise an implicit distribution right in relation to cinematographic adaptations and reproductions.[188] The TRIPS Agreement does provide a specific right to prevent importation, especially of 'pirated' copyright goods (as well as 'counterfeit' trademarks).[189] The WIPO Internet Treaties are the first international instruments which explicitly provide for a general distribution right in relation to literary and artistic works, performances and phonograms. The right is defined as 'making available to the public of originals and copies' of such works as tangible objects.[190]

Under EU copyright law, all authors and related rights owners can exercise the right of distribution subject to the doctrine of exhaustion, namely, the first sale or transfer of the ownership of the physical product inside the Eurozone with the rights holder's consent will exhaust that right. Thus, international exhaustion does not apply.[191] EU copyright jurisprudence is continuously shaping the right of distribution, and the related exhaustion doctrine. In *Dimensione Direct Sales Srl v. Knoll International SpA*, the CJEU extended the scope of the distribution right, holding that the right may be infringed by the mere advertising or offer for sale of protected works even where the work is not sold or transferred. Thus, the mere act of offering copies of a copyright work for sale can be tantamount to breaching the distribution right.[192]

The rental right is, in principle, an exception to the exhaustion/first sale doctrine discussed below. US copyright law, for instance, recognises rental right in phonorecords and computer programs.[193] Within the EU, the rental right is available to all authors of all types of works (save works of applied art and works of architecture); performers in respect of fixation of performances; producers in relation to phonograms or films, and computer programs. A unique feature of the EU rental right is that authors and performers have a non-waivable equitable right of remuneration in

---

[187] P.S. Morris, 'Beyond Trade: Global Digital Exhaustion in International Economic Regulation' (2013) 36 *Campbell L. Rev.* 107; S. Ghosh, 'The Implementation of Exhaustion Policies: Lessons from National Experiences, ICTSD Issue Paper No. 40', 2013.

[188] Berne Convention, Art 14(1).

[189] TRIPS Agreement, Arts 44(1), 50(1)(a) and 51; see Ricketson and Ginsburg, *supra* note 63, paras 11.77 *et seq.*

[190] WCT, Art 6; WPPT, Arts 8 and 12 and Agreed Statements.

[191] EU Copyright in the Information Society Directive 2001/29/EC, Art 4(1), (2); Rental Right Directive, Art 9; Software Directive, Art 4(1)(c), (2); Database Directive, Arts 5(c), 7(2)(b).

[192] C-516/13.

[193] 17 U.S.C. §109(b)(1)(A).

relation to their rental rights for phonograms and cinematographic works. The right applies even where the economic rights (including the rental right) have been assigned to the phonogram or film producer.[194]

Controversially, the rental right was introduced as a mandatory global right within the TRIPS Agreement, albeit only in relation to computer programs, cinematographic works and sound recordings. Authors and phonogram producers have the right to prohibit the commercial rental of originals or copies of computer programs/films (authors) and sound recordings (producers).[195] The WIPO Treaties subsequently confirmed the following beneficiaries of the rental right: (i) authors of computer programs, cinematographic works, and works embodied in phonograms; (ii) phonogram producers in relation to phonograms; (iii) performers in relation to performances fixed in phonograms.[196] One should note the slight anomaly whereby the exhaustion principle does not apply to rentals, lease or lending since possession via these mechanisms is not tantamount to ownership; thus, the copyright owner specifically retains his rental right after the first sale of the product.

The *droit de suite* (or resale royalty right) refers to the author's right to a share in the proceeds of subsequent sales of his original work with reference to the original form (physical copy) in which the work is embodied.[197] Having originally arisen in France in the nineteenth century, and being finally adopted in 1920, the original rationale of the right is that artists usually only benefit from the proceeds of the first sale of the original work, and do not have a share in subsequent proceeds of the original work, unlike authors of literary and musical works who benefit from mass reproduction of their works. This is especially so when artists acquire reputation and standing, but rarely benefit from the increase in value of their original work. The *droit de suite* attempts to remedy this position by allowing artists to take a share in subsequent sales of their work.[198]

The resale royalty right found its way into the 1948 Berne Convention revision, which provides a resale royalty right in relation to original works of art and original manuscripts of writers and composers. The Convention further stipulates a proviso in respect of this right: an author can claim the *droit de suite* in a Union country only if the legislation in the country to which the author belongs so permits, and only to the extent permitted by the country where this protection is claimed.[199] Within the EU, the Resale Royalty Directive introduces a pan EU-wide right which adopts the Berne Convention norm – it applies to all works of fine and visual art, re-sold by an art market professional i.e., galleries, auction houses or art dealers, for a minimum price of €1,000. Thus, the following sales will not qualify: private sales, or such sales involving non-copyright industrial designs (or non-copyright works of applied art), or sales held in non-EEA countries, or

---

[194] Rental Directive 2006/115/EC, Arts 3, 4, 5; and Software Directive, Art 4(c).

[195] TRIPS Agreement, Arts 11, 14.

[196] WCT, Art 7; WPPT, Arts 9, 13.

[197] Ricketson and Ginsburg, *supra* note 63, para 11.53.

[198] R. Plaisant, 'Droit de Suite and Droit Moral under the Berne Convention Conference' (1986) 11 *Colum.-VLA J.L. & Arts* 157; J.L. Duchemin, *Le Droit de Suite des Artistes* (1948).

[199] Berne Convention (1971 Paris Act), Art 14*ter*. For more on the right, see E. Ulmer, 'The "Droit de Suite" in International Copyright Law' (1975) 6 *IIC* 12.

those involving non-EEA citizens.[200] In the US, the right is not available under federal copyright law, but is available under some state laws.[201]

4.6.3   Exhaustion of rights

There is currently no accepted norm on the nature and extent of the doctrine on exhaustion, and countries favour one of three types of exhaustion: national; regional (as adopted within the EU); and international (as adopted by New Zealand, and perhaps the US *ex post* the *Kirstaeng* decision, discussed below). The TRIPS Agreement clearly leaves it to individual WTO member states to adopt their own exhaustion rules.[202] Both WIPO Treaties vaguely limit the distribution right to the first sale of such works. Thus, the WCT states as follows:

> Nothing in this Treaty shall affect the freedom of Contracting Parties to determine the conditions, if any, under which the exhaustion off the right in paragraph (1) applies after the first sale or other transfer of ownership of the original or a copy of the work with the authorization of the author.[203]

Although EU law, as discussed above, does not recognise international exhaustion but rather regional exhaustion, the CJEU in the highly controversial decision of *UsedSoft v. Oracle International* recognised that the exhaustion doctrine can apply in relation to computer software sold as digital downloads within the EU: specifically, when there is an authorised download of the software from the proprietor's website, coupled with the grant of a perpetual licence. The court considered such licences to be, in effect, a 'sale', which was thus subjected to the exhaustion doctrine; moreover, a subsequent acquirer of the software, especially on a second-hand market, would be considered a lawful acquirer.[204]

In the *Art&Allposters* decision,[205] authorisation had been granted for the reproduction and sale of images on posters, but not necessarily in the canvas form; the defendant argued that it was allowed to transfer such images off paper on to canvas as the distribution right had been exhausted by the first sale of the posters on the EU market, with the consent of the copyright owners. The

---

[200] Resale Royalty Right Directive 2001/84/EC.

[201] D.E. Shipley, 'Droit De Suite, Copyright's First Sale Doctrine and Preemption of State Law' (2017) 39 *Hastings Comm. & Ent. L.J* 1.

[202] TRIPS Agreement, Art 6.

[203] WCT, Art 6(2); the rule is subsequently applied to performances and phonograms in Arts 8(2), 12(2) WPPT.

[204] Case C-128/11 *UsedSoft GmbH v. Oracle International Corp* [2012] ECDR 368; see A. Nicholson, 'Old Habits Die Hard? UsedSoft v. Oracle' (2013) 10:3 SCRIPTed. The main controversy arises from whether the *UsedSoft* decision can be applied *mutatis mutandis* across the whole spectrum of copyright works, as the decision was made under the Computer Programs Directive 2009/24, which is a *lex specialis* within EU copyright law. See also the slightly different position in relation to back-up copies – Case C-166/15 *Ranks v. Finanšu un economisko noziegumu izmeklēšanas prokuratūra* [2017] ECDR 12; S. Wolk, 'CJEU Holds the Reproduced Copies Cannot be Resold' (2017) 39(2) *EIPR* 125.

[205] Case C-419/13.

CJEU held that the exhaustion of the right only applies to tangible objects, relying on both the EU Copyright in the Information Society Directive, and the WCT. It is implied by the decision that should an object be transformed into another medium, or even digitised, any prior authorised distribution or release into the marketplace will be annulled, and the distribution right will not be exhausted.

Under US law, the right of distribution is available to all copyright works which are distributed 'by sale or other transfer of ownership, or by rental, lease or lending'. The right is subjected to the exhaustion principle, which is codified in the Act, allowing the owner of a lawfully made copy of a protected work to dispose of that copy.[206] In 2013, the US Supreme Court in *Kirtsaeng v. Wiley Publishing*[207] determined the basic rules of the first sale doctrine in relation to text books. A Thai student had imported large quantities of text books which were manufactured and marketed lawfully at a low price in Thailand, for resale at a higher price in the US. The Court held that there had been no infringement of the importation and distribution rights, as the first sale doctrine applied; moreover, there was no geographic limits on the doctrine, thus recognising international exhaustion at least for in-copyright second-hand books.

There is no clear global trend in respect of a rule of law for digital goods such as e-books and downloaded digital music. In Europe, all eagerly await the CJEU decision in the *Tom Kabinet* decision.[208] The case involves the online Dutch marketplace 'Tom Kabinet' for used and DRM-free e-books. Consumers who wish to sell e-books on the platform have to declare that they legally acquired their copies and that they would delete their existing copies after uploading a further copy to the platform. The digital platform added watermarks to the e-books after they were purchased. Whilst the national courts ruled that the resale of used e-books was permissible, on referral to the CJEU, the Advocate General has advised that the supply of e-books by downloading online for permanent use is covered by the right of communication to the public, rather than by the distribution right. In other words, and unless the CJEU decides otherwise, the exhaustion rule will not apply to e-books for the purposes of a resale market. In coming to this conclusion, it is clear that the Advocate General struggled with prior case law, as well as the WIPO Copyright Treaty and its implementation within EU copyright law. Interestingly, the Advocate General admitted that the right of communication, whilst not being capable of exhaustion, could nevertheless be limited in the digital context (such as in the case of hypertext and framing links), as discussed below.[209]

---

[206] US Copyright Law, ss 106(3), 109.

[207] *Kirtsaeng v. John Wiley & Sons, Inc*, 568 US 519 (2013); see also *Quality King v. L'anza*, 523 U.S. 135 (1998).

[208] Case 263/18, *Nederlands Uitgeversverbond, Groep Algemene Uitgevers v. Tom Kabinet Internet BV, Tom Kabinet Holding BV, Tom Kabinet Uitgeverij BV*, Advocate General's Opinion, 10th September 2019, ECLI:EU:C:2019:697.

[209] See also C-174/14 – *Verenmging Openbare Bibliotheken v. Stichting Leenrecht*, CJEU, 2016, where the court held that public libraries which lawfully acquired e-books could copy such e-books to a server and allow users to download a copy to a personal computer. For a comparative review of digital exhaustion in the US and EU, see L. Determann, 'Digital Exhaustion: New Law from the Old World' (2018) 33(1) *Berkeley Tech L.J.* 177; W. Kerber, 'Exhaustion of Digital Goods: An Economic Perspective' (2016) 8 *Intellectual Property Journal* 149.

4.6.4   Communication to the public, broadcasting and making available[210]

As discussed above, the right of communication was recognised early under eighteenth-century French copyright law, and variations of this right currently exist under the Berne Convention,[211] TRIPS Agreement and WIPO treaties.[212] At the EU level, this right can be found under the Information Society Directive.[213] It should be kept in mind that international instruments do not prevent contacting states from implementing national versions of minimal rights.[214] One of the earliest versions of the right arises from Article 11*bis*, Berne Convention, which offers a margin of appreciation as to how the right is implemented in national laws. Moreover, the right is not equally applied to all works under the Berne Convention, and the scope of protection is different depending on the type of the work. The Berne notion of communication is further complemented and clarified with the introduction of 'the making available right' under the WIPO Treaties, for application to the online environment.[215] The disjointed application of the right under the Berne Convention is rectified under the WIPO Treaties, and the communication right is equally applicable to all types of work. Both treaties include the same technology-neutral wording: 'making available in such a way that public may access at any place and at a time individually chosen by them', with the intention of keeping the scope of this right wide enough for the online transmissions.[216]

In the US, communication activities are treated mainly under the exclusive right of distribution.[217] A case involving the indexing and providing thumbnails of illegally posted images was handled by discussing the criteria for distribution and public display rights.[218] In other US cases involving making available of works, it was held that the distribution does not have to actually take place but it should be more than just authorisation and it is not required to prove the knowledge or intent of the infringers.[219]

The CJEU, on the other hand, has been actively construing the communication to the public right, and has to this extent attracted some criticism. First, a broad interpretation of the right is in danger of intersecting with other rights including the reproduction, rental, lending, and distribution rights. Secondly, the 'new public' criterion has also been criticised as being in conflict with international treaties and EU Directives.[220] Its predecessor, the 'new audience' concept, had been specifically

---

[210] The authors are grateful to Ms Pinar Oruc for her invaluable research work in this section.

[211] Berne Convention for the Protection of Literary and Artistic Works, Arts 11, 11*bis*, 11*ter*, 14, 14*bis*.

[212] WCT, Art 8; WPPT, Arts 2, 10, 14, 15.

[213] EU Copyright in the Information Society Directive, Art 3.

[214] J. Reinbothe and S. Von Lewinski, *The WIPO Treaties on Copyright* (2nd ed., Oxford University Press, 2015), 135.

[215] Ibid., 129.

[216] The EU Copyright in the Information Society Directive also includes similar technology-neutral wording in Art 3.

[217] US Copyright Law, s 106(3).

[218] *Perfect 10, Inc v. Amazon.com Inc*, 508 F 3d 1146 (9th Cir, 2007).

[219] *Hotaling v. Church of Latter-Day Saints*, 118 F 3d 199, 203 (4th Cir, 1997).

[220] P. Torremans, 'When the Court of Justice of the European Union Sets about Defining Exclusive Rights: Copyright *quo vadis?*', in Torremans, *supra* note 149; N. Cordell and B. Potts, 'Is the CJEU using Communication to the Public to

rejected in the travaux of Berne Convention as being too complex. On the other hand, one must note that Article 11*bis*, Berne Convention which introduces the elusive concept of communication into copyright law originates from an antiquated understanding of technology: as terrestrial broadcasting. Thus, commentaries on the interpretation of Article 11*bis* should not constrain the modern notion of the right of communication. Thirdly, the CJEU's approach in the *Svensson* decision has been specifically criticised – the decision appears to exhaust the communication right in respect of works that are freely available online, as it is assumed that posting material online without restrictions is an 'implied license' authorising all communication to public.[221] Finally, the CJEU has been criticised for not making a distinction between hyperlinking, deep linking and framing (namely, the former providing the location of something, without communicating its content, whereas the latter two forms of linking directly bring the content to the user).[222]

The right covers three main activities: communication to public (the general act including the following two); broadcasting (simultaneous reception); and making available (individual communication at a time and place chosen by the audience). In setting out the scope of the right, the CJEU has identified further complementary factors which are 'not autonomous and are interdependent' – we discuss them below.[223]

Communication: transmission or making available

The CJEU interprets the concept of 'communication to the public' rather broadly, and the following acts (done without authorisation) were held to fall within the ambit of the right: offering a pay-per-view TV service;[224] disseminating musical works in live circus performances;[225] installing TV sets and playing ambient music in a hotel;[226] re-transmitting football games for public house customers;[227] offering an internet TV broadcasting service to show programmes;[228] installing radio and TV sets in spa rooms;[229] providing links to newspaper articles found online;[230] radio broadcast

---

Harmonise Accessory Liability across the EU?' (2018) 40 *EIPR* 289; P.B. Hugenholtz and S.C. van Velze, 'Communication to a New Public? Three Reasons Why EU Copyright Law Can Do Without a "New Public"' (2016) 47 *IIC* 797.

[221] ALAI, 'Report and Opinion on a Berne-Compatible Reconciliation of Hyperlinking and the Communication to the Public Right on the Internet' (2015); B. Clark and S. Tozzi, '"Communication to the Public" under EU Copyright Law: An Increasingly Delphic Concept or Intentional Fragmentation?' (2016) 38 *EIPR* 715.

[222] ALAI, ibid.

[223] Case C-162/10 *Phonographic Performance (Ireland) Ltd v. Ireland* [2012] 2 CMLR (29) 895, para 42.

[224] Case C-89/04 *Mediakabel BV v. Commissariaat voor de Media* EU:C:2005:348; [2005] ECR I-4891.

[225] Case C-283/10 *Circul Globus Bucureşti v. UCMR - ADA* ECLI:EU:C:2011:772.

[226] Case C-306/05 *Sociedad General de Autores y Editores de España (SGAE) v. Rafael Hoteles SA* ECLI:EU:C:2006:764; [2007] ECDR 2.

[227] Joined Cases C-403/08 & C-429/08 *Football Association Premier League Ltd v. QC Leisure & Murphy v. Media Protection Services Ltd* EU:C:2011:631; [2012] ECDR 8.

[228] Case C-607/11 *ITV Broadcasting Ltd v. TVCatchup Ltd* ECLI:EU:C:2013:147; [2013] ECDR 9.

[229] Case C-351/12 *Ochranny svaz autorsky pro prava k dilum hudebnim os (OSA) v. Lecebne lazne Marianske Lazne as* EU:C:2014:110; [2014] ECDR 25.

[230] Case C-466/12 *Svensson v. Retriever Sverige AB* EU:C:2014:76; [2014] ECDR 9.

in cafés and restaurants;[231] installing televisions for patients in the waiting room of a rehabilita-tion clinic;[232] hyperlinking to illegally published photographs;[233] selling a multimedia player that allows the content from third-party streaming websites to be watched on television screens;[234] retransmitting an original broadcast;[235] and indexing metadata to allow users to search and share protected works via peer-to-peer network.[236]

There are further rules: for instance, the public need to be at a different location, so that it is different from 'public performance'; the concept does not include live performances or direct presentation; while a simple reception of a programme does not constitute communication, the mere act of making available is sufficient (thus, a communication to the public still occurs even if the customers do not switch on the televisions in the hotel rooms).[237]

Deliberate 'intervention' of a user

The communication in question would not have taken place without the deliberate intervention, which is beyond technical means or beyond increasing the quality of the transmission.[238] For example, the customers could be already in the area of the broadcast but they would not have enjoyed it without the intervention of the hotel, the public house proprietor or the rehabilitation clinic operator.[239]

The legal concept of 'public'

When determining whether there is a public, there are certain fundamental rules and parameters. The private nature of the location does not change the fact that it is still communication to the public, as it can take place in a time and place chosen by the audience. It was held that even if the communication is made available on a pay-per-view basis to a limited audience by using a code, it is still a television broadcast and cannot be interpreted as 'provided on individual demand'.[240] The cumulative effect is taken into consideration.[241] Thus, for example, the CJEU has decided that hotel customers quickly succeed each other, leading to a fairly large number of people.[242] If the unau-thorised communication is made via different technical means to a public, such as a retransmission

---

[231] Case C-151/15 *Sociedade Portuguesa de Autores CRL v. Ministério Público and Others* ECLI:EU:C:2015:468.

[232] Case C-117/15 *Reha Training Gesellschaft für Sport- und Unfallrehabilitation mbH v. Gesellschaft für musikalische Aufführungs- und mechanische Vervielfältigungsrechte eV* ECLI:EU:C:2016:379; [2017] ECDR 1.

[233] Case C-160/15 *GS Media BV v. Sanoma Media Netherlands BV and Others* ECLI:EU:C:2016:644; [2016] ECDR 25.

[234] Case C-527/15 *Stichting Brein v. Jack Frederick Wullems, also trading under the name Filmspieler* ECLI:EU:C:2017:300; [2017] ECDR 14.

[235] Case C-138/16 *Staatlich genehmigte Gesellschaft der Autoren, Komponisten und Musikverleger registrierte Genossenschaft mbH (AKM) v. Zurs.net Betriebs GmbH* EU:C:2017:218; [2017] ECDR 15.

[236] Case C-610/15 *Stichting Brein v. Ziggo BV* ECLI:EU:C:2017:456; [2017] ECDR 19.

[237] *SGAE* [2007] ECDR 2 at para 43.

[238] *ITV v. TVCatchup* [2013] ECDR 9 at para 30.

[239] *SGAE* [2007] ECDR 2 para 42; *FAPL* [2012] ECDR 8 at para 195; *Reha Training* [2017] ECDR 1 at para 46.

[240] *SGAE* [2007] ECDR 2 at para 51; *Mediakabel* [2007] ECDR 2 at para 32.

[241] *Mediakabel* [2007] ECDR 2 at para 37; *Filmspieler* [2017] ECDR 14 at para 44.

[242] *SGAE* [2007] ECDR 2 at paras 38–39.

of a terrestrial television broadcast via internet,[243] then a 'new public' is not needed. However, if the unauthorised communication is made via the same technical means, there must be a 'new public' namely a public which was not taken into consideration by the rights holder when they authorised the communication.

It should be noted that the criterion of a 'new public' is an EU phenomenon, and does not have a basis in international instruments. Article 11*bis*(1) of the Berne Convention, for instance, requires the author's authorisation for a 'communication made by an organization other than the original one'; this has been interpreted by the CJEU as meaning that 'such a transmission is made to a public different from the public at which the original act of communication of the work is directed, that is, to a new public'.[244]

Hyperlinks

Further interpretation of the concept of 'public' was attempted in the *Svensson* decision. If providing a hyperlink directs users to a content that is already freely available, then there is no 'new public'; however, if the hyperlink circumvents an existing restriction, then there is a 'new public', which will require further authorisation.[245] Moreover, if the work is posted illegally and if the person knows or ought to have known of the illegality, the Court will hold such an act as constituting an unauthorised act of communication to the public.[246] It was held that selling a media player with pre-installed hyperlinks to illegally published content meant that there was the knowledge of illegality, especially because it was also mentioned in the advertisement of the player.[247] The 2019 Copyright Directive, which extends the rights of reproduction and communication to cover online use of press publications by ISPs, specifically allows hyperlinks to press publications.[248]

Profit

Although motivation of profit is not required for the act to be interpreted as 'communication to a public',[249] the CJEU has nevertheless considered profit as a factor. Thus, the existence of TV sets affects the pricing of hotel rooms, the broadcasting in a public house attracts more customers,[250] the broadcasting of television programmes in a rehabilitation clinic provides a diversion for the patients and contributes to the establishment's attractiveness.[251] Conversely, the availability of

---

[243] *ITV v. TVCatchup* [2013] ECDR 9 at para 26.

[244] *SGAE* [2007] ECDR 2 at para 40; *FAPL* [2012] ECDR 8 at para 197; *OSA* [2014] ECDR 25 at para 31; *Reha Training* [2017] ECDR 1 paras 57–61.

[245] *Svensson* [2014] ECDR 9.

[246] *GS Media* [2016] ECDR 25 at paras 49–51.

[247] *Filmspieler* [2017] ECDR 14 at paras 49–50.

[248] Art 15(1).

[249] *SGAE* [2007] ECDR 2 at para 44; *ITV v. TVCatchup* [2013] ECDR 9; [2013] FSR 36 at para 35.

[250] *SGAE*, ibid.; *FAPL* [2012] ECDR 8 at para 205.

[251] *Reha Training* [2017] ECDR 1 at para 63.

, does not increase the business of a dentist clinic because such patients attend clinics for treatment and listening to broadcasts is not something they actively chose.[252]

Other rights

A new breed of laws was also introduced under the WIPO Internet Treaties which give protection to rights holders who use technological measures to protect their copyright works[253] and who use digital rights management systems[254] embedded in most digital versions of creative works today which allow owners to keep track of the distribution and usage of copyright works.

4.6.5   Duration of economic rights

The minimum term of protection is the life of the author plus 50 years thereafter under international copyright law. However, there is no ceiling on the maximum term of protection, and the rules vary from country to country. Thus, Japan has a copyright term of life plus 50 years, Indian copyright law protects its works for a term of life plus 60 years, the US, EU and Australia have copyright terms of life plus 70 years, while Mexico has a term of protection of life plus 100 years. Moreover, there are the anomalies and idiosyncrasies within each nation's laws, which either extend protection indefinitely or refuse protection absolutely. Other exceptions relate to unpublished works, laws, and neighbouring rights. Note the rather quixotic decision which held that sound recordings of performances made in England during the 1930s were protected under New York state common law copyright until 2067, despite copyright having expired in these recordings throughout the world including under US federal copyright law.[255] Another anomalous area is in relation to moral rights. Despite the cessation of economic rights, moral rights are perpetual in certain countries such as France and Egypt, in which case literary and artistic property in works are never truly in the public domain.[256] Note the 2005 French Supreme Court decision, which confirmed that the unauthorised sequel to Victor Hugo's work *Les Misérables* would be allowed to be published on principle – but such sequels must respect the moral rights of the deceased Victor Hugo by not 'denaturing' the author and his work.[257]

Authorial works

Since the inception of copyright in the eighteenth century, there has been a constant expansion of the duration of copyright protection. Take for example the UK, where the maximum term was

---

[252] It is a neighbouring rights case but provides insight on the 'public' criterion. *SCF v. Del Corso* [2012] ECDR 16 at paras 97–100.

[253] WCT, Art 11; WPPT, Art 18.

[254] WCT, Art 12; WPPT, Art 19.

[255] *Capitol Records, Inc. v. Naxos of America, Inc.*, 45 NY 3d 5540 (NY, 2005), the common law right extends only to the right to prevent duplication and publication.

[256] French Intellectual Property Code, Art L. 121-1; 2002 Law n°82/2002 on Intellectual Property (Egypt), Chapter III.

[257] *Société Plon and another v. P. Hugo and the Société des Gens de Lettres*, Court of cassation (1st civil chamber), 30 January 2007; [2007] 4 ECDR 205.

28 years under the first copyright law, which was then extended to the term of t'
in 1814, and then in response to heavy authorial lobbying, was further extended to lite pius ஜ. -
years in 1842.[258] A parallel effort to extend terms occurred on European soil; the French Decree of
1791 held that the heirs or successors in title of the author should be proprietors of the works for
five years after the death of the author, whilst the Prussian law of 1837 provided for protection for
life plus 30 years.[259]

The Berne Convention adopted the international standard of life of the author plus 50 years
post-mortem auctoris, which was subsequently adopted by the TRIPS Agreement. Therefore, the *de
jure* international standard for the term of protection of an author's works is the life of the author
plus 50 years. In more recent years, there has been a concerted effort to expand the international
norm from life plus 50 to life plus 70 years through the following measures: the EU adoption of the
life plus 70-year term,[260] the subsequent adoption of this new term by the US,[261] and the imposition
of the life plus 70-year formula through free trade agreements. The trend towards the life plus 70
term of protection has been followed in, inter alia, Singapore, Australia, and Chile.[262]

Where countries apply a term in excess of the Berne rule, Union countries are free to apply
the comparison of terms test namely the term of protection is governed by the law of the country
where protection is claimed. The term of protection cannot exceed the term fixed in the country
of origin of the work (unless there are provisions stating otherwise in the country where protection is claimed). There are exceptions to this basic rule for certain categories of works under the
Berne Convention, which is further applied within the TRIPS Agreement and the WIPO Treaties.
Regarding films, there is no international rule and Berne Union countries have two options. They
can either adopt the general term of life plus 50 years, or they may provide protection for 50 years
after the work has been made available to the public, or, if not made available, then 50 years after
the making of such a work (Art 7(2), Berne Convention). In relation to photographic works and
works of applied art, the minimum term of protection is 25 years from the making of the work (Art
7(4), Berne Convention). The WCT however obliges all signatories (including those belonging to
the Berne Union) to provide the normal term of life plus 50 years for photographs. Under EU law,
films are treated as authored works and are protected for 70 years after the death of the last of the
following persons to survive, whether or not these persons are designated as co-authors:

(i)   principal director;
(ii)   the author of the screenplay;
(iii)   the author of the dialogue; and
(iv)   the composer of music specifically created for use in the cinematographic and audiovisual work.

---

[258] UK Copyright Act 1814; UK Copyright Act 1842 (the Talfoud Act); for a discussion on authors' lobbying to get the term
of protection extended, see S. Eilenberg, *Strange Power of Speech: Wordsworth, Coleridge and Literary Possession* (Oxford
University Press, 1992), Chapter 8.

[259] J.A.L. Sterling, *World Copyright Law* (Sweet & Maxwell, 1998), para 11-02.

[260] EU Term Directive 2006/116/EC.

[261] US Copyright Law, s 302.

[262] Singapore Copyright Act 1987; Australian Copyright Law; Chile Law 19914 (implementing the FTA with US (2003)).

Entrepreneurial works

Under the 1961 Rome Convention it was provided that performers, phonogram producers and broadcasters should have protection for at least 20 years from when the fixation of the phonogram and performance was made (or from when the performance took place), or when the broadcast took place. The TRIPS Agreement and the WPPT extended the term of protection for performers and phonogram producers to 50 years from the date of fixation or performance, though the term of protection for broadcasters remains at 20 years.

Under EU copyright rules, phonogram producers can now claim 70 years protection from when the sound recording is made, or first published; a similar 70-year term of protection is available to performers in relation to the fixation of their performances in a phonogram, from lawful publication or communication to the public. The term of protection for broadcasters is 50 years from the initial making of the broadcast. EU law also confers a 50-year term of protection to film producers from first fixation or first publication or first communication of the work. A more modern type of right is the two-year 'publishers' right' granted to press publishers established within the EU whereby they can exercise the rights of reproduction and communication to the public for the online use of their publications by 'information society service providers'.[263]

4.7 MORAL RIGHTS[264]

Historically, moral rights have allowed the author to safeguard the provenance of her work, as well as her personality and reputation. One of the earliest pronouncements on moral rights arises in the English decision of *Millar v. Taylor*[265] where Lord Mansfield referred to the inherent common law authorial rights of paternity, integrity and divulgation in the pre-Statute of Anne era. In his judgment, Lord Mansfield emphasised the core elements of authorial rights as comprising the right to reap 'pecuniary profit' as well as a right to control 'use of his own name', to control 'the correctness of his own work', to 'retract errors' or to 'cancel a faulty edition'. These were important as Mansfield subsequently emphasises that the printing of such imperfections will be to the author's disgrace. And yet, despite this early identification of moral rights within common law,

---

[263] Rome Convention, Art 14; TRIPS Agreement, Art 14; EU Term Directive 2006/116/EC; EU Performers Term Directive 2011/77/EU; EU Copyright in the Digital Single Market 2019/790.

[264] For a more detailed discussion on this area, see Ricketson and Ginsburg, *supra* note 63, Chapter 10; R. Platt, 'A Comparative Survey of Moral Rights' (2009/2010) 57 J. *Copyright Soc'y U.S.A.* 951; E. Adeney, *The Moral Rights of Authors and Performers: An International Comparative Analysis* (Oxford University Press, 2006); D. Vaver, 'Moral Rights Yesterday, Today and Tomorrow' (1999) *Int J Law Info Tech* 270; A. Dietz, 'Moral Rights and the Civil Law Countries' (1994–95) 19 *Colum. VLA J.L. & Arts* 199; N. Walravens, 'La protection de l'oeuvre d'art et le droit moral de l'artiste' (2003) 197 *RIDA* 3; Z. Radojokovic, 'The Historical Development of "Moral Right"' (1966) *Copyright* 168; S. Strömholm, 'Le droit moral de l'auteur en droit allemand, français et scandinave avec un aperçu de l'evolution internationale' in *Etude de droit comparé* (3rd vol., Stockholm, 1973); A. Dietz, 'Legal Principles of Moral Rights (Civil Law)', General Report, ALAI Congress, Anvers, 1993.

[265] (1769) 9 Geo. 3 B.R. 2303; (1769) 98 ER 201.

there was no direct protection for moral rights in the UK, and by extension, in other common law countries until the mid-twentieth century; instead, it was (and still is in the US) claimed that such rights were available within the common law regimes by virtue of contract or tort laws.[266] In contrast, moral rights norms evolved jurisprudentially in France during the nineteenth century, despite the absence of statutory provisions. An 1814 decision saw the author being granted a right to prevent unauthorised amendments of his texts by the publishers to whom the manuscript was submitted; subsequent decisions saw the courts widening the right of integrity to allow authors to control a work even after the transfer of his economic rights, or the outright sale of the work.[267] German moral rights, conversely, arose from legal doctrine deriving from Kant, Fichte and other German jurists. Moral rights were situated within individual rights, to be enjoyed alongside economic rights. Due to the personal aspects of these rights, the German approach was to dictate that all authors' rights – both economic and moral – could never be alienated from the originator.

By the twentieth century, the European civil law countries pushed for the adoption of moral rights within the international arena, and the 1928 Rome Conference of the Berne Convention adopted the *de minimis* threshold namely the rights of attribution and integrity.

4.7.1 Monist and dualist systems

Are moral rights separable from the economic rights of the author? This historical debate has resulted in two current schools of tradition, with Germany and Austria following the monist approach and France, Italy, Spain and other Francophone countries adopting the dualist approach.

Article L.113–1 of the French IP Code sets out that the author's rights will consist of both moral and economic rights. The two rights exist independently of each other, as is evidenced by the fact that the transfer of economic rights does not derogate from the author's moral rights. The independence of the two rights categorises the classic French author's rights system as 'dualist', with moral rights being rendered inalienable and perpetual under the law, while the economic rights of the author can be dealt with separately and are limited in duration.[268]

In contrast, within the 'monist' countries, moral rights are considered to be intertwined and inseparable from the economic rights. Accordingly, an author's moral rights in a work terminates when the term of protection for economic rights cease. There are further consequences to adopting the monist approach: as moral rights are considered inalienable and such rights are linked with economic rights, full transfer or assignment of economic rights are not recognised under the monist system.[269]

---

[266] G. Dworkin, 'Moral Rights and the Common Law Countries' (1994) *Australian Intell. Prop. J.* 5.

[267] *Billecocq v. Didot*, Trib. Civ. Seine (France), August 17, 1814, reprinted in A.-Ch. Renoard, 2 *Traité des Droit d'Auteurs*, 332 (1839); *Teyssèdre v. Garnier*, Trib. Paris, 6 April 1842, as cited in Ströholm, ibid., 122.

[268] French Intellectual Property Code, Arts L.122-1, L.131-4, 131-6, 131-7; see also the French decision in *Asphalt Jungle* Cour de cassation, Cass 1e civ, May 28, 1991, Bull Civ I, No 172 holding that the moral right is a matter of public policy and that the moral right provisions constitute a part of international private law which apply to everyone regardless of their national origin.

[269] G. Davies and K. Garnett (eds), *Moral Rights* (Sweet & Maxwell, 2016), para 3-001.

4.7.2   International rules

Article 6*bis*, Berne Convention provides for two moral rights, namely (i) the right of attribution, whereby the author has the right to have her name associated with the work created, and (ii) the right of integrity, whereby the author has the right to object to any mutilation or deformation or other modification of, or other derogatory action in relation to, the work which would be prejudicial to the author's honour or reputation. The Berne provision further provides that these rights shall, after the author's death, be maintained at least until the expiry of the economic rights. There is much flexibility as the Convention confirms that the means of redress for safeguarding the moral rights are governed by the legislation of the country where protection is claimed. This has historically allowed common law countries to avoid the specific implementation of moral rights within copyright, arguing that similar protection was available to authors under defamation or contract laws.[270] The Berne provision has also been construed to allow the waiver of moral rights.[271] The WIPO Internet Treaties further substantiate these rights by adopting the two moral rights, as well as extending the rights of attribution and integrity in respect of live and recorded aural performances to performers.[272]

Conversely, the TRIPS Agreement, while adopting all the main provisions of the Berne Convention, specifically excludes Article 6*bis* on moral rights.[273] There are two main justifications for the exclusion of moral rights within the TRIPS Agreement. First, it is argued that moral rights play no role within an international trade agreement due to their elusive nature as compared to economic rights violations.[274] This is not overly convincing as the right of communication is proving impossible to define and control within both US and CJEU jurisprudence. The second, more muted, argument is that moral rights have remained a thorny issue for the US and its questionable claim that its domestic copyright law is in compliance with its obligations under Article 6*bis*, Berne Convention. This view is further substantiated by section 3(b) of the US Berne Convention Implementation Act 1988 which idiosyncratically declares that the adherence of the US to the Berne Convention does not affect the US domestic law on moral rights. The exclusion of moral rights under the TRIPS Agreement offers the US another layer of protection against international approbation.[275]

4.7.3   National laws

The French Intellectual Property Code declares that moral rights attach to the author, and by

---

[270] J. Ginsburg, and J.M. Kernochan, 'One Hundred and Two Years Later: the US Joins the Berne Convention' (1988) 13 *Columbia-VLA Journal of Law and the Arts* 1.

[271] Ricketson and Ginsburg, *supra* note 63, paras 10.17–10.18, citing German Copyright Law, s 29(1) as allowing specifically defined waivers; a more famous provision is s 87, UK Copyright Law, where all moral rights can be waived, other than the right of attribution.

[272] WPPT, Art 5.

[273] TRIPS Agreement, Art 9(1).

[274] Ricketson and Ginsburg, *supra* note 63, para 10.41.

[275] J. Drexl, 'Constitutional Protection of Authors' Moral Rights in the European Union – Between Privacy, Property and the Regulation of the Economy', in K. Ziegler (ed.), *Human Rights and Private Law* (Oxford: Hart Publishing, 2007).

implication, to the author's personality. Specifically, under the Intellectual Property Code will enjoy the 'right to respect for his name, his authorship and his work'.[276] Jurisprudential doctrine has translated this rather vague principle into four specific categories of rights: the right to disclosure; the right to reconsider or retract a work; the right to claim authorship (the right of attribution), and finally, the right to object to derogatory treatment of the work (the right of integrity).

Other EU member states have a similar set of fundamental rights. German copyright law declares in a general sense that the author will be protected in respect of his 'intellectual and personal relationship with his work'. The Act specifically then names three rights: the right of disclosure, the right of paternity, and the right of integrity.[277] The British copyright law recognises the rights of attribution (including against false attribution), integrity, and a limited right of privacy in relation to commissioned photographs.[278]

At the other end of the spectrum is the thin protection afforded under the US federal copyright law. Three specific moral rights are accorded (the rights of integrity, attribution and destruction) to one set of beneficiaries, namely, authors of works of visual art.[279]

Attribution and naming

The paternity or attribution right allows the author to have his authorship, and – in French-inspired legislation – his title, recognised 'in clear and unambiguous fashion'.[280] The right of attribution allows the author to choose whether to assert his authorship and have his name/title acknowledged on the work; or whether to exercise his right to withhold his name and to have the work published anonymously or pseudonymously. It also allows the author to prevent misattributions, misleading attributions (where the extent of the author's contribution is misrepresented), and false attributions (where the author's name is placed on a work he did not create, or on a mutilated version of his work).[281]

Integrity and destruction

The right of integrity allows the author to object to all sorts of distortions, mutilations or modifications of the work including interpretations, additions, deletions, changes, imperfections, which are a result of reproduction techniques, including poor or wrong colours in the case of artistic works. Examples of instances where national courts have held that the integrity right has been infringed include unauthorised Christmas ribbon decorations tied to flying geese sculptures,[282] the dismantling

---

[276] French Intellectual Property Code, Art L.121-1.

[277] German Copyright Law, Arts 11 *et seq.*

[278] UK Copyright Law, ss 77–89.

[279] US Copyright Law, ss 101, 106A. Visual arts are defined to mean paintings, drawings, prints, sculptures or photographs, and only if such works exist in a single copy or in a limited edition of 200 copies that are signed and numbered by the author.

[280] Ricketson and Ginsburg, *supra* note 63, para 10.19.

[281] French Intellectual Property Code, Art 121-1; German Copyright Law, Art 13.

[282] *Snow v. Eaton Centre*, (1982) 70 CPR (2d) 105 (Ontario Supreme Court), held infringement of the sculptor's integrity right as ribbons distorted the work.

and sale of a painted refrigerator by the purchaser,[283] the enactment of the play *Waiting for Godot* by female actors, against the author's specific instructions that all roles be played only by males,[284] and placing songs within a compilation of recordings with an extreme right-wing presentation.[285]

There is great divergence in the interpretation of this right. First, most jurisdictions, adopt the Berne Convention standard and require that the author show there has been prejudice to his honour or reputation.[286] French copyright law, however, does not require the author to prove that the acts in question prejudice his honour or reputation, nor does the author have to justify his reasons for refusing to tolerate such acts.

Secondly, the scope of the right of integrity is limited in Germany and UK where courts employ an objective test relying on impartial evidence as to whether the treatment has been derogatory enough for infringement to take place. Thus, under German law an author has the right to prohibit any distortion or any other mutilation of his work, which would harm his intellectual or personal interest in the work. The right is infringed by any act that threatens or harms his or her honour and reputation, which is objectively determined with reference to evidence of harm to the author. In *Oberammergau Passion Plays*, the German Federal Court held that modifications of a 1930s-created set design did not constitute a breach of the author's right of integrity. In determining whether the impairment to the set designs constituted a prejudice to the legitimate interests of the author, the court weighed the interests of the author against those of the adapter, concluding that authorial interests would be given less weight decades after his death than during his lifetime.[287] The opposite is true in France where the author's opinion is the final arbiter as to whether there has been a breach of right: the general test employed by the courts is whether an act has denatured the ethic of the work (*dénaturer l'éthique de l'oeuvre*).[288]

Thirdly, the right of integrity gives the French or German author the right to oppose every use of the work in a context that denigrates the meaning of it, even without alteration or modification of the work;[289] whereas under UK and common law systems, the law requires that there be derogatory

---

[283] *Bernard Bufet Refrigerator*, CA Paris, 1re ch. (France), May 30, 1962, J.C.P., 1963, II, 12989, on appeal to Cass. 1re civ., July 6, 1965, (1965) 47 RIDA 221, an injunction was granted against the purchaser of the refrigerator preventing him from dismantling the panels and selling them separately; the panels had been decorated by the painter Bernard Bufet; held that the author had the moral right to prevent his work from being denatured or mutilated, even after the disclosure or sale of the work to the public.

[284] *Godot* TGI Paris, 3e ch. (France), 15 Oct. 1992: RIDA 1/1993, p.225. The opposite conclusion was reached in the Netherlands (President Rechtbank Haarlem, 29 April 1998: AMI 1998/4, p.83, annotated by Cohen Jehoram).

[285] *Neo-Fascist Slant in Copyright Works*, OLG Frankfurt-am-Main (Germany), 1994, [1996] ECC 375.

[286] For British law, see *Confetti Records v. Warner Music UK* [2003] EWHC 1274.

[287] *Oberammergau Passion Plays*, German Federal Court, October 13, 1988; [1989] GRUR 10; For UK, see *Tidy v. Trustees of the Natural History Museum and another* [1996] 39 IPR 501 (UK High Court), holding that to be derogatory, the treatment concerned – a reproduction of cartoons in reduced size in this case – must amount to a distortion or mutilation of the plaintiff's work, or must otherwise [be] prejudicial to the honour or reputation of the plaintiff's work. In order to prove the latter, the court would apply an 'objective test of reasonableness'.

[288] *Chaplin v. Chatelus* TGI Paris, January 24, 2000; (2000) 186 RIDA 305, note by Kéréver at 235.

[289] TGI Paris, 1re ch. (France), 15 May 1991: RIDA 2/1992, p.209, infringement to use Massenet's religious music as background for a publicity movie that highlighted the strengths of a project developer, despite having not altered or adapted

'treatment' of the work in that the work must be deleted from or altered somewhat. For nations have elevated the right of integrity to the upper echelons of constitutional and public policy laws.[290] The opposite is also true when the exercise of the right is curtailed by fundamental freedoms.[291]

Finally, does the moral right of integrity include the right to prevent the destruction of the copyright work? The issue is at its most contentious when the rights of the author clash with those of a real property owner – this usually occurs when an artistic work is situated in a public or private space, or affixed to a building, belonging to a third party. One of the most explicit rules of law in this matter derives, ironically, from the US federal copyright law in relation to works of visual art: an author has the right to prevent 'any destruction of a work of recognised stature, and any intentional or grossly negligent destruction of that work'.[292] In the well-publicised decision *Cohen v. G&M Realty* involving the planned destruction of the 5Pointz building in New York, the US courts positively affirmed the moral rights of street and graffiti artists (who had been covering the building with their artworks since the 1990s) to prevent the destruction of the building. The court not only recognised graffiti as copyright-protected art but also held that the destruction of the building by its owners constituted a breach of the artists' moral rights. In doing so, the judge was cognisant of the difficulty of interpreting the statutory requirement that the right is only applicable to works of recognised stature: this was done by giving rather substantial weight to the artists' expert testimony regarding the technical skill employed in the creation of each work, the importance of 5Pointz as an 'aerosol art mecca', and the considerable stature accorded the graffiti and street art from art world academics and professionals.[293]

The situation is not so clear cut under other laws. In Germany, there are no statutory provisions granting a right to prevent destruction. The courts have, at times, recognised that the right of integrity should extend to cover preventing destruction of art works; this is, however, subject to proving that the author's interests have been damaged. Moreover, the courts in the past have bewilderingly noted that in order to balance the rights of the owners of conflicting property rights,

---

the music; *Neo-Fascist Slant in Copyright Works*, OLG Frankfurt-am-Main (Germany), 1994, [1996] ECC 375, author's moral right of integrity infringed by situating songs in a compilation of recordings comprising extreme right-wing music.

[290] *Barbelivien v. Agence Business*, Cass. 1re civ., January 28, 2003 (2003) 196 RIDA 414, French Supreme Court held that the inalienable nature of the right of integrity of the work is a principle of public policy; *Amar Nath Sehgal v. Union of India (UOI) and Anr.*, High Court of Delhi, 117(2005) (30) PTC 253(Delhi), Court held that defendant had violated not only the plaintiff's moral right of integrity in the mural sculpture, but also violated the integrity of the work in relation to the cultural heritage of the nation.

[291] *Les Misérables*, Cass. 1re civ., 30 Jan. 2007; RIDA 2/2007, p.249; CA Paris, 4e ch., 19 Dec. 2008: RIDA 2/2009, p.444, the French Supreme Court ruled that the moral right to integrity was not absolute, and that the freedom to create restrains the author or his heirs from objecting to the creation of a sequel work created at the end of the economic right in the work.

[292] US Copyright Law, s 106A; a similar provision is available under Swiss Copyright Law 1992, Art 15.

[293] *Cohen et al. v. G&M REALTY L.P. et al.*, Case No. 13-CV-05612(FB) (RLM) (EDNY, 2018); see also *Carter v. Helmsley-Spear Inc.*, 861 F. Supp. 303, 325 (SDNY, 1994); 71 F 3d 77 (2d Cir, 1995) setting out the key factors in deciding what constitutes a work of stature.

the owners of the material (or building) in which the copyright work is incorporated may have to destroy the copyright work itself in order to preserve the author's reputation.[294]

Divulgation and retraction

These two rights are not specifically recognised under international copyright law, although several civil law countries, including France and Germany recognise them. Under French copyright law, the divulgation right vests in the author the right to disclose his work and to determine the method and conditions of such disclosure. In the famous *Whistler* decision, the French Supreme Court determined that the author's moral right of divulgation outweighed his contractual obligation to deliver the painting.[295] The divulgation right also allows the author to complete a work, even when it is being commissioned by a third party who decides to not go ahead with the work.[296] It is arguable that the divulgation right is somewhat akin to the economic right of first distribution or first publication, available in all jurisdictions.[297]

The right of retraction allows the author to reconsider or correct his work, or to withdraw his work from circulation, even after publication of the work. An author who has transferred his economic rights is thus given the option to reconsider and retract his transfer. However, the right is limited and is unusually in favour of the transferee. Not only must the author indemnify the transferee for any prejudice caused, he must further offer the transferee the right of first publication under the original terms of the agreement should the author thereafter wish to continue with the publication of the work.

---

[294] See A. Dietz, 'Letters from Germany' (1984) *Copyright* 438 citing *Rock Island with Sirens* decision (79 RGZ 397/401, Reichsgericht, June 8, 1912) where the defendant had commissioned the author to paint a mural on the stairway of his home; upon completion and having disliked the naked sirens depicted within the artwork, the defendant had them painted over with clothing. The Court held that the author had the right to present his work to the public In its original form; on the other hand the purchaser of the art work had a right to either sell or destroy the work; he had no right, however, to modify the work; similarly, in the *Decorated Building* decision (LG Munich 1, December 8, 1981), the owner of a building had the author's decorations on the exterior of the building removed. The court held that the author's moral rights could be respected only if the modifications were reversed and the decorations restored; in the alternative, the owner should destroy the remaining parts of the work so as to not affect the author's reputation.

[295] French Intellectual Property Code, Art L.121-2; *Whistler* decision, Cass. 1re civ., 14 March 1900: DP 1900, 1, p. 497, note by Planiol.

[296] *Dubuffet v. Regie Nationales des Usines Renault*, Jan 8, 1980, Cass. 1re civ., RIDA April 1980, 154, A. Francon obs.; March 16, 1983, Cass civ Ire, RIDA July 1983, 80, the French Supreme Court held that the Renault Company, which had commissioned Dubuffet to create a sculpture, could not withdraw the commission after Dubuffet had already commenced construction. See also *Bouvier v. Cassigneul*, Cass. Crim., December 13, 1995; (1996) 169 RIDA 306, where the defendant found and sold early works of an artist, who had not wished them published; the court held the defendant liable of infringing the right of divulgation.

[297] Although the right of disclosure was contained in the original draft for Art 6*bis* Berne Convention, it was removed because of common law countries' concerns that that right could not be reconciled with publishing agreements – see M.-C. Janssens, 'Invitation for a "Europeanification" of moral rights', in P. Torremans (ed.), *Research Handbook on Copyright Law* (2nd ed., Cheltenham: Edward Elgar Publishing, 2017).

4.7.4   Duration of moral rights

The Berne Convention provides for two moral rights, and states that these rights shall, after the author's death, be maintained at least until the expiry of the economic rights. The WIPO Treaties adopt a similar approach, although extending moral rights to performers. As discussed above, the term of moral rights depends particularly on whether a state follows the monist or dualist approach. Under the dualist concept, economic and moral rights have different terms of protection, where moral rights tend to be perpetual in duration; under the monist approach, moral and economic rights will expire at the same time.

4.8   LIMITATIONS AND EXCEPTIONS

4.8.1   The 'three-step' test

The three-step test made its first appearance in the 1967 Stockholm revision of the Berne Convention and was initially only applicable to the right of reproduction. Since then, it has been transplanted into the TRIPS Agreement, the 1996 WIPO Internet Treaties, the Beijing Audiovisual Treaty, and the Marrakesh Treaty. The wording of the three-step test varies slightly from treaty to treaty; the limited version under Article 9, Berne Convention reads that a Union country may 'permit the reproduction of such works in certain special cases, provided that such reproduction does not conflict with a normal exploitation of the work and does not unreasonably prejudice the legitimate interests of the author'. The expansive version under Article 13, TRIPS, states that 'Members shall confine limitations and exceptions to exclusive rights to certain special cases which do not conflict with a normal exploitation of the work and do not unreasonably prejudice the legitimate interests of the rights holder.' The three-step test has also been incorporated into regional and national laws, as well as EU bilateral and regional trade agreements.[298]

The key concepts within those three steps (namely, special cases, normal exploitation of the work, and unreasonably prejudice the legitimate interests) have been interpreted by the WTO panel decision regarding the exceptions under the US Copyright Act which allowed restaurants, bars and shops to play radio and TV broadcasts without paying licensing fees. The WTO panel held the exceptions to breach Article 13, TRIPS, and laid down several guidelines as to the interpretation of the three-step test.[299]

First, the three requirements are applied cumulatively. Secondly, the panel offered an extremely literal explanation of the term 'special'; it means 'having an individual or limited application

---

[298] Berne Convention, Art 9(2); TRIPS Agreement, Art 14; WCT, Art 10; WPPT, Art 16; Marrakesh Treaty, Art 11; InfoSoc Directive 2001, Art 5(5). See also M. Senftleben, *Copyright, Limitations and the Three-Step Test. An Analysis of the Three-Step Test in International and EC Copyright Law* (The Hague: Kluwer Law International, 2004); Ricketson and Ginsburg, *supra* note 63, paras 13.03 *et seq.* and 13–97 *et seq.*

[299] Report on Section 110(5) of the United States Copyright Act, WT/DS160/R, 15 June 2000. For an analysis of the

or purpose' and hence an exception or limitation should be limited in its field of application or exceptional in its scope. However, there is no need to identify explicitly each and every possible situation to which the exception could apply, provided that the scope of the exception is known and particularised.[300] On the facts, the US limitation did not qualify under the first condition as a substantial majority of eating and drinking establishments and close to half of retail establishments were covered by the exemption – this meant that the exemption did not qualify as a 'certain special case' within the meaning of the first condition of Article 13, TRIPS.

In respect of the second step, the limitation must be considered in light of the explicit statement in several copyright instruments that the scope of protection, especially in the case of the right of reproduction, extends to protecting the work 'in any manner or form'. Thus, for example, the usual example of the type of activity that constitutes 'normal exploitation' is photocopying of a 'very large number of copies' for a particular purpose; however, it may also be that in the case of a musical score, the making of even one copy of one of the orchestral parts for use in a school might be regarded very differently from the making of a number of copies of part of a short story for a class of students.[301] The WTO panel was clear that not every use of a work conflicts with a normal exploitation of that work. Instead, it held that an exception or limitation to an exclusive right in domestic legislation:

> Rises to the level of a conflict with a normal exploitation of the work (i.e., the copyright or rather the whole bundle of exclusive rights conferred by the ownership of the copyright), if uses, that in principle are covered by that right but are exempted under the exception or limitation, enter into economic competition with the ways that right holders normally extract economic value from that right to the work (i.e., the copyright) and thereby deprive them of significant or tangible commercial gains.[302]

On the facts of the case, the panel found that the exception, in some cases, was exempting 70 per cent of the targeted users from paying a licence fee. Moreover, there appeared to be no overwhelming public interest or policy reason why these groups of users should be exempted from payment (as opposed to other users of the same type of copyright works).

In respect of the key phrase in step three, namely 'unreasonably prejudice the legitimate interest of the owner', the ethos was rationalised during the 1967 Stockholm proceedings. It was argued that as long as an equitable remuneration was paid to the author, large numbers of copies for use may not unreasonably prejudice the author. Moreover, it was thought that a small number

---

decision, see M. Ficsor, 'How Much of What? The "Three-Step Test" and its Application in Two Recent WTO Dispute Settlement Cases' (2002) 192 RIDA 110–251; cf C. Geiger, D. Gervais and M. Senftleben, 'The Three-Step Test Revisited: How to Use the Test's Flexibility in National Copyright Law' (2014) 29 *American University International Law Review* 581–626, arguing that the WTO panel interpretation may be too restrictive.

[300] WTO Report WT/DS160/R.

[301] Ricketson and Ginsburg, *supra* note 63, paras 13.15 *et seq.*

[302] Ibid.

of copies made for individual or scientific use should not incur any payment even.[303] This appears to suggest that where an act, hitherto permitted, threatens to lead to unreasonable prejudice to the rights owner, member states can either introduce absolute exceptions or compulsory licensing. The WTO panel was reticent as to the exact scope of the third condition, but did address inconclusively an intriguing question: who can enforce the legitimate interests of right holders of various WTO members in panel proceedings within the WTO dispute settlement system? The panel held that there was no indication in the wording of Article 13 of TRIPS, that the assessment of the nature of the prejudice caused to the legitimate interests of the right holder should be limited to the right holders of the member that brings forth the complaint.

The EU Information Society Directive contains an exhaustive list of exceptions and limitations that, save for the mandatory exception for temporary acts of reproduction, all member states are free to transpose or not into their own legal systems. The Directive also subjects the list of exceptions and limitations to the three-step test.[304] Not all member states have adopted the test into their national laws (for example, Germany and the UK), while other member states have specifically included the whole three-step test into their national copyright laws (such as Spain).[305] The difficulty with this rather schizophrenic approach is that the three-step test has evolved from an international norm addressed to governments to one that is applied by national judges in order to test the parameters of national copyright exclusions.[306] According to a recent analysis of the cases from the CJEU, it is suggested that the three-step test within Article 5(5) is not addressed solely to the legislatures of the Member States, but also to national courts.[307]

4.8.2   Public interest and the three-step test

It is an accepted notion that copyright cannot be absolute, and this was emphasised by the Chairman of the first 1884 Berne Conference, Numa Droz, in his closing speech:

---

[303] Records of the Intellectual Property Conference of Stockholm, June 11–July 14 1967, Vol. 1, 883.

[304] InfoSoc Directive 2001, Art 5. The test is also incorporated into Art 10(3) of the Rental and Lending Rights Directive 2006/115/EC.

[305] For the status of the implementation of the Directive, see B. Lindner and T. Shapiro (eds), *Copyright in the Information Society: A Guide to National Implementation of the European Directive* (Cheltenham: Edward Elgar Publishing, 2011).

[306] P.B. Hugenholtz and R.L. Okediji, 'Conceiving an International Instrument on Limitations and Exceptions to Copyright. Final Report, available at http://www.eifl.net/sites/default/files/resources/201409/conceiving_an_international_instrument_on_limitiations_and_exceptions_to_copyright.pdf. See also 'Declaration on a Balanced Interpretation of the "Three-Step Test" in Copyright Law', initiated by four well-known copyright scholars: C. Geiger, J. Griffiths, R. Hilty and U. Suthersanen, available at http://www.ip.mpg.de/ww/en/pub/news/declaration_on_the_three_step_.cfm.

[307] R. Arnold and E. Rosati, 'Are National Courts the Addressees of the InfoSoc Three-Step Test?' (2015) 10(10) *Journal of Intellectual Property Law & Practice* 741–9. See Case C-117/13 *Technische Universität Darmstadt v. Eugen Ulmer KG* [2014] ECDR 23; Case C-351/12 *Ochranný svaz autorský pro práva k dílům hudebním, os (OSA) v. Léčebné lázně Mariánské Lázně* EU:C:2013:749, where the CJEU has held that exceptions and limitations must be construed in light of Art 5(5).

> [...] consideration also has to be given to the fact that limitations on absolute protection are dictated, rightly in my opinion, by the public interest. The ever-growing need for mass instruction could never be met if there were no reservation of certain reproduction facilities, which at the same time should not degenerate into abuses.

Copyright law, by allowing for exceptions or limitations, is based on the tenet that certain types of usages do not allow right holders to extract any economic value, let alone normal or significant or tangible values or gains. Should the three-step test be considered solely from an economic perspective? Should the public interest policies and objectives of Articles 7 and 8, TRIPS be also considered? (See Chapter 3.4.2.) A more teleological approach would then ensure that where circumstances dictate, the public interest in securing freedoms and rights (in order to create wealth) requires a broader approach to the three-step test. Moreover, it is arguable that the panel decision can be looked on as being much broader as limitations or exceptions would only be deemed unacceptable if the use was in 'economic competition'. It is clear that a literal interpretation of the three-step test is narrow and has the power to exclude many limitations and exceptions. It is clear also that some domestic courts are already looking at the three-step test as a means of testing traditional defences against the new digital landscape. It is argued here that domestic courts should avoid this literal approach and adopt alternative interpretative methods. As a matter of principle, it cannot be right to concede that any limitation which allows competitive usage of the work falls foul of the three-step test.

Ricketson's study on the three-step test is relevant here.[308] His view is that the second step cannot be interpreted from a solely economic perspective as this would mean 'very little, if any, work left for the third step' to perform. Moreover, he acknowledges that the great bulk of uses that fall within the three-step test could, in a narrow and economic interpretation, be regarded as being within the scope of the normal exploitation of a work. Ricketson argues that the three-step test, especially at the second stage, must consider 'non-economic normative' factors such as the balance to be achieved between rights holders' interest and the needs of society and culture. Finally, he advocates a teleological (evolutionary) approach by concluding that the three-step test is dynamic and should not become a 'grandfathering' clause that confers an immunity for all time on an exception under national law.

Countries can apply these broad principles in a manner, which suits their own constitutional, development and socio-economic needs. It is indisputable that the three-step test narrows the freedom of legislators to create a broad and general exception; the test is also a recognition, however, that copyright is limited inherently by the public interest, and that exceptions and limitations must exist. Can the test be construed in such a way as to allow for a more positive rights approach so that developing countries can implement clear exceptions, which allow full access to educational and scientific information? This seems possible considering the later versions of this test under

---

[308] S. Ricketson, *The Three-Step Test, Deemed Quantities, Libraries and Closed Exceptions – A Study of the Three-Step Test in Article 9(2) of the Berne Convention, Article 13 of the TRIPS Agreement and Article 10 of the WCT, with Particular Respect to its Application to the Quantitative Test in Subsection 40(3) of the Fair Dealing Provisions, Library And Educational Copying, the Library Provisions Generally and Proposals for an Open Fair Dealing Exception* (Centre for Copyright Studies Ltd, 2002).

the TRIPS Agreement (which refers to competing and complementary objectives and purposes) or the WCT (referring to the need to maintain a balance between the rights of authors and the larger public interest, particularly education, research and access to information), or the Marrakesh Treaty (referring to flexibility if required by the economic situation, and the social and cultural needs of contracting parties).[309] It has been argued that the abstract criteria of the three-step test allows us to view it as a proportionality test where we can use all the different abstract factors to balance competing interests.

A 2012 Spanish Supreme Court decision, for instance, has done exactly this: the court emphasised that copyright:

> Is neither an absolute right (i.e. the owner must endure any ius usus inocui by third parties) nor immune to the general principles of the law (i.e. good faith, prohibition of abuse of right), and that the three-step test must be read not only as a 'restrictive' instrument for the interpretation and application of the limitations but rather as a flexible clause to allow for these doctrines and principles of law to be taken into account when interpreting and applying the copyright law.[310]

4.8.3   Limitations and exceptions under international law

The international conventions, adopting the Berne Convention approach, do not set out a general category of defences and excepted uses (private use, or fair use); rather they list the types of subject matter which do not need to be protected (discussed above), or enumerate specific permissible activities in relation to certain types of works, though some activities are only allowed subject to compensation to authors and owners. Ricketson and Ginsburg term the latter as 'use limitations', a term which sits in delightful contrast to that employed by copyright sceptics in relation to the same excepted activities, namely 'user rights'. Under the Berne Convention one suggested typology of limitations and exceptions existing under national copyright legislation is as follows:[311]

- quotations – of published works provided that their making is compatible with fair practice, and the extent does not exceed that justified by the purpose;
- teaching purposes – use of literary or artistic works in publications, broadcasts or sound or visual recordings for teaching purposes, provided the use is compatible with fair practice;

---

[309] Compare the evolving public interest objectives within international copyright law: Art 1, Berne Convention, with Arts 7 and 8, TRIPS Agreement, the Preamble to the WCT, and Art 12, Marrakesh Treaty. See Geiger, Gervais and Senftleben, *supra* note 299, 626.

[310] Sentencia n.172/2012, of 3 April 2012, Spanish Supreme Court, Civil Chamber; discussed in R. Xalabarder, 'Spanish Supreme Court Rules in Favour of Google Search Engine [...] and a Flexible Reading of Copyright Statutes?' 3 (2012) JIPITEC 162.

[311] Berne Convention, Arts 2*bis*(2), 10, 10*bis*, 11*bis*(2), 13(2), 17; Lewinski, *supra* note 83, 1151–172; Ricketson and Ginsburg, *supra* note 63, paras 13.31 *et seq.*

- press and reporting purposes – reproduction by the press, broadcasting or communication to the public by wire (cabling) of newspaper articles on current, economic, political or religious topics; reproduction for the purpose of reporting current events;
- miscellaneous restrictions including compulsory licences in relation to recording of musical works or broadcasting of works, ephemeral recordings of broadcasts, contributions to films and competition law.

The TRIPS Agreement and the WIPO Treaties incorporate these specific limitations and exceptions from the Berne Convention, and further widen the three-step test to apply to all economic rights. Of course the list above is the minimum set of limits one expects in member states' countries, many of them being optional. Otherwise, signatory countries are free to introduce national variations of the list above and other types of exclusions, subject to the three-step test.

UK and Commonwealth – fair dealing

The key query is whether the taking has been fair or within accepted public interest rationales. This was recognised as early as 1802 by Lord Ellenborough C.J. in *Cary v. Kearsley* where he held that anyone may 'fairly adopt part of the work of another: he may so make use of another's labours for the promotion of science, and the benefit of the public'. What was important, he emphasised, was whether *animus furandi* was present.[312] Many of the early pre-twentieth-century decisions confirmed that the scope of copyright protection did not extend to a 'real and fair abridgement' made by third parties; this was later extended to allow quotations and criticisms of the copyright work.[313] With time, the 'fair abridgement' exception had morphed into the 'fair use' defence. With the publication of the 1911 Copyright Act, the judicially-forged exceptions were consolidated in the statutory fair dealing defence.[314]

Nearly 170 years later, Lord Denning MR noted in *Hubbard v. Vosper* that it was impossible to define what is 'fair dealing' although he set down the following enduring guidelines:[315]

(i)   the defence is not confined to published works, but can apply to the publication of unpublished works;

---

[312] *Cary v. Kearsley* (1802) 170 ER 679 at 680.

[313] *Gyles v. Wilcox* (1741) 2 Atk 141; *Wilkins v. Aitkin* (1810) 17 Vesey, 422; *Whittington v. Wooler* (1817) 2 Swan 428; *Mawman v. Tegg* (1826) 2 Russ 385; *Bell v. Whitehead* (1839) 8 LJ Ch 141; for a summary of inconsistency thrown up by the early court decisions, see W.A. Copinger, *The Law of Copyright in Works of Literature and Art, etc.* (6th ed., 1927), 134 *et seq.* Also see D. Vaver, 'Abridgments and Abstracts: Copyright Implications' (1995) *EIPR* 225; L. Bently, 'Copyright and the Death of the Author in Literature and Law' (1994) 57 *MLR* 973.

[314] 'Fair use' was the accepted nomenclature in common law copyright law, emanating from a line of UK jurisprudence although upon codification the adopted term was 'fair dealing'. For an account of this and the repercussions, see A. Katz, 'Debunking the Fair Use vs. Fair Dealing Myth: Have We Had Fair Use All Along?' available at https://osf.io/preprints/lawarxiv/26vjt/download.

[315] *Hubbard v. Vosper* [1972] 2 QB 84, 98.

(ii) 'fair dealing' is a question of degree and must be a matter of impression, with the court looking to the number and extent of quotations and extracts;

(iii) was the defendant's use of the work for comment, criticism or review as opposed to rival or
competitive use?;

(iv) if a defendant has the reasonable defences of fair dealing and public interest, they should not
be restrained from publication by interlocutory injunction because such a defendant 'if he is
right, is entitled to publish it: and the law will not intervene to suppress freedom of speech
except when it is abused'.[316]

The 'fair dealing' defence is available for the following purposes: non-commercial research; private study; criticism; review; quotation; reporting current events; caricature, parody or pastiche;
illustration for non-commercial teaching purposes.[317] Further limitations under UK copyright law,
which are not subjected to the fair dealing formula, include the following specific and tailored provisions: making temporary copies which are transient and incidental (the mandatory EU exception); making copies for text and data analysis for non-commercial research; incidental inclusion;
copies for the disabled; extracts for educational anthologies; educational exceptions; library and
archival exceptions; legal deposit, and orphan works.[318]

US – fair use

The US doctrine of 'fair use', codified in section 107 of the US Copyright Act, allows any fair use of
a work for all sorts of purposes (beyond the stipulated examples). In determining whether the use
made is a fair use the factors to be considered shall include:

1. the purpose and character of the use, including whether such use is of a commercial nature
or is for nonprofit educational purposes;

2. the nature of the copyrighted work;

3. the amount and substantiality of the portion used in relation to the copyrighted work as a
whole; and

4. the effect of the use upon the potential market for or value of the copyrighted work.

This is not an exhaustive enumeration of factors, and other factors may prove to have a bearing
upon the determination of fair use. The courts have acknowledged that while all the four factors
are important considerations, market effect as directed by the fourth factor is probably the most
crucial one. The US Supreme Court held in *Harper & Row, Publishers, Inc v. National Enterprises* that
the fair use exception should:

[…] come into play only in those situations in which the market fails or the price the

---

[316] Ibid., 94–7.

[317] UK Copyright Law, ss. 29, 30, 30A, 32 *et seq.* For a discussion, see C. Waelde et al., *Contemporary Intellectual Property*
(3rd ed., Oxford University Press, 2016), 175–88.

[318] UK Copyright Law ss 29 *et seq.*; Waelde et al., ibid., 188–96.

copyright holder would ask is near zero. [...] In the economists' view, permitting 'fair use' to displace normal copyright channels disrupts the copyright market without a commensurate public benefit.[319]

Another key factor is whether there has been transformative use of the work. In *Campbell v. Acuff-Rose Music Inc*, the Supreme Court acknowledged that although transformative use is not absolutely necessary for a finding of fair use:

> The goal of copyright, to promote science and the arts, is generally furthered by the creation of transformative works. Such works thus lie at the heart of the fair use doctrine's guarantee of breathing space within the confines of copyright, and the more transformative the new work, the less will be the significance of other factors, like commercialism, that may weigh against a finding of fair use.[320]

The Court further elaborated on the four factors. In relation to the first factor, the central purpose is to determine 'whether the new work merely supersede[s] the objects of the original creation, or instead adds something new, with further purpose or different character, altering the first with new expression, meaning, or message'. The second factor requires a court to consider 'the value of the materials used', recognising that 'some works are closer to the core of intended copyright protection than others'. Purely factual works are further from the core of copyright protection, although there are gradations, for example, between 'directories' and 'elegantly written biographies'. The third factor requires a court to analyse 'not only [...] the quantity of the materials used, but [...] their quality and importance, too'.

   In assessing the fourth factor, courts must 'consider not only the extent of market harm caused by the particular actions of the alleged infringer, but also whether unrestricted and widespread conduct' like that of the defendant 'would result in a substantially adverse impact on the potential market for the original'. Moreover, the 'enquiry must take account not only of harm to the original but also of harm to the market for derivative works'.[321] In the more recent decision *The Authors Guild Inc, et al. v. Google, Inc*[322] the Second Circuit court confirmed that the fair use provision is broad enough to include new types of activities such as digital scanning, text extraction and data mining (discussed further in Chapter 12).

EU law

The Copyright in the Information Society Directive[323] sets out an exhaustive enumeration of the exceptions and limitations that member states can introduce into national law. Only one of the

---

[319] *Harper & Row, Publishers, Inc v. National Enterprises*, 471 US 539 (S Ct, 1985); and re-confirmed in *Steward v. Abend* 14 USPQ 2d 1614 (S Ct, 1990) and *Campbell v. Acuff-Rose Music Inc* 510 US 569; 114 S Ct 1164; 29 USPQ 2d 1961.

[320] *Campbell v. Acuff-Rose Music Inc.* ibid.

[321] Ibid., 578–90.

[322] *Authors Guild v. Google, Inc*, 804 F 3d 202 (2d Cir, 2015); 954 F Supp 2d 282 (SDNY, 2013).

[323] Directive 2001/29/EC (the InfoSoc Directive).

exceptions is mandatory, with the others being optional, and with all exceptions having to comply with the three-step test.[324] Although EU member states have the freedom to pick and choose from the list of optional defences, they do not have the freedom to introduce any new defence. The main excepted acts are:

(i) temporary reproduction which are transient to technological processes, without any independent economic significance;
(ii) reprography and private copying;
(iii) library, educational, museum and archival reproduction for non-commercial purposes;
(iv) activities for teaching and research purposes;
(v) parody, pastiche and caricature; and
(vi) reporting current events or quotations for criticism or review.

There are further minor and quixotic exceptions such as use during religious celebrations, ephemeral broadcasts and minor analogue exceptions. The 2019 Copyright in the Digital Single Market Directive[325] introduces several new mandatory exceptions. First, a text and data mining exception has been provided in relation to the reproduction right, the database right, and the press publishers' right (newly introduced under this 2019 Directive) for reproductions and extractions made by research organisations and cultural heritage institutions for the purposes of scientific research.[326] Secondly, the 2019 Directive clarifies that the existing scope of limitations under EU law should also be applicable in relation to online, distance and cross-border teaching activities.[327] Finally, there are new provisions in relation to heritage preservation and out-of-commerce works. Exceptions will be obligatory in order to allow cultural heritage institutions to make copies of works permanently in their collections, in any format or medium, for the purposes of preservation of works.[328] Thirdly, the 2019 Directive mandates states to introduce exceptions so as to allow such heritage institutions to make available, for non-commercial purposes, out-of-commerce works or other subject matter that are permanently in their collections (on satisfaction of several conditions).[329]

We discuss the rationales and scope of education and cultural exceptions further in Chapter 12.

---

[324] Ibid., Art 5.

[325] Directive (EU) 2019/790 of the European Parliament and of the Council of 17 April 2019 on copyright and related rights in the Digital Single Market and amending Directives 96/9/EC and 2001/29/EC, OJ L 130/92, 17.5.2019. This legislation courted much controversy since its inception in 2016, with over 1,000 amendments from European Parliament members having been tabled during its passage.

[326] Ibid., Arts 2(2), 3, 4, 7.

[327] Ibid., Arts 5, 7.

[328] Ibid., Arts 2(3), 6, 7.

[329] Ibid., Art 8.

5
Patents

As copyright is for literary and artistic works, patents are for inventions – whatever 'inventions' are. As legal documents, patents normally comprise two parts. The first comes at the front and at a minimum comprises the title of the invention, the names of the inventors and an abstract that briefly summarises the invention. The second is the specification. The specification is made up of: (i) a description, which is likely to contain both text and diagrams or drawings; and (ii) one or more claims. In Europe, the description part of the specification tends first to explain the background to the invention, in doing so 'mapping' the prior art. It then presents the problem to which the invention is addressed and the solution being offered. After this, it explains how to carry out the invention. This must all be done in a way that is sufficiently clear and descriptive for a person of normal skill in the relevant technical field to be able to repeat the invention,[1] and that clearly supports the validity of the totality of what is claimed.[2] The claims set the boundaries for the monopoly right. It should be noted at the outset that what Europeans and most other non-Americans would call a patent is frequently referred to by Americans as a utility patent. This may be confusing to some especially those living in countries which provide for second-tier patents often called utility models (see Chapter 10). Utility patents and utility models are completely different. The reason why utility patent is a commonly used term is that the US provides two other IP rights that despite being called patents and appearing in the same part of the United States Code (Title 35) are distinct and different: plant patents and design patents.

The next two sections set out a brief economic history of patent law, especially in relation to two factors. First, patent systems were established ostensibly to fulfil public policy objectives relating to economic and technological progress. Second, these laws were bound to vary as a result of the different developmental opportunities and aspirations of countries, the perspectives of interest groups most able to influence legislatures, and 'path dependence'.[3]

5.1   ORIGINS

The Republic of Venice passed a patent law in 1474, whose underlying purpose was to attract men

---

[1] European Patent Convention, Art 83.

[2] Ibid., Art 84. In the UK, see *Biogen Inc v. Medeva Plc* [1996] UKHL 18.

[3] Path dependence refers to a situation in which apparent anomalies result from decisions made in the past intended to fulfil objectives or solve problems that have become irrelevant. Once the feature in question becomes established it can persist when no longer necessary (or even when sub-optimal from an economic efficiency perspective) and exert a strong influence on the evolutionary trajectory of a given institution, technology, law, or economic system.

'from divers parts' with the incentive of a ten-year monopoly right to their 'works and devices'.[4] The moral interest of inventors and the wider societal benefits were treated as complementary. Thus, in preventing others from building them and taking the inventor's honour away, it was believed that 'more men would then apply their genius, would discover, and would build devices of great utility to our commonwealth'.[5] The public interest was also upheld by a provision allowing for government use.

The next significant legislative development in patent law, and one whose influence was far more enduring, came in 1624 with the English Statute of Monopolies.[6] In reality, its primary purpose was to prohibit monopolies rather than to promote invention, a policy which can be traced back to the landmark decision in *Darcy v. Allen* (or The Case of Monopolies).[7] The court held that the grant to Darcy of an exclusive right to manufacture and sell playing cards was invalid as it contravened common law principles prohibiting monopolies by inhibiting a traditionally lawful trade. The 1624 Statute was also in order to encourage continental craftsmen to settle in the country.[8]

Monopoly grants were declared illegal except 'the true and first inventor or inventors' of 'any manner of new manufactures within this realm' as long as 'they be not contrary to the law, nor mischievous to the state, by raising prices of commodities at home, or hurt of trade, or generally inconvenient'. Such inventors could acquire a patent or grant allowing up to 14 years' monopoly protection, a period equalling the duration of two consecutive apprenticeships. The exclusions reflect concerns at the time about the chaos that might arise due to high commodity prices and unemployment caused by new labour-saving devices.[9] This is not unrelated to the modern European patent law contrary to *ordre public* exclusion (see below). Strict novelty was not required since courts interpreted the purpose of granting patents as being to introduce new trades to England whether or not they were 'novel' elsewhere in the world.[10] It is unlikely to be entirely coincidental that at this time

---

[4] E. Kaufer, *The Economics of the Patent System* (Chur: Harwood Academic Publishers, 1980), 5–6; J. Kostylo, 'Commentary on the Venetian Statute on Industrial Brevets (1474)', in L. Bently and M. Kretschmer (eds), *Primary Sources on Copyright (1450–1900)*, www.copyrighthistory.org; J. Phillips, 'The English Patent as a Reward for Invention: The Importation of an Idea' (1982) 3(1) *Journal of Legal History* 71–9.

[5] Patent Law of Venice, translated by F.D. Prager in his own translation of an article by G. Mandich. F.D. Prager, 'Venetian Patents 1450–1550' (1948) 30(3) *Journal of the Patent Office Society* 176–7.

[6] Officially, 'An Act concerning Monopolies and Dispensations with penall Lawes and the Forfeyture thereof'.

[7] 11 Co Rep 84, 77 Eng Rep 1260 (1603); the court did not hand down any judicial opinion and much reliance (and criticism) is made on Edward Coke's own reports. See J.I. Corré, 'The Argument, Decision and Reports of *Darcy v. Allen*' (1996) 45 *Emory L.J.* 1261.

[8] C. MacLeod, 'The Paradoxes of Patenting: Invention and its Diffusion in 18th and 19th Century Britain, France, and North America' (1991) 32(4) *Technology and Culture*, 885–911, 891.

[9] C. MacLeod, *Inventing the Industrial Revolution: The English Patent System, 1660–1800* (Cambridge: Cambridge University Press, 2009), 18–19.

[10] This was already an accepted norm in the early case of *Darcy v. Allin*, *supra* note 7, which determined that 'the introducer of a new trade into the realm, or of any engine tending to the furtherance of a trade, is the inventor'. A later 1691 patent dispute (*Edgeberry v. Stephens*) clarified that 'if the invention be new in England, a patent may be granted though the thing was practised beyond the sea before; for the statute speaks of new manufactures within this realm; so that if they be new here, it is within the statute; for the Act intended to encourage new devices useful to the kingdom,

England was less advanced technologically than near neighbours France and the Netherlands.[11] The 1624 Statute was amended several times but remained in force – albeit in amended form – until 1977 when the UK patent system was overhauled to make it compatible with the 1973 European Patent Convention. Courts in Australia and New Zealand continue to rely on the language of the Statute of Monopolies as guidance as to how far the scope of 'invention' may be stretched.[12]

The original role of US federal patent (and copyright) law was to implement Article 1 section 8 of the Constitution, which empowers Congress 'to promote the Progress of Science and useful Arts, by securing for limited Times to Authors and Inventors the exclusive Right to their respective Writings and Discoveries'. Prior to this, several state patent laws had existed conferring a 14-year term of protection; however without inter-state reciprocity or recognition, the system was untenable and in 1790, the first US federal patent law was passed. Three things are noticeable: first, that it was intended from the start that the patent system should be accessible to all classes of society and not just to the moneyed classes; secondly, that patent applications were to be filed in the name of individual inventors irrespective of actual ownership; and finally, that in giving statutory expression to the Constitutional clause, the US became the first country not to allow patents of importation.[13] The inventor really had to be the first to invent. As the Supreme Court stated in 1818, perhaps the first time it dealt with issues of substantive patent law, 'the discovery must not only be useful, but new; it must not have been known or used before in any part of the world'.[14] The 1836 Patent Act, in requiring substantive examination of applications (see also below), was arguably the first modern patent law in the world. Its official title nods to the Constitution: 'An act to promote the progress of useful arts, and to repeal all acts and parts of acts heretofore made for that purpose.' Although this law did not discriminate between US and foreign inventors with respect to the examination or the extent of rights granted, foreign applicants had to pay much higher fees, highest of all if they were British. Such discrimination was abolished in 1861 for nationals of countries whose laws were non-discriminatory towards Americans.

The 1791 French patent law in relation to 'Useful Discoveries' awarded property rights to the authors of such inventions. The law, which was enacted in the midst of the French Revolution,

---

and where learned by travel or study, it is the same thing'.

[11] W.R. Cornish, *Intellectual Property: Patents, Copyright, Trade Marks and Allied Rights* (4th ed., London: Sweet & Maxwell, 1999), 111.

[12] *National Research Development Corporation v. Commissioner of Patents* [1959] HCA 67; (1959) CLR 252; *D'Arcy v. Myriad Genetics Inc* [2014] FCAFC 115; *D'Arcy v. Myriad Genetics Inc* [2015] HCA 35. For discussion, see J.C. Lai, 'A Tale of Two Histories: The "Invention" and its Incentive Theory', in J.C. Lai and A.M. Dominicé (eds), *Intellectual Property and Access to Im/material Goods* (Cheltenham: Edward Elgar Publishing, 2016), 94–120; also S. Hubicki and B. Sherman, 'We Have Never Been Modern: The High Court's Decision in National Research Development Corporation v. Commissioner of Patents', in A.T. Kenyon, M. Richardson and S. Ricketson (eds), *Landmarks in Australian Intellectual Property Law* (Port Melbourne: Cambridge University Press, 2009), 73–96.

[13] Z.B. Khan, 'Intellectual Property and Economic Development: Lessons from American and European History', London: Commission on Intellectual Property Rights, 2002; E.C. Walterscheid, *The Nature of the Intellectual Property Clause: A Study in Historical Perspective* (Hein, 2002), 310.

[14] *Evans v. Eaton* 16 US (3 Wheat) 454.

is noteworthy for having also acknowledged the moral interests of inventors, albeit elevated to a human right, and the wider societal benefits of the law:

> Considering that every new idea, whereof the manifestation or the development may become useful to society belongs originally to him who has conceived it; and that it would be to attack the rights of man in their essence, not to regard a discovery in industry (in useful arts and manufactures) as the property of its author.[15]

The author's right to his *découverte industrielle* was deemed a property right that the law must 'protect and render sacred'. Right holders did not have to be inventors. As with the Statute of Monopolies, they could be importers of other people's inventions with or without their consent. Second, once a patent was awarded protected goods had to be made (or 'worked' in patent law parlance) domestically. If owners imported them instead the patent could be forfeited. In addition, it was prohibited to patent the same invention in other countries. While the incorporation of author's rights into patent law did not endure, Paris Convention Article 4*ter* provides a related attribution right, stating that 'the inventor shall have the right to be mentioned as such in the patent' (see below).

The German Patent Act (*Reichspatentgesetz*) of 1877 followed the US example by establishing an examination system. In other respects it was quite different, giving rights to the first applicant to file (as opposed to the US' first to invent which was not abandoned statutorily until the America Invents Act, 2011 – see below), providing for pre-grant publication and the opportunity to formally oppose a patent, and vesting rights in 'applicants' who were likely to be corporations rather than independent inventors. Elsewhere, registration systems – which granted patents without the need to convince a specialist that the documentation submitted with the application described a genuine invention – were the norm. Some European countries, though, managed without a patent law for much of the nineteenth century.

5.2   TOWARDS THE MODERN ERA

5.2.1   A social contract

The modern system of patents for inventions has some fundamental characteristics that make it different from earlier patent systems which were, in essence, mainly monopoly privileges relating to trade in certain commodities. The first major step towards the modernisation of patents came with the adoption of the notion that patents represent a bargain in which inventors are granted limited monopoly rights by the government on behalf of society in exchange for the

---

[15] Reproduced in Annex D, Select Committee, *Report of the Select Committee on the Law Relative to Patents for Inventions*, Parliamentary Papers III (Command Paper 332), 1829. On the historical context of the 1791 legislation and its legacy, see F. Savignon, 'The French Revolution and Patents' (1989) *Industrial Property* 391–400.

disclosure of technical information.[16] Lord Mansfield may have been the first jurist to formulate this view of patents as an information-for-monopoly transaction when he pronounced, in a 1778 case, that:

> The law relative to patents requires, as a price the individual should pay the people for his monopoly, that he should enrol, to the very best of his knowledge and judgment, the fullest and most sufficient description of all the particulars on which the effect depended, that he was at the time able to do.[17]

In doing so he laid out the now conventional explanation of patents that they are a bargain in which inventors are granted time-limited monopoly rights by the government on behalf of society in exchange for the disclosure of technical information that is presumed to advance scientific and technological development. This understanding of the essential nature of the patentable invention contrasts with its original guise as no more nor less than a trading monopoly over a 'thing', typically (if one goes far enough back) neither truly novel nor even inventive.

For Biagioli, this essential feature of the modern-day patent evolved historically as national governance evolved from absolutism to liberalism.[18] This seems highly plausible. On the other hand, his claim that 'modern patent law has come to construe the patented invention as a text'[19] seems like an assertion that patented inventions have become purely immaterial as far as the law is concerned,[20] implying also that the inventor had become someone who may be characterised 'as a right-bearing author'.[21] The inventor may be an author of sorts, but she is not the author of the patent specification, which is not a copyright-protectable work of literature but 'an inscribed verbal act'[22] that is anonymous yet personal. It has remained personal despite the mid-nineteenth-century emergence of patent attorneys charged with writing the patent on behalf of the inventors, a task that many conducted with great skill, as they still do. Artificial intelligence has not yet made patent attorneys redundant. However, somewhat paradoxically, this did not diminish the standing of inventors as geniuses who continued to be celebrated as both inventors and authors of their

---

[16] M. Fisher, 'Enablement and Written Description', in R.L. Okediji and M.A. Bagley (eds), *Patent Law in Global Perspective* (New York: Oxford University Press, 2014), 243–83, 250–52.

[17] *Liardet v. Johnson*, [1778] 1 WPC 52 at 54. For a similar statement from the United States: *Lowell v. Lewis* 15 F Cas 1018, 1020 (1817). On the origins of the disclosure requirement in the United States and France, see A. Pottage and B. Sherman, *Figures of Invention: A History of Modern Patent Law* (Oxford: Oxford University Press, 2010), 54–60.

[18] M. Biagioli, 'Patent Specification and Political Representation: How Patents Became Rights', in M. Biagioli, P. Jaszi and M. Woodmansee (eds), *Making and Unmaking Intellectual Property: Creative Production in Legal and Cultural Perspective* (Chicago: University of Chicago Press, 2011), 25–39.

[19] Ibid., 31.

[20] This sounds rather like Lord Hoffmann's assertion that 'an invention is a piece of information'; *Merrell Dow Pharmaceuticals Inc v. HN Norton & Co Ltd* [1995] UKHL 14 (26 October 1995), para 28.

[21] Biagioli, *supra* note 18, 32.

[22] K. Swanson, 'Authoring as Invention: Patent Protection in the Nineteenth-Century United States', in Biagioli, Jaszi and Woodmansee, *supra* note 18, 25–39, 41–54, 41.

patents (see below). Nonetheless, the fact remains that the rhetorical power of the Mansfieldian formulation of the patent bargain is deeply rooted and persistent.

Another critical point to make about this view of inventions as texts is that certain inventions in complex fields, including those claiming life forms, are irreducible to a mere written text, as if they are recipes for a meal, even with the support of a deposited biological sample (as required for many biological inventions), and that for owners this is not without advantages. With such categories of invention, the text may play no more than a limited role in terms of asserting the patent including litigation. It is perfectly possible to make an invention – and get sued for doing so – without any reference to the patent specification. Thus, the US Supreme Court justices recently held unanimously that a farmer had infringed a company's patent covering genetically modified seeds by the act of reproducing seed on-farm from plants grown from seeds he had acquired legally (see Chapter 17).[23] Accordingly, he had 'made' the invention despite doing nothing other than planting second-generation seed on his land and letting nature do the bulk of the remaining work. According to the dictionary definition of 'to make', though, the Court was perfectly correct. But this is far away from other inventions where one really would have to read the patent text in order to re-make the invention as disclosed. For this particular patent infringer, the specification provided no useful scientific or legal instruction. Would-be infringers largely comprised consumers able to reproduce merely by normal cultivation practices and not just commercial scientific competitors.

5.2.2   Examination and litigation

A second step in the modernisation of patent law came with the introduction of the requirement that patent applications be examined to ensure that the specification describes a genuine invention. As mentioned, the 1836 US Patent Act was itself quite innovative in that it required all applications to be examined by the patent office for novelty and usefulness. Gradually, other countries followed suit, the first being Germany through the 1877 *Reichspatentgesetz*. With such notable exceptions as the Netherlands (since 1995) and South Africa (where shifting to examination is currently under consideration), most countries today either have examination systems or are members of regional organisations responsible for examining patent applications and granting either bundles of national patents, such as the European Patent Organisation, or single unitary ones like the *Organisation Africaine de la Propriété Intellectuelle*.

The third step came with the confirmation that the patentable bar should be kept low enough to capture the incremental inventions flooding out of the corporate research and development (R&D) facilities of the Second Industrial Revolution. In late-nineteenth-century Germany, which had become dominant in the field of synthetic dyestuffs, the industry became concerned about whether or to what extent it should be considered inventive to apply known processes to make new dyes through fairly uncreative chemical 'tinkering'. The problem was not resolved until an 1889 Supreme Court case relating to the Congo decision. Its long-term significance makes it worth discussing in some detail. Congo Red was an azo dye, the process for making of which was patented by Paul Böttiger, a former Bayer chemist. Sold to AGFA, it became a very profitable product.

---

[23] This is the *Bowman v. Monsanto* case discussed in Chapter 14.

Carl Duisberg at Bayer came up with a chemically very similar dye albeit more brilliant in colour than Congo Red called Benzopurpurin 4B and filed a patent. AGFA and Bayer agreed not to challenge each other's patents and made an arrangement by which AGFA held both patents but both companies would be able to commercialise the two dyes.[24]

Subsequently, a small firm called Ewer & Pick began selling both products made by a slightly different process. AGFA sued for infringement and Ewer & Pick counter-sued to have the patents nullified. Some very eminent chemists provided written or oral testimony that the patents should be made void, including Heinrich Caro of BASF who argued that so lacking in inventiveness was Congo Red that one of his young lab assistants would be able to make it just by reading the title of the patent. Duisberg, representing Bayer, cleverly responded that his assistants could also make BASF's dyes merely by reading the titles of the patents. This was to make the point that if Congo Red were unpatentable then so would the azo dyes generally be too. Such an outcome would obviously have been highly undesirable for both firms.

Duisberg's defence of the patent won the day. But the most important outcome was the fashioning by the court of the 'new technical effect' doctrine, which softened the requirement of true inventiveness in certain cases where the result was a product with 'unexpected and valuable technical qualities'. The 'element of surprise' factor continues in Europe to be relevant, albeit not always decisive, to considerations of non-obviousness and inventive step (see below). The latter has led to much uncertainty since an agreed definition of 'technical' continues to elude inventors, practitioners and jurists (see the discussion on this below). According to one account:

> The court argued that the process for making Congo red, lacking any inventiveness of its own, would as such not have been patentable. In this case, however, the application of the general method resulted in a dyestuff of undoubted technical and commercial value. Its unexpected and valuable technical qualities more than compensated for the lack of inventiveness of the process. In other words, the court said that, if the requirement of utility is particularly emphasized, it is no longer necessary to look at whether the requirement of inventiveness is also satisfied.[25]

5.2.3 Corporate patenting

The Court's decision had great long-term importance. First, it enabled the bigger firms to amass large patent holdings for inventions based on their organised research programmes. In consequence, it became economically more feasible for chemical firms to invest in organised, large-scale, in-house research and development. Second, it was a key stage in a gradual change in perception shared by industry, the patent office and the courts from one that treated invention as a

---

[24] For an account of the decision, and the background to the dye industry lawsuits, see J.P. Murmann, *Knowledge and Competitive Advantage: The Coevolution of Firms, Technology and National Institutions* (New York: Cambridge University Press, 2003); also, H. van den Belt and A. Rip, 'The Nelson-Winter-Dosi Model and Synthetic Dye Chemistry', in W.E. Bijker, T.P. Hughes and T. Pinch (eds), *The Social Construction of Technological Systems* (Cambridge, MA: MIT Press, 1989).

[25] Belt and Rip, ibid., 154.

solitary activity inspired – so it was often said – by individual genius, to one that considered it as a collective and almost routine corporate endeavour. In 1891 German patent law was reformed and incorporated the new technical effect doctrine, which is now part of modern European patent law.

In the post-Second World War period, the emerging American pharmaceutical industry seeing the possibility of making unprecedented profits from antibiotics screened through increasingly routine procedures, faced similar uncertainty since it was questionable whether they could get patents for natural products discovered through what had become well-known procedures. Successful lobbying by the American pharmaceutical industry achieved the incorporation in the 1952 Patent Act of helpful language in order, inter alia, to ensure that antibiotics discovered through techniques of systematic screening could be patented. 'On behalf of their pharmaceutical industry clients, New York Patent Bar Association members drafted a Bill and were able to get it introduced in Congress, and this, supplemented by other Bills and pressures, brought about the changes they wanted.'[26] Essentially, the non-obviousness criterion was incorporated into patent law in a particular way that meant 'patentability shall not be negatived by the manner in which the invention was made'. This phrase was intended to keep the invention threshold from drifting too high. According to its underlying purpose it was successful.[27]

Overturning the flash of genius test in the US (see below)[28] and limiting the inventiveness threshold in Europe had a number of consequences. First, the collective and cumulative innovations of large firms could more securely be protected. Second, businesses could more easily surround their products with large portfolios of patents for related inventions. Third, firms were better able to secure returns from investments in expensive research and development. As a result of these consequences, the larger ones were encouraged to create large in-house R&D structures.

5.2.4   Patents as business assets

Patents seem nowadays to function in the modern economy primarily as rather impersonal business assets; like stocks and shares they are a form of intangible capital and are frequently bought, sold, licensed, cross-licensed and pooled. They are not usually owned by individual peoples but by corporations. Patent licensing is very important for small firms which may be poorly placed to exploit their invention in the marketplace. As for large firms, some of them can amass huge revenues not just from generating new patent-protected products, but from licensing patents to other firms

---

[26] W. Kingston, 'Removing Some Harm from the World Trade Organisation' (2004) 32(2) *Oxford Development Studies* 309–20, 310.

[27] G.S. Rich, 'The Vague Concept of "Invention" as Replaced by Sec. 103 of the 1952 Patents Act' (1964) 46(12) *Journal of the Patent Office Society* 855–76, 860. It should be mentioned that this was not the view of the Supreme Court, which in 1966 considered that the 1952 Act did not change 'the general level of innovation necessary to sustain patentability'. At the same time, though, the Court admitted that the intention of 'the last sentence of § 103' was 'to abolish the test [...] announced in the controversial phrase "flash of creative genius"'. *Graham v. John Deere*, 148 USPQ (BNA) 459 (1966).

[28] In a controversial 1941 judgment (*Cuno Engineering Corp v. Automatic Devices Corp* (1941) 314 US 84), the US Supreme Court denied the patentability of a mechanical device on the grounds that the inventor's skill had not 'reached the level of inventive genius which the Constitution authorizes Congress to award'.

interested in exploiting the inventions in the marketplace. It is the alienable nature of patents that enables them to function as currency in knowledge transactions. But if patent laws are essentially public policy instruments centred upon inventors and their inventions, how did this modern function and character emerge?

The way patents have been justified in different countries has always depended to some extent at least on the level of industrial development – and also to whom one speaks. Over the years, states have granted patents for a variety of public policy purposes such as to encourage the immigration of craftsmen, to reward importers of foreign technologies, to reward inventors, to create incentives for further inventive activity, to encourage the dissemination of new knowledge, and to allow corporations to recoup their investments in research and development. From a public policy perspective, each of these justifications is as legitimate as the others depending on a country's economic circumstances among other factors.[29] Nonetheless, as with other forms of intellectual property (especially copyright), justice-based arguments for stronger and better enforced rights are also frequently deployed, and such claims can carry strong moral force. After all, many people would consider it just as immoral for somebody to copy an inventor's useful new gadget and claim it as his or her own as to similarly misappropriate somebody's new novel, song or painting.

In theory, patents are tools for economic advancement that should contribute to the enrichment of society through: (i) the widest possible availability of new and useful goods, services and technical information that derive from inventive activity; and (ii) the highest possible level of economic activity based on the production, circulation and further development of such goods, services and information. In pursuit of these aims, inventors are able to protect their inventions through a system of property rights – the patent system. Once these have been acquired, the owners seek to exploit them in the marketplace. The possibility of attaining commercial benefits, it is believed, encourages innovation. But, after a certain period of time, these legal rights are extinguished and the now unprotected inventions are freely available for others to use and improve upon.

Another common way to interpret the modern patent system focuses more on intangible elements, fundamentally on knowledge as opposed to the goods that embody them. Accordingly, patents are a regulatory response to the failure of the free market to achieve optimal resource allocation for new knowledge that has practical application of potential or actual commercial value. This interpretation sits neatly within the public interest school of regulation, according to which one of the roles of the state is to resolve market failures. Thus, 'patents are designed to create a market for knowledge by assigning propriety rights to innovators which enable them to overcome the problem of non-excludability while, at the same time, encouraging the maximum diffusion of knowledge by making it public'.[30] This explanation for patents assumes that knowledge is a public good. This assumption was nicely articulated by Thomas Jefferson who wrote that the

---

[29] For an interesting discussion of how the justifications of patents have evolved over time, see J.C. Lai, 'The Changing Function of Patents: A Reversion to Privileges?' (2017) 37(4) *Legal Studies* 807–37.

[30] P. Geroski, 'Markets for Technology: Knowledge, Innovation and Appropriability', in P. Stoneman (ed.) *Handbook of the Economics of Innovation and Technological Change* (Oxford and Malden: Blackwell, 1995), 90–131, 97; also, K.J. Arrow, 'Economic Welfare and the Allocation of Resources in Invention', in NBER, *The Rate and Direction of Innovative Activity* (Princeton: Princeton University Press, 1962).

'peculiar character' of an idea is that 'the moment it is divulged, it forces itself into the possession of everyone, and the receiver cannot dispossess himself of it', and also that 'no one possesses the less, because every other possesses the whole of it'. He then went on to explain that 'he who receives an idea from me, receives instruction himself without lessening mine; as he who lights his taper at mine receives light without darkening me'.[31]

One of the reasons why patents are so controversial is that the intellectual property incentive, as far as it actually works, functions by restricting use by others of the protected invention for a certain period. Yet follow-on innovation by others is more likely to happen if use is not restricted. Thus a balance between private control over the use of technical information and its diffusion needs to be struck. Where the line should be drawn is very difficult to determine, but the ideal location is likely to vary widely from one country to another, and, one may argue, from one business sector to another. In countries where little inventive activity takes place, free access to technical information may well do more to foster technological capacity building than providing strong private rights over such information. In fact, technological capacity building may at certain stages of national development be best achieved by requiring foreign technology holders to transfer their technologies on generous terms rather than by trying to encourage domestic innovation by making strong legal rights available to all. This point applies to those developing countries that have attained a reasonable capacity to adopt and benefit from such technologies. Countries with very limited capacity have far less to gain from free access to technologies. This suggests that developing countries should be careful not to make the rights too strong in relation to the extent of enforceability of the rights and the absence or relative lack of limitations and exceptions to patentable subject matter – at least until their economies are more advanced. Historical evidence indicates that several present-day developed countries, rightly or wrongly, took such a policy decision in the past.[32]

Patents are temporary exclusionary rights that are alienable. As such, owners can exploit them in various possible ways. For example, as legal property rights, patents themselves can be sold or licensed even before a product based on the invention has been developed. More advantageously, they can be converted into market monopolies if the invention so protected results in a commercial product and depending on certain factors such as the relationship between the invention and the product, which may actually be protected by more than one patent, and the extent to which substitute products exist on the market. The public goods explanation for patents posits that the possibility of acquiring such commercial advantages encourages both investment in inventive knowledge and the research and development needed to turn inventions into marketable innovations.

But that is not all. Information about the invention as revealed in the patent and by the invention itself is, into the bargain, diffused throughout the economy. In this context, it is helpful to conceive of a patent as a contract between the holder and the government on behalf of the citizenry.

---

[31] Letter to Isaac McPherson written on 13 August 1813, and reprinted in A.A. Lipscomb and A.E. Burgh (eds), *The Writings of Thomas Jefferson* (Washington, DC: Thomas Jefferson Memorial Association, 1903).

[32] H-J. Chang, *Kicking away the Ladder: Development Strategy in Historical Perspective* (London: Anthem, 2002); G. Dutfield and U. Suthersanen, 'Harmonisation or Differentiation in Intellectual Property Protection? The Lessons of History' (2005) 23(2) *Prometheus* 131–47. Also see the discussion on minor innovations in Chapter 10.

The holder receives an exclusive right over his or her invention in exchange for the payment of fees and – which is much more important – for disclosing the invention to others. (So we are back with Lord Mansfield.) Without a patent, the inventor would have no incentive to disclose it. This would be a loss for society if such lack of protection left the inventor with no alternative but to keep it secret. Such an alternative is a feasible option in several technological fields including biotechnology. But it is also true that many kinds of product would upon examination readily betray the invention[33] that brought it into existence.

As for the creation of markets for knowledge, it might be useful here to explain why these are considered beneficial and how patents are thought to bring them into being. The explanation relates to the common situation that many patent holders are poorly placed to exploit their invention in the marketplace. Take the case of a creative but small company lacking the funds to develop and commercialise new products based upon its inventions. If such products are desirable for consumers, failure to commercialise would be a loss for society. But if the company owns a patent, a wealthier company may wish to license or buy the patent secure in the knowledge that the invention is legally protected. And if the invention were kept secret, how would bigger companies know about it? The disclosure of information and presentation in published patent documents makes it possible for prospective users to find inventions of interest and then to approach their owners.

It is interesting to note that controversy surrounding the patent system is far from new. During the nineteenth century, patents came under attack. Ironically, free market economists and infant industry protectionists could be found on both sides of the debate. In 1869, Holland abolished its patent system for mixed reasons; both pro-free trade ideology and infant industry protectionism influenced the government's decision. Britain came close to following its example, citing especially Byzantine patent procedures. Indeed, *The Economist* confidently predicted its demise in a June 1869 editorial (in the same year as the Dutch abolition), declaring with its customary confidence: 'It is probable enough that the patent laws will be abolished ere long.'[34]

Views from the business sector as to the efficacy of patents were mixed. The inventor-industrialist Sir Henry Bessemer, who was granted about 120 patents between 1838 and 1883, was sufficiently positive about the law to claim that 'the security offered by patent law to persons who expend large sums of money […] in pursuing novel invention, results in many new and important improvements in our manufactures'.[35] But other entrepreneurs of the era were less confident. The great Victorian engineer Isambard Kingdom Brunel actually refused to patent any of his inventions. As he expressed it:

---

[33] In this context the word 'invention' refers to the act of bringing a new thing into existence rather than to the thing itself.

[34] Quoted in F. Machlup and E. Penrose, 'The Patent Controversy in the Nineteenth Century' (1950) 10(1) *Journal of Economic History* 1–29, 1. For the 1869 *Economist* leader, and other primary sources, see R.A. Macfie, *Recent Discussions on the Abolition of Patents for Inventions in the United Kingdom, France, Germany and the Netherlands* (Longmans, 1869); For a grand overview on the multi-faceted relationship between patent and innovation, see R. Cullis, 'Technological Roulette: A Study of the Influence of Intrinsic, Serendipitous and Institutional Factors on Innovation in the Electrical, Electronic and Communications Engineering Industries' (PhD thesis, University of London, 2004).

[35] Quoted in J. Mokyr, *The Lever of Riches: Technological Creativity and Economic Progress* (New York: Oxford University Press, 1990), 248.

I believe the most useful and novel inventions and improvements of the present day are mere progressive steps in a highly wrought and highly advanced system, suggested by, and dependent on, other previous steps, their whole value and the means of their application probably dependent on the success of some or many other inventions, some old, some new [...] Without the hopes of exclusive privileges, I believe that a clever man would produce many more good ideas, and derive much more easily some benefit from them.[36]

5.2.5   The 'inventor'

As discussed above, patents in the commercial world serve as impersonal business assets to be bought, sold and licensed. Despite this, the patent system cannot quite let go of the personal: every patentable invention is still deemed to be attributable to one or a few human beings. To the public the inventor works alone. In actuality, the inventor is probably not working alone and is likely to be an employee having to assign her or his invention (see section 5.2.8 on employee inventions). As with authorship, the figure of the inventor has been the focus of a certain amount of critical attention. In addition to legal scholars, historians and philosophers of science have engaged in debates surrounding such questions as the nature, role and standing of the 'inventor' as original creator, and whether inventions can genuinely be attributed to one or a small group of identifiable persons to the exclusion of others.

Herein lies a puzzle: with a growing acceptance of inventing's collective nature, the role of business and other establishments in providing the inventive environment, and the corporate ownership of patents, one might have expected the names of inventors to disappear from patent documents, leaving only the names of the firms or other institutions that paid and stocked the labs, hired the scientists, applied for the patents, and took ownership of them once granted. And yet, inventors did not disappear. Despite this transformation from personal property to business asset, we still name each member of the small group of individuals who are most closely associated with the invention described. Indeed, the individual inventor today has just as prominent a place on patent documents as in the past, albeit accompanied more often as not with the names of one or more colleagues. This section examines this paradox.

5.2.6   Collective or individual inventions?

The Second Industrial Revolution of the late-nineteenth century leading up to the First World War, pioneered largely by Germany and the US, is associated with a number of phenomena favouring more collective – and potentially anonymous – conceptions of the inventive act, and a diminished autonomy for inventors. These are: (i) the emergence of corporate in-house research and development; (ii) the professionalisation of science with teams of well-trained employee scientists; and (iii) the industrial application of the scientific knowledge coming out of laboratories manned by

---

[36] A. Buchanan, *Brunel: The Life and Times of Isambard Kingdom Brunel* (London and New York: Hambledon and London, 2002), 177.

this new scientific-worker class. 'Heroes of invention'[37] never did disappear from the public gaze or from the journalistic imagination.[38] But team invention became increasingly the norm during the twentieth century, and a legally well-recognised one at that. This trend has endured notwithstanding the significant role that entrepreneur-inventors continue to play in the modern economy.

Patent law and management came to reflect these developments. Increasingly, patents were owned not by the inventors but the companies employing them and to whom they were assigned. Accordingly, patents were ceasing to be personal property, at least in any general sense. Instead, they were changing into a class of business asset used by firms for two ends: (i) to actively and strategically control information and industrial processes and products embodying this information; and (ii) to negotiate access to the valuable information, processes and products of others.[39]

In the US, the constitutional exhortation to secure rights to 'authors and inventors' was a potential threat to the emergent scientific research-based corporations, although evidence suggests that it did little, if any, harm to the corporate bottom line. Indeed, it took quite a long time, by the end of the 1920s, for formal corporate control to be finally achieved through contract.[40] But already the courts had become amenable: 'It was in the twentieth century, when judges imagined firms as originators, or at least as essential incubators, of the idea, that the position of the inventive employee changed.'

That change in thinking required a significant re-imagining of the status and nature of inventors',[41] and was in the nature of a shift in the perception of such people as autonomous exemplars of free labour, to subordinate workers forming part of a large innovation system. But already, from the late-nineteenth century we start to see patent individualism being balanced, as it is today, by the freedom of companies to require employees to assign their inventions to those paying their wages. This was assisted by a view that the law, as in Britain, generally required from successful patent applications no great feats of personal inspiration. Thus, the Supreme Court in *Hotchkiss v. Greenwood*, which crafted the criterion of non-obviousness, required an invention to be 'something more akin in terms of ingenuity than the work of a skilled mechanic' but did not expect any sparks of extraordinary brilliance.[42] Israel, in an essay on Edison, points out that credit tended to be given

---

[37] C. MacLeod, *Heroes of Invention: Technology, Liberalism and British National Identity 1750–1914* (Cambridge: Cambridge University Press, 2007).

[38] The '*great inventors*' of the past are still revered. *Science* magazine reported that 'the 2012 Lemelson-MIT Invention Index [which] surveyed Americans aged 16 to 25'. Asked 'who they thought was the greatest innovator of all time, 54% of the 1,000 respondents named the inventor and holder of more than 1,000 U.S. patents – taking a bite out of second-place holder and Apple Inc. co-founder Steve Jobs, who weighed in at 24%.' That holder of over 1,000 patents was Thomas Edison. (3 February 2012) 335(6068) *Science* 508.

[39] The long career of Thomas Edison as inventor and entrepreneur reflects this transition. See P. Israel, '"Claim the Earth": Protecting Edison's Inventions at Home and Abroad', in S. Arapostathis and G. Dutfield (eds), *Knowledge Management and Intellectual Property: Concepts, Actors and Practices from the Past to the Present* (Cheltenham: Edward Elgar Publishing, 2013), 19–43.

[40] C. Fisk, *Working Knowledge: Employee Invention and the Rise of Corporate Intellectual Property, 1800–1930* (Chapel Hill: University of North Carolina Press, 2009).

[41] Ibid., 249.

[42] *Hotchkiss v. Greenwood*, 52 US 11 How. 248 248 (1850).

more to people who conceptualised inventions, as so frequently did Edison, rather than those technicians, frequently employees, who found out how to reduce concept to practice.[43] The decision in *US v. Burns* made it lawful for employees to be required to assign their patents.[44]

However, US courts were unable for a long time to shake off the idea of the individual inventive genius, perhaps a consequence of the long shadow cast by Thomas Edison. The Supreme Court was not immune from this tendency. In 1941, in *Cuno Engineering v. Automatic Devices*, America's highest court formulated the 'flash of creative genius test' to the consternation of many in industry.[45] Things were to change drastically in 1952, though, when the US overhauled its patent legislation and consequently this became no longer good law; indeed, that was intended. The non-obviousness requirement was incorporated into the statute in the form of the new section 103(a) (see below). This was subsequently interpreted by both Patent Office and courts to mean that, as in the German *Congo Red* case discussed earlier, no great inspiration was necessary in the means employed to achieve the inventive result, and this obviously suited industry.[46] Intriguingly, and probably not coincidentally, by this time therapeutic revolutions in such areas as antibiotics and hormones had taken off and there was undoubtedly some concern that discoveries arising from sometimes quite routine screening and isolation processes would be found unpatentable on obviousness grounds.[47] The new law helped ensure that industry had nothing to worry about in this regard.

Nonetheless, the inventors' names stubbornly remain on the patents. In 2001 the US Court of Appeals for the Federal Circuit still felt moved to pronounce that 'An expectation of ownership of a patent is not a prerequisite for a putative inventor to possess standing to sue to correct inventorship under § 256 [Correction of named inventor].'[48] Accordingly, true inventors with a legitimate interest in an invention have recourse in cases of deliberate exclusion of their name even when they have no ownership rights to the patent.

5.2.7   The right to be named

This is not tantamount to admission of a broad moral right of attribution. But we need to consider the Court's decision in light of the long-standing requirement in section 115 of the Patent Act that 'The applicant shall make oath that he believes himself to be the original and first inventor'. It is true that the America Invents Act, 2011 has changed the language slightly to accommodate the US's new adherence to the first-to-file principle, the most important difference in the present context being the deletion of the words 'and first' after 'original'. Nonetheless, that the US held out

---

[43] Israel, in Arapostathis and Dutfield, *supra* note 39, 27.

[44] *United States v. Burns*, 79 US 12 Wall 246 246 (1870). For discussion, see W. Kingston, *Beyond Intellectual Property: Matching Information Protection to Innovation* (Cheltenham: Edward Elgar Publishing, 2010), 51.

[45] *Cuno Engineering Corp v. Automatic Devices Corp*, 314 US 84 (1941).

[46] Kingston *supra* note 44, 54; D.P. Miller, 'Intellectual Property and Narratives of Discovery/Invention: The League of Nations' Draft Convention on "Scientific Property" and Its Fate' (2008) 46 *History of Science* 299–342, 319.

[47] G. Dutfield, *Intellectual Property Rights and the Life Science Industries* (Singapore: World Scientific, 2009); Kingston, ibid.

[48] *Chou v. University of Chicago*, 254 F 3d 1347 (Fed Cir, 2001).

for so long against first-to-file testifies to the high importance placed for so long on ensuring that nobody but the true inventor could file a patent. According to the Court:

> Chou [the plaintiff] argues that a reputational interest alone is enough to satisfy the requirements […] That assertion is not implausible. After all, being considered an inventor of important subject matter is a mark of success in one's field, comparable to being an author of an important scientific paper. Pecuniary consequences may well flow from being designated as an inventor. However, we need not decide that issue because Chou has alleged a concrete financial interest in the patent, albeit an interest less than ownership.[49]

The UK Patents Act is quite explicit in its implementation of Article 4*ter* of the Paris Convention, added to the 1934 revision which provides for the inventor's right of attribution: 'The inventor shall have the right to be mentioned as such in the patent.'[50] There is no provision for the right to be waived, as there is, oddly enough, in the country's copyright law for authors:

> The inventor or joint inventors of an invention shall have a right to be mentioned as such in any patent granted for the invention and shall also have a right to be so mentioned if possible in any published application for a patent for the invention and, if not so mentioned, a right to be so mentioned in accordance with rules in a prescribed document.[51]

It seems axiomatic that a work of literature must have an author. Even so, Anglo-American copyright law enables the author to disappear to be replaced by the corporation. This is achieved in the US through the work for hire doctrine, and in other common law systems, the author can – and is frequently encouraged to – waive her moral rights including the right of attribution (see Chapter 4). Yet the inventor has not experienced a similarly ignominious fate despite the corporatisation and collectivisation of invention (and the patent systems) of the past 150 years. There is no invention for hire doctrine where inventors' names disappear as there is work for hire in the US – despite the fact most inventing is literally done for hire, or at least in the course of employment.

Of course, some scepticism about the whole notion of the invention (and the inventor) is perfectly legitimate. Generally speaking, wolfpacks and termites' nests notwithstanding, humans are inherently collaborative creatures to a degree that is not common in the animal world: all creative manifestations stem from a greater or lesser degree from the wisdom of crowds rather than the genius of a few. Arguably, that is how most human innovation has been conducted since pre-history, and in such a scenario there would most commonly be no moral imperative to single out certain people. Indeed, it might actually be immoral to do so. As early as 1941, Charles Kettering of

---

[49] Ibid.

[50] Union Internationale pour la Protection de la Propriété Industrielle, *Actes de la Conférence Réunie a Londres du 1er Mai au 2 Juin 1934*, Berne: Bureau de l'Union Internationale pour la Protection de la Propriété Industrielle.

[51] UK Patents Act, s 13(1).

General Motors commented that 'a one-man invention isn't very possible these days', and opined that it would be unfair to single out individuals for collective attainments.[52]

Wherever the truth lies, we nearly all believe there is such a thing as inventing just as there is literary authorship. We are not ready to erase inventors either from popular discourse or from law and policy. The same goes for authors. Even those who purport to disbelieve in the author as one who creates something nobody else could are happy to place their names on their writings express- ing this opinion (we know of no postmodernists querying the notion of the author or proclaiming her or his death to have disclaimed their own authorship). In the present climate, naming the inventor does seem eminently fair and culturally appropriate in most industrialised societies. Even if one rejects the traditional heroic inventor model as being mostly mythical, one can hardly deny the presence of a person or small group of people close enough to the inventive conception and its practical reduction to be named as inventors, and who deserve to be acknowledged. As long as such people can be identified with at least some semblance of reasonableness, it is difficult to ar- gue, logically or morally, that they should not at the very least be named in the patent. Nonetheless, how 'invention' (and for that matter 'authorship') are conceived is a matter of interpretation that cannot be wholly objective. Undoubtedly patent law influences our notion of what an invention is, just as certain views as to what an invention is shapes its legal definition. The vast majority of all valuable patents are owned by corporations, not individual inventors. Consequently, inventors' moral right of attribution looks like a fair quid pro quo that can do no harm to businesses and which satisfies a general sense that it is just.

There may be strategic reasons too. If corporations invent rather than nameable individuals, the patent system becomes nothing more than a business monopoly in the eyes of the public. Having the names of individuals on patents gives moral legitimacy to the system that it may otherwise lose, even when the companies employing them are the actual owners. It also provides immense propaganda value:

> By the end of the twentieth century, corporate intellectual property ownership became the norm and individual invention and authorship the exception. The late twentieth-century erasure of the natural person's name from the responsibility for innovation has dehuman- ized intellectual property and the ideas and work embodied in it. Yet the moral claims of corporations as intellectual property rights holders still are not as persuasive as the claims of individuals.[53]

Moreover, the inventor function serves the practical purpose of pinning the invention in space and time in a way that would be much harder if invention were anonymised. If all else fails, who better

---

[52] Quoted in L. Owens, 'Patents, the "Frontiers" of American Invention, and the Monopoly Committee of 1939: Anatomy of a Discourse' (1991) 32(4) *Technology and Culture* 1076–93; see also, D.F. Noble, *America by Design: Science, Technology, and the Rise of Corporate Capitalism* (New York: Alfred A. Knopf, 1979).

[53] Fisk, *supra* note 40, 252.

to give substance to, and defend, an invention's existence and location than the persons named on the patents?[54]

5.2.8   Patent ownership and employee inventions

In Europe, a patent belongs to the inventor (or the co-inventors) or his/her successor in title.[55] In Europe, as elsewhere, the inventor is often an employee, in which case the right to the patent depends on the law of the state in which the inventor is employed. In the UK and Germany, for instance, if an invention is made in the course of the employee's normal duties, the national patent laws vest *ab initio* ownership in the employer, while giving employee-inventors a right to claim compensation should the invention be a success or of outstanding benefit to the employer.[56] This area is becoming of increasing importance, due of course to the proliferation of university inventions.[57]

In Europe, the European Patent Convention leaves the regulation of employee inventions entirely to national law. In the UK, which as mentioned affirms the attribution right of inventors, an employee's invention belongs to the employer in two specific instances namely if the invention was made: (i) in the course of the normal duties of the employee or in the course of duties falling outside his normal duties, but specifically assigned to him, and the circumstances in either case were such that an invention might reasonably be expected to result from the carrying out of his duties; or (ii) in the course of the duties of the employee and, at the time of making the invention, because of the nature of his duties and the particular responsibilities arising from the nature of his duties he had a special obligation to further the interests of the employer's undertaking.[58] These rules apply not only to patents granted nationally under the UK patent law, but also to granted European Patents (UK) under the EPC. Prior to the 1977 Act, the position of employee inventors was a matter under common law.[59]

---

[54] An excellent high-profile example is Nobel laureate Kary Mullis's defence of the two key patents on polymerase chain reaction (PCR), which he is usually credited with inventing. The Northern California district court upheld both patents. See *E.I. Du Pont de Nemours & Co. v. Cetus Corp.*, 19 USPQ 2d 1174 (N.D. Cal. 1990).

[55] European Patent Convention, Arts 60–61, 71–74.

[56] See UK Patents Act 1977, ss 7, 39–43; E. Pakuscher, 'Rewards for Employee Inventors in the Federal Republic of Germany – Part 1' (1981) 11 *EIPR* 318.

[57] W.R. Cornish, 'Rights in University Inventions' (1992) 13 *EIP*; for the US perspective, see S. Cherensky, 'A Penny for their Thoughts System', Prepared for the WIPO Conference on the International Patent System, Geneva, 25–27 March 2002; R. Sagar and A. Nagarsheth, *Ownership of Employee Inventions and Remuneration: A Comparative Overview* (London: Intellectual Property Institute, 2006).

[58] UK Patents Act 1977, s 39(3). As to what constitutes the normal duties of an employee, the courts have elaborated that in addition to the written contract, an employee's duties can be further implied by the court based on his actual work circumstances. *Re Harris' Patent* (1985) RPC 19; *LIFFE Administration and Management v. Pavel Pinkava* [2007] RPC 30 (CA, UK).

[59] *Worthington Pump v. Moore* (1903) RPC 41, 49, confirming the common law master-servant position vis-à-vis employee inventions, namely that:

The mere existence of a contract of service does not per se disqualify a servant from taking out a Patent for an

However, the employee-inventor may appeal to the patent-granting office or the courts for compensation if the invention and/or the patent 'is of outstanding benefit to the employer'[60] and that consequently 'it is just that the employee should be awarded compensation to be paid by the employer'.[61] Compensation may be payable even if there is a contract of assignment or other agreement awarding benefits to the inventor if it is deemed 'inadequate in relation to the benefit derived by the employer from the invention or the patent for it (or both)'.[62] In the first UK judgment to award compensation to employees, the High Court in *Kelly & Chiu v. GE Healthcare Ltd*,[63] clarified that 'outstanding' meant 'something special' or 'out of the ordinary' and more than 'substantial', 'significant' or 'good'. The benefit had to be something more that would normally be expected to arise from the duties for which the employee was paid.

In Germany employee-inventions are governed by the Act on Employees' Invention. As a general rule, inventions are owned by the inventor. As in Japan (see below), inventions are of two types: 'service' or 'free'. Service inventions are made by an employee during the course of his employed and are based on the nature of the work. In such cases, an employer does have a right to claim such inventions within four months and unless any agreement is made to the contrary, will generally be deemed to have done so.[64] All other types of inventions are categorised as free inventions, which belong to the employee-inventor, although notification should be given to the employer who has, after a period of time, a right to claim a licence to the invention under reasonable conditions. If no claim is made after this period, the invention will remain a free invention. Whether one is service or free can be a matter for contestation between employer and employee. With respect to service inventions, employers are entitled to claim the invention wholly, or else partially, in which case ownership is retained by the inventor. The latter case is not necessarily disadvantageous to the employer who will still be entitled to a non-exclusive licence subject to a royalty and will not be responsible for the costs incurred in filing patents. As in Britain, statutory remuneration is provided. In Germany, this is calculated on the basis of Ministry of Labour guidelines and applies where employers claim the invention without restriction.[65] The way the law is structured resolves the conflict between German labour law, which stipulates that the work of an employee belongs to his employer and the German patent law under which the rights to the patent are vested in the inventor.[66]

---

invention made by him during his term of service, even though the invention may relate to subject-matter germane to and useful for his employers in their business, and that, even though the servant may have made use of his employer's time and servants and materials in bringing his invention to completion, and may have allowed his employers to use the invention while in their employment […].

[60] Patents Act, 1977, s 40 (as amended).

[61] Ibid.

[62] Ibid.

[63] *Kelly & Chiu v. GE Healthcare Ltd* [2009] RPC 12; *Shanks v Unilever Plc and ors* [2019] UKSC 45.

[64] German Act on Employee Inventions, *Gesetz über Arbeitnehmererfindungen* (ArbEG), Art 6.

[65] Ibid., s 9; see also D. Harhoff and K. Hoisl, 'Institutionalized Incentives for Ingenuity: Patent Value and the German Employees' Invention' (2007) 36(8) *Research Policy* 1143–62.

[66] R. Sagar, 'UK, France, Germany and Japan: With Record-Breaking Decisions, is the Inventor King?', unpublished paper on file with the author, 2012.

In Japan, employee inventions are, similar to Germany but unlike the UK, normally owned in the first instance by the employee. However, those inventions made in the course of an employee's duties, known as 'service' inventions, are pre-assignable by contract. However, where such pre-assignment is applied, the employee has a statutory entitlement to a 'reasonable remuneration'. As a matter of general practice, remuneration sums are provided for in employment contracts or in internal company regulations. But following a number of legal challenges made by employees to the sums provided, the Patent Law was revised in 2004 to give companies more legal certainty subject to the performance of employer-employee consultations on standards for remuneration.[67]

In the US, there are generally three different types of inventions in relation to employee-created works, resulting in different default rules under common law:

- specific-inventive employees who are hired/employed to invent, and in such cases employers expect to own the inventions;
- non-inventive employees who are not employed to create, and in such cases employers do not have any claims to the ownerships of their inventions;
- general-inventive employees who perform general 'research or design work', such as software engineers, and in such cases employees are encouraged to 'pursue his or her creative instincts, even though they may diverge from assigned work'; in such cases, it is not immediately clear who is entitled to own the invention as it may fall outside the scope of employment.[68]

The common law is also generally supportive to the employer where there is no contract, though individual state laws differ markedly. There is no provision for remuneration in the statutory law except for federal government employees. However, US companies tend to provide their own internal reward schemes for employees.[69]

5.3   PROTECTABLE SUBJECT MATTER

In patent law and practice, if subject matter is not expressly excluded in the statutes or the case law, it is likely to be included. This is subject of course to the protection criteria being met, and its accordance with the classification scheme in use and these are very flexible. Deciding to allow may be subject to other considerations such as doctrines and tests applied by granting offices and courts. Accordingly, in recent times the idea of synthesising something, isolating and purifying a natural product, or of genetically modifying a living thing is seen as a highly creative act and one deserving of a patent on the basis that it is an original human-made thing resulting from

---

[67] Ibid.

[68] R.L. Gullette, 'State Legislation Governing Ownership Rights in Inventions Under Employee Invention Agreements' (1980) 62 *J. Pat. Off. Soc'y* 732, 733; P.A. Howell, 'Whose Invention is it Anyway? Employee Invention-Assignment Agreements and their Limits' (2012) 8 *Wash. J.L. Tech & Arts* 79, 84–5.

[69] Howell, ibid., 89 *et seq*.

the application of extraordinary skill or insight, effort and investment, or that it has some wider utility or applicability even if it was stumbled across by a happy accident. Whether it was a stroke of genius or a fluke, required huge investments or none, a patent is the appropriate reward or encouragement in this field as in others. Once the criteria are met, patent law is blind with respect to labour, expense, genuinely creative thought, socio-economic significance, or to the lack of these. It is established law that it makes no difference how the inventor came up with the invention or how ground-breaking it may or may not be in terms of the technological or utilitarian progress it may represent:

> [...] in point of law, the labour of thought, or experiments, and the expenditure of money, are not the essential grounds of consideration on which the question, whether the invention is or is not the subject-matter of a patent, ought to depend. For if the invention be new and useful to the public, it is not material whether it be the result of long experiments and profound research, or whether by some sudden and lucky thought, or mere accidental discovery.[70]

The US adopts a similar stance. The principles and rules of patent law:

> [...] secure to the inventor a monopoly in the manufacture, use, and sale of very humble contrivances, of limited usefulness, the fruits of indifferent skill, and trifling ingenuity, as well as those grander products of his genius which confer renown on himself, and extensive and lasting benefits on society.[71]

5.3.1   Patentable inventions

Patents provide inventors with legal rights to prevent others from making, using, selling or importing their inventions for a fixed period, nowadays normally 20 years subject to regular payment of renewal fees. Applicants for a patent must satisfy a national or regional[72] patent issuing authority that the invention described in the application is new, susceptible of industrial application, and that its creation involved an inventive step or would be unobvious to a typically skilled practitioner. The patent system recognises inventions of various forms. In Europe the following are possible:

- Things (products).
- Methods and processes.
- New purposes (new advantages of old things used in an old way).
- Selection patents.
- New uses for old things.

---

[70] *Crane v. Price and Others* (1842) 1 Web 393.

[71] *Morton v. New York Eye Infirmary* (17 F 879, 1862 Dec 01).

[72] Such regional authorities include the European Patent Office, the Eurasian Patent Office and the Office of the African Regional Industrial Property Organization.

Patents claiming new things are highly desirable for inventors since they cover any use of the product including those as yet undiscovered. They also cover any method of making it. A patent protecting only a new process protects any product arising from it, but not the same product manufactured by a different process. While process patents tend to be less valuable than product patents, breakthrough process inventions can be highly lucrative such as the patent on the recombinant DNA technique (see Chapter 14). Product by process claims are possible too in which the product claims are restricted to the new method disclosed to make it. In Europe there is no need for the product itself to be new. In contrast, Canada does not allow such claims where the product itself is old or obvious.[73]

New (non-medical) advantage, or novelty of purpose, patents are controversial. The patentability of new advantages was considered doubtful in Europe until the ruling of the Enlarged Board of Appeal (EBA) of the European Patent Office in *Mobil/Friction reducing additive*.[74] Mobil's patent application relating to a friction-reducing additive in lubricating oil already used to inhibit rust formation claimed the use of the additive for reducing friction. According to Mobil, this particular useful advantage was previously unknown. The fact that the substance in question was being used in the same way as before did not, according to the EBA, render the advantage unpatentable. In contrast, pre-EPC British case did not allow claims to new purposes per se. The hugely authoritative Blanco White remarked in the 1974 edition of his treatise that for something to be patentable, 'there must be a new way of using it as distinct from merely use with a different end in view', though he did accept that 'the patenting of a "new use" is ordinarily a mere matter of selecting a form of claim appropriate to the case'.[75] He also stated as follows:

> An extreme case of a specification claiming nothing that is 'new or alleged to be new' is found where the article or process claimed is old: the alleged invention consisting merely in the discovery that an old article or process is useful for a particular new purpose, and the alleged distinction in the claims from what is old consisting merely in an indication that the article or process is claimed 'for' that purpose. Such claims are invalid: a thing is not made a different thing by a statement that it is used for a particular purpose or with a particular end in view. Patents are not granted for the mere discovery that a particular known thing has hitherto unknown properties [...]. There must be a new way of using it as distinct from merely use with a different end in view.[76]

We now raise the question of whether chemical (including pharmaceutical) inventions differ from mechanical inventions in specific ways that require the law to treat them in a special way in terms of the scope of protectable subject matter and/or the way that novelty should be applied. Thus, so-called selection patents respond to a problem that is common in chemistry research. Frequently,

---

[73] D. Vaver, *Intellectual Property Law: Copyright, Patents, Trade-marks* (2nd ed., Toronto: Irwin Law, 2011), 293.

[74] *Mobil/Friction reducing additive*, G2/88 [1990] EPOR 73.

[75] T.A. Blanco White, *Patents for Invention and the Protection of Industrial Designs* (4th ed., London: Stevens and Sons, 1974), 1–208.

[76] Ibid.

a researcher will find that a particular useful effect will be shared by thousands of related compounds. Consequently, an inventor may disclose a very large number of chemicals, some of which may turn out to have other useful attributes. But by disclosing them, the researcher will already be precluded from filing subsequent claims on individual members of the group of chemicals already disclosed.

In an influential 1930 British patent case, *I.G. Farbenindustrie* argued that while its patent claimed a selection of substances that had been disclosed in an earlier patent, the selection shared certain beneficial and hitherto unknown properties. According to the court, such a patent may be valid if:

1. the selection is based on some substantial advantage to be gained by the use of the selected members;
2. all the selected members possess this advantage; and
3. this advantage must be of a special character peculiar to the selected group.[77]

The specificity of chemical inventions is evident in another way that was recognised many decades ago. In furtherance of the early post-war effort under the auspices of the Council of Europe to harmonise substantive patent law, a European Committee of Experts on Patents was set up. In a study produced in 1951, the Committee stated that:

> [...] a new mechanical part, for example a special kind of screw or valve, may well have many different applications, but in general they are immediately foreseeable once the nature and function of the device have been explained, whereas, although the process of 'tailoring molecules' i.e. designing a new chemical product with a view to achieving certain definite properties for a particular application, may be said to have begun, it is still in general the case that a new chemical compound is first prepared (perhaps with some definite object in view, perhaps by accident) and is then applied to a variety of different uses.[78]

As long as patents mainly protected mechanical devices for single applications there was little controversy about the existence or reach of product patents. A mousetrap is for catching mice and that is all it is for. A new coffee lid is for keeping hot drinks warm and preventing spilling but not for anything else.[79] But once the question arose of whether chemical substances such as drugs and natural products could be patented, the situation changed. For example, a patented gene may

---

[77] *IG Farbenindustrie's patents* (1930) 47 RPC 289.

[78] Committee of Experts, Resolutions adopted by the Session of the Committee of Experts on Patents held at The Hague on 2nd to 9th July 1951, CM/WP IV (51) 27, 4, quoted in J. Pila, *The Requirement for an Invention in Patent Law* (Oxford: Oxford University Press, 2010), 166.

[79] One should not go too far in singling out chemistry as a special case. Creative multiuse contrivances far removed from chemistry are hardly uncommon in human societies. To randomly take one example, the Aboriginal spear-thrower used by people in the Australian Western Desert also serves as a fire-starter, a woodworking tool, a tray, a musical instrument, a tool for clearing land for campsites, and a guide to recalling the locations of sites such as waterholes. T. Ingold, *The*

turn out to perform many functions of which the initial discoverer who is the patent owner may be aware of only one. A new drug patented as a cure for cancer may later be found to cure heart disease. One may reasonably question, on grounds both of fairness and of public policy, whether the person who discovers one use of a product she has invented or made available to the public for the first time should continue to enjoy such a right to classes of product that can be highly versatile. But one may also wonder whether the discovery of a new use for something invented earlier, perhaps by somebody else, entitles the person responsible to a legal monopoly that is just as long.

While the above statement from 1951 was used to argue in favour of allowing compulsory licensing, it also leads to an important and very different policy response: that different uses of a known chemical product can also be sources of economic value that may be deserving of separate patent rights. Indeed, this policy approach was in fact adopted and is very suitable for business if not necessarily for consumers.

As it gets harder and more expensive for the pharmaceutical industry to discover new therapeutic substances, companies have increasingly directed research to finding new uses for old drugs. It is largely due to the demands of this industry that old substances for which a first or additional use has been discovered can be patented for such new use. Justifications from science can be argued for. In the past, some synthetic dyes turned out to have anti-infective attributes and such discoveries benefited the public.[80] As for additional uses, aspirin, sold initially as a painkiller and febrifuge, has for example turned out to have several unrelated medical applications.[81] As we will see in Chapter 13, second and further use patents have been more controversial than first use patents but they are certainly possible despite the medicine's absence of physical novelty.

5.3.2 Invention v. discovery

In his magisterial history of science,[82] David Wootton shows that the word 'discover' entered the English language from Portuguese (*discobrir*) in which its literal meaning clearly was 'to uncover'. This took place around the time of Columbus's arrival in the Americas, as it became known, which, famously, he failed to recognise as somewhere other than part of Asia. Up to that time, its meaning was distinct from that of the Latin verb *invenio*. Soon afterwards, the meaning of 'discovery' was expanded also to express a claim to priority. With a tendency also to translate *invenio* as 'to discover', this led to a merging of the meaning of the two words. This is hardly surprising given the latter word's etymology: in, meaning 'into' or 'upon', and *venire*, meaning 'come'.[83] Columbus

---

Perception of the Environment: Essays in Livelihood, Dwelling and Skill (London and New York: Routledge, 2000), 367.

[80] Of these, perhaps the most important was Prontosil Red. In 1932, Gerhard Domagk discovered that the substance, which became the first sulphonamide drug, inhibited streptococcal infections. The active part of the chemical, sulphanilamide, though, did not have dyeing qualities. It was a prodrug. J.E. Lesch, *The First Miracle Drugs: How the Sulfa Drugs Transformed Medicine* (New York: Oxford University Press, 2007).

[81] D. Jeffreys, *Aspirin: The Story of a Wonder Drug* (London: Bloomsbury, 2004).

[82] D. Wootton, *The Invention of Science: A New History of the Scientific Revolution* (London: Penguin Books, 2015), see especially Chapter 3 – 'Inventing Discovery'.

[83] This suggests that we might have had more legal certainty had we adopted 'innovation' in place of 'invention' as a means

himself used *invenio* for his achievement although, as mentioned just before, he was ignorant that the lands he visited were a completely separate landmass. He was at least correctly aware that he had found out a new route (analogous one might suggest to claiming as patently novel a new process to make a known thing). This was a time when Europeans who had long believed that everything significant to be known was already known were beginning to appreciate the novelty of innovations like gunpowder, the printing press and the compass, none of which the ancients had ever come up with. This new notion of discovery and the realisation of the significance of the 'discovery' of America were simultaneous. The 'invention' of science came quite soon after. According to Wootton none of this is coincidental, but that is another story.

Nonetheless, in popular parlance discovery and invention tend to be considered as different from each other though there is a certain blurring when it comes to the natural sciences including biology. The fact that the US expressly allows discoveries as well as inventions to be patented seems rather startling from a European perspective, at least those of us who are not patent attorneys; the latter tend to be quite unfussy about this. In fact, 'in the early republic there was a considerable dispute as to whether "discovery" and "invention" were to be considered synonymous'.[84] One view is that when the US Constitution was drawn up there was no clear difference in meaning between the two words – hence its authorisation to Congress to secure 'Inventors the exclusive right to their [...] discoveries'. There is no mention at all of inventions, only discoveries. According to the US Congress's Committee on Patents in its 1930 report on the then new Plant Patent Act:

> At the time of the adoption of the Constitution the term 'inventor' was used in two senses. In the first place the inventor was a discoverer, one who finds or finds out. In the second place an inventor was one who created something new. All the dictionaries at the time of the framing of the Constitution recognized that 'inventor' included the finder out or discoverer as well as the creator of something new. Thus Sheridan in 1790 defined 'inventor' as 'A finder out of something new,' and 'invention' as 'discovery.' [...] The distinction between discovering or finding out on the one hand and creating or producing on the other hand, being recognized in the dictionaries current at the time of the framing of the Constitution, it is reasonable to suppose the framers of the Constitution attributed to the term 'inventor' the then customary meaning.[85]

This may or may not be entirely correct. Samuel Johnson's famous late-eighteenth-century dictionary, which was known to much of the American intelligentsia,[86] identified a clear distinction between

---

to separate what merits protection from unprotectable discoveries, derived as it is from the Latin *nova*, meaning 'new'. That said, though, innovation is also used in various ways to the extent that we currently lack a consensus on its precise meaning.

[84] E.C. Walterscheid, *The Nature of the Intellectual Property Clause: A Study in Historical Perspective* (Hein, 2002), 310.

[85] Committee on Patents, 'Report' (1930) *Journal of Heredity* 319–22, 357–61, 359.

[86] Three framers of the Constitution, Washington, Jefferson and Franklin, all had copies. Even in recent years US Supreme Court judges have relied on Samuel Johnson for guidance on the meaning of words adopted in the constitution. J. Lynch, 'Dr. Johnson's Revolution', *The New York Times*, 2 July 2005.

inventor and discovery, the former producing a new thing, the latter being the act of finding or revealing something hidden or secret. Discovery brought nothing new to the world even if it made something available for the first time. In due course the US adopted quite a strict requirement of novelty so that patents of importation were excluded. Perhaps this rendered unnecessary the drawing of a clear distinction between discovery and invention, at least during that era. In *Evans v. Eaton*, for example, counsel for Oliver Evans claimed in the lower court that one can discover without inventing, and that in mentioning 'discoveries', the constitutional framers and Congress intended that patents for importation be provided in order to reward people whose introductions benefit the country:

> A plant unknown may be discovered, or a new use of a known plant, by diligence and search, without invention. A new and useful principle of law in nature may, by expensive and laborious researches or experiments, be discovered, though the aid of invention may be necessary to apply them to useful purposes [...]. Did neither the framers of the constitution, nor congress, contemplate a reward for such expensive and patriotic labours to promote the welfare of his fellow citizens?[87]

That court and the Supreme Court rejected this stating that what mattered was that the invention or discovery be novel and original. In doing so, both courts omitted to contemplate possible semantic or legal distinctions between discovery and invention.

Nonetheless, none of this made for generally applicable rules and in the absence of clear set-in-stone meaning courts had to take the initiative in order to decide on the disputes set before them. Undoubtedly there is a difference between mere discovery and a discovery that really does bring new knowledge to the fore. Simon Bolivar, the famous liberator of South America, recognised this when he called the German scientist and explorer Alexander von Humboldt, who travelled there more than three centuries after Columbus, 'the true discoverer of South America'.[88] In one early case, the court required that a 'discovery' must at least 'amount to the contrivance or production of something which did not exist before; or in other words, to an invention'.[89] In the later decision of *Morton v. New York Eye Infirmary*, the judge declared that:

> It is only when the explorer has gone beyond the mere domain of discovery, and has laid hold of the new principle, force, or law, and connected it with some particular medium or mechanical contrivance, by which, or through which, it acts on the material world, that he can secure the exclusive control of it under the patent laws.[90]

Modern US patent law still does not formally differentiate between invention and discovery, both of which are patentable. This hardly makes for clarity either. Logically a discovery conventionally

---

[87] Quoted in Walterscheid, *supra* note 84, 333.

[88] P. Watson, *The German Genius: Europe's Third Renaissance, the Second Scientific Revolution, and the Twentieth Century* (London: Simon & Schuster, 2010), 177.

[89] *In re Kemper*, 14 F Cas, 286, 288 (DC Cir, 1841).

[90] *Morton v. New York Eye Infirmary* (17 F 879, 1862 Dec 01).

defined makes something available to the public for the first time that has always been there. If so one might argue that it passes the novelty test on the basis of first availability to the public and this is in fact how 'natural' products came to be deemed patentable. But this does not seem entirely satisfactory. In most jurisdictions, merely disclosing some novel insight about natural phenomena such as gravity, relativity, quantum effects, biological evolution, in vivo protein synthesis or disease causation is not inventing. Things that have been found and claimed as such are likewise unpatentable, although as we will see this is a much less clear-cut matter. We might call these laws of nature, natural phenomena, or principles. Either way they are not inventions. The Higgs boson is unpatentable irrespective of the enormous cost of building, managing and operating CERN, the facility where its existence was confirmed. Those who find no meaningful distinction would probably call them mere discoveries, whereas those who hold that the words have quite different meanings in the patent law context and that patents only protect inventions have less use for the word 'mere': discovery is discovery. Either way most would agree that invention is discovery plus something. The trouble is, what that 'something' must amount to is hardly a straightforward question, and we are not getting any closer to a consensus. Agreeing on how big must be the mental step, the physical transformation, or the degree of human control over nature to fulfil the requirements for a patent, is a sizeable challenge to jurisprudential consistency and international harmonisation.[91] As we will see the US and European positions are, if anything, diverging. To make matters more complicated, the difficulties are not confined to the life sciences of chemistry but also engineering, the physical sciences and computing.

One highly significant nineteenth-century English case is *Neilson v. Harford*.[92] It concerned a patent registered in 1828 'for the improved application of air to produce heat in fires, forges, and furnaces, where bellow or other blowing apparatus are required'. In itself the invention, while extremely practical, appears on its face to be no more than an application of a physical phenomenon, the patent itself comprising instructions for the more efficient utilisation of air in a common industrial process. The court considered the matter carefully but ended up upholding the patent:

> It is very difficult to distinguish it from the specification of a patent for a principle, and this at first created in the minds of some of the court much difficulty; but after full consideration, we think that the plaintiff does not merely claim a principle, but a machine embodying a principle, and a very valuable one.

Oddly, the US Supreme Court has relied on this case, which it first cited in an 1853 judgment involving the patentability of Samuel Morse's electromagnetic telegraphs,[93] to recalibrate the 'inventive application' principle, whose origins may be traced to the 1948 *Funk Bros. Seed Co. v. Kalo*

---

[91] For an excellent and very detailed treatment of such conceptual difficulties, especially – but not exclusively – in the context of the US Plant Patent Act, see Pottage and Sherman, *supra* note 17, 153–82.

[92] *Neilson v. Harford* 1 Web PC 295 (1841). For an excellent contextualised discussion on the Neilson patent and the background to it, see D.P. Miller, 'Of Patents, Principles, and the Construction of Heroic Invention: The Case of Neilson's Hot Blast in Iron Production' (2016) 160 *Proceedings of the American Philosophical Society* 361–422.

[93] *O'Reilly v. Morse* 56 US 62 (S Ct, 1853).

Inoculant case discussed below, in a way that appears to raise rather than lower the patentability bar (see *Parker v. Flook*; also *Mayo v. Prometheus*, discussed below and in Chapter 14).[94]

In Britain, courts have likewise struggled with the question of whether once you have your 'mere' discovery you can patent a practical embodiment even when the latter is an obvious application of the former. Prior to its adherence to the European Patent Convention, the real distinction to be drawn was between a discovery and a manufacture. In a 1903 case, the judge explained it thus:

> Discovery adds to the amount of human knowledge but it does so only by lifting the veil and disclosing something which before had been unseen or dimly seen. Invention also adds to human knowledge, but not merely by disclosing something. Invention necessarily involves also the suggestion of an act to be done, and it must be an act which results in a new product, or a new result, or a new process, or a new combination for producing an old product or an old result.[95]

Nowadays, to favour a generous stance towards patentability is to say that where there is a technical contribution, the obviousness of the application of the discovery is not necessary as long as the discovery itself is novel and unobvious, and when that disclosure (such as of genetic information) points to an industrial application: the invention and the discovery, the former patentable, the latter (still) not, may yet be treated as two different things even when there is no inventive step between them.

In the life sciences field, *Genentech Inc.'s Patent* took this position. It seems reasonable to ask in such situations where the excluded subject matter (here discoveries) is new, unobvious and suggesting of an industrial application, whether there are justifications for granting patents to such matter. From her reading of the Genentech decision, Pila identifies a number of reasons for justifying such an approach. Among these are the rather intriguing perspective that such inventions in the fields of chemistry and biotechnology essentially concern not so much physical stuff but 'information of novel and practical significance'. But there is also a policy objective. The decision reflects a willingness 'to relax the standards of inherent patentability' to pursue patent law's goal of 'encouraging socially useful innovation [...] by focusing not on what subject matter takes from an excluded item, but rather on what it gives to the public'.[96] This may well be reasonable in certain cases, and falling back on public policy justifications for patent law is of course nothing new. But applying it in (excluded) subject matter decisions can support quite opposite outcomes, ones less favourable to patent applicants and owners. Moreover, there is an arguable case that courts should not get involved at all in relaxing standards of inherent patentability but leave it up to legislators. As it is there is quite a lot of such relaxation going on in the pharmaceuticals field as we will see in Chapter 13. Admittedly, even relatively trivial pharmaceutical inventions stand a good chance of having more public utility than yet another variation on the theme of 'coffee lid'.

---

[94] J.A. Lefstin, 'Inventive Application: A History' (2016) 67(2) *Florida Law Review* 565–648.

[95] *Reynolds v. Herbert Smith & Co Ltd* (1903) 20 RPC 123.

[96] Genentech Inc.'s Patent, [1989] R.P.C. 147 (C.A.), Pila, *supra* note 78, 259–60.

5.3.3   Excluded subject matter

In continental Europe, and in contrast to the US and Great Britain, statutorily defined exceptions have been very common, although they have been reduced in recent years. The most common of these was medicines and foods. The first German patent law, for example, excluded 'inventions the realization of which are contrary to law or morals', and 'inventions of articles of food, drinks and medicine as well as of substances manufactured by a chemical process in so far as the inventions do not relate to a certain process for manufacturing such articles'.[97] This was largely because private (especially foreign) monopolies for such basic essentials were considered to conflict with the public interest. Such a view has deep roots in European society. With respect to drugs, protection may have been denied also so that the public would not be deceived into thinking that because an ineffective or dangerous drug had been patented, its use had been endorsed by the government.[98] Excluding the patenting of drugs persisted until quite recently in several European countries. Pharmaceutical products became patentable in France only in 1960, in Ireland in 1964, in Germany in 1968, in Switzerland in 1977, in Italy and Sweden in 1978, and Spain in 1992. In Japan, they became patentable in 1976. Interestingly, a few developing countries acted in the reverse direction. For example, in the late 1960s and early 1970s Brazil and India passed laws to exclude pharmaceuticals as such from patentability (as well as processes to manufacture them in Brazil's case). TRIPS compliance, though, has required these countries to change direction again. India finally allowed drugs to be patented, albeit with some continuing restrictions, in 2005.

Europe and 'technical effect'

Modern European patent law lays out the exclusions and exceptions in fairly explicit form. Article 52(2), European Patent Convention (EPC)[99] ('patentable inventions') provides a list of subject matters that are not to be regarded as inventions, as such:

(a)   discoveries, scientific theories and mathematical methods;
(b)   aesthetic creations;
(c)   schemes, rules and methods for performing mental acts, playing games or doing business, and programs for computers;
(d)   presentations of information.

Article 52(2) does not read as a positive exclusion clause but rather as a negative definition of what constitutes an invention. It should be emphasised that these exclusions apply only to the extent to which a European patent application or European patent relates to such subject matter or activities 'as such'. One area in which this phrase has caused much consternation is computer programs (and to a certain extent, business methods). On the one hand, the written law is clear and no patent protection can be granted to computer programs. The reason for the exclusion of

---

[97] Section 1, Patent Law. Dated 25 May 1877, *Reichs-Gesetzblatt* (Imperial Law Journal) No. 23, 501.

[98] A.M. Lewers, 'Composition of Matter' (1922) 4(11) *Journal of the Patent Office Society* 530–53, 530.

[99] European Patent Convention 2000 (EPC 2000) as adopted by decision of the Administrative Council of 28 June 2001.

programs for computers as such is that, like discoveries, scientific theories, mathematical methods and presentations of information, they are presumed to be not of a technical nature. The German legacy (see the *Congo Red* case discussed earlier) demands that patentability under European law requires a specific technical application, whatever that is.

On the other hand, for the past 30 years the European Patent Office has interpreted the law so as to grant patent protection to computer-implemented inventions[100] as long as they are novel, inventive and make a technical contribution. It should be noted here that the EPO tends to treat technical contribution as an inherent patentability matter whereas technical effect may form part of the inventive step analysis, though there have been inconsistencies as the EPO and British courts have considered technical contribution in the context of inventiveness, that is, non-obviousness, and also sufficiency and novelty.[101] It may not go too far to suggest that it requires an effort of heroic proportions to identify consistency or purpose in the meaning and usage of the terms 'technical contribution', 'technical character and 'technical effect' in European patent law practice. Neither does it seems possible to be able to differentiate any of these terms with other commonly used ones like 'heart of the invention' and 'inventive concept', the latter incidentally 'enjoying' a revival in the US in the *Alice* decision.[102]

Legal uncertainty on this matter has been exacerbated by the divergent approaches of national patent offices vis-à-vis the EPO as to what constitutes a 'computer-implemented invention' (CII) and a business method and to what extent disclosures and claims to a mix of patentable and statutorily excluded items are sufficiently 'technical' to fulfil the invention requirement. One attempt by the European legislators to clarify and harmonise the issue came to naught in 2005.

The EPO has become quite liberal such that an invention deemed to be 'technical' fulfils the invention requirement even if it falls entirely within excluded subject matter. The so-called 'any hardware' approach, arising from a Technical Board of Appeal (TBA) decision in 2001 and since then expanded, currently operates in this way.[103] The UK is stricter about granting patents to CIIs. In a case decided in 2007, the UK Court of Appeal adopted and applied the following test suggested by the UK Intellectual Property Office, which places the technical query at the end not the beginning (as with current EPO practice), and does not allow patents where the technical contribution is solely related to excluded subject matter:[104]

1.   properly construe the claim (i.e., decide what the monopoly is);
2.   identify the actual contribution (in substance, not form);
3.   ask whether it falls solely within the excluded subject matter; and
4.   check whether the actual or alleged contribution is actually technical in nature.

---

[100] T208/84 *Vicom*, T26/86 *Koch*, T115/85 *IBM*, T935/97 *IBM* and T1173/97 *IBM*.

[101] *Triazoles/AgrEvo* T939/92; *IBM/Computer Program Product* T1173/97; *Eli Lilly v. Human Genome Sciences* [2008] RPC 29.

[102] *Alice Corp v. CLS Bank International*, 134 S Ct 2347 (2014). For a frank meditation on the vagueness of 'technical' (and of 'invention' and 'discovery') (see *CFPH LLC* [2005] EWHC 1589 (Pat)). For an excellent discussion comparing the US with Europe see S. Thambisetty, '*Alice* and "Something More": The Drift towards European Patent Jurisprudence' (2016) 3(3) *Journal of Law and the Biosciences* 691.

[103] *Pension Benefit Systems Partnership* [2001] T931/96.

[104] *Aerotel v. Telco Holdings* [2006] EWCA Civ 1371 (UK CA).

A subsequent case affirmed this approach while suggesting that the steps can be ordered differently and that the third and fourth can be merged.[105] Of course, part of the reason why there has been a real push to patent software in some way or another is that the Americans do it and that the US was, until recently, quite permissive. The difference between the US and EU position is partly due to the fact that the European patent system requires an invention to be of a technical character – and this is difficult to show where computer programs are concerned. US patent law merely requires that the invention uses a computer or software, and this is sufficient to make it technical, as long as useful, concrete and tangible results are provided. Admittedly this has become difficult to comply with in light of recent decisions.

Ordre public and morality

Article 53, EPC states that patents should not be granted in respect of:

(a)   inventions the commercial exploitation of which would be contrary to 'ordre public' or morality, provided that such exploitation shall not be deemed to be so contrary merely because it is prohibited by law or regulation in some or all of the Contracting States;

(b)   plant or animal varieties or essentially biological processes for the production of plants or animals; this provision shall not apply to microbiological processes or the products thereof.

The latter is due to the existence of a separate IP right for plant breeding and the lack of demand for IP protection among animal breeders. With respect to the former, the true meaning and potential extent of the ordre public/morality exclusions are somewhat unclear. In French civil law, 'ordre public' has a wider meaning than 'public order' and is more akin to 'public policy'. The origins of the exclusion can be traced back to the English Statute of Monopolies (see above), from where it found its way into the Paris Convention, the French Revolution, and thirdly to other international agreements which sought to leave certain sensitive issues to national governments to decide upon including most recently the TRIPS Agreement.[106] However, as Parthasarathy and Walker explain 'it is only in the wake of activist challenges that it gained the association with the ethical dimensions of patent law that it has now'.[107]

The qualification to the Article 53(a) exception requires an explanation. Essentially, the fact that the publication or commercial exploitation of an invention is prohibited is insufficient in itself to render it unpatentable on ordre public or morality grounds. Take the example of a pharmaceutical. Although drugs can be patented upon their initial discovery, their sale is normally prohibited until such time as their developers are able to demonstrate to a state drug regulator that they are safe and effective. So this provision cannot be used to reject a drug patent application or delay its grant because its safety and effectiveness have yet to be proven. Nor can it be used to revoke a patent if it subsequently turns out that the drug is unsafe or ineffective.

---

[105] Symbian v. Comptroller-General of Patents [2008] EWCA Civ 1066 (UK CA).

[106] TRIPS Agreement, Art 27(2); see S. Parthasarathy and A. Walker, 'Observing the Patent System in Social and Political Perspective: A Case Study of Europe', in R.L. Okediji and M.A. Bagley (eds), Patent Law in Global Perspective (New York: Oxford University Press, 2014), 321–43, 326.

[107] Ibid.

On the other hand, to reject a patent application on *ordre public* or morality grounds for an invention whose publication or exploitation is not prohibited by law or regulation would not be permissible. So such prohibition appears to be a necessary but not sufficient condition for the refusal to grant a patent on these grounds.[108]

Under Article 53(c), EPC, 'methods for treatment of the human or animal body by surgery or therapy and diagnostic methods practised on the human or animal body' are unpatentable. Ostensibly, this is on the grounds of not being susceptible of industrial application. But that is unlikely to be the sole reason. It is generally considered undesirable for physicians and surgeons to be sued for patent infringement for acts in the course of their work. This implies morality (or ethics) is a factor in this exclusion too. (For further discussion on the exclusion see Chapter 13.)

US and 'laws of nature'

According to US Patent Act, section 101:

> Whoever invents or discovers any new and useful process, machine, manufacture, or composition of matter, or any new and useful improvement thereof, may obtain a patent therefor, subject to the conditions and requirements of this title.

In other words, a patentable invention may be a process, machine, manufacture or composition of matter. The process need not be new in the sense that a new use of a known process may be patentable. Thus, the US has had no statutory subject matter exceptions to patentability, except for one introduced in 2011 that essentially codified existing internal patent office policy: 'notwithstanding any other provision of law, no patent may issue on a claim directed to or encompassing a human organism'. Does this (virtual) absence of statutory subject matter exclusions necessarily make for clarity? And does it allow the US patent system to readily accommodate discoveries arising from new technologies like biotechnology and information and communication technologies? Probably the best answers are 'no', and 'not necessarily'.

Although it is well-established that patents are not available for laws of nature, physical phenomena or abstract ideas, the concept of 'laws of nature' is a misleading metaphor which is vague and problematic. Although it has earlier origins, the term as we understand it now is rooted in seventeenth-century natural philosophy and a theology that saw God as a divine universal legislator whose laws were perfect and intelligible but who personally had little time for daily interventions bestowing blessings, curses and punishments from on high that would bend or completely break those laws.[109] The usage of 'laws of nature' appears either for referring to a set of descriptions of the

---

[108] For further discussion, see N.P. de Carvalho, *The TRIPS Regime of Patent Rights* (London, The Hague, New York: Kluwer Law International, 2002), 170–75.

[109] For excellent treatment of 'laws of nature' that brings together history, philosophy and theology, see J.H. Brooke, *Science and Religion: Some Historical Perspectives* (Cambridge: Cambridge University Press, 1991). Of course, how we have often credited discoverers of 'laws of nature' and 'natural phenomena' impliedly turns the discoverer into the inventor of the law as if to usurp God's dominion over the universe. Thus, we have Newton's laws of motion, Hooke's law of elasticity, and Boyle's law. Of course, patent law accepts no such presumptuousness: discoverers of laws of nature cannot acquire patents on 'their' laws.

universe that are true as far as we know, or else it is applied to certain principles about universal 'natural phenomena' that scientists have revealed and generally agree upon. The two are quite different. But whichever meaning is adopted, law is inherently societal and has nothing to do with the way we think the world is – or with how the universe actually is.

Accordingly, 'law of nature', useful as it may be for science, arguably has no place in patent law which concerns human inventions and whether there is novelty, non-obviousness and of course utility or industrial application. It is right that $E=mc^2$ should not be patentable; but a discovery of a universal principle accepted by the majority of people 'skilled in the art' as being true has by itself no practical usefulness in the commercial or industrial sense and therefore fails one of the basic patentability criteria.

The Supreme Court in the 1972 decision of *Gottschalk v. Benson*[110] indicated that 'an algorithm, or mathematical formula, is like a law of nature, which cannot be the subject of a patent'. The use of a simile to link algorithms and formulae with laws of nature, cited with approval in *Parker v. Flook*,[111] seems unsatisfactory. In the latter case, the Supreme Court opined that:

> Even though a phenomenon of nature or mathematical formula may be well known, an inventive application of the principle may be patented. Conversely, the discovery of such a phenomenon cannot support a patent unless there is some other inventive concept in its application.

In considering eligibility on the basis of there being an inventive 'application' or 'concept', non-obviousness must be treated as a completely separate criterion. In *Mayo v. Prometheus*, the claimed correlation between metabolite levels and the likelihood of a particular dose of thiopurine being harmful or ineffective is of course a natural phenomenon but there is nothing 'natural' about placing thiopurine in one's body. Methods are inherently abstract and to the extent they fail to have a physical embodiment or application, insofar as that should matter, Europe's industrial application criterion seems to deal with that better than the even vaguer US utility. This is all rather puzzling.

Part of the problem is the failure to distinguish between discovery and invention (discussed extensively above), which the US's statutory language in section 101 hardly helps with. But it is far from being an eligibility issue alone, or even at all. Doubtless, a quantifiable method of optimising a drug dose for an individual patient is a genuinely useful and novel technique. However, the problems with the two patents appear to be quite simple. Indeed, there are reasons to find them unpatentable that have little to do with the 'inventions' being essentially natural in the way the Court held them to be. Applying the normal criteria would have been sufficient without stretching 'natural-ness' so far as it did. First, the correlation between the level of such metabolites and the likelihood a particular dose of thiopurine being harmful or ineffective was already known albeit with less precision. Second, the patents claim a set of instructions to doctors, which in themselves are obvious. In the US, the question of whether there is industrial applicability does not of course arise. Other high-profile cases[112] have assisted little in clarifying eligibility of products and

---

[110] *Gottschalk v. Benson* 409 US 63 (S Ct, 1972).

[111] *Parker v. Flook* 437 US 584 (S Ct, 1978).

[112] For example, *Bilski v. Kappos* 561 US 593.

methods, and it seems fair to say that the US patent system is currently experiencing quite a large degree of confusion about what is and is not patentable.

Unfortunately, and to be fair to US courts, they are stuck with the fact that the exclusion of laws of nature, natural phenomena, and abstract ideas seems to be settled law laid down by a line of fairly consistent, albeit frequently confusing to read, Supreme Court decisions. What has struggled to become settled law is how to impose the exclusions in specific cases or to come up with a coherent generally applicable test. In *Mayo v. Prometheus*, the Supreme Court arguably contributed nothing to legal certainty by taking on the case. The Court could at least have unpacked the meaning of 'laws of nature', which might have been helpful. Judge Breyer adopted the word 'principle' in a futile effort to clarify the meaning or possible legal significance of the law of nature exclusion.[113] Doing so made little difference. Subsequent interim guidelines issued by the United States Patent and Trademark Office (USPTO) for its examiners, taking into account this and other recent Supreme Court cases, have done little to assuage concerns about lack of legal clarity. Perhaps the EPC's Article 52 list of exclusions including discoveries and scientific theories is marginally clearer for patent examiners and helps to preclude baffling court decisions. At least we can probably agree on what a scientific theory is.

It is certainly true that the 'laws of nature' doctrine allowed the patenting of DNA sequences, but other types of subject matter presented real difficulties. In 1980, about the same year that DNA sequences were first being claimed, the US Supreme Court in 1980 ruled by a narrow majority in *Diamond v. Chakrabarty* (as discussed in Chapter 14) that a man-made oil-eating bacterium produced by Anand Chakrabarty, an employee of General Electric, could be classed as a 'composition of matter' or a 'manufacture', and therefore could be treated as a patentable invention. Initially, the PTO had rejected the patent claims directed to the micro-organism itself on the basis that it was a product of nature. On appeal, the Court of Customs and Patent Appeals overturned the patent rejection. According to the Supreme Court's majority opinion, the Congress had 'recognized that the relevant distinction was not between living and inanimate things, but between products of nature, whether living or not, and human-made inventions'. It also pointed out that Congress's intention at the time of the passage of the 1952 US Patent Act was for statutory subject matter to 'include anything under the sun that is made by man'. Consequently, Congress construed terms like 'manufacture' and 'composition of matter' broadly enough that life-form inventions could be patented without need for further legislation.

In 1985, the PTO Board of Patent Appeals and Interferences accepted (in *ex parte Hibberd*)[114] the patentability of plants, seeds and plant tissue cultures. Radical as this might have seemed at the time, as early as 1813 a published statement on what the author deemed to be eligible subject matter had included 'the discovery of an unknown plant and its uses' and 'the discovery of new uses of a known plant'.[115] Nonetheless, the decision did not permanently settle the question of

---

[113] *Mayo Collaborative Services v. Prometheus Laboratories, Inc.* 566 US (2012). The Court cited, inter alia, the old English case *Neilson v. Harford* (discussed above), *Parker v. Flook* 437 US 584 (S Ct, 1978), and *Gottschalk v. Benson* 409 US 63 (S Ct, 1972).

[114] 227 USPQ (BNA) 443 (Bd Pat App & Int 1985).

[115] O. Evans (writing under the pseudonym of P.N.I. Elisha), 'Patent Right Oppression Exposed; Or, Knavery Detected. In

whether or not plants are patentable. In 2001, the Supreme Court finally confirmed the legality of patents on plants.[116]

In 1987, the PTO Board produced another ground-breaking ruling in relation to patenting nature (in *ex parte Allen*) concerning a patent application on polyploid oysters.[117] Although the patent was rejected, the ruling established that multicellular organisms were patentable. A year later the first ever animal patent was granted for 'a transgenic nonhuman mammal' containing an activated oncogene sequence. The patent is commonly referred to as the oncomouse patent, since it describes a mouse into which a gene has been introduced which induces increased susceptibility to cancer (see Chapter 14).

The Supreme Court clarified the application of the 'laws of nature' principle in relation to computer programs in *Diamond v. Diehr*. The patent in question was on a process for curing synthetic rubber, which involved the use of a mathematical formula and a programmed digital computer. The PTO had refused the patent on section 101 grounds, essentially that those steps in the process carried out by a computer under control of a stored program constituted non-statutory subject matter. But its decision was reversed by the Court of Customs and Patent Appeals. The Supreme Court's majority opinion referred to the earlier *Gottschalk v. Benson* but clarified that 'it is now commonplace that an application of a law of nature or mathematical formula to a known structure or process may well be deserving of patent protection'. Consequently, the Court held that where:

> A claim containing a mathematical formula implements or applies that formula in a structure or process which, when considered as a whole, is performing a function which the patent laws were designed to protect (for example, transforming or reducing an article to a different state or thing), then the claim satisfies the requirements of § 101.[118]

As for the validity of methods of doing business, these too were considered unpatentable for many years on the basis of a series of court decisions going back to 1908. However, in assessing the validity of a software-related invention the Court of Appeals repudiated this judicially created exception for business methods.[119] In doing so, the Court argued that these earlier decisions forming the basis for the exception had not in fact established the inherent unpatentability of business methods under section 101. Rather, they had denied the validity of patents for such reasons as that they were merely mathematical algorithms and were therefore abstract ideas, or that the 'inventions' in question lacked novelty. In sum, according to the Court, a business claim should be treated by the PTO in the same way as any other process claim.

In 2014 in *Alice v. CLS*, the Supreme Court applied a two-step eligibility test (in relation to claims about a computer-implemented, electronic escrow service for assisting financial transactions) based upon its earlier decision in *Mayo v. Prometheus*. The first step asks whether the claims 'are

---

an Address to Unite all Good People to Obtain a Repeal of the Patent Laws', Philadelphia, 1813. Quoted in Walterscheid, *supra* note 84, 363.

[116] *J.E.M. Ag Supply, Inc. v. Pioneer Hi-Bred Int'l., Inc.* 534 US 124 (2001).

[117] 2 USPQ 2d (BNA) 1425 (Bd Pat App & Int 1987).

[118] *Diamond v. Diehr* 450 US 175 (1981).

[119] *State Street Bank & Trust Co v. Signature Financial Group, Inc.* 47 USPQ 2d 1596, 1604 (Fed Cir, 1998) 149 F 3d 1368.

directed to a patent-ineligible concept'. If so, the next step – citing *Prometheus* – is to ask 'whether the claim's elements considered both individually and "as an ordered combination," "transform the nature of the claim" into a patent-eligible application'. Behind the test is a long-running concern about 'pre-emption', that is, about patent law not inhibiting future discovery by tying up laws of nature, which form the 'basic tools', or 'building blocks', of human ingenuity, science and technology. The *Mayo* test has now been adopted by the USPTO for computer-implemented inventions including business methods.[120] Alongside this, for inventions that might fall afoul of the natural product, laws or principles of nature, or natural phenomena exclusions, following *Diamond v. Chakrabarty* and *AMP v. Myriad*, inventions must have 'markedly different characteristics' (see Chapter 17).

5.4   CRITERIA FOR PROTECTION

As we have seen, applicants for a patent must satisfy a national or regional patent issuing authority that the invention described in the application is new, susceptible of industrial application (or 'useful' in the US), and that its creation involved an inventive step or would be unobvious to a skilled practitioner.

5.4.1   Novelty

The European Patent Convention considers an invention 'to be new if it does not form part of the state of the art' on the priority date, which is 'held to comprise everything made available to the public by means of a written or oral description, by use, or in any other way, before the date of filing of the European patent application'.[121] This indicates that inventions which are publicly available may form the state of the art whether or not they have been described in writing or even orally. Thus a patent on a drug metabolite was anticipated (and thus invalidated) not by use of the prodrug disclosed in an earlier patent by clinical triallists, but by written description. The first patent showed how that prodrug could be used to therapeutic effect and the mere naming of the metabolite in the 'language' of chemistry was insufficient in itself to form a separate invention.[122] Secret or ignorant prior use is not novelty destroying. And since ignorance is not a defence, unknown use can be infringing. With respect to description, the European Patent Office Technical Board of Appeal has ruled that, 'the concept of novelty must not be given such a narrow interpretation that only what has already been described in the same terms is prejudicial to it [...] There are many ways of describing a substance'.[123]

Furthermore, the TBA subsequently found that it may not necessarily be the case that for novelty to be destroyed, 'all the technical characteristics combined in the claimed invention need to

---

[120] *Mayo Collaborative Services v. Prometheus Laboratories, Inc.* 566 U.S. (2012); *Alice Corp. v. CLS Bank International* 134 S. Ct. 2347 (2014). Thambisetty, *supra* note 102, 691.

[121] EPC, Art 54.

[122] *Merrell Dow v. HN Norton* [1995] UKHL 14.

[123] *Diastereomers*, Case No. T 12/81 – 3.3.1, EPO Technical Board of Appeal.

have been communicated to the public or laid open for public inspection'.[124] According to Bently and Sherman:

> It has long been recognised that the information disclosed by a product is not limited to the information that is immediately apparent from looking at the product. Importantly, the information available to the public also includes information that a skilled person would be able to derive from the product if they analysed or examined it.[125]

However, to demonstrate lack of novelty, a person skilled in the art would have to be able to discover the composition or the internal structure of the product and reproduce it without 'undue burden'.[126]

How foreign prior art may be used in determining if the novelty of an invention varies from one legal jurisdiction to another. In some countries inventions cannot be patented if prior knowledge, use or publication exists anywhere in the world. This is the case for Europe. Elsewhere, only unpublished foreign use or knowledge cannot be taken into account in prior art searches. But in a few countries, only domestically held knowledge, use or manufacture is accepted. These different conceptions of novelty may respectively be referred to as absolute novelty, mixed novelty and local novelty.[127]

Until recently, in the US undocumented knowledge held only in foreign countries did not form the state of the relevant art, meaning the US was a mixed novelty jurisdiction.[128] Although an applicant was not allowed to receive a patent if 'he did not himself invent the subject matter sought to be patented',[129] there were concerns that this loophole sometimes allowed people to copy such undocumented foreign knowledge and claim they had come up with a new invention. However, the America Invents Act, 2011 has switched the US to global novelty. Section 102 now states that 'a person shall be entitled to a patent unless (a) the claimed invention was patented, described in a printed publication, or in public use, on sale, or otherwise available to the public before the effective filing date of the claimed invention'.

---

[124] *Thomson/Electron tube*, Case No. T 953/90, EPO Technical Board of Appeal; 13 EPOR 415.

[125] L. Bently and B. Sherman, *Intellectual Property Law* (2nd ed., Oxford: Oxford University Press, 2004), 419–20.

[126] 'Where it is possible for the skilled person to discover the composition or the internal structure of the product and to reproduce it without undue burden, then both the product and its composition or internal structure becomes state of the art'. Availability to the public – Decision of the Enlarged Board of Appeal, G01/92 (18 December 1992). 8 EPOR 241.

[127] US Patent Law, s 102(f); P.W. Grubb, *Patents for Chemicals, Pharmaceuticals and Biotechnology* (Oxford: Clarendon Press, 1999), 54.

[128] US Patent Law s 102:

  A person shall be entitled to a patent unless:

  (a) the invention was known or used by others in this country, or patented or described in a printed publication in this or a foreign country, before the invention thereof by the applicant for patent; or

  (b) the invention was patented or described in a printed publication in this or a foreign country or in public use or on sale in this country, more than one year prior to the date of the application for patent in the United States.

[129] See US Patent Law, s 102(f).

5.4.2   Industrial application or utility

Industrial application is in most cases a relatively undemanding criterion. Article 57 EPC states that 'an invention shall be considered as susceptible of industrial application if it can be made or used in any kind of industry, including agriculture'. In effect, an invention lacking a practical application is unlikely to be patentable. If it has one, then it will probably pass the industrial applicability test.

As set out by the judgment in a recent UK Supreme Court case,[130] the EPO's Technical Board of Appeal applies as many as 15 principles for determining the presence of an industrial application in the patent disclosure. The four general principles are as follows:

(i)   The patent must disclose 'a practical application' and 'some profitable use' for the claimed substance, so that the ensuing monopoly 'can be expected [to lead to] some [...] commercial benefit' (citing EPO cases T 0870/04, T 0898/05).

(ii)   A 'concrete benefit', namely the invention's 'use [...] in industrial practice' must be 'derivable directly from the description', coupled with common general knowledge (citing EPO cases T 0898/05, T 0604/04).

(iii)   A merely 'speculative' use will not suffice, so 'a vague and speculative indication of possible objectives that might or might not be achievable' will not do (citing EPO cases T 0870/04, T 0898/05).

(iv)   The patent and common general knowledge must enable the skilled person 'to reproduce' or 'exploit' the claimed invention without 'undue burden', or having to carry out 'a research programme' (citing EPO cases T 0604/04, T 0898/05).

In the US, the operative term is 'useful'.[131] Although usefulness appears to be a less demanding requirement, it is possible for a claimed invention to pass the test of industrial applicability in Europe but to fail the analogous test in the US. As one jurist commented:

> One can imagine a product or a process giving an answer to a technical problem, or involving steps of technical nature, but without any utility: such an invention, patentable according to the European system, shall not be patentable according to the American system.[132]

The US Supreme Court in *Brenner v. Manson* required that utility must be substantial, and the invention must be fully developed.[133] The Court famously stated in this context that 'a patent is not a hunting license. It is not a reward for the search, but compensation for its successful conclusion'. The current US law generally requires that utility be 'sufficiently specific, substantial and credible'

---

[130] *Human Genome Sciences v. Eli Lilly* [2011] UKSC 51, para 107.

[131] US Patent Law, s 101.

[132] A. Gallochat, 'The Criteria for Patentability: Where are the Boundaries?' Prepared for the WIPO Conference on the International Patent System, Geneva, 25–27 March 2002.

[133] *Brenner v. Manson* 383 US 519 (1966).

in line with the test fashioned by the USPTO in 2001 to deal with gene patent applications.[134] It is noteworthy that US patent law does not exclude patents on the grounds of disclosing or claiming 'immoral' inventions. However, years back courts found a way to keep morally questionable inventions out of the patent system, such as those intended to poison people or facilitate gambling: to declare them lacking in utility.[135]

In recent years Canada adopted a particularly stringent application of utility for certain cases: the so-called 'promise doctrine'. Section 2 of the Canadian Patent Act defined an invention as: 'any new and useful art, process, machine, manufacture or composition of matter, or any new and useful improvement in any art, process, machine, manufacture or composition of matter'.[136] Whereas in Europe (discussed in detail in Chapter 13) the 'plausibility doctrine' requires that in validity decisions the credibility of the invention on the basis of the patent disclosure be assessed, the promise doctrine goes further, requiring that where the utility of the invention is in the form of an explicit promise made in the claims, the latter must be demonstrated or soundly predicted.[137] This imposes quite a heavy obligation, at least in some fields of technology like pharmaceuticals where the 'journey' from initial discovery to commercial product is quite distant and the full consequences of further experimentation and testing cannot realistically be foreseen. This can make a promise of utility a somewhat hazardous commitment that inventors would prefer not to have to make in any definitive way. Ironically, without a promise (or a statement interpreted by the courts as being a promise), the utility requirement in Canada has been undemanding. Australia is somewhat similar in this regard, suggesting that Canada was by no means an outlier.[138] In one high-profile Australian Federal Court case, Justice Beach offered the following questions in testing for usefulness: 'What has the patentee promised for the invention as described in the relevant claim? Is the promise useful? Has that promise been met?'[139]

However, in 2017, the Supreme Court of Canada nullified the doctrine on the basis that it is 'unsound', 'incongruent' with the Patent Act, and 'excessively onerous'.[140] Instead, the Court declared, 'every invention pertains to a single subject-matter, and any single use of that subject-matter that is demonstrated or soundly predicted by the filing date is sufficient to make an invention useful for the purposes of' the relevant section of the statute. 'To require all multiple uses be met for the patent's validity to be upheld, has the potential for unfair consequences.' The correct test was: first, courts

---

[134] USPTO, 'Utility Examination Guidelines', Federal Register 66(4); 1092–99, 2001; *ICOS Corp/Novel/V28 seven transmembrane receptor* [2002] 6 OJEPO 293; *Aeomica Inc* BL O/286/05. S. Thambisethy, 'Legal Transplants in Patent Law: Why Utility is the New Industrial Applicability' (2009) 49 *Jurimetrics Journal* 195.

[135] For a critical view on the adequacy moral utility doctrine, see M.A. Bagley, 'Patent First, Ask Questions Later: Morality and Biotechnology in Patent Law' (2003) 45(2) *William and Mary Law Review* 469.

[136] Canada Patent Law.

[137] *Pfizer Canada Inc v. Mylan Pharmaceuticals ULC*, 2011 FC 547 (Federal Ct, Canada).

[138] E.R. Gold and M. Short, 'The Promise of the Patent in Canada and Around the World' (2014) 30 *Canadian Intellectual Property Review* 35.

[139] *Streetworx Pty Ltd v. Artcraft Urban Group Pty Ltd* [2014] FCA 1366 (Fed Ct, Australia), para 340.

[140] *AstraZeneca v. Apotex*, 2017 SCC 36 (S Ct, Canada); E. Crowne, 'Promises not Kept: Supreme Court of Canada Abandons Promise Doctrine' (2017) 12(10) *Journal of Intellectual Property Law & Practice* 816–17.

must identify the subject matter of the invention as claimed in the patent. Second, courts must ask whether that subject matter is useful – is it capable of a practical purpose (i.e., an actual result)? A mere scintilla of utility that relates to any use of the subject matter of the claimed invention will suffice. To some commentators this is somewhat concerning particularly given that Canada has quite undemanding obviousness and enabling disclosure requirements by international standards, and that the promise doctrine was reducing opportunities to 'game' the patent system.[141]

5.4.3   Inventive step

It is possible for an invention not to be new, capable of industrial application, or even be useful. But without an inventive step that is unobvious to the average skilled person there can be no invention in the first place. Having said this, it can be extremely difficult if not impossible to be perfectly consistent and objective about this. 'Step' is of course a metaphor implying some kind of cognitive 'distance' needing to be overcome.[142]

UK and EPO approaches

What is inventive step and how does one go about deciding whether it is present or not? One thing to underline from the start is that nowadays it is not about creativity per se. In the British context, Nicholls VC presents its meaning in about as clear a way as is possible:

> […] the criterion for deciding whether or not the claimed invention involves an inventive step is wholly objective. It is an objective criterion defined in statutory terms, that is to say whether the step was obvious to a person skilled in the art having regard to any matter which forms part of the state of the art […] We do not consider that it assists to ask whether 'the patent discloses something sufficiently inventive to deserve the grant of a monopoly'. Nor is it useful to extract from older judgments such as 'that scintilla of invention necessary to support a patent'. The statute has laid down what the criterion is to be: it is a qualitative test not a quantitative test.[143]

Inventive step or non-obviousness is perhaps the most difficult criterion to assess and to be objective about. This is especially the case given that for historical reasons, as discussed earlier, no great leap of creative genius is expected. Indeed, no creativity whatsoever needs to be supplied. Consequently, in the US, as in the UK, the person having ordinary skill in the art, who is the nominal determiner of non-obviousness, is still presumed a rather dull unimaginative fellow, a type in

---

[141] Richard Gold (McGill University), personal communication to G. Dutfield, 1 July 2017 (on file with author).

[142] For a discussion on the varying standards of inventiveness under Australian, UK and US laws, see A. Monotti, 'Divergent Approaches in Defining the Appropriate Level of Inventiveness in Patent Law', in C. Ng, L. Bently and G. D'Agostino (eds), *The Common Law of Intellectual Property: Essays in Honour of Professor David Vaver* (Oxford: Hart Publishing, 2010), 177–98.

[143] *Mölnlycke v. Procter & Gamble* [1994] RPC 49, 112.

Britain quite recently referred to by a judge as 'a nerd' albeit 'not a complete android'.[144] Or as was hardly less impolitely stated in an earlier case, which also considered the obviousness or otherwise of so-called 'mosaicing':

> [...] the hypothetic addressee is a skilled technician who is well acquainted with workshop technique and who has carefully read the relevant literature. He is supposed to have an unlimited capacity to assimilate the contents of, it may be, scores of specifications but to be incapable of scintilla of invention. When dealing with obviousness, unlike novelty, it is permissible to make a 'mosaic' out of the relevant documents, but it must be a mosaic which can be put together by an unimaginative man with no inventive capacity.[145]

It is also meant to be technology neutral. Like many attempted qualitative judgements, especially in areas that can be highly technical and having also to take on board important public policy considerations, being objective can be no easy task. It is especially important for courts to avoid the unfairness of hindsight bias. As stated by Arnold J: 'The fact that, after the event, it is easy to see how the invention could be arrived at by starting from an item of prior art and taking a series of apparently simple steps does not necessarily show that it was obvious at the time.'[146]

Article 56 of the EPC states that 'an invention shall be considered as involving an inventive step if, having regard to the state of the art, it is not obvious to a person skilled in the art'. But drawing the line between the obvious and non-obvious may be no easy matter. To do this in an objective manner, the EPO has adopted what is called 'the problem and solution approach', which seeks to answer whether the solution offered in the patent would have been obvious to a person skilled in the art on the priority date.[147] In the case in which the approach was initially adopted, the Technical Board of Appeal accepted, in the light of fresh experimental evidence presented by the appellants, the 'surprising' nature of the improvement described in the patent application.[148] It is worth noting here that even where the result is surprising, the claimed invention may be still obvious if the activities leading to it were routine and success at some point was to be expected.[149] The UK approach is slightly different in that the evaluation of obviousness is based on a four-step test, first laid out in 1985 by the Court of Appeal. These are to:

1.   Identify the inventive concept embodied in the patent.
2.   Assume the mantle of the normally skilled but unimaginative addressee in the art at the priority date and to impute what was common general knowledge in the art in question.
3.   Identify what, if any, differences exist between the matter cited as being 'known and used' and the alleged invention.

---

[144] Jacob LJ, in *Rockwater v. Technip France & Anor* [2004] EWCA Civ 381.

[145] *Technograph v. Mills & Rockley* [1972] RPC 346, 355.

[146] *Glenmark Generics & Others v. Wellcome Foundation* [2013] EWHC 148 (Pat).

[147] G.S.A. Szabo, 'The Problem and Solution Approach in the European Patent Office' (1995) 26 *IIC* 457.

[148] *Bayer/Carbonless Copying* T1/80 [1979–85] B EPOR 250.

[149] *Actavis Group PTC EHF & Anor v. Teva UK Ltd & Ors* [2017] EWCA Civ 1671.

4.   Ask whether, viewed without any knowledge of the alleged invention, those differences constitute steps, which would have been obvious to the skilled man or whether they require any degree of invention.[150]

The skilled individuals whose 'mantle' the courts must assume may in fact entail a multidisciplinary team as opposed to a single 'skilled but unimaginative addressee'.[151] Parties to a dispute may disagree as to the disciplines of those forming the team in which case the task for judges is to determine the specialisms of these nominal team members.[152]

Also influential is the so-called *Pozzoli* test,[153] which is basically a restatement of the *Windsurfing* questions, and which forms the following revised structured approach:

1.   Identify the notional 'person skilled in the art'.
2.   Identify the relevant common general knowledge of that person.
3.   Identify the inventive concept of the claim in question or if that cannot readily be done, construe it.
4.   Identify what, if any, differences exist between the matter cited as forming part of the 'state of the art' and the inventive concept of the claim or the claim as construed.
5.   Viewed without any knowledge of the alleged invention as claimed, do those differences constitute steps which would have been obvious to the person skilled in the art or do they require any degree of invention?

Interestingly, in one British case, the judge applied both the *Pozzoli* test and the EPO's problem-solution approach, which may or may not be a sign of things to come.[154] Another test applied in some relevant cases is 'obvious to try', which relates to the last part of the *Windsurfing/Pozzoli* test. The enquiry is whether there was or was not a fair expectation of success in trying something out such as combining known element A with known element B (and perhaps also with C and D) to come up with an invention. Without that fair expectation, the invention is not obvious.[155] On this matter, British courts and the EPO appear to be closely aligned.[156]

---

[150] *Windsurfing v. Tabur Marine* [1985] RPC 59, 73-4. See A. Griffiths, 'Windsurfing and the Inventive Step', (1999) *IPQ* 160; P. England, 'Inventive Step in Europe and the UPC' (2018) 13(7) *Journal of Intellectual Property Law & Practice* 534.

[151] *Osram v. Pope* (1917) 34 RPC 369.

[152] *Medimmune v. Novartis* [2011] EWHC 1669 (Pat), paras 375–379. On how to determine the composition of the team: *Schlumberger Holdings Ltd v. Electromagnetic Geoservices AS* [2010] EWCA Civ 819, [2010] RPC 33; *Merck Sharpe and Dohme Ltd v. Shionogi & Co Ltd* [2016] EWHC 2989 (Pat).

[153] *Pozzoli v. BDMO SA* [2007] EWCA; also see current UK IP Office's *Manual of Patent Practice*, Section 3.01 et seq.

[154] *Teva UK Ltd. v. Boehringer Ingelheim Pharma GmbH & Co KG* [2015] EWHC 2963 (Pat).

[155] Initially formulated by Diplock LJ in *Johns-Manville Corporation's Patent* [1967] RPC 479; see also *Medimmune v. Novartis* [2011] EWHC 1669 (Pat), paras 377–378.

[156] T296/93 *Biogen/Hepatitis B* [1995] OJ EPO 627 at para 7.4.4.

US approach

In the US, section 103 of the Patent Act provides for non-obviousness as follows:

> A patent may not be obtained though the invention is not identically disclosed or described as set forth in section 102 of this title, if the differences between the subject matter sought to be patented and the prior art are such that the subject matter as a whole would have been obvious at the time the invention was made to a person having ordinary skill in the art to which said subject matter pertains. Patentability shall not be negatived by the manner in which the invention was made.

Arguably, the seminal case in that country is *Graham v. John Deere*,[157] in which the Supreme Court expressed its opinion concerning the meaning of section 103. Accordingly, the obviousness or non-obviousness of an invention should be assessed by:

1.   determining the scope and content of the prior art;
2.   ascertaining the differences between the prior art and the claims at issue; and
3.   resolving the level of ordinary skill in the pertinent art resolved.

The Court went on to indicate that secondary considerations could be used to clarify the circumstances surrounding the origin of the subject matter sought to be patented, and which might serve as confirmations of non-obviousness. Such considerations could include commercial success, long felt but unmet needs, and failure of others to come up with the same invention. The latter appear to shut the door on hindsight bias, whereas the other considerations appear to encourage it. The need for an invention disclosed in a patent may not be at all evident. It has been claimed that the worth of the DNA amplification technique known as polymerase chain reaction that was patented and subsequently sold for $300 million was not at all evident at the time it was invented. And its extraordinary commercial success came some years after the patent was granted as new applications for it were devised.

Since then higher courts (and the USPTO) have applied a non-obviousness test commonly referred to as teaching-suggestion-motivation test (TSM) to combine the prior art. The test has been criticised for lowering the bar to an excessive degree, such that what would be obvious according to the *Graham* assessment could be found non-obvious and undeserving of a patent monopoly. However, the 2007 decision in *KSR International v. Teleflex* appears to have raised the obviousness bar again.[158] In that decision, the US Supreme Court reaffirmed the *Graham* factors and stated that the Circuit courts had erred in applying the TSM test in an overly rigid and formalistic way; the test was merely one of numerous rationales that could be used to determine obviousness. For those concerned about the poor quality of many issued US patents, this is a welcome decision, though it has not been universally praised and subsequent decisions have not apparently added a great deal of clarity.

---

[157] *Graham v. John Deere*, 148 USPQ (BNA) 459, 1966.

[158] *KSR International v. Teleflex*, 127 S Ct 1727 (2007); also see Section 2141, Examination Guidelines for Determining Obviousness Under 35 USC 103 [R-08.2017] in USPTO *Manual of Patent Examining Procedure*, Ninth Edition, Revision 08.2017. Last Revised January 2018.

5.5   SCOPE OF PROTECTION

5.5.1   Fence posts v. sign posts

The claims set the boundaries for the monopoly right. The scope of the claims should be no broader than the information disclosed in the description. In the patent law of the US and the UK, the claims define the scope of the invention by placing 'fence posts' around it. In order to place the fence posts as far apart as possible, patent drafters will try to anticipate all conceivable embodiments and variants of the invention so that others will be unable to 'invent around' the patent. In some other jurisdictions, such as Germany, the claims are meant to provide 'sign posts' for the invention so that the inventive step is defined and patent examiners can more clearly identify what is new about the invention.

The European Patent Convention reflects a compromise between fence post and sign post claiming.[159] But it must be remembered that 'European' patents are in actuality separate national patents. It follows that infringement cases must be tried in national courts. Consequently, it is perfectly possible for a British court to find an EPO-granted patent not infringed and/or invalid but for a German court to find it infringed and valid. Nonetheless, the EPC and EPO practice have quite substantially harmonised national patent laws in Europe, including how patent claims are interpreted. Thus, with regard to interpretation of claims, the Protocol on the Interpretation of Article 69 of the EPC 2000 seeks to strike a compromise between the relatively strict interpretation of claims traditionally applied by UK courts and the broader approach employed in Germany which sees claims as guidelines rather than strict boundaries. Nonetheless, interpretation of claims for the purpose of 'mapping' the scope of a patent and considering whether acts close to the 'boundaries' invade its 'territory' and therefore infringe continues to be a tricky matter for courts. Until the 1980s, British courts interpreted claims literally but then they began to construct claims purposively,[160] according to which the primary challenge for the court was that of assessing what the person skilled in the art would understand the claims to mean.[161] In 2017, the Supreme Court in *Actavis v Eli Lilly* has shifted again, accepting the German (and US') doctrine of equivalents. According to the Court (para 54):

> A problem of infringement is best approached by addressing two issues, each of which is to be considered through the eyes of the notional addressee of the patent in suit, i.e. the person skilled in the relevant art. Those issues are: (i) does the variant infringe any of the claims as a matter of normal interpretation; and, if not, (ii) does the variant nonetheless infringe because it varies from the invention in a way or ways which is or are immaterial?

---

[159] On the UK, see *EMI v. Lissen* (1939) 56 RPC 23 (UK HL). Comparing the UK and Germany, see M. Fisher, *Fundamentals of Patent Law: Interpretation and Scope of Protection* (Oxford and Portland: Hart Publishing, 2007), 7–8. For discussion on US patent law, see D. Burk and M. Lemley, 'Fence Posts of Sign Posts? Rethinking Patent Claim Construction' (2009) 157 *University of Pennsylvania Law Review* 1743–99.

[160] *Catnic Components Ltd v. Hill & Smith Ltd* (1982) RPC 183.

[161] *Improver Corporation v. Remington Consumer Products Ltd* [1990] FSR 181; also, *Kirin-Amgen v. Hoechst Marion Roussel Ltd* [2004] UKHL 46.

Perhaps it goes without saying that assessing 'immateriality' may not be at all straightforward.[162]

5.5.2   Rights conferred

Article 28 of the TRIPS Agreement presents the rights conferred in a succinct manner and in doing so reflects common practice nationally. Accordingly, in the case of a product patent, third parties cannot without the owner's consent make, use, offer the product for sale, sell, or import it for those purposes. As regards a process patent, third parties cannot use the process or use, offer for sale or sell the product obtained directly by that process or import it for those purposes. This language is very similar to section 154 of the US Patent Act.

The European Patent Convention, however, does not lay out the rights conferred. These are left to the national jurisdictions. However, the Community Patent Convention, which has still not been implemented, defines the rights in a detailed manner.[163] Some countries have drawn upon the language of the EPC in their national laws. One such country is the UK, where the rights conferred are presented in the context of what it means to infringe a patent. Section 60 of the UK Patents Act 1977 states that the following acts done without the patent owner's consent are infringing:

(a)   where the invention is a product, he makes, disposes of, offers to dispose of, uses or imports the product or keeps it whether for disposal or otherwise;

(b)   where the invention is a process, he uses the process or he offers it for use in the United Kingdom when he knows, or it is obvious to a reasonable person in the circumstances, that its use there without the consent of the proprietor would be an infringement of the patent;

(c)   where the invention is a process, he disposes of, offers to dispose of, uses or imports any product obtained directly by means of that process or keeps any such product whether for disposal or otherwise.

In addition to these, a person also infringes a patent if without the owner's consent he:

Supplies or offers to supply in the United Kingdom a person other than a licensee or other person entitled to work the invention with any of the means, relating to an essential element of the invention, for putting the invention into effect when he knows, or it is obvious to a reasonable person in the circumstances, that those means are suitable for putting, and are intended to put, the invention into effect in the United Kingdom.[164]

---

[162] *Actavis UK Ltd v. Eli Lilly & Co* [2017] UKSC 48 (UK); for the US, see *Warner-Jenkinson v. Hilton Davis* 520 US 17 (1997) (US).

[163] CPC, Arts 25 and 26.

[164] As one might expect, these rules have evolved over time. According to one rather old work on patent law, the exclusive right over making (and vending) only applies to product inventions, whereas the exclusive right to use mainly applies to processes. P.C. Rushen, *A Critical Study of the Form of Letters Patent for Inventions* (London: Stevens and Sons, 1908), 66.

The European patent: still a bundle of national rights? Towards patents having unitary effect

As should be clear, currently, the most important patent instrument in Europe is the European Patent Convention of 1973, which was revised in 2000. According to the Convention, a so-called 'European patent' is in actuality a bundle of national patents that when granted become valid and enforceable in each national territory. However, reform is underway.

The EPC is the culmination of a 30-year process in developing a European patent system starting with France and the Benelux countries and continuing by way of the Council of Europe.[165] Contrary to what many people might assume it is not an EU treaty, and membership is not confined to the 28 EU members. Thus Turkey, Serbia, Macedonia (FYRM), Iceland and Albania are among those making up the 38 contracting states. Moldova, Morocco, Tunisia and (oddly perhaps) Cambodia have agreed to accept granted European patents as valid in their countries, at the request of applicants, through bilateral validation agreements. Although patents granted by the European Patent Office in Munich are commonly referred to as European patents this is not strictly correct. They are separate national patents valid in each member state. Enforcement, renewal and litigation are matters for national law. The validity of recently issued patents can be challenged at the EPO.

At the time of writing, the EU is seeking to provide for a unitary European patent. At present the options for inventors seeking protection in Europe are either to file separately in each country as required, or to apply for a so-called 'European patent' through the EPO which as mentioned leads to a bundle of granted national patents. However, a third way is pending which is for owners of an EPO-granted patent to request that it have 'unitary effect'. What does this mean in actual practice? According to Article 5 of the Agreement on a Unified Patent Court (UPC):

1. The European patent with unitary effect shall confer on its proprietor the right to prevent any third party from committing acts against which that patent provides protection throughout the territories of the participating member states in which it has unitary effect, subject to applicable limitations.
2. The scope of that right and its limitations shall be uniform in all participating member states in which the patent has unitary effect.

The relevant instruments to make this a reality are awaiting the required ratifications. These are as follows:

•   Council Decision of 10 March 2011 authorising enhanced cooperation in the area of the creation of unitary patent protection (2011/167/EU).
•   Regulation (EU) No 1257/2012 of the European Parliament and of the Council of 17 December 2012 implementing enhanced cooperation in the area of the creation of unitary patent protection.

---

[165] Parthasarathy and Walker, *supra* note 106, 321–43.

- Council Regulation (EU) No 1260/2012 of 17 December 2012 implementing enhanced cooperation in the area of the creation of unitary patent protection with regard to the applicable
  translation arrangements.
- Agreement on a Unified Patent Court, 2013.

The UK's recent decision to leave the EU without (at the time of writing) any exit strategy has
caused a certain amount of confusion, although we expect the unitary system to come into existence with or without the UK's participation. The UK government has issued some guidance notes in
the Technical Notice to deal with two alternative situations namely if the UPC does not come into
force, and if it does. In the former situation, despite the UK having ratified the UPC Agreement, this
will not take effect in UK and there will be no changes in UK law (in the hypothetical *ex post* exit
scenario). In the latter situation where the UPC is ratified, the UK will apparently 'explore' whether
it should remain within the UPC and the unitary system. The Notice also gives several reassurances
to business that all existing rights and licences will remain in force, and that pending applications
for patents, plant variety rights and supplementary protection certificates will be continued.[166]

5.5.3   Duration

European Patent Convention, Article 63 establishes a patent term of 20 years from the filing date.
This is repeated in the TRIPS Agreement and is now the global standard. Why 20 years and not,
say, 15 or 25 years, and for all industrial sectors? This is an example of political convenience trump-
ing economic logic. When governments undertake to harmonise regulatory standards it may be
politically difficult for any of them to accept levels less favourable to powerful interest groups than
the present ones. This is especially the case when, as in IPRs, the economic stakes are so high
for private industry. The progressive strengthening of domestic intellectual property standards
results from the lobbying pressure of interest groups which stand to gain the most economically.
Governments will usually find it more politically palatable to raise intellectual property standards
than to lower them, since opponents are unlikely to be so well-organised or resourced. Since the
minimum patent term in Europe – as apparently elsewhere – was 20 years, it was expedient to
choose this term rather than a lower one.

   As for the decision to make patent terms equal for all industries, economic rationality also
had nothing to do with it. After all, product life cycles within different industrial sectors can vary
tremendously. Some products may have an average life cycle duration that is shorter than the time
it takes for a patent to be granted.[167] In the pharmaceutical sector the situation is very different.
Aspirin, for example, recently celebrated its centenary, while many other health products may be
marketable for several decades. But interest group politics may not provide the complete explanation either. As one commentator sees it, a standardised term 'would preserve the notion that intellectual property was indeed an area of real framework law which applied across the economies of

---

[166] *Guidance Patents if there's no Brexit deal*, UK Department for Business, Energy and Industrial Strategy, September 2018.

[167] B.H. Hall and R.M. Ham, 'The Determinants of Patenting in the US Semiconductor Industry, 1980–1994', Presented at
the NBER Patent System and Innovation Conference, Santa Barbara, California, January 1999.

member states and did not constitute a form of sector-specific "industrial" policy which it would be if many sectoral-based periods of protection were possible'.[168] In a similar vein, Merges argued in a submission to a US Senate Committee that the *raison d'être* of the patent system would be undermined if the rights granted varied according to specific industries:

> Patents issue every day for devices ranging from the proverbial mousetrap to super-conductors and man-made organisms [...] In the eyes of the patent system [...] all inventors are created equal [...] Indeed, it is this equal treatment which distinguishes a true patent system from a series of ad hoc awards to inventors.[169]

In some jurisdictions the 20-year term can under certain circumstances be extended for pharmaceutical products. In the US, the 1984 Drug Price Competition and Patent Term Restoration Act (usually referred to as 'the Hatch-Waxman Act') allows patent term extensions of up to five years to compensate for the restriction on the effective protection term because of the time needed to acquire the Food and Drug Administration's marketing approval. In exchange, generic firms only need to file a so-called Abbreviated New Drug Application (ANDA) with the Food and Drug Administration (FDA) for their equivalent drugs, rather than go through extensive clinical trials to demonstrate the safety and efficacy of their version of the soon to go off-patent medicine. Second, the legislation incorporated the so-called 'Bolar exemption', which meant that certain acts performed before the expiry date of the patent that would normally infringe it are allowed as long as they are related to seeking FDA approval and do not constitute commercial use. The Bolar exemption was named after a court case involving Hoffman LaRoche and a generic producer called Bolar,[170] and has been incorporated into the patent laws of several countries.[171] In the European Community, for example, the rules provide that generic companies may use the original producer's data to obtain their own regulatory approval after eight years even if the patent is still in force. But the generic version cannot be marketed until ten years after the date of the original product's first marketing, or longer since generic companies are likely to opt to wait until after the expiry of any patents.[172]

The World Trade Organization has determined that Bolar exemptions, or regulatory review exceptions to be more formal, do not conflict with the TRIPS Agreement. However, a stockpiling exception is not allowable.[173] Thus, the regulatory review exception as provided in the following

[168] G.B. Doern, *Global Change and Intellectual Property Agencies* (London and New York: Pinter, 1999), 46.

[169] R.P. Merges, 'Contracting into Liability Rules: Intellectual Property Rights and Collective Rights Organizations' (1996) 84(5) *California Law Review* 1293–386, 1315.

[170] *Roche Products Inc v. Bolar Pharmaceutical Co, Inc,* 221 USPQ 937 (Fed Cir, 1984).

[171] See C.M. Correa, 'Protecting Test Data for Pharmaceutical and Agrochemical Products under Free Trade Agreement', in P. Roffe, G. Tansey and D. Vivas-Eugui, *Negotiating Health: Intellectual Property and Access to Medicines* (London: Earthscan, 2006), 81–96; M.P. Pugatch, 'Intellectual Property, Data Exclusivity, Innovation and Market Access', in Roffe et al., ibid., 97–132.

[172] Directive 2004/27/EC of the European Parliament and of the Council of 31 March 2004 amending Directive 2001/83/EC on the Community code relating to medicinal products for human use.

[173] WTO, '*Canada – Patent Protection of Pharmaceutical Products. Complaint by the European Communities and their Member*

subsection of Canada's Patent Act was deemed by a dispute settlement panel as not conflicting with TRIPS:

> It is not an infringement of a patent for any person to make, construct, use or sell the patented invention solely for uses reasonably related to the development and submission of information required under any law of Canada, a province or a country other than Canada that regulates the manufacture, construction, use or sale of any product.

On the other hand, this subsection, which provided for a so-called stockpiling exception, was held to be in conflict with TRIPS:

> It is not an infringement of a patent for any person who makes, constructs, uses or sells a patented invention in accordance with subsection (1) to make, construct or use the invention, during the applicable period provided for by the regulations, for the manufacture and storage of articles intended for sale after the date on which the term of the patent expires.

In 1992, the European Council adopted a Regulation requiring EU countries to provide monopoly rights for medicinal products beyond the life of the basic patents protecting them, to make up for the time taken to secure marketing authorisation.[174] These rights are known as supplementary protection certificates (SPCs). Applications by a patent holder for an SPC must be made to the national patent offices within six months of receiving marketing authorisation for the drug in question in that country. The maximum possible extension period is, as in the US, five years. They used to be available only for human or veterinary medical products authorised for the first time. However, they are now available for existing chemical entities where these are the subject of a patent on a different use.[175]

5.6   LIMITATIONS AND EXCEPTIONS

As we saw earlier, patents may be considered as tools for economic advancement that should contribute to the enrichment of society. In reality, though, balancing the interests of inventors, users of other people's inventions and society as a whole in the design of patent systems is extremely difficult.

Among the safeguards commonly made available to ensure that patent rights do not overprotect at the expense of users and the public are what may be referred to as defences to infringement. We feel that the word 'defences' downplays the fact that these limitations to rights are an essential part

---

States. Report of the Panel' [WTO document WT/DS114/R, 2000].

[174] Council Regulation (EEC) No 1768/92 of 18 June 1992 concerning the creation of a supplementary protection certificate for medicinal products. A similar regulation was passed in 1996 for plant protection products (Regulation (EC) No 1610/96 of the European Parliament and of the Council of 23 July 1996 concerning the creation of a supplementary protection certificate for plant protection products).

[175] Case C-130/11 *Neurim* of 19 July 2012.

of the balance we need to ensure present generation intellectual property owners are not afforded excessively strong rights to inhibit would-be follow-on inventors and to constrain important human and market-based freedoms. These include private use and experimental use limitations and other possible provisions allowable as long as they comply with Article 30 of the TRIPS Agreement's three-step test. There are also public interest measures that may be deployed to restrict the enjoyment of full patent rights for a greater good, such as compulsory licensing and government use provisions.[176] Outside patent law, competition law may also come into play.

5.6.1   Private and experimental use

European countries tend to provide defences to infringement in their statutes in the form of limitations to the rights conferred. The most important ones are (i) private and non-commercial use, and (ii) experimental use. These tend to conform to the Community Patent Convention.[177] For example, the UK Patents Act 1977 provides a list of defences to infringement.[178] The general defences to an act that would otherwise constitute infringement as laid out in section 60(5) include if it is done privately and for purposes which are not commercial, and if it is done for experimental purposes relating to the subject matter of the invention. It should be noted that the two defences are separate. Recent court decisions in Europe have tended to interpret the experimental use exception quite broadly. In consequence, the exception is able to cover commercial as well as non-commercial acts. As Cornish explains in his survey of European court decisions, 'even if the concern initiating the trials is a commercial organisation, the exception may apply if the immediate purpose is to discover more about the properties of the invention. The courts will no longer insist that that motivation must be "solely" or "exclusively" to gain more scientific knowledge'.[179] This approach seems sensible and much better accommodates the present reality that universities and businesses increasingly collaborate, that it is difficult to separate out pure and applied science, and that it is far from obvious where to draw the line between commercial and non-commercial research.

In the US, the scope of the common law experimental use exemption attracted critical attention as a result of the judgment in *Madey v. Duke University*.[180] The judgment gave rise to concerns that the US may have gone too far in interpreting the exemption into a state of virtual non-existence, and that in doing so it may well hinder universities from conducting the basic research upon which subsequent commercially oriented research so often depends, and which the private sector cannot be relied upon to carry out all by itself.[181] In the opinion of the Court of Appeals for the Federal

[176] WIPO Standing Committee on the Law of Patents, 'Exclusions from Patentability and Exceptions and Limitations to Patentees' Rights, A Study Prepared by L. Bently, B. Sherman, D. Barbosa, S. Basheer, C. Visser, R. Gold, Geneva: WIPO [SCP/15/3 – Annex I], 2010.

[177] CPC, Art 27.

[178] UK Patents Act 1977, s 60(5).

[179] W.P. Cornish, 'Experimental Use of Patented Inventions in European Community States' (1998) 29 *IIC* 735, 753.

[180] *Madey v. Duke University*, 64 USPQ 2d 1737 (Fed Cir, 2002).

[181] For examples of how basic research carried out in universities, hospitals and government research agencies contributed

Circuit, despite a university's non-profit status, its apparently non-commercial projects 'unmistakably further the institution's legitimate business objectives'. As long as such projects are 'not solely for amusement, to satisfy idle curiosity, or for strictly philosophical inquiry', then they do not qualify for the experimental use defence.

The TRIPS Agreement makes no reference to private or experimental use. Instead it incorporates a modified form of the Berne Convention's three-step test. Accordingly, Article 30 permits WTO members to provide limited exceptions to the rights conferred provided that: (1) such exceptions do not unreasonably conflict with a normal exploitation of the patent; and (2) do not unreasonably prejudice the legitimate interests of the patent owner, taking account of the legitimate interests of third parties.

5.6.2   Compulsory licensing and government use

Compulsory licensing and government use measures, which allow third parties or the government to use a patented invention for a royalty or fee, are provided in some countries' laws, though not necessarily in their patent laws, for such purposes as:

- to deal with a situation in which a patent owner is unwilling to work his invention;
- to satisfy an unmet demand from the public for a patented product;
- to introduce price-reducing competition for important but expensive products, for example, some drugs;
- to deal with a situation in which refusal to license a patent, or the imposition of unreasonable terms, is preventing the exploitation of another invention which is of technical or economic importance;
- to prevent abuses of patent rights including by breaking up competition-inhibiting monopolies and cartels;
- to prevent the creation of potential competition-inhibiting monopolies and cartels.

In international law, compulsory licensing provisions arose as a compromise between those countries that preferred to have patents revoked in cases of non-working and other nations that were less keen to interfere with the freedom of patent owners to set up manufacturing facilities where they pleased. Conflict arose between two groups of countries. The first group consisted mainly of the most advanced industrialised countries who considered it unreasonable and unrealistic to require patent holders to set up manufacturing facilities in every domestic market. The second group was made up mostly of less industrially advanced countries seeking to protect their emerging industries. Supporters of the latter position increased in number during the 1960s. This was because many newly independent countries joined the Paris Union, and these tended to be much less interested in using IPRs to generate their own technologies than in acquiring useful technologies from foreigners.

---

to major biomedical revolutions, see G. Dutfield, *Intellectual Property Rights and the Life Science Industries: A Twentieth Century History* (Aldershot: Ashgate, 2003).

The original 1883 Paris Convention text stated that 'the patentee shall remain bound to work his patent in conformity with the laws of the country into which he introduces the patented objects'. But subsequent revisions strengthened the rights of patent holders in this respect, principally by providing for compulsory licensing as a sanction for non-working, albeit without completely excluding the possibility of revocation. According to the current text of the convention, 'a compulsory licence may not be applied for on the ground of failure to work or insufficient working before the expiration of a period of four years from the date of filing [...] or three years from the date of the grant of the patent, whichever period expires last'. Such a licence must be non-exclusive and non-transferable, and an application for one 'shall be refused if the patentee justified his inaction by legitimate reasons'.

Compulsory licensing provisions are very common. 'About one hundred countries recognised some form of non-voluntary licensing in their patent laws by the early 1990s'.[182] Canada, between 1969 and 1992, granted 613 licences for the manufacture or importation of medicines.[183] National patent laws in Europe tend to provide for compulsory licensing and government use. Despite this, the grant of compulsory licences has generally been quite rare in the developed countries, and has become much less so, perhaps mostly for ideological and political reasons. In the developing countries, the most high-profile granting of non-voluntary licences has involved pharmaceuticals.

In the US, on the other hand, while the patent law contains no reference to compulsory licensing, for much of the twentieth-century American courts had few qualms about using compulsory licensing in response to abuses by patentees including antitrust violations. The Federal Trade Commission has also issued compulsory licensees when regulating corporate mergers and acquisitions.[184] In addition, government measures have been invoked on occasions, usually for national defence purposes, but also to reduce drug prices and in pursuit of environment protection and economic development. It is rather ironic, then, that today the US actively discourages other countries from resorting to compulsory licensing.

The TRIPS Agreement provides some detailed provisions concerning compulsory licensing. Because of their relevance in particular to access to medicine, they are discussed in Chapter 13.

5.7   TRADE SECRETS

Frequently the patent system is justified on the basis that if it were unavailable inventors would resort to secrecy. This sounds plausible for inventions that could not easily be reverse engineered. However, it is highly misleading if it leaves people to assume that secrecy is only employed as a second-best solution to the challenge of how best to appropriate valuable research findings, discoveries and technical creations. In fact it is rarely an either/or choice. Businesses use both in

---

[182] J. Reichman and C. Hasenzahl, 'Non-Voluntary Licensing of Patented Inventions: Historical Perspective, Legal Framework under TRIPS, and an Overview of the Practice in Canada and the United States of America', Issues Paper 5. UNCTAD-ICTSD Project on IPRs and Sustainable Development, 2002, 12.

[183] Ibid., 4.

[184] Ibid., 19.

their intellectual property management strategy – as they have done since the nineteenth century.[185] There is no multilateral treaty referring specifically to trade secrets. However, the TRIPS Agreement covers trade secrecy in the section on 'undisclosed information', which is a broader concept than trade secrets and the arguably less narrow (but still related to trade secrecy) concept of know-how.[186] The inclusion of undisclosed information in TRIPS was strongly opposed by developing countries that did not consider confidential information to be a form of intellectual property. However, Switzerland and the US, concerned to safeguard trade secrets internationally, successfully persuaded other governments to accept their proposal for such protection. Because no previous convention provides for protection of undisclosed information, the strategy adopted by the two countries was to argue that such protection is a necessary measure for countries to fulfil their obligations to suppress unfair competition as required by Article 2 of TRIPS, which requires members to comply with various parts of the Paris Convention including the provisions dealing with unfair competition.

Members must enable natural and legal persons to prevent 'information lawfully within their control from being disclosed to, acquired by, or used by others without their consent in a manner contrary to honest commercial practices'. Acts contrary to honest commercial practices that are mentioned include breach of contract and breach of confidence. To be protected, information must be secret (that is, not generally known among or readily accessible to persons within the circles that normally deal with the kind of information in question); have commercial value because it is secret; and have been subject to reasonable steps to keep it secret. Members, by virtue of Article 39.3, are also required to prevent disclosure of data that pharmaceutical and agrochemical producers must submit to the government as conditions for approval of the marketing of new products. This provision is discussed Chapter 13.

In the EU, trade secrecy is provided by the Directive on the Protection of Undisclosed Know-How and Business Information (Trade Secrets Directive). The counterpart legislation in the US is the Defend Trade Secrets Act (DTSA). With respect to the protection of data submitted as a condition for marketing approval, these come under separate regulations. It can be argued that trade secrets do not serve the public interest as well as patents. This is because, while society may benefit from availability of the product or technology associated with a trade secret, this kind of intellectual property right keeps technical information that would be disclosed in a patent application outside the public domain. Nevertheless, effective trade secrecy protection is widely considered to be essential for encouraging technology transfer.[187] It is also important for the seed industry, since it is commonly used to protect the inbred parent lines of hybrids, since if these are accessed by competitors, the same hybrids could easily be developed by these rivals.

---

[185] J. Mercelis, 'Corporate Secrecy and Intellectual Property in the Chemical Industry through a Transatlantic Lens c. 1860–1930' (2016) 82 *Entreprises et Histoire* 32–46.

[186] On how the concept of trade secrecy superseded know-how, at least in the US juridical context (if not necessarily in the business one in that country or elsewhere), see D. O'Reagan, 'Know-how in Postwar Business and Law' (2017) 58(1) *Technology and Culture* 121–53.

[187] J.H. Barton, 'New Trends in Technology Transfer', ICTSD-UNCTAD Issue Paper No 18, Geneva: ICTSD-UNCTAD, 2007.

6
Trade marks

6.1   EARLY PROTECTION OF TRADE MARKS

There is very early evidence of the usage of marks and devices to distinguish goods of one trader from another. Branding, for instance, has been in use to mark slaves, animals and goods since the early Minoan, Egyptian, Mesopotamian, Etruscan and Chinese civilisations.[1] From medieval times, marks were used by various guilds to police the quality of the goods produced by guild members, and to protect members from competitors. After the demise of guilds, marks were still used by traders and manufacturers, especially with the growing numbers of shop-merchants and specialised goods shops, which sprang up in the latter part of the eighteenth century, hallmarking the Industrial Revolution.

This period brought about several economic and social changes. One of the most important changes to make an impact on the evolution of trade marks was the emergence of a large consumer class in the newly formed industrial cities.[2] This new class was armed with spending power, and a social ambition to emulate the upper classes.[3] A wide range of new consumer goods was introduced to meet this rapidly growing demand. Increasingly, retailing and advertising techniques were modernised and intensified to increase sales. There had been advertising of some sort since the seventeenth century; however, with the removal of official restrictions on printing in 1695, the eighteenth century saw the number of individual advertisements printed in the newspapers running into millions; supplemented by a proliferation of shop signs, handbills and trade cards.[4] 'Over time, as consumers started to realise that some marks indicated a particular manufacturer, and in turn goods of a certain standard, the nature of the mark changed from being a source of liability to become an indicator of quality.'[5]

In Europe, courts had begun began to recognise the legal effect of 'marks' by the sixteenth century and held that if another trader were allowed to use the same sign, this would allow a fraud to

---

[1] K. Shao, 'Look at my Sign – Trademarks in China from Antiquity to the Early Modern Times' (2005) 87 *Journal of the Patent and Trademark Office Society* 654; F. Schechter, *The Historical Foundations of the Law Relating to Trade Marks* (Columbia University Press, 1925), 38–77; D. Wengrow, 'Prehistories of Commodity Branding' (2008) 49(1) *Current Anthropology* 7.

[2] Wengrow establishes that this phenomenon had already occurred back in Mesopotamian times, ibid.

[3] This was especially true of Londoners – M.D. George, *London Life in the Eighteenth Century* (Penguin, 1925), Chapter 4; E.W. Gilboy, 'Demand as a Factor in the Industrial Revolution', in A.H. Cole (ed.), *Facts and Factors in Economic History* (Harvard University Press, 1932), 620–40.

[4] J. Styles, 'Manufacturing, Consumption and Design', in J. Brewer and R. Porter (eds), *Consumption and the World of Goods* (London: Routledge, 1993), 540.

[5] L. Bently and B. Sherman, *Intellectual Property Law* (2nd ed., Oxford: Oxford University Press, 2004), 810.

be committed on the public. This basis for protection was eventually to become, under the British Courts of Chancery, the basis of the action for 'passing off' to protect a trader who had developed a reputation or goodwill in a particular sign or symbol.[6] An early decision described it thus:

> A man is not to sell his goods under the pretence that they are the goods of another man; he cannot be permitted to practise such a deception, nor to use the means which contribute to that end. He cannot therefore be allowed to use names, marks, letters or other indicia, by which he may induce purchasers to believe that the goods which he is selling are the manufacture of another person.[7]

By the late-nineteenth century, Britain had introduced a system of registration of marks,[8] especially as there was already judicial recognition of the 'trade mark' and its value. Lord Westbury, for instance, in a pre-registration decision described a trade mark as '[…] a brand which has reputation and currency in the market as a well-known sign of quality; and that, as such, the trade mark is a valuable property […] and may be properly sold with the works'.[9] The notion that a manufacturer who places on his goods a particular mark can prevent others from using the same mark to sell similar goods similarly appeared for the first time in American jurisprudence in the middle of the nineteenth century.[10]

6.2   TOWARDS A MODERN ERA

Phillips notes astutely that:

> Trade mark law and practice as we know it today more or less started afresh in the mid-1990s, with the establishment of the internationally accepted TRIPS norms, the implementation of the Community trade mark and Madrid Protocol systems, and the introduction of Federal anti-dilution laws in the United States.[11]

---

[6] Ibid., 811. *Blanchard v. Hill* (1742) 2 Atk 485, which was probably one of the earliest recorded trade mark infringement actions brought before an equity court.

[7] *Perry v. Truefitt* (1842) 6 Beav 66; 49 ER 749.

[8] Trade Mark Registration Act 1875 which gave the registered proprietor the right to the exclusive use of the mark in respect of the specified goods.

[9] *Hall v. Barrows* (1863) 4 De GJ & S 150; 12 WR 322.

[10] *Thomson v. Winchester*, although the court did not use the word 'trademark', relying instead on the general tort of fraud, 36 Mass (19 Pick) 214 (Sup Ct, 1873).

[11] J. Phillips, *Trade Mark Law: A Practical Anatomy* (Oxford University Press, 2003), 14. The relevant instruments Phillips refers to are Directive 89/104/EEC on trade marks, 21 December 1988; Community Regulation EC No. 40/94 on the Community Trade Mark, 20 December 1993 that have recently been amended by the EU trade marks reform package; and the Protocol relating to the Madrid Agreement concerning International Registration of Marks 1989. For discussion on anti-dilution laws in the US and elsewhere, see I.R. Simon Fhima, *Trade Mark Dilution in Europe and the United States* (Oxford University Press, 2011).

The Paris Convention for the Protection of Industrial Property (see Chapter 2) provides international protection for industrial property including trade mark rights. In relation to trade marks, service marks, trade names and well-known marks, the Convention extends its rules on national treatment and priority rules. This is also extended to the protection of marketers against unfair competition and the protection of flags and armorial bearings. All countries that are parties to TRIPS have national registration systems for trade marks. The procedural aspects of applying for registration vary from country to country, and below we set out the salient points under the European Union registration system and the international Madrid/ Protocol system.

6.2.1   EU trade mark registration

The EU Trade Mark Regulation (EUTMR; until recently the Community Trade Mark Regulation)[12] establishes a unitary right that has equal effect throughout the territory of the European Union. The EU Trade Mark (EUTM) can be registered, transferred, surrendered or revoked only for the whole European Union. Registration is made with a single application to the EU Intellectual Property Office (EUIPO).[13] It is still possible, of course, to obtain national trade mark registration in individual EU member states, but all national trade mark offices and courts are bound by EU laws, and they take into account the decisions of the EUIPO and the European courts.

Applications can be filed in any official language of the EU but must indicate a second language from the five EUIPO languages, namely English, French, German, Italian and Spanish. The applicant is also required to provide for the classes of goods and services that registration is sought for. An international system for categorising groups and services was established in 1957 with the Nice Classification System that provides for 45 groups of goods and services under which applicants can register their trade marks. The Nice classifications provides quite general class headings for the goods and services which led to the question whether an applicant's reference to the general class heading would cover all goods and services under the general group heading. This would potentially widen the scope of protection as goods or services could be covered that the trade mark holder was not intending to use in the course of trade.

The Court of Justice of the European Union (CJEU) decision in *CIPA v. Registrar of Trade Marks* ('*IP Translator*' decision) shed light on this question. It established that 'the goods and services for which the protection of the trade mark is sought (are) to be identified by the applicant with sufficient clarity and precision to enable the competent authorities and economic operators, on that basis alone, to determine the extent of the protection conferred by the trade mark'. The decision

---

[12] The European Trade Mark system as a whole is currently undergoing several changes. The European Parliament passed a Trade Mark reform package on 15 December 2015. For instance, the former Community Trade Mark was renamed into EU Trade Mark to reflect the changes that the Treaty of Lisbon brought.

[13] Pursuant to the changes that the EU trade marks reform package will bring, the former Office for the Harmonisation in the Internal Market (OHIM) that administered the former Community Trade Mark was renamed the European Union Intellectual Property Office (EUIPO) on 23 March 2016.

means that the use of the general class headings was still possible as long as they were as accurate and precise as possible.[14]

The Office examines each application according to certain formalities, entitlement and absolute grounds. The application is published for opposition or observation purposes, and oppositions must be filed within three months following the publication. The decisions of the Office are subject to an appeal before the Board of Appeal, and from there, to EU Courts, i.e., the General Court and the CJEU. For infringement proceedings, jurisdiction is based on the member state of the defendant's domicile or establishment, or the plaintiff's domicile or establishment; and if there is no such state, then jurisdiction is awarded to the Spanish EU Trade Mark Courts. Being a unitary right, decisions on infringement etc. are enforceable throughout the EU without further proceedings.

The EU trade mark framework additionally entails the EU Trade Mark Directive. This instrument was used to harmonise national trade mark laws within the member states of the EU and was recently updated in similar lines as the EU Trade Mark Regulation. The Directive mirrors the provisions of the EU Trade Mark Regulation closely which means that a coherent TM system within the EU and its member states has been established. This is furthermore heightened by the fact that the European courts have jurisdictions over both the Directive and the Regulation.

6.2.2 International registration

The oldest international filing system is the Madrid Agreement for International Registration. The Agreement is an arrangement between some of the members of the International Union aiming to facilitate protection in multiple jurisdictions by providing a common route for obtaining and administering a registration in multiple jurisdictions. 'International Registration' does not result in a common or unitary right but only in a bundle of independent rights arising from registration in each national jurisdiction (rather like the PCT). Despite its age, not many countries are parties to the Agreement, non-parties including the US, Japan and the UK.

The Protocol to the Madrid Agreement, established in 1989, is similar but independent from the Madrid Agreement. The scope of the Protocol is to provide an alternative and more attractive way of routing an application to many destinations. The Protocol is administered by WIPO. International registration will still only provide a bundle of national registrations which are subject to national laws. However, international registration under the Protocol is based either on application or registration in the country of origin, and the applicant must indicate the countries where a territorial extension of the basic registration is being sought. Application is then transferred to the Bureau (that is, WIPO) and following examination and publication, it is communicated to the designated territories. There is a provision which makes the international registration vulnerable to a central attack for a period of five years. However, the owner of the fallen registration has the right to file for an independent registration of the mark in the other territorial offices within a three-month period following cancellation of the international registration and with the priority of the original registration.

---

[14] C-307/10 (19 June 2012) (ECJ), para 64; also see Phillips, *supra* note 11, 45–6.

6.2.3   Rationalising trade marks[15]

Origin

The accepted and traditional role of a trade mark is to act as an 'indicator of origin'. Phillips further notes that trade marks can function in two distinct ways: to identify the actual physical origin of the goods/services; and to guarantee the identity of the origin of the goods/services. The first type relates to the ancient function of trade marks, that is, to designate that goods come from a particular manufacturer. This function, that is, the use of the trade mark to indicate the actual source of the product, has not been accepted by the CJEU as the proper justification of a trade mark. Instead, the Court has opted for the second function as being the sole justification for trade mark protection, that is, 'to guarantee the trade mark as an indication of origin'.[16] The CJEU confirmed and expanded this view:

> Moreover, according to the case-law of the Court, the essential function of a trade mark is to guarantee the identity of the origin of the marked product to the consumer or end-user by enabling him, without any possibility of confusion, to distinguish the product or service from others which have another origin, and for the trade mark to be able to fulfil its essential role in the system of undistorted competition [...] it must offer a guarantee that all the goods or services bearing it have originated under the control of a single undertaking which is responsible for their quality.[17]

Goodwill and quality

The more American perspective of the role of the trade mark is that a trade mark 'is merely one of the visible mediums by which the good will is identified, bought and sold, and known to the public'.[18] Indeed, some have argued that a trade mark is more than a mere symbol of goodwill but rather it is 'an agency for actual creation and perpetuation of goodwill'.[19] Thus, consumers purchase a trade-marked product because it guarantees quality. According to perhaps the most often-cited American trade mark historian, Schechter, the role of the mark is then to 'identify a product as satisfactory and thereby to stimulate further purchases by the consuming public'.[20]

---

[15] For a comprehensive review, see A. Griffiths, *An Economic Perspective on Trademark Law* (Cheltenham: Edward Elgar Publishing, 2011).

[16] Recital (8), EUTMR as amended; and *Hag II*, (1990) CMLR 571, 608 (ECJ).

[17] *Philips Electronics NV v. Remington Consumer Products* [2002] 2 CMLR 1329 (ECJ), para 30; see also Case C-349/95 *Loendersloot* [1997] ECR I-6227, paras 22 and 24; and Case C-39/97 *Canon* [1998] ECR I-5507, para 28; and Case C-206/01 *Arsenal Football Club plc v. Matthew Reed* [2003] ETMR 227 (ECJ), para 48.

[18] *Coca-Cola Bottling Co. v. Coca-Cola Co.*, 269 F 796 (D Del, 1920).

[19] F. Schechter, 'The Rational Basis of Trade Mark Protection' (1927) 40 *Harvard Law Review* 813, 818; H. Norman, 'Schechter's The Rational Basis of Trade Mark Protection Revisited', in N. Dawson and A. Firth (eds), *Trade Marks Retrospective* (Sweet & Maxwell, 2000), 192; S.M. Maniatis, 'Trade Mark Rights: A Justification Based on Property' (2002) 6 *IPQ* 123.

[20] Schechter, ibid.

Communication and advertising

Trade marks serve not only to identify and differentiate products in the marketplace, but also to differentiate their purchasers or wearers. Trade marks have become 'fashion statements'.[21] Trade marks can convey a variety of messages and information to the consumer, and to the public. 'Fashion trade marks do much more than simply indicate the origin or quality of manufactured products. They enable consumers to buy goods that speak to the world and declare: "this is the sort of person I am"'.[22]

Indeed, modern business itself has cynically utilised this ability of a trade mark to be a conveyor and purveyor of lifestyle messages and has transformed them into sales rhetoric. Nike, for example, owes its enormous success not only to the performance of its shoes but to its apparent allegiance to 'young' values and the firm has done much to enhance this creed, which includes embracing politically correct language in relation to its manufacturing methods. The same applies, uncynically one hopes, to trade marks such as Fair Trade and Cafédirect which constantly emphasise 'fair' trading practices. The packaging of both brands of coffee positively glow with philanthropic maxims including the following: 'A better deal for coffee growers'; 'Guarantees a better deal for Third World Producers'; 'All Cafédirect growers are always paid a good minimum price to cover the cost of production however low the international market falls'.

Competition and investment

A primary economic role of the trade mark is to enable competitors to guard against unfair trading or competition. Consumers rely on trade mark law to protect the distinctive power of the mark so that it can convey information in a more efficient manner. The market as a whole relies on the law to regulate the use of trade marks so as to protect against confusion in the marketplace which would severely compromise consumer choice. Trade mark owners also rely on trade mark law to prevent other competitors misappropriating or tarnishing their business goodwill. Trade mark law in Europe may now even extend to not just protecting the trade mark as such but moreover the 'brand' behind the mark.[23]

The traditional 'indicator of origin' function sets down merely one parameter of trade mark law. If one investigates EU trade mark law, for instance, one can find that the Trade Mark Directive is replete with provisions which operate to protect the marketplace, including the rights of other market traders vis-à-vis a trade mark owner, rather than being solely concerned with protecting the trade mark owner against diminution of goodwill caused by confusion. After all, trade mark theory constantly emphasises that protection is necessary to correct the market failure which may

---

[21] Phillips, *supra* note 11, 27.

[22] Ibid.

[23] The CJEU decision in *L'Oréal v. Bellure* [2010] RPC 1 arguably extended trade mark protection to brand value which has been criticised. See, for instance, D. Gangjee and R. Burell, 'Because You're Worth It: L'Oréal and the Prohibition on Free Riding' (2010) 2 *Modern Law Review* 282–304; and L. McDonagh, 'From Brand Performance to Consumer Performativity: Assessing European Trade Mark Law after the Rise of Anthropological Marketing' (2015) 4 *Journal of Law and Society* 611–36.

result if one allows others to misappropriate distinctive signs.[24] A final succinct restatement of the function of the trade mark system is proffered by Phillips. He states that the function in every developed economy is to establish an equilibrium of creative tension between the following interests: trade marks owners, competitors and other non-competing market players, and finally consumers of both the trade-marked goods, and other consumers.[25]

6.3   PROTECTABLE SUBJECT MATTER

There are many advantages to gaining trade mark protection including the fact that the term of protection is theoretically infinite and the criterion of protection can be perceived to be less onerous than that under copyright, patent and some of the *sui generis* laws. This chapter concentrates on European trade mark law for two reasons. First, the legislation is analogous to the TRIPS Agreement in certain core definitions (subject matter and scope of protection). Second, this regional jurisdiction has seen an incredible amount of jurisprudence emanating from the CJEU in the last 15 or more years and reveals a complex and fluctuating area of policy and law.[26] Where relevant and deemed interesting, reference is also made to US trademark[27] law.

6.3.1   Definition

Trade mark law, as governed by the EU Trade Mark Regulation and Directive, adopts an expansive notion of trade mark:

> Any signs, in particular words, including personal names, or designs, letters, numerals, colours, the shape of goods or of the packaging of goods, or sounds, provided that such signs are capable of distinguishing the goods or services of one undertaking from those of other undertakings; and being represented on the Register of European Union trade marks, ('the Register'), in a manner which enables the competent authorities and the public to determine the clear and precise subject matter of the protection afforded to its proprietor.[28]

---

[24] U. Suthersanen, 'The European Court of Justice in Philips v. Remington – Trade Marks and Market Freedom' (2003) 7 *IPQ* 257; W.M. Landes and R.A. Posner, *The Economic Structure of Intellectual Property Law* (Belknap Press/Harvard University Press, 2003), Chapter 7; A. Kur, 'Trade Marks Function, and Don't They? CJEU Jurisprudence and Unfair Competition Principles' (2014) 45 *IIC* 434.

[25] Phillips, *supra* note 11, 32.

[26] A. von Mühlendahl et al., *Trade Marks in Europe: A Practical Jurisprudence* (3rd ed., Oxford University Press, 2016).

[27] Note that the term used in the US is 'trademark', while in the UK and Europe we use 'trade mark'. TRIPS and the relevant WIPO treaties follow the US in this regard.

[28] EU Trade Marks Directive, Art 3; Directive of the European Parliament and of the Council of 16 December 2015 to Approximate the Laws of the Member States Relating to Trade Marks (2015/2436/EU); Council Regulation (EC) No 207/2009 of 26 February 2009 on the European Union Trade Mark (as amended), Art 4.

A similarly wide definition is available under Article 15, TRIPS Agreement:

> Any sign, or any combination of signs, capable of distinguishing the goods or services of one undertaking from those of other undertakings, shall be capable of constituting a trademark. Such signs, in particular words including personal names, letters, numerals, figurative elements and combinations of colours as well as any combination of such signs, shall be eligible for registration as trademarks. Where signs are not inherently capable of distinguishing the relevant goods or services, Members may make registrability depend on distinctiveness acquired through use. Members may require, as a condition of registration, that signs be visually perceptible.

From both definitions, it is clear that trade mark protection is not limited to names or visual signs or even three-dimensional shapes, but also includes any sensory marks which are perceptible to the human senses such as olfactory and aural signs. Examples of protected trade marks include the three-dimensional shape of chairs, the colours used on drugs, shoes and chocolates, the sound of advertising jingles or roaring animals, and the scent of perfumes and toothbrushes.

It should be noted that some laws, such as the EU trade mark regime, require some form of representation of the trade mark. This criterion is not compulsory under the TRIPS Agreement.[29] Until recently, the sign had to be capable of being represented graphically under EU trade mark law. This is rather similar to the fixation criterion as required in some countries. Initially, the former graphical representation requirement used to be less onerous bearing in mind that 'exotic' or 'non-traditional' marks such as smell marks were registered. In one tribunal decision, it was held that the description of the mark as 'the smell of fresh cut grass' in relation to tennis balls was an adequate representation of the mark.[30] However, this practice was made obsolete with the *Siekmann* decision of the CJEU.[31] In that decision, the applicant wished to register an olfactory mark which was described as 'balsamically fruity with a slight hint of cinnamon'. The CJEU held that graphical representation required a sign to be clear, precise, self-contained, easily accessible, intelligible, durable and objective. These seven criteria became to be known as the 'Siekmann 7'. The *Siekmann* decision ultimately made it more difficult for exotic trade marks such as smells, taste and sound marks to overcome the threshold of 'graphical representation'. A description of the smell was held not to be sufficiently clear, precise and objective.[32] In relation to sound marks, the graphic representation of sounds must be made either by musical notation (with stave, clef, notes and rests), or by a sonogram with a timescale and a frequency scale.[33] In this line, OHIM has been accepting mp3 files for sound marks since 2005.[34]

---

[29] TRIPS Agreement, Art 15.

[30] *Vennootschap Onder Firma Senta Aromatic Marketing's Application*, [1999] ETMR 429 (OHIM – Second Board of Appeal).

[31] Case C - 273/00 *Ralf Sieckmann v. Deutsches Patent und Markenamt* 12 December 2002.

[32] Ibid., para 70.

[33] Case R-781/1999–4 *Metro Goldwyn-Mayer Lion Corp's Application* [2004] ETMR 24 (roar of a lion); *Shield Mark* [2004] ETMR 33 (first nine notes of Ludwig van Beethovens 'Für Elise').

[34] *Decision No EX-05-3*, 10 October 2005 (concerning electronic filing of sound marks) available at http://oami.europa.eu/en/office/aspects/pdf/ex05-3.pdf.

The aforementioned EU trade marks reform package, however, deleted the graphical representation requirement from the Regulation and the Directive. It will from now on suffice for the sign to be 'represented on the register in a manner which enables the competent authorities and the public to determine the clear and precise subject matter of the protection afforded to its proprietor'.[35] This will arguably make the registration of exotic trade marks in Europe significantly easier.

6.3.2   Criteria of protection and excluded subject matter

First, there are absolute legal bars, meaning legal thresholds that exclude marks inherently not distinctive, and those that cannot be protected on public interest grounds. In most cases, however, a trade mark can overcome the absolute bar if its owner shows that the mark has acquired distinctiveness through actual use. This means that consumers have become accustomed to associate the trade mark with a particular producer over the years. A simple yet classic example is the word 'Apple': 'apple' used on a box containing apples would have a descriptive meaning, and would not be allowed as a trade mark; 'Apple' printed on a computer has acquired a distinctive and trade mark meaning, and denotes the source of the computer. Second, EU trade mark law sets out relative legal bars which are thresholds that exclude inherently distinctive trade marks which nevertheless cannot be protected because they conflict with an earlier mark or sign which belongs to another trader. In brief, the absolute legal bars exclude five categories of trade marks, which we will look at in turn:

- marks which are devoid of any distinctive character;
- marks which are descriptive;
- marks which are generic;
- marks which comprise certain types of shapes;
- marks which are refused on general grounds of morality and public policy.

In order to fulfil its function as a trade mark, the sign must be capable of distinguishing goods and services; that is, the mark must have 'distinctive character'. Under EU trade mark law, the distinctiveness of a mark depends, to a certain extent, on what marks are barred from trade mark protection as they are deemed not to be able to work as trade marks. EU trade mark law generally discards such marks which are devoid of distinctive character, that are descriptive or generic. These three categories should be seen to be elaborations of the general notion that a mark should be distinctive to be protected as a trade mark.

Devoid of distinctive character
The first absolute bar under the European law is that a trade mark must not be 'devoid of any distinctive character'.[36] The CJEU has interpreted it to mean that all trade marks 'must be capable of identifying the product as originating from a particular undertaking and thus distinguishing it

---

[35] EUTMR, Art 4(b).

[36] Phillips, *supra* note 11, 86–98.

from other undertakings'.[37] A more wordy explanation was offered by the British court in relation to the equivalent provision within the UK Trade Marks Act 1994:[38]

> What does devoid of any distinctive character mean? I think the phrase requires consideration of the mark on its own, assuming no use. Is it the sort of word (or other sign) which cannot do the job of distinguishing without first educating the public that it is a trade mark? A meaningless word or a word inappropriate for the goods concerned ('North Pole' for bananas) can clearly do. But a common laudatory word such as 'Treat' is, absent use and recognition as a trade mark in itself [...] devoid of any inherently distinctive character.

Single letters, numbers, and colours per se without any unusual or fanciful features generally would be devoid of any distinctive character, since they are considered to be in the public domain and form part of the store of signs available to all traders.[39] Furthermore, the relevant average consumers would perceive signs such as colours or shapes rather to be of decorative or appealing nature and not necessarily to designate origin.[40]

A sign is devoid if it is 'commonly used in trade in connection with the presentation of goods or services or in respect of which they could be used in that way', as such a sign will not enable consumers to distinguish the goods or services.[41] Another example is the mark AD2000, which was rejected on the ground that it was devoid of any distinctive character. It was held that although an idiosyncratic combination of letters and figures might well possess a distinctive character, the term 'AD2000' was not an idiosyncratic combination as most people when seeing or hearing the mark would think of the year. In the court's view, a sign possessed distinctive character when it was endowed either by 'nature' or 'nurture' with the capacity to communicate the fact that the goods are those of a particular undertaking.[42]

Descriptive marks

The second absolute legal bar to registration is in respect to trade marks which consist exclusively of signs or indications which may serve in trade to designate the kind, quality, quantity, intended purpose, value, geographical origin, time of production of the goods or of rendering of the service, or other characteristics of the goods or service (descriptive marks).[43] The policy rationale is

---

[37] Joined Cases C-53/01, C-54/01, C-55/01 *Linde AG, Winward Industries, Rado Watch Co Ltd* [2003] ETMR 963, para 47.

[38] *British Sugar plc v. James Robertson & Sons Ltd* [1996] RPC 281.

[39] *Ty-Nant Spring Water Ltd's Trade Mark Application* [1999] ETMR 974, OHIM, Third BoA.

[40] Case C-144/06 P *Henkel* ECLI:EU:C:2007:577, para 36, in relation to shape marks:

> Average consumers are not in the habit of making assumptions about the origin of products on the basis of their shape or the shape of their packaging in the absence of any graphic or word element, and it could therefore prove more difficult to establish distinctiveness in relation to such a three-dimensional mark than in relation to a word or figurative mark.

[41] Case T-79/00 *Rewe-Zentral v. OHIM (Lite)* [2002] ECR II-705.

[42] *Allied Domecq plc's Application: AD2000 Trade Mark* (1997) RPC 168.

[43] EUTMR, Art 7(1)(c).

clear: other traders need to access such words in order to describe their own goods and services, unless there is convincing evidence that the market has attached a secondary meaning to the word. Examples of descriptive terms which would be denied protection, unless there is evidence of acquired distinctiveness, include: (i) terms indicating kind, quality or quantity of the goods or services such as 'best', 'good', or 'Frootloops' for cereal preparations containing fruits; (ii) terms informing the intended purpose of the product such as 'Get Thin' for weight loss products or 'Biomild' for yoghurt being mild and organic; (iii) terms indicating value such as 'Bargain' or 'Super'; (iv) terms indicating geographical origin of the product or service such as 'Argentine Beef' for butchers;[44] and (v) terms indicating the time of production of goods or rendering of services such as '24-hour online'. The EUIPO has further special guidance in relation to language and transliterations in relation to the official EU languages (for example, excluded Greek words would extend to Latin characteristics, or Cyrillic alphabet).[45]

A key decision in this area from the CJEU is the *Windsurfing Chiemsee* decision.[46] The key issue was whether a local company, called Windsurfing Chiemsee, based at a location close to Chiemsee, the largest lake in Bavaria, could be allowed to claim the word 'Chiemsee', which was used on its clothing, and which was part of its registered graphic trade mark. The defendants sold similar goods in a town situated near the shores of the Chiemsee lake, and its goods also bore the designation 'Chiemsee', but it was depicted in a different graphic form from that of the trade marks which identified Windsurfing Chiemsee's products. The defendants contended that the word 'Chiemsee' was an indication which designates geographical origin and must consequently remain available to all traders operating in that region and should not be capable of protection. The CJEU held that the underlying purpose of the trade mark law was to ensure that geographical names remained available for use by all:

> [...] it is in the public interest that they remain available, not least because they may be an indication of the quality and other characteristics of the categories of goods concerned, and may also, in various ways influence consumer tastes by, for instance, associating the goods with a place that may give rise to a favourable response.[47]

There were, the Court held, two exceptions to this rule:

1. Where a geographical name had, through use, become associated with a particular product, and in assessing the extent of distinctive character, the authorities should evaluate all available evidence and were entitled to resort to a national opinion poll in cases of difficulty.

---

[44] Of course, it is open to countries to provide, by way of derogation from this provision, that signs or indications which serve to designate the geographical origin of the goods may constitute collective marks or GIs – see Chapter 8.

[45] *Guidelines for Examination Of European Union Trade Marks*, EUIPO, Part B Examination Section 4, Chapter 4 Descriptive Trade Marks Article 7(1)(C) EUTMR, 01/10/2017.

[46] Joined Cases C108/97 and C109/97 *Windsurfing Chiemsee Produktions und Vertriebs GmbH v. Boots und Segelzubehör Walter Huber; and v. Attenberger* [1999] ETMR 585.

[47] Ibid., para 35.

2. Where there was currently no association in the minds of the average consumer with the name in question, and in assessing this, one could take into account the extent of familiarity with the name among the appropriate class of persons, characteristics of the place identified by the name, and the nature of the goods.

This area of law is in a state of confusion which, according to some writers, is the result of a series of decisions by the CJEU. The subsequent CJEU case was *Procter & Gamble Co. v. OHIM (Baby Dry)*[48] where the Court held that the term 'Baby Dry' was registrable and not descriptive of the essential characteristics of goods in question which were disposable nappies. Despite the fact that the words 'Baby Dry' were partly descriptive of one of the essential characteristics of the goods (that is, nappies keep a baby dry), the CJEU upheld the registration of 'Baby Dry' as a trade mark for nappies because of the 'unusual syntactical juxtaposition' of the words Baby and Dry, adding that it was not a normal way for English speakers to refer to nappies. In a subsequent decision, *OHIM v. Wrigley (Doublemint)*,[49] the CJEU held that 'Doublemint' was a purely descriptive mark. Confusingly, the Court held that although 'Double' and 'Mint' in combination gave rise to a variety of possible meanings, the resultant word was descriptive. The Court referred to the public interest basis of the provision, citing the *Windsurfing* decision as stating the authoritative position, and failed to mention the *Baby Dry* decision.[50]

Generic marks

The third absolute bar denies registration to trade marks which consist exclusively of signs or indications which have become customary in the current language or in the bona fide and established practices of trade.[51] Examples include '4 Star ****' for brandy or hotels, or the picture of grapes for wine. The reasoning is that such generic marks do not allow the 'relevant public to repeat the experience of a purchase, if it proves to be positive, or to avoid it, if it proves to be negative, on the occasion of a subsequent acquisition of the goods or services concerned'.[52] Sometimes, a trade mark can lose its distinctiveness and be expunged from the trade mark register due to 'genericide', namely the loss of trade mark through uncontrolled over-use. More famous examples include aspirin, heroin (both ex-Bayer registered marks for drugs), Monopoly (ex-Parker Brothers registered mark), cornflakes, escalator, linoleum, yo-yo – all of which have inadvertently entered the public domain in most countries.[53] The basic warning for trade mark owners is that they have to play a proactive role in ensuring that their mark does not fall into public usage, as the perception of the end-user is the decisive factor.[54]

---

[48] Case C-383/99 P, (2002) ETMR (3) 22.

[49] Case C-191/01P, (2003) ETMR (88) 1068.

[50] J. Davis, 'The Need to Leave Free for Others to Use and the Trade Mark Common', in J. Phillips and I. Simon (eds), *Trade Mark Use* (Oxford: Oxford University Press, 2005), 30–45; Phillips, *supra* note 11, 78–84.

[51] EUTMR, Art 7(1)(d).

[52] *Best Buy Concepts v. OHIM* [2004] ETMR 19 (Court of First Instance). For further discussion, see Phillips, *supra* note 11, 76–8 and 169–87.

[53] J.D. Ingram, 'The Genericide of Trademarks' (2004) 2 *Buffalo Intellectual Property Law Journal* 154.

[54] Case C-409/12 *Backaldrin Österreich The Kornspitz Co GmbH v. Pfahnl Backmittel* GmbH EU:C:2014:130 (CJEU), para 39.

Acquired distinctiveness

Finally, it needs to be borne in mind again that some inherently undistinctive, descriptive or generic marks can acquire distinctiveness through use and be registered according to Article 7(3) EUTMR. This means that the applicant has been successful in 'convincing' consumers that the sign now works as a trade mark, i.e., an indicator of source. This requires that the sign must have been previously used and 'in consequence of such use, [that] the relevant class of persons actually perceive the goods or services, designated exclusively by the mark applied for, as originating from a given undertaking'.[55]

In the *Windsurfing Chiemsee* decision, the CJEU has elaborated that the assessment of whether a sign has acquired distinctiveness can be based on the following factors:

> The market share held by the mark; how intensive, geographically widespread and long-standing use of the mark has been; the amount invested by the undertaking in promoting the mark; the proportion of the relevant class of persons who, because of the mark, identify goods as originating from a particular undertaking; and statements from chambers of commerce and industry or other trade and professional associations.[56]

This means that marks which are inherently devoid of distinctive character, descriptive or generic can be registered albeit not being inherently distinctive. However, signs that are immoral or shapes which are functional (discussed below) cannot be saved by acquired distinctiveness. It would be against the respective policy consideration if such marks could be rendered registrable through acquired distinctiveness.

Functional marks

Under Article 7(1)(e), EU Trade Mark Regulation (CTMR), a sign will not be registered as a trade mark if it consists exclusively of:

(i)   the shape, or another characteristic, which results from the nature of the goods themselves;

(ii)   the shape, or another characteristic, of goods which is necessary to obtain a technical result (for example, the head of a screwdriver; the shape of a ball; the shape of a wheel);

(iii) the shape, or another characteristic, which gives substantial value to the goods (for example, an elaborate bottle for perfume).

Article 7(1)(e), EUTMR acts as a bastion of control for shape marks. What is its *raison d'être*? One simple explanation is that the legislature constructed this provision so as to minimise areas of cumulative protection between patent, design and trade mark laws, and part of the role of this clause is to prevent trade mark proprietors obtaining permanent monopolies in functional engineering

---

[55] Case C-215/14 *Société des Produits Nestlé SA v. Cadbury UK Ltd* (2015) ECLI:EU:C:2015:604, para 64.

[56] *Windsurfing Chiemsee, supra* note 46, para 51.

designs and shapes. However, in *Philips v. Remington*,[57] the CJEU held that the rationale of this exclusion is to prevent anti-competitive protection in relation to 'technical solutions' or 'functional characteristics of a product'.[58] The exclusion of functional shapes in European trade mark law is intended to:

> [...] prevent the protection conferred by the trade mark right from being extended, beyond signs which serve to distinguish a product or service from those offered by competitors, so as to form an obstacle preventing competitors from freely offering for sale products incorporating such technical solutions or functional characteristics in competition with the proprietor of the trade mark.[59]

Article 7(1)(e)(i) EUTMR bars trade marks that exclusively consist shapes or another characteristic from being protected where these would result from the nature of the goods themselves. This exclusion appeared to be barring such characteristics produced by nature.[60] However, this provision brought some difficulties when the characteristics of the object in question were designed by man, i.e., not by nature. It could then be argued that this exclusion would only apply when the designer had no real alternative in creating the shape as it was only then resulting from the nature of the goods.

The CJEU has recently given some guidance to this issue in *Hauck GmbH & Co. KG v. Stokke A/S*.[61] The case involved the famous Tripp Trapp chair for children. The Court held that the first indent should not only apply to such shapes or characteristics provided by nature or are the result of legal standard setting.[62] It rather held that 'shape which results from the nature of the goods themselves' means that shapes with essential characteristics *which are inherent to the generic function or functions of such goods must*, in principle, [must] also be denied registration' (emphasis added).[63]

The first indent of Article 7(1)(e) relates very much to the second one that excludes such trade marks that consist exclusively of shapes or characteristics that are necessary to obtain a technical result. There, the question of how alternative shapes that have the same technical effect could render the shape in question not exclusively having such effect was raised and was a main point in *Philips Electronics*, discussed above. The Court, however, held that the fact that alternative shapes existed would not on its own suffice to overcome the exclusion of Article 7(1)(e)(iii).[64] The *LEGO* decision

---

[57] *Philips Electronics NV v. Remington Consumer Products*, [1998] RPC 283 (UK EWHC); [1999] RPC 809 (UK EWCA); [2002] CMLR 1329 (AGO and ECJ); cf *Ide Line AG v. Philips Electronics NV* (1997) ETMR 377 (Swedish District Ct.); U. Suthersanen, 'The European Court of Justice in Philips v. Remington – Trade Marks and Market Freedom' [2003] 3 *IPQ* 257.

[58] Recently reaffirmed by the CJEU in: Case C-30/15 P *Simba Toys GmbH & Co KG v. EUIPO* [2016], para 39.

[59] *Philips Electronics NV, supra* note 57, para 78.

[60] Lord Aldous referred to the shape of a banana as an example of shapes resulting from the nature of goods. *Philips v. Remington* [1999] RPC 809, 820 (UK).

[61] Case C-205/13 *Hauck GmbH & Co KG v. Stokke A/S, Stokke Nederland BV, Peter Opsvik and Peter Opsvik A/S*.

[62] Ibid., para 24.

[63] Ibid., para 25.

[64] *Philips Electronics NV, supra* note 57, para 81.

by the CJEU further stipulates that the existence of previous patent protection for the shape in question could be an indicator of the functionality of the shape.[65] While Article 7(1)(e) seeks to bar registration of shapes as trade marks that are the result of the nature of the goods and that serve the function of the product, it also renders shapes unregistrable which give substantial value to the object. The General Court has held that iconic loudspeakers of the Danish firm Bang & Olufsen fall within Article 7(1)(e) (iii) EUTMR.[66] The Court held that the specific shape was emphasised by the applicant himself and was used in advertising, hence giving substantial value to the shape.

Public interest

Additionally, marks can be refused protection due to general public interest reasons, namely: (i) the mark is contrary to public policy or accepted principles of morality; or (ii) the mark is of such a nature as to deceive the public (for instance as to nature, quality or geographical origin of goods); or (iii) the mark comprises a specially protected emblem.[67] Thus, the word 'Orwoola' for woollen goods may be excluded on the specific ground that it is descriptive, and also on the more public interest ground that the mark would be deceptive if the goods were not 100 per cent wool. Another example is 'Eurolamb' which was refused registration on the ground that it was deceptive if the meat originated outside Europe, and descriptive should the meat actually come from Europe. Similarly, if the meat was not lamb, then 'Lamb' was deceptive, and if it was, the term was descriptive![68]

Relative grounds for refusal

Distinctive trade marks that have overcome the statutory bars that the absolute grounds for refusal provide but nevertheless conflict with earlier trade marks or with any other rights which exist in the sign may be declared invalid. In contrast to absolute grounds discussed above, relative grounds are not examined *ex ante* by the EUIPO. After publication of the registration of a trade mark an opposition proceeding can be initiated before the Office challenging the registration of the trade mark. This is meant to make the registration process swifter and cheaper while right holders of earlier trade marks are in a better position to 'police' registrations which conflict with their rights. Such conflict with earlier rights may occur where the subsequently registered sign:

- is identical to an earlier registered mark, in relation to identical goods; or
- is identical or similar to an earlier registered mark, in relation to identical or similar goods, and if there is confusion including a likelihood of association;
- is identical or similar to a registered famous mark, in respect of either similar or dissimilar goods, and if unfair advantage is taken of or is detrimental to the distinctive character or repute of the famous mark (anti-dilution).[69]

---

[65] Case C-48/09 P, *Lego Juris v. OHIM* [2010] ECR I-8403, para 85.

[66] Case T-508/08 *Bang & Olufsen v. OHIM*, General Court, 6 October 2011.

[67] EUTMR, Art 7(1)(f)–(e). Where a trade mark has been registered in bad faith it can be declared invalid pursuant to Art 52 EUTMR.

[68] *BOCM Pauls Ltd and Scottish Agricultural College's Application* [1997] ETMR 420; Phillips, *supra* note 11, 67–73.

[69] EUTMR, Art 8 (1), (5).

The relative grounds for refusal mirror the provisions dealing with trade mark infringement, and thus Article 8 EUTMR is analogous to Article 9 EUTMR on infringement. Thus, most of the discussion in the next section is applicable here.

6.4   SCOPE OF PROTECTION AND DURATION

Article 16(1), TRIPS Agreement states the following in relation to the scope of trade mark protection:

> The owner of a registered trademark shall have the exclusive right to prevent all third parties not having the owner's consent from *using* in the course of trade identical or similar signs for goods or services which are *identical or similar* to those in respect of which the trademark is registered where such use would result in a *likelihood of confusion*. In case of the use of an identical sign for identical goods or services, a likelihood of confusion shall be presumed. The rights described above shall not prejudice any existing prior rights, nor shall they affect the possibility of Members making rights available on the basis of use. (Emphasis added)

As is clear from the italicised terms in the paragraphs above, the TRIPS provision is analogous to the scope of protection offered under Article 9 (2) EUTMR where the trade mark proprietor has the right to prohibit anyone who in the course of trade uses:

(i)   a sign which is identical with an earlier trade mark in relation to goods or services which are identical with those for which it is registered (double identity);

(ii) a sign which is identical with or similar to an earlier trade mark and is used in relation to goods or services similar to those for which the earlier mark is registered, and there exists a likelihood of confusion on the part of the public (confusing similarities).

Thus, these are the key elements in two different scenarios:

- double identity, where one must show unauthorised use of an identical mark on identical goods;
- confusing similarities, where one must show unauthorised use of an identical/similar mark on identical/similar goods,[70] and a likelihood of confusion.[71]

---

[70] As mentioned above, trade mark registration for a mark is conferred in relation to one or several classes of goods or services. Importantly, trade mark protection does not confer protection against unauthorised use of the mark for all types of goods, or in all areas of commerce. In normal cases, trade mark protection is likely to be limited by the class of goods or services for which the mark has been registered for. In infringement cases, courts will compare the goods used by the defendants to the goods specified by the trade mark registration.

[71] This criterion is missing in double identity cases because the legislator wanted to provide absolute protection in double identity cases, i.e., the clear-cut counterfeit cases (see Recital (8) EUTMR).

The following discussion focuses on European case law in order to give a bird's eye view of the law, and a flavour of the increasing complexity in this area. It should briefly be noted that the term of protection for trade marks is very dependent on individual countries. Under Article 18 TRIPS, the minimum term of protection is a term of no less than seven years, with the registration being renewable indefinitely.

6.4.1   Trade mark infringement

Trade mark infringement occurs when there has been unauthorised use of a sign. What does 'use' actually signify? There are no guidelines within the TRIPS Agreement though the European legislation does offer a non-exhaustive list of activities that can constitute unauthorised use:

(a)   affixing the sign to the goods or to the packaging thereof;
(b)   offering the goods, putting them on the market, or stocking them for those purposes under the sign, or offering or supplying services thereunder;
(c)   importing or exporting the goods under the sign;
(d)   using the sign as a trade or company name or part of a trade or company name;
(e)   using the sign on business papers and in advertising;
(f)   using the sign in comparative advertising in a manner that is contrary to Directive 2006/114/ EC of the European Parliament and of the Council.[72]

Other types of unauthorised uses which would probably constitute infringement of the mark include use of a mark on a website, applying to register another's trade mark, and even invisible use such as use of the mark in a metatag.[73] The CJEU, for instance, has held that advertisers using the Google AdWord function may be liable for trade mark infringement.[74]

Use in the course of trade

A trade mark is only infringed if there is unauthorised use 'in the course of trade'. In *Arsenal v. Reed*,[75] the famous football club, said to be quite popular in certain parts of North London, owned several trade marks including 'Arsenal' and 'Arsenal Gunners' in respect of articles of clothing and sports-wear. Mr Matthew Reed sold several items of clothing, including scarves, bearing these marks, with a disclaimer located at his stall that certain products were not official merchandise of the club. One argument was that these marks were badges of support, loyalty and affiliation, and did not indicate the trade origin of the merchandise; hence, it could be said that Reed's use

---

[72] EUTMR, Art 9(3), as amended.

[73] See generally Phillips, *supra* note 11, Chapters 7 and 17.

[74] C-236/08, C-237/08 and C-238/08 *Google France v. Louis Vuitton; GF v. Viaticum; GF v. CNRRH* [2010] ETMR 30. Such AdWords are paid advertisements which are displayed next to or above the search results as so-called 'sponsored links' when Google users type the keyword into the search engine bar.

[75] Case C-206/01 *Arsenal Football Club plc v. Matthew Reed* [2002] ETMR 227 (ECJ).

of the signs was non-trade mark use.[76] The CJEU rejected this view and instead held that the use of Arsenal's marks by Reed was such as to create the impression that there was a 'clear possibility' that some consumers would draw a link, in the course of trade, between the goods concerned and the trade mark proprietor. This was so despite the disclaimers on Reed's stall that the goods were not all Arsenal official merchandise. Rather the CJEU focused on the issue that some consumer may come across the goods away from the stall which rendering the disclaimer futile.[77] The Court therefore found that a post-sale confusion of consumers as to the origin of the goods bearing the sign may occur.

The case was remanded back to the UK courts. The first instance judge, despite the clear line given by the CJEU, chose nonetheless to find Reed not guilty of trade mark infringement on the grounds of non-trade mark use, holding that only trade mark use can constitute an infringing 'use' of a trade mark. On appeal to the UK Court of Appeal, it was held that this was an erroneous application of the CJEU's guidelines, and that registration of a trade mark gave the proprietor a property right, and not merely a right to stop 'trade mark use'. As long as the unauthorised 'use' jeopardised the essential function of the trade mark (i.e., as a guarantee of origin of the merchandise), such use would constitute unlawful use.[78]

In the subsequent case of *Opel v. Autec*,[79] the CJEU has held that the origin function may not be affected where the defendant's use was only decorative. Opel, the car manufacturer, registered its logo for toys and objected to the Autec's use of its logo for an Opel scale model car. The Court, however, held that the origin function would not be affected where the relevant public would 'not perceive the sign identical to the Opel logo appearing on the scale models marketed by Autec as an indication that those products come from Adam Opel or an undertaking economically linked to it'.[80]

Double identity

In the English case *British Sugar v. Robertson*,[81] the claimant had registered the mark 'Treat' for dessert sauces and syrups, whereas the defendant made and sold a toffee-flavoured spread called 'Robertson's Toffee Treat'. The primary issue was whether the Robertson product was a dessert sauce/syrup, and hence identical to the claimant's goods, or was it a spread? It was held that the 'Toffee Treat' was not a dessert sauce or syrup, but it was a 'jam', as it was packed in jam jars and supermarkets regarded it as a spread rather than as a dessert. The Court suggested several factors which would be useful in gauging whether products were identical: the respective uses and users

---

[76] This was the holding of the first instance court – *Arsenal Football Club plc v. Matthew Reed* [2001] ETMR 77.

[77] *Arsenal v. Reed*, para 57.

[78] *Arsenal Football Club plc v. Matthew Reed* [2002] EWHC 2695 (Ch); [2003] EWCA 696. See R. Sumroy and C. Badger, 'Infringing "Use in the Course of Trade": Trade Mark Use and the Essential Function of a Trade Mark', in Phillips and Simon, *supra* note 50, 163–80.

[79] Case C-48/05 *Adam Opel AG v. Autec AG* [2007] ECR I-1017 (ECJ).

[80] Ibid., para 24. The CJEU followed the explanation by the referring court that the relevant consumers would be used to scale model cars and would place extreme importance to the absolute fidelity to the original. This would not create consumer confusion as to the origin of the replica cars.

[81] (1996) RPC 281.

of the respective goods or services; the physical nature of the goods or acts of services; the respective trade channels through which the goods or services reach the market; and the extent to which the respective goods or services are competitive.

In the more recent English decision of *Supreme Petfoods v. Henry Bell & Co*,[82] the court trawled through all the more recent decisions emanating from the CJEU before categorising the following types of factors and uses under the 'double identity' scenario:

1. Six conditions must be shown for the scenario to apply: (i) there must be use of a sign by a third party within the relevant territory; (ii) the use must be in the course of trade; (iii) it must be without the consent of the proprietor of the trade mark; (iv) it must be of a sign which is identical to the trade mark; (v) it must be in relation to goods or services which are identical to those for which the trade mark is registered; and (vi) it must affect, or be liable to affect, one of the functions of the trade mark.[83]

2. Normal cases, namely the defendant uses the identical mark in relation to the same goods, and it is presumed to lead to confusion. In these cases, strong protection is important for trade mark owners against counterfeiting (see *Arsenal v. Reed* discussed above). This particular use interferes with the origin function of the trade mark; however, it may not necessarily interfere with the other functions of a trade mark (for example, quality, communication, investment and advertising).

3. Exhaustion of rights cases, where the trade mark owner is battling against imports from outside the EEA, and where the defendant's use does not necessarily interfere with any trade mark function other than it is the rights holders' prerogative to decide where to first release trade marked goods.

4. Honest concurrent use cases, where there is no adverse effect on the origin function, though there may be detrimental effects on the other functions. In any event, the defendant has to prove that he is entitled to use.

5. Keyword advertising cases, where the origin function of the mark is adversely affected.

Confusing similarities

In *Sabel v. Puma*,[84] Puma were registered proprietors of two pictorial trade marks depicting large cats in various bounding and leaping positions. The mark was registered for leather goods and articles of clothing. Subsequently, Sabel applied to register their mark which depicted a bounding cheetah, with the word 'Sabel' for leather and imitation leather products, and clothing. The CJEU was asked

---

[82] *Supreme Petfoods v. Henry Bell & Co* [2015] EWHC 256 (Ch) – the judgment, albeit 208 paragraphs, is a *tour de force* of the recent CJEU and UK jurisprudence on the functions of trademark, and infringement.

[83] Citing: Case C-206/01 *Arsenal Football plc v. Reed* [2002] ECR I-10273 at para 51; Case C-245/02 *Anheuser-Busch Inc v. Budějovický Budvar np* [2004] I-10989 at para 59; Case C-48/05 *Adam Opel AG v. Autec AG* [2007] ECR I-1017 at paras 18–22; Case C-17/06 *Céline SARL v. Céline SA* [2007] ECR I-7041 at para 16; Case C-62/08 *UDV North America Inc v. Brandtraders NV* [2009] ECR I-1279 at para 42; and Case C-487/07 *L'Oréal SA v. Bellure NV* [2009] ECR I-5185 at paras 58–64.

[84] Case C-251/95 *Sabel BV v. Puma AG, Rudolf Dassler Sport* (1997) ECR I-6191, I-6224.

to determine the scope of trade mark protection, especially in relation to the test for determining the likelihood of confusion. Specifically, would the mere association which the public might make between the two marks, through the idea of a 'bounding feline', justify refusing protection to the 'Sabel' mark for products similar to those on the list of articles covered by Puma's priority mark?

The CJEU held that the test for trade mark protection is whether there is a 'likelihood of confusion' which includes the 'likelihood of association'; the two notions are not alternatives but rather complementary concepts. To find trade mark infringement, some degree of confusion on the part of the public is essential. Moreover, likelihood of confusion should be appreciated globally, taking into account all the factors relevant to the case, such as visual, aural and conceptual similarity of marks. The Court further noted that the ordinary consumer normally perceives the mark as a whole and does not necessarily analyse each element of the mark, adding that the more distinctive and strong the mark, the greater the likelihood of confusion.

This approach was further approved by the CJEU in *Canon Kabushiki Kaisha v. Metro-Goldwyn Meyer*[85] which involved two near-identical marks in relation to similar goods in Germany. Canon was the proprietor of the 'Canon' trade mark in relation to video recorders and cameras, whereas the defendant wanted to register 'Cannon' for video film cassettes. The German Supreme Court noted that the two marks were phonetically equivalent, and that the first registrant, Canon, had a strong market reputation. However, the German Court also noted that, paradoxically, the strong similarity may not result in actual consumer confusion as the German public did not view both sets of goods as deriving from a common source.

The CJEU disagreed, holding that despite a lesser degree of similarity between the goods of the two parties, where the marks are very similar, and where the earlier mark and its reputation is distinctive, the first mark should prevail. Taking a 'global' account of the mark meant that marks with highly distinctive character, either per se or because of their market reputation, enjoyed a broader scope of protection than marks with less distinctive character as already mentioned in *Sabel v. Puma*. Here, the important issue is whether the public believes that the goods come from the same undertaking or from economically linked undertakings, irrespective of the fact that the public is not confused as to the place of production of goods.

In reality, however, the decisions appear rather quixotic. Note the following examples: 'Bud' and 'Budmen' (similar marks); 'Giorgio Aire' and 'Miss Giorgi' (dissimilar); 'Mystery' and 'Mixery' (similar); 'Viagra' and 'Viagrene' (similar); 'Asterix' and 'Starix' (dissimilar); 'Oxbridge' and 'Bridge' (similar).[86] As Bently and Sherman accurately state: 'these counter-examples are a useful reminder that the rulings are fact-specific, so previous decisions are helpful only to provide a sense of the standards being applied; they have virtually no value as precedents'.[87]

---

[85] Case C-39/97 (1999) ETMR 1.

[86] Case T-129/01 *Jose Alejando SL v. OHIM* [2003] ECR II-2251; Case T-156/01 *Laboratoires RTB, SL v. OHIM* [2003] ECR II-2789 (ECJ); Case T – 99/01 *Mystery Drinks GmbH v. OHIM* [2004] ETMR (18) 217; *Pfizer v. Eurofood Link (UK)* [2000] ETMR 187; Case T-311/01 *Les Editions Albert Rene v. OHIM* [2003] ECR II-426; *Dunsford-Wesley v. Manufacturas Antonio Gassol SA*, R310/2000-4. Some of these examples are set out in Bently and Sherman, *supra* note 5, 982–3.

[87] Bently and Sherman, ibid., 983.

6.4.2   Protection of well-known marks

Article 6*bis*, Paris Convention sets out the following:

> (1) The countries of the Union undertake […] to refuse or to cancel the registration, and to prohibit the use, of a trademark which constitutes a reproduction, an imitation, or a translation, liable to create confusion, of a mark considered by the competent authority of the country of registration or use to be *well known* in that country as being already the mark of a person entitled to the benefits of this Convention and used for identical or similar goods. These provisions shall also apply when the essential part of the mark constitutes a reproduction of any such well-known mark or an imitation liable to create confusion therewith. (Emphasis added)

Article 16(2) and (3), TRIPS Agreement augment this scope of protection for well-known marks:

> (2) Article 6bis of the Paris Convention (1967) shall apply, mutatis mutandis, to services. In determining whether a trademark is *well-known*, Members shall take account of the knowledge of the trademark in the relevant sector of the public, including knowledge in the Member concerned which has been obtained as a result of the promotion of the trademark.
>
> (3) Article 6bis of the Paris Convention (1967) shall apply, mutatis mutandis, to goods or services which are *not similar* to those in respect of which a trademark is registered, provided that use of that trademark in relation to those goods or services would indicate a connection between those goods or services and the owner of the registered trademark and provided that the interests of the owner of the registered trademark are likely to be *damaged by* such use. (Emphasis added)

Basically, these TRIPS provisions supplement the protection for well-known marks required by Article 6*bis* of the Paris Convention, and emphasise that the provisions must be applied also to services. Second, it is required that knowledge in the relevant sector of the public acquired not only as a result of the use of the mark but also by other means, including as a result of its promotion, be taken into account. Furthermore, the protection of registered well-known marks must extend to goods or services which are not similar to those in respect of which the trade mark has been registered, provided that its use would indicate a connection between the parties.

Similarly, the EUTMR states that the proprietor of a trade mark with reputation is entitled to prevent all third parties not having his consent from using in the course of trade, in relation to goods or services, any sign where:

> (a) The sign is identical with, or similar to, the EU trade mark irrespective of whether it is used in relation to goods or services which are identical with, similar to or not similar to those for which the EU trade mark is registered, where the latter *has a reputation* in the Union and where use of that sign without due cause *takes unfair advantage of, or is detrimental to*, the distinctive character or the repute of the EU trade mark.[88] (Emphasis added)

---

[88] EUTMR, Art 9(3).

This provision significantly expands the protection for trade marks with reputation. While trade marks are protected against confusing uses by similar marks as we discussed above, they additionally receive protection from uses that do not relate to raising confusion of consumers. The harm that the provision is protecting against is threefold: first, it protects against such uses that erode the distinctiveness of a trade mark with reputation which is referred to as 'blurring'; second, it prevents such uses of the trade mark which would taint the reputation and goodwill associated by the mark by using it in relation to products of unsavoury quality or characteristics (referred to as 'tarnishment'); finally, the provision also protects the right holder from third parties free-riding on the reputation of the mark.

In order to receive this additional layer of protection it must be shown that the mark acquires reputation in the EU. In *General Motors Corporation v. Yplon*,[89] the CJEU had to determine the notion of reputation in relation to the word mark 'Chevy' for motor vehicles which the defendants were using in respect of detergents and cleaning products. The defendants were based in Belgium and claimed that the mark 'Chevy' had no reputation in the Benelux region.

The Court held that a mark would have a reputation where it was known by a significant part of the public concerned by the products covered by the trade mark. This 'public' could be, depending on the product or service marketed, either the public at large, or a more specialised group of public (for example, traders in a specific sector). The national courts should, in order to determine the reputation of the mark, take into consideration relevant facts such as: market share held, intensity, geographical extent, duration of use, and the size of investment made by the undertaking promoting it. Moreover, the reputation should exist in a substantial part of the member state, or region.[90] The US trade mark law, as we shall see below, also protects famous trade marks.

Infringing uses that are detrimental to the distinctiveness of a mark with reputation are referred to as blurring. It occurs where the defendant harms the unique character of the mark by using the mark on similar and particularly on dissimilar products without authorisation. Such use would ultimately impair the selling power of a mark with reputation and has been referred to as 'the death by a thousand cuts'.[91] Schechter, who wrote a seminal article of this particular harm,[92] provides a good example to explain the harm concerned in a hearing before the US Congress: 'If you allow Rolls-Royce Restaurants, and Rolls-Royce cafeterias, and Rolls Royce Pants and Rolls-Royce candy, in ten years you will not have a Rolls-Royce mark anymore.'[93]

Uses that are detrimental to the reputation of a mark are referred to as tarnishment and are much easier to conceive. The action protects against the use of the mark in association with products that could contain an unsavoury connotation. The CJEU has held this to occur where 'the goods or services offered by the third party possess a characteristic or a quality which is liable

---

[89] Case C-375/97, [1999] 3 CMLR 427.

[90] See also Case C-301/07 *Pago Intl v. Tirolmilch* [2009] ECR I-9429, where the CJEU has held that the relevant reputation within the EU can be established where the mark has reputation in a single member state (there Austria).

[91] B. Beebe, 'A Defense of the New Federal Trademark Antidilution Law' (2006) 4 *Fordham Intellectual Property, Media & Entertainment Law Journal* 1163, footnote 102.

[92] Schechter, *supra* note 19, 813.

[93] Hearings before the Congressional Committee on Patents, 72nd Congress, 1st Session 15 (1932).

to have a negative impact on the image of the mark'.[94] An example here is the use of the 'Enjoy Cola-Cola' slogan in its typical script to display 'Cocaine' on T-Shirts which was discussed in a US case.[95]

The final harm that the provision protects against is where the unauthorised use by the defendant takes unfair advantage of the mark with a reputation. These cases cover uses that would free-ride on or misappropriate the reputation of the other mark. Here, the mark as such is not harmed but rather the reputation or image is unfairly transferred to the products or services of the unauthorized user.[96] The leading case here, the already mentioned case *L'Oréal v. Bellure*[97] which related to smell-alike perfumes, was criticised for significantly expanding the scope of protection for trade mark holders unduly.

6.4.3   Limitations and defences

TRIPS Agreement, Article 17, sets out the 'trade mark' version of the three-step test (which in fact stops at two steps rather than the whole three): 'Members may provide limited exceptions to the rights conferred by a trademark, such as fair use of descriptive terms, provided that such exceptions take account of the legitimate interests of the owner of the trademark and of third parties.'

The EUTMR offers more specific lines of defences:

1.   An EU trade mark shall not entitle the proprietor to prohibit a third party from using, in the course of trade:
    (a)   the name or address of the third party, where that third party is a natural person;
    (b)   signs or indications which are not distinctive or which concern the kind, quality, quantity, intended purpose, value, geographical origin, the time of production of goods or of rendering of the service, or other characteristics of the goods or services;
    (c)   the EU trade mark for the purpose of identifying or referring to goods or services as those of the proprietor of that trade mark, in particular, where the use of that trade mark is necessary to indicate the intended purpose of a product or service, in particular as accessories or spare parts.

All the above uses by the third party must be done in in accordance with 'honest practices in industrial or commercial matters'.[98] The CJEU has interpreted the latter proviso in markedly different ways: in one case, use was not in accordance with honest practices if it gives the impression of a commercial connection between the parties, or takes unfair advantage of its distinctive character or discredits or denigrates the mark; in another case, the Court held that honest use depends on

---

[94] *L'Oréal v. Bellure, supra* note 83, para 40.

[95] *Coca-Cola v. Gemini Rising* 346 F Supp 1183; 175 USPQ 56 (EDNY, 1972).

[96] *L'Oréal v. Bellure, supra* note 83, para 40.

[97] Ibid.

[98] EUTMR, Art 12.

whether the user understood that objectively the public would see a link between the second use and the trade mark use.[99]

The US trade mark law has a case-made fair use doctrine whereby an unauthorised use of another's trade mark will not infringe it if three conditions are fulfilled, namely:

1. the trade mark proprietor's product or service must be one which is not readily identifiable by the defendant if he does not make use of the trade mark;
2. only so much of the trade mark may be used as is reasonably necessary to identify the product or service; and
3. the user must do nothing that would, in conjunction with the mark, suggest sponsorship or endorsement by the trade mark holder.[100]

6.5 UNITED STATES TRADE MARK LAW

The general principles under US trade mark law are analogous to EU trade mark law as discussed above; however, there are important differences. This section discusses briefly the most salient divergences between the two jurisdictions.

Trade marks are protected either under the federal statute, namely the Lanham Act (15 USC, ss 1051–1127), under states' statutory law, and common laws. Indeed, there is no need for registration to obtain rights in the mark as long as legitimate use has been made of the mark. Owning a federal trade mark registration does have some advantages including the legal presumption of the registrant's ownership of the mark, the right to use the mark nationwide in relation to the goods and/or services listed in the registration, and the ability to bring an action concerning the mark in federal court.

6.5.1 Distinctiveness

Under the Lanham Act, a trade mark consists of 'any word, name, symbol, or device, or any combination thereof [… used] to identify and distinguish […] goods […] or] services'.[101] This definition includes all sorts of marks consisting of words, logos, and product designs and configurations, trade dress, sound marks, and even scents for toothbrushes – as long as these marks act as an indicator of source. This means that a trade mark must be distinctive in order to be registrable in the US. Similarly to the situation in the EU, a trade mark can be inherently distinctive or can acquire distinctiveness through use (which is also referred to as 'secondary meaning' in US trade mark law).

Case law has provided several categories of marks that are arranged in an ascending order as to

---

[99] Case C-228/03 *The Gillette Company and Gillette Group Finland Oy v. LA-Laboratories Ltd Oy* [2005] ECR I-2337, para 32; Case C-245/02 *Anheuser-Busch Inc. v. Budějovický Budvar, národní podnik* [2004] ECR I-10989, paras 59–60 respectively. See also I. Simon, 'The Public Interest in European Trade Mark Law' (2017) *IPQ* 311.

[100] Phillips, *supra* note 11, 222.

[101] Lanham Act, s 45 (15 USC, § 1127).

their origin-identifying ability.[102] Arbitrary,[103] fanciful[104] or suggestive[105] marks may be inherently distinctive, while descriptive signs need to show acquired distinctiveness in order to be registered. Such secondary meaning arises over time after consumers have repeatedly encountered the trade mark[106] and relate it to the undertaking behind the mark. 'Exotic' trade marks, such as sounds, colours[107] and shapes, are generally required to demonstrate secondary meaning. This is because they are 'not immediately recognizable as source identifiers'.[108] Trade dress, i.e., the distinctive features of a product's packaging or of the product configuration, itself can also be protected as a trade mark. The US Supreme Court has, for instance, discussed whether the interior design of a restaurant can receive trade mark protection.[109] The same court, however, held in *Wal-Mart Stores v. Samara* that product packaging may be inherently distinctive while product design must show secondary meaning:

> The attribution of inherent distinctiveness to certain categories of word marks and product packaging derives from the fact that the very purpose of attaching a particular word to a product, or encasing it in a distinctive packaging, is most often to identify the source of the product. […] In the case of product design, as in the case of color, we think consumer predisposition to equate the feature with the source does not exist. Consumers are aware of the reality that, almost invariably, even the most unusual of product designs-such as a cocktail shaker shaped like a penguin-is intended not to identify the source, but to render the product itself more useful or more appealing.[110]

The final category, generic marks, however, cannot be protected as trade marks; thus descriptive signs can become protectable should they acquire secondary meaning but this option is not offered to generic signs.[111]

---

[102] *Abercrombie & Fitch Co. v. Hunting World*, 537 F 2d 4 (2nd Cir, 1976).

[103] Abitrary terms are commonly used, dictionary terms. They are however used in a manner where they do not describe the goods in question in any way.

[104] Fanciful terms have no dictionary meaning as they are invented terms. 'Xerox' for copying devices or 'Kodak' for photographic equipment are examples for fanciful trade marks.

[105] Suggestive terms are neither descriptive nor fanciful but range between these two categories. A court explained that: '[a] term is suggestive if it requires imagination, thought and perception to reach a conclusion as to the nature of goods. A term is descriptive if it forthwith conveys a immediate idea of the ingredients, qualities or characteristics of the goods.' See *Stix Products, Inc v. United Merchants & Mfrs*, Inc., 295 F Supp. 479 (SDNY 1968). An example for a suggestive term is 'Penguin' for refrigerators (connotating a cold climate).

[106] Mary LaFrance, *Understanding Trademark Law* (2nd ed., Lexis Nexis, 2009), 47.

[107] *Qualitex Co v. Jacobsen Products Co*, 514 US 159 (S Ct, 1995) at 162–3.

[108] LaFrance, *supra* note 106, 68.

[109] *Two Pesos, Inc v. Taco Cabana, Inc*, 505 US 763 (S Ct, 1992).

[110] *Wal-Mart Stores, Inc. v. Samara Brothers, Inc.* 529 US 205 (S Ct, 2000), 212–13.

[111] 15 USC § 1052(f); *CES Publishing Corp v. St. Regis Publications, Inc*, 531 F 2d 11 (1975); *Bayer Co v. United Drug Co*, 272 F 505 (2d Cir, 1921), 'aspirin' held to be generic; *DuPont Cellophane Co v. Waxed Products Co*, 85 F 2d 75 (2d Cir), cert. denied, 299 US 601 (S Ct, 1936), 'cellophane' held to be generic.

6.5.2 Functionality doctrine

Trade marks that are functional are also barred from having trade mark protection even where they have acquired distinctiveness.[112] The rationale for excluding such marks corresponds to the one we have already discussed with regard to the exclusion of certain shapes or other characteristics as stipulated in Article 7(1)(e) of the EUTMR. The US Supreme Court has provided a definition and explanation of the doctrine of functionality:

> In 'general terms, a product feature is functional,' and cannot serve as a trademark, 'if it is essential to the use or purpose of the article or if it affects the cost or quality of the article,' that is, if exclusive use of the feature would put competitors at a significant non-reputation-related disadvantage.[113]

There are two variations of the functionality doctrine in US trade mark law: utilitarian and aesthetic functionality. Utilitarian functionality is given where a feature serves a useful purpose for that product. Examples for such functional features are the dual-spring design mechanism for keeping outdoor signs upright in adverse wind conditions[114] or the colour black for boat motors by making them appear smaller.[115] Such features, however, should be protected by patent law where applicable and not by trade mark law. The Supreme Court explains that:

> It is the province of patent law, not trademark law, to encourage invention by granting inventors a monopoly over new product designs or functions for a limited time, 35 U.S.C. §§ 154, 173, after which competitors are free to use the innovation. If a product's functional features could be used as trademarks, however, a monopoly over such features could be obtained without regard to whether they qualify as patents and could be extended forever (because trademarks may be renewed in perpetuity).[116]

Aesthetic functionality, on the other hand, is a complicated and controversial doctrine in US trade mark law. It occurs where a feature of a product (colour or other ornamentation) leads to a competitive advantage due to its aesthetic appeal rather than its utility.[117] A case that showcases aesthetic functionality nicely and highlights its complexity relates to the red-lacquered soles of Christian Louboutin. His 'Red Sole Mark' was held to have acquired secondary meaning and received federal registration in 2008. In 2011, Louboutin learned that Yves Saint Laurent America was applying red soles to their shoes and filed for trade mark infringement seeking a preliminary injunction. The District Court held for YSL. It stated that in the fashion industry, single-colour

---

[112] Lanham Act, s 2 (15 USC, § 1052 (e) (5)); *Qualitex Co v. Jacobson Prods Co, supra* note 107, 165.

[113] *Qualitex Co v. Jacobson Prods Co,* ibid.

[114] *Traffix Devices, Inc v. Marketing Displays, Inc,* 532 US 23 (S Ct, 2001).

[115] *Brunswick Corp v. British Seagull Ltd,* 35 F 3d 1527, 32 USPQ 2d 1120 (Fed Cir, 1994).

[116] *Qualitex Co v. Jacobson Prods Co, supra* note 107, 164–5.

[117] *Wallace Int'l Silversmiths, Inc v. Godinger Silver Art Co,* 916 F 2d 76 (2d Cir, 1990); J. Gilson and A. Gilson LaLonde, 'Cinnamon Buns, Marching Ducks and Cherry-Scented Racecar Exhaust: Protecting Nontraditional Trademarks' (1995) 95(4) *Trademark Reporter* 789.

marks are inherently 'functional' and that any such registered trade mark would likely be held invalid by applying aesthetic functionality.[118] Such rule would effectively deny trademark protection to any use of a single colour on an item of apparel. The appeal against this decision by the Second Circuit held that the District Court erred in denying any form of trade mark protection for colours as this would contradict the precedent in *Qualitex* by the US Supreme Court.[119]

6.5.3   Confusion

The Lanham Act provides protection of registered[120] and unregistered[121] trade marks against confusion and therefore establishes a similar regime as in Europe. Trade mark infringement occurs where the defendant's false representation is likely to cause confusion to consumers. In assessing whether such likelihood of confusion has been created courts in the US have applied multi-factor tests. The Second Circuit has, for instance, established the so-called Polaroid factors:[122]

1.   The strength of the senior (i.e., the right holders' mark).
2.   The degree of similarity between the two marks.
3.   The proximity of the products or services.
4.   The likelihood that the prior owner will 'bridge the gap'.[123]
5.   Evidence of a likelihood of confusion.
6.   The defendant's good (or bad) faith in adopting the sign.
7.   The quality of the defendant's goods or services.
8.   The sophistication of buyers.

The US federal law also protects famous trade marks as follows:

> Subject to the principles of equity, the owner of a famous mark that is distinctive, inherently or through acquired distinctiveness, shall be entitled to an injunction against another person who, at any time after the owner's mark has become famous, commences use of a mark or trade name in commerce that is likely to cause dilution by blurring or dilution by tarnishment of the famous mark, regardless of the presence or absence of actual or likely confusion, of competition, or of actual economic injury.[124]

---

[118] *Christian Louboutin SA v. Yves Saint Laurent America Inc*, 778 F Supp. 2d 445 (SDNY, 2011).

[119] *Christian Louboutin SA v. Yves Saint Laurent America Inc*, 696 F 3d 206, 218 (2d Cir, 2012). For a full discussion, see J. Hughes, 'Non-Traditional Trademarks and the Dilemma of Aesthetic Functionality', in I. Calboli and M. Senftleben (eds), *The Protection of Non-Traditional Marks: Critical Perspectives* (Oxford University Press, 2018), Chapter 5.

[120] Lanham Act, s 32 (15 USC, § 1114).

[121] Ibid., s 43(a) (15 USC, § 1125(a)).

[122] *Polaroid Corp v. Polard Elecs. Copr*, 287 F 2d 492, 495 (2d Cir).

[123] This relates to the question whether the trade mark holder would expand his business into the market of the alleged defendant.

[124] Lanham Act, s 43(c)(1) (15 USC, § 1125(c)(1)).

Thus, unlike traditional trade mark principles, where the likelihood of confusion among consumers must be shown, dilution recognises injury to a trade mark proprietor in cases where there is no such confusion, for example, if someone started selling 'Kodak' bicycles or 'Coca-Cola' pianos, it would injure the distinctiveness of the 'Kodak' and 'Coca-Cola' trade marks by blurring[125] its distinctiveness even if there were no evidence that any consumers actually thought the bicycles or pianos came from the film or drinks corporations. All a trade mark proprietor need do is show that the defendant's mark is likely to cause dilution of the famous mark. Moreover, the law allows a trade mark proprietor to sue by way of a 'dilution by tarnishment' cause of action, which is defined as 'association arising from the similarity between a mark or trade name and a famous mark that harms the reputation of the famous mark'.[126]

The code additionally specifies when a mark is considered famous. This is the case when it is 'it is widely recognized by the general consuming public of the United States as a designation of source of the goods or services of the mark's owner'.[127] The situation in the US must therefore be contrasted with that in the EU where 'niche fame' can already render a trade mark famous.[128] The Lanham Act further stipulates that some uses will constitute non-infringing 'fair use' of the mark, including using the famous mark in comparative advertising, in a non-commercial manner and in news reporting and commentary.[129]

6.6   THE COMMON LAW ACTION OF PASSING OFF

A passing off action allows a trader to prevent another trader from passing their goods off as if they

---

[125] 'Blurring' is a legal concept, and is defined as an 'association arising from the similarity between a mark or trade name and a famous mark that impairs the distinctiveness of the famous mark'; Lanham Act, s 43(c)(2)(B); (15 USC, § 1125(c)(2)(B)). The statutory provision directs courts to consider all relevant factors in determining a likelihood of dilution by blurring, including:

1. The degree of similarity between the mark or trade name and the famous mark.
2. The degree of inherent or acquired distinctiveness of the famous mark.
3. The extent to which the owner of the famous mark is engaging in substantially exclusive use of the mark.
4. The degree of recognition of the famous mark.
5. Whether the user of the mark or trade name intended to create an association with the famous mark.
6. Any actual association between the accused mark or trade name and the famous mark.

[126] Lanham Act, s 43(c)(2)(C); (15 USC, § 1125(c)(2)(C)). For a further study on this, see K.R. Whittaker, 'Trademark Dilution in A Global Age' (2006) 27 *Univ. Pennsylvania Journal of International Economic Law* 907; I. Simon, 'Dilution in the United States and European Union (and Beyond) Compared, Part I: International Obligations and Basic Definitions' (2006) 1 *Oxford Journal of Intellectual Property Law and Practice* 406–12, and 'Part II: Testing for Blurring' (2006) 1 *Oxford Journal of Intellectual Property Law and Practice* 649–59.

[127] Lanham Act, s 43(c)(2)(A); (15 USC, § 1125(c)(2)(A)).

[128] Case C-375/97 *General Motors Corporation v. Yplon* [1999] 3 CMLR 427.

[129] Lanham Act, s 43(c)(3); (15 USC, § 1125(c)(3)).

were the first traders. A nineteenth-century English definition of this form of action was given earlier in this chapter.[130] It is a common law action, rather than one based on statute law, and hence is moulded by case law.[131] It is to be distinguished from unfair competition law as exists under civil law jurisdictions, and as set out in Article 6*bis*, Paris Convention (see below).

Briefly, the law today is employed to stop any misrepresentation in the course of trade to prospective customers calculated to injure the business goodwill of another trader and that causes actual damage. There are two valid definitions of what constitutes passing off. In the early classic formulation set out in the *Advocaat* case,[132] Lord Diplock held that five characteristics must be present in order to create a valid cause of action for passing off:

(i)   a misrepresentation;
(ii)   made by a trader in the course of trade;
(iii)   to prospective customers of his or ultimate consumers of goods or services supplied by him;
(iv)   which is calculated to injure the business or goodwill of another trader (in the sense that this is a reasonably foreseeable consequence); and
(v)   which causes actual damage to the business or goodwill of the trader by whom the action is brought or (in a *quia timet* action) will probably do so.

A later re-formulation of this classic test was offered by Lord Oliver in the *Jif Lemon* decision[133] where he stated that in order to succeed in an action for passing-off, a claimant must show that:

(i)   the claimant had goodwill;
(ii)   a misrepresentation had been made by the defendant, that would be likely to deceive the public; and
(iii)   the misrepresentation would be likely to damage the claimant.

It should be emphasised that the action for passing off is not concerned with copying or slavish imitation (as under unfair competition law) and these acts per se are not considered unlawful outside the recognised intellectual property laws. This was forcefully stated in the *Roho* decision: 'There is no tort of copying. There is no tort of taking a man's market or customers. Neither the market nor the customers are the plaintiff's to own. There is no tort of making use of another's goodwill as such. There is no tort of competition.'[134]

---

[130] *Perry v. Truefitt* (1842) 6 Beav 66, 73.

[131] The ability to bring a common law action for passing off, in addition to an action based on registered trade marks, is specifically preserved under some statutes – see, for example, 1994 Trade Marks Act (UK), s 2(2).

[132] *Erven Warnink BV v. J Townsend & Sons (Hull) Ltd* [1979] AC 731; [1979] FSR 397.

[133] *Reckitt & Colman v. Borden (Jif Case)* [1990] 1 All ER 873; [1990] RPC 340.

[134] *Hodgkinson & Corby Ltd and Roho Inc v. Wards Mobility Services Ltd* [1995] FSR 169; U. Suthersanen, 'Case Comment' (1995) *Journal of Business Law* 197.

TRADE MARKS

This sentiment is echoed in other judgments emanating both from the High Court and the Court of Appeal,[135] and also from other common law jurisdictions.[136] Rather, the law on passing off emphasises the notions of confusion to and deception of consumers. In the *Jif Lemon*[137] case, the plaintiff was held to have established a trading reputation in lemon juice sold in plastic containers which looked like life-sized lemons. The defendant sold lemon juice in similarly shaped lemon containers, and although the two containers bore dissimilar marks ('Jif' as opposed to 'RealLemon'), the court held that passing off had been established. The House of Lords proceeded to offer a re-formulation of the test of passing off:

> First, he must establish a goodwill or reputation attached to the goods or services which he supplies in the mind of the purchasing public by association with the identifying 'get-up' (whether it consists simply of a brand name or a trade description, or the individual features of labelling or packaging) under which his particular goods or services are offered to the public, such that the get-up is recognised by the public as distinctive specifically of the plaintiff's goods or services. Secondly, he must demonstrate a misrepresentation by the defendant to the public (whether or not intentional) leading or likely to lead the public to believe that goods or services offered by him are the goods or services of the plaintiff [...] Thirdly, he must demonstrate that he suffers, or in a *quia timet* action, that he is likely to suffer damage by reason of the erroneous belief engendered by the defendant's misrepresentation that the source of the defendant's goods or services is the same as the source of those offered by the plaintiff.[138]

With these principles in mind, it is clear that different considerations arise in the action for passing off – the element of confusion is insufficient, and it must be shown that the plaintiff has a sufficient trading reputation which will lead consumers, acquiring the defendant's products, into thinking that they are securing the goods of the plaintiff. Moreover, the product or its get-up or packaging must have some distinguishing feature upon which his trading reputation is founded.[139]

It should be noted that the action of passing off does not only protect the goodwill of a single trader. Rather, goodwill can also be held by a group of traders by what is known as 'extended passing off'. This means that the producers of Champagne,[140] Swiss Chocolate[141] or Greek cheese[142] can

---

[135] With regard to the passing off claim that was brought forward within the *L'Oréal v. Bellure* litigation, Lord Justice Jacob again rejected 'the invitation to invent a tort of unfair competition' – *L'Oréal S.A. v. Bellure N.V. and others*, [2007] EWCA Civ 968, para 142.

[136] *Cadbury Schweppes v. Pub Squash*, [1981] RPC 429 (Privy Council); *Moorgate Tobacco v. Phillip Morris*, [1985] RPC 219 (Australian High Court).

[137] *Reckitt & Colman v. Borden* [1990] RPC 340, HL.

[138] Ibid., 499.

[139] *Edge v. Nicolls* [1911] AC 693, HL.

[140] *J Bollinger & Ors v. Costa Brava Wine Co Ltd (No 2)* [1961] 1 WLR 277.

[141] *Chocosuisse Union des Fabricants Suisse de Chocolat v. Cadbury Ltd* [1999] RPC 826.

[142] *Fage UK Ltd and another v. Chobani UK Ltd and another* [2014] EWCA Civ 5 [37].

have shared goodwill in the name or other distinctive feature of their products.[143] The Court of Appeal has recently described when such extended passing off occurs:

> [A] geographical name has become so distinctive of particular goods made in that geographical area that its use in relation to other goods amounts to a misrepresentation which is calculated to lead to the deception of members of the public and to cause damage to those traders who enjoy a goodwill in their businesses of supplying goods which are in fact made in that area.[144]

But extended passing off does not only apply against geographical misrepresentations but also to a specific quality or characteristic of a product as discussed in the abovementioned *Advocaat* case. Important in proving misrepresentation is the public's perception of the way the term is used.[145] This means that where UK customers would understand Greek cheese as being produced in Greece, then a US made cheese labelled as 'Greek cheese' involves a material misrepresentation.[146]

6.7   TRADE MARKS AND UNFAIR COMPETITION

6.7.1   Rationale

Unfair competition is a broad concept, and its relationship to intellectual property goes far beyond its relevance to trade mark law and passing off. Nonetheless, since trade marks play a huge role in marketing goods and services, we will deal briefly with unfair competition here.

One view as to the function of unfair competition law is that it acts as a corollary to competition law. While competition law protects the institution of competition as the chosen order of the marketplace, unfair competition theory regulates the behaviour of the various competitors with regard to their behaviour in the marketplace. This is in tandem with the view that unfair competition law relates to the conduct of an imitator, rather than what is imitated.[147]

The second view holds that unfair competition should not be ethics-based but rather should determine whether or not the result of the competitor's behaviour hinders or stifles the competitive process of differentiation and imitation. This view upholds the sanctity of consumer welfare as the prime consideration, as opposed to upholding moral standards within the marketplace. From this perspective, imitation products on the market may reflect the dishonest business practices of the imitator but should be regarded also as being economically beneficial to the consumer in bringing the price of the product down and in forcing standardisation of the product.[148]

---

[143] Bently and Sherman, *supra* note 5, 878.

[144] *Fage UK Ltd, supra* note 142, para 37.

[145] Bently and Sherman, *supra* note 5, 883.

[146] *Fage UK Ltd and another v. Chobani UK Ltd and another* [2013] EWHC 630 (Ch) [136].

[147] U. Suthersanen, *Design Law in Europe* (London: Sweet & Maxwell, 2000), 402.

[148] Ibid.

6.7.2 Definitions

Most WTO member states do have a general unfair competition law which is based on fault or wrongdoing, as set out in Article 10*bis* of the Paris Convention. Any infringement of an intellectual property right invariably involves fault or wrongdoing on the part of the imitator. The difficulty lies in that in addition to regulating the conduct of the imitator in order to maintain a fair marketplace, unfair competition laws can also indirectly serve as a means of conferring proprietary rights. In this manner, rather than market regulatory mechanisms, the law is seen as an important supplement to intellectual property protection.

In this way, one can understand the reasoning behind the classification of unfair competition under Article 1(2), Paris Convention as part of the industrial property regime. Article 10*bis*, Paris Convention goes further and defines the concept of 'unfair competition' as 'any act of competition contrary to honest practices in industrial or commercial matters'.[149]

According to the Paris Convention, acts of confusion, of denigration and of misleading indications are specifically prohibited:[150]

1. All acts of such a nature as to create confusion by any means whatever with the establishment, the goods, or the industrial or commercial activities, of a competitor.
2. False allegations in the course of trade of such a nature as to discredit the establishment, the goods, or the industrial or commercial activities, of a competitor.
3. Indications or allegations the use of which in the course of trade is liable to mislead the public as to the nature, the manufacturing process, the characteristics, the suitability for their purpose, or the quantity, of the goods.

The TRIPS Agreement incorporates the substantive provisions of the Paris Convention by reference and explicitly mentions Article 10*bis* in the sections dealing with geographical indications and undisclosed information.[151] Specifically, WTO members must provide legal means to prevent any use of geographical indications that would constitute unfair competition. Also, members must ensure effective protection against unfair competition with respect to undisclosed information.

6.7.3 Confusion and slavish imitation

The prohibition of acts which create confusion with distinctive signs, products or services of the competitor is the basis of this classical rule against unfair competition. One can even find this rule under the common law action for passing off. The prohibition of confusion may supplement existing laws for the protection of distinctive signs. However, national laws of many countries do differ in one important feature: the nexus between unfair competition law and trade mark protection. The question arises of whether these two laws co-exist in a cumulative, supplementary, or mutually exclusive manner.

---

[149] Paris Convention, Art 10*bis* (2).

[150] Ibid., Art 10*bis* (3).

[151] TRIPS Agreement, Arts 22–4, 39.

In principle, products that are not, or are no longer, protected by IPRs may be freely copied and imitated. Unfair competition law should not extend the boundaries of intellectual property legislation. However, the circumstances in which such copying is done may amount to unfair competition. Many European countries, for instance, prohibit the slavish copying of goods if such reproduction leads to a deception of consumers as to the origin of the product. These cases can be addressed under the topic of causing confusion (see above). Furthermore, systematic copying or copying made possible by a breach of confidentiality is also considered not to be 'fair' market behaviour.

Different opinions exist, however, whether and to what extent elements such as confusion, slavish imitation or parasitic behaviour should be taken into account. Under French law, for example, the law adopts three different stances simultaneously.[152] German law does address slavish imitation where this entails the undue exploitation of the claimants' reputation.[153]

A first view is that copying an item in the public domain cannot amount to fault and it is not a civil wrong to reproduce an unprotected object even if damage is caused. A further element such as confusion is required. The second contrary notion is that the slavish reproduction of a product in the public domain is wrong if this is done with a view to creating a confusion in the public concerning the origin of products sold, and indeed, the mere fact of slavish imitation demonstrates an intention to cause confusion, and a fault should be inferred. The final position is that the taking of fruits of another's industry and investment is unjust enrichment and therefore, unfair competition law should be invoked on the basis of parasitic competition 'concurrence parasitaire'.[154]

The second and third approaches pose a serious problem. This is that unfair competition law can usurp patent, copyright and trade mark laws by either conferring or extending protection of inventions, works and marks.

---

[152] Suthersanen, *supra* note 147, 403–6.

[153] M. Mimler, 'The Aspects of Unfair Competition within the Apple v. Samsung litigation in Germany' (2013) 3 *Queen Mary Journal of Intellectual Property* 176–84.

[154] Kamperman Sanders views *concurrence parasitaire* as a synthesis of traditional French law on unfair competition and unjust enrichment, A. Kamperman Sanders, *Unfair Competition Law: The Protection of Intellectual and Industrial Creativity* (Oxford: Clarendon Press, 1997), 29.

7
Design intellectual property

7.1   ORIGINS[1]

> Design means [...] a conception or suggestion or idea of a shape or of a picture or of a device or of some arrangement which can be applied to an article by some manual, mechanical or chemical means. It is a conception, suggestion, or idea, and not an article, which is the thing capable of being registered [...] it is a suggestion of form or ornament to be applied to a physical body.[2]

This struggle to derive a legal definition of design should be contrasted with the more realistic acceptance of a bifurcated legal order based on a historical schism in how we view the creation of things:

> Modern bourgeois culture made a sharp division between the world of the arts and that of technology and machines; hence culture was split into two mutually exclusive branches: one scientific, quantifiable and 'hard', the other aesthetic, evaluative and 'soft'. [...] the word design formed a bridge between the two. It could do this since it is an expression of the internal connection between art and technology.[3]

Most objects live in the nebulous and grey area where multiple definitions of the object and their purpose exist. Most objects are also designed, configured, and shaped to promise and sell a lifestyle. Creators understand that the object must be designed in such a way as to tell a story, using elements of functionalism or symbolism or aestheticism. Consumers understand that objects can be throwaways, vital spare parts within complex products, or perhaps even investments.

This notion of design encompasses technical or biological inventions, geographical and fashion works, engineering or architectural design documents, and packaging. The concept can stand true irrespective of the mode of production, or the nature of the substrate manifesting the design, or the purpose of the creator, or the context of the use. Thus, standing as they do at the junction of art

---

[1] The section summarises the following works: U. Suthersanen, *Design Law in Europe* (Sweet & Maxwell, 2000); U. Suthersanen, *Design Law: European Union and United States* (Sweet & Maxwell, 2010); N. Pevsner, *The Pioneers of Modern Design – From William Morris to Walter Gropius* (Penguin, 1960); W. Ashworth, *A Short History of International Economy Since 1850* (Longman, 1987); P. Mantoux, *The Industrial Revolution in the Eighteenth Century – The Outline of the Beginnings of the Modern Factory System in England* (Methuen University Paperbacks, 1964 (re-publication of the original 1928 edition)); L. Jardine, *Wordly Goods – A New History of the Renaissance* (London: Macmillan, 1996); and J. Heskett, *Industrial Design* (London: Thames & Hudson, 1980).

[2] *Dover v. Niirnberger Celluloidwaren Fabrick Cebriider Wolff* (1910) 27 RPC 498, 503.

[3] Vilém Flusser, *The Shape of Things – A Philosophy of Design* (Reaktion Books, 1999), 18–19.

and industry manifesting themselves in many different sectoral markets and guises, 'designs' pose considerable challenges within the intellectual property spectrum. The hybrid nature of a product, as fashion icons, as museum exhibits, as collectors' items, as practical everyday objects, as trade marks and trade dress, and as industrial functional products, has made legal categorisation difficult. The stance of demarcating a manufactured object into the copyright-art hemisphere, on the one hand, and into the industrial property/applied art/commerce hemisphere, on the other hand, has had a real effect on the commercial market.

For example, unlike Germany and France with their strong protective ethos in relation to designer fashion and furniture, the UK (until recently) and the US have been sources for reproduction designer furniture, often made without licences from the original designers, and manufactured elsewhere. On both sides of the Atlantic, 'designer' objects can be sourced for a fraction of the cost of the original as such unauthorised reproductions are lawful. The dilemma has also, to a certain extent, shaped intellectual property law typology, so that designs are perceived as industrial property, functional models, industrial designs, drawings, and artistic works. Accordingly, protection for designs is possible under all intellectual property regimes, including *sui generis* design, copyright, trade mark, patent and unfair competition laws.

7.1.1 The artist-craftsman

Design as a profession is influenced largely by the dynamic economic conditions which historically have driven constant metamorphoses of the artist from a designer, to an industrialist, and back again to an artist.

The traditional view is that the discipline of design arose from the field of arts and crafts. The difference between a seventeenth-century pattern-maker and a modern industrial designer is less one of the nature of their respective creative activities than of the economic, technological and social constraints within which the activity is performed. The notion of 'industrial design' was alien in the medieval world where art and industry were unified in concept and in practice, and where cultured and leisurely patrons were served by a class of equally cultured and guild-trained craftsmen.[4] No demarcation between art and industry was necessary for several reasons. First, there was a lack of tooling and production capabilities to make goods on a mass scale. Second, the income level of the general population could not support a large consumer product industry in the medieval market system. Third, the absence of a large consumer market was bolstered by the handicraft production system. Each finished article was made individually, leading to high costs per unit product – the main clientele came from the church, the court and the merchant ranks. Furthermore, from the mid-fifteenth century onwards, it was an established rule that the possession of collectible *objets d'art* was an indication of individual worth in society. There was no real pressure on the European craftsmen to

---

[4] W. Duchemin, *Protection of the Works of Artist-Craftsmen – Study for EC Commission*, SPADEM (Société de la Propriété Artistique et des Dessins et Modèles), 1976 (CT - XII/905/76-E), 29; Pevsner, *supra* note 1, 45. On design history and its relationship with industrialisation and consumerism, see F. Braudel, *Civilization and Capitalism 15th–18th Century*, Volume 1 (The Structures of Everyday Life), Volume 2 (The Wheels of Commerce), Volume 3 (The Perspective of the World) (London: Collins, 1981, 1982, 1984).

adopt a consumer-orientated approach.[5] However, it would not be accurate to portray the pre-Industrial Revolution era as one where the artist-craftsmen were totally inured to market forces. The gentle erosion of the secure and protected domain of the artist-craftsmen had begun during the seventeenth century. There was an expansion of trade routes and commercial opportunities that led to a slow growth in output among the craft trade. A pattern began to emerge whereby the general craftsman shifted his skills towards specialisation as a measure to secure a competitive edge.[6]

Several factors in the nineteenth century contributed to the growing importance of design. First, the growth in supply and demand for goods created competitive pressures that led to demands for product innovation, notably in the application of some characteristic feature or aspect of skill to distinguish a product and attract the interest of customers.[7] Second, the furious pace of inventions and innovations enabled new manufacturing techniques, with greater production units at lower costs, thus encouraging and catering for a growing consumer market. A third influential factor was the massive organisational changes which occurred in the production process, heralding the arrival of the mass manufacturer. Although the factory system had existed in some form or other prior to the nineteenth century, it primarily functioned as a source of luxury goods.[8] The previous manufacturing process whereby goods were made from start to finish by a single craftsman was to evolve into a process whereby goods were being produced in a series of stages by different specialists. This phenomenon was already noted at the turn of the eighteenth century, Adam Smith observed that one factor which accounted for the increase in the quantity of work was the invention of a 'great number of machines which facilitate and abridge labour, and enable one man to do the work of many'. The addition of the designing stages in the manufacturing process gave rise to the profession of designers or 'art-workers' who 'translated the ideas of fine artists into mass production'.[9]

The fourth and perhaps, most important, factor was the emergence of a large consumer class – a result of rises in real wages and shifts in public taste. To cope with the new social climate of acquisition, a wide range of new consumer goods was introduced, with the assistance of retailing and advertising.[10] Advertising literature began exhorting the design as a means of selling the

---

[5] Braudel, ibid., The Structures of Everyday Life, 283, 303; Mantoux, *supra* note 1, 30–31; Jardine, *supra* note 1, 72; J. Heskett, 'Industrial Design', in H. Conway (ed.), *Design History* (London: Routledge, 1992), 118.

[6] Jardine, ibid., 74–7; Heskett, *supra* note 1, 11.

[7] For a similar situation arising in the twentieth century, see S.Z. Wang, 'Chinese Modern Design: A Retrospective', in D. Doordan (ed.), *Design History – An Anthology* (Cambridge, MA: MIT Press, 1995). The author notes that the rising income levels of the Chinese people have resulted in them rejecting poorly designed, old-fashioned products; instead, there is a tendency to seek better-quality and better-looking products, 237–8.

[8] Braudel, *The Wheels of Commerce*, 298–302; and E.W. Gilboy, 'Demand as a Factor in the Industrial Revolution', in A.H. Cole (ed.), *Facts and Factors in Economic History: Articles by Former Students of Edwin Francis Gous* (Cambridge, MA: Harvard University Press, 1932), 620–40.

[9] A. Smith, *An Inquiry into the Nature and Causes of the Wealth of Nations* (London: Henry Growde, 1904), 9; P. Sparkes, *An Introduction to Design & Culture in the Twentieth Century* (London: Allen & Unwin, 1987), 4; J. Styles, 'Manufacturing, Consumption and Design', in J. Brewer and R. Porter, *Consumption and the World of Goods* (London: Routledge, 1993), 527–53.

[10] For example, to cope with the growing demand in Britain for neo-classical furnishings, and in the absence of genuine

product, as it still does. The traditional ornament and decoration which were used as an expression of the craftsman's skill in working precious and delicate materials were ignored. There was a change of emphasis in the design of the products from artistic exclusivity to commercial acceptability. At times, considerable effort was expended to make simple articles look more intricate, and therefore more expensive. The era was one of indiscriminate application of ornament, widening the gulf between art, style and function.

7.1.2 Evolution of national laws

Early intellectual property laws can be viewed as a cog within the prevailing mercantilist economic policies namely a system of incentives to introduce and support important industries, especially the textile industry. The first design-related regulation is the 1711 Lyon local regulation, which conferred protection to silk design patterns, akin to a copyright/misappropriation approach.[11] Subsequent design laws in France and England were also short-lived measures that were more concerned with offering immediate relief within the textile design industry against copying or misappropriation.[12]

With the Industrial Revolution, manufactured objects were viewed increasingly as utilitarian and functional objects, made by the new mechanical technologies. The artist/craftsman had metamorphosed into a nameless industrial worker making mass-produced objects. The massive organisational changes wrought by the Industrial Revolution, coupled with new manufacturing techniques, with greater production units at lower costs, catered for the growing consumer market. Competitive pressures led to demands for product innovation, notably in the application of some characteristic feature or aspect of skill to distinguish a manufactured product and attract the interest of customers.

For the next 300 years, a taxonomic approach was adopted in relation to the legal protection of design, as reflected in the design/art/craft schisms. While the 'aesthetic effect' of manufactured goods was something to be rewarded and protected, the fact that the effect was tied to the utility of the product made legislators' concern shift from the protection of the 'art', to the protection of the 'decorative art' or 'applied art' which had to be balanced against allowing such copying to preserve and promote competition.[13]

---

antique sculptures and vases, substitute products were provided for. The Wedgewood/Boulton sales phenomenon is a good example of this point – see A. Forty, *Objects of Desire-Design and Society since 1750* (London: Thames and Hudson, 1986), 17–41; Heskett, *supra* note 1, 15–17.

[11] Ordinance of the Consuls of Lyons (1711), approved by the Council of State (1712) and registered in Parliament (1717), as discussed in F. Prager, 'History of Intellectual Property From 1545 to 1787' (1944) 26 (11) *JPTOS* 711–60; and L.E. Miller, 'Innovation and Industrial Espionage in Eighteenth Century France: An Investigation of the Selling of Silks Through Samples' (1999) 12 *Journal of Design History* 271–92; Suthersanen, 2000, *supra* note 1, 43–4.

[12] Law of 18 March 1806 (France); Act for the Encouragement of the Arts of Designing and Printing of Linens, Cottons, Calicoes and Muslin, 1787, 27 Geo. 3, c. 38 (UK).

[13] *Gorham Mfg Co v. White*, 81 US (14 Wall) 511 (S Ct, 1872), the first US Supreme Court decision in design law which stated that the 'acts of Congress which authorize the granting of patents for designs were plainly intended to give encouragement to the decorative arts'.

A parallel regime of IPRs – design law – was the norm by the late-nineteenth century as the legislative solution to accommodate the rights of creators while promoting a product competitive market. Design law was considered more suitable for manufactured objects circulating within the general products market for several reasons, including the fact that it had higher thresholds of protection (often novelty), and that it offered a much shorter duration of protection as compared to copyright law. This would have the effect of releasing the industrial object from the grasp of IP law into the public domain. This policy subsequently became one of the cornerstones of judicial decisions in some countries (including the UK and Germany) as to why manufactured objects should be discriminated against under copyright law, namely, to avoid the usurpation of the *sui generis* design regime.

If we turn to look at the situation in the US, a similar dilemma arises in relation to the copyright/design overlap. In order to fill the perceived gap between copyright protection for authors, and patent protection for inventors, the first design patent statute was enacted in 1842 within the general patent scheme. Recent studies show that the early proposals were 'a direct descendant of British copyright and design registration law',[14] although the final law orientated towards a more patent paradigm due to extrinsic circumstances.[15] In 1902, the ambit of the design patent statute was extended to 'any new, original, and ornamental design for an article of manufacture', which remains the essential statutory rule under the current patent law.

7.1.3   Modern designs and rationales

The various rationales for design protection indicate that a major impetus in introducing IP protection for design is the belief that design plays a role in promoting and maintaining competition and innovation within a market economy.[16] A basic rationale for the protection of design is to reward the designer's creativity and to provide incentives for future contributions. The conundrum lies not in justifying its protection, but in boxing a designed product into the intellectual property categories.

Objects play various different roles. A pair of spectacles is both a medical appliance and a fashion accessory: they should be hardy and fit for the purpose of corrective vision, but they also modify the appearance and may connote scholarly maturity or being 'cool'. Many of the rationales for not accepting industrial objects as beaux arts are no longer convincing in our current society. Some manufactured objects eschew practicality to embrace value and emotion-laden sentiments of beauty, aesthetics and pleasure. Other manufactured objects, albeit destined to be anonymous mass-produced objects, are still passionately created 'by people who spend a lot of time worrying about injection moulding, or about the precise degree of curve needed to blunt the sharp edges of a monitor screen'.[17]

---

[14] J. Du Mont and M. Janis, 'The Origins of American Design Patent Protection' (2013) 88 *Indiana Law Journal* 837, 860–61.

[15] As the research shows, the extrinsic factors included the need for a newly constructed US Patent Office for a new revenue stream derived from design patent registrations, ibid., 864–8.

[16] D. Ullman, *The Mechanical Design Process* (New York: McGraw-Hill, 1992), 3, '[…] it has been estimated that 85 percent of the problems with new products – not working as they should, taking too long to bring to market, costing too much – is the result of poor design process'.

[17] D. Sudjic, *The Language of Things* (London: Penguin, 2009), 31.

Indeed, many today advocate that design is the art of our age, with the current trend ι industrial objects as a reflection of the cultural identity of society today as is evidenced by th Victoria and Albert Museum's collection of Dr Martens shoes or the New York Metropolitaι. um of Modern Art's collection of Hilti chairs or typewriters.

A fashion object may be transformed into a powerful medium of information conveying political and social messages. The Dutch Court of The Hague understood this when it allowed the artist Nadia Plesner to incorporate an exact reproduction of a Louis Vuiton Audra handbag in her mural painting entitled Dafurnica, inspired by Picasso's Guernica. Despite the IPRs subsisting in the design of the bag, the artist's right to freedom of expression allowed her to usurp the original intent of the creators and employ the object as a symbol to contrast poverty and consumptive tastes.[18]

Of course, part of the problem is the knee-jerk reaction to demarcate between copyright, design, trademark and patent laws. In the UK decision of *British Leyland Motor Corporation v. Armstrong Patents Co Ltd*, a case dealing with the scope of protection of technical drawings depicting an exhaust pipe, the UK court's instinctive stance was that it is anomalous for manufacturers of 'purely functional objects' to have a monopoly under copyright law when the object is not patentable or registrable as a design.[19] The concern as to the anti-competitive effects of copyright protection is that the creativity imbued within a three-dimensional manufactured object is manifested physically.

The 2011 UK decision in *Lucasfilm Ltd. v. Ainsworth*[20] is another clear example of why this approach may be short-sighted and unreflective of the modern role of industrial objects in everyday life. One of the primary issues in the case was whether the Imperial Stormtrooper helmet as used in the original Star Wars films could qualify as an artistic work. The court's view was clear: the helmet was functional only as the equipment of the 'stormtrooper' soldier, and moreover, this was all the creator had intended. In thus concluding, the court did not look at other factors which their brethren courts in the EU have done in recent times. If they had, it would have been clear to them that far from merely functioning as the equipment of soldiers in a film, the Stormtrooper helmet manifests itself in diverse forms in the amorphous world of fashion, symbolism, culture and image identifiers. For instance, there are countless websites retailing Star Wars paraphernalia and costumes where one can purchase a Stormtrooper helmet to suit every age, taste and budget. If one wished an 'original' Stormtrooper helmet cast from the 'original Ainsworth' mould (namely those made using the original moulds used to cast the first helmets utilised in the original Star Wars movies, hence explaining, in part, the consternation and resulting lawsuit from Lucasfilm Inc in this case), it would cost between £500 and £1,000.

One appreciates the aversion to protecting patentable inventions under copyright law, and thus bypassing the strict thresholds of protection under patent law (namely novelty and inventive step). As we see from the discussion below on the principles of *sui generis* law, the usual determinants as to whether protection should be granted are: (i) functionality; and (ii) the intention of the creator. When one is dealing with everyday objects, the main 'function' may lie in its visual significance and product differentiation – and in this way, many 3-D designs also function as trade marks (see Chapter 6).

---

[18] *Louis Vuitton SA v. Nadia Plesner* [2011] ECDR 4.

[19] *British Leyland Motor Corp v. Armstrong Patents Co Ltd* [1986] UKHL 7 (27 February 1986).

[20] *Lucasfilm Ltd. v. Ainsworth* High Court [2008] EWHC 1878 (Ch), [2008] ECDR 17; Court of Appeal, [2009] EWCA Civ 1328; [2010] ECDR 6; Supreme Court, [2011] UKSC 39, [2011] 6 ECDR 21.

An object may look functional but this can be a deliberate deception by the object designers to seduce the user in a crowded field of technology. One jurist ascribes this characteristic of design to compete in both the market for artistic works and the general products market as a result of a two-market conundrum, which 'facilitates extension of the generous modalities of copyright law into the general product market for which it was not designed'.[21] EU design law is premised on similar ideas which acknowledge design to be a 'marketing tool of ever-increasing importance' and a 'significant aspect of modern culture'. In defining the need for an effective regime of protection within the Community, the European Commission similarly trumpeted the importance of the influence of good design on the competitiveness of the economy.[22] Under US law, the rationale for *sui generis* design patent protection is clear from the first Supreme Court decision in this area. In *Gorham Mfg Co. v. White*, the Court held that design patent law:

> Were plainly intended to give encouragement to the decorative arts. They contemplate not so much utility as appearance, and that, not an abstract impression or picture, but an aspect given to those objects mentioned in the acts […] The law manifestly contemplated that giving certain new and original appearances to a manufactured article may enhance its saleable value, may enlarge the demand for it, and may be a meritorious service to the public.[23]

Others have argued that the US design patent regime was constructed as a response to technological innovation, namely the increasing incorporation of design features into mass-manufactured consumer products. As opposed to the European impetus for early design legislation which arose primarily from the textile industry, the main American petitioners for increased protection in relation to designs were the cast-iron producers.[24]

7.2 INTERNATIONAL LAW

7.2.1 De minimis rules

Once design law was viewed as the vehicle of protection for industrially manufactured objects, an inchoate set of international and national policies started to mushroom within international and national copyright laws. In respect of the former, the position is still primarily governed by the 1886 Berne Convention which adopted an expansive definition of protectable subject matter, and

---

[21] J. Reichmann, 'Legal Hybrids between Patent and Copyright Paradigms' (1994) 94(8) *Columbia Law Review* 2432, 2461.

[22] Legal Review on Industrial Design Protection in Europe, European Commission, June 2016, available at https://ec.europa.eu/growth/content/legal-review-industrial-design-protection-europe-0_en, para 2.

[23] 81 US (14 Wall) 511 (S Ct, 1872), 524–5; confirmed in *Egyptian Goddess, Inc v. Swisa, Inc*, 543 F 3d 665, 670 (Fed Cir, 2008) (en banc). Beebe similarly suggests that the primary purpose of design patents is to incentivise product differentiation – see B. Beebe, 'Intellectual Property Law and the Sumptuary Code' (2010) 123 *Harvard Law Review* 809, 862–64.

[24] Du Mont and Janis, *supra* note 14, 837, 848–54.

is, in turn, supported by the 1883 Paris Convention for the Protection of Industrial Property and the 1994 TRIPS Agreement.

Article 2(1) of Berne Convention for the Protection of Literary and Artistic Works specifies that Union countries must protect 'literary and artistic works' which includes 'every production in the literary, scientific and artistic domain, whatever may be the mode or form of its expression', which in turn, include 'works of drawing, painting, architecture, sculpture, engraving and lithography', 'works of applied art', and 'illustrations, maps, plans, sketches and three-dimensional works relative to geography, topography, architecture or science'. The inclusive definition above should be read together with Article 2(7) of the Convention that states:

> [...] it shall be a matter for legislation in the countries of the Union to determine the extent of the application of their laws to works of applied art and industrial designs and models, as well as the conditions under which such works, designs and models shall be protected.

The issue of whether 'works of art applied to industrial purposes' should be included within the scope of the copyright law had been a matter of much contention at preceding Berne revision conferences and was finally adopted in Brussels (1948). It is clear that attempts to bring designed objects under the umbrella of full artistic copyright protection under the Berne Convention was not entirely successful. Due to the insistence of the UK (and countries which followed her non-cumulative approach), the Convention further provided that works protected in their 'country of origin solely as designs and models' were only entitled to in other Union countries to such 'special protection' as accorded to designs and models; the unusual position of the designs/works of applied art category was further emphasised by the suspension of mandatory rules on term of protection, with 25 years being the bare minimum length of copyright protection.[25] A celebrated example of a national law, which availed itself of this exception, was the British provision on artistic works that are industrially applied.[26]

Subsequent international IP instruments did not clarify matters, with the 1883 Paris Convention (on industrial property) being another contender for objects, under the separate classifications of 'designs and utility models'. However, the mode or criteria of protection, whether by a registered design regime or by copyright, was left entirely to the discretion of member states.[27] An analogous treatment can also be recognised in the TRIPS Agreement 1994, which adopts the Berne position while obliging WTO states to give a minimum standard of protection, and suggesting specifically that copyright protection may be the best approach for the protection

---

[25] Berne Convention (1971 Paris revision), Arts 2(7), 7(4). See also S. Ricketson and J. Ginsburg, *International Copyright and Neighbouring Rights: The Berne Convention and Beyond* (2nd ed., Oxford: Oxford University Press, 2005), paras 1.14, 3.11, 3.38.

[26] The provision can be seen in various forms in the 1911 Copyright Act, 1956 Copyright Act and the 1988 Copyright, Designs, Patents Act.

[27] Paris Convention, Arts 1(2), 5*quinquies*; the categories entered the Convention under the 1925 Hague Revision Conference; see also G. Bodenhausen, *Guide to the Application of the Paris Convention for the Protection of Industrial Property* (Geneva: BIRPI, 1967), 73–4, 86.

of textile designs. No definitions of 'applied art' or 'industrial design' are offered in any of these instruments.[28]

The differences between the Berne-copyright approach and the Paris-industrial property approach are numerous. Under copyright law, protection is automatically accorded, without the need for formalities nor registration. An anti-copying right is granted, for the term of the author's life plus 50 years, on original designs. The position under *sui generis* design law is less uniform under the international agreements, resulting in a more varied design law landscape:

(i)   registered design (or design patent) systems offering an exclusive 25-year right to novel designs, although many jurisdictions require additional criteria such as originality, distinctiveness or individual character (discussed below);

(ii)   unregistered design protection systems offering a short-lived anti-copying right within design or copyright or *sui generis* laws with modified rules as under the EU/UK design regimes discussed below, or under the US semiconductor chip law, or under the US vessel hull law;[29]

(iii) a cause of action based on liability rules and unfair competition law, as under the US trade dress regime,[30] or under Japanese and Korean unfair competition laws.[31]

Of course, there is always the possibility of claiming protection for the shape of a product through trade mark, and even patent or utility models laws.

---

[28] TRIPS Agreement, Arts 9(1), 25 and 26.

[29] A modified copyright approach was adopted in the 1984 US Semiconductor Chip Protection Act, s 902, US Copyright Law Chapter 9. This legislation is historically interesting as it shifted the protection of scientific innovation from patent law to the design/copyright spheres. To be protectable, topography design must be original, and it cannot consist 'solely of designs that are staple, commonplace, or familiar in the semiconductor industry, or variations of such designs, combined in a way that, considered as a whole, are not original'. A variation of this legal formula was subsequently adopted by the UK in its 1988 unregistered design rights regime for all types of functional designs, and then the EU in relation to its unregistered Community Design Right. The second type of industry-specific law is the US Vessel Hull Design Protection Act, s 1201(a), US Copyright Law Chapter 12 – which resulted from rather bizarre lobbying endeavours by the boat industry. Protection is granted for ten years to an original design of a vessel hull, vessel plug or vessel mould which makes the vessel attractive or distinctive in appearance to the purchasing or using public. Originality is defined thus: 'the result of the designer's creative endeavour that provides a distinguishable variation over prior work, pertaining to similar articles which is more than merely trivial and has not been copied from another source'. Excluded are staple, commonplace designs dictated solely by a utilitarian function of the article that embodies it.

[30] Suthersanen, 2000, *supra* note 1. Chapter 12.

[31] Unfair Competition Prevention Act 2015 (Japan); Unfair Competition Prevention and Trade Secrets Act (Korea). See also *Slowfood-Korea, Inc v. Gil-Soo Kim and Hyung-Yak Lee*, Korean Supreme Court, 2016Da229058, 21 Sept 2016, a shop's appearance, including the logo, outdoor signage, indoor layout, and other decorative elements are protected trade dress, as reported in *Lexology*, March 14, 2017.

7.2.2 International registration

The Hague Agreement Concerning the International Registration of Industrial Designs frames the international registration of designs. The Agreement was adopted in 1925 but despite modernising and expansive revisions under the 1934 London Act, and the still effective Hague Act 1960, the Agreement proved rather ineffective until the more recent revisions under the Geneva Act 1999 which enticed more major countries to join, including the EU as a whole, the US and Japan. Insofar as the EU is concerned, applicants have a choice of either designating protection for the whole of the EU (thus gaining a unitary Community Registered design), or by designating individual EU member states who are themselves members of the Hague Agreement (for example, France, Germany and most recently in 2018, the UK).[32]

Currently, the Hague Agreement comprises two of the latter acts, namely, the 1960 Hague Act and the 1999 Geneva Act. Both consist of a different set of legal provisions, and signatories are free to choose whichever act they are party to – except in the case of international intergovernmental organisations which can only become party to the Geneva Act. An applicant can file a single application with WIPO, either directly or through any of the 67 contracting parties, to obtain registered design protection in one or more than one jurisdiction. The Agreement also allows proprietors to record changes or to effect renewals through a single procedural step. The rights themselves, however, are covered by the national laws of the designated countries.

The international registration framework, which has been compared to the Madrid Protocol for trade marks, is favourable in that it provides protection in up to 82 territories currently, through a single application and set of fees. Applications may include up to 100 designs, provided they all belong to the same class of the Locarno International Classification for Industrial Designs. Applications are in English, French or Spanish, and must contain one or several reproductions of the design. On the other hand, WIPO only examines the application as to formalities – all substantive examinations are carried out by the national or regional offices. A similar process applies for applications for invalidity or infringement. Thus, the single design application will have to pre-empt possible challenges and opposition if it is designated for multiple jurisdictions with disparate rules of protection.

7.3 ARTISTIC COPYRIGHT IN THE EU

7.3.1 EU jurisprudence

The European journey in design legislation can be traced back to the 1960s when initial attempts to harmonise IP laws in the original six member states led to a report recommending that uniform rules could and should be adopted at the Community level. The report also underlined the

---

[32] Design Regulation, Art 106.

difficulty of undertaking legislative harmonisation due to the substantial differences that charac-terised the laws of the member states in the area.[33]

International ambivalence in relation to the copyright/design law interface helps one to appre-ciate the fact that the European legal landscape has historically been a patchwork of laws repre-senting various modes and standards of protection for designs, under both copyright and design laws. Although France and the UK had historically protected designs, the legal approach between these two historical models was clearly divided by the end of the nineteenth century.[34] At one end of the spectrum were countries such as France where the growing jurisprudential view was that all objects, especially fashion items, whether classified as pure art or manufactured industrially, de-served the same treatment under copyright law[35] – the so-called cumulative protection approach, as opposed to the partial or non-cumulative approaches. At the doubting end of the spectrum was the UK, which had tentatively extended copyright protection beyond the print medium to busts and sculptures from 1798.[36] However, a parallel scheme of protection under a *sui generis* system was deemed more acceptable for industrial objects,[37] whereas truly artistic works (or fine arts) would continue to fall within the purview of copyright law.[38]

In between the two historical extremes of cumulative and non-cumulative protection, stood the rest of the EU countries. Some member states' copyright laws, such as the Benelux area, veered to-wards the French position. Others took a more vigorous stance against cumulative protection. For example, the jurisprudential and legislative history of Italy, Germany and the UK clearly indicated a conscious policy decision to demarcate between copyright law, and the *sui generis* design regime, by employing various legal tools (for example, creativity, artistic merit or separability) to ensure that copyright protection was limited to a small number of truly artistic and creative designs. This latter policy arises from two bases: a historical abhorrence to extending copyright to 'industrial' objects; and a fear that untrammelled copyright protection can lead to anti-competitive barriers, especially in relation to functional aspects of a product design.[39]

The conflict between national positions was scrutinised by the CJEU in *Titus Donner*[40] where it was confirmed that EU law, including the free movement principle, has no effect on cross-

---

[33] 1962 Report of the Working Party on Industrial Designs, as cited in *Fundación Española para la Innovación de la Artesanía (FEIA) v. Cul de Sac Espacio Creativo SL and Acierta Product & Position SA*, Advocate General's Opinion, C-32/08, 26 March 2009, para 2.

[34] S. Ricketson and U. Suthersanen, 'The Design/Copyright Overlap: is there a Resolution', in N. Wilkof and S. Basheer, *Overlapping Intellectual Property Rights* (Oxford University Press, 2012), 159–87.

[35] *Robin v. Romagnesi*, Cour de Cassation. 17 November 1814, available at *Primary Sources on Copyright (1450–1900)*, http://copy.law.cam.ac.uk/record/f_1814; for a subsequent confirmation, see Cass. Civ. 2 August 1854, D.P. 1854, 1, p. 395 cited in A. Lucas and H.J. Lucas, *Traité de la Propriété littéraire et artistique* (Paris: Litec, 1994), para 74.

[36] Models and Casts of Busts Act, 1798 (38 Geo. III, c.71); Sculpture Copyright Act 1814 (54 Geo. III, c. 56).

[37] Copyright and Designs Act 1839 II (2 & 3 Vict c 17); Utility Designs Act 1843, which protected designs incorporating functional features; Patents, Trade Marks and Registered Designs Act 1883.

[38] Fine Art Copyright Act, 1862, 25 & 26 Vict., c. 68.

[39] Suthersanen, 2000, *supra* note 1, Chapter 9.

[40] Case C-5/11 *Criminal proceedings against Titus Donner* [2012] ECLI:EU:C:2012: 370.

border transactions, as long as aspects of national intellectual property laws remain unharmonised. Here, the German rights holder employed the EU harmonised right of distribution and national criminal sanctions to stop the distribution of furniture made in Italy, but sold and distributed to German customers, via the accused's company. As the Advocate General noted, the German courts had considered all the items to be copies of copyright protected works of applied art; whereas in Italy the items were either unprotected under national copyright law or copyright in them was unenforceable in practice during the relevant period. The CJEU's view was that EU law could not impede national copyright provisions, including criminal sanctions, where the goods are marketed for a particular national market, namely Germany, in light of the unharmonised state of affairs.

Two landmark decisions in *Flos v. Semararo*[41] and *Cofemel v. G-Star*[42] sees the CJEU ending the long-running saga within the EU as to whether industrially manufactured objects can be copyright works: they can be. In *Flos*, the Court held that the law could not be 'interpreted as meaning that Member States have a choice as to whether or not to confer copyright protection for a design protected by a design right registered in or in respect of a Member State if the design meets the conditions under which copyright protection is conferred'.[43] This was further confirmed in *Cofemel* where the Court held that for a design to be original, it is both necessary and sufficient for the work to reflect the personality of the author as manifested from her free and creative choices. Where, however, technical considerations, rules or other constraints leave no room for the exercise of such creative freedom, then the design cannot constitute an original work.[44]

7.3.2 National landscapes

Since the overhaul of her copyright law in 1988,[45] the UK has constructed a complex legal structure in order to restrain the inadvertent anti-competitive consequences of protecting functional designs, especially in relation to motor vehicles. Following the CJEU's decision in *Flos*, the UK government re-considered its stance on copyright protection of industrially applied artistic works, and amended.[46] The result is that 'artistic works' will now be protected by copyright law for the full term of protection, irrespective of whether such works are industrially manufactured. This surprising turn of events has prompted criticism of the UK's and indeed, the CJEU's interpretation of the principle of cumulation.[47] While there is reference to the *Flos* decision in the rationale for the repeal of the durational exception, the British government does not specifically cite this decision as the basis for its volte face on its copyright/design policy. Instead, it is claimed that:

[41] Case C-168/09 *Flos SpA v. Semeraro Casa e Famiglia SpA* [2011] ECDR 8.

[42] Case C-683/17 *Cofemel – Sociedade de Vestuário SA v G-Star Raw CV*, [2019] ECLI:EU:C:2019:721.

[43] Discussing Design Directive 98/71, Art 17, *Flos SpA v. Semeraro*, ibid., para 36; See also Case C-198/10 *Cassina SpA v. Alivar Srl and Galliani Host Arredamenti Srl* 9 Sept 2011.

[44] *Supra* note 42, paras 30–31.

[45] UK Copyright Law, ss 1, 4; see U. Suthersanen, 'Copyright and Industrial Objects: Aesthetic Considerations and Policy Discriminations', in D. Halbert and M. David (eds), *Sage Handbook of Intellectual Property* (Sage, 2015).

[46] Enterprise and Regulatory Reform Act 2013, s 74, repealing CDPA 1988 (UK), s 52.

[47] L. Bently, 'The Return of Industrial Copyright' [2012] 10 *EIPR* 654.

A company which makes 'furniture design classics' has claimed that it loses more than EUR 250 million per year in international turnover due to copies and that a significant proportion of that loss is attributable to the UK legislation which differs from that in other EU states.[48]

Citing evidence from manufacturers of classic design furniture, including *Flos*, *Cassina*, and *Knoll*, the government further stated that it had been told that all the significant internet importers into the EU from the Far East of the replicas use the UK as a staging post to take advantage of her relaxed copyright.[49] The effect of the *Flos* decision is clear in the more recent Italian jurisprudence. Since 2001, designs are now eligible for copyright protection in Italy if they 'possess in themselves creative character and artistic value'.[50] In order to determine whether the object has an inherent aesthetic and creative character, the courts look to external indicia for a confirmation of such qualities in the design. In the *Panton Chair* decision for instance, the Milan Court of Appeal held that the 'artistic value' had to be assessed objectively, and that:

> A particular indicator of the artistic value of a design work is the fact that some cultural institutions have commonly recognised it to emanate from or be the expression of trends and influences of art movements, beyond the intentions and awareness of its author, having regard to both the intrinsic value and the representation and communication ability that a work of art has, and is recognised to have, by a circle of persons not limited to the consumers of that specific product.[51]

This line of analysis was also applied in the *Flos* decision which was remanded back to the Court of Milan. The court, this time round, considered the following factors in order to ascertain the 'artistic value' of the Arco lamp: whether there was widespread appreciation of the work in the cultural and institutional sector (for example, critics, cultural institutions, museums), irrespective of the fact that it is of daily use; *Flos's* evidence that a consensus had been reached among cultural and institutional fields on the 'Arco' lamp's ability to represent the trends of the post-war Italian industrial design; the fact that the 'Arco' lamp had been included in the collection of the New York Museum of Arts and Design for over ten years.[52] This has been further codified by the Italian Supreme Court in *Metalco SpA v. City Design SpA*, namely that designs can enjoy copyright protection subject to presence of 'artistic value' which can be proven from three objective factors:

---

[48] 'Copyright protection for designs', HMG Impact Assessment, 15.5.2012, available at http://www.legislation.gov.uk/ukia/2013/1053/pdfs/ukia_20131053_en.pdf.

[49] Ibid.

[50] Italian Copyright Law, Art 2(10).

[51] *Vitra Patente AG v. High Tech s.r.l.*, Case No 1983/2007, Court of Milan, September 13, 2012; see A. Barbieri and F. De Santis, 'Copyright Protection of Design: Approach of Italian Courts and Italian Law after ECJ's Decision in Flos vs Semeraro', 2012, available at http://www.portolano.it/2012/10/copyright-protection-of-design-approach-of-italian-courts-and-italian-law-after-ecjs-decision-in-flos-vs-semeraro/.

[52] *Cassina v. High Tech S.r.l.*, Court of Milan, July 7, 2011; *Flos/Arco* decision, Court of Milan, September 20, 2012; Suthersanen, *supra* note 45, Chapter 29.

1.   the institutional and cultural, and evidenced by the display of the work in museums and ex-
     hibitions, the publication in non-commercial dedicated journals, the participation in artistic
     events, the awards received, the reviews of experts in the relevant field, etc.;
2.   the commercialisation of the design in the art market and not just in purely commercial
     markets, or the higher value gained by the design in the purely commercial market;
3.   the creation of the design by a famous artist.[53]

In light of the *Cofemel* decision discussed above, it remains to be seen whether the Italian courts
will change this approach of requiring 'artistic value'. The German position has also changed
considerably. It was the case under German law that it would have been possible to gain simultaneous protection under both its *droit d'auteur* and *sui generis* design law if the work fulfils the criteria of protection under both laws, and if the work attains certain judicially determined artistic
standards. This position is not derived from any specific legal position but rather from a long
line of jurisprudence commencing with the 1911 decision of the Supreme Court in *Schulfraktur*
which held that while there is no absolute or fixed frontier between artistic works (protected
under *droit d'auteur* law) and designs (protected under design law), the difference between them
was a difference of degree which was determined, more or less, by the aesthetic quality of the
work. The position has been re-affirmed on many occasions by the Supreme Court which has
held that industrially manufactured objects (or as termed under German law 'works of applied
art') had to conform to a higher degree of creative individuality, authorial freedom and aesthetic
considerations in order to gain copyright protection.[54] It is not the art expert's opinion which is
paramount, but:

> [...] the aesthetic impression that the work communicates according to the assessment of a
> person sensitive to and, to a certain extent, familiar with art. In the process, account must be
> taken of the conditions at the time of the creation of the work.[55]

---

[53] *Metalco SpA v. City Design SpA*, Case No 23292/2015, Suprema Corte di Cassazione, Sezione I Civile, 13 November
2015. See M. Bellia, 'Italy: comment on Metalco – top-tier design, copyright protection and the assessment of the artistic
value requirement under Italian law' [2016] 47(7) *IIC* 875. Other member states have changed their approach to embrace
cumulative protection of designs under both copyright and design, Slovenia, Spain, Netherlands, Finland, Denmark,
Austria and Sweden as long as designs show a 'marked artistic character' test. Legal Review on Industrial Design
Protection in Europe, European Commission, *supra* note 22, 95–6.

[54] The statutory requirement under Art 2(2), German Copyright Law is that copyright will be conferred on works which
show the 'author's own intellectual creations'. *Cf Silberdistel*, BGH, June 22, 1995, GRUR 1995, 581; (1997) 28 *IIC* 140,
mass-produced silver thistle earrings served a utilitarian purpose and were works of applied, rather than pure, art;
further confirmation of this principle is also to be found in the following German Supreme Court decisions: *Mecki-Igel*,
BGH, GRUR 1958, 500 (501); *Stahlrohrstuhl* BGH, GRUR 1961, 635 (638). See also U. Suthersanen, 'Breaking Down the
Intellectual Property Barriers' (1998) 3 *IPQ* 267, 272.

[55] Suthersanen, *supra* note 45, 545, citing OLG Hamburg, 3 May 2001, 3 U 130/00, GRUR 2002, 419 (Move); [2003] 34
IIC 461, 462.

This attitude has changed dramatically in light of the *Flos* decision, with the German Supreme Court holding that the level of creativity required for works of applied art will be no higher than that required for works of fine art. It is thus sufficient 'that they attain a level of creativity that allows a public that is open to art and relatively familiar with views on art justifiably to speak of "artistic" creation [...]'.[56]

7.3.3   Resolving two rights: community design

Copyright protection sits alongside *sui generis* design law which is governed by a Community Design Regulation and a Design Directive. The latter sets out a two-tier regulatory framework.[57] To accommodate the different needs of varying design sectors (from toys to textiles to fashion to light engineering to optical to automotive), the Design Regulation creates a unitary protection system within the EU by offering two pan-EU design rights: (i) the registered Community design right, an exclusive right for up to 25 years (based on five-year renewable periods); and (ii) the unregistered Community design right, an anti-copying right which offers a less extensive, automatic, three-year right.

Irrespective of the form of protection, the Community Design Right has equal effect throughout the EU, and would not normally be subject to transfer, surrender or invalidity declarations, except in respect of the whole EU region. Designers who have opted initially for a national registered right, and who subsequently wish to venture into the EU trading arena armed with a wider right, may rely (if applicable) on their national filing dates to acquire a priority right for a registered Community design; or even acquire priority rights beyond the EU region in Contracting States of the Paris Convention or the Hague Agreement.[58] The Design Directive harmonises the substantive rules of national registered design laws, and the national registered design systems co-exist in parallel with the Design Regulation. The areas of harmonisation include protectable subject matter, conditions of protection, scope of protection, and validity. Matters which are left to member states include rules on the following: ownership, registration, procedures and remedies.[59]

---

[56] *Independent Toy Designer v. Toy Manufacturer, Geburtstagszug/'Birthday Train'*, German Federal Supreme Court, I ZR 143/12, 13 November 2013; Case Comment, IIC 2014, 45(7), 831–4.

[57] Design Directive 98/71/EC of the European Parliament and Council of 13 October 1998 on the legal protection of design [1998] O.J. L289; Council Regulation (EC) 6/2002 of 12 December 2001 on Community designs (OJ EC No L 3 of 5.1.2002, p. 1), amended by Council Regulation No 1891/2006 of 18 December 2006 amending Regulations (EC) No 6/2002 and (EC) No 40/94 (OJ EC No L 386 of 29.12.2006, p. 14).

[58] Paris Convention for the Protection of Industrial Property of March 20, 1883, (1979 revision); Geneva Act of the Hague Agreement concerning the international registration of industrial designs (1999).

[59] For a detailed report on the current EU Community design framework see Legal Review on Industrial Design Protection in Europe, European Commission, *supra* note 22.

7.4 ARTISTIC COPYRIGHT IN THE UNITED STATES

7.4.1 Early jurisprudence

While there was no doubt of the constitutional basis for protecting designs under copyright laws, the earliest recorded statutory protection for copyright works in the US under the 1790 Act shows that protection only extended to maps, charts, books and prints. Thereafter, protection was extended under the Copyright Act of 1870 to include, inter alia, 'engraving, cut, print, or photograph or negative thereof, or of a painting, drawing, chromo, statute, statuary, and of models or designs intended to be perfected as works of the fine art'. The phrase 'works of fine arts' was to prove to be elusive due to the uneasiness of courts as to the demarcation line between 'fine art' and industrially-based artistic works. A major reason for this dilemma arose from US Supreme Court's ruling in *Baker v. Selden*, which had denied copyright protection to blank book-keeping forms due to the utilitarian nature of the work. Should works of 'fine arts' similarly exclude articles, which exuded a utilitarian nature?[60]

The dilemma has been, inconclusively, addressed in three landmark Supreme Court decisions. First, we have an early-twentieth-century decision in *Bleistein v. Donaldson Lithographing Co*, which concerned the issue of whether copyright protection could be granted to chromolithographs used primarily as posters for circus advertisements. Essentially, the court deprecated an analysis of 'works of fine arts' based purely on artistic merit; instead, it recommended a non-discrimination approach. Justice Holmes's dicta is a salutary warning against courts (and legislators) embracing the 'aesthetic' criterion as a means of determining artistic copyright protection:

> It would be a dangerous undertaking for persons trained only to the law to constitute themselves final judges of the worth of pictorial illustrations, outside of the narrowest and most obvious limits. At the one extreme some works of genius would be sure to miss appreciation. Their very novelty would make them repulsive until the public had learned the new language in which their author spoke. It may be more than doubted, for instance, whether the etchings of Goya or the paintings of Manet would have been sure of protection when seen for the first time. At the other end, copyright would be denied to pictures which appealed to a public less educated than the judge. Yet if they command the interest of any public, they have commercial value – it would be bold to say that they have not an aesthetic and educational value – and the taste of any public is not to be treated with contempt.[61]

The Copyright Act 1909 thereafter extended copyright protection to three-dimensional artefacts by including within the scope of copyrightable works: 'works of art; model or designs for works

---

[60] US Constitution, Art. 1, s 8, cl. 8.; US Copyright Act of May 31, 1790, Ch. 15, 1 Stat. 124; Act of April 29, 1802, ch. 36, 2 Stat. 171; US Copyright Act of July 8, 1870, ch. 230, s 86, 16 Stat. 198, 212 (repealed 1916); *Baker v. Selden* 101 US 99 (S Ct, 1879).

[61] *Bleistein v. Donaldson Lithographing Co*, 188 US 239 (S Ct, 1903) at 251–2.

of arts'.[62] Nevertheless, a dichotomy grew between the legal notions of art and industrial designs which led to the denial of copyright protection to industrially manufactured products, until the Supreme Court intervened in the second landmark decision.

In *Mazer v. Stein*, the prevailing dichotomy between art and utility was demolished, the *Bleistein* standard was re-established thus enabling copyright protection for works of applied art. Faced with the question as to whether an artist's intention to put the artistic work to industrial use disentitled the work to copyright protection (namely to use the Balinese-inspired dancing figurine as a mass-produced lamp-base), the Supreme Court held that the:

> Individual perception of the beautiful is too varied a power to permit a narrow or rigid concept of art […] [D]ichotomy of protection for the aesthetic is not beauty and utility but, art for the copyright and the invention of original and ornamental design for design patents […] We find nothing in the copyright statute to support the argument that the intended use or use in industry of an article eligible for copyright bars or invalidates its registration. We do not read such a limitation into the copyright law.[63]

7.4.2 The separability doctrine[64]

Having accepted that copyright protection extends to articles which incorporate utilitarian aspects, the Copyright Office and courts adopted the separability doctrine, which was eventually codified in the 1976 Copyright Act. The latter also explicitly recognises useful articles (thereby somewhat codifying *Mazer v. Stein*). The current copyright law thus protects 'pictorial, graphic and sculptural works' which include:

> Works of artistic craftsmanship insofar as their form but not their mechanical or utilitarian aspects are concerned; the design of a useful article, as defined in this section, shall be considered a pictorial, graphic, or sculptural work only if, and only to the extent that, such design incorporates pictorial, graphic, or sculptural features that can be identified separately from, and are capable of existing independently of, the utilitarian aspects of the article.[65]

---

[62] 1909 Act, 35 Stat 1075 s 5(g).

[63] *Mazer v. Stein*, 347 US 201 (S Ct, 1954), 214, 218. The Supreme Court referred, in particular, to the British copyright decision in *King Features v. Kleeman* [1941] 58 RPC 207, where the intention of the designer was relevant under the Copyright Act 1911 but was limited by the court to the time when the work was created.

[64] The difficulty of the doctrine is wittily critiqued in Charles E. Colman, 'The History and Doctrine of American Copyright Protection for Fashion Design: Managing Mazer' (2016) 7 *Harvard Journal of Sports & Entertainment Law* 151; and 'Thomas Dreams of Separability' (2018) 9 *Harvard Journal of Sports & Entertainment Law* 83.

[65] 17 USC § 101. The separability criterion is applied only to a 'useful article', namely 'an article having an intrinsic utilitarian function that is not merely to portray the appearance of the article or to convey information'.

The US legislators expounded on the separability doctrine, stating that:

> Unless the shape of an automobile, airplane, ladies' dress, food processor, television set, or any other industrial product contains some element that, physically or conceptually, can be identified as separable from the utilitarian aspects of that article, the design would not be copyrighted [...].[66]

The Court of Appeals for the Second Circuit has been the primary agent in expanding the 'conceptual separability' doctrine. Thus, in *Kieselstein-Cord v. Accessories by Pearl, Inc*, the Court conceded that the artistic aspects of the designer belt buckles could not be physically separable from the utilitarian features. However, since the buckles were detachable and could be used as separate pieces of jewellery, the Court held that the 'primary ornamental aspect of the Vaquero and Winchester buckles is conceptually separable from their subsidiary utilitarian function'.[67]

In this author's view, the instability of the dizzying conceptual separability doctrine has been glaringly exposed in the third landmark Supreme Court decision in 2018.[68] In *Star Athletica LLC v. Varsity Brands, Inc*,[69] far from resolving the disparate approaches, the Court resolved that the clothing designs were copyright protected, but on differing grounds, accompanied by a strongly argued dissenting opinion. The majority opinion is that an artistic feature of the design of a useful article is eligible for copyright protection:

> If the feature (1) can be perceived as a two- or three-dimensional work of art separate from the useful article and (2) would qualify as a protectable pictorial, graphic, or sculptural work either on its own or in some other medium if imagined separately from the useful article.[70]

Justice Ginsburg, while concurring that the designs were copyrightable, opined that the Court had unnecessarily engaged with the separability doctrine; in her view, the designs were not of useful articles, but were reproduced on useful articles. In their dissenting judgment, Justices Breyer and Kennedy argued that the clothing designs were not eligible for copyright protection as the design was not separable from the useful article since 'extracting the claimed features would necessarily bring along the underlying useful article'.

---

[66] 'Protection of Ornamental Designs of Useful Articles', in (1976) HR Rep No 94-1476, 55.

[67] *Kieselstein-Cord v. Accessories by Pearl, Inc* 632 F 2d 989 (2nd Cir, 1980), 993.

[68] See *Carol Barnhart Inc v. Economy Cover Corp*, 773 F 2d 411 (2nd Cir, 1985); *Brandir International Inc v. Cascade Pacific Lumber Co*, 834 F 2d 1142 (2nd Cir, 1987); *Pivot Point International, Inc*, 372 F 3d 913 at 931 (7th Cir, 2004); *Galiano v. Harrah's Operating Co, Inc*, 416 F 3d 411 (5th Cir, 2005).

[69] *Star Athletica LLC v. Varsity Brands, Inc*, 137 S Ct 1002 (S Ct).

[70] Ibid., 1016.

7.5   DESIGN LAW

7.5.1   *De minimis* standards under TRIPS

Under the TRIPS Agreement, no attempt is made to define what constitutes industrial designs, albeit textile designs are specifically mentioned; hence, the notion of 'industrial design' as employed in the TRIPS Agreement can refer to all types of aesthetic, useful and functional designs including subject matter protected as 'works of applied art' (specifically referred to in Art 12 of the Agreement), or 'works of artistic craftsmanship' under copyright law, or even as utility models. In relation to textile designs, members must protect textile designs either through design or copyright laws.[71]

The TRIPS Agreement provides that protection should be given to 'independently created industrial designs that are new or original'. WTO members may also provide that designs are not new or original if the designs do not differ significantly from known designs or combinations of known design features. Members can also adopt additional criteria.[72] Thus, under EU law, protection is granted to designs which fulfil the twin criteria of novelty and individual character, and under the US design patent regime, protection is accorded to any 'new, original, and ornamental design for an article of manufacture'.[73]

There are no compulsory provisions as to excluded subject matter or limitations and exceptions to protection under the TRIPS Agreement, although the Agreement offers members an optional mandate. Under Article 25(1), TRIPS Agreement, members may exclude designs which are 'dictated essentially by technical or functional considerations'. Members are thus free, as is the case under the UK unregistered design right system, to grant protection to both aesthetic and functional designs.[74] Should countries wish to tailor the regime to meet the demands of domestic firms, they can do this too. Thus, the EU's design laws have adopted a specific 'interconnections' exclusion clause, while the British/Hong Kong copyright laws limit copyright protection of functional design drawings and works of applied art.[75]

Under the Agreement, the minimum term of protection is ten years although there is no guidance on whether this term is to be computed from the date of filing (if any) or the date of issue. This provision is also taken to refer only to situations where *sui generis* design law is the only means of protection. If a WTO member opts for copyright protection of industrial designs, the duration of protection should be governed by the Berne Convention. The general rule for copyright is that the duration of protection must be 50 years pma. The exceptions to this include works of applied art – Berne signatories remain free to provide for a shorter duration of protection, as long as a minimum term of 25 years from the making of the work is granted.[76]

---

[71] TRIPS Agreement, Art 25(2).

[72] TRIPS Agreement, Art 25(1).

[73] EU law: Design Directive 98/71/EC, Arts 3–5; Community Design Regulation 6/2002, Arts 4–6; US law: US Patent Law, s 171.

[74] UK Copyright Law, ss 213 *et seq.*

[75] For example, UK Copyright Law, ss 51 and 52.

[76] Berne Convention, Art 7(4).

7.5.2   Definition of design and product

EU design law defines 'design' as follows: 'the appearance of the whole or a part of a product resulting from the features of, in particular, the lines, contours, colours, shape, texture and/or materials of the product itself and/or its ornamentation'.

This definition of design, anchored in the appearance of the whole or part of the product, may include any element which can be perceived by the human senses such as the weight or flexibility or the tactile impressions given by the designed product. At the outset, it is clear that there is no qualitative requirement of artistic merit or aesthetic quality.[77] The European Commission had also initially expressed the view that the definition should be wide enough to cover any economic value attached to the appearance of the product, and that the 'texture' of a product should be included if a 'particular impression is made to the sense of touch'.[78] Current jurisprudence points to some uncertainty as the inclusion of such elements has caused confusion. Is the legal notion of design limited to visual perceptibility, with texture and material being relevant only insofar as they impact on the visual appearance? While the definition does not state that the design must be visible to the naked eye, EU law does stipulate that where design protection is claimed for internal mechanisms (such as the 'under the bonnet' parts of motor vehicles), these will only qualify for protection if they pass a visibility test.

Finally, if the definition of design is read in conjunction with the recitals, the EU General Court has held that the definition of design is clearly restricted to 'visible elements', 'the product's appearance', and 'the visible parts of the products or parts of products'. It is also noteworthy that features of a design which cannot be derived from the design representation in a clear, precise and objective manner should not form part of the protectable subject matter.[79] This view is further supported by the statement of the Advocate General in *PepsiCo Inc*, that the protection of designs under the Design Regulation 'takes into account only the visual impression which the designs produce on the informed user'.[80]

Under US design law, there is no definition of 'design' within the statute, and resort has to be made to the guidelines adopted by the courts, and USPTO.[81] In summary, protection is accorded to 'visual characteristics embodied in or applied to an article'; which include the following: ornamental designs of all kinds including surface ornamentation as well as configuration of goods; visual characteristics embodied in or applied to an article, or aspect displayed by the article; appearances presented by the article which creates an impression through the eye upon the mind of the observer. The issue of visibility also arises under US law, and the current position is that protection will not be accorded to designs which only remain visible in their ultimate end use which is primarily functional, or to designs which are not visible in its normal and intended use (showing that its appearance is not a matter of concern).[82]

---

[77] Design Directive, Recital (14).

[78] EC Green Paper on the Legal Protection of Industrial Design, June 1991, III/F/5131/91/EN, para 5.4.7.2 (EC Green Paper).

[79] Case T-494/12 *Biscuits Poult SAS v. OHIM* ECLI:EU:T:2014:757.

[80] C-281/10 P *PepsiCo Inc v. Grupo Promer Mon Graphic SA*, AG's Opinion, [2011] ECDR 12, para 73.

[81] US Patent Law, s 171; USPTO Manual of Patent Examining Procedure (MPEP), 9th ed., 08.2017.

[82] *In re Webb*, 916 F 2d 1553 (Fed Cir, 1990); for a further discussion, see Suthersanen, 2010, *supra* note 1, Chapter 10.

7.5.3   Criteria of protection – the EU position

Novelty

Within EU law, a design shall be considered new if no identical design has been made available to the public before the date of filing of the application for registration or, if priority is claimed, the date of priority. Factors taken into consideration include: the degree of the designer's freedom in developing the design; the application of a known design to a new product or medium or the fact that the design is a novel arrangement or configuration of known design features. Note however that the European design law embraces 'relative novelty', as opposed to an absolute or universal degree of novelty. We discuss this disclosure provision below.

Another consideration is the grace period of 12 months preceding the filing date or the priority date, within which designs could be tested in the market without endangering the novelty of the design. The grace period is in respect of any disclosure of the design made by the designer, his successor in title or any third party. The grace period is also available in relation to any disclosure of the design which is the result of abusive conduct. During this period, the design proprietor will be able to claim the Community unregistered design right.[83]

Individual character

A design shall be considered to have individual character if the overall impression it produces on the informed user differs from the overall impression produced on such a user by any design which has been made available to the public before the date of filing of the application for registration or, if priority is claimed, the date of priority. In assessing individual character, the degree of freedom of the designer in developing the design shall be taken into consideration.[84] Several issues arise.

First, the test reinforces the notion that the design must be considered in its entirety. Irrespective of the number of detailed differences which exist between the design under review and the prior design, if the overall impression is one of similarity, the subsequent design will not have individual character.

Second, it is difficult to see how the test of individual character can be carried out unless the informed user relates his impression of the design to a relevant product or trade environment; in other words, the user must be informed as to a particular design as employed within a specific product market. The criterion of individual character is gauged by the hypothetical informed user. The early commentaries suggest that, in line with the 'design is a marketing tool' theory, the informed user will normally, though not necessarily, be the end consumer or purchaser of the product.[85] The CJEU has confirmed that the concept of informed user:

> Must be understood as lying somewhere between that of the average consumer, applicable in trade mark matters, who need not have any specific knowledge and who, as a rule, makes no direct comparison between the trade marks in conflict, and the sectoral expert, who is an expert

---

[83] Design Directive 98/71/EC, Art 6(2); Community Design Regulation 6/2002, Art 7(2).

[84] Design Directive 98/71/EC, Arts 3–5; Community Design Regulation 6/2002, Arts 4–6.

[85] EC Green Paper, *supra* note 76, para 5.5.6.2.

with detailed technical expertise. Thus, the concept of the informed user may be understood as referring, not to a user of average attention, but to a particularly observant one, either because of his personal experience or his extensive knowledge of the sector in question.[86]

A practical definition of the informed user, summarising the current jurisprudence of the CJEU and the EU IP Office, was laid out in *Samsung v. Apple*:[87]

(i)   she is a user of the product in which the design is intended to be incorporated, not a designer, technical expert, manufacturer or seller;

(ii)   however, unlike the average consumer of trade mark law, she is particularly observant;

(iii)   she has knowledge of the design corpus and of the design features normally included in the designs existing in the sector concerned;

(iv)   she is interested in the products concerned and shows a relatively high degree of attention when she uses them;

(v)   she conducts a direct comparison of the designs in issue unless there are specific circumstances or the devices have certain characteristics which make it impractical or uncommon to do so;

(vi)   she merely perceives the designs as a whole and does not analyse details, nor observes in detail minimal differences which may exist.[88]

Third, the assessment must take into account the designer's freedom in developing the design. In relation to the freedom of the designer, the General Court has held that this must be considered in light of standardisation of certain features due to the constraints imposed by technical function and by any statutory requirements applicable to the product.[89] The General Court, in *Grupo Promer Mon Graphic v. OHIM*, held that:

> [T]he designer's degree of freedom in developing his design is established, inter alia, by the constraints of the features imposed by the technical function of the product or an element thereof, or by statutory requirements applicable to the product. Those constraints result in a standardisation of certain features, which will thus be common to the designs applied to the product concerned.

The General Court in this decision also noted that other constraints may be placed on the designer which should be taken into account such as cost, safety for the end-user, and fitness for purpose.[90]

---

[86] Case C-281/10P *PepsiCo Inc v. GrupoPromer Mon Graphic SA* ECLI:EU:C:2011:679.

[87] *Samsung v. Apple* UK Court of Appeal [2012] EWCA 133, paras 39–51.

[88] Summarising EU jurisprudence in Case C-281/10P, *PepsiCo Inc v. GrupoPromer*, supra note 86, paras 54–55, 59; Case T9/07 *GrupoPromer Mon Graphic SA v. OHIM* ECLI:EU:T:2010:96, para 62; Case T-153/08 *Shenzen Taiden/OHIM* ECLI:EU:T:2010:248, para 46.

[89] Ibid.

[90] *GrupoPromer Mon Graphic SA v. OHIM*, supra note 88.

Since then, the Court has further clarified that in order for a design to be considered to have individual character, the overall impression which that design produces on the informed user 'must be different from that produced on such a user not by a combination of features taken in isolation and drawn from a number of earlier designs, but by one or more earlier designs, taken individually'.[91]

Current position.

Disclosure proviso

EU design law creates a legal nexus between the following concepts: novelty, overall impression; informed user; existing design corpus; nature of the product; the industrial sector to which the design belongs. The reference to product nature and industrial sector is made more difficult by the fact that the scope of protection is linked to the design itself, and not to the product to which the design is applied or incorporated into. Moreover, the law is clear in that the scope of protection, unlike trade mark law, is not linked to the indication of product or class within the registered design application.[92] The disclosure provision tempers these open-ended queries by setting out that a disclosure will not be taken into account if the said disclosure events 'could not reasonably have become known in the normal course of business to the circles specialised in the sector concerned, operating within the Community', before the filing or priority date.[93]

The EU legislators have termed this proviso as the 'safeguard clause' against the perceived danger that design rights could be subject to invalidation challenges mounted by potential infringers claiming that antecedents could be found in remote places or museums of which the European industry could not possibly be aware.[94] It is hard to envisage, in this era of communications and of cross-fertilisation of cultural concepts, of many areas which would be inaccessible to European industrial sectors. This is especially true of furniture, textile, homeware and fashion industries which habitually scout designs from Asian, African and South American continents: for example, should furniture manufacturers in the Community be considered to be reasonably aware of the latest Japanese or Korean futon designs? Should casual beachwear designers be assumed to be aware of exhibitions in North American boating communities?

Within EU jurisprudence, it is clear that disclosures do not need to take place within the EU. Prior sales of Crocs shoes in the US or food processor designs in China would constitute valid acts of disclosure. Thus, in *Holey Soles Holdings Ltd v. Crocs Inc*, the EUIPO took into account of sales of Crocs shoes in the US, and display of such shoes in a US international boat show. Their view was that the North American market was an important one in which the Community circles specialised in the 'clogs' industry operate and monitor in the normal course of business.[95] In *Kirschenhofer v. WS Teleshop International*, it was held that disclosures of prior designs in China was important due to the volume of trade between China and Europe.[96]

---

[91] Case C-345/13 *Karen Millen Fashions Ltd v. Dunnes Stores* ECLI:EU:C:2014:2013.

[92] Design Directive, Recital (13), Art 6; Design Regulation, Recital (14), Arts 7, 10, 36(6).

[93] Design Directive, Art 6; Design Regulation, Art 7.

[94] European Parliament Opinion, [1995] OJ C287/157; Economic and Social Committee Opinion [1994] OJ C388/9.

[95] *Holey Soles Holdings Ltd* [2008] ECDR 8 OHIM (Invalidity Decision); *Crocs Inc v. Holey Soles Holdings Ltd*, [2010] ECDR 11; *Samsung Electronics and Others v. Apple Inc*.

[96] *Kirschenhofer GmbH v. WS Teleshop International Handels GmbH*, Third Board of Appeal OHIM, July 11, 2007.

7.5.4 Criteria of protection – the US position

Under the US design patent law, protection is for 'any new, original and ornamental' design. In addition to this, designs have to satisfy the non-obviousness requirement that applies to utility patents.[97]

New and original

The novelty requirement of patentability is expressed as including designs which are known or used publicly in the US, or which have been described in print worldwide, before the application. The exception is in relation to disclosures made within a year of the filing date by the designer or by another authorised person. US design law adopts the same standard of novelty as under the utility patent law: 'The degree of difference [from the prior art] required to establish novelty occurs when the average observer takes the new design for a different, and not a modified, already-existing design.'[98]

The requirement of originality is similar to that under copyright law: a design will be considered original as long as the patentable ornamental features originated with the patent applicant and was not copied from others who are not named as inventors of the design.

Ornamentality and aestheticism

An ornamental feature or design is one which was 'created for the purpose of ornamenting' and cannot be the result or merely a by-product of functional or mechanical considerations. In *LA Gear Inc v. Thom McAn Shoe Co* the Federal Circuit held that in determining whether a design is primarily functional or primarily ornamental the claimed design is viewed in its entirety, 'for the ultimate question is not the functional or decorative aspect of each separate feature, but the overall appearance of the article, in determining whether the claimed design is dictated by the utilitarian purpose of the article'.[99]

Over the years, courts have further introduced an aesthetic analysis when considering the ornamentality requirement. The Supreme Court has held that a design, to be patentable, 'must present an aesthetically pleasing appearance that is not dictated by function alone'.[100] In *Bliss v. Gotham Indus, Inc* the Court held that a bottle pitcher could not possibly be ornamental as it 'does not appeal to the eye as a thing of beauty, does not relate more to appearance and to matters of ornament than to utility and does not appeal to the aesthetic emotion'.[101] Similarly, in *Wabern Packaging Indus, Inc v. Cut Rate Plastic Hangers, Inc* the Second Circuit court held that a design patent 'has been defined to include an article that is ornamental, a product of aesthetic skill and artistic conception'.[102]

---

[97] US Patent Law, ss 101, 102, 103, and 171.

[98] *In re Bartlett* 133 USPQ 204 (CCPA, 1962), 205.

[99] *LA Gear Inc. v. Thom McAn Shoe Co* 25 USPQ 2d 1913 at 1917 (Fed Cir, 1993).

[100] *Bonito Boats, Inc v. Thunder Craft Boats, Inc,* 489 US 141, 148 (1989).

[101] *Bliss v. Gotham Indus, Inc,* 137 USPQ 189 (9th Cir, 1963).

[102] *Wabern Packaging Indus, Inc v. Cut Rate Plastic Hangers, Inc,* 210 USPQ 777 (2nd Cir, 1981).

A more elaborate guideline was given in *Design, Inc v. Emerson Co* in respect of the design of an insulated beverage container and carrier:

> The primary feature which is most striking to the casual observer is its featurelessness. Although it is not an object which is displeasing to the eye, it is far from what could be considered a thing of beauty. There is nothing either artistic or aesthetic about it. One who sees it does not take delight in its creation. It is an item which is more likely to be stored in a kitchen closet rather than on display in one's living room. The design embodied in the Schroeder patent is, therefore, not ornamental.[103]

Non-obvious

An early interpretation was set out by the Supreme Court in *Graham v. John Deere Co*, holding that obviousness had to be determined with reference to 'the scope and content of the prior art to be determined; differences between the prior art and the claims at issue; and the level of ordinary skill in the pertinent art resolved'.[104] The challenging query is from whose perspective is obviousness judged from? The normative rule is that a design is obvious if a designer of ordinary skill would have found the claimed design obvious in light of the prior art.[105] In *Laverne*, the Court adopted a less strict threshold i.e., the 'ordinary intelligent man':

> Yet the clear purpose of the design patent law is to promote progress in the 'art' of industrial design and who is going to produce that progress if it is not the class of 'competent designers'? We cannot equate them with the mechanics in the mechanic vs. inventor test for patentability. Correspondingly, we cannot solve the problem here, obviousness, by using for our basis of comparison the inventor class in the field of industrial design [...].[106]

However, this test has been reframed considerably and the current test for determining obviousness is 'whether the design would have been obvious to a designer of ordinary skill who designs articles of the type involved'.[107]

---

[103] *Design, Inc v. Emerson Co*, 168 USPQ 519 (SD Tex, 1970).

[104] 383 US 1 (S Ct, 1966), 17.

[105] *Titan Tire Corp v. Case New Holland, Inc*, 566 F 3d 1372, 1383 (Fed Cir, 2009), 1380–81.

[106] *In re Laverne* 356 F 2d 1003 (CCPA, 1966) at 1006.

[107] *In re Carter*, 213 USPQ 625 (CCPA, 1982); *In re Nalbandian* 211 USPQ 782 (CCPA, 1981); *cf Int'l Seaway Trading Corp v. Walgreens Corp*, 589 F 3d 1233, 1240 (Fed Cir, 2009).

7.5.5   Excluded subject matter – EU position

Under the EU law, design protection will not be granted to the following subject matter:[108]

1.   features of appearance of a product which are solely dictated by its technical function;
2.   features of appearance of a product which must necessarily be reproduced in their exact form and dimensions in order to permit the designed product to be mechanically connected to or placed in, around or against another product so that either product may perform its function (the interoperability exclusion);
3.   designs which are contrary to public policy or to accepted principles of morality.

Functionality

While no distinction is to be maintained between aesthetic and functional designs, the EU legislators recognised that the protection of certain functional designs can give rise to unduly restrictive effects on legitimate competition and technological innovation.[109] The reasoning is that certain features of functional designs should be excluded, but other more ambivalent features which are both functional and have market appeal (whether because it is pleasant to look at or fashionably functional) should be protected. In light of the complete befuddle that existed prior to this decision, the CJEU's formulation in the landmark decision of *Doceram*[110] should have been a welcome clarification, especially as the EU national courts, together with the EUIPO, have grappled with three separate approaches.

The first approach – the Amp or causality approach – was adopted by the (then) UK House of Lords in the decision of *Amp Inc v. Utilux Pty Ltd*.[111] The House of Lords held that the test was whether every single feature of the shape of the product in question was dictated by the function 'in the sense of being attributable to or caused by or prompted by' the product's function. In deciding whether a design was dictated by functional considerations, what is relevant is not whether the feature is the sole feature which may achieve the technical function, but whether the sole reason for using the feature is the technical function it provides. It is irrelevant, in this line of analysis, to consider whether there are alternative shapes which achieve the same function; indeed, the existence of other alternative configurations implies that the need to achieve the product's technical function was the only relevant factor when the feature in question was selected.

The second approach – multiplicity of forms approach – dictates that if other forms of a product exist that are capable of fulfilling the same technical function, the product's design may enjoy protection, 'since that range of forms shows that in such a case the product's designer was not constrained by the function, but was free to opt for any one of those forms when developing the design'.[112] This approach, initially popularised by the French courts, has been adopted by several

---

[108] Design Directive, Arts 7–8, Community Design Regulation, Arts 8–9.

[109] Community Design Regulation, Recital (10).

[110] Case 395/16, *Doceram GmbH v CeramTec GmbH*, ECLI:EU:C:2017:779 (AGO); ECLI:EU:C:2018:172 (CJEU).

[111] *Amp v. Utilux* (1972) RPC 103.

[112] Advocate General's Opinion, *Doceram, supra* note 110.

member states' courts including the UK, France, Germany, and Spain.[113] The analysis is narrow and, in most cases, there will always be an alternative shape or means of achieving the technical function.

The third approach was put forward by the EUIPO in the *Lindner* decision – the objective observer approach.[114] This approach dictates that a design is eligible for protection as long as 'aesthetic considerations' are relevant. While very much akin to that adopted in UK in the *Amp* decision, this perspective assesses the matter from the viewpoint of a 'reasonable observer': 'from the standpoint of a reasonable observer who looks at the design and asks himself whether anything other than purely functional considerations could have been relevant when a specific feature was chosen'.

In *Doceram*, the CJEU has upheld the latter approach but with modifications. In its view, the functionality exclusion:

> [...] must be interpreted as meaning that in order to determine whether the features of appearance of a product are exclusively dictated by its technical function, it must be established that the technical function is the only factor which determined those features, the existence of alternative designs not being decisive in that regard.[115]

However, the Court offered further dicta, including declaring firmly that while the visual aspects of the design remain a decisive factor, 'it is not essential for the appearance of the product in question to have an aesthetic aspect'. Moreover, in order to determine this, a court should take account of all the objective circumstances relevant to each individual case, without resorting to the hypothetical perceptions of an 'objective observer'. Far from clarifying matters, the Court held that a range of factors should be assessed including: the design at issue; the objective circumstances indicative of the reasons which dictated the choice of features of appearance of the product concerned; information on its use; and the existence of alternative designs which fulfil the same technical function, provided that those circumstances, data, or information as to the existence of alternative designs are supported by reliable evidence.[116]

What is clear is that the CJEU has rejected any reference to 'aesthetic considerations'; and while we may not employ the concept of an 'objective observer' test, one must still wade through a list of 'objective' factors, including the multiplicity of forms analysis. Moreover, this decision now aligns the interpretation of the functionality exclusions within the EU for both trade mark and design laws. Whether this is the right approach is debatable.[117]

---

[113] *Legal Review on Industrial Design Protection in Europe*, European Commission, *supra* note 22, 86–8.

[114] Case R 690/2007-3 *Lindner Recyclingtech v. Franssons Verkstäder*, Invalidity Division, 3 April 2007; (OHIM Board of Appeal, 22 October 2009), [2010] ECDR 1.

[115] Case 395/16, *Doceram GmbH v. CeramTec GmbH supra* note 110, para 32.

[116] Ibid., para 38.

[117] See Chapter 6. Some may argue that the notion of functionality must be viewed differently within design and trade mark laws. This, for example, was the historical approach and confirmed within EU jurisprudence in Case C-299/99 *Koninklijke Philips Electronics NV v. Remington Consumer Products Ltd* ECLI:EU:C:2001:52 (AGO – paras A30–A34); ECLI:EU:C:2002:377 (CJEU). See U. Suthersanen, 'Excluding Designs (and Shape Marks): Where Is the EU Court of Justice Going?' (2019) 50(2) *IIC – International Revue of Intellectual Property and Competition Law* 157–60.

Interoperability

The EU interoperability exception applies to such design features which hinder the interoperability of products of different makes. Such features enable one designed product to be 'mechanically connected or placed in, around or against another product so that either product may perform its function'. The exclusion will probably not apply to the whole design of the product but only to those features which actually physically interface with another product.[118]

The legislative hearings show that the provision is aimed primarily at the spare parts, aftermarkets and peripheral markets. There is an increasing tendency for manufacturers in certain product sectors to rely on IPRs protection to control the aftermarkets such as the motor vehicle, printer cartridge or reprographic or coffee cartridges industries. Many other industries do not have similar problems with respect to independent producers due to, perhaps, a wider degree of standardisation in peripheral parts in these sectors.[119]

It can be argued that the interconnection provision, by attempting to create a level playing field for independent parts manufacturers, assumes a task more appropriately dealt with under the general principles of competition law. Conversely, the argument is that the dismal lack of success under competition law to curb the market practices of car manufacturers has inevitably led to the adoption of the interconnection provision within the EU design system.[120] This issue is discussed further below.

An idiosyncratic proviso is that the interoperability exclusion does not apply to modular designs, that is, such designs destined for modular systems, and which by their nature must fit together or be capable of assembly.[121] Examples of such modular systems include modular toy systems such as building blocks or tiles for children, or Lego bricks or modular furniture such as desks and tables, which may consist of a number of smaller tables that can be assembled in alternative configurations. The law rationalises protection of modular systems (including mechanical fittings) stating that the mechanical fittings of modular products may constitute 'an important element of the innovative characteristics of modular products and present a major marketing asset [...]'.[122]

Morality and public policy exclusions

This provision adopts a moral stance and denies protection to designs which are contrary to public policy or to accepted principles of morality. The rule emanates from a reluctantly accepted

---

[118] Directive, Art 7(2); Regulation, Art 8(2).

[119] The European Commission admitted that its main concern, in implementing its interoperability exclusion is the spare parts industry in the automotive sector, *Hearings on the Green Paper*, Working Paper no. 3, Brussels, 25–26 June 1992, III/F/5252/92. It appears from the Commission's Report that other industries, such as, the consumer electronics sector, did not evince similar problems.

[120] EC Green Paper, *supra* note 78, 63–4.

   To ensure 'interoperability' and competition in the spare part after market in respect of a wide range of household articles, motor vehicles, consumer electronics etc, it appears advisable to exclude from protection those features of a design which would have to be reproduced necessarily in their exact form and dimensions in order for the component part to fit into the complex product for which it is intended.

[121] Directive, Art 7(3); Regulation, Art 8(3).

[122] Design Directive, Recital (15); Design Regulation, Recital (11).

international policy in IP law of not according protection where public morality is offended or if the protection is against public policy.[123] Arguments for including such a clause within an IP regime range from environmental to socio-political. The inclusion of such a clause is probably harmless, although it has potential to upset the unitary concept of a European design law. It is difficult to anticipate standards for either public policy or morality at any given time; the concept is not only linked closely to the moral climate of the era but is also highly dependent on the cultural and sociological climate of individual states.

A design can be totally unacceptable in one member state and yet be considered protectable as a work of art or design in another – nevertheless, the unitary character of the registered Community design means that it is enough that a design is found contrary to public policy in at least part of the EU for the design to be refused registration throughout the whole region. The EUIPO's guidelines on the matter are:

> The safeguard of public policy may be relied on to refuse a Community design application only if there is a genuine and sufficiently serious threat to a fundamental interest of society [...] Designs which portray or promote violence or discrimination based on sex, racial or ethnic origin, religion or belief, disability, age or sexual orientation will be refused on that account [...].[124]

Similarly, the EUIPO's Guidelines on the morality exclusion advise that designs will be excluded if: '[...] they are perceived as sufficiently obscene or offensive from the perspective of a reasonable person of normal sensitivity and tolerance Bad taste, as opposed to contrariety to morality, is not a ground for refusal'.

7.5.6   Excluded subject matter – US position

Under US law, there are no specific excluded subject matter barring the jurisprudence on non-ornamental and functional designs. The USPTO guidelines note that functionality may be an inherent aspect in all articles of manufacture, and both design and utility patents may reside in a single article of manufacture if the invention resides both in its utility and ornamental appearance.[125] Despite the absence of statutory basis, the USPTO and the judiciary have managed to forge and develop a functionality doctrine within design patent law, in an attempt to prevent the circumvention of patent law by technically dictated designs.

This is through the ornamentality requirement, which is determined by asking the following question: is the design in question solely governed by the function of the article of manufacture? If the functional or mechanical characteristics of the article dictates the primary purpose

---

[123] TRIPS Agreement, Art 27(2); European Patent Convention, Art 53(a); Paris Convention for the Protection of Industrial Property of 20 March 1883 (1979 Stockholm version), Art 6 *quinquies*(b)(iii).

[124] Section 4.2.2, *Guidelines for Examination of Registered Community Designs*, European Union Intellectual Property Office (EUIPO), 1.10.2017, citing Case C-54/99 *Église de scientologie* EU:C:2000:124, para 17.

[125] USPTO Manual of Patent Examining Procedure, 9th ed., 08.2017, s 1502.01.

functionality

of the design, a design patent will not issue.[126] A classic case in point is *Best Lock v. Ilco* where the court was faced with a design patent for a key blade blank. It was held to be invalid as the design was dictated solely by the key blades's function of having to fit within its corresponding keyway. Every feature of the design was dictated by functional considerations.[127] More specific guidance was given in *Power Controls Corp v. Hybrinetics, Inc* where the Federal Circuit court held that a clam shell type packaging which was used to encase a dimmer switch was primarily functional rather than ornamental. In considering whether the design is primarily functional, 'the purposes of the particular elements of the design necessarily must be considered'.[128] How does the court determine whether the design is functional? The usual test is to determine whether alternative designs are available in the particular product market. If so, then a design may not be dictated solely by function. In *Avia Group International v. LA Gear California*, the Federal Circuit held that the design patents for shoes patterns were valid and not functional: 'If the functional aspect or purpose could be accomplished in many other ways that is [sic] involved in this very design, that fact is enough to destroy the claim that this design is primarily functional.'[129]

In a more detailed discussion of the functionality doctrine, the Federal Circuit in *LA Gear Inc. v. Thom McAn Shoe Co* recently rejected the notion that the existence of competing products in the product's market environment immediately signalled that the design configuration was ornamental, rather than functional. Instead, reminiscent to the recent stance in the EU, the Circuit court suggested a multi-faceted test:

> The design of a useful article is deemed to be functional when the appearance of the claimed design is dictated by the use or purpose of the article. If the particular design is essential to the use of the article, it cannot be the subject of a design patent [...] In determining whether a design is primarily functional or primarily ornamental the claimed design is viewed in its entirety, for the ultimate question is not the functional or decorative aspect of each separate feature, but the overall appearance of the article, in determining whether the claimed design is dictated by the utilitarian purpose of the article [...] When there are several ways to achieve the function of an article of manufacture, the design of the article is more likely to serve a primarily ornamental purpose.[130]

7.5.7   Scope and duration of protection

Registered or unregistered right
As previously discussed, registration is not a necessary pre-requisite in order to obtain protection

---

[126] *Bentley v. Sunset House Distrib Corp*, 149 USPQ 152 (9th Cir, 1966).

[127] *Best Lock v. Ilco Unican*, 94 F 3d 1563 at 1555–1556 (Fed Cir, 1996).

[128] *Power Controls Corp v. Hybrinetics, Inc*, 806 2d 234 (Fed Cir, 1986).

[129] *Avia Group International Inc v. LA Gear California Inc*, 7 USPQ 2d 1548 at 1553 (Fed Cir, 1988).

[130] *LA Gear Inc. v. Thom McAn Shoe Co* 25 USPQ 2d 1913 at 1917 (Fed Cir, 1993); see U. Suthersanen, 2010, *supra* note 1, Chapter 10.

[handwritten: Beneficial for small scale business fashion field.]

within the EU – the designer can opt for an unregistered Community design right which confers a three-year anti-copying right.

If exclusive design protection is desired, the design proprietor must apply for registration within 12 months of the design being made available to the public. If registration is applied for, the holder of a registered Community design right will be granted an exclusive right to use the design or any design included within the scope of protection, and to prevent any third party from copying or using such a design. 'Use' is defined to cover, in particular, the making, offering, putting on the market, importing, exporting or using of a product in which the design is incorporated or to which it is applied, or stocking such a product for those purposes.[131] The duration of protection will be for an initial period of five years, which is renewable for four further periods of five years, up to a maximum of 25 years.

If, on the other hand, the proprietor opts for the unregistered Community design right, a right against copying is conferred. Moreover, the anti-copying right is limited in that it will not be effective where use is deemed to result from 'copying the protected design if it results from an independent work of creation by a designer who may be reasonably thought not to be familiar with the design made available to the public by the holder'. The unregistered Community design right arises automatically and lasts for a period of three years only from the date on which the design was first made available to the public within the Community.

[handwritten: Take steps to indicate availability date as this serves as proof of life.]

Scope of protection

Article 10 of the Community Design Regulation states:

1. The scope of the protection conferred by a Community design shall include any design which does not produce on the informed user a different overall impression.
2. In assessing the scope of protection, the degree of freedom of the designer in developing his design shall be taken into consideration.

The scope of protection conferred by the law is identical in relation to both registered and unregistered rights. As stated above, the test for assessing infringement is very much linked to that of individual character. In *Procter & Gamble Co v. Reckitt Benckiser (UK) Ltd* it was held that the court should consider the design and alleged infringement with a reasonable degree of care and at the same level of detail, characterising the impression given by each. The test to be applied is whether the overall impressions of the registration and alleged infringement are different but does not require them to be clearly different. The Court gave the following guidelines:

(i)   Compare the designs in respect of their various features taken individually and in respect of the weight (or importance) of the various features according to their influence on the overall impression.
(ii) Identify similarities and differences.

---

[131] Design Regulation, Art 19. See Suthersanen, ibid., Chapter 6, paras 6-046 *et seq.*

(iii) Identify the most important features of the two designs because the informed user focuses his or her attention primarily on such features.[132]

(iv) If the most important visual parts of the designs at issue do not give a different overall impression, then consider whether the other parts of the designs are sufficiently different in appearance or importance to change the impression given by the main elements.

The test is not easy to apply as the UK Supreme Court decision in *PMS International Group plc v. Magmatic Ltd* has shown, and much relies on how the design is depicted within the registration itself. Thus, an unadorned line drawing of a product design (showing only the contours of the design) may claim a wider scope of protection than a detailed CAD-assisted drawing or photograph which, by depicting the shape as well as the surface pattern and material used, may narrow the scope of protection.[133]

The scope of protection conferred by the law is identical in relation to both registered and unregistered rights. As stated above, the test for assessing infringement is very much linked to individual character.

Excluded from the scope

The Community design right will not extend to several acts including: acts done privately and for non-commercial purposes; acts done for experimental purposes; and acts of reproduction for the purposes of making citations or of teaching, provided that such acts are compatible with fair practice and do not unduly prejudice the normal exploitation of the design.[134]

The CJEU has considered the provision in *Nintendo Co Ltd v. BigBen Interactive*, holding that third parties could use images of goods protected by registered community designs for specific commercial purposes. Here, the defendants were allowed to use protected images of Nintendo's Wii consoles to demonstrate the compatibility of Nintendo's products with those of the defendant as this was an example of 'making citations'.[135]

Spare parts (the repair defence)

As we have seen from above, component parts of product are protectable subject matter though some aspects are excluded *ab initia* (for example, interconnections and functional designs). In addition to these exclusion clauses, the law provides an additional qualification to protection whereby a Community design right will not subsist in a design, 'which constitutes a component part of a complex product used within the meaning of Article 19(1) for the purpose of the repair of that complex product so as to restore its original appearance'.[136]

---

[132] *Procter & Gamble Co* [2007] ECDR 4; A. Carboni, 'Design Validity and Infringement: Feel the Difference' [2008] *EIPR* 111.

[133] [2016] UKSC 12.

[134] Design Regulation, Art 20.

[135] Cases C-24/16 and C-25/16 *Nintendo Co Ltd v. BigBen Interactive GmbH, BigBen Interactive SA* [2018] ECDR 3.

[136] Design Regulation, Art 110.

The CJEU has attempted to set some guidelines as to the interpretation of the 'repair clause' in the *Audi/Porsche v. Acacia* decision.[137] The defendants made and sold wheel rims designed to replicate those of major car brands. The rims were stamped with the indication 'NOT OEM' so as to warn consumers that the parts did not originate from the 'Original Equipment Manufacturer'. The CJEU's view was that the repair defence would not be available if the replacement part does not correspond, in terms of its colour or its dimensions, to the original part, or if the appearance of a complex product was changed since it was placed on the market. Moreover, spare parts manufacturers have a duty of diligence to inform other users and consumers that the design is not theirs, and that it is intended exclusively for the purpose of repair, and that the component parts cannot be used for other purposes.

The national jurisprudence on the above clause, and the interrelation between competition law and the doctrine of repair for component parts is well discussed in the European Commission's 2016 Legal Review on design protection. The Review's study reveals that there is a disparate national approach within the EU. Where countries have introduced a repair clause, the majority view is that the clause only applies to 'must match' designs, namely, such designs whose appearance is dependent on the appearance of the entire product, for example, a car.[138]

---

[137] Joined Cases C-397/16 and C-435/16, ECLI:EU:C:2017:992, CJEU, 20 December 2017.

[138] Legal Review on Industrial Design Protection in Europe, European Commission, *supra* note 22, para 6.2. Australia has also introduced a repair defence in relation to registered designs under its Designs Act 2003 (Australia). The defence has been recently considered in *GM Global Technology Operations LLC v. SSS Auto Parts Pty Ltd* [2019] FCA 97, Federal Court of Australia, 11 February 2019 (holding that spare parts can be acquired for both repair and enhancement purposes).

8

Geographical indications[*]

8.1 ORIGINS

Geographical indications (GIs) are place names registered for use by commercial makers of certain products for which spatial origin is regarded or claimed as a defining characteristic. Typically these include wines, spirits and other beverages such as beers and mineral waters, agricultural products and foods, minerals, and hand-crafted products and small-scale manufactures. GIs are unusual for two reasons.

Unlike the other IPRs covered in TRIPS and in previous multilateral treaties, the term is completely new in international law, first seeing the light of day during the Uruguay Round in proposals made by the European Community and by Switzerland. Admittedly, the related terms like indications of source and appellations of origin are much older, being included in the 1891 Madrid Agreement and in the 1958 Lisbon Agreement.[1] However, the 'geographical indication', of which

---

[*] We dedicate this chapter to Dwijen Rangnekar (1965–2015), an expert on geographical indications whose recent and far too premature death was a very sad loss to friends, family and to the world of intellectual property.

[1] Madrid Agreement on the Repression of False or Deceptive Indications of Source in Goods 1891; Lisbon Agreement

indications of source and appellations of origin may be considered a subset, is much more recent.[2] Indeed, it was only in July 1992 that the European Community itself adopted a Regulation[3] supplementing protection made available earlier for wines and spirits. Under this Regulation, the European Commission established a register of protected designations of origin and protected geographical indications. As we will see, the Regulation, which is no longer in force, proved to be controversial internationally.

The second unusual feature of GIs is that, unlike patents, copyright or trade marks, they are not themselves a discrete and universally accepted category of IP right. The TRIPS definition says little about what a GIs regime should actually look like and more than 25 years later, the legal concept of GIs remains somewhat fuzzy. How WTO members should provide the legal means to protect such indications is 'strategically vague', allowing for much flexibility. Accordingly, there are diverse ways by which an indication of geographical origin, and the product so indicated, may be protected legally. This gives WTO members broad scope to draw up implementing laws and regulations as they see fit.

8.1.1   Rationales

In a report for the International Trade Centre, Giovannucci, et al. point to the pros and cons of GIs, and offer four conditions for success which are generally applicable also to collective and certification trademarks.[4] On the one hand, they 'can offer a comprehensive framework for rural development since they can positively encompass issues of economic competitiveness, stakeholder equity, environmental stewardship, and socio-cultural value'. On the other, especially if the GI is poorly designed or inadequately governed, 'badly managed GIs can be dominated by limited political interests or just a few enterprises. In some cases, GIs can exclude the poorest producers or even stimulate inappropriate outcomes such as the dissolution of traditional practices or the destruction of biodiversity'. As for the conditions for success, the authors of the above report offer the following:

---

for the Protection of Appellations of Origin and their International Protection 1958; D. Gervais, *The TRIPS Agreement: Drafting History and Analysis* (2nd ed., London: Sweet & Maxwell, 1998), 188.

[2] The phrase 'geographical indications of origin' was used by Robin Jacob, subsequently a British court of appeals judge, in an article published in 1980. But its common usage nowadays is obviously due to TRIPS and to more recent EU law. R. Jacob, 'The Protection of Geographical Indications of Origin in the United Kingdom', in H.C. Jehoram (ed.), *Protection of Geographic Denominations of Goods and Services* (Alphen aan den Rijn and Germantown: Sijthoff and Noordhoff, 1980), 135–48.

[3] Council Regulation (EEC) No 2081/92 on the Protection of Geographical Indications and Designations of Origin for Agricultural Products and Foodstuffs. The Regulation does not cover wines and spirits, which continue to be treated separately.

[4] D. Giovannucci, T. Josling, W. Kerr, B. O'Connor and M.T. Yeung, *Guide to Geographical Indications: Linking Products and their Origins* (Geneva: International Trade Centre, 2009). Available at http://legacy.intracen.org/publications/Free-publications/Geographical_Indications.pdf.

1. Strong organisational and institutional structures to maintain, market, and monitor the GI. The core processes of: (i) identifying and fairly demarcating a GI; (ii) organising existing practices and standards; and (iii) establishing a plan to protect and market the GI all require building local institutions and management structures with a long-term commitment to participatory methods of cooperation.

2. Equitable participation among the producers and enterprises in a GI region. Equitable is here defined as the participating residents of a GI region sharing reasonably in not only costs and benefits but also in the control and decisions regarding their public assets.

3. Strong market partners committed to promote and commercialise over the long term. Many of the GI market successes are the result of mutually beneficial business relations via which consistent market positioning and effective commercialisation have led to a long-term market presence.

4. Effective legal protection including a strong domestic GI system. Carefully chosen protection options will permit effective monitoring and enforcement in relevant markets to reduce the likelihood of fraud that can compromise not only the GI's reputation but also its legal validity.

There is sufficient experience now to demonstrate that GIs have the potential to promote certain goods that can generate income for local communities and small-scale producers in developing countries. But GI regimes can be complicated. The market alone cannot regulate the system and ensure it works for the benefit of all stakeholders especially the poorer ones. For one thing, GIs are not private rights (unless they are in the form of trade marks), and can thus be seen as public assets. Moreover, a certain amount of state involvement may be necessary for a registration system to operate and in case small producer associations lack the capacity to police misuse of the indication in foreign markets. These features may lead some communities to opt for collective trade mark protection. Trade marks are private property, and their registration is more likely to be inexpensive, straightforward and un-bureaucratic once the mark itself has been created by the community association that will make the application. Indeed, this is why an association representing indigenous communities inhabiting the Potato Park in highland Peru has recently chosen to eschew seeking GI protection in favour of developing its own mark which it is currently using, so far with some success.[5]

The production specifications are of vital importance if consideration is to be given to the needs of local producers, the importance of capturing as much of the production chain to keep as much of the value in the region as possible (but taking into account possible capacity deficiencies), and the vital need to maintain the integrity of the indication. However, a certain amount of flexibility should be allowed.

---

[5] A. Argumedo, 'Collective Trademarks and Biocultural Heritage: Towards New Indications of Distinction for Indigenous Peoples in the Potato Park, Peru', International Institute for Environment and Development, 2013. Available at http://pubs.iied.org/16528IIED.html.

8.1.2   Multiple regimes

Different countries may well protect them under original and specific (*sui generis*) GI laws, as in the EU and India. But they may alternatively – or additionally – be protected largely or completely under either of the following: an appellation (or designation) of origin regime; trademark law, or in some countries influenced by English law under the common law tort of passing off as with unregistered trademarks; or indirectly through unfair competition law.

They could in fact be embedded within areas of law and regulation other than IP according to the underlying purpose of protecting them, such as: consumer protection rules relating to trade descriptions or food product labelling; cultural heritage regulations and policies; or rural development regulations and policies. Even urban planning has been employed to protect a de facto GI. Savile Row in London is famous for its high-quality suits. Arguably, the appeal and prestige of purchasing a Savile Row suit is enhanced by the street's ambience which derives from its unique character conveying a sense of exclusivity. In 2016, the street was granted protected status by the local city council to prevent it from becoming indistinguishable from other streets such as by allowing major and non-local chain stores to locate there.[6]

The role of the state may be minimal, simply providing the legal framework and granting rights. Or else the state may be directly involved in overseeing the regulation and enforcement of GIs. Thus, GIs are not a type of IP as is the patent, copyright or trade mark. Perhaps it is best to think of 'geographical indication' as a convenient catch-all term for a variety of mostly currently-existing laws and regulations concerning products that are differentiated by possessing features or a reputation attributable to their spatial origins. In this sense, GIs have a much longer history than the term itself.

What we can say with certainty is that like *sui generis* plant variety protection (and its international incarnation as UPOV – see Chapter 9), GIs are of European origin. Indeed, it is no secret that the reason for their inclusion in the Uruguay Round of trade negotiations of the late 1980s and early 1990s that lead to the establishment of the WTO was a direct consequence of proposals made by the European Community and by Switzerland.

France

Probably the longest established GIs regime is the French appellations of origin system for products considered to be distinctively local due to a combination of traditional know-how and highly localised natural conditions.[7] Early renditions of the regulatory system have been traced back to the medieval rules in relation to Bordeaux wine producers including the *privilége de la descente* (forbidding non-Bordeaux wine producers operating on the wine market during certain preferential calendar periods) and the *privilége de la barrique* (forbidding the unauthorised use of the 'Bordeaux' appellation on barrels, as the Bordeaux producers were entitled to superior wood barrels). Early laws were reflective of the two concerns of wine producers not only in Bordeaux, but Armagnac and Champagne regions, namely: (i) the need to stop counterfeit wines; and (ii) the

---

[6] City of Westminster, 'Unique Status of Savile Row Safeguarded by Council'. Available at https://www.westminster.gov.uk/unique-status-savile-row-safeguarded-council.

[7] D. Gangjee, *Relocating the Law of Geographical Indications* (Cambridge: Cambridge University Press, 2012), 77–115.

genericide of important geographical names. It is arguable that these early French laws focused on the need to protect consumers against misleading information as to the product origin – and thus diluting the value of place names – as opposed to conferring property rights based on quality and terroir.[8] The laws were modernised under the 1905 Law which protected consumers from trade and contract frauds, including fraudulent labelling especially in relation to the origin of the product. It became truly effective only from the mid-1930s when the Bordeaux winegrowers' associations lobbied successfully for the Decree of 30 July 1935 which introduced the AOC system – discussed below – which not only patrolled counterfeiting and market control, but also controlled quality and production volume.[9]

Today, the French government agency (INAO – *Institut National de l'Origine et de la Qualité*) is in charge of regulating French agricultural products with its multi-tiered certification schemes including *Appellations d'Origine Contrôlée* (AOC) – the French term for Protected Designations of Origin (PDOs), *Agriculture Biologique* (for organic foods), and *Label Rouge* (a French-derived system for high quality goods). The validation (except for *Label Rouge*) protects producers of wines, spirits, dairy and agricultural products, whose goods are renowned for their distinctive qualities and geographic origins, from those who would undermine or exploit their good reputation by making false claims. Applications are made by producer associations, and these are scrutinised by committees of inquiry composed of members of the national committee and expert appointees who may draw up production conditions that users of the indication must comply with. The INAO, the committees, and the associations cooperate to make the system of accreditation, management and enforcement, operate effectively.[10] In relation to the Bordeaux wines, for instance, the producers hold, inter alia, seven different AOCs and one GI (Fine Bordeaux), depending on the grape variety within the Bordeaux region. There are similar regimes in Italy, Spain and Switzerland among other European countries.

In countries like the US and the UK, GIs tend to be protected under trade mark law. In the US, for example, Idaho potatoes and Florida oranges are protected as certification marks. The US and Australia, both as it happens important wine producers, have argued that trade marks are in fact sufficient to protect GIs. Indeed, the popular view in the US is that there is nothing wrong with selling locally made products using words like Champagne and Chablis as long as there is no deception as to origin (see below). Indeed, such GI scepticism is supported by the food industry's Consortium for Common Food Names, influential think-tanks like the Cato Institute,[11] and the

---

[8] Early laws include the Law of July 28, 1824 (prohibiting use of place names except by authorised wine producers), Law of 1857 (on marks); Law of January 11, 1892. M. Blakeney, *The Protection of Geographical Indications: Law and Practice* (Cheltenham: Edward Elgar Publishing, 2014), 4–5; L.E. Simon, 'Appellations of Origin: The Continuing Controversy' (1983) 5 *Nw. J. Int'l L. & Bus.* 132, 137; and L.C. Lenzen, 'Bacchus in the Hinterlands: A Study of Denominations of Origin in French and American Wine-labeling Laws' (1968) 58 *TMR* 145, 175.

[9] A. Stanziani, 'French Collective Wine Branding in the Nineteenth–Twentieth Centuries', in D. Gangjee (ed.), *Research Handbook on Intellectual Property and Geographical Indications* (Cheltenham: Edward Elgar Publishing, 2016), 13–45.

[10] F. Roncin, 'The Protection of Geographical Indication', in L. Bérard et al. (eds), *Biodiversity and Local Ecological Knowledge in France* (Paris: CIRAD, IDDRI, IFB and INRA, 2005), 175–80.

[11] K.W. Watson, 'Reign of *Terroir*: How to Resist Europe's Efforts to Control Common Food Names as Geographical

government[12] which is now actively countering the influence of the European GIs regime though bilateral trade negotiations. One point of consistency with trade marks, though, is that when a once local product becomes generic it can no longer be protected.

Stilton and Harris Tweed

Stilton is a popular British cheese that is made by hand using a recipe that is at least 300 years old.[13] The cheese is named after a small town in the East Midlands located on the old Great North Road from London to the North. In the old days, horses for the stagecoaches would be changed there. At the Bell Inn, travellers would be served a local cheese that became commonly known as Stilton. In 1727, Daniel Defoe, the author of Robinson Crusoe in his published A Tour through the Whole Island of Great Britain mentioned passing through Stilton, 'a town famous for cheese'. In fact the way he described his dining with the local cheese ('which is called our English Parmesan') is hardly enticing, served as it was 'with the mites, or maggots round it, so thick, that they bring a spoon with them for you to eat the mites with, as you do the cheese'.

    Stilton cheese has been protected by a certification trade mark since 1966 and has been a European 'Protected Designation of Origin' (PDO) since 1996, which very conveniently ensures protection throughout the European Union. The owner of the mark is the Stilton Cheesemakers' Association, which was founded in 1936 to look after the interests of the producers and to ensure that standards are maintained at licensed dairies. Six of the eight dairies are members of the Association, the other two being licensees of the trade marks and the PDO. The marks are the word 'Stilton' and the logo of the Association which includes a cylindrical block of cheese with a slice missing and a crown on top.

    In order to use the name 'Stilton', a cheese must:

(i)   be made only in the three counties from local milk which is pasteurised before use. These counties are Leicestershire, Derbyshire and Nottinghamshire;

(ii)   be made only in a traditional cylindrical shape;

(iii)   be allowed to form its own crust or coat;

(iv)   be un-pressed;

(v)   have delicate blue veins radiating from the centre;

(vi)   have a taste profile typical of Stilton.

Clearly, the cheese market is a highly competitive one. Since the prestige of British cheese, excellent as much of it is, is not especially high in Europe or elsewhere, marketing such a product is a serious challenge. In this respect, the Association has been successful. Stilton is not only popular in the UK but is exported to about 40 countries.

    Harris Tweed is a cloth made in the Scottish islands of Lewis, Harris, Uist and Barra, which

---

Indications' (Policy Analysis No 787), CATO Institute, 2016.

[12] Office of the United States Trade Representative, *2016 Special 301 Report*, USTR, 2016.

[13] Stilton Cheesemakers' Association, available at http://www.stiltoncheese.com/; T. Hickman, *Stilton Cheese: A History* (Amberley Publishing, 2012); M. Rippon, 'What is the Geography of Geographical Indications?' (2014) 46 *Area* 154–62.

together form a large part of an area known as the Outer Hebrides.[14] It is handwoven and made from wool that is spun and dyed in the Outer Hebrides. This area of Scotland has been known for producing fine quality cloth for several centuries. While mechanisation during the Industrial Revolution transformed production in other areas, the Outer Hebrides continued to make cloth entirely by hand, and it remains to a large extent a cottage industry. From the mid-nineteenth century, this cloth became popular throughout the UK. At the time, the methods used were as follows:

> The raw material, wool, was produced locally and part of it would have been used in its natural uncoloured state, the rest was dyed. In the 19th century vegetable dyes were used. Following dyeing, the wool was mixed, the shade being regulated by the amount of coloured wool added; then it was oiled and teased; the latter process involves pulling the wool apart to open out the fibres. The next part of the preparation, carding, results in the fibres of the wool being drawn out preparatory to spinning. This was a very lengthy process followed by spinning carried out on a familiar spinning-wheel by women. Until the turn of the century a very early type of handloom was used for weaving with a manually operated shuttle. The final process is finished where the tweed is washed and given a raised compact finish. Those involved in this process were often accompanied by songs in Gaelic. (Harris Tweed Authority Website)[15]

Around the beginning of the twentieth century, a degree of modernisation took place and production increased in consequence. Following a meeting of producers in 1906, the Harris Tweed Association was established three years later to apply for a trade mark that would help the producers compete in a market in which industrial spinning mills able to mass-produce cloth were threatening to force out the small producers. The Harris Tweed mark, which was granted in 1909, comprises the words 'Harris Tweed' with an orb and a Maltese cross and has since become very well known. The official definition of Harris Tweed then was 'a tweed, hand-spun, hand-woven and dyed by the crofters and cottars in the Outer Hebrides'.

In 1934, the trade mark definition was changed to the following: 'Harris Tweed means a tweed made from pure virgin wool produced in Scotland, spun, dyed and finished in Outer Hebrides and hand-woven by the islanders at their own homes in the Islands of Lewis, Harris, Uist, Barra and their several purtenances and all known as the Outer Hebrides'. This of course allows for increased production while ensuring that it was still at least to some extent a tradition-bound cottage industry, albeit less so than before.

Production reached a peak of 7.6 million yards in 1966, but subsequently began to contract as Harris Tweed became less fashionable. Moreover, the British textiles industry, once the world's largest, was about to begin shrinking in the face of competition from lower cost producers overseas. In order to be more competitive, it was felt necessary to retrain weavers, introduce tougher standards and better meet new demands, including for softer, lighter cloth. In 1993, the UK

---

[14] Most of the information presented here comes from the website of the Harris Tweed Authority. Available at http://www.harristweed.org.

[15] This text is no longer on the website, but can be read at https://smartsofyork.co.uk/harris-tweed/.

government came to the producers' aid by passing legislation, the Harris Tweed Act. The law set up the Harris Tweed Authority, a statutory body, in place of the Harris Tweed Association. Under Part III of the Act, Harris Tweed's latest definition is as follows:

> Harris Tweed means a tweed which has been hand woven by the islanders at their homes in the Outer Hebrides, finished in the islands of Harris, Lewis, North Uist, Benbecula, South Uist and Barra and their several purtenances (The Outer Hebrides) and made from pure virgin wool dyed and spun in the Outer Hebrides.

Unlike Stilton, the future of Harris Tweed is less secure, hence the need felt by the government to take legislative action. Stilton, on the other hand, has not needed to resort to state intervention. This point highlights the fact that GIs and certification trade marks for traditional goods are useless without good standards of quality control and marketing, and up-to-date information on markets including foreign ones if the products are to be exported. But even then, success is far from guaranteed.

8.2   GLOBAL RULES ON GEOGRAPHICAL INDICATIONS

8.2.1   WTO–TRIPS Agreement

Geographical indications are defined in the TRIPS Agreement as 'indications which identify a good as originating in the territory of a Member, or a region or locality in that territory, where a given quality, reputation, or other characteristic of the good is essentially attributable to its geographical origin'. WTO members are required to permit legal action enabling traders to prevent: (a) the designation or presentation of a good (such as a trademark) that suggests, in a manner that misleads the public, that the good in question originates in a geographical area other than the true place of origin; and (b) any use which constitutes unfair competition. Article 23, TRIPS deals solely with wines and spirits, which are subject to additional protection. This evidences how far the European wine and spirit-exporting countries were willing to go to pursue their economic interests with respect to such goods.

In November 2001, the WTO members attending the Doha Ministerial Conference agreed 'to negotiate the establishment of a multilateral system of notification and registration of geographical indications for wines and spirits by the Fifth Session of the Ministerial Conference'.[16] However, there is continuing absence of consensus on what should be the legal effects of registration, and on the scope of the allowable rights and freedoms of non-registering producers. There have also been differences concerning the modalities of the negotiations. The EU has proposed incorporation of the issue into agricultural talks. Others prefer to join discussion with

---

[16] By virtue of Ministerial Declaration, para 18, which is based on Art 23.4 of TRIPS but with the addition of spirits.

talks on disclosure of origin in patents. With respect to the possible extension of the enhanced protection of GIs to products other than wines and spirits, the Ministerial Declaration acknowledged that issues related to this matter would be addressed in the Council for TRIPS. At the time of writing, there is still no consensus on whether TRIPS should be amended or not, and on the modalities of negotiations.

There are further controversies. One is the issue of the relationship with trade marks. The US protects GIs through trade marks and does not wish to see any diminution of the rights of trade mark owners. The EU is generally unconcerned about co-existence difficulties between the two IP rights. In addition, there are differences about long-term use of GIs by other producers where there is no deception as to true origin. The US would like such prior use to be permitted. Indeed, its position is that there is nothing wrong with 'Californian Champagne', whereas the Europeans wish to have a broad anti-dilution approach that would prevent such unconfusing usage of a word like Champagne for any product, not just sparkling wines.

It is fair to say that GIs have been a source of friction between Europe and the European settler states whose people of European origin took their Old World plants, animals, foods, beverages and place-names with them (see below for further discussion). Other countries' views on GIs are affected by such matters as their perceptions about the influence GIs might have on their main export products. Among those countries that have expressed support for the additional protection for products other than wines and spirits are the EU, India, Jamaica, Kenya, Madagascar, Morocco, Pakistan, Switzerland, Thailand, Tunisia and Turkey. Opponents include Argentina, Australia, Canada, Chile, Colombia, Guatemala, New Zealand, Panama, the Philippines and the US.

In the WTO dispute in relation to the European law on GIs, Australia and the US initiated a complaint against the European methods of protecting GIs, which it was alleged was incompatible with the TRIPS Agreement.[17] One aspect of this dispute concerned Article 17 TRIPS which allows members to provide 'limited exceptions' such as 'fair use of descriptive terms' to use of trademarks, provided that such exceptions take account of the interests of the trademark owner and third parties.

Australia and the US argued that the 'fair use' example suggested that exceptions were to be confined to those circumstances where third parties needed to use the mark, such as for denominative purposes, but not to indicate commercial trade origin. Under US domestic law as set out above, the 'fair use' defence which permits the good faith use of a mark to describe the geographical origin of goods is not available if the use is 'as a mark'.[18] European jurisprudence, on the other hand, has held that a defendant's use of a GI that also denoted trade origin and was confusingly similar to an earlier registered trade mark could fall within the defence allowing for use in accordance with 'honest practices' of indications of the geographical origin of goods, with the emphasis being on the 'honesty' of the trader.

---

[17] WTO Panel Report, *European Communities – Protection of Trademarks and Geographical Indications for Agricultural Products and Foodstuffs*, WT/DS174/R, 2005.

[18] S.H. Klein, and N.C. Norton, 'The Role of Trade Mark Use in US Infringement, Unfair Competition and Dilution Proceedings', in J. Phillips and I. Simon (eds), *Trade Mark Use* (Oxford University Press, 2005), 329–40.

The dispute panel did not fully accept the position of Australia and the US, and adopted a formalistic interpretation of the TRIPS Agreement, holding that the EC Regulation was a permissible exception under Article 17, TRIPS. However, the Panel did concur with the complainants' view that the Regulation violated the national treatment provision in TRIPS by discriminating against foreign nationals seeking to have their GIs registered in Europe. Since then the European GIs regime has been overhauled twice, in part to satisfy the Panel's interpretation of TRIPS, with Regulations implemented in 2006 and then in 2012 (see below).

Several WTO members do not consider a special GIs regime of the kind existing in the EU to be necessary. A few of them have other concerns too, such as the possibility that an existing trade mark with a similar or identical name to a GI will have diminished protection. The stalemate in WTO negotiations on GIs has led a number of European countries to shift forum to WIPO, ensuring their demands have been incorporated into a revised Lisbon Agreement (see below).

8.2.2   European *sui generis* GI regimes

Europe has the most elaborate GI regime in the world, covering wines,[19] spirits,[20] agricultural products and foodstuffs. Regulation No 1151/2012 governs the latter two types of product, which are the most relevant ones to the current controversies and discussions below.[21] The Regulation has three types of registered GI. These are: (i) protected designations of origin (PDOs); (ii) protected geographical indications (PGIs); and (iii) traditional specialities guaranteed (TSGs). It is worthwhile looking at these in some detail because despite Europe's relative wealth and longer experience in the use of GIs, their objectives appear on the face of it to be consistent with those that small-scale producers in developing countries might also consider relevant and important. Thus, the preamble of Regulation 1151/2012 has the following to say:

> Operating quality schemes for producers which reward them for their efforts to produce a diverse range of quality products can benefit the rural economy. This is particularly the case in less favoured areas, in mountain areas and in the most remote regions, where the farming sector accounts for a significant part of the economy and production costs are high. In this way quality schemes are able to contribute to and complement rural development policy.

---

[19] Commission Regulation (EU) No 401/2010 of 7 May 2010 amending and correcting Regulation (EC) No 607/2009 laying down certain detailed rules for the implementation of Council Regulation (EC) No 479/2008 as regards protected designations of origin and geographical indications, traditional terms, labelling and presentation of certain wine sector products.

[20] Regulation (EC) No 110/2008 of the European Parliament and of the Council of 15 January 2008 on the definition, description, presentation, labelling and the protection of geographical indications of spirit drinks and repealing Council Regulation (EEC) No 1576/89.

[21] Council Regulation (EC) No 1151/2012 of 21 November 2012 on quality schemes for agricultural products and foodstuffs.

PDOs and PGIs

Article 5 of the same Regulation provides definitions of PDOs and PGIs. A designation of origin is:

A name which identifies a product:
(a) originating in a specific place, region or, in exceptional cases, a country;
(b) whose quality or characteristics are essentially or exclusively due to a particular geographical environment with its inherent natural and human factors; and
(c) the production steps of which all take place in the defined geographical area.

A geographical indication is:

A name which identifies a product:
(a) originating in a specific place, region or country;
(b) whose given quality, reputation or other characteristic is essentially attributable to its geographical origin; and
(c) at least one of the production steps of which take place in the defined geographical area.

The definitions look quite similar but we can see that the requirements for a PDO are somewhat different in two senses. First, there is a link between the product and the inherent natural and human factors which characterise it and effectively make it a distinct product. PGIs also place a lot of emphasis on geography but it is mere place-origin that counts rather than any special environmental or human influences. Moreover, with PGIs the responsibility of geography for the specialness of the product is expressed in less absolute terms: 'attributable to' rather than 'exclusively due to'. Second, PDOs require that production, processing and preparation of the product all take place in the geographical area, while PGIs require just that at least one production step be carried out in the area. Like patents and trademarks, PDOs and PGIs must be registered. The Regulation explains the procedures for doing this. Once registered, the official EU symbol denoting a PDO or PGI must be used on the labelling, but only for products originating in the EU. Those coming from outside the EU area, such as Café de Colombia, are not required to use the symbol.

An intriguing question here is that of what is permissible when a PDO is an ingredient of an unrelated type of product. A real example is a foodstuff containing champagne called 'Champagner Sorbet' that was considered in early 2018 by the CJEU. It was ruled that: (i) where such a PDO forming part of the name of the product is for an ingredient that corresponds to the product specification for that PDO; and (ii) that the product has 'a taste attributable primarily to the presence of that ingredient in the composition of the foodstuff', use of the PDO as part of the product's name 'does not constitute misuse, imitation or evocation' and is therefore permitted.[22]

It is possible to oppose any indication. However, when governments forward applications to the Commission, they tend to be registered whether or not they are particularly rigorously prepared or indeed whether they necessarily stand up to serious critical examination. Some controversial

---

[22] Case C393/16 *Comité Interprofessionnel du Vin de Champagne v. Aldi Süd Dienstleistungs-GmbH & Co.OHG* ECLI:EU:C:2017:991.

indications have been registered and even survived litigation when objective observers would not necessarily have expected such an outcome. Two such examples are feta cheese, which is a PDO, and the PGI on the Cornish pasty.

Feta is a white cheese stored in brine and made from sheep's milk or a mix of sheep's and goat's milk from local breeds and made using traditional methods. It was registered in 2002 as a cheese made in certain areas of Greece. As is often the case with GIs, the product has for quite some time been produced elsewhere. The question then arises as to whether it is fair to grant a GI when a reasonably objective case could be made for its having become a generic term for damp salty, white sheep or goat milk cheese, and that the public was not misled into thinking that non-Greek feta is really Greek. Nonetheless, in 2005, the CJEU, perhaps mistakenly, ruled it illegal for any cheese produced outside Greece to be called 'feta', despite the fact that in Denmark, Germany and France locally made cheeses with the word 'feta' in the name had been sold for several decades. Feta is not in fact the name of a place but is the Greek – but Italian-derived – word for 'slice'.[23]

A pasty is a type of meat and vegetable pie commonly associated with the English county of Cornwall, which is one of the poorest parts of the country suffering from the consequences of the closing down of its mining industry and cultural erosion including loss of its own language. In 2011, 'Cornish pasty' was granted PGI status recognising it as an important aspect of the county's 'culinary heritage', and acknowledging also that: (i) the general public tends to associate pasties with Cornwall; and (ii) that pasty making does seem to be taken quite as seriously there as compared to other parts of England where they were also made. On the other hand, 'Cornish' pasties have been produced outside the county for a very long time and there is no particular reason to suppose that making them in Cornwall and from ingredients sourced within the county results in a product that is different in quality or in any other way from pasties made elsewhere. After all, it is not regarded as a particularly high-quality product and no special skill is required to make them. Indeed, there is some documentary evidence to suggest that pasties originate not from Cornwall but the neighbouring county of Devon although this is far from being widely known.[24] Despite this, once registered all existing producers outside Cornwall had either to cease or to phase out their use of the indication. They can of course continue to call their products pasties; they just have to discontinue using the work 'Cornish'. Whatever the true origin, there is little doubt that the county that most people associate pasties with is Cornwall. Moreover, to the best of our knowledge producers of pasties in Devon have not sought to make origin-based claims of their own.

TSGs

The objective of the Traditional Specialities Guaranteed (TSGs) scheme is 'to safeguard traditional methods of production and recipes by helping producers of traditional product in marketing and communicating the value-adding attributes of their traditional recipes and products to consumers'.[25] With regard to criteria, Article 18.1 states that:

---

[23] Joined Cases C-465/02 and C-466/02 *Federal Republic of Germany and Kingdom of Denmark v. Commission of the European Communities* [2005] ECR I-09115.

[24] BBC, 'Devon Invented the Cornish Pasty', *BBC News* [Online], 2006.

[25] Regulation (EC) No 1151/2012, *supra* note 21, Art 17.

A name shall be eligible for registration as a traditional speciality guaranteed where it describes a specific product or foodstuff that:

(a) results from a mode of production, processing or composition corresponding to traditional practice for that product or foodstuff; or

(b) is produced from raw materials or ingredients that are those traditionally used.

Being 'traditional' means: 'proven usage on the domestic market for a period that allows transmission between generations; this period is to be at least 30 years'. There are two interesting points to mention here. First, becoming traditional does not appear to be very long even though this is five more years than in the previous 2006 Regulation. Second, this minimum period for traditionality appears to be turning into the EU standard. Thus, the EU's regulation on traditional herbal medicines also requires a similar 30-year period of use.[26]

It is not necessary that they be produced in a particular area. This feature makes TSGs rather interesting. After all, many indigenous peoples have been forced to inhabit areas other than their original territories yet traditional products continue to be made. Two European examples of TSG products are Traditionally Farmed Gloucestershire Old Spots Pork and Pizza Napoletana. These two names can be used by producers anywhere in Europe: there is no requirement to produce only in Gloucestershire or Naples; but only those products produced according to the specifications laid out by the TSG can actually use the mark. In the former case, the TSG is controlled by the Gloucestershire Old Spots Pig Breeders Club. As for the latter, two associations in the city of Naples applied for the TSG, with three organisations made responsible for verifying compliance with the specification.

Scope of protection

What acts by third parties are right holders, permitted users or other interested parties entitled to prevent? Article 13.1 (Protection) of the Regulation protects against various acts including the following:

- any *misuse, imitation or* evocation, even if the true origin of the products or services is indicated or if the protected name is translated or accompanied by an expression such as '*style*', '*type*', '*method*', '*as produced in*', '*imitation*' or similar, including when those products are used as an ingredient;
- any other false or misleading indication as to the provenance, origin, nature or essential qualities of the product that is used on the inner or outer packaging, advertising material or documents relating to the product concerned, and the packing of the product in a container liable to convey a false impression as to its origin. (Emphasis added)

As for TSGs, Article 24 protects the name 'against any misuse, imitation or evocation, or against any other practice liable to mislead the consumer'. However, in common with certification trade marks (but not collective marks), use by others is not precluded. Under Article 23: 'A name registered as

---

[26] Directive 2004/24/EC on traditional herbal medicinal products, which allows marketing subject to proof of safety and quality, as well as evidence of a 30-year period of traditional use.

a traditional speciality guaranteed may be used by any operator marketing a product that conforms to the corresponding specification', although it is not necessary that the name itself be protected: exclusivity is only in reference to the TSG symbol or the 'traditional specialities guaranteed' phrase. It depends on whether the producer group concerned has requested that the name of the product be reserved. For this request to be granted, Article 21 allows as a ground for opposition that the name not already be 'used in a lawful, renowned and economically significant manner for similar agricultural products or foodstuffs'.

It should be clarified that, notwithstanding the feta case suggesting otherwise, once a local product becomes generic it can no longer be protected. This has been the fate of such products named after places as Cheddar cheese and Dijon mustard, which can now be produced anywhere. One would suppose that once a product becomes generic there is no going back. And yet reclaiming the indication may not be totally impossible. A partial re-localisation has been achieved, for example, with Cheddar cheese. There is now a PDO on 'West Country Farmhouse Cheddar'. However, the permitted area of production is far larger than the village of Cheddar.

Moreover, with political will and sympathetic courts, products that supposedly have become generic in some territories can sometimes be re-localised outside and within the jurisdiction. This has been the case for sherry, a fortified wine named by linguistically challenged English people after a district of Spain called Jerez.[27] 'Cyprus sherry', sold under that name since the 1930s, has thus been renamed 'Cyprus fortified wine'. The naming of South African fortified wines as sherry and port had to be phased out under the terms of the 1999 EU-South Africa free trade agreement,[28] according to which all exporting under those names had to cease within eight years, with domestic sale having to end within 12 years.[29] Another good example is the aforementioned feta cheese.

At the time of writing, the European Commission is consulting with a view to a possible instrument to extend the scope of GIs to non-agricultural products such as regional handicrafts. In fact, some European countries such as France already provide GI protection for industrial products and crafts.[30]

8.2.3   The revised Lisbon Agreement

The 1958 Lisbon Agreement for the Protection of Appellations of Origin and their International Registration provided for a system of mutual legal recognition of appellations of origins registered with the International Bureau of WIPO. As mentioned above, the appellation of origin is a

---

[27] Similarly, 'blue denim' is a corruption of *'bleu de Nîmes'*.

[28] Agreement on Trade, Development and Cooperation between the European Community and its Member States, of the one part, and the Republic of South Africa, of the other part.

[29] O'Connor and Co, 'Geographical Indications and TRIPs: 10 Years Later [...] A Roadmap for EU GI Holders to Get Protection in other WTO Members', Report commissioned by the EC, 2007, available at http://trade.ec.europa.eu/doclib/docs/2007/june/tradoc_135088.pdf, 10–11.

[30] *Décret no 2015-595 du 2 juin 2015 relatif aux indications géographiques protégeant les produits industriels et artisanaux et portant diverses dispositions relatives aux marques*; G. Moretti, 'The Registration of Geographical Indications for Non-Agricultural Products in France and its Impact on Proposed EU Legislation' (2016) 38(11) *EIPR* 686–96.

category of what subsequently became known as a geographical indication. Under this Agreement, the appellation of origin is 'the geographical name of a country, region, or locality, which serves to designate a product originating therein, the quality and characteristics of which are due exclusively or essentially to the geographical environment, including natural and human factors'.[31] The 'exclusively or essentially' part of the definition plus mention of 'natural and human factors' makes it closely equivalent to the European PDO. One big difference is that the Lisbon Agreement 1958 makes no mention of type of product (wine, spirit, food, beverage, etc.). The country of origin is the country whose name, or the country in which is situated the region or locality whose name, constitutes the appellation of origin which has given the product its reputation.[32] Article 3, the language of which was incorporated into TRIPS by virtue of Article 23.1, states as follows: 'Protection shall be ensured against any usurpation or imitation, even if the true origin of the product is indicated or if the appellation is used in translated form or accompanied by terms such as "kind," "type," "make," "imitation", or the like.'

The difference with TRIPS is that whereas the latter confines its application to wines and spirits, the anti-dilution clause of the Lisbon Agreement (Art 3) is not limited to any particular kind of product. Contracting parties may refuse protection of a registered appellation if they state a reason for doing so. Iran, for example, has refused to protect registered appellations for alcoholic beverages. Several developing countries are parties to the Lisbon Agreement 1958, with six having registered appellations.[33]

In May 2015, the Lisbon Agreement was revised and extended to include geographical indications. This new version of the Agreement ('the Geneva Act') reflects very much the interests of the existing membership and the EU. Thus, the revised Agreement adds the word 'denomination' to its definition of appellation of origin and then follows this with the TRIPS definition of geographical indication.[34] The revised version also now allows for the possibility of joint applications from countries sharing the same geographical areas. Thus, in theory, the possibility arises of Peru and Chile making joint applications to register pisco (see below) or India and Pakistan to register basmati rice – subject obviously to these pairs of countries agreeing to take such an approach.[35]

The revised Agreement also provides provisions combating the dilution and genericide of appellations or indications. Thus, parties must provide legal means to prevent use of the appellation or indication 'in respect of goods that are not of the same kind as those to which the appellation of origin or geographical indication applies or services', if the use 'would be likely to damage their interests' or where, because the reputation of the appellation/indication, the use would be 'likely to impair or dilute in an unfair manner, or take unfair advantage of, that reputation'.[36] It also retains

---

[31] Lisbon Agreement, Art 2(1).

[32] Ibid., Art 2(2).

[33] These are Algeria, Cuba, Mexico, North Korea, Peru and Tunisia.

[34] Lisbon Agreement for the Protection of Appellations of Origin and Geographical Indications (Geneva Act, 2015), Art 2; A.G. Micara, 'The Geneva Act of the Lisbon Agreement for the Protection of Appellations of Origin and their International Registration: An Assessment of a Controversial Agreement' (2016) 47(6) *IIC* 673.

[35] Lisbon Agreement, Geneva Act, Art 5.

[36] Ibid., Art 11.1(a)(ii).

the 'true origin indicated' protection of the original Agreement including the 'kind, type, make, imitation, or the like' language that expands the breadth of protection and to all protected products.

In relation to the anti-genericide provision, the revised Agreement states that 'registered appellations of origin and registered geographical indications cannot be considered to have become generic in a Contracting Party'.[37] This means, for example, that as long as Champagne is protected in France it can never become treated as generic outside Europe. If the US were to sign up to Lisbon instruments, they would not be able to allow US producers from purveying their own Champagne. And Vietnam would no longer be able to reject Champagne as a GI, as it has done, on the ground that it is a generic name in that country.

One final innovation is that intergovernmental organisations can now become parties to the Lisbon system. This would of course allow organisations like the EU to join. Overall, then, the Lisbon system, from which WTO negotiators borrowed text for the TRIPS Agreement, has returned the compliment, selectively borrowing language from TRIPS in order to present some parties with the possibility to achieve elsewhere what they cannot get agreement to at the WTO.

8.3   A PRO-DEVELOPMENT IPR?

Despite the fact they are in TRIPS largely at the instigation of the European Commission and certain EU member states, GIs have for several years been promoted as a concession to developing countries that they ought to take advantage of. Supposedly, they provide the means by which developing countries can use IP to protect categories of local rural knowledge that they possess in abundance. In particular, the EU and the Swiss government are very keen to promote GIs worldwide by arguing that this part of TRIPS can potentially provide substantial gains for developing countries. This seems plausible when one considers that GIs are especially appropriate for the produce of small-scale producers and cultivators, and, it should be underlined here, not just for foods and beverages but also for handicrafts and other hand-made items.[38]

Many developing countries are rich in traditional knowledge having applications in agriculture, food production and small-scale manufacturing. So GIs would appear to have real potential in terms of developing and exploiting lucrative markets for natural products including those manufactured by resource-poor farming communities. Such countries tend to favour the extension of the additional protection to cover all products, not just beverages. Are they right to be so pro-GI with respect to products they wish to export? Possibly so, but caution should be exercised. At present the potential of GIs for developing countries is somewhat speculative because this type of IPR has been used only in a few countries outside Europe. Moreover, many GIs have quite small markets, and a relatively small number are traded internationally.

Other developing countries do not have an abundance of traditional knowledge and are key exporters of products that compete with well-established GI-protected goods coming from Europe. For those countries, GIs may be considered a threat and not an opportunity. Indeed, some such

---

[37] Ibid., Art 12.

[38] W. Moran, 'Rural Space as Intellectual Property' (1993) 12(3) *Political Geography* 263–77.

countries are understandably concerned that the present enthusiasm for GIs among Europeans is really about protectionism. For example, New World developing country wine producing countries like Chile and Argentina and also South Africa are competitors with Europe, and tend to be unhappy about the privileged status of wines and spirits because this serves the interests of their Old World competitors. Many of the place names in these countries originated in Europe. Some developed countries, such as Australia, feel the same way.

Evidently, a substantial majority of EU GIs do come from relatively poor areas of Europe. Given the premium prices achieved by the more successful indications, it may indeed reasonably be asserted that 'GIs have the potential to generate value-added products for farmers in depressed areas'.[39] A frequently cited example is Comté cheese from the French Jura mountain region. When protected as a GI in 1993 'the cheese enjoyed a 20 per cent price differential over Emmenthal produced in Switzerland which is not GI protected. By 2003 this had risen to 46 per cent and production of Comté had risen by 3 per cent a year'.[40]

What of developing countries? The vast majority (about 90 per cent) of GIs are from the OECD countries. Consequently, developing country experiences are quite limited. But this is not to say these countries have been completely inactive. Indeed, Chile protected the grape brandy product 'Pisco' (see below) as early as 1943 requiring the name be reserved 'for an "eau de vie" produced in a certain region of the country'.[41]

Several developing countries have provided for the registration of GIs in the form of designations or appellations of origin. To name a few: Brazil, Cuba and Mexico in Latin America, and Algeria and Tunisia in North Africa. These are to a large extent wines, spirits, foodstuffs and agricultural products, and tobacco products, though some of them also provide for handicrafts and small-scale manufactures. Brazil has two types of GI: Denominations of Origin and Indications of Source of which by August 2016, 17 and 40 respectively had been registered. Interestingly GI protection in Brazil is available for services. Oddly, a science park in Recife called Porto Digital has indication of source protection for its software services. The EU has given substantial attention to trade and development relations with the more than 70 countries of the African, Caribbean and Pacific (ACP) Group of States. The ACP countries (minus Cuba) and the EU and its member states signed the Cotonou Agreement, a lengthy development cooperation partnership instrument detailing the commitment on the part of each of the parties 'to work together towards the achievement of the objectives of poverty eradication, sustainable development and the gradual integration of the ACP countries into the world economy'.[42] Chapter 5, on trade-related areas, contains an article on IP that makes explicit reference to GIs. It stresses cooperation, technical assistance and

---

[39] S. Bowen, 'Development from Within? The Potential for Geographical Indications in the Global South' (2010) 13(2) *Journal of World Intellectual Property* 231–52, 234.

[40] J. Watson and J. Streatfeild, 'The Starbucks/Ethiopian Coffee Saga: Geographical Indications as a Linchpin for Development in Developing Countries', Policy Note 3, Uppsala: Nordic Africa Institute, 2008.

[41] E.D. Aracama Zorraquin, 'The Protection of Geographic Denominations in South America', in Jehoram (ed.), *supra* note 2, 93–6, 94.

[42] Partnership Agreement between the Members of the African, Caribbean and Pacific Group of States of the one part, and the European Community and its Member States, of the other part, second revision, June 2010, Preamble.

envisages the possibility of engaging in further agreements on protection of GIs and trademarks for certain products.

8.3.1   India

India was one of the first developing countries to pass a TRIPS-compliant law on geographical indications.[43] The Indian government appeared to have been motivated to do so by: (i) a notorious US patent relating to basmati rice, as well as trademarks being granted claiming the 'mati' part of the word in combination with other prefixes; (ii) concerns about the substantial quantity of tea being falsely labelled as Darjeeling; and (iii) a conviction that GIs are suitable for many products in which India has a competitive advantage. According to this law, an applicant to register a GI may be: 'Any association of persons or producer or any organization or authority established by or under any law for the time being in force representing the interest of the producers of the concerned goods, who are desirous of registering a geographical indication in relation to such goods.'[44]

Despite the complexity of the procedure for acquiring a GI in India, 301 had been registered by 25 October 2017. There are 86 for agricultural products, 176 for handicrafts, 20 for manufactured goods including beverages, 12 for foodstuffs, six textiles and one natural good (a mineral). Here are a few examples: Darjeeling Tea (the very first registered), Basmati Rice, Bhalia Wheat, Mahabaleshwar Strawberry, Nashik Grapes (agricultural products); Channapatna dolls and toys, Hand-made Carpet of Bhadohi; Mysore Silk (handicrafts); Feni, Mysore Sandalwood Oil, Nashik Valley Wine (manufactures); and Hyderabad Haleem (foodstuffs). There are 11 foreign registrations in India, all of which are foods or beverages including: Champagne (France), Napa Valley (USA), Parma Ham (Italy), Peruvian Pisco (Peru) and Scotch Whisky (UK). While the benefits of the system have been uneven, and it is of course still early days, a recent review suggests there have been successes.[45] One of the problems is that often the GI applicant is a state government entity that is not involved in actual production, whereas local producers must individually register with the national government office in Chennai before being permitted to use the indication.[46]

8.3.2   Jamaica

Jamaica is another country that has been active, although the slowness in implementing legislation is fairly typical. Diplomatically, Jamaica is very pro-GI. It is a supporter of extending additional protection of GIs at the WTO. Until recently, only certification marks were available to protect Jamaican GIs. However, Jamaica has now opted for a *sui generis* GI law. In 2009, its Protection of Geographical Indications Act entered into force along with the implementing regulations. The legislation is closely based on the language of TRIPS Articles 22–24 and accordingly provides a higher

---

[43] Geographical Indications of Goods (Registration and Protection) Act of 1999 (India).

[44] Ibid., s 11(1).

[45] K. Das, 'Prospects and Challenges of Geographical Indications in India' (2010) 13(2) *Journal of World Intellectual Property* 148–201.

[46] P. Ganguli, personal communication, 17 June 2016.

level of protection for wines and spirits and a lower level for all other products. The government intends to change that so that the heightened level is available to all products without discrimination. In order to develop a workable infrastructure for the GI system, the government has received technical assistance from the Swiss Federal Intellectual Property Institute.

One of Jamaica's best-known products is its 'Blue Mountain coffee', which is protected in many countries by a certification trademark. It is a high-value product whose quality is directly attributable to local climatic and soil conditions. There are said to be large quantities of coffee being mislabelled as Blue Mountain including in countries where a certification trademark has been granted. Another problem is the sale of blends that include Blue Mountain along with other coffees. There is a strong intention to protect Blue Mountain as a GI under the new law and it is hoped that by doing so it will be easier to take effective legal action in these key overseas markets. Two other products that should be registered soon are 'Jamaica Rum' and 'Jamaica Jerk', a type of seasoning for meats, originally pork but nowadays also poultry and fish. The coffee and rum producers are already organised into associations. This makes it easier for them to take advantage of having use of a GI and taking control over the whole production chain from growing the raw materials to packing or bottling the finished product. The Jerk producers, however, do not have a well-established association. The Bureau of Standards of Jamaica will perform the role of monitoring the production process and maintaining quality.

8.3.3   Spirits of the South: Feni, Tequila and Pisco

Nonetheless, it remains the case that few developing country GIs are registered in any part of the world both in absolute and relative terms with only a small number of them having any indications at all. A number of empirical studies on GIs in developing countries have been conducted that highlight the practical possibilities and challenges, while allowing for comparison with other GIs. It is to these that the discussion now turns.

Feni is an alcoholic beverage produced in Goa in India and generally associated with that part of the country. In 2009 it was registered as a GI jointly by the Department for Science and Technology of the government of the state of Goa and a producer association called the Goa Cashew Feni Distillers and Bottlers Association. In line with the rules operating in India, the applicants need to submit detailed specifications containing 'historical information about Feni in Goa, details of the materials and techniques of feni distilling and chemical analysis of the liquor'.[47] Producers and bottlers obviously have a common interest in being about to take advantage of the Feni GI and prevent others whose product does not comply with the specifications but who may wish to pass it off as Feni from doing so. But they are also competitors whose interests may not be identical. Given the stakes involved, it is obviously important that those intending to benefit from the GI are able to agree on the specifications and on any future modifications to them that may become necessary. Indeed, as with other longer-existing GIs in the world, characteristics of the product and manufacturing techniques and conditions will not remain the same indefinitely but will evolve.

---

[47] D. Rangnekar, 'Geographical Indications and Localisation: A Case Study of Feni', ESRC/University of Warwick, 2009. Available at http://papers.ssrn.com/sol3/papers.cfm?abstract_id=1564624.

Such evolution may entail the abandonment of some long-established cultural norms where these hinder the scale-up of production to meet increased market demand. Obviously, securing the integrity of the indication during such change is a vital consideration.

Specifications may vary in terms of how far they include bottling, packing or preparing the product for sale and consumption. Extending local control by covering every stage from cultivation of raw materials to production and presentation of the good to the final consumer is obviously highly desirable if the capacity is available to do it. For example, in Europe, Parma Ham must be sliced and packaged in the designated area in order to be indicated as Parma Ham. The sale of Parma-indicated ham that was sourced appropriately but that was sliced and packaged elsewhere was the subject of a 2003 case at the European Court of Justice in which the Consorzio del Prosciutto di Parma (Consortium of Parma Ham) prevailed against Asda, a British supermarket chain.[48] Returning to Feni, Rangnekar suggests that in the interests both of maintaining quality and enhancing local economic returns, the specification could be modified to require the main ingredient, cashew apples, to be sourced locally while permitting greater flexibility in terms of ingredients, distillation processes and alcoholic strength.

Reconciling the interests of all stakeholders while ensuring that fair returns go to the poorest is a far from simple matter, especially when a product is commercially successful and large corporations dominate production and distribution. In the case of Feni it is too early to say much about this.

In recent years, Tequila, which is the oldest non-European GI, has seen huge growth in production, revenues and quality.[49] And yet, the three main groups involved in the agave-Tequila supply chain, the farmers, the distillers and the bottlers and distributors have not benefited equally, as we will see. So how far should the interests of producers and consumers take into account both: (a) local communities and their skills and methods; and (b) conservation and sustainable use of biodiversity where there may be a conflict between sustainability and the interests of brand owners in meeting demand for the product? While the precision of the specification is hugely important given the need to protect the integrity of the product, the production requirements can be drawn up in a way that is both too excessively liberal and unduly inflexible. Tequila provides an excellent case study in this regard.

In some respects Tequila is a victim of its own success which has been particularly detrimental to local small-scale cultivators and craft producers and, arguably, to the environment. First, as with other popular products there has been pressure to expand geographical boundaries to allow for increased overall production and blending. Indeed, this is what has happened with Tequila and it has undermined the applicability – at least in respect of this product – of the whole idea of *terroir* as the primary source of its defining specialness.

Second, under US pressure, the Mexican government decided not to ban the bulk export of Tequila Mixto for bottling outside the country. This went against the interests of many farmers,

---

[48] Case C-108/01 *Consorzio del Prosciutto di Parma and Salumificio S. Rita SpA v. Asda Stores Ltd & Hygrade Foods Ltd*, ECJ, 20 May 2003.

[49] C. Martineau, *How the Gringos Stole Tequila: The Modern Age of Mexico's Most Traditional Spirit* (Chicago: Chicago Review Press, 2015).

distillers and government officials concerned about the loss of jobs and diminished ability to maintain quality control over the product. Indeed, many growers (*jimadores*), who do all of the harvesting manually, using methods that go back generations, are getting old and not being replaced.[50] As Bowen put it, 'the continued exportation of tequila in bulk, despite opposition by the Mexican government, which holds the rights of the GI, reflects the power that the US-based importers and bottlers hold in the tequila industry, as well as the increasingly multinational ownership of the major tequila companies'.[51] Some Mexican Tequila firms owned by transnational corporations were also content for it to be exported in bulk.

Third, while it is true that 100 per cent blue agave Tequilas are available, mixtos need only contain 51 per cent blue agave with the remaining source of sugar content coming from other types of plant especially sugar cane. Allowing use of sugar from cane rather dilutes the distinctness of tequila as a type of spirit. But this reduction in the required blue agave content suited the large producers as it lowered costs and made sugar supplies more reliable.[52]

With respect to undue flexibility, only one variety of the blue agave species *Agave tequilana* can be used. In consequence, many other agave types are no longer being grown, some of which could have been used without jeopardising quality or geographical integrity. This encourages the spread of monocultures.

Of course, certain forms of differentiation within the indication are unproblematic, such as Tequila's five age categories: Joven, Reposado, Añejo and Extra Añejo. Similarly, the Scotch Whisky GI accommodates product differentiation into single malts, vatted malts, and blended whiskys that mix the product of two or more distilleries.

In concluding her critical study on tequila, Bowen points to some major challenges to using GIs in developing countries for the benefit of the local stakeholders. The fundamental need is for strong legislation backed up by state involvement. The objectives of the regime should not focus narrowly on promoting the product and preventing misappropriation; rather, they should target rural development and local empowerment, and seek to prevent co-optation by transnational corporations. The more distant and powerful supply chain actors must not be allowed to shift the norms in directions that marginalise and disenfranchise the local people and dilute the indication and the reputation of the product for short-term gain. The production regulations need to be drawn up with the full participation of the local stakeholders who need to be involved in any decisions on revising production norms. This highlights a wider issue that small farmers throughout the world tend, through no fault of their own, not to be well represented as an interest group, a situation exacerbated as government generally intervene less and less in rural development matters.

---

[50] H. Ellis-Petersen, 'In Mexico's Tequila-Making Heartland an Age-Old Craft is in Danger of Dying Out, *The Guardian*, 29 May 2015.

[51] Bowen, *supra* note 39, 239; J. Larson, 'Relevance of Geographical Indications and Designations of Origin for the Sustainable Use of Genetic Resources', Report commissioned for the Global Facilitation Unit for Underutilized Species, Rome, 2007. Available at http://www.underutilized-species.org/Documents/PUBLICATIONS/gi_larson_lr.pdf.

[52] J. Santilli, *Agrobiodiversity and the Law: Regulating Genetic Resources, Food Security and Cultural Diversity* (London: Earthscan, 2012), Chapter 13.

The grape brandy Pisco highlights another possible complication: that two or more countries may claim the same indication on the basis that each has a similar or identical product of the same name and for which they claim to be the country of origin. This is by no means unusual. As mentioned earlier, 'Pisco' has been protected in Chile for many decades, as it has been in Peru since 1990. Chile's early designation is despite the fact that Pisco is a city and province of the neighbouring country of Peru where the drink originates. Chilean and Peruvian Pisco differ in terms of definition, grape type, alcoholic content, and (obviously) designated growing area, and this does not make cooperation between the two countries at all easy. In India, the Peruvian government's application to register 'Pisco' was opposed by Chile. Accepting that the word was used in both countries, the registrar accepted the indication 'Peruvian Pisco'. In Thailand, on the other hand, Peru has succeeded in registering 'Pisco' as a GI.[53] Peru has registered 'Pisco' as an appellation of origin under the Lisbon Agreement 1958 but several state parties to the Agreement have indicated their intention of refusing the appellation on their territories mostly because they accept Chile's right to market their drink under the same name.

In Europe, the government of Peru has registered 'Pisco' under the relevant EU Regulation on spirits.[54] According to the technical file submitted with the European GI application,[55] there are three types differentiated by type of grape and fermentation level: Pisco Puro, Pisco Acholado and Pisco Mosto Verde. As far as 'capturing' the whole supply chain, the file goes quite far claiming 'all the stages of processing "Pisco", from growing the vine, processing the grape and bottling the final product, are carried out in the "Pisco" -making area'. The area is far more expansive than the city or province of Pisco, covering numerous provinces and departments.

Chile has also had successes in getting trade parties to accept the designations 'Pisco' and 'Chilean Pisco', mostly through bilateral trade agreements. While cooperation including sharing the indication would appear to be the obvious way forward, agreeing on common specifications and regulations may prove to be extremely difficult. The same may be said for basmati rice, a commercially successful product that is grown in both India and Pakistan and protected as a GI in the former country. In both cases, achieving such cooperation is not just a technical challenge, but a political, social and cultural one too.[56] The two countries are yet to agree on a definition of what basmati rice in terms of its origin actually is.

---

[53] Trademark Office, Department of Intellectual Property, Ministry of Commerce of Thailand, *Notice of Registration of Geographical Indications Gazette (Thailand)* 1(1), 2005. Available at http://www.ecap-project.org/archive/fileadmin/ecapII/pdf/en/information/thailand/gazettes/GI_Gazette_1__English.pdf.

[54] Regulation (EC) No 110/2008 of the European Parliament and of the Council on the definition, description, presentation, labelling and the protection of geographical indications of spirit drinks and repealing Council Regulation (EEC) No 1576/89.

[55] European Commission 2011, *Main Specifications of the Technical File for 'Pisco'* (2011/C 141/16). *Official Journal of the European Union* 12 May. Available at http://eur-lex.europa.eu/LexUriServ/LexUriServ.do?uri=OJ:C:2011:141:0016:0018:EN:PDF.

[56] D. Rangnekar and S. Kumar, 'Another Look at Basmati: Genericity and the Problems of a Transborder Geographical Indication' (2010) 13(2) *Journal of World Intellectual Property* 202–30.

If it proves impossible to cooperate on the definition, what we have are two different products having the same name. The issue of homonymous products is covered in TRIPS, but only for wines. Accordingly, co-existence of both indications must be allowed. How this is to be done is left up to WTO members, but the producers concerned must be treated equitably and consumers must not be misled.[57]

---

[57] Agreement on Trade-Related Aspects of Intellectual Property Rights, Art 23.3.

9

Plant intellectual property

In 1950s' Europe, the question arose of whether and how to protect innovations in the form of improved cultivated plants. From the start it proved to be a complex and controversial matter. The United States Plant Patent Act had protected asexually reproduced plants since 1930,[1] and still does. But this legislation had little if any international influence – other countries did not line up to follow the US example.[2] Patents had occasionally been granted on plants in a few European

---

[1] As revised in 1954, the Plant Patent Act makes plant patents (as opposed to utility (ordinary) patents and design patents) available to 'whoever invents or discovers and asexually reproduces any distinct and new variety of plants, including cultivated sports, mutants, hybrids, and newly found seedlings, other than a tuber propagated plant or a plant found in an uncultivated state, may obtain a patent thereof, subject to the conditions and requirements of this title.' US Patent Law Sec. 161. What is and is not an 'uncultivated state' is not necessarily such a clear-cut matter (*In re Beineke* 690 F 3d 1344 (Fed Cir, 2012)).

[2] G.E. Bugos and D.J. Kevles, 'Plants as Intellectual Property: American Practice, Law, and Policy in a World Context' (1992) 7 *Osiris* 75–104; G. Dutfield *Intellectual Property Rights and the Life Science Industries: A Twentieth Century History*

countries but it was hardly common.[3] Initially, there were severe doubts expressed as to the patentability of scientifically bred plants due to the lack of inventiveness. This left the options either of leaving them legally unprotected or else of creating a *sui generis* alternative to patents. Many countries have since then, and for a number of different reasons, opted for the *sui generis* alternative. More recently, with the increased adoption of gene technologies to transform plants through the insertion of traits that are not 'native' to plants, or at least not to those particular recipient crops, and to accelerate conventional breeding approaches through such means as marker-assisted selection, the role of patents and their effects on the freedoms of both breeders and farmers has attracted critical attention. This chapter focuses on the best-known *sui generis* system available while seeking to make sense of the complexities and controversies of the past 60 years since high-level discussions began on legal protection of plant varieties, in light of the long history of agriculture.

To date, the only plant variety protection (PVP) system with international recognition is the one defined under the International Convention for the Protection of New Varieties of Plants – whose contracting parties form an association known in the original French as the *Union pour la Protection des Obtentions Végétales* (UPOV).[4] UPOV is legally separate from, but has a close relationship with, the World Intellectual Property Organization (WIPO) which houses the secretariat (the UPOV Office) in its Geneva headquarters. Officially, UPOV's mission is 'to provide and promote an effective system of plant variety protection, with the aim of encouraging the development of new varieties of plants, for the benefit of society'. Thus, as an IPR specifically for protecting new plant varieties, PVP has important implications for the improvement of plants grown in field, garden and orchard. But its significance goes far beyond this. PVP relates also to agricultural and food policy, food security, rural development, and biodiversity and genetic resource conservation.

As we will see, UPOV started off as very much a West European club. The Convention was largely conceived and designed by and for European breeding interests in a way that balanced these interests with those of farmers and operated alongside and in harmony with seed regulations. Agriculture ministries, rather than ministries of trade or industry, were also involved in discussions on the need for objectives and basic features of the UPOV system. In its early years the Convention applied exclusively to European countries. These same European breeding interests continue to be intimately involved in the operations of the Convention and of the Union, and have also played important roles in encouraging more and more countries to join UPOV. By the end of 1995, the year that the World Trade Organization (WTO) was established, there were only 29 members, mostly developed countries. This reflects the reality that in many developing countries, especially in Africa, private sector involvement in plant breeding and seed supply was quite limited. Moreover, in many of these countries small-scale farming communities were, and often still are, responsible for much of the plant breeding and seed distribution, as they have been

(Aldershot: Ashgate, 2003), Chapter 7; C. Fowler, *Unnatural Selection: Technology, Politics, and Plant Evolution* (Yverdon: Gordon and Breach, 1994); and A. Pottage and B. Sherman, *Figures of Invention: A History of Patent Law* (Oxford: Oxford University Press, 2010).

[3] Dutfield, ibid., 184.

[4] International Convention for the Protection of New Varieties of Plants, 1961, as revised at Geneva on 1972, 1978 and 1991.

for centuries. Consequently, until recently there would have been few domestic beneficiaries of a PVP system apart from the public institutes for agricultural research. However, many developing countries are now members of the Union and parties to the Convention. As of the February 2019, UPOV has 75 members including the European Union (EU) and the 17-member state *Organisation Africaine de la Propriété Intellectuelle* (OAPI), with the majority of the membership now comprising developing countries or former communist nations.[5]

9.1   PLANT INNOVATION

9.1.1   An ancient practice

The development and diffusion of innovations of the kind IP law now protects occupies merely the most recent episode in the 12,000-year-long agricultural history of the world. Domestication of ecoregions, landscapes, ecosystems and species across the habitable world through agriculture among other subsistence and livelihood practices, both deliberate and through unconscious processes of co-evolution, leading to the present era now commonly referred to as the Anthropocene, comes in many guises. Many if not most of these guises are far from visible or obvious to the casual observer, and indeed are still being discovered (or in some cases rediscovered).[6] For some scientists, wild plants are better recast as 'wild' plants,[7] or as non- or semi-domesticated plants, the different punctuation or words serving to acknowledge that plants assumed to be unmanaged and uncultivated may well in fact fall within the domestication continuum.[8] Just because people leave their fields to collect them – often for their nutritional or medicinal benefits – does not mean they just happen to be lying around there. Indeed, some of the world's most 'natural'-looking places are actually domesticated landscapes and have been for a very long time.[9]

Admittedly, human transformation of nature has never been more deliberate, faster or more in-

---

[5] The membership list is available on the official UPOV website (www.upov.int).

[6] On the Amazon, one of the regions that has proved hardest for Europeans to identify as an area under domestication possibly for millennia, see C. Levis et al., 'How People Domesticated Amazonian Forests' (2018) 5 *Frontiers in Ecology and Evolution* 1–21.

[7] G.S. Cruz-Garcia, 'Management and Motivations to Manage "Wild" Food Plants. A Case Study in a Mestizo Village in the Amazon Deforestation Frontier', in *Front. Ecol. Evol.* 5:127. doi: 10.3389/fevo.2017.00127.

[8] Ethnoecological studies demonstrate that in some parts of the world there is not always a sharp line that can be drawn between domesticated varieties and 'wild' plants, but more of a continuum. D.A. Posey, 'Diachronic Ecotones and Anthropogenic Landscapes in Amazonia: Contesting the Consciousness of Conservation', in W. Balée (ed.), *Advances in Historical Ecology* (Columbia University Press, 1998), 113; D.A. Posey, 'Utilizing Amazonian Indigenous Knowledge in the Conservation of Biodiversity: Can Kayapó Management Strategies be Equitably Utilized and Applied?', in F. Arler and I. Svennevig (eds), *Cross-Cultural Protection of Nature and the Environment* (Odense University Press, 1997), 119–33.

[9] The term 'domesticated landscape' was coined by Douglas Yen. D.E. Yen, 'The Domestication of Environment', in D.R. Harris and G.C. Hillman (eds), *Foraging and Farming: The Evolution of Plant Exploitation* (London: Unwin, 1989), 55–78.

tense than it is today as innovation becomes more and more organised, systematic and reduction-ist. But does this truly mean that humans now have mastery over nature? Or to put it another way, has science enabled human agency to stamp out nature's agency, reducing the latter to tame pas-sivity? It is certainly the case that innovation and the property claims associated with it imply the possibility to disassociate human agency from the agency of nature, privileging the former whilst overlooking and even denying ecosystems and plants 'their own creativity and temporality'.[10] This is, at least in some part, a conceit; and perhaps even an illusion. However flawed, belief in such a disassociation, or at least in its ability to underpin convenient legal fictions, supplies a foundation upon which plant intellectual property legal frameworks have been constructed.

Ever since the birth of agriculture, and possibly even before then, humans have not been passive in accepting nature as we found it. The Neolithic adoption and spread of agriculture transformed the biosphere, turning untamed wildernesses into farmlands. Farming and crop improvement were carried out by the same people and in the same places: by farmers on the farm or other areas where cultivation took place impermanently. From Neolithic times, farmers have set aside some of their harvested seeds for replanting. They selected such seeds, whether consciously or unintentionally, on the basis that the plants producing them possessed desirable traits such as high yields, disease resistance, or drought or frost tolerance. Over the generations, this practice resulted in ever increas-ing quantities of locally adapted varieties known as 'landraces', 'folk varieties' or 'farmers' varieties'.

We prefer the latter term because 'landrace' implicitly pays insufficient credit to the role of genera-tions of farmers, while 'folk' suggests old age and quaintness whereas local farmers' varieties can also be new. Ecologically speaking, agriculture involves arresting natural succession processes at a very early stage. By preventing the maturation of ecosystems, invasive species, often grasses like wheat, rice, barley and maize, remain dominant instead of giving way to trees as would otherwise happen without humans to prevent it by weeding, tilling and (in some places) burning. Wild plants and an-imals became domesticated ones, initially by becoming 'camp followers' taking advantage of the op-portunities provided by human habitation to spread on to the disturbed terrain and scavenge for food. While human selection ultimately had a massive effect, 'domestication' in its early stages was not something that humans 'did'. Rather it was a normal evolutionary response to the formation of new ecological niches resulting from human settlement and activity that selectively advantaged individ-uals with certain traits. Such traits included tameness in certain animals and opportunism in plants.

In time, humans would have preferred plant species that were edible and individuals tended to put their energies more into vegetative growth and seed production than in developing complex and extensive root systems.[11] Here human selection would have come into play. Much, much later, the will and capability to improve the world with a little hard work and ingenuity came to be seen by Europeans as one of the hallmarks of a civilised society. From the Enlightenment, successful 'improvers' of nature such as Thomas Fairchild (died 1729), who produced the first known artificial hybrid, Fairchild's Mule, and Robert Bakewell (died 1795), the famed livestock breeder, and US plant breeder Luther Burbank (died 1926), began to be honoured with credit, fame, and eventually with property rights.

---

[10] C. Fullilove, *The Profit of the Earth: The Global Seeds of American Agriculture* (Chicago: University of Chicago Press, 2017), 5.

[11] S. Budiansky, *The Covenant of the Wild: Why Animals Chose Domestication* (New York: William Morrow, 1992).

9.1.2   Traditional farming and breeding

The separation of the two activities of farming and breeding is very recent historically. In some parts of the developing world, though, it has hardly begun. In late-nineteenth-century North America and Europe, a marked divergence emerged between the occupation of farming and of seed production. Those engaged in the latter were selecting from the existing materials to increase their share in a growing market in commercial seed. This commercial crop improvement was empirical and experimental but with a growing scientific basis in mathematics applied to selection methods. Very soon after the 1900 rediscovery of Mendel's insights into the laws of heredity, scientists sought to apply genetics to crop improvement. According to conventional accounts, this led in good historically linear fashion to the directed development of 'pure lines' of self-pollinating crops. Pure lines, a term coined by Danish botanist Wilhelm Johannsen, are uniform, breed true to type and contain consistent and identifiable traits that can be transferred to other plants. According to Pistorius and van Wijk, 'while Mendelian breeding allowed for a controlled mixing of genetic characteristics, pure line breeding offered a practical method to "fix" them in succeeding generations'.[12] It must be said here that debate continues as to how far the notion of the pure line truly transformed breeding practices and whether it was all that crucial in attracting new commercial interest in crop improvement.[13] A deeper discussion falls beyond the scope of this book. Suffice it to say that plant variety protection is implicitly founded upon a pure line-derived conception of breeding practices and of what the 'new plant variety' by definition is.

Nowadays, the inputs for crop improvement work largely include earlier varieties that themselves were previously developed by the same improvement techniques. These form a large proportion of the stock of breeding material already in wide circulation among breeders. Thus, much plant breeding centres on the mixing or 'shuffling' of traits that are either known about already or else can be identified in easily accessible and well-characterised plant material. However, inputs also include varieties acquired from seed collections newly or only recently circulated as breeding material. In addition, varieties hitherto found within and around the fields of local and indigenous cultivators may also be used. In certain cases, such human populations inhabit areas within the centres of origin and diversity of major crops such as rice, wheat, maize and potatoes as were initially identified by the great early-twentieth-century Russian geneticist Nikolai Vavilov. The centres, therefore, are strategically important in terms of food security, conservation, and commercial activity in plant breeding and commercial biotechnology. Realisation of this importance has left an indelible mark on international law.

As environmental historian Courtney Fullilove has argued, 'cultivated seeds are not products of nature but deep-time technologies, domesticated some 10,000–12,000 years ago and improved by successive generations of farmers'.[14] In terms of their social character, 'seeds are not stable objects,

---

[12] R. Pistorius, and J. van Wijk, *The Exploitation of Plant Genetic Information: Political Strategies in Crop Development* (CABI Publishing, 1999).

[13] D. Berry, 'The Plant Breeding Industry after Pure Line Theory: Lessons from the National Institute of Agricultural Botany' (2014) 46 *Studies in History and Philosophy of Biological and Biomedical Sciences* 25–37.

[14] Fullilove, *supra* note 10, 1.

but contested artefacts, classified according to variable logics of science, heritage, and property'.[15] This matters a great deal both for the application of IP law and for the appropriate way to treat farmers especially those who are custodians of agricultural biodiversity. With respect to the former, it follows that the ways plant breeders conceptualise their work, their role, and the extent to which they intervene in and control nature is very important. Of course, how they have done so has changed over the decades and not only on scientific grounds. Intellectual property and commercialisation are implicated too in how breeders frame what they do and seek to shape the applicable legal framework. As science historian Berris Charnley explains:

> In the 1950s and 60s, despite the US Plant Patent Act 1930 and UPOV, and the legal arguments around inventorship behind such legislation, many plant breeders still saw themselves as stewards of somewhat natural variability, rather than as inventors. The varieties they produced had to be constantly maintained, otherwise a variety might 'run out', becoming heterogeneous and unruly. This stewardship role – enshrined in breeders' practices – was a key selling point in catalogues which proclaimed the length of time varieties had been maintained and purified [...] Over the decades since mid-century the variety has slowly been ossified as a fixed and discrete unit. Variability has been recast within acceptable boundaries which do not threaten a variety's integrity. In the years since 1980, this conception of variety has in turn been displaced as the product of plant breeding by allegedly fixed identifiable entities around which intellectual property could be circumscribed, without the need for maintenance – DNA sequences.[16]

This refusal to countenance the inevitability of natural variability is, Charnley argues, a fiction, demonstrating once again that human mastery over nature is at best partial and short-lived. In the present context one needs to be aware of some wider implications: 'The law's recent focus on DNA sequences, as though they were static and unchanging over time, degrades the importance of stewardship roles (especially those conducted by small scale farmers in maintaining land races).'[17] We continue the discussion on agricultural biotechnology in Chapter 14. Despite what one might assume from this, plant variety protection has definitely not reached a state of redundancy.

9.1.3 Innovation in breeding

What do plant breeders actually do for which IPRs are deemed to be a just reward? Plant breeding is in fact a very laborious and time-consuming process. It takes about seven to ten years to get from the first cross to the marketable variety. The first task is to determine the objectives of the breeding programme. One obvious goal is to produce varieties with higher yields, but there are many other

---

[15] Ibid., 5.

[16] B. Charnley, 'Cui bono? Gauging the Successes of Publicly-funded Plant Breeding in Retrospect', in C. Lawson and B. Charnley (eds), Intellectual Property and Genetically Modified Organisms (Cheltenham: Edward Elgar Publishing, 2015), 23–4.

[17] Ibid., 24.

possible objectives such as the development of varieties with added or improved characteristics such as pest or disease resistance, drought tolerance, responsiveness to inputs such as fertilisers and pesticides, improved consumption or food-processing characteristics, and compatibility with mechanised harvesting. A major challenge for breeders is to respond on the one side to the requirements of varying farming conditions, and on the other hand to the need to develop varieties that can be sold widely. Furthermore, they increasingly have to respond to the ever-changing demands of conglomerate seed and chemical companies, food-processing companies, and supermarket chains.

The basic conventional technique is known as 'crossing and selecting', which involves crossing two or more parent lines or varieties with desirable traits to produce multiple offspring. Of these, the best plants are selected and allowed to breed again. Also, the best ones are selected for breeding and the process is repeated a number of times. After eight to 12 generations, an improved variety is produced that breeds true and is ready to be planted by farmers.

But breeding is rarely this simple in terms of goals or activity. For one thing, there may be an inherent trade-off in the sense that the objectives of higher yields and convenience for farmers can lead to breeders selecting and breeding crops with lower nutritional quality. This situation has been referred to as 'the breeder's dilemma'.[18] For another, a new variety may be derived from 50 or more parental lines. Also, a variety used in the breeding programme may be the source of only one desirable trait and many undesirable ones. So how does the breeder incorporate this single trait into his or her new variety while excluding the others? To explain in the simplest terms, let us call plants from the parent line or new variety into which the single trait is to be introduced 'Group A'. We shall then call members of the 'donor' plants (which could well be a wild or semi-domesticated relative) 'Group B'. These Group B plants, then, are the source of just one desirable trait out of many unwanted ones, for which as little as one gene may be responsible. For the breeder to transfer this trait without the undesirable ones, he must first cross Group A and Group B plants and then 'back-cross' those offspring containing the trait with plants from Group A. This is repeated through the generations, selecting plants that retain the trait and back-crossing them with Group A plants. In time, the proportion of genes from Group B plants contained in the offspring goes down in conventional selection systems from 50–50 in the first generation to a negligible figure.

These approaches generally work well with crops like wheat, rice and sorghum that self-fertilise. These tend to be genetically stable and consequently breed true. But of course harnessing that basic plant characteristic to advantage first requires carrying out many crossings. Doing this is hardly a simple matter: it is necessary to prevent self-fertilisation when it is the plant's 'natural inclination' to do just that. Be that as it may, as with humans and animals, inbreeding for cross-pollinators such as maize, pearl millet and cruciferous crops like cabbages and oilseed rape can be deleterious. This is not such a problem for plants that can reproduce – or be reproduced – asexually, such as vines, apple trees and potatoes, where the genetics are fixed through this reproduction system: once a new variety has been bred, it can be multiplied through vegetative forms of propagation, whether cuttings, grafts or tubers. But for cross-fertilising seed crops, the breeder must find another approach.

---

[18] C.E. Morris and D.C. Sands, 'The Breeder's Dilemma – Yield or Nutrition?' (2006) 24(9) *Nature Biotechnology* 1078–80.

Maize breeders in the early-twentieth century came up with a solution by applying the redis-covered principles of Mendelian genetics. George Shull, an experimental breeder working at a US government research centre, managed to induce the characteristic of (what he called) 'heterosis' in the corn plants resulting from his cross-breeding of inbred lines. This phenomenon, commonly referred to as 'hybrid vigour', which is still not fully understood,[19] is manifested in heightened yields of seeds resulting from the first cross. The additional advantage that hybrid varieties provide a uniform crop compared to the open pollinated populations became apparent with large-scale agricultural mechanisation. But because they are hybrids, the harvested seed does not give rise to true to type offspring and the maximum yield enhancements thus last only for a single generation. These resulting plants tend to be 'segregated', reflecting the characteristics of the grandparents. So while farmers stand to benefit from seeds providing this hybrid vigour, they need to buy seeds at the beginning of every planting season to enjoy equally productive future harvests. This necessity to buy seed was and continues to be a boon for the seed companies that could correct a major risk factor in seed production, namely that seed markets are generally anti-cyclic, that is, after a good harvest – when the seed producer has good stocks – farmers save their seed and the demand for seed is high when seed production conditions have been poor. Hybrids create a stable seed market.

Unfortunately for breeders (and presumably for commercial farmers especially those with large holdings), hybridisation does not work easily if at all for some of the most economically important crops such as wheat. This of course presents problems for breeders. Plants are self-reproducing. With no law to prevent it, there is nothing to stop farmers from replanting harvested seed, or even multiplying seed for the purpose of selling it in competition with the breeder (assuming this would be more profitable for them than selling harvested produce). This is of course where IPRs come in.

Other techniques like tissue and cell culture development have been used for several decades. These enable scientists to regenerate large numbers of plants that are genetically identical and free from disease. These techniques do not replace conventional breeding but can improve its efficiency. More recently molecular biology introduced new opportunities in breeding, either to make conventional breeding more efficient and effective (marker-assisted selection) or by moving foreign genes into the breeding materials (genetic engineering) not just from other plant species, but from completely different forms of life. For example, scientists have succeeded in inducing in-sect resistance in crops like corn and cotton by inserting genes from a soil microbe called Bacillus thuringiensis that is toxic for certain insects. (Interestingly – and to the consternation of some people – the Bt protein and the genetic material coding for its production in the plant is regulated in the United States as a pesticide.) Plant genetic modification techniques include direct gene transfer into tissue cultures using bacteria like Agrobacterium tumifaciens or viruses as carriers of the foreign DNA, and such devices as high-velocity 'gene guns' which shoot DNA-containing 'bullets' into cell nuclei. The new science of genomics is being used to identify useful genes and their functions in the plants which contain them, and new gene editing tools are now being used. The latter raises interesting regulatory issues which fall beyond the scope of this book. For more discussion on GM crops and intellectual property, see Chapter 14.

---

[19] Z.J. Chen, 'Genomic and epigenetic insights into the molecular bases of heterosis' (2013) 14 *Nature Reviews Genetics* 471–82.

9.1.4   Food and traditional farming

The hyper-abundance of food products in the developed world and the reduction of mass hunger in a few developing countries are largely attributable to modern agriculture including the varieties in common use bred by public and private sector breeders. Legitimate concerns about overconsumption and the low-quality diets of many people should not be used to gainsay this important point. However, despite its potential for huge social welfare enhancement, generating revenues from plant breeding is a challenge. For varieties that breed true, meaning they have consistent traits that persist generation by generation, farmers and even amateur gardeners can save, clean and replant or sell seeds. Asexually-reproducing species can be mass-copied through techniques such as cutting and grafting. In response, technology, intellectual property and contract law as applied through use of licenses that purchasing seed dealers and farmers must agree to (which for the latter may be more restrictive than PVP rules) may be deployed so that breeders can derive revenue from plant varieties which they have developed.

Plant innovation is inherently cumulative based on incremental improvements on what already exists. Much of what exists goes back thousands of years and has generally been freely available for everyone's benefit. Admittedly, modern field-crop breeders are not usually reliant on traditional farmers' varieties on an everyday basis, except when they are starting up new breeding programmes. Even then, this reliance is likely to diminish over time as they focus ever more on the recycling of modern varieties.[20] However, local farmers' varieties and wild relatives of crops continue to be extremely important for integrating new traits or new variants of known traits (for example, disease resistance) and their continued use and existence is essential for breeders and local/indigenous communities alike.[21] As conservers through use and improvers themselves, many so-called 'traditional' cultivators provide an essential service to breeders and to those of us who do not farm and need others to provide sustained food security.

Indeed, global food security can be enhanced by encouraging their use and by ensuring that access to them be kept open, subject to the rules and principles of the 2001 FAO International Treaty on Plant Genetic Resources for Food and Agriculture, which establishes a multilateral system of facilitated access to plant genetic resources but respects national sovereignty and requires benefit sharing. The Treaty also provides certain safeguards for the rights of farmers – thus, Article 9 deals with the protection of traditional knowledge, benefit sharing, participation in decision-making, and freedoms to save, use, exchange and sell farm-saved seed and propagating material. The latter raises potential conflict issues with patents and PVP but the enjoyment of these freedoms is 'subject to national law and as appropriate'.

---

[20] Some genetic technologies might in fact counteract this trend.

[21] Regarding farmers' varieties: M. Halewood and I. Lapeña, 'Farmers' Varieties and Farmers' Rights: Challenges at the Crossroads of Agriculture, Taxonomy and Law', in M. Halewood (ed.), *Farmers' Crop Varieties and Farmers' Rights: Challenges in Taxonomy and Law* (Routledge, 2016), 1–24; N.P. Louwaars and W.S. De Boef, 'Integrated Seed Sector Development in Africa: A Conceptual Framework for Creating Coherence between Practices, Programs and Policies' (2012) 26 *Journal of Crop Improvement* 39–59; Concerning wild relatives: N.P. Castañeda-Álvarez et al., 'Global Conservation Priorities for Crop Wild Relatives' (2016) 2(16022) *Nature Plants*; M. Montenegro, 'Banking on Wild Relatives to Feed the World' (2016) 16(1) *Gastronomica: The Journal of Critical Food Studies* 1–8.

What of innovation in traditional agricultural systems, which persist in vast areas of the inhabited world, especially in the developing countries? There is a tendency to write off traditional small-scale systems as being obsolete, maladaptive and generally unproductive. One of the main reasons why we fail to respect traditional agriculture is perhaps that the word 'traditional' implies a rootedness to the past as if that is its defining and only feature. In fact, the 1992 Convention on Biological Diversity (see Chapter 15) refers to the 'knowledge, innovations and practices of indigenous and local communities embodying traditional lifestyles'. It is unfortunate that 'innovations' has largely been left out of the discourse. To suggest that traditional knowledge is old and therefore lacks novelty is an unhelpful presumption. It may well be true that these systems alone will never support today's global population of which more than half is now urban dwelling, and that modern intensive agriculture based on high-yielding varieties and large doses of chemical inputs is vital. Nonetheless, they should not be disparaged. Indeed, they are the main providers of food security in many developing countries, and as mentioned their sustainable production and use of agricultural biodiversity is a boon for all humans.

So-called 'traditional farmers' can also be highly innovative in the face of fluctuating and unpredictable environmental conditions. Indeed, not all farmers' varieties are ancient; neither are they all 'traditional': sometimes there is cross-breeding with modern varieties,[22] including in India genetically modified ones.[23] Anthropologist Paul Richards explains, for example, how Mende farming communities in Sierra Leone continue effectively to manage agricultural genetic diversity, experiment on-farm with traditional and modern rice varieties and to produce their own varieties whose performance is often better than those provided by extension services.[24]

There are very good reasons why such innovation should be allowed to persist and not interfered with by inappropriate and monopolistic intellectual property laws and seed regulations including compulsory seed lists like the European Agricultural and Vegetable Common Catalogues. The intellectual property laws may have this effect if they narrow or eliminate the privilege of farmers to replant and exchange saved seed. Seed regulations may do so if they require that the only cultivated varieties sown by farmers be those on an official seed list, and that farmers' varieties be mainly or entirely excluded from it for failing to meet strict, inflexible criteria.[25] Unfortunately, in many parts of the world, workable local agricultural systems have been modified and distorted, and thereby

---

[22] N. Kingsbury, *Hybrid: The History and Science of Plant Breeding* (University of Chicago Press, 2009), 65–6.

[23] G.D. Stone, 'The Birth and Death of Traditional Knowledge: Paradoxical Effects of Biotechnology in India', in C. McManis (ed.), *Biodiversity and the Law: Intellectual Property, Biotechnology and Traditional Knowledge* (London: Earthscan, 2007), 207–38.

[24] P. Richards, 'Casting Seeds to the Four Winds: A Modest Proposal for Plant Genetic Diversity Management', in D.A. Posey (ed.), *Cultural and Spiritual Values of Biodiversity* (Nairobi: UNEP and IT, 1999), 315–6.

[25] Halewood, *supra* note 21. The EU does provide for limited derogations allowing for the cultivation and marketing of certain locally adapted and threatened agricultural varieties, or landraces – Commission Directive 2008/62/EC of 20 June 2008 providing for certain derogations for acceptance of agricultural landraces and varieties which are naturally adapted to the local and regional conditions and threatened by genetic erosion and for marketing of seed and seed potatoes of those landraces and varieties; Commission Directive 2009/145/EC of 26 November 2009 providing for certain derogations, for acceptance of vegetable landraces and varieties which have been traditionally grown in particular

rendered ineffective.[26] One should not be romantic about traditional agriculture, if for no other reason than that many of these systems have been degraded through no fault of the local people themselves and no longer function as they did. Population increases, the spread of market economies with the introduction of export crops and Green Revolution technologies, all-too-prevalent assumptions that Western techniques and methods such as high-input monocultural agriculture are superior to local ones like intercropping, the imposition of inappropriate laws and regulations by governments, and war, are all factors in this.

Nonetheless, original agricultural systems are intact in many areas of the world. Moreover, some good results have been achieved by reviving the use of traditional crop species and introducing modern post-harvesting technologies that ironically can enhance the viability of 'old' varieties and species for the benefit of farmers and consumers.[27] Clearly, we should not throw out the baby with the bathwater. On the other hand, some countries rely heavily on cultivating and exporting non-traditional crops and their produce. For example, Kenya depends heavily on trade in tea, coffee, and horticultural produce including vegetables and cut flowers. These products are extremely important not just as sources of foreign exchange but also employment and income for rural people. Ornamental varieties are normally bred in Europe, and the breeding firms may be insistent that they be intellectual property protected in the developing country where they are planted and from where they are exported. Argentina and Brazil are also large exporters of non-native agricultural produce such as soybean, wheat and coffee. Nonetheless, the interaction of traditional knowledge with agricultural techniques applied to local or exotic crops is fertile ground for innovation in many parts of the world.

9.1.5   The emergence of the commercial seed industry

During the nineteenth-century westward expansion of the US, the government sought to encourage settlement. One way to do this was to entrust the farmers themselves with the selection, breeding and multiplication of seed. To this effect, the Patent Office, first, and then the US Department of Agriculture (USDA), provided farmers with free seed packets for them to experiment with. At the time, the seed industry was small and insignificant. Farmers used these seeds and those introduced by the immigrants arriving in the US to breed varieties adapted to suit their own needs and the local ecological conditions. The number of such varieties increased enormously. Later these farmer-bred and selected crop varieties formed the basis of the public and private sector breeding programmes.

Fowler argues that the separation of farming from breeding, the undermining of the customary practice of seed saving in the case of hybridised crops, and the commodification of the seed cannot be explained by advances in plant breeding science and technology alone.[28] When scientifically bred

---

localities and regions and are threatened by genetic erosion and of vegetable varieties with no intrinsic value for commercial crop production but developed for growing under particular conditions and for marketing of seed of those landraces and varieties.

[26] D. Brokensha, 'What African Farmers Know', in Posey, *supra* note 24, 309–12.

[27] J.-F. Cruz, 'Fonio: A Small Grain with Potential' (2004) March *LEISA Magazine* 16–17.

[28] C. Fowler, *Unnatural Selection: Technology, Politics, and Plant Evolution* (Yverdon: Gordon and Breach, 1994).

seeds came onto the market, subsistence agriculture had largely been replaced by commercial farming anyway. Mechanised harvesting and the consolidation of land-holdings had made seed selection non-viable compared to the greater convenience of purchasing mechanically cleaned seed from dealers. And, since most farmers were no longer improving seeds themselves, the attraction of selecting and replanting was declining even before scientifically bred varieties were becoming widely available.

In 1890, 596 firms were involved in commercial seed production. Having formed a business association called the American Seed Trade Association (ASTA) a few years earlier, they were becoming active in defending their interests. One of ASTA's early campaigns was to stop the government from providing farmers with seeds. This failed for lack of support from the public and Congress, many of whose members sent seed packets to constituents. However, during the first two decades of the twentieth century, the government increasingly sent seeds only of the most common varieties to farmers, while passing on the more exotic germplasm to the government experiment stations and colleges. A later campaign by ASTA from the First World War onwards was to oppose the saving of seed by the farmers.

Shortly after the First World War, the Secretary of Agriculture decided that the USDA would henceforth support research aimed at the development of hybrids and ending farmer participation in breeding programmes. The implications of the emergence of corn hybrids for private sector breeding cannot be underestimated. Several of the world's major twentieth-century seed companies first came to prominence through their successful breeding of hybrid corn varieties. Many of these old seed companies are now owned by large transnational corporations like Monsanto, Syngenta and DuPont.

Contrary to the US situation, virtually all the cultivable land in nineteenth-century Europe had been farmed for a very long time. Most of those major crops whose origins were exotic, like wheat, rye, maize, potatoes and tomatoes, had become well-established and integrated into local farming systems for centuries or even millennia. Although some such crops were vulnerable to devastating diseases due to widespread genetic uniformity (most notoriously potatoes), European farmers developed a huge range of varieties over the centuries to suit local conditions. European governments generally did not find it necessary to encourage farmers to breed new varieties themselves as in the US case.

Introducing new species and formal experimental breeding were carried out first by wealthy landowners, and from the early-twentieth century by the small family seed firms. These firms descended from farmers who made it their main business to provide seed for other farmers and who then started breeding programmes to better meet the requirements of their customers. As in the US, public research institutions and universities were also carrying out breeding work which benefited the emerging private plant breeding sector.

9.2   THE UPOV CONVENTION

9.2.1   History

Crop improvement has gone on for at least 10,000 years almost entirely before there had ever been patents or plant variety protection and when open access regimes are assumed to have been the norm.[29] Even the advent of scientific breeding methods, which has dramatically increased the pace of crop improvement, preceded the availability of plant intellectual property. Before the 1960s, then, IP protection of plant varieties was uncommon. With very few national regimes, European breeder associations were instrumental in UPOV's existence. Two organisations were deeply involved in the creation of the UPOV Convention: (i) the International Association for the Protection of Intellectual Property (AIPPI), which largely comprises lawyers with a pro-industry stance; and (ii) the International Association of Plant Breeders (ASSINSEL), forerunner to today's International Seed Federation. Both took the strategic view that the lack of intellectual property norms specifically for plants needed to be resolved internationally.

In 1956, ASSINSEL's members called for a conference to consider the possibility of developing a new international instrument for protecting plant varieties, requesting the French government to organise it.[30] That conference, which took place the following year, established the basic principles of plant variety protection as later incorporated into the UPOV Convention. Only European governments were invited, mainly representatives of agriculture ministries. These agreed to set up a Committee of Experts, charged with the following tasks: (a) studying the legal problems arising out of the protection of the breeder's right as defined by the Conference; (b) giving as precise formulations as might be appropriate of the basic technical and economic principles laid down by the Conference; and (c) preparing the first draft of an international convention for submission to a later session of the Conference itself. The Committee met twice before appointing a Drafting Group to develop a legal text. One of the important issues the Committee had to decide upon was whether the convention would be incorporated into the general framework of the Paris Convention, or whether a separate convention was necessary. It decided in favour of the latter but recommended that the new office administering the convention should work closely with the *Bureaux Internationaux Réunis de la Protection de la Propriété Intellectuelle* (BIRPI), which subsequently became WIPO's International Bureau.

The second meeting of the International Conference for the Protection of New Varieties of Plants took place in November 1961, with 12 European countries being invited, as were BIRPI, the FAO, the European Economic Community, the Organisation of Economic Co-operation and Development (OECD), and other business associations including ASSINSEL, AIPPI, the *Communauté Internationale des Obtenteurs de Plantes Ornementales de Reproduction Asexuée* (CIOPORA), and the *Fédération Internationale du Commerce des Semences* (FIS).[31] Since then ASSINSEL, FIS and the new International Seed Federation (comprising the merged ASSINSEL and FIS) along with CIOPORA and the International Chamber of Commerce have played key roles in shaping the evolution of the UPOV Convention through its various revisions. All of these were and remain organisations headquartered in Europe.

There were few existing models for drawing up a PVP system. However, it appears that the drafting of the Convention did draw in part on the German Law of 27 June 1953 on the Protection

---

[29] This is a common assumption, but one should not overstate the case. Open access did prevail, but it was not universally applied and not at all times, even at the local level.

[30] A. Heitz, 'The History of Plant Variety Protection, in UPOV, *The First Twenty-five Years of the International Convention for the Protection of New Varieties of Plants* (UPOV, 1987), 82.

[31] FIS later merged with ASSINSEL to form the International Seed Federation.

of Varieties and the Seeds of Cultivated Plants. This Law offered legal protection for 'useful' new varieties that were 'individualised' (read: distinct) and 'stable'.[32] In turn, this law was derived from non-intellectual property seed regulations. As explained by plant breeder Gregory Sage (2002), these 'began as consumer protection regulations specifying aspects such as germination capacity, freedom from disease, levels of admixture and trueness to type'.[33] Indeed, legally separate but complementary seed regulations continue to exist alongside PVP in many parts of the world and in some cases these require commercial farmers to use only registered seed.

9.2.2   UPOV and plant variety protection

Compared to some other important international agreements on intellectual property, such as TRIPS and the Paris Convention on the Protection of Industrial Property, the UPOV Convention's provisions are detailed and specific. In order to join the Union, countries are supposed to have a plant variety protection (PVP) law already in place, or minimally a draft legislation, and this is normally scrutinised by UPOV in case there are provisions that conflict with the Convention.

The most substantial revisions took place in 1978 and 1991 and these are discussed and compared below. But first it is important to note that the French word '*obtention*' in the name of the Union and the Convention is significant since it indicates that rights can be acquired not just by those who breed new varieties in the classic sense of creating new varieties by crossing and selecting sexually reproducing plants, but also by those who improve plants based on the discovery and selection of mutants or variants found in a population of cultivated plants. Thus, UPOV 1991 clarifies that a breeder is the person 'who bred, or discovered and developed, a variety'. In doing so, this latest revision is consistent with the original intent of the Convention to protect varieties that may not be attributable entirely to the application of scientific breeding. At the same time, it represents a divergence from patent law which professes not to allow mere discoveries to be protected.

Eligibility

What is a 'plant variety', and how may it be distinguished, for the purposes of intellectual property protection, from a 'plant'. This is very important given the increased application of genetic engineering to crop research and the fact that in some jurisdictions, plants are patentable but plant varieties are only protectable under national PVP systems. The original UPOV 1961 defined 'plant variety' as including 'any cultivar, clone, line, stock or hybrid which is capable of cultivation'. The UPOV 1978, which several countries are still contracting parties to, defines the scope of protection as the breeder's right to authorise the following acts: 'the production for purposes of commercial marketing; the offering for sale; and the marketing of the reproductive or vegetative propagating material, as such, of the variety'. The 1991 revision contains a more detailed definition, according to which a plant variety is:

---

[32] 'The [1953 German] Seed Law played a substantial part in the making of the UPOV Convention', Heitz, *supra* note 30, 75.

[33] G.C.M. Sage, 'Intellectual Property, Agriculture and Genetic Resources'. Commission on Intellectual Property Rights Feb. 2002. (Unpublished paper on file with authors.)

A plant grouping within a single botanical taxon of the lowest known rank, which grouping, irrespective of whether the conditions for the grant of a breeder's right are fully met, can be,

- defined by the expression of the characteristics resulting from a given genotype or combination of genotypes,
- distinguished from any other plant grouping by the expression of at least one of the said characteristics, and
- considered as a unit with regard to its suitability for being propagated unchanged.[34]

To be eligible for protection under the UPOV system, plant varieties must be new, distinct, stable and uniform. To be new, the variety needs not necessarily to be so in the absolute sense, but not to have been offered for sale or marketed, with the agreement of the breeder or his successor in title, in the source country, or for longer than a limited number of years in any other country. To be distinct, the variety must be distinguishable by one or more characteristics from any other variety whose existence is a matter of common knowledge anywhere in the world, implicitly including among traditional farming communities. Compared to UPOV 1978, the requirement in the most recent version has been relaxed somewhat. It does this by dropping the phrase 'by one or more important characteristics' after the word 'distinguishable'.

To be considered as stable, the variety must remain true to its description after repeated reproduction or propagation. Accordingly, it must have a certain level of uniformity which avoids change in the variety through genetic drift. This requirement also shows the specific nature of the UPOV system since the uniformity requirement cannot practically be the same for species with different ways of reproduction; self-fertilising species can be much more uniform than cross-fertilising crops. Uniformity requirements are made relative instead, that is, a new variety should be uniform when compared to the varieties of the same species. This means that when the plant breeding techniques were refined, the uniformity requirement gradually increased, placing it beyond the reach of farmer-breeders who may select in landraces to develop new varieties.

Unlike patents, there is no disclosure requirement. Generally, applicants are required to submit the plant material, which may be used by a government institution (or a private institution authorised by the government to conduct this role) to demonstrate stability and homogeneity through planting trials, also known as 'DUS examinations'. Some countries do not undertake DUS examinations, and benefit from the exchange of examination results among UPOV members. The Office of UPOV hopes this will get easier once there is a full harmonisation of examination procedures at the various national and regional PVP offices. It is by no means a simple matter for a country to set up a PVP system from scratch including running the field trials. The technical assistance available from the UPOV system may therefore be quite useful, although there are reasonable concerns that this harmonisation contributes to a creeping PVP rule uniformity that may not suit many developing countries.

---

[34] Art 1(vi), UPOV (1991 revision).

Scope of PVP rights

The UPOV 1991 extends the scope of the breeders' rights in two ways. First, it increases the number of acts for which prior authorisation of the breeder is required. These include 'production or reproduction; conditioning for the purpose of propagation; offering for sale; selling or other marketing; exporting; importing; stocking for the above purposes'. Second, such acts are not just in respect of the reproductive or vegetative propagating material, but also encompass harvested material obtained through the use of propagating material, and so-called essentially derived varieties.

However, the right of breeders both to use protected varieties as an initial source of variation for the creation of new varieties and to market these varieties without authorisation from the original breeder (the 'breeders' exemption') is upheld in both versions. This represents a major difference with patent law, which normally has a very narrow research exemption.[35] At this point it is worth mentioning that many plant breeders are concerned about the effects of patents on free access to plant genetic resources including varieties bred by others.

One further feature of the Convention to add is that there are rules concerning denomination. The applicants must provide a name for the variety and this must be used in trade. This obviously helps to avoid confusion in the marketplace. The applicant does not become owner of the denomination, which must be used indefinitely, that is, after the PVP right on the variety so denominated has expired. Thus, the denomination is not a brand name but a non-proprietary generic name.

One difference between UPOV 1978 and UPOV 1991 is that the latter extends rights to varieties which are essentially derived from the protected variety. So the breeder of PVP-protected variety A has the right to demand that the breeder of variety B secure his or her authorisation to commercialise B if it was essentially derived from A. The main idea here is that breeders should not be able to acquire protection too easily for minor modifications of extant varieties produced perhaps through cosmetic breeding or genetic engineering, or free-ride without doing any breeding of their own, problems that the increased application of biotechnology in this field appeared likely to exacerbate.[36]

Beyond resolving these particular issues, but related to them, the provision was also intended to ensure that patent rights and PVP rights operate in a harmonious fashion in jurisdictions where plants and their parts, seeds and genes are patentable and access to these could be blocked by patent holders. Such a practice would undermine one of the main justifications for PVP protection, which is that breeders should be able to secure returns on their investments but without preventing competitors from being able freely to access breeding material. It should be noted here that the PVP-issuing office will not itself determine whether a variety is essentially derived from an earlier one. This will be left to the courts. So far, only three courts, two in the Netherlands and one in Israel, have been called upon to make such a determination.[37]

---

[35] V. Prifti, *The Breeder's Exception to Patent Rights: Analysis of Compliance with Article 30 of the TRIPS Agreement* (Springer, 2015).

[36] J. Sanderson, *Plants, People and Practices: The Nature and History of the UPOV Convention* (Cambridge: Cambridge University Press, 2017), 215–29.

[37] *Asteé Flowers BV v. Danziger 'Dan' Flower Farm*, Case 198763, Court of The Hague (13 July 2005); *Danziger 'Dan' Flower Farm v. Asteé Flowers BV* (105.003.932/01, Court of Appeal, The Hague (2009); *Danziger v. Azolay & Asteé Flowers*

In the EU, the 1998 EU Directive on the Legal Protection of Biotechnological Inventions seeks to make PVP and patents operate more harmoniously by providing that where the acquisition or exploitation of a PVP right is impossible without infringing a patent, or vice versa, a compulsory licence may be applied for. If issued, the licensor party will be entitled to cross-license the licensee's patent or PVP right. Subsequent legislation in Germany and France restored the breeder's exemption in that it explicitly allows breeders to use genetic materials that include patented components for further breeding. When the new variety contains the patented component, however, consent has to be sought for the marketing of that new variety; when the patented component is 'bred out' of the material, the patent holder has no rights in the new variety.

While PVP is assumed to provide a weaker monopoly than do patents, one could also argue the opposite. Article 28, TRIPS lists five acts by third parties in relation to a patent that require the holder's authorisation: making, using, offering for sale, selling, or importing. The UPOV 1991 list of acts requiring such authorisation includes not just importing but also exporting. Thus, in the early 1990s, Argentinean strawberry plant growers could not export their plantlets to Europe because foreign PVP-holding licensees did not want these plantlets to compete with ones already produced in Europe.

UPOV 1991 extends protection from at least 15 years to a minimum of 20 years. This later version is silent on the matter of double (that is, both patent and PVP) protection. Allowing double protection without any restriction was to ensure that the intellectual property practices of the US and Japan, which allowed such double protection, would be fully compliant with UPOV. Nonetheless, most countries expressly forbid the patenting of plant varieties, including all European countries, where it has caused some legal uncertainty.

Louwaars sums up the key changes introduced in UPOV 1991:

- the restriction of the farmers' privilege (see below) to the saving of seed of a restricted number of crops 'taking into account the interest of the breeder' instead of a broad interpretation of the 'non-commercial use' article. This outlaws the exchange of seed of protected varieties among farmers;
- a slight limitation of the breeder's exemption which allows for rights that go beyond the limits of an individual variety (but avoiding the large-scale stacking of rights in the patent system) in the case of 'essentially derived varieties';
- possibilities to claim rights on the harvested product when the breeder has not had a reasonable opportunity to claim rights (read: royalties) on the harvested product, which deals with what is called 'parallel imports' in the patent systems.[38]

Farmers' privilege

The seed industry generally dislikes the farmers' privilege. Firms prefer fresh purchases for every planting season. There is no reference in UPOV 1978 to the right of farmers to re-sow seed

---

001228/03, District Court, Tel Aviv-Jaffa (5 March 2009).

[38] N. Louwaars, 'Policy and Institutions for Intellectual Property Rights for Seed System Development: Comparing Industrialized and Developing Countries.' Paper presented at the Asian Productivity Organisation Seminar on Intellectual Property Rights in Agriculture, Faisalabad, Pakistan, 3–7 April 2006.

harvested from protected varieties for their own use (often referred to as 'farmers' privilege'). The Convention establishes minimum standards such that the breeder's prior authorisation is required for at least the three acts mentioned above. Thus, countries that are members of the 1978 version of the Convention are free to uphold farmers' privilege or eliminate it. All UPOV member countries implemented the exemption for 'private and non-commercial use' under the UPOV Act of 1978 so as to include the re-sowing and in some cases the local exchange or sales of seed.

However, this was not the case in ornamental crops in the Netherlands, where a stronger protection was deemed necessary. Conversely, in the US this was interpreted very widely, resulting in practice in sales of farm-saved seed being allowable to a level where it would contribute less than 50 per cent of total farm income, thus resulting in large quantities of seed being 'brown bagged' to the detriment of the commercial interests of the breeder.

UPOV 1991 is more specific about this. Whereas the scope of the breeder's right includes production or reproduction and conditioning for the purpose of propagation, governments can use their discretion in deciding whether to uphold the farmers' privilege which includes only the use of saved seed on the same farm (and thus excludes any type of exchange or sale of such seed). Thus, the breeder's right in relation to a variety may be restricted 'in order to permit farmers to use for propagating purposes, on their own holdings, the product of the harvest which they have obtained by planting […] the protected variety'.[39] UPOV 1991 obliges UPOV members who opt to retain the privilege to take account of 'the legitimate interests of the breeder'.[40]

The extent of the 'farmers' privilege' varies quite widely. France had no farmers' privilege at all with the exception of tender wheat, but the country now fully provides the privilege under the EU Regulation. The latter, however, safeguards all interests by ensuring 'that the breeder receives equitable remuneration'. Accordingly, the Regulation restricts farmers' privilege to certain crops, and breeders must be remunerated through the payment of royalties unless they are small farmers, in which case they are exempted.[41] The US' PVP rules are less strict in this regard albeit stricter than previously when brown-bagging was even permitted: seed saving must be restricted to the amount necessary for on-farm replanting. But it is still unclear how the legitimate interest of the breeder is provided given that royalty payments on farm-saved seed are not required.

9.3   UPOV AS A GLOBAL INSTITUTION

UPOV is in fact one element of a genetic resource property 'regime complex' that includes a number of instruments and cannot be considered in total isolation. The WTO–TRIPS Agreement requires member states to provide 'effective intellectual property protection for plant varieties'. The

---

[39] UPOV 1991, Art 15.

[40] Ibid., Art 15(2).

[41] EU Regulation 2100/94 on Community Plant Variety Rights, linked with Article 17(2), UPOV 1991; the European Community's patent rules also require that farmers' privilege be provided and defined under the same terms as the above EU Regulation. Art 11, EU Directive on the Legal Protection of Biotechnological Inventions. G. Würtenberger, P. Van Der Kooij, B. Kiewiet and M. Ekvad, *European Union Plant Variety Protection* (2nd ed., Oxford: Oxford University Press, 2015).

WTO allows governments quite a lot of choice in how they put this requirement into effect: TRIPS negotiators elected not to mention the UPOV Convention, allowing for possibilities other than joining UPOV. WTO members may extend patent protection to cover plant varieties and provide no other form of IP protection. Alternatively, they may choose to keep conventional plant breeding out of the patent system, as in Europe. In the latter case, though, TRIPS requires a *sui generis* IP regime for plant varieties. Another important agreement is the aforementioned FAO International Treaty on Plant Genetic Resources for Food and Agriculture, which contains important provisions relating to the rights of farmers that should be taken into account when governments draw up their PVP rules. The Convention on Biological Diversity is also important – it requires that access to genetic resources be conducted on the basis of terms mutually agreed between the user and authorities representing the provider country and that benefits arising from their use be shared fairly and equitably. Similar requirements apply to the knowledge, innovations and practices of indigenous and local communities embodying traditional lifestyles.

9.3.1   The UPOV Office

UPOV is legally separate from WIPO and is not part of the United Nations. Despite UPOV's formal distance from WIPO, the two have a close relationship. The UPOV Office is located in the WIPO building in Geneva, where UPOV meetings are also held. WIPO services the Office. And by formal agreement, the Director-General is the Secretary-General of UPOV with the power to approve the appointment of the Vice Secretary-General. The latter oversees the day-to-day operations of UPOV.

The present relationship between WIPO and UPOV is defined by the 1982 WIPO/UPOV Agreement.[42] Much of the Agreement concerns the various administrative and practical tasks that WIPO must undertake for UPOV. These are not free of charge: UPOV is required to pay WIPO 'for any service rendered to, and any expenditure incurred on behalf of, UPOV'. Article 3 affirms the 'complete independence' of WIPO's International Bureau and the UPOV Office in respect of the exercise of their functions. What is behind this legal independence from WIPO despite their having such a close and practically dependent relationship? Going back in time, UPOV was not unanimously welcomed. AIPPI, though by no means opposed to PVP, was especially firm in its criticisms of the Convention and the formation of UPOV and expressed preference for incorporating PVP rules within the Paris Convention for the Protection of Industrial Property, now administered by WIPO and previously by BIRPI.[43]

The Office of UPOV is very small with a current full-time staff of fewer than ten people involved in the substantive technical work of the Union. This small group consists of people with backgrounds in such fields as agricultural economics, agronomy, plant breeding and law. The highest body within the UPOV system is the Council, which comprises one representative of each of the member states and has an elected President and Vice-President. Regular sessions of the Council

---

[42] UPOV, *Agreement between the World Intellectual Property Organization and the International Union for the Protection of New Varieties of Plants* signed on Nov. 26, 1982. [UPOV/INF/8].

[43] UPOV (1974) *Actes des Conférences Internationales pour la Protection des Obtentions Végétales* 1957–1961, 1972, 114; AIPPI, Annuaire 1961. *Compte-rendu de la Réunion du Comité Exécutif à Ottawa*, 1961.

take place once a year, but in recent years the Council has tended to meet twice, once in October and once in March or April. Countries that have signed but not ratified the Convention can send observers. The Council is subject to rules of procedure of which the latest version was adopted in 1982.[44] Below the Council is the Consultative Committee. Since 1988, this Committee has been delegated decision-making powers 'concerning the granting of observer status to non-governmental organizations'.[45] The Consultative Committee normally holds closed sessions restricted to members of the Union. Next down the hierarchy are two committees: the Legal and Administrative Committee and the Technical Committee.

9.3.2 Membership

UPOV membership has expanded rapidly since the establishment of the WTO and the proliferation of bilateral trade agreements. 45 of its 74 current members joined after 1995. UPOV can no longer be seen as a European 'club' if the membership is anything to go by. But active participation is another matter. The most obvious barrier to entry is that PVP is a highly technical and scientific area of IP law involving specialised field-testing procedures and requiring knowledge of biological and agricultural sciences including genetics and agronomy. Nonetheless, PVP is not a uniquely complex area of IP law.

UPOV's initially gradual expansion may have served a useful purpose for the older (i.e., European) members of the Union. An attempt to expand more rapidly in its first two decades might have led to the entry of 'outsiders' who may then have worked to change the culture in certain ways, such as by pushing UPOV to accept national PVP regimes not fully consistent with UPOV's rules. This view may be somewhat cynical. But it is quite plausible that such a long consolidation period helped make it easier to absorb the recent membership expansion without threatening the leadership of the established custodians. Prospective UPOV members, whether states or intergovernmental organisations of which the EU is the only one, are required to request an analysis of their law or draft law from the UPOV Council before they can join. If the law is deemed compliant with UPOV and has entered into force (but not necessarily been technically implemented), the government or intergovernmental organisation can proceed to ratify the Convention, thereby becoming an UPOV member. If modifications are deemed by the Council or Office as necessary for compliance, these must be effected before ratification is allowed.[46]

Obviously, this enables existing members of UPOV (and the UPOV Office) to impose a fairly strict conformity requirement upon new ones and may quite possibly give those members able and willing to be assertive a degree of leverage over the legislatures of applicant countries. Indeed, the UPOV Office plays an essential role in 'guiding' the aspiring member through the membership

[44] UPOV, 'Rules of Procedure of the Council as of Oct. 15, 1982'. [UPOV/INF/7].

[45] UPOV, 'Rules Governing the Granting of Observer Status to States, Intergovernmental Organizations and International Non-Governmental Organizations in UPOV Bodies and Access to UPOV Documents', adopted by the Council on October 7, 2005. [C/39/13].

[46] UPOV, 'Guidance on How to Become a Member of UPOV', adopted by the Council at its 43rd ordinary session on October 22, 2009. [UPOV/INF/13/1].

procedure including the assessment of 'conformity' of its law with the UPOV Convention and pre-pares the recommendation on this matter to the Council. Comments made on laws of prospective members are not publicly available.

Why do countries join UPOV, and what role does the Office of UPOV and the Council play in shaping countries' views on PVP that dispose them to seek UPOV membership? One obvious factor is Article 27.3(b) of TRIPS, which requires WTO Members to 'provide for the protection of plant varieties either by patents or by an effective sui generis system or by any combination there-of.' TRIPS does not specify UPOV as providing the '*sui generis*' alternative to patents. Any 'effective' PVP regime is possible. But the UPOV Office has been actively discouraging deviating from the UPOV norms. Thus, in a position statement based on an intervention by UPOV before the WTO's Council for TRIPS, it is stated that 'the plant variety protection system established on the UPOV Convention meets the requirements of Article 27.3(b) of the TRIPS Agreement'.[47]

So far this is perfectly reasonable. But the statement goes on to state this: 'the introduction of a system which differs significantly from the harmonized approach based on the UPOV Convention will raise questions with regard to the implementation of the TRIPS Agreement'. For countries unsure of where their interests lie with respect to IP protection in the field of plant breeding but anxious to avoid being criticised by the US and EU for failing to meet their TRIPS commitments, this is quite a powerful statement.

UPOV's mission receives a great deal of support from powerful nations. Nowadays, both the US through its free trade agreements and the EU by way of its economic partnership agreements are pressing developing country parties to these agreements to commit themselves to applying for UPOV membership, or if they are already UPOV members to provide patent protection for plants. Moreover, technical assistance programmes sometimes stress UPOV-conformity with no proper evaluation of how PVP should benefit the country as a whole. To make matters worse, such programmes may be carried out without consulting at all the local stakeholders such as farmers' groups, public sector breeding institutions and local seed companies. It should be borne in mind that some technical assistance coming from the developed world is intended to serve primarily the interests of businesses in those same parts of the world. To express this plainly, the intent is mostly about protecting the PVP rights of developed country businesses in the devel-oping world rather than about helping the developing countries to produce their own varieties to protect.

International harmonisation based on UPOV's standards, whether in terms of statutory law, implementation rules or of testing procedures, is something that the UPOV community is very keen on, and the UPOV Office has been more than willing to play its part as an advocate. Some-times this has provoked controversy. A good example is the PVP section of the 1999 Revised Ban-gui Agreement, signed by the African OAPI group.[48] Most OAPI members are least-developed

---

[47] UPOV, 'International Harmonization is Essential for Effective Plant Variety Protection, Trade and Transfer of Technology', UPOV Position based on an intervention in the Council for TRIPS, on 19 September, 2002.

[48] Annex 10 provides for PVP, *Accord Portant Revision de l'Accord de Bangui du 2 Mars 1977 Instituant une Organisation Africaine de la Propriété Intellectuelle*, signed by the 16-member state-strong *Organisation Africaine de la Propriété Intellectuelle* (OAPI).

countries that did not have to fully implement TRIPS until 1 January 2006 (and now are not re-quired to until 1 July 2021). WIPO, the UPOV Office and the French intellectual property office (INPI) played key roles in the preparation, adoption and ratification of this instrument, which came into force in 2002 and 'applies automatically as national law in each of the OAPI member states that ratifies the agreement', and was intended to be fully TRIPS compliant, as well as being entirely consistent with the UPOV 1991.[49] And although WIPO, UPOV and INPI had input into draft texts, at 'no point in the Bangui revision process was there any formal interstate negotiation of the draft text'.[50] Moreover:

> [...] neither the OAPI Secretariat, member states, or international donors undertook any substantive empirical assessments to substantiate expectations about the prospective gains or to identify the distribution of potential losses from the revised Agreement. While it is true that the OAPI Secretariat forwarded the draft text to national intellectual property offices, there is no record of any substantive written comments from member states to the OAPI Secretariat [...].[51]

UPOV 1991 was deemed a politically convenient model for the OAPI Secretariat to get its member states to adopt whether or not it was beneficial for them in any other ways, 'the OAPI Secretariat advised its members that UPOV offered a law that member states could take 'off the shelf' and that the development of an alternative sui generis law, would be a time-consuming and impractical endeavour'.

It is worth noting in this context that not one developing country UPOV member that joined under the 1978 Act has elected to 'upgrade' to UPOV 1991.

9.4 ALTERNATIVES TO UPOV

The question of whether and how IPRs over plant varieties can contribute to food security and to the transfer of high-value and high-yielding field and horticultural varieties including fruits, vegetables and ornamentals is much debated. UPOV 1991 has been criticised on the grounds of providing too weak protection compared to patents, too strong protection vis-à-vis farmers, and also for being insufficiently flexible. We make no effort to assess the evidence for or against UPOV and offer no new empirical evidence to what others have provided.[52] What we can say is that an

---

[49] C. Deere, *The Implementation Game: The TRIPS Agreement and the Global Politics of Intellectual Property Reform in Developing Countries* (Oxford: Oxford University Press, 2009), 253.

[50] Ibid., at 261.

[51] Ibid.

[52] W. Jaffé and J. van Wijk, 'The Impact of Plant Breeders' Rights in Developing Countries: Debate and Experience in Argentina, Chile, Colombia, Mexico and Uruguay', Ministry of Foreign Affairs, 1995; N. Louwaars, et al., 'Impacts of Strengthened Intellectual Property Rights Regimes on the Plant Breeding Industry in Developing Countries: A Synthesis of Five Case Studies'. A study commissioned by the World Bank, Wageningen University, 2005; S. Smith, S. Lence,

ideal plant variety IP regime needs to provide incentives and attract research investment in at least two directions. First, and most importantly, towards supporting breeding targeted to the nutritional needs of the whole populace without unduly disrupting existing traditions and farming systems. Secondly, to support the development of non-food or luxury food crops for sale on national and international markets that can generate wealth that to the greatest extent possible is captured at local and national levels. How far the UPOV system is able to support such aspirations across a diversity of developing countries remains a matter for further research.

There are reasonable concerns that the UPOV system fails to provide sufficient flexibilities for developing countries to fashion optimal PVP regimes that accommodate their own specific plant improvement needs.[53] Unfortunately, the Union and its institutional set-up appear to inhibit debate on appropriate rules for an increasingly diverse membership that includes developed, developing and least-developed countries.

Even in Europe the benefits of plant IP should not entirely be taken for granted especially given that patenting and PVP are both available for plant innovation there, and may not operate together in a harmonious fashion. A recent study by Louwaars et al. is broadly uncritical on the effects of PVP in the European context, stating that PVP: 'makes a positive contribution to innovation and hardly causes restrictions'.[54] But it does raise concerns about the dangers of patents: (i) accelerating corporate concentration with few new market entrants to counter this; (ii) encouraging strategic behaviour contrary to the public interest; and (iii) restricting access to breeding material and eliminating farmers' privilege, thereby undermining the effective workings of PVP. It is noteworthy that this study was conducted in the Netherlands, which has a long experience of providing IP protection for plant varieties, has resident breeding institutions that are major users of foreign PVP systems and thus benefit from the globalisation of UPOV's norms, and that as a EU member state is subject to rules that to some extent at least have sought to maintain a separate but cooperative relationship between the patent and PVP systems.

The existence of the UPOV system does not preclude non-UPOV members adopting other PVP regimes as long as these are 'effective' according to Article 27.3(b), TRIPS Agreement. But while some non-UPOV *sui generis* systems have been established in recent years (for example, in India

D. Hayes, J. Alston and E. Corona, 'Elements of Intellectual Property Protection in Plant Breeding and Biotechnology: Interactions and Outcomes' (2016) 56 *Crop Science* 140–11; *UPOV Report on the Impact of Plant Variety Protection*, UPOV, 2005.

[53] T. Adebola, 'Access and Benefit Sharing, Farmers' Rights and Plant Breeders' Rights: Reflections on the African Model Law' (2019) 9(1) *Queen Mary Journal of Intellectual Property* 105–21; C. Oguamanam, 'Breeding Apples for Oranges: Africa's Misplaced Priority over Plant Breeders Rights' (2015) 18(5) *Journal of World Intellectual Property* 165–95. It is also arguable that the UPOV Convention is not entirely consistent with other instruments forming the international genetic resources regime complex and that national plant IP laws should take greater account of the provisions of the FAO International Treaty and the CBD than UPOV allows. See T. Adebola, 'Examining Plant Variety Protection in Nigeria: Realities, Obligations and Prospects' (2019) 22(1–2) *Journal of World Intellectual Property* 36–58.

[54] N. Louwaars et al., *Breeding Business: The Future of Plant Breeding in the Light of Developments in Patent Rights and Plant Breeder's Rights* (Wageningen University, 2009), 56.

and Thailand[55]) developing countries are more often opting for UPOV membership than exploring other approaches. Frequently, developing countries agree to apply for UPOV membership – or adopt UPOV 1991 compatible legislation – in their trade agreements with the US, the EU, Japan and the European Free Trade Association. The decision to do this is part of the price to be paid for enhanced access for other goods to developed world markets. Given the increasing competition among developing countries to access these markets, meaning the share of access is spread among more and more countries (or a few dominant ones like China), it is uncertain that this price is worth paying. In addition, technical assistance programmes funded or implemented by agencies representing or influenced by commercial breeders can result in PVP rules that may comply with the latest version of the UPOV Convention but are in no way tailored to the local conditions.

The obvious alternative to the UPOV system is simply to eschew any special regime and extend the scope of patentable subject matter to include plants and plant varieties, an option that TRIPS permits. There are a number of reasons why this is probably inadvisable for most countries. For one thing, the normal extent of the private and experimental use exemptions in patent law are extremely and inappropriately narrow for plant breeding and would likely stifle innovation and create excessively strong monopolies.

Given the specificities of plant breeding and innovation in this field, it makes much sense to provide a special regime if one is to be provided at all. UPOV has some advantages over patents. It provides some legal clarity where patents do not: whereas a single product may be protected by numerous patents, any plant variety is covered by a single PVP certificate. Unsurprisingly, there is far less litigation than with patents. That the UPOV system was designed with and for the European plant breeding community does not automatically make it unsuitable elsewhere. But adaptations to what may be very different economic, social and agricultural, and environmental conditions are probably necessary. Interestingly, India, Thailand and Malaysia, all UPOV non-members, have PVP systems based on the 1978 Act but which arguably diverge in certain ways, such as by conditionally allowing farmers' sale of seed or allowing farmers' varieties to be protected even when they fail to meet the conventional criteria.

What does seem inadvisable for many countries is to follow the US, Australia, Japan and South Korea in allowing plant varieties to be doubly protected by patents and PVP. The interaction between patent law and PVP law is challenging enough without the additional legal uncertainties for plant breeders of there being double protection which, while legal under the UPOV Convention, is nonetheless contrary to its spirit.

In this context, plant variety right applications of large agricultural biotechnology firms like Monsanto submitted in the US are quite revealing in this regard. For example, Monsanto declared that a soybean variety forming the subject matter of application number A1026742 granted a certificate in 2013 from the US Department of Agriculture was 'covered under one of more of' a total of nine US patents (see Chapter 16). The variety itself is also the subject of a separate patent

---

[55] For India, see M. Kochupillai, *Promoting Sustainable Innovations in Plant Varieties* (Springer, 2016), 79–147; for Thailand, see P. Lertdhamtewe, 'Plant Variety Protection in Thailand: The Need for a New Coherent Framework' (2013) 8(1) *Journal of Intellectual Property Law and Practice* 33; R. Kanniah, 'Plant Variety Protection in Indonesia, Malaysia, the Philippines and Thailand' (2005) 8(3) *Journal of World Intellectual Property* 283.

application. Of course, just because Monsanto claims that its variety is covered by these patents does not necessarily mean that it is, or that the patent on the variety will necessarily be granted. It is not for the granting office to verify whether the scope of the monopolies provided by each and every one of these patents actually encompasses the variety. It should be noted that PVP provides an additional exclusive right that patent laws generally do not have, that of exporting. It has been plausibly argued that this right is an export restriction inconsistent with GATT 1994.[56] In other words, UPOV Convention – in this specific regard – conflicts with WTO law.

Plant breeding has not been made obsolete by biotechnology; it is just as vital as ever. And as long as there is private investment in breeding, there will be interest in IP protection. Admittedly, IP may also be useful for the public sector as it seeks to protect its own innovations for the public good, and to generate research income through licensing. Nonetheless, most interest in securing protection comes from the business sector. But what if there is not much private investment in the first place? Will the availability of PVP make a difference? There is no compelling evidence that the existence of PVP alone will stimulate the establishment of private sector plant breeding enterprises, though it may well encourage the growth of an industry that already exists.[57] What the empirical evidence does lead us to expect is that the vast majority of PVP applications in developing countries will come from foreigners, at least in the early years.

Creating institutions that in the short term at least are primarily occupied in protecting developed world assets in the developing world is not inherently a bad thing for the latter countries if that is the price to be paid for the transfer of valuable improved genetic material and associated technology to the developing countries and the price is not unduly exorbitant. Local stakeholders' respect for the PVP system in place will undoubtedly be influenced by the effectiveness of enforcement and the maintenance of reasonable limitations and exceptions to the fullest extent allowed by UPOV. But in the longer term the image of PVP will be enhanced when they have IP of their own to defend. As long as PVP is about protecting the rights of foreigners alone, one cannot assume that local firms, breeders and farmers will feel any compelling moral reasons for observing IPRs in the varieties they use.

UPOV statistics show a steady global growth in applications, alongside a proportionate overall increase in foreign applications. There is clear evidence of developed country-based seed companies becoming more interested in developing country markets, sometimes taking over domestic firms (as in Argentina), or using foreign territories for producing their plants for exportation. Often such plants are ornamentals or out-of-season vegetables for the European and North American markets. For example, out of 482 PVP applications in Kenya from 1997 to 2003, 247 were for roses, all of which were foreign bred.[58] Rangnekar adds some additional information concerning applications and grants for that country: 'by 2004, just over 45 per cent of the PBRs [i.e., PVP] applications were for flowers and vegetables. And, foreign breeders dominate by accounting for 57

---

[56] M. Kennedy, 'Export Restrictions in Plant Breeder's Rights' (2018) 20(4) *Journal of International Economic Law* 883–903.

[57] World Bank, *Intellectual Property Rights: Designing Regimes to Support Plant Breeding in Developing Countries*. World Bank Agriculture and Rural Development Dept., 2006, available athttp://siteresources.worldbank.org/INTARD/Resources/IPR_ESW.pdf.

[58] UPOV, *UPOV Report on the Impact of Plant Variety Protection*. Geneva: UPOV, 2005, 55.

per cent of the applications and 79 per cent of the grants'.[59] Whether foreign applicants are shifting breeding operations to developing countries in order to adapt their varieties to local conditions, which might be a very good thing for these countries, cannot be revealed by these statistics alone.

While some developed countries, of which New Zealand is a good example, may have a large proportion of non-resident applications the higher cost of protected seed and the need to pay royalties and licensing fees is unlikely to impose such heavy burdens on the national economy, local seed suppliers or commercial farmers as compared to poorer nations. For developing countries, which are more likely than developed countries to have a big shortfall in resident applications as compared to non-resident ones, such additional costs may be quite burdensome. This matter does require case-by-case analysis: much depends on the kinds of plant for which foreign applications are most common.

Even if those developing countries with an established domestic private sector experience a growth in investment thanks to PVP, public sector breeding is still likely to be of vital importance. It is not a realistic or sensible policy to depend on the private sector to do all the work. Public sector crop improvement is the norm in most parts of the world. Private investment in breeding is less ubiquitous although important especially in North America and Western Europe. In a great many developing countries hardly any seed companies exist to carry out in-country breeding. Many low-income farmers may not even benefit from such breeding if it is targeted purely to commercial sectors. Nonetheless, cash crops can be an important source of income for farming communities and the national economy. Public sector breeding may be highly relevant here too. While private investment may be useful in making up for cuts in government spending on crop improvement programmes, it does not automatically make sense for public breeders to be kept away from commercially oriented breeding as a matter of policy. There is no guarantee that the private sector will step into the breach to take advantage of the elimination of public sector competition even with the availability of PVP.

---

[59] D. Rangnekar, 'Geneva Rhetoric, National Reality: The Political Economy of Introducing Plant Breeders' Rights in Kenya' (2013) 19(3) *New Political Economy* 359–83.

10
Utility models and innovation patents

There has been, in the last two decades, a growing belief within the intellectual property fraternity as to the desirability for and the relevance of a further tier of patent-like protection within the general intellectual property framework. Such laws, usually referred to as utility model or innovation patent laws, are considered to be conducive to innovation and growth in highly diverse national economic settings. Thus, within established, developed economies, alternative *sui generis* regimes are viewed as a means of ameliorating the way that patent law in certain respects is less 'friendly' to small- and medium-sized enterprises (SMEs) than to large corporations. In addition, legal and economic scholars have praised the utility model regime as a necessary facet in promoting a sustainable development space to help weaker industrialising economies promote indigenous innovation especially in nationally important socio-economic sectors.[1]

A key issue is whether second-tier patent protection should be promoted in certain countries or regions on the grounds that it does a better job in those places than patents of enabling a more robust and pro-innovation ecosystem that achieves economic and sustainable growth.[2] This leads us to the following question: even if the deficiencies of the traditional patent system can be effectively

---

[1] The term innovation is akin to the Schumpeterian approach – J. Schumpeter, *Business Cycles* (New York and London: McGraw-Hill, 1939), vol 1, 84; and W. Kingston, *The Political Economy of Innovation* (The Hague: Martin Nijhoff Publishers, 1984), Chapters 1 and 3.

[2] U. Suthersanen and G. Dutfield, 'Utility Models and Other Alternatives to Patents', in U. Suthersanen, G. Dutfield and K.B. Chow (eds), *Innovation without Patents: Harnessing the Creative Spirit in a Diverse World* (Cheltenham: Edward Elgar Publishing, 2007), 18 *et seq.*

resolved, are there still good reasons to introduce a second-tier patent law alongside reformed standard patent laws? In other words, does their value lie solely in their ability to deal with the inadequacies – at least in certain contexts – of patent law; or are they intrinsically beneficial IPRs that can be justified on their own terms?

10.1 SECOND-TIER PATENTS WITHIN A GLOBAL LEGAL FRAMEWORK[3]

Historically, second-tier rights have been in force in some jurisdictions for at least 160 years. From 1985 to 2000, such rights were introduced in at least 25 jurisdictions which did not have them previously. Approximately 70 countries now provide second-tier patent protection resembling utility model protection in some form or another, including countries with highly successful innovation strategies, notably Japan, South Korea, China and Germany. Nevertheless, it is still far from being a widely recognised or implemented species of law; conversely, other countries which manifest a similar economic history of innovation, including the US, the UK, Singapore, Sweden and Canada have not embraced any such regime.[4]

10.1.1 Definition and protectable subject matter

It should be noted from the start that the term 'utility model' law has morphed, over the years, into a generic term referring to a second-tier patent system which grants a property right to a certain class of invention, quickly and cheaply. It is ostensibly a registered IPR which confers exclusive protection for a technical invention. It resembles a patent in that the invention must be new and should display a measure of inventive achievement. Unlike patents however, utility models are often granted without prior examination to establish novelty and/or inventive step. Thus, protection can be obtained more rapidly and cheaply, but the protection conferred will be commensurately less secure.

There is no universal nomenclature for this type of hybrid right. Australian law, for example, has alternatively referred to them as 'petty patents', and then as 'innovation patents'. They are called

---

[3] The following discussion is based on: Australian Advisory Council on Industrial Property, *Review of the Petty Patent Systems*, 1995; M.D. Janis, 'Second Tier Patent Protection' (1999) 40 *Harv. Int'l L.J.* 151; U. Suthersanen, 'Incremental Inventions in Europe: A Legal and Economic Appraisal of Second-tier Patents' (2001) *J. Bus. L.* 319; U. Suthersanen, 'Utility Models and Innovation in Developing Countries', UNCTAD-ICTSD Project on IPRs and Sustainable Development (2006), available at http://unctad.org/en/docs/iteipc20066_en.pdf; I. Png and A. Hu, *Protection of Sub-Patentable Inventions in Singapore* (Singapore IP Academy, 2014); Suthersanen, Dutfield and Chow (eds), *supra* note 2; Australian Government, Advisory Council on Intellectual Property, 'Review of the Innovation Patent System' (May 2015), available at https://www.ipaustralia.gov.au/sites/g/files/net856/f/final_report.pdf; H.-P. Brack, 'Utility Models and their Comparison with Patents and Implications for the US Intellectual Property Law System', Boston College Intellectual Property & Technology Forum (2009), available at http://bciptf.org/wp-content/uploads/2011/07/13-iptf-Brack.pdf.

[4] A list of countries and regions with utility model protection can be found on the World Intellectual Property Organization (WIPO) website, available at http://www.wipo.int/sme/en/ip_business/utility_models/where.htm.

'utility innovations' in Malaysia, 'utility certificates' in France, 'short-term patents' in Belgium, though the prevailing term remains 'utility models' as used in Germany and China. International instruments refer to them synonymously as utility certificates, utility models, and utility certificates of addition.[5] Some systems define utility models as incorporeal subject matter including technical concepts or inventions or devices; while others anchor their definitions to three-dimensional forms and exclude plants, methods, biological and pharmaceutical products. A few countries offer second tier protection which, is akin to patent protection, without prior examination and for a shorter duration. The Australian experience, discussed in detail below, shows how conceptually slippery the construction of the law can be in relation to indigenous innovation.

From a global perspective, identifiable common traits within national 'utility model' regimes, include the following traits: (i) the laws confer registered, exclusive rights on the proprietor of the right (as opposed to an anti-copying or automatic rights); (ii) novelty is a criterion in all systems, although the standard of novelty varies from universal novelty to local novelty; (iii) there is usually no substantive examination of applications. The major points of divergence are:

1. *Subject matter* under protection – some utility model laws protect only the three-dimensional form while others extend the umbrella of protection to cover all technologies and processes but exclude controversial subject matter such as pharmaceutical or biological substances, or plant varieties.[6] A majority of utility model laws simply adopt the domestic patent law definition of protectable subject matter. The current German Utility Model Act, for example, is the archetypical second tier regime within a developed nation, where protection can extend to all inventions with important exceptions, including methods, processes or biotechnological inventions.[7]

2. *Granting procedure* – many systems adopt a simple registration procedure with cursory examination; while a few implement a detailed examination process. In practice, some examining offices offer an optional detailed search facility with the payment of supplementary fees. Other jurisdictions expressly call for a detailed search on validity to be carried out on the commencement of civil proceedings.[8]

3. *Substantive criteria* – herein lies the greatest disparity between the utility model systems. While all major utility model systems adopt the criterion of novelty, the level of novelty required ranges from universal novelty, to relative novelty, to domestic novelty. A second criterion is usually, though not always, imposed in the form of inventiveness or usefulness. Again, the standard employed for the level of inventiveness varies greatly. There is also a significant propensity within current utility model laws to link the definition of the utility model with an element of industrial application.

4. *Scope of protection* – a final element of divergence is the duration which can vary from six years (as in France) to ten years (for example, in Germany, Korea and Spain), to 15 years (Brazil); with varying restrictions on the specifications and claims of the utility model right.

---

[5] PCT, Art 2; and Agreement for the International Patent Classification 1971, Art 2.

[6] For example, Czech Republic, Hungary and Spain (under the new Spanish Patent Act No. 24/2015, wef 2017).

[7] German Utility Model Act, 1986, s 1(2), (3).

[8] Under the new Spanish Patent Act No. 24/2015, wef 2017.

10.1.2 International rules

The absence of a transnational pattern is reflected in the lack of international norms regarding the nature and extent of a second-tier patent regime. The Paris Convention, for example, states: 'The protection of industrial property has as its object patents, utility models, industrial designs, trade marks, service marks, trade names, indications of source or appellations of origin, and the repression of unfair competition.'

Countries are free to formulate or reject utility model protection as they see fit; should a country introduce a utility model regime, it can tailor such a regime to exclusively adapt to local socio-economic conditions and infrastructure. Nonetheless, it should also be noted that Paris Union countries which have a utility model regime cannot discriminate against a foreign rights holders in terms of recognition and enforcement of such utility models.[9] Reciprocal national treatment will also apply for select international principles including the right of priority, the importation and forfeiture clauses, and the compulsory licensing arrangements.[10] However, the Paris Convention is silent on the definition, nature and scope of the right and protection. It should be further noted that those countries that do adopt national utility model systems tend to extend the relevant provisions of the PCT as well as the International Patent Classification (IPC), thus allowing international applications to be made for utility model or other second-tier systems.[11]

The TRIPS Agreement fails to establish any further benchmark for this form of protection, although it is arguable that by incorporating the main provisions of the Paris Convention, it extends the WTO dispute settlement system to utility models. Thus, should WTO members formulate second-tier protection regimes, the national treatment obligations under the Paris Convention and the TRIPS Agreement would be enforceable under the WTO dispute settlement regime.[12] A consideration of other international arenas reveals that despite the recalcitrance of international instruments to engage with utility models, these rights are being increasingly recognised within the intellectual property chapters of free trade agreements (FTAs) or as investment under some international investment agreements (IIA).[13]

---

[9] Paris Convention, Art 2(1); G.H.C. Bodenhausen, 'Guide to the Paris Convention (1968), Guide to the Application of the Paris Convention for the Protection of Industrial Property, as Revised at Stockholm in 1967' (WIPO, 1969) 29.

[10] Paris Convention, Arts 4(E)(1), 4(E)(2), 5A, 5D and 11 respectively.

[11] PCT, Art 2 clarifies that references to an 'application' shall be construed as references to applications for patents for inventions, inventors' certificates, utility certificates, utility models, patents or certificates of addition, inventors' certificates of addition, and utility certificates of addition. Art 2, of the Agreement for the International Patent Classification 1971, for example, covers not just patents for invention, but also inventors' certificates, utility models and utility certificates. The Agreement facilitates the retrieval of patent documents in order to conduct effective novelty searches and determine the state of the art.

[12] TRIPS Agreement, Arts 1(2), 2(1).

[13] For example, the EU–CARIFORUM European Partnership Agreement, and the Japan–Indonesia Economic Partnership Agreement, and the Germany–Pakistan Bilateral Investment Agreement. See H. Grosse Ruse-Khan, *Utility Model Protection in Pakistan – An Option for Incentivising Incremental Innovation*, A WIPO-commissioned report (2015) 14–15; H. Grosse Ruse-Khan, 'The International Legal Framework for the Protection of Utility Models', Max Planck Institute for

10.2 JUSTIFYING SECOND-TIER PATENTS

Intellectual property laws have been criticised for being 'a drain on learning and source of market power that is inimical to development'.[14] Valid or not, policy and economic rationales underpin the limits placed on national patent law ensuring that not all inventive activities are embraced as being worthwhile of protection. Inventions must fulfil certain criteria under a rigorous examination procedure, while other types of subject matter are excluded *ab initio* from the patent regime so as to support complementary, and sometimes, conflicting policies in maintaining public domain, competition, health and education. Simply put, it is now accepted that the monopoly privileges and exclusivity arising from patents invariably effect other public spheres, and the rigorous eligibility standards are essential to prevent excessive patenting. Conversely, there are several cogent reasons for introducing utility model laws, and the following discussion explores three main rationales: (a) curing the defects of the national patent system; (b) preventing free-riding and encouraging innovation, especially in relation to SMEs; and (c) improving the legal environment in developing countries.

10.2.1 'Curing' patent law

In 1843, the first known second-tier patent system was introduced in the UK's Utility Designs Act in response to criticism of the Victorian British patent system as being administratively complex, with insuperable costs. The law protected the 'shape or configuration of useful articles of manufacture'.[15] In similar vein, the German utility model system emerged in 1891 as a backlash against the stringent German patentability standards, especially its level of inventive step.[16] Arguably, the introduction of a *sui generis* law was perhaps the inevitable solution in these two newly industrialised nations in order to resolve the deficiencies of their patent systems, especially in terms of cost, speed and ease. Indeed, British history continues to show that an ineffective utility model system, which fails to grapple with the patent problem is doomed to failure, and by 1919, the British utility model experiment concluded. Instead, Britain eventually replaced the lacuna in protecting minor innovations in 1989 with its own national *sui generis* unregistered design right – a system which protects functional three-dimensional shapes, using much lower criteria (see Chapter 7 on design).

Intellectual Property & Competition Law Research Paper No. 12–10 (October 2012).

[14] See discussion in Chapter 2, section 2.3.2. K. Maskus, *Private Rights and Public Problems: The Global Economics of Intellectual Property in the 21st Century* (Peterson Institute for International Economics, 2012), 234.

[15] 6 & 7 Vict. ch. 65; M.D. Janis, 'Second Tier Patent Protection' (1999) 40 *Harvard International Law Journal* 151, 156; L. Bently and B. Sherman, 'The United Kingdom's Forgotten Utility Model: The Utility Designs Act of 1843' (1997) 3 *IPQ* 265; Charles Dickens, *The Poor Man's Tale of a Patent*, 1850, reproduced and annotated in J. Phillips, *Charles Dickens and the 'Poor Man's Tale of a Patent'* (Oxford: ESC, 1984).

[16] U. Suthersanen, 'Utility Models and Innovation in Developing Countries', UNCTAD-ICTSD Project on IPRs and Sustainable Development, 2006, 15; P.A. Cummings, 'From Germany to Australia: Opportunity for a Second Tier Patent System in the United States' (2010) 18(2) *Michigan State Journal of International Law* 297, 303.

It is unarguable that a *sui generis* regime is useful in resolving or avoiding the deficiencies of the current patent system, especially in terms of cost and speed of securing protection. One commentator lists the advantages of utility model registration in comparison to patents in Germany, as including: lower costs; lower thresholds in relation to novelty and inventiveness; quicker registration procedure; strategic means of obtaining full protection during the intermediate period between publication and actual grant of a patent.[17] This type of reasoning can be easily extrapolated across other established, developed countries, where utility model law is viewed as a means of ameliorating the worst effects of patent law.

Nevertheless, is this a sufficient basis for the introduction of yet another IPR, notably as the right in question appears to undermine essential facets of the current patent law such as lowering the thresholds of examination and dispensing with substantial examinations? IPRs are predicated on the notion that inventions and creative works are in the public domain unless such works fulfil various thresholds such as novelty or inventive step (in the case of patents), originality or distinctiveness (in the cases of copyright or trade mark). Partly in deference to the high societal costs imposed by the conferral of a proprietary right, which will stifle competition for a short duration, and partly to forestall duplication of patent protection for identical or similar inventions, the examination system is a major element of the patent regime. The justifications of the traditional patent law are re-confirmed during the examination process. Providing second-tier rights for inventions that fail to meet such standards undermines both the public-private boundary and the doctrinal bases of IPRs.

The worrying concern is that utility model laws can result in barring the entry of both new and competing substitutive products, especially so in capitalist market-based economies where it is generally accepted that all market actors, including competitors, follow-on creators and consumers, should be allowed to freely use such public domain works which fall short of the required standards.[18] Developing countries, in particular, should be cautious in broadening protection to cover all types of innovations – irrespective of whether they are minor and low-cost innovations, or whether they involve complex and cutting edge technologies such as biological and pharmaceutical products.

Indeed, there is a reasonable concern that larger market players may use utility models as a means of circumventing the more stringent criteria under the patent system and overuse the system in ways that make it hard for SMEs to compete. Certainly, the lack of substantive examination prior to grant will give rise to uncertainty for third parties when conducting infringement searches to ascertain what valid rights exist in a particular field of technology, which may act as an additional barrier to competitors and lead to abusive behaviour by foreign applicants.

Perhaps we should accept the desirability of a differentiated patent policy in respect of different types of inventive activities. This was clear, for example, when the failed EU Directive for utility model was under consideration. While condoning lower standards of protection for various inventive activities, the Commission Proposal also excluded protection of biological or pharmaceutical inventions within the utility model system. This exclusion was rationalised on two grounds:

---

[17] Brack, *supra* note 3.

[18] F.M. Scherer and D.R. Ross, *Industrial Market Structure and Economic Performance* (Houghton Mifflin, 1990), 577–8.

such subject matters call for lengthy preparation before being placed on the market and should therefore be given patent protection that lasts longer than utility model protection. Secondly, the Commission conceded that these sectors are complex areas in which property rights involving no examination as to novelty or inventive step are out of place.[19]

The resulting issue then is how we distinguish between various innovations. It may be that this will be dependent on the innovative capacity of each country, which in turn will depend on the particular industrial sector in focus.

10.2.2 Incremental innovation and SMEs

The nature of inventive efforts has evolved from technological breakthroughs to a greater focus on inventions that are incremental in nature; broadening patent protection to encompass such incremental innovations can be an accepted patent policy under certain circumstances, especially in encouraging follow-on inventors to secure rights on their cumulative improvements. A corollary factor is that in some countries, more innovations, both of the breakthrough and incremental varieties, emanate from local SMEs than from larger multinational conglomerates. Such inventions tend to have a lower standard of inventiveness, are prime candidates for free-riding activities by competitors and deserve new hybrid IPRs.

It is argued that *sui generis* regimes have historically improved the legal environment for incremental innovation, and consequently are good for the national economy. A related reason why utility models may be good for SMEs is that the cost factor may inhibit them from using the patent system as much as they would desire. First, such firms are often engaged in an ongoing process of innovation and adaptation. This is the case particularly in relation to those industries which are concerned, not so much with revolutionary technological breakthroughs, but more with incremental innovation. And it is in these latter areas where unfair, slavish copying is rife.[20] Secondly, more breakthrough and incremental varieties of innovation emanate from SMEs than from larger multinational conglomerates. Finally, it has been argued that the utility model regime offers the ideal cost-effective protection to SMEs who cannot afford the expensive patent system.

Nascent industries exhibit high levels of product innovation as firms attempt to settle on the primary characteristics and architectures of their new offerings. A realistic perspective of today's industrial society shows, however, that the process of innovation is nuanced and varies dramatically across different industries and throughout product life cycles. Howard and Guile's model for market competitiveness offers one reasonable rationale for this behaviour namely that all successful commercialisations have three distinct stages: technology-enabled commercialisation; design-driven

---

[19] Art 4(b) and (c) of the Commission Proposal of 12 December 1997 for a European Parliament and Council Directive approximating the legal arrangements for the protection of inventions by utility model, COM(1997) 691 final.

[20] Thus, the proposed EU directive on utility models was rationalised on the need for a rapid and cheap protective regime for minor innovations in the following industries: toy manufacturing, clock and watchmaking, optics, microtechnology and micro mechanics – *Green Paper on the Protection of Utility Models in the Single Market*, COM(95) 370 final, July 19, 1995, 16.

commercialisation; and market-driven commercialisation.[21] Technology-enabled commercialisation is driven by revolutionary scientific or technical discoveries, with little emphasis or understanding of the market for resulting products of the technology. We can see this in the field of bio-technology, pharmaceuticals and computing, but not necessarily in areas including mechanics and electronics.

This is to be contrasted with the incremental innovation that occurs when firms engage in de-sign-driven and market-driven commercialisation. Once a concept has been proven in the market, competition shifts to price, performance, utility, ergonomic and aesthetic design features; the ability of the product to maintain its market status relies on further improvements to the product. These last two stages of design and market-driven commercialisation correlate with the reasons why countries introduce the second-tier patent system. Thus, the majority of inventions today are incremental in nature, which though novel, exhibit a modicum of inventiveness; and these incremental products are open to imitation when their product is placed on the market. Moreover, the majority of innovators in most economic infrastructures receive no encouragement or incentive for continued development.

The theoretical rationale for utility models derives from the fact that most welfare-enhancing inventions are cumulative in nature and that many of them are sub-patentable in the sense that the novelty and inventive step requirements are too high for the patent system to accommodate them. Instead, the patent system is geared towards major technological breakthroughs, which are not an everyday occurrence. For example, the European Commission argued for the introduction of a pan-EU utility model law as it felt the need for a rapid and cheap protective regime for minor innovations in the following industries: toy manufacturing, clock and watchmaking, optics, micro-technology and micromechanics. A more recent 2015 study acknowledges this view: the picture in the wider public has therefore emerged of the utility model being an IP tool for the 'small inventor and his/her small inventions'.[22]

National policy makers who wish to introduce utility model laws on this basis should note that much is dependent on the economic status of the country in question. For example, what is the percentage of SMEs within the country or region? And how much innovation that is important to that region's economy emanates from these SMEs? It may be that many innovations emanate from SMEs as opposed to from larger multinational conglomerates. Or that SMEs have a heavy presence in small or emergent industries that are concerned, not so much with revolutionary technological breakthroughs, but more so with cumulative innovation. If this is so, it is important to gauge whether the current national patent regime is attuned to the needs of SMEs and the types of inventions they produce. In the recent 2015 report on the economic impact of utility model laws in the EU, it was shown that SMEs did not use utility model as a primary protection tool – instead the function of utility model was as an 'auxiliary IP tool in environments where patents are important'.[23]

---

[21] W.G. Howard Jr. and B.R. Guile, 'Profiting from Innovation', in N. Rosenberg, R. Landau and D. Mowery (eds), *Technology and the Wealth of Nations* (Stanford University Press, 1992), 397 *et seq.*

[22] A. Radauer, C. Rosemberg, O. Cassagneau-Francis and H. Goddar, 'Study on the Economic Impact of the Utility Model Legislation in selected Member States – Final Report', *Study of Technopolis & Boehmert on behalf of the European Commission*, April 2015, available at http://www.technopolis-group.com/wp-content/uploads/2015/09/ET0415184ENN_002.pdf.

[23] Ibid., 18.

This may be the case in mature economies, but can this conclusion be transplanted to emerging and developing nations?

10.2.3 Developing economies and indigenous innovation

Legal and economic scholars have argued that an effective utility model regime, involving low levels of novelty and limited periods of protection, can supply the critical policy and legal space to promote sustainable development practices and to help struggling economies promote indigenous innovation. Through adaptation, imitation, and incremental innovation, firms in developing economies can acquire knowledge and harness invaluable 'learning-by-doing' experience.[24]

It is argued that strong patent laws can stifle innovation at low levels of economic development as most innovation and inventions are specific to local market circumstances.[25] The argument is that weaker IPRs would be more beneficial as this would allow the local absorption of foreign innovations. This is, as some of the studies indicate, especially beneficial for relatively innovative developing countries with cottage and fledgling industries. Historically, countries such as Japan, South Korea and Taiwan have used this combination of weak IPRs and second-tier regimes to start and sustain a steep technological learning curve.[26]

A recent review of the patent system by the Sri Lankan IP office, for example, advocated that the national economic strategy would be best served and improved with the introduction of a five-year utility model right, in parallel with the patent system.[27] The Indian government has also released its own report which suggests that the introduction of a utility model regime in India will encourage useful and low-cost innovations which may have commercial value for a limited time period, especially from SMEs.[28] Brazil, the Philippines and Malaysia[29] are further current examples as to how national utility model regimes can help nascent industries gain a stronghold in certain sectors. Domestic producers in Brazil, for example, have protected local adaptations of foreign farm machinery technology through the utility model regime; the utility model regime was shown to have enabled local producers to win a dominant share of the market away from foreign producers of the farm machinery. Another study demonstrated that utility models in the Philippines stimulated the adaptation of rice threshers.[30]

---

[24] Y.K. Kim, K. Lee, W.G. Park and K. Choo, 'Appropriate Intellectual Property Protection and Economic Growth in Countries at Different Levels of Development' (2012) 41(2) *Research Policy* 358.

[25] C. Fink and K.E. Maskus (eds), *Intellectual Property and Development: Lessons from Recent Economic Research* (World Bank/Oxford University Press, 2005), 299.

[26] N. Kumar, 'Technology and Economic Development: Experiences of Asian Countries', Commission on Intellectual Property Rights, 2002, London.

[27] A. Perera, 'Adminstration of the Patent System in Sri Lanka: A Critical Appraisal' (2014) 43 *Comm. L. World Rev.* 344, 354.

[28] Government of India – Department of Industrial Policy and Promotion, *Discussion Paper on Utility Models*, 13 May 2011, paras 26–40, Annex I.

[29] Suthersanen, Dutfield and Chow (eds), *supra* note 2, 169–76.

[30] Fink and Maskus (eds), *supra* note 25, 299; R.E. Evenson and L.E. Westphal, 'Technological Change and Technology Strategy', in J. Behrman and T.N. Sinivasan (eds), *Handbook of Development Economics* (Elsevier, 1995), 2249–50.

10.3 LEGAL TRANSPLANTS AND EXPERIMENTS

10.3.1 China and Japan

The transplantation of the utility model framework is most visible in China.[31] Utility model protection is accorded to 'any new technical solution relating to the shape, structure, or their combination, of a product, which is fit for practical use'.[32] The standard for inventiveness is lower than that required for patents, and applications are examined *ex officio* as to compliance with formalities only.[33] The positive impact of the utility model regime on China has been strenuously claimed including, inter alia, the following: increased usage of utility models has contributed to rising labour productivity in the country; utility models have had a significant impact on the Total Factor Productivity from 1988 to 2009, and individual inventors and SMEs in particular, although also large companies to some extent, in China have benefited from technological learning opportunities afforded by using utility models.[34]

On the other hand, some commentators believe that despite its value, the utility model system in China is problematic. The absence of examination makes it especially difficult to guarantee the quality or level of inventiveness involved in a utility model and consequently, disputes have occurred. It is suggested that this could only be resolved by providing a corresponding search report.[35] Moreover, it has been alleged that utility models are granted to local 'inventors' for inventions imported from overseas and that the local owners sometimes assert their rights against the original inventors.[36]

Much does depend on the innovation culture of the country. Take Japan for example. She was the first Asian country to introduce utility model protection, with the system dating from 1905 and directly transplanted from German law. It is undoubtedly a prime example of a country that used utility models to improve its technological capacity and boost its indigenous incremental innovation, but markedly changed the structure in order to suit an increasingly higher innovative climate.

---

[31] D. Prud'homme, 'Utility Model Patent Regime "Strength" and Technological Development: Experiences of China and other East Asian Latecomers' (2017) 42 *China Economic Review* 50; P. Yu, 'Intellectual Property, Economic Development, and the China Puzzle', in D. Gervais (ed.), *Intellectual Property, Trade and Development: Strategies to Optimize Economic Development in a TRIPS Plus Area* (Oxford University Press, 2007), 173–220; N. Lee, 'Intellectual Property Law in China – From Legal Transplant to Governance', in N. Lee, N. Bruun and M. Li (eds), *Governance of Intellectual Property Rights in China and Europe* (Cheltenham: Edward Elgar Publishing, 2016), 5–19.

[32] PRC Implementing Regulations of 12 December 1992, Art (2).

[33] PRC Patent Law of 12 March 1984, as revised 1992, Art 22(3).

[34] D. Prud'homme, *supra* note 31, citing several empirical studies from 2002 to 2011.

[35] S. Guo, 'The Development and Perspective of Intellectual Property in the People's Republic of China' (1997) *IPQ* 151.

[36] Suthersanen, *supra* note 3, 39; B. Spurgeon, 'The New Chinese Counterfeit Game', *International Herald Tribune* (14 November 2004). Abuse of the utility model system is also reported in the US International Trade Commission Report, *China: Intellectual Property Infringement, Indigenous Innovation Policies, and Frameworks for Measuring the Effects on the U.S. Economy*, 2010.

Current studies show that there has been a steady drop in applications for registrations from 1980 onwards.[37] Various reasons can be suggested. First, the Japanese government revised the utility model law and introduced a 'no examination' rule, while curtailing the duration of protection from ten to six years. One commentator states that these revisions constituted barriers to obtaining injunctive relief, and a loss of confidence as to the validity of non-examined rights.[38] Secondly, the amount of patents applied for increased during this same period which saw a decline for utility models – suggesting a shift in the Japanese innovation culture from incremental innovation (during the immediate post-war years to the 1980s), to more radical innovation thereafter.[39]

Finally, the patent regime was reformed in 1987 to eliminate the single claim requirement – thus making the patent regime more attractive. Maskus and McDaniel suggest that the utility model experiment in Japan was extremely important as it bolstered 'technology diffusion through utility model applications'. Thus, they conclude, utility models:

> Had a positive impact on Japan's post-war productivity growth. Further, there was an important indirect impact of applications for invention patents, reflecting more fundamental industrial invention, through their stimulation of follow-on utility model applications, which were quickly diffused into commercial use.[40]

10.3.2 Australia[41]

The Australian experience is instructive in revealing how conceptually slippery the transplantation, construction and judicial implementation of second-tier laws can be in relation to innovation. Australian national IP policy embraced the second-tier scheme in 1979 when the 'petty patent' was introduced as a specific form of protection for indigenous inventions with a short commercial life. The key features were: universal novelty but with a local prior art examination, a six-year term of protection, process and chemical/biochemical inventions specially being excluded, and a limited scope of protection. This was, thus, a classic utility model right.

The origins of the petty patent system lay in dissatisfaction with the design right system, which did not protect functional designs. The legislature decided that a petty patent system was necessary to contribute to an environment of growth within the national boundaries – one rationale was that it would encourage small business to invest and operate in another market; another was that

---

[37] H. Odagiri, A. Goto, A. Sunami and R. Nelson, 'Introduction', in H. Odagiri, A. Goto, A. Sunami and R. Nelson (eds), *Intellectual Property Rights, Development, and Catch-Up – An International Comparative Study* (Oxford University Press, 2010), 1–28; U. Suthersanen, 'Utility Models: Do they really Serve National Innovation?', in J. Drexl and A.K. Sanders, *The Innovation Society and Intellectual Property* (Cheltenham: Edward Elgar Publishing, 2019), 2–24.

[38] C. Heath, 'Utility Model Law', in *Encyclopaedia of Japanese Law from 1868* (Brill Publishing, 2002). Parties have the possibility of requesting Technical Opinions, especially prior to commencing infringement proceedings.

[39] E. Mansfield, 'Industrial R&D in Japan and the United States: A Comparative Study' (1988) 78 *Am. Econ. Rev.* 223–28.

[40] K.E. Maskus and C. McDaniel, 'Impacts of the Japanese Patent System on Productivity Growth' (1999) *Japan and the World Economy* 557–74.

[41] For an expanded discussion, see Suthersanen, *supra* note 37.

the regime would help limit importation of copies. This conclusion was partly due to the nature of the Australian economic infrastructure as it was a net importer of technology and much innovation was based on improvements and innovative effort.[42]

However, the system has had limited success in meeting its intended objectives. Although the main users of the petty patent system are Australian individuals and SMEs, the number of applications made for petty patents remained small. One dissatisfaction with the system was that the requirement of inventiveness was similar to that of a standard patent. After a governmental consultation and review of the system, the decision was to retain the second-tier system but to tailor the law to meet the expectations of the local industry, and to foster more indigenous innovation, especially in relation to the level of inventiveness, the duration of the right and the scope of prior art.[43] Thus, in 2001, the second-tier system was revised to lower the threshold of inventiveness, and the system was re-established as the 'innovation patent' system. The newly reformed innovative step was subsequently defined in a 2008 Federal Court of Australia's decision in *Delnorth*. The Court determined that the threshold for innovation patents was set lower than the threshold for standard patents. While this was something that was anticipated by the legislature and the industry, the Court went further to hold that an 'innovative step' allows even obvious enhancements to be patented.[44]

With this lowered level of inventiveness, concerns arose that this regime was being used for strategic or tactical purposes to protect higher-level inventions, rather than to stimulate innovation within SMEs. The consequences were, in hindsight, predictable: evergreening practices, since the low threshold allows certain users to extend the effective term of the patent monopoly of a previously patented invention by claiming for obvious or very incremental modifications; and developing patent thickets by filing divisional innovation patents for minor (and obvious) variants of the main patented invention, leading possibly to more time and expense involved in opposition applications. A final concern was the rise of innovation patent applications in particular technological areas – specifically, electrical devices and engineering (a 350 per cent rise), information technology (a 390 per cent rise) and pharmaceuticals (a 560 per cent rise). The 2015 Australian Advisory Council on IP concluded that it was 'unable to obtain adequate empirical evidence as to whether the system does or does not stimulate innovation in Australian SMEs'.[45]

The Australian experience offers a list of highly pertinent queries for countries considering introducing the utility model regime. For instance, the Australian government's report stated that the continuation of the system would not guarantee that in the long run Australian SMEs will be the primary beneficiaries of such protection – as foreign companies were increasingly taking advantage of the innovation patent system. In such circumstances, it would become difficult to

---

[42] Advisory Council on Industrial Property, 'Review of the Petty Patent System', Australian Industrial Property Organisation, 1995, 24.

[43] Ibid., Chapter 5.

[44] *Dura-Post (Aust) Pty Ltd v. Delnorth Pty Ltd* [2009] FCAFC 81; interpreting s 7, Australian Patents Act.

[45] Australian Government's Advisory Council on Intellectual Property, 'Review of the Innovation Patent System – Final Report (May 2015), 8, 28, 36–39. See also Australian Government – IP Australia, 'Innovation Patents – Raising the Step', Consultation Paper (2012).

identify the market failure that an innovation patent is addressing. More challenging is its final concern as to whether the system costs more than the benefits it generates:

> Which incremental technological developments will not occur if protection is not given via a level of innovation approach as opposed to a level of invention approach? Alternatively, which of such developments will not be worked in Australia as a consequence of a lack of protection at the sub-patent level? On the other hand, if other incremental technological developments are stymied by innovation patents and those developments that do receive an innovation patent would have occurred in any event without the grant of such protection, the Australian economy would be incurring costs without obtaining any significant counter-vailing benefit.

The Australian government has agreed to phase out the innovation patent system – although to date, the regime continues.[46]

---

[46] Australian Government – Productivity Commission 2016, *Intellectual Property Arrangements, Inquiry Report No. 78*, 23 September 2016. Also see *Australian Government Response to the Productivity Commission Inquiry into Intellectual Property Arrangements*, August 2017. Links to the various reports are available at https://www.ipaustralia.gov.au/about-us/legislation/ip-legislation/intellectual-property-laws-amendment-productivity-commission-response-part-1-and-other-measures-act.

PART III
SHIFTING CONTOURS

11
Human rights and intellectual property

11.1 INTERDEPENDENCE OF RIGHTS

The nature and level of interaction between human rights and IPRs in the international and national spheres has grown rapidly in the last few decades. This chapter examines the relationship between these two legal fields in an increasingly complicated and controversial policy arena comprising UN bodies, international and national norms, industry policies and public welfare measures.

The primary ethos in the discourse, we believe, should be to strive towards a socially-optimal balance in law and policy while taking full account of fundamental rights and freedoms. This is undoubtedly difficult as the human rights and freedoms frameworks represent an intertwined and inter-dependent set of compromises between different constituencies. While a perfect balance is probably unattainable, it is arguable that the human rights perspective should, at the end of the day, wholeheartedly embrace economic, social and rights as much as political and civil ones promoting a more communitarian and humane society. The discourse as to the linkages between the different rights is not new. The seventeenth-century philosopher John Locke had already noted that natural law obliges us individuals 'to preserve the rest of mankind' by abstaining from harming another's 'life, health, liberty or possessions'.[1] The latter four areas today constitute fundamental freedoms under both the International Covenant on Civil and Political Rights (ICCPR) and the International Covenant on Economic, Social and Cultural Rights (ICESCR). As aptly summarised by the Nobel Laureate Sen:

> [...] we also have to understand the remarkable empirical connection that links freedoms of different kinds with one another. Political freedoms (in the form of free speech and elections) help to promote economic security. Social opportunities (in the form of education and health facilities) facilitate economic participation. Economic facilities (in the form of opportunities for participation in trade and production) can help generate personal abundance as well as public resources for social facilities. Freedoms of different kinds can strengthen one another.[2]

There is a viable case for arguing that future debates on IPRs should be reframed from a human rights perspective.[3] Such a re-contextualisation enables us to focus on the details of the balance required including, inter alia: (i) rewarding authors and inventors; (ii) ensuring the dissemination of technological, scientific, health, educational and traditional knowledge; and (iii) recognising the obligations of non-state actors including publishers, pharmaceutical companies and networking technologies. This balancing act also requires us to note the different political and moral stances adopted by diverse stakeholders on several questions. Here are just a few: what are the correct mechanisms for satisfying the rights of traditional knowledge holders in the face of activities aimed at exploiting a nation's genetic and informational resources in the interests of economic growth? What rights do indigenous groups have to control their knowledge and cultural resources, including in cases where such knowledge and resources are shared with other groups that may inhabit lands separated by national frontiers? Is there a class of activities (such as scientific and educational use) which should be *ab initio* excluded from the effects of IPRs? Or should IPRs be open to protect any practical knowledge, cultural work, signs and designs without discrimination?

One can restate such dilemmas by highlighting the internecine conflict between the different rights, depending on whether the conferment of a registered IPR will encroach upon the existing public domain and thus rights of others to use the intangible thing, or whether the IP has already been created in which case other fundamental freedoms, such as the right to health or education,

---

[1] J. Locke, *Second Treatise of Civil Government (1690)*, Chapter 2, para 6.

[2] A. Sen, *Development as Freedom* (New York: Knopf, 1999), 3–4, 10–11; also R. Howse and M. Mutua, 'Protecting Human Rights in a Global Economy: Challenges for the World Trade Organisation', in H. Stokke and A. Tostensen (eds), *Human Rights in Development Yearbook 1999/2000* (Kluwer Law International, 2001), 51.

[3] UN Economic and Social Council, Commission on Human Rights, Sub-Commission on the Promotion and Protection of Human Rights, 'Intellectual Property Rights and Human Rights: Report of the Secretary General'. 14 June 2001 [Document E/CN.4/Sub.2/2001/12]. Also L.R. Helfer, 'Toward a Human Rights Framework for Intellectual Property' (2006/2007) 40 *U.C. Davis L. Rev.* 971; L.R. Helfer, 'Human Rights and Intellectual Property: Conflict or Coexistence?' (2003) 5 *Minn. Intell. Prop. Rev.* 47.

will constitute an interference with the fundamental right to property.[4] This interdependence has further been recognised by the UN in various reports and documents, with Resolution 2000/7 on intellectual property and human rights concluding that:

> [...] since the implementation of the TRIPS Agreement does not adequately reflect the fundamental nature and indivisibility of all human rights, including the right of everyone to enjoy the benefits of scientific progress and its applications, the right to health, the right to food and the right to self-determination, there are apparent conflicts between the intellectual property rights regime embodied in the TRIPS Agreement, on the one hand, and international human rights law, on the other [...].[5]

It has been argued that the rights created through the enactment of IP laws are instrumental rights, and such rights should serve the interests and needs of citizens (such access to science and health), failing which such IP laws are close to transgressing the basic principles of human rights laws. The 2005 Geneva Declaration on the Future of the World Intellectual Property Organization[6] also brought attention to the need to consider alternative IP policy approaches that promote and protect the social and cultural rights of others. The claims by indigenous groups to traditional knowledge and cultural expressions have further highlighted how the third-generational rights can be deployed as bases for IPRs in traditional knowledge and traditional cultural expressions (see Chapter 15).

This may be an exaggerated view as it can be equally argued that more recent international IP instruments, such as the TRIPS Agreement and the WIPO copyright treaties, do recognise that some balance is required between property and authorial rights on the one hand, and social and economic welfare, public health and education, on the other. The preamble to the WIPO Treaties, for example, recognises the need to maintain a balance between the rights of authors, performers and phonogram producers and 'the larger public interest, particularly education, research and access to information'. The debates surrounding patented drugs and access to essential medicines further indicate a growing awareness of the inherent mechanisms within Articles 7 and 8, TRIPS Agreement to accommodate social and welfare freedoms. The European Commission has similarly alluded to the need for an IP regime to incentivise innovation which is indispensable for 'ensuring food security, containing climate change, dealing with demographic change and improving citizens' health'.[7]

---

[4] A. Peukert, 'The Fundamental Right to (Intellectual) Property and the Discretion of the Legislature', in C. Geiger (ed.), *Research Handbook on Human Rights and Intellectual Property* (Cheltenham: Edward Elgar Publishing, 2015), 140.

[5] UN Economic and Social Council, Commission on Human Rights, Sub-Commission on the Promotion and Protection on Human Rights, *Intellectual Property and Human Rights*, Resolution 2000/7, 17 August 2000, paras 1–2 (hereinafter Resolution 2000/7).

[6] Available at http://www.cptech.org/ip/wipo/genevadeclaration.html.

[7] Preamble to WCT, and preamble to WPPT; 'Communication from the Commission, "A Single Market for Intellectual Property Rights"', Brussels, 24 May 2011, COM (2011) 287 final, 3.

11.2 CLASSIFICATIONS OF RIGHTS

Human rights can be defined as 'a set of claims and entitlements to human dignity, which the existing international regime assumes will be provided (or threatened) by the state'.[8] The Universal Declaration of Human Rights (UDHR), which was adopted and proclaimed by the General Assembly of the United Nations in 1948, offers a broader notion based on an ethical rights-based society which focuses on the 'just distribution of material and non-material advantages'. This approach seeks to guarantee everyone a dignified livelihood with opportunities for personal attainment.[9] It is debatable whether all the rights are of equal ranking and priority. The 1966 international covenants – the ICCPR and the ICESCR – split civil and political rights from socio-economic ones spawning two generations of rights. This is somewhat reflected in the European framework where the European Convention on Human Rights (ECHR) incorporates most of the civil and political rights, while the European Social Charter incorporates the socio-economic rights; the EU Charter of Fundamental Rights protects both first- and second-generation rights within a single instrument.[10]

The first classical bastion of rights (civil and political rights) enjoins states to abstain from interfering with personal freedom, including the rights to life, liberty and human dignity, and the right of political participation and democratic governance. The right to human dignity, in particular, has influenced the contours of IPRs to a certain extent. Take for instance, the EU Directive on the Legal Protection of Biotechnological Inventions which states that: 'patent law must be applied so as to respect the fundamental principles safeguarding the dignity and integrity of the person'. The difficulty of applying moral norms within patent law is clear in *Oliver Brüstle v. Greenpeace e. V* where the EU Court of Justice struggled with the concepts of morality and invention as applied to human embryonic and stem cell research.[11] On a more positivist note, the right of dignity and personal development underpins moral rights (within copyright law) in some countries such as Germany (see Chapter 4).

The second generation of rights (social, economic and cultural rights) obliges public authorities to take active measures to provide an incubating environment by granting rights in various social-economic and cultural activities. There are, as we shall see below in relation to IPRs, several conflicts especially in relation to property, access to science and culture, labour, health, and education. The interdependence between social and economic rights was noted in the early 1769 decision of *Millar v. Taylor* where the Court recognised that a perpetual or indefinite copyright would lead to anti-competitive practices, excessive pricing, and would further go against the

---

[8] A. Brysk, 'Transnational Threats and Opportunities', in A. Brysk (ed.), *Globalization and Human Rights* (University of California Press, 2002), 1.

[9] S. George, 'Globalizing Rights?', in M. Gibney (ed.), *Globalizing Rights: Oxford Amnesty Lectures* (Oxford University Press, 2003), 17–18.

[10] Charter of Fundamental Rights of the European Union, 2012/C 326/02, OJ C 326, 26.10.2012, 391–407. For a sceptical view of splitting civil/political rights from economic/social/cultural rights, see J. Donnelly, *Universal Human Rights in Theory and Practice* (Cornell Univ. Press, 2003), 27 *et seq.*

[11] Recital (16), EU Directive 98/44 on the legal protection of biotechnological inventions, 6 July 1998, OJ L213/1; also Universal Declaration on the Human Genome and Human Rights, UNESCO 1997; Case C-34/10 *Oliver Brüstle v. Greenpeace e.V.* [2011] – see Chapter 14.

'natural rights of mankind in the exercise of their trade and calling', as it would restrain the natural right to labour of printers and booksellers.[12]

The third and relatively recent category (collective rights) represents complex composite and collective rights including the right to membership in a cultural or indigenous community, the right to a clean and healthy environment, and the right to development or self-determination.[13] The third generation of rights has had a renewed relevance in current debates on the protection and misappropriation of traditional knowledge and traditional cultural heritage, as well as on the access and benefit-sharing rules in relation to the exploitation of genetic and plant resources.[14] The drafting history of the UDHR also suggests that some of the motivations behind various individual rights stem from a more communitarian basis. For instance, Article 27, UDRH (discussed below) not only guarantees moral and economic benefits for authors, but also more societal rights such as the right to share in the benefits of science. Morsink notes that the inspiration and support for such socio-economic and cultural freedoms came from the more socialist South American states.[15]

11.3　INTERNATIONAL HUMAN RIGHTS AND TRIPS

As discussed below, our critique highlights the difficulties faced by the legislator in drawing rules in relation to human rights vis-à-vis intellectual property. Part of this problem lies in the fact that the rights discussed can be viewed as being there for the benefit of individuals and the community as a whole. Even if we accept that legislators and courts should adopt a more human-rights approach, the pertinent query is: what should such an approach entail? This query is especially crucial in light of the WTO–TRIPS Agreement (see Chapter 3).

It used to be that international trade law and international human rights law rarely interacted, but rather co-existed within an extremely broad global framework of legal and regulatory norms. It is arguable that neither WTO law nor the 1966 covenants make explicit references to human rights or international trade law respectively.[16] Nevertheless, out of the 164 WTO members that

---

[12] *Millar v. Taylor*, (1769) 9 Geo 3. BR 2303, 2393 *et seq.*

[13] Brysk, *op cit*, 3.

[14] ICESCR, the UN Declaration on the Rights of Indigenous Peoples, recognising the right of indigenous peoples to self-development and law making, and the CBD as contextualised by the Nagoya Protocol, recognising the right to fair and equitable benefits from the use of plant and genetic resources: G. Dutfield and U. Suthersanen, 'Traditional Knowledge and Genetic Resources: Observing Legal Protection through the Lens of Historical Geography And Human Rights' (2019) 58 *Washburn Law Journal* 399; B. Tobin, *Indigenous Peoples, Customary Law and Human Rights* (Abingdon: Routledge, 2014), 3–5.

[15] J. Morsink, *The Universal Declaration of Human Rights: Origins, Drafting and Intent* (Philadelphia: University of Pennsylvania Press, 1999), 139; the suggestion of the communitarian ethos in Art 27(1) is further substantiated by Art 1 of UNESCO's Declaration of Principles of International Co-operation.

[16] H. Hestermeyer, 'Economic, Social and Cultural Rights in the World Trade Organization: Legal Aspects and Practice', in E. Riedel and G. Giacca, *Economic, Social, and Cultural Rights: Contemporary Issues and Challenges* (Oxford: Oxford University Press, 2014), 260–86.

have undertaken to implement the minimum standards of IP protection under the TRIPS Agreement, about 85 per cent of the membership have also ratified the ICESCR on economic, social and cultural rights. Such members thus have a dual obligation to implement the minimum standards of the TRIPS Agreement bearing in mind their human rights obligations.

Moreover, as the effects of the TRIPS Agreement begin to manifest themselves, we need to re-evaluate the relationship between these trade policies, and the social and constitutional values of countries, especially those with emerging economies. Various UN Special Rapporteurs' reports and General Comments on the rights to food, education, health, science and a cultural life have been issued in the past three decades, many of which highlight the incongruous partnership between intellectual property and human rights.[17] In order to articulate clearly the cause-and-effect linkage between excessive pricing, access to science and culture, and property rights, the reports have discussed three specific examples.

First, the reports refer to the worryingly strong copyright laws under the TRIPS Agreement which, it is claimed, will indirectly allow corporations to control access to essential textbooks in developing countries; which in turn can affect educational access as well as data-mining activities for research purposes (see Chapter 12). Secondly, it is alleged that the current TRIPS provisions on patent laws may result in a denial of public access to affordable health care and essential drugs, especially in relation to HIV medicines. This was specifically linked to the media and diplomatic controversy in South Africa in relation to the HIV/AIDs crisis where a clear linkage was made between the right to health, high pricing of drugs, and the existence of medical patents (see Chapter 13). Thirdly, a similar concern was expressed in relation to TRIPS provisions on plants and plant varieties which are deemed by several countries to have negative consequences for the livelihoods of farming communities, and potentially conflict with the right to food (see Chapter 9).

11.3.1 The UN resolutions on TRIPS

Traditionally, some WTO members have instituted and maintained the balance between property rights of individuals and corporations, and the individual's rights to science, culture and education, or to wider societal rights in relation to national innovation goals, public or environmental health. This has been done by implementing limitations and exceptions within IPRs or by introducing wide public-policy exceptions or by allowing compulsory licences, thereby allowing third parties to offer substitute IP goods, either at zero or low pricing.[18] The policy of state autonomy in

---

[17] CESCR General Comment No 12: The Right to Adequate Food (Art 11); CESCR General Comment No 13: The Right to Education (Art 13); CESCR General Comment No 14: The Right to the Highest Attainable Standard of Health (Art 12); General Comment No 17: The Right of Everyone to Benefit from the Protection of the Moral and Material Interests Resulting from any Scientific, Literary or Artistic Production of Which He or She is the Author (Art 15, Para 1 (c) of the Covenant). Also of import and discussed below are the Special Rapporteur documents.

[18] Examples include Art 53(a), European Patent Convention, the notion of *ordre public* includes the protection of the environment – *Plant Genetic Systems* T356/93 (1995) EPOR 357; M. Azam, 'The Experiences of TRIPS-compliant Patent Law Reforms in Brazil, India and South America and Lessons from Bangladesh' (2014) 7(2) *Akron Intellectual Property Journal* 61, in relation to compulsory licence provisions for public interest/health reasons; G. Van Overwalle, 'The

delineating its national laws in line with its own priorities is also in line with the Declaration on the Right to Development:

> States have the right and the duty to formulate appropriate national development policies that aim at the constant improvement of the well-being of the entire population and of all individuals, on the basis of their active, free and meaningful participation in development and in the fair distribution of the benefits resulting therefrom.[19]

The United Nations committees have reacted with several reports and statements in relation to the TRIPS Agreement. For example, UN Resolution 2000/7 entitled Intellectual Property Rights and Human Rights identifies the following areas of conflict between human rights and intellectual property: (i) impediments resulting from the application of IPRs to the transfer of technology to developing countries; (ii) the consequences of plant variety rights and the patenting of genetically modified organisms for the enjoyment of the basic right to food; (iii) the reduction of control by communities especially indigenous communities over their own genetic and natural resources and cultural values, leading to accusations of 'biopiracy'; (iv) the restrictions on access to patented pharmaceuticals and the implications for the enjoyment of a basic right to health.[20]

Resolution 2000/7 calls on all states and intergovernmental bodies to reaffirm their commitments toward the achievement of international human rights norms, and to adopt a human rights approach to the development of international IP regimes. In the following year the UN adopted Resolution 2001/21 which pushed the agenda of the necessity of intellectual property regimes protecting all human rights with especial emphasis on the rights to health and food.[21] Resolution 2001/21 further recommended an analysis into: (a) whether the patent 'as a legal instrument' was compatible with the promotion and protection of human rights; and (b) the impact of the TRIPS Agreement on the rights of indigenous peoples. According to a further 2001 Report, governments should be reminded of the primacy of human rights obligations over economic policies and agreements. Indeed, this report identifies that the IP regime contained in the TRIPS Agreement might be a means of operationalising Article 15, ICESCR (discussed below) as long as the grant and exercise of those rights promotes and protects human rights.[22]

This corresponds to the view of some jurists, especially Petersmann, that there is no conflict between a universally recognised human right and a commitment ensuing from an international

---

Implementation of the Biotechnology Directive in Belgium and its Aftereffects. The Introduction of a New Research Exemption and a Compulsory License for Public Health' (2006) 37 *International Review of Intellectual Property and Competition Law* 889.

[19] Declaration on the Right to Development, UN Doc. A/RES/41/128, Art 2(4); ICESCR, Art 1(2); and UDHR, Art 1(2).

[20] Resolution 2000/7, *supra* note 5.

[21] *Intellectual Property Rights and Human Rights*, UN Commission on Human Rights, Sub-commission on the Promotion and Protection of Human Rights, Resolution 2001/21, UN Doc. E/CN.4/Sub.2/Res/2001/ 21 (2001) [hereinafter Resolution 2001/21].

[22] Para 15, *The Impact of the TRIPS Agreement on the Enjoyment of all Human Rights*, report of the High Commissioner for Human Rights, UN Doc. E/CN.4/Sub.2/2001/13 (2001).

trade agreement since 'the trade regime recognizes that human rights are fundamental and prior to free trade itself'.[23] A human rights approach to interpreting obligations under the TRIPS Agreement would strike the public-private balance by setting international human rights laws above international economic laws; this was further emphasised at the 2003 WTO Ministerial Conference which highlighted the right to health, the availability of pharmaceuticals, the protection of economic, social and cultural rights in areas such as health, education, the protection of the environment, the rights of indigenous people over their traditional knowledge, and the grant of IPRs over genetic resources.[24]

11.3.2 The social purpose within TRIPS

The WTO is not a 'self-contained' legal regime but is now recognised to be part of the international community of legal norms. As such, it should be interpreted 'in good faith in accordance with the ordinary meaning to be given to the terms of the treaty in their context and in the light of its object and purposes'.[25] The main object and purpose of the WTO–TRIPS Agreement is to be found in Articles 7 and 8 of the TRIPS Agreement (as well as the preamble). Article 7 clarifies that IPRs are not an end in themselves. Instead, IP protection and enforcement 'should contribute to the promotion of technological innovation and to the transfer and dissemination of technology, to the mutual advantage of producers and users of technological knowledge and in a manner conducive to social and economic welfare, and to a balance of rights and obligations'. Article 8(1) reminds member states that there is an institutional policy space within the Agreement which enables tailor-made national IPRs – 'to protect public health and nutrition, and to promote the public interest in sectors of vital importance to their socio-economic and technological development'. The provision is somewhat circular as national measures must be consistent with the Agreement.

The two provisions are unusual in being the first provisions in international IP instruments which have clear socio-economic objectives and policies. In this, there is some correlation between Articles 7 and 8, TRIPS and other international instruments such as the ICESCR and the CBD/Nagoya Protocol, in promoting economic development, transfer of technology, social welfare, nutritional and health needs, and so forth.[26] A key issue is whether Articles 7 and 8 allow Member states to transgress trade-related IP rules for human rights-related principles, or whether states can only limit the scope of IP rules as per the various three-step tests within the TRIPS

---

[23] Resolution 2000/7, para 3; E.U. Petersmann, 'The WTO Constitution and Human Rights' (2000) 3 *Journal of International Economic Law* 19; E.U. Petersmann, 'Human Rights and International Economic Law in the 21st Century. The Need to Clarify their Interrelationships' (2001) 4 *Journal of International Economic Law* 3.

[24] 'Human Rights and Trade'. OHCHR Paper for the 5th WTO Ministerial Conference, Cancún, Mexico, 10–14 September 2003, 6–16.

[25] WTO, '*United States – Import Prohibition on Certain Shrimp and Shrimp Products*', AB-1998-4, 12 October 1998. [Document WT/DS58/AB/R]; Vienna Convention on the Law of Treaties, Art 31(3).

[26] UNCTAD-ICTSD, *Resource Book on TRIPS and Development* (Cambridge: Cambridge University Press, 2005) 130; Appendix to the Nagoya Protocol.

Agreement;[27] or whether these provisions offer vague non-binding guiding principles. One UN report on the impact of the TRIPS Agreement on human rights acknowledges the tension stating that if a human rights approach was adopted, it would place the 'promotion and protection of human rights, in particular those in ICESCR, at the heart of the objectives of intellectual property protection, rather than only as permitted exceptions that are subordinated to the other provisions of the Agreement'.[28]

The saga that arose in relation to patent protection of essential medicines (see Chapter 13) can provide insights as to the ambit of Articles 7 and 8. The Doha Ministerial Declaration on the TRIPS Agreement and Public Health states that these provisions can and should be 'interpreted and implemented in a manner supportive of the WTO Members' right to protect public health and, in particular, to promote access to medicines for all'.[29] This, it is submitted, is a correct construction of the TRIPS Agreement in light of Article XX, GATT 1994 which also overrides trade rules for public order and health reasons.[30]

Pushing this interpretation further, we submit that Articles 7 and 8 give member states the mandate to take whatever steps they need to protect their citizens' health and educational expectations and interests. These two provisions arguably carve out a human rights mandate by providing a neat linkage between IPRs and public health, nutrition, education, environment, innovation and development. A generous interpretation of Articles 7 and 8 is that a balance must be struck between the public and private interests of IP producers, users and society within the international legal order. For example, Article 8(2), read with Article 40, TRIPS on anti-competitive measures, can be the basis for allowing states to legitimately construct laws which pursue indigenous public policy objectives, thus enabling limitations which lead to unreasonable trade practices or which adversely affect technology transfer, or be the bases for placing cultural, educational, health, free speech and development considerations on a par with, if not above, IPRs.[31]

The balance of rights and powers within the TRIPS document does not reflect the asymmetry within newer trade agreements such as the Comprehensive and Progressive Agreement for Trans-Pacific Partnership (which require TRIPS-plus intellectual property protection), or such as the free-trade agreements between US or the EU with other third parties (where the IP provisions can overwhelm economic growth and development, including access to affordable medicines). As the UN Special Rapporteur on patent policy astutely notes:

---

[27] The various three-step rules are articulated in: Arts 13 (copyright), 17 (trademarks), 26(2) (designs), and 30 (patents) TRIPS; for a review, see A. Christie and R. Wright, 'A Comparative Analysis of the Three-Step Tests in International Treaties' (2014) 45(4) *International Review of Intellectual Property and Competition Law* 409.

[28] *The Impact of the TRIPS Agreement on the Enjoyment of all Human Rights, Report of the High Commissioner for Human Rights*, UN Doc. E/CN.4/Sub.2/2001/13 (2001).

[29] Paras 4 and 5(a), Doha Declaration on the TRIPS Agreement and Public Health, WT/MIN (01)/DEC/W/2 of 14 November 2001.

[30] General Agreement on Tariffs and Trade, Art XX(a) and (b).

[31] For more discussion on the wider significance and legal effect of Arts 7 and 8, see A. Slade, 'Articles 7 and 8 of the TRIPS Agreement: A Force for Convergence within the International IP System' (2011) 14(6) *Journal of World Intellectual Property* 413–40.

Although exclusions, exceptions and flexibilities are fully part of international intellectual property law, such as the TRIPS Agreement, they remain optional from the perspective of trade law. From the perspective of human rights, however, they are often to be considered as obligations.[32]

11.4 RIGHTS OF AUTHORS AND INVENTORS

11.4.1 The 'IP' clause

Article 27, UDHR states that everyone has the following rights: 'to participate in the cultural life of the community', 'to enjoy the arts and to share in scientific advancement and its benefits', and 'to the protection of the moral and material interests resulting from any scientific, literary or artistic production of which he is the author'. Although the Declaration is not legally binding, the provision does nevertheless offer this universal moral precept to 'every individual and every organ of society'.[33] A similar prescription can be found in numerous other instruments[34] including Article 15, ICESCR:

1. The States Parties to the present Covenant recognize the right of everyone:
   a. To take part in cultural life;
   b. To enjoy the benefits of scientific progress and its applications;
   c. To benefit from the protection of the moral and material interest resulting from any scientific, literary or artistic production of which he is the author.

The two provisions offer a delicate balance between public and private interests, with the traditional interpretation being that the provisions promote access to scientific and cultural knowledge and objects, while guaranteeing the protection of those 'authors' (which extends to all those involved in creative activities, including scientists, designers, breeders, etc.) of scientific and cultural goods, without specifying the modalities of such protection. The drafters of Article 27(2) UDHR expressed their intentions thus: 'Authors of all artistic, literary, scientific works and inventors shall retain, in addition to just remuneration of their labour, a moral right on their work and/or discovery which shall not disappear, even after such a work shall have become the common property of mankind.'[35]

Similarly, the drafting history of Article 15(1)(c) ICESCR reveals that the provision was intended to guarantee a moral right to the scientist and the artist, against plagiarism, theft, mutilation

---

[32] Para 71, *Cultural Rights*, Human Rights Council Document A/70/279, 4 August 2015 (Shaheed Patent Report).

[33] Opening paragraph of Proclamation, and Second Preamble, UDHR. See Morsink, *supra* note 15, Chapter 2.

[34] American Declaration of the Rights and Duties of Man of 1948, Art 13.2; Art 14.1(c), of the Additional Protocol to the American Convention on Human Rights in the Area of Economic, Social and Cultural Rights of 1988 ('Protocol of San Salvador').

[35] Commission on Human Rights, second session, Report of the Working Group on the Declaration on Human Rights, E/CN.4/57, 10 December 1947, 15; A. Plomer, 'The Human Rights Paradox: Intellectual Property Rights and Rights of Access to Science' (2013) 35(1) *Human Rights Quarterly* 160 *et seq.*, discussing the drafting history of Art 27, UDHR.

and unwarranted use.[36] The ICCPR does not offer a positive basis for the protection of IPRs, but it does guarantee protection against arbitrary or unlawful interference with privacy, and against attacks on honour and reputation, thus arguably providing the bases for trade secret, confidentiality and moral rights rules.[37] Further indirect guarantees for personality and reputational rights can be found in the provision dealing with freedom of expression.[38]

This international prescription forms our universal understanding of creators' rights within a human rights framework, especially within national and regional laws. Within these general obligations, several queries then arise: How does the law enable creators' rights? Should authors and inventors be accorded rights of property or recognition (via IP regimes, moral rights or other liability-based rules), or specific rights of remuneration (which can include prizes and non-assignable equitable rights of remuneration)? Should all knowledge holders be guaranteed such rights?

11.4.2 Intellectual property as a 'right to property'

It has been argued that Article 15(1)(c) ICESCR does not guarantee a property right nor a monopoly rent, but 'only basic material compensation for effective costs incurred in developing a new scientific, literary, or artistic production and to foster a decent standard of living'.[39] This is understandable given that rights are often vested in multinational corporations, and more so when one reviews the relationship between the WTO–TRIPS Agreement and the UN-based human rights instruments.

One finds muted support for property rights within the drafting history of Article 27 UDHR. Accounts record an agreement between the French, Mexican and Cuban delegates that the notion of 'intellectual property rights' should be included in the declaration as this would recognise the right to own property and the right to work as being universal norms.[40] Indeed, the French chair of the working group on the Declaration, René Cassin, who was concurrently working on the 1948 revision of the Berne Convention and the inter-American Bogota Declaration (in relation to patents and copyrights), had initially proposed recognition of the author's and scientist's 'spiritual

---

[36] M. Green, 'Drafting History of the Article 15(1)(c) of the International Covenant', UN Document E/C.12/2000/15 (Oct. 9, 2000), 7–8; A. Chapman, 'Approaching Intellectual Property as a Human Right: Obligations Related to Article 15 (1) (c)' (2001) XXXV(3) *Copyright Bulletin* 4.

[37] ICCPR, Art 17; Berne Convention (for moral rights), Art 6*bis*; Paris Convention (for trade secrets laws), Art 10*bis*. Also see the right of an inventor to be named, Chapter 5.

[38] ICCPR, Art 19(2).

[39] P. Cullet, 'Human Rights and Intellectual Property Protection in the TRIPS Era' (2007) 29(2) *Human Rights Quarterly* 403, 409. For arguments that intellectual property rights should be recognised as 'intellectual monopoly privileges', rather than as human rights: G. Tansey, *TRIPS with Everything: Intellectual Property in the Farming World* (Food Ethics Council, 2002); C. Raghavan, *Recolonization. GATT, the Uruguay Round & the Third World* (Zed Books/Third World Network, 1990), 115–16; Submission of Quaker United Nations Office/Friends World Committee Consultation, in UN Human Rights Council, Sub-Commission on the Promotion and Protection of Human Rights, 'Economic, Social and Cultural Rights: Intellectual Property Rights and Human Rights: Report of the Secretary-General Addendum', 3 July 2001 [Document E/CN.4/Sub.2/2001/12/Add.1].

[40] Plomer, *supra* note 35, 171.

and moral rights'. Perhaps in keeping with this ethos, the signatories of the Berne Union adopted a non-binding Declaration on the centennial anniversary of the Berne Convention (on copyright) to the effect that: 'copyright is based on human rights and justice and that authors, as creators of beauty, entertainment and learning, deserve that their rights in their creation be recognized and effectively protected both in their own country and in all other countries of their world'.[41]

Albeit the ambiguous legal status of this Declaration, it is arguable that the Berne Convention obliges member states to accord a limited property right, and expressly subjects copyright rules to human rights norms. Moreover, some regional instruments have extended the remits of the property right to intangible and intellectual property.[42] The European Court of Human Rights, for instance, has confirmed that not only is this right of property to be enjoyed by both natural and legal persons, but it also undeniably includes 'intellectual property', in relation to patents, copyrights and trade marks.[43] Within the EU, the right to property within the ECHR and the specific right to intellectual property within Article 17(2), EU Charter on Fundamental Rights, have elevated IP as constituting an important element not only within a human rights regime but within the EU constitutional framework. The CJEU has interpreted the law as imposing positive obligations to protect intellectual property and that intellectual property is constitutionally guaranteed, especially in relation to their 'social function'.[44] In a recent judgment, *Coty Germany*, the CJEU further noted that EU states have a positive obligation to ensure that a legal owner of IPRs can exercise its right to information under enforcement regulations. Despite the obvious conflicts with provisions guaranteeing privacy and personal data, the Court held the IPR holders' right to information as being critical in enforcing effective remedies, especially in relation to 'the fundamental right to intellectual property'.[45]

---

[41] Solemn Declaration, adopted in the 1986 Centenary Assembly of the Berne Union, reprinted in whole in 'Cérémonies du Centième Anniversaire de la Convention de Berne', (1986) 22 *Copyright* 367; for the view that Cassin's strong beliefs in the rights of authors and inventors were situated in the Lockean belief of reward, see Plomer, ibid., 172.

[42] American Convention on Human Rights, Art 21; American Declaration on the Rights and Duties of Man, Art XXIII; and European Convention for the Protection of Human Rights and Fundamental Freedoms, 20 March 1952 (ECHR), Art 1, Protocol No 1.

[43] *Smith Kline and French Laboratories Ltd v. The Netherlands*, App No 12633/87, 4 October 1990, ECtHR, for patents; *Balan v. Moldova*, App No 19247/03, 29 January 2008, ECtHR, for copyright; *Anheuser-Busch Inc v. Portugal*, App No 73049/01, 11 January 2007, ECtHR, for trade mark; and also L. Helfer, 'The New Innovation Frontier? Intellectual Property and the European Court of Human Rights' (2008) 49 *Harvard International Law Journal* 1.

[44] Case C-277/10 *Martin Luksan v. Petrus van der Let*, EU:C:2012:65, emphasising the 'social function of property' aspect; Case C-275/06 *Productores de Música de España (Promusicae) v. Telefónica de España SAU* ECLI:EU:C:2008:54, setting out the proportionality/balancing test in relation to copyright; Case C-461/10 *Bonnier Audio*, EU:C:2012:219; Case C-70/10 *Scarlet Extended*, EU:C:2011:771; Case C-314/12 *UPC Telekabel Wien* EU:C:2014:192.

[45] Case C-580/13 *Coty Germany* EU:C:2015:485, interpreting personal data and privacy rights under EU Directives 2002/58/EC on personal data and the protection of privacy [2002] OJ L 201, and Directive 95/46/EC on personal data and on the free movement of such data [1995] OJ L 281; M. Husovec, 'Intellectual Property Rights and Integration by Conflict: The Past, Present and Future' (2016) 18 *Cambridge Yearbook of European Legal Studies* 239.

11.4.3 A critique on General Comment No 17

General Comment No 17 is a paradoxical elaboration of the 'intellectual property' clause within Article 15.1(c) ICESCR. First, the General Comment defines the subject matter of Art.15(1)(c) broadly to include 'creations of the human mind', 'scientific productions', 'innovations, including knowledge, innovations and practices of indigenous and local communities', and 'literary and artistic productions'.[46] However, despite this wide notion of creativity, the lack of reference within the Comment to the concept of inventors and 'inventions' is noticeable, especially as this is the core subject matter of protection under international and national patent laws, and there are references throughout the General Comment on patent law. Moreover, from the negotiating history of the UDHR, we can see that 'authors' was meant to include inventors within its intended meaning.[47]

Secondly, although the Comment recognises that authors should receive some sort of protection, it contends that such human rights in this context do not 'necessarily reflect the level and means of protection found in present copyright, patent and other intellectual property regimes'. Instead, the Comment states that Article 15(1)(c) can be satisfied by other means.[48] Historically, this is undoubtedly true as protection for authors and inventors has always been satisfied by a variety of mixed legal regimes including liability rule regimes and criminal laws. These 'other' laws do not, however, exist in a legal lacuna. They only function as protection for authors and inventors by referencing existing international norms which recognise various enforceable rights for creators.[49] The Comment's disapproval of 'intellectual property law' as a means of realising Article 15(1)(c) is surprising since it does not reflect the plethora of national IP laws with strong deontological and constitutional bases justifying natural rights of creators – based on human dignity, personal development or labourer rights.[50] This is especially so considering the provenance of this provision within the UDHR.[51]

---

[46] *General Comment, No 17 – The Right of Everyone to Benefit From the Protection of the Moral and Material Interests Resulting From any Scientific, Literary or Artistic Production of Which He or She is the Author*, UN ESCOR, Comm on Econ, Soc and Cult Rts, UN Doc. E/C.12/GC/17 (2006) [hereinafter General Comment 17] paras 7–8.

[47] G. Dutfield, 'Collective Invention and Patent Law Individualism, 1877–2012; Or, the Curious Persistence of Inventor's Moral Right', in S. Arapostathis and G. Dutfield (eds), *Knowledge Management and Intellectual Property: Concepts, Actors and Practices* (Cheltenham: Edward Elgar Publishing, 2013), 109–23, 118.

[48] General Comment 17, *supra* note 46, paras 2–3, 7 and 10.

[49] For example, the US has maintained that it satisfies its obligations under Art 6*bis*, Berne Convention, which obliges Berne Union countries to implement moral rights, despite the absence of express moral rights language under her national copyright law, through tort and unfair competition laws. See at E. Schéré, 'Where is the Morality? Moral Rights in International Intellectual Property and Trade Law' (2018) 41 *Fordham International Law Journal* 773.

[50] See Chapter 2. The civil law perspective has always been that the protection of authors and inventors are both economic *and* cultural issues, with pecuniary and humanistic elements imbibed in both sets of laws protecting works and inventions. Most civil law countries do have provisions, for example, which espouse the notion that benefit-sharing where the invention or work is of substantial benefit to the owner/employer/exploiter.

[51] The drafting history of this provision's predecessor i.e., Art 27, UDHR, shows that the Working Committee was not only aware of the inherent 'human rights' of authors and scientists, but also of the existing IP laws during this period. Morsink, *supra* note 15, 220–22.

Thirdly, Comment No 17 rightly recognises that IP laws are economic instruments conferred by states to protect business and corporate interests. Conversely, the General Comment also recognises intellectual property law as being 'a social product with a social function', which imposes obligations on states to 'prevent unreasonably high costs for access to essential medicines, plant seeds or other means of food production that could undermine the rights of large segments of the population to health and food'.[52]

Finally, the Comment recognises the link between the author and his work within the concept of 'moral interests', as well as the linkages between IPRs and other human rights under international and regional instruments due to their economic dimensions including the rights to gain one's living, to adequate remuneration, to an adequate standard of living, and to property.[53]

This was perhaps a lost opportunity for the drafters of the General Comment to invite nations and legislators to consider the inherent humanistic and societal characteristics existing within national and regional intellectual property instruments. We submit that a more constructive rights-based approach to Article 15(1)(c) is that the provision serves as a mandate for creators to claim a 'right' to intellectual property as a human right vested in individual creators. As such, this would have allowed various types of creators and communities to claim a *de minimis* non-waivable right to benefit sharing in any exploitation of their works. Moreover, rather than deny human rights status to IPRs, a more palatable perspective would accept that IP laws are evolving economic and social constructs which should include several fundamental values such as:

- compulsory benefit-sharing safeguards including an inalienable and equitable right of remuneration for creators, whether employees, authors or indigenous groups;[54]
- inalienable moral rights recognising the human dignity and personality of creators;[55]
- a commensurate degree of 'public domain' space within national IP frameworks to accommodate the linkages with other fundamental rights to education, health and development.

This perspective would help in two continuing dilemmas: labour rights of employees/freelancers, and traditional knowledge. In relation to the former, there are far too few measures within current IP laws controlling corporate ownership or protecting any ensuing benefits for employee creators. This is further troubling in light of ever-increasing terms of protection, the expanding subject matter of protection, the inclusion of restrictive covenants within hiring contracts, and the attempts to evergreen IPRs within the entertainment, chemical and engineering fields.

---

[52] General Comment 17, *supra* note 46, paras 2 and 35.

[53] Ibid., paras 13–14, referring to Arts 6.1, 7(a), and 11.1, ICESCR, and the UDHR respectively.

[54] Authors and performers, for example, are entitled to an inalienable equitable right of remuneration under EU copyright law in relation to the rental right (Council Directive 92/100/EEC); and to moral rights of attribution and integrity under international copyright law (WCT and WPPT).

[55] For instance, French copyright law implements Art 6*bis*, Berne Convention as perpetual, inalienable and imprescriptible rights (see Chapter 4, section 4.7); and Art 4*ter*, Paris Convention recognises that inventors have the right to be recognised or named on the patent (see discussion in Chapter 5, section 5.2.5). Moreover, it is clear that the moral rights of creators was envisioned as being part of the UDHR Arti 27 package – Morsink, *supra* note 15, 219 *et seq.*

A human-rights base for work done by authors and scientists within the General Comment would help to counter the prevailing custom of vesting *ab initio* ownership in employers in respect of employee-created works and inventions. Such an approach could have gone further to promote more robust measures to ensure a fair and equitable benefit or compensation for creative authors and scientists.

This approach, for instance, is tacit in the later report by the UN Special Rapporteur in relation to copyright:

> Unlike copyrights, the human right to protection of authorship is non-transferable, grounded on the concept of human dignity, and may be claimed only by the human creator, 'whether man or woman, individual or group of individuals'. Even when an author sells their copyright interest to a corporate publisher or distributer, the right to protection of authorship remains with the human author(s) whose creative vision gave expression to the work.[56]

In relation to traditional knowledge, our suggested perspective would certainly be helpful to indigenous groups and local communities struggling for recognition of rights within other international instruments. For instance, one can employ this recommended approach to Article 15(1)(c) as a basis for arguing that the fair and equitable benefit sharing provision within the CBD-Nagoya Protocol, especially in relation to traditional knowledge, should be perceived as conferring inalienable rights to indigenous peoples and communities.[57]

Such a stance within a joint framework comprising international intellectual property and human rights norms would also encourage countries and inter-governmental organisations to interpret IP laws more holistically, taking into account other fundamental freedoms, and perhaps even employing the European proportionality doctrine (see above). It should also be noted that a version of the proportionality doctrine is advocated by the UN Special Rapporteur in relation to Article 15(1)(a) and patent policy, namely, that where patent law places a limitation on the rights to health, food, science and culture, states should demonstrate that 'the limitation pursues a legitimate aim, is compatible with the nature of this right and is strictly necessary for the promotion of general welfare in a democratic society', with the least restrictive measure being adopted.[58] We now turn to the UN reports on Article 15. We believe the latter underpin our views that the General Comment is not the conclusive explanation of whether authors and inventors have definitive human rights.

---

[56] Report of the Special Rapporteur in the field of cultural rights, Farida Shaheed: *Copyright Policy and the Right to Science and Culture*, Human Rights Council Document A/HRC/28/57, 24 December 2014 (Shaheed Copyright Report), para 28.

[57] For the link between rights and the Nagoya Protocol, see E. Morgera, 'Fair and Equitable Benefit-Sharing at the Cross-Roads of the Human Right to Science and International Biodiversity Law' (2015) 4(4) *Laws* 803; Dutfield and Suthersanen, *supra* note 14.

[58] Shaheed Patent Report, *supra* note 32, para 100.

11.5 CULTURAL AND SOCIETAL RIGHTS

11.5.1 Right to culture and science

Cultural rights are inseparable from human rights, as recognised in Article 27(1), UDHR; Article 5 of the 2001 UNESCO Declaration on Cultural Diversity; Article 15(2), ICESCR and the 2005 UNESCO Convention on the Protection and Promotion of the Diversity of Cultural Expressions. The rights can be defined as the right of access to, participation in and enjoyment of culture. This includes the right of individuals and communities to understand, access, utilise, conserve, disseminate and develop cultural heritage and cultural expressions, as well as to benefit from the cultural heritage and cultural expressions of others. It also includes the right to participate in the identification, interpretation and development of cultural heritage, as well as in the implementation of safeguarding policies and programmes. According to Morsink's account of the drafting history of Article 27, UDHR, there was no disagreement in relation to the notion that everyone has a right, including those who did not participate in creating them, to enjoy the benefits of artistic and scientific advancements.[59]

The ICESCR recognises at a general level that a nation's social and economic development is realised by improving methods of production, conservation and distribution of resources through technical and scientific knowledge and by developing efficient systems so as to achieve efficient development and utilisation of resources.[60] To this end, Article 15(2)–(4), ICESCR juxtapose cultural, scientific and research purposes and freedoms against the need to protect a creator's interests under Article 15(1)(c). It should be obvious that this grouping of rights urges states to consider the balance between the commercial and cultural needs of creators, and the communitarian and public interest needs of societies comprising of users, researchers, scientists and future generation of creators and innovators. Article 15(3) is also noteworthy in emphasising the importance of respecting academic freedom.[61] A delegate in an early drafting session declared that the right of everyone to enjoy the benefits of science:

> Implied the dissemination of basic scientific knowledge, especially knowledge best calculated to enlighten men's minds and combat prejudices, coordinated efforts on the part of States, in conjunction with the competent specialized agencies, to raise standards of living, and a wider dissemination of culture through the processes and apparatus created by science.[62]

That the balance between the two rights embedded in Article 15, ICESCR (namely intellectual property and the right to access culture and science) would be difficult to achieve is acknowledged by Green in her advisory paper to the UN nearly 40 years later:

---

[59] Morsink, *supra* note 15, 219.

[60] ICESCR, Art 11.2.

[61] General Comment No 13: The right to education (Article 13 of the Covenant); see Chapman, *supra* note 36.

[62] UN Econ. and Social Council, CESCR, *Implementation of the International Covenant on Economic, Social, and Cultural Rights: Drafting History of the Article 15(1)(c) of the International Covenant on Economic, Social, and Cultural Rights*, UN Doc. E/C.12/2000/15 (Oct. 9, 2000) (by Maria Green), 7–8.

We face a world with issues that the drafters of the ICESCR could never have envisaged, from an AIDS epidemic reigning in one part of the world while the drugs that could help are largely owned in another, to scientifically engineered non-reproducing crops, to scientists 'bio-prospecting' for traditional knowledge whose ownership does not fit into existing patent definitions.[63]

The 2005 UNESCO Cultural Diversity Convention adopts the approach that IPRs should be subservient to demands concerning culture and development. The objectives of the Convention include the reaffirmation of sovereign rights of states to elaborate cultural policies with a view both 'to protect and promote the diversity of cultural expressions' and 'to create the conditions for cultures to flourish and to freely interact in a mutually beneficial manner'.[64] There is recognition that cultural expressions may have to be anchored to market mechanisms for the purposes of dissemination, especially in relation to 'cultural activities, goods and services' which are the products of creativity. Such products are different from other global goods and services.[65] Although not an international human rights instrument in the strict, technical sense, the Cultural Diversity Convention has guiding principles which do explicitly espouse several human rights principles. In contrast to IP treaties, the Convention embraces a holistic perspective and attempts to highlight several alternative ways whereby some balance can be achieved between competing, though not necessarily conflicting, rights and goals including IPRs, development and indigenous peoples' rights – for example, two of the mechanisms discussed within the Convention are noteworthy, namely the provisions promoting benefit-sharing and the setting up of the International Fund for Cultural Diversity.[66]

The boundaries of all these rights and entitlements are broad, and are continuously re-defined in political and legal spheres, with reference to other rights. In the next section we turn to the Special Rapporteur's conclusions in relation to the right of access to science and culture vis-à-vis IPRs.[67]

11.5.2 UN Special Rapporteur on copyright

The Special Rapporteur Shaheed emphasised the weak bargaining position of human authors vis-à-vis corporate ownership, and the restrictive contracts imposed on authors which can result in reduced profits to authors. The report also highlights various aspects of national copyright laws

---

[63] Ibid., 13.

[64] UNESCO Cultural Diversity Convention 2005, Art 1.

[65] Ibid., Art 2; A. Khachaturian, 'The New Cultural Diversity Convention and its Implications on the WTO International Trade Regime: A Critical Comparative Analysis' (2006) 42 *Texas International Law Journal* 191, 194.

[66] Ibid., Arts 2.6, 13.

[67] Report of the Special Rapporteur in the field of cultural rights, Farida Shaheed: (i) *The right to enjoy the benefits of scientific progress and its applications*, Human Rights Council, Document A/HRC/20/26, 14 May 2012 (Shaheed Cultural Report); (ii) *Copyright policy and the right to science and culture*, Human Rights Council Document A/HRC/28/57, 24 December 2014 (Shaheed Copyright Report); (iii) *Cultural rights*, Human Rights Council Document A/70/279, 4 August 2015 (Shaheed Patent Report).

which promote 'the human right to protection of authorship': copyright reversion from corporate owners to human authors; a right of remuneration, *droit de suite*, statutory licensing schemes which ensure a share of collected royalties for authors (such as the public lending right). Thus the report urges a nuanced copyright policy, where 'strong' copyright laws do not necessarily offer authorial protection but where exceptions and limitations could be expanded in order to 'empower new creativity, enhance rewards to authors, increase educational opportunities, preserve space for non-commercial culture and promote inclusion and access to cultural works'. The report is especially favourable to statutory licensing schemes which ensure compulsory, non-waivable remuneration.[68]

The report quite accurately notes the influential role of international copyright treaties in that the latter instruct signatory countries to treat copyright protection as mandatory obligations but tend to treat exceptions and limitations as optional. It suggests that in order to assure the right to science and culture, a policy change should incorporate a mandatory minimum list of exceptions and limitations in international copyright instruments, especially those national provisions which have become accepted as global norms (such as quotations, personal use, archival and storage reproduction, data mining exceptions, parody et al.),[69] including a new international treaty on exceptions and limitations. Unsurprisingly, the three-step test (as established under Art 9(2), Berne Convention and Art 13, TRIPS Agreement) comes under considerable criticism. To this end, it should be noted that the EU regional copyright law has started to grapple with some of these issues namely out-of-print books and data mining exceptions.[70] In addition to the normal voluntary and compulsory licensing routes, the report embraces the open licensing route, including Creative Commons, Free Art License, GNU General Public License and open access publishing – so as to create a 'cultural commons'.

Finally, despite its sceptical stance towards strong copyright protection, the report reverses this outlook in relation to the rights of indigenous peoples and proposes that states adopt measures to ensure 'the right of indigenous peoples to maintain, control, protect and develop their intellectual property over their cultural heritage, traditional knowledge, and traditional cultural expressions'.[71] (See Chapter 15.)

11.5.3 UN Special Rapporteur on patent, health, food and environment

The main concern within the report was the effect of patent protection of technologies on the various rights to health, to access to science and culture, to education, and to food and a sustainable environment. This was highlighted in relation to new technologies such as energy, agrochemical,

---

[68] Shaheed Copyright Report, *supra* note 56, 9–11.

[69] Ibid., 13; R. Okediji, 'The International Copyright System: Limitations, Exceptions and Public Interest Considerations for Developing Countries', ICTSD Issue Paper No 15 (2006). Available at http://unctad.org/en/Docs/iteipc200610_en.pdf.

[70] See Chapter 4.

[71] Shaheed Copyright Report, *supra* note 56, 21.

pharmaceutical, nanotechnology and synthetic biology.[72] The report concedes that patent protection is crucial for providing corporate incentives to invest in new technologies and to bring them into the marketplace, and for furthering national socio-economic development. Nevertheless, the report decries as simplistic any conclusion which equates IPRs as being beneficial within all industries in all countries as the effects of IPRs are country-dependent, depending on the technological capacity and industrial profile of individual nations.

The linkage between patents, pharmaceutical industries and public interest is discussed in great detail in the Special Rapporteur's report on the right to health.[73] Of particular interest is the concern in relation to the 'evergreening' of patents by pharmaceutical companies, namely, obtaining new patents on existing patented medicines by making minor innovative changes.[74] As one can surmise, the evergreening phenomenon delays the entry of competitive generic medicines into the market; moreover this problem is not confined to patents but also utility models. In relation to the right of health, it is well documented that patent protection allows the rights holder to either prevent access to medicines or to allow access under unreasonable or impracticable pricing schemes. A human rights framework should make innovations essential for a life with dignity accessible to everyone, with enabling mechanisms to protect public interests critical to health, agriculture and housing.[75] In summary, the Rapporteur argues for a patent regime which enables developing countries and least developed countries (LDCs) to use TRIPS flexibilities to enable access to medicines and to facilitate the entry of generic medicines including: developing local technical and manufacturing capabilities; excluding new or second medical use patents; allowing certain uses including research, experimental and educational activities; adopting international exhaustion and parallel importation; compulsory licensing; adopting competition measures to prevent the abuse of the system. Moreover, developing countries and LDCs are exhorted to avoid introducing TRIPS-plus standards or to enter into TRIPS-plus FTAs.

There are several examples of WTO members using the TRIPS flexibilities in favour of health. Moreover, the Indian and US Supreme Court decisions in the *Glivec* and *Myriad* cases[76] indicate how patent law can be interpreted to exclude certain types of subject matter. Countries have subjected health-related patents to re-examination (Brazil), or to disclosure of origin requirements (Peru) or to compulsory licensing (Brazil, Ecuador, India, Indonesia, Malaysia and Thailand in relation to HIV/AIDS-related medicines, cardiovascular, cancer and hepatitis medicines), or have refused enforcement (LDCs have declined to enforce patents on medicines).[77]

---

[72] These concerns were already noted in the Shaheed Cultural Report, *supra* note 67, paras 26 and 29.

[73] Anand Grover, *Report of the Special Rapporteur on the Right of Everyone to the Enjoyment of the Highest Attainable Standard of Physical and Mental Health*, UN Human Rights Council, Document A/HRC/11/12, 31 March 2009, paras 17–93.

[74] Ibid., para 34; H.P. Hestermeyer, *Human Rights and the WTO: The Case of Patents and Access to Medicines* (Oxford University Press, 2007).

[75] Shaheed Patent Report, *supra* note 32, paras 48–50.

[76] These cases, both of which have major implications for access to medical products and services are discussed in subsections 13.2 (*Glivec*) and 14.4 (*Myriad*).

[77] Ibid., paras 77–86.

11.5.4 Indigenous peoples, local communities, property rights and benefit sharing

Is there a specific right within the human rights framework to the protection of bio-cultural heritage of indigenous peoples and local communities, and if yes, should it be realised via the intellectual property regime? The pertinent sections within the 2005 UNESCO Cultural Diversity Convention recognises a broad range of potential IP works including traditional knowledge and the knowledge systems of indigenous peoples as a source of intangible and material wealth, and traditional cultural expressions, and other cultural goods and services. It also notes the importance of IP rights as an incentive to cultural creativity. The Convention then obfuscates matters by housing these concerns and principles within a human rights framework including the freedom to create, disseminate and distribute, the rights to access and benefit for development interests, freedom of expression, information and communication, and the need for the sustainable development for present and future generations.[78] These are lofty aims, indeed which are further boosted by the UN Declaration on the Rights of Indigenous Peoples (UNDRIP). The latter states that indigenous peoples 'have the right to maintain, control, protect and develop their intellectual property'.[79]

These instruments have formed the bases for the current international discourse on genetic resources, traditional knowledge and traditional cultural expressions. From the human rights perspective, it is not immediately clear whether there is indeed a positive 'right to intellectual property protection' of indigenous bio-cultural heritage, and if so, whether the right is based on a positive right of property. Or whether the bases for the right lies within Article 15(1), or can be sought in the wider right of indigenous peoples to self-determination, their right to maintain and develop their culture and their struggle for cultural survival.[80]

The rationale for rights vesting in indigenous peoples is manifold. General Comment 21 on the rights of everyone to 'take part in cultural life'[81] argues strongly for their 'right to maintain, control, protect and develop' all manifestations of indigenous peoples, their heritage and their sciences. Examples of protectable matter include traditional knowledge, traditional cultural expressions, human and genetic resources, seeds, medicines, knowledge of the properties of fauna and flora, oral traditions, literature, designs, sports and traditional games, and visual and performing arts.[82] Unlike General Comment 17 (discussed above) which does not equate authorial rights to intellectual property law, General Comment 21 calls upon both international and national intellectual property regimes to widen their parameters to 'take into account the concerns of indigenous peoples and local communities'.

Interestingly enough, the recent Special Rapporteur's reports advocate states adopt laws to protect and develop 'their intellectual property over their cultural heritage, traditional knowledge,

---

[78] UNESCO Cultural Diversity Convention 2005, preamble, Arts 2.1, 2.6, 2.7, 4.3, 6.1 and 6.2(g), 7.

[79] UNDRIP, Art 31, para 1. Also see Arts 5, 8, and 10–13.

[80] Shaheed Patent Report, *supra* note 67, para 37.

[81] General comment No 21: Right of Everyone to Take Part in Cultural Life (Article 15, para 1 (a), of the International Covenant on Economic, Social and Cultural Rights) (2009).

[82] Ibid. General Comment No 21, paras 36–37, making reference to UNDRIP, Arts 11–13.

and traditional cultural expressions'. The Special Rapporteur's patent report pushes for much wider boundaries than perhaps traditional IPRs allow. The Shaheed Patent Report calls for the availability of measures and remedies to allow indigenous peoples and communities to control their biocultural heritage; and to prohibit unethical and/or unlawful appropriation of indigenous heritage through patents. Needless to say, there are also calls to ensure the right of attribution (including within patent applications) and adequate compensation, with particular emphasis on the interconnectivity between IPRs and the utilisation of traditional knowledge and cultural expressions, and genetic resources within the international law framework citing the CBD and the subsequent Nagoya Protocol.[83]

Thus, despite the stance of General Comment No 17 (discussed above), there is a strong contention within the other human rights instruments and reports that there is an indisputable mandate for vesting property rights in indigenous peoples and local communities, and that this group of stakeholders have the right to develop their IP as part of the right to development. This does not necessarily mean that the recognition of IP can ameliorate their difficulties and concerns, and that IPRs are the main means of redressing compensation claims. This rather depends on how we view the term 'intellectual property'. The use of the term by the various human rights-based organisations might suggest a reduction of traditional and local knowledge rights to a conventional legal taxonomy comprising patent, copyright, trademark, design, trade secret, and geographical indications. However, in this highly specific context, such a construction would be misleading. Human rights law, of which the UNDRIP is a key instrument, clearly plays a greater role in formulating the rights of indigenous peoples than intellectual property so construed. The institutions, customs, traditions, and systems of such peoples comprise norms that are relevant to access and to the use by others of their cultural heritage, TK, cultural expressions, as well as their local resources such as seeds and medicinal plants. A much broader conception of 'intellectual property' is envisaged. Support for indigenous peoples' land and territorial and resource rights in the Declaration strengthens their ability to impose their own norms on others entering their lands.

Moreover, if we accept that the resources of indigenous peoples and local communities are part of the wider debate on environmental concerns and sustainable development, which are unquestionably of vast value, and that considerations of land and cultural values should play a part in capturing the needs of the indigenous and local communities, then the legally holistic UNDRIP is arguably the more appropriate legal instrument within which we can capture myriad strands including property rights, and a feasible access and benefit-sharing framework.[84]

---

[83] Shaheed Copyright Report, *supra* note 56, para 117; Shaheed Patent Report, *supra* note 32, paras 43 and 114–116.

[84] Dutfield and Suthersanen, *supra* note 14, 432 *et seq.*; UNCTAD, *The Convention on Biodiversity and the Nagoya Protocol: Intellectual Property Implications: A Handbook on the Interface between Global Access and Benefit Sharing Rules and Intellectual Property* (Geneva, 2014). Also see Chapter 15.

12
Education and cultural heritage

What measures, if any, are available under international intellectual property laws that can accommodate and enhance rather than undermine public interest concerns such as the rights to education and to benefit from science and culture? How can society have access to the vast amounts of digitised texts, data and cultural assets at a reasonable (or even at no) cost, while ensuring a commensurate payment to creators and corporate producers of IP goods? Should we incorporate the human rights-based balancing proportionality test so as to ensure that all sectoral interests and needs are taken into account? A key issue is whether WTO member countries can take advantage of the flexibilities provided in existing international treaties to establish exceptions for research, educational, scientific and even commercial usage of informational goods.

The traditional view focuses on the right of creators and producers to adequate remuneration or compensation, emphasising that all exceptions or limitations, irrespective of their public interest bases, must be interpreted narrowly. The converse position is that a more positivist perspective should be employed in interpreting IP laws. If there are discernible linkages between individual IP clauses and fundamental human rights, such clauses should then be interpreted within a broader public interest framework, taking into account the relevant educational, cultural or developmental needs. In this respect, perhaps the WIPO Development Agenda will be useful in promoting IP policies that prioritise the economic knowledge needs of the public, especially in relation to developing countries.

One suggestion is to introduce an international public interest rule within IP law. It is clear that 'public interest' must be taken into account with declarations and interpretive statements emphasising the public's interest in access to knowledge and culture, and asserting that states must give primacy to human rights over IP rights in cases of conflict.[1] Provisions within the International Bill on Human Rights and the UN Convention on the Rights of the Child are recognised within national copyright laws of several countries which have recognised the link between copyright law and educational needs. The 1996 Internet Treaties expressly recognise the need to maintain a balance between the rights of creators and producers, and 'the larger public interest, particularly education, research and access to information'.[2]

12.1 TWENTIETH-CENTURY POLICY LANDSCAPE

12.1.1 Intellectual property disruptions

The current nature of IP law is often accepted as being the necessary and efficient means by which to capture the economic value of creative works when exploited in various modes. The law is nevertheless in flux as courts and legislatures have begun to interpret IP laws as a means to attain social good, especially in accessing education, research and culture. This is particularly true when we see the modern jurisprudential and legislative solutions in relation to digital libraries, data mining, and orphan works. These changes are partly due to several global disruptions.

The first disruption is the unprecedented expansion of protected subject matter due to the open-ended international rules on what constitutes IP. The parameters of protection can potentially cover almost any object from oral, visual, textual and even olfactory works, grounded in the physical and analogue world (such as music, photographs, films, designs and even scents), to digital manifestations of such works (such as computer programs, electronic databases, computer-generated and AI works), to genetic resources, plant varieties, geographical indications, traditional knowledge and cultural expressions. The list of protectable works includes derivative works, web platforms, networked technologies, performances, phonograms, broadcasts, non-creative photographs, published editions of previously unpublished works, and new critical editions of public domain works or scientific writings. This expansion of subject matter is paralleled by the growing term of protection for several IP rights. This in turn is exacerbated by the lowering

---

[1] L. Helfer, 'Regime Shifting: The TRIPS Agreement and New Dynamics of International Intellectual Property Lawmaking' (2004) 29 *Yale J. Intl L.* 1, 49 *et seq.*; U. Suthersanen, 'Towards an International Public Interest Rule? Human Rights and International Copyright Law', in J. Griffiths and U. Suthersanen (eds), *Copyright and Free Speech: Comparative and International Analyses* (Oxford: Oxford University Press, 2005), 117.

[2] Preambles to WCT and WPPT.

of protection thresholds across the IP framework, as well as attempts to evergreen an IP right by claiming supplementary protection through unfair competition or through hybrid IP rights.[3]

The second disruptive challenge to current IP laws arises from the impact of technology on established patterns of production, distribution and consumption of informational goods. The advent of the internet, cloud computing and high-speed broadband, coupled with the increasing availability of individual computing power has expanded access to and usage of informational products, especially cultural, scientific and academic works. Technology enables digitisation of works and facilitates access to such works. Technology can be further harnessed to control and monitor access and exploitation of works, and even (theoretically at least) to calculate, collect and distribute any royalties payable.

With the convergence of the digital and internet spheres, a third possible disruptive factor is the growing sense of entitlement from today's global citizenry. This generation of Millennial and Generation Z users expect access to streaming and cloud services, digital libraries, databases comprising seminal and new research and innovation, e-Health hubs, etc. The current hyperbole as to 'Big Data' further fuel the expectations of research and business communities as to the value of extracting data as in text and data mining activities which enable new derivative markets and increased efficiencies in public services. This view is aptly summed up by the European Commission in justifying more new copyright rules: 'The internet and digital technologies are transforming our world. But existing barriers online mean citizens miss out on goods and services, internet companies and start-ups have their horizons limited, and businesses and governments cannot fully benefit from digital tools.'[4]

A fourth disruptive factor is that new technological markets and goods challenge traditional concepts of property. Users, in both developed and developing countries, are not only concerned with excessive pricing of digital goods and services but are also questioning whether lawfully bought digital goods are subject to ordinary rules on ownership (as in the case of e-books, software and 3D printed objects). There are different jurisprudential approaches worldwide as to whether the doctrine of exhaustion/first sale doctrine applies (in the national and international contexts) to digitised IP goods in the same manner as analogue goods (discussed below), as well as to self-replicating technologies including modified life-forms.

12.1.2 Scholarly publishing

For countries with public education systems which are primarily dependent on foreign materials, international copyright law can appear hostile to attempts to extract and use copyrighted protected works at zero or little cost. Pricing issues can be a matter of concern for both developing and developed nations. As discussed in Chapter 2, it is acknowledged within economic theory that IP protection

---

[3] Examples include: the widening of IPRs (the term of patents from 14 years to 20 years, and the term of copyright from 28 years to 50–70 years *pma*); the attempt to protect pharmaceutical data, for example, under Art 39, TRIPS Agreement; or attempts to claim protection for factual or minor innovations under national utility model or *sui generis* database rights.

[4] European Commission Fact Sheet, *Commission Publishes Mid-Term Review of the 2015 Digital Single Market Strategy*, 10 May 2017.

should be limited in circumstances where the IP holder gains an excessive control over a specific product market, and where the consumer is left with no alternative competing substitute product.

In relation to scholarly publishing, the underlying problem is the fact that academic journals are an atypical information good. A 2015 study indicates that five publishers account for more than half of today's published scholarly journal output, across the humanities and sciences. Within scholarly publishing, academic authors provide journal articles without financial compensation; publishers do not pay for quality control in the form of peer review; and the reading consumer is not affected by price increases as the purchases are made by academic libraries with specific budgets. As the study notes: 'Because purchase and use are not directly linked, price fluctuations do not influence demand [...] Due to the publisher's oligopoly, libraries are more or less helpless, for in scholarly publishing each product represents a unique value and cannot be replaced.'[5] With the advent of electronic publishing, costs have become marginal as the associated costs with printed material have virtually disappeared (for example, typesetting, printing, and distribution costs). In economic terms:

> Printed journals can be considered as rival goods – goods that cannot be owned simultane-
> ously by two individuals – online journals are non-rival goods: a single journal issue that has
> been uploaded by the publisher on the journal's website can be accessed by many researchers
> from many universities at the same time. The publisher does not have to upload or produce
> an additional copy each time a paper is accessed on the server as it can be duplicated ad in-
> finitum, which in turn reduces the marginal cost of additional subscriptions to 0. In a system
> where the marginal cost of goods reaches 0, their cost becomes arbitrary and depends merely
> on how badly they are needed, as well as by the purchasing power of those who need them.[6]

One can imagine more extreme scenarios where the publishing oligopoly is the sole source of crucial scientific, medical or legal data worldwide, with the power to charge non-competitive prices for access and distribution of such data. The result is that universities and research libraries can get locked into purchasing bulk subscription packages in order to avail certain key journals. While this may be the affordable option for well-endowed universities and research centres, high-pricing schemes can pose an impossible hurdle for state institutions from impoverished regions and countries.

Unsurprisingly, contractual licences based on copyright laws are key tools in controlling initial access to research works, and subsequent distribution of the works, whether through the old-fashioned reprographic method or through making available digital extracts of books or electronic journals. Where a copyright work is available for educational copying under an educational exception, it may still be that such copying is curtailed where licences are available or that compensation

---

[5] V. Larivière, S. Haustein and P. Mongeon, 'The Oligopoly of Academic Publishers in the Digital Era' (2015) 10(6) PLoS ONE, e0127502. doi:10.1371/ journal.pone.0127502, 11–12, indicating that in terms of profit and market shares in 2013, Reed-Elsevier, Wiley-Blackwell, Springer, and Taylor & Francis were within the top five publishers within the NMS (natural and medical sciences) and SSH (social sciences and humanities) fields, with the American Chemical Society being a fifth within NMS, while the fifth most prolific publisher in SSH was Sage Publications.

[6] Ibid., 12.

is gathered via equipment levies. In this respect, collective management organisations (CMOs) have become an essential practical and economic ingredient within any copyright regime, and blanket licensing is a key strategy with which reprographic copying in the educational sector is controlled.[7] The blanket licence obliterates the need to determine whether the usage in question is inside or outside the fair use or fair dealing exceptions. For an institutional user, it is more expedient to be directed to one entity which manages the rights in relation to a specific category of work, thus saving it from incurring transaction costs in terms of search and negotiation in obtaining licences from different authors in respect of different works.

For developing countries, however, the establishment and maintenance of CMOs involves high transactional costs the burden of which should, if possible, be placed on rights owners rather than states or institutional users. Highlighted problems include obtaining permission from publishers for works excluded from the licence repertoire; foreign currency payments; multiple licences for translations into different local dialects; digitisation fees; and differential contractual terms from different publishing houses which are superimposed on local copyright laws.[8]

12.1.3 Post-colonial copyright reforms

The twentieth century witnessed the decolonisation and independence of a large number of newly independent African and Asian countries. A major priority within these young nations was the building of schools and hospitals, accompanied by the need to provide readily accessible and affordable educational and scientific materials and instruction. The main concern was (and still is) the fact that consumers in the Global South have lower purchasing power compared to those in the North. Thus, a book which would cost US$20 in the US would cost approximately US$14 in India, and US$45 in South Africa.[9]

Embedded within these priorities was the stance that existing copyright norms within the Berne Convention had to be changed due to the inherent bias towards rights owners in developed countries. Some countries also felt that the Western countries had a responsibility to assist their former colonial dominions. Altbach, a scholar in education and publishing policies, puts forward a similar argument:

> Those who control knowledge distribution have a responsibility to ensure that knowledge is available throughout the world at prices that can be afforded. I do not advocate overthrowing

---

[7] U. Suthersanen, 'Copyright and Educational Policies: A Stakeholder Analysis' (2003) 23(4) *Oxford Journal of Legal Studies* 585.

[8] A. Story, *Study on Intellectual Property Rights, the Internet, and Copyright* (Commission on Intellectual Property Rights, 2002), on education; S. Schlatter, 'Copyright Collecting Societies in Developing Countries: Possibilities and Dangers', in C. Heath and A. Kamperman Sanders (eds), *New Frontiers of Intellectual Property Law* (IIC Studies, 25, Hart, 2005), 53–69.

[9] For critical analyses on copyright, education and development, see M. Chon, 'Distributive Justice and Intellectual Property: Intellectual Property "From Below": Copyright and Capability for Education' (2007) 40 *U.C. Davis Law Review* 803; and A. Rens, A. Prabhala and D. Kawooya, *Intellectual Property, Education and Access to Knowledge in Southern Africa* (ICTSD-UNCTAD-TRALAC, 2006).

the copyright system, or even weakening it. I do argue for a broader understanding by publishers of their responsibilities in an unequal world.[10]

The Indian government voiced a more forthright position in stating that 'the high production costs of scientific and technical books standing in the way of their dissemination in developing countries could be substantially reduced if the advanced countries would freely allow their books to be reprinted and translated by underdeveloped countries'.[11] One can trace the earliest calls for this socialist approach to 'access to knowledge' in a 1967 speech by Fidel Castro:

> It was not the intellectual property of the authors or the spiritual product but of those who on the market paid with money on the barrel and at any price. Those who had the book monopoly generally paid low prices for that product of intelligence. They had the right to sell the books at the price they considered proper. [...] We feel that what man's intelligence has created should be the patrimony of all mankind. Who pays Cervantes his royalties for intellectual property? Who pays Shakespeare? [...] As of now, we say that we renounce all rights to our intellectual property and that (since) things are settled between the Cuban intellectual producer and the Cuban Government, our country renounces all rights to intellectual property. This means our books may be freely printed anywhere in the world, (applause) while we at the same time consider ourselves to have the right to do the same.[12]

During the reform period, leading up to the 1971 Paris revisions, the Universal Copyright Convention (UCC) was briefly the preferred international copyright instrument. Administered by UNESCO, and perceived as being more developing country friendly, the UCC was more accommodating and flexible than the author-centric Berne Convention, with fewer mandatory requirements and lower durations and thresholds of protection. First, countries could introduce any limitation or exception as long as these provisions did 'not conflict with the spirit and provisions of this Convention', and if the state gave a 'reasonable degree of effective protection to each of the rights' to which exception was made. This is to be compared to the three-step test within the Berne Convention.[13] Secondly, the UCC limited the right of translation which was the bane of many developing countries who were eager for the opportunity to translate books into indigenous and dialect languages.[14]

Several reform attempts were made during the 1950s and 1960s to modernise the Berne Convention. Developing countries wanted clear concessions for educational and translation uses of

---

[10] P. Altbach, 'The Subtle Inequalities of Copyright: Power without Responsibility' (1992) 3(3) *Logos* 144, 148.

[11] C.F. Johnson, 'The Origins of the Stockholm Protocol', (1970) 18 *Bulletin of the Copyright Society of the USA* 91. For a lively discussion of India's ambivalent attitude to the Berne Convention, see T.P. Reddy and S. Chandrashekaran, *Create, Copy, Disrupt: India's Intellectual Property Dilemmas* (Oxford University Press, 2017), 115–39.

[12] 'Castro Delivers Speech at Guane Ceremony', Havana Domestic Television and Radio Services, April 1967, English translation, available at http://www1.lanic.utexas.edu/project/castro/db/1967/19670430.html.

[13] Universal Copyright Convention, Art IV*bis*(2); *cf*, Berne Convention, Art 9(2); and TRIPS Agreement, Arts 13 and 30.

[14] Universal Copyright Convention, Art 5.

copyright materials. This issue had been raised in the 1967 Stockholm Revision Conference (leading to the Stockholm Protocol) but was heavily resisted by authors' organisations, publishers, and other rights holders in the developed world. Their view was that 'the Protocol constitutes a sacrifice of the rights of authors in developed countries and jeopardizes the best interests of authors in developing countries'.[15] One may view the 1971 Paris revisions to both the UCC and the Berne Convention as an acceptance of some fundamental principles such as educational and teaching exceptions, and compulsory licensing for the reproduction and translation of works in developing countries.[16]

One of the major changes wrought in the world copyright system during this period of reform was the introduction of a right of reproduction, and a provision allowing certain exceptions to this 'new right', namely the three-step test. Introduced for the first time in international IP law in the 1967 Stockholm revision to the Berne Convention, the three-step test has now come to represent the core basis for any national limitation to all IP rights within the TRIPs Agreement. An unanswered query is whether the three-step test, when incorporated into national and regional laws, is addressed to contracting nations or should courts embark on such a test when determining limitations and exceptions in all contexts.[17]

12.2 EDUCATION AND COPYRIGHT

What exactly is meant by 'educational use'? There are national laws throughout the world drawing the boundaries of this defence through a variety of means and phrases. Some countries have expressly broad provisions which allow any use of a work, whether by means of reproduction, communication, distribution, and whether it is for personal use or mass copying for the purposes of classroom or university use. Other jurisdictions specifically only allow non-profit educational use though with the advent of fee-paying schools and higher educational institutions, the boundaries between commercial and not-for-profit activities are increasingly blurred. A further difficulty is that most of the existing educational exceptions, drafted in the pre-digital, pre-internet and pre-cloud system eras, have become obsolete and inapplicable. Many have argued for 'free' copying where educational institutions and schools are allowed to copy and communicate published or publicly available materials for non-commercial educational purposes without compensation or statutory licensing schemes. Added within this mix is the call by libraries and archives to be able to copy materials for educational or archival uses, or to be able to migrate contents from existing formats to newer formats, or to be allowed to digitise existing materials so as to make them more accessible to the wider public. And e-books have added another dimension to this legal uncertainty.

---

[15] General Assembly of ALAI, 23 April 1968, Paris, reproduced in (1968) *Copyright* 189. For a full account of the Stockholm Protocol and its aftermath, see S. Ricketson and J. Ginsburg, *International Copyright and Neighbouring Rights: The Berne Convention and Beyond* (Oxford: Oxford University Press, 2005), Chapter 14.

[16] These concessions are to be found in the Appendix to the Berne Convention, and within Arts V*bis*, V*ter* and V*quarter*, Universal Copyright Convention.

[17] In relation to the EU region, R. Arnold and E. Rosati, 'Are National Courts the Addressees of the InfoSoc Three-Step Test?' (2015) 10(10) *Journal of Intellectual Property Law & Practice* 741.

The notion of education is constantly re-purposed to mean 'the educational need of society' to access all knowledge housed within an educational or cultural institution including for the purposes of teaching, scholarship, data and textual mining, preservation, conservation and culture. This approach has allowed schools, universities and libraries to argue that they are vested with a public interest mandate to digitise all works within their collections so as to make them accessible to all, and to also preserve them for future generations. Some would argue that this mandate can also extend to non-commercial activities of profit-making companies such as the Google Cultural Institute.

12.2.1 Berne Convention

Article 10(2), Berne Convention provides the necessary mandate for permitting reproduction for educational purposes:

> It shall be a matter for legislation in the countries of the Union, and for special agreements existing or to be concluded between them, to permit the utilization, to the extent justified by the purpose, of literary or artistic works by way of illustration in publications, broadcasts or sound or visual recordings for teaching, provided such utilization is compatible with fair practice.

Due to its ambiguous meaning, Article 10(2) Berne Convention has limited value in the modern world. The provision may not, for instance, allow local community adult education courses or adult literacy campaigns, distance learning programmes, and translation of materials. Translating works for little or nil cost is especially important in Africa and India where many countries and regions have more than 30 different languages and dialects.[18] It is also not clear what the phrase 'to the extent justified by the purpose' means. It is arguable that it places a limit on the amount that may be copied from any given work. Thus, for instance, it may be difficult to argue that a whole work must be copied in order to convey the information required for teaching purposes. On the other hand, one could argue that Article 10(2) permits the preparation of compilations anthologising all or parts of a variety of works for teaching purposes. The qualification that the use should be compatible with fair practice suggests that one has to refer back to the three-step test – discussed below in relation to the TRIPS Agreement.

The Berne Appendix further exemplifies the failure of the Berne Convention to assuage developing countries' fears as to paying unsustainable prices for educational materials. The Appendix was to be the post-colonial panacea to the international copyright crisis. It would allow compulsory licensing in relation to the mass reproduction and translation of works for educational purposes. It would act as an incentive to authors and publishers to engage with their counterparts in other countries. It could also act as a bargaining tool for developing countries to enable a degree of practical cooperation with the possibility of establishing an affordable book supply system in

---

[18] A. Story, 'Burn Berne: Why the Leading International Copyright Convention Must be Repealed' (2003) 40(3) *Houston Law Review* 763, 781, 798.

developing countries. Theoretically pragmatic and noble,[19] the reality is that the Appendix has many limitations. First, it is so highly detailed and complicated that it exceeds the original Berne Act in length. Second, although the Appendix does permit the invocation of a compulsory licence of works if voluntary negotiations over translations and reproduction rights are not successful, the provisions are extremely complex. Third, the Appendix only extends to translation and reproduction rights, and does not apply to broadcasting or other communication rights – hence online transmission of works does not come within the exceptions. Fourth, the Appendix contains no provisions for free educational use or for any reduction in duration of copyright.[20] The general consensus is that no more than nine developing countries have used the Appendix.

IP rights holders had argued during the 1990s that international copyright laws had to be revisited in order to accommodate the new technologies. The result is the increase in the set of rights vested in authors and the creative industries. Despite the anxieties regarding access to IP protected works for educational and knowledge purposes, especially within a digital and connected environment, the copyright laws in most developing countries reflect the international standard of protection without much divergence. There has been, in recent times, a discernible shift towards interpreting international copyright law as accommodating wider educational usage without compensation, especially in Canada and India.

12.2.2 Three-step test

The TRIPS Agreement incorporates the Berne Convention *in toto* including the Appendix. It also introduces a wider three-step test with which all WTO members must comply when introducing limitations and exceptions. The three-step test comprises a triptych of constraints on the limitations and exceptions to rights under national copyright laws. It was first applied to the exclusive right of reproduction under Article 9(2) of the Berne Convention. Since then, it has been transplanted into the TRIPS Agreement and the two WIPO Internet Treaties. As we have noted previously, the three-step test for copyright under the TRIPS Agreement calls for special circumstances, exceptions which do not conflict with the normal exploitation of the work, and exceptions which do not unreasonably prejudice the legitimate interests of the rights holder.[21] When applying the three-step requirement in this area, key considerations are whether mass copying for classroom teaching is allowed, and whether any educational use by individuals or educational institutions requires compensation.

---

[19] Appendix to the Berne Convention, Special Provisions Regarding Developing Countries (1971 Paris Act of the Berne Convention). Specifically, the Appendix provides that, subject to compensation to the copyright owner, there is a possibility of granting non-exclusive and non-transferable compulsory licensing in respect of: (i) translation for the purpose of teaching, scholarship or research; and (ii) reproduction for use in connection with systematic instructional activities, of works protected under the Convention. See Ricketson and Ginsburg, *supra* note 15, paras 14–49 *et seq.*

[20] Ricketson and Ginsburg, ibid. To read the different positions of countries and NGOs regarding the Appendix during its passage, see https://www.keionline.org/book/berne-convention/1971-appendix-to-the-berne-convention-special-provisions-regarding-developing-countries.

[21] See Chapter 4.8 for a full discussion on the three-step test.

Exceptions that are specifically directed to educational activities have been said to pass the first step of being directed towards 'certain special cases'.[22] However, some of the above activities may also fall foul of the next two steps. For instance, mass photocopying of educational materials will arguably conflict with the authors' or publishers' normal exploitation of the work. Similarly, mass reproduction followed by a non-payment of compensation can be considered as unreasonably prejudicing the legitimate interests of the rights holder.[23] On the other hand, it is also equally arguable that some of the above activities would not conflict with the rights holder's normal exploitation if it can be shown that the rights holders have failed to provide the work to correspond to market demand, or that the work, although available in the marketplace, is inaccessible in terms of cost and thus poses obstacles to the dissemination of knowledge.

A pro-development approach is to argue that Article 13, TRIPS allows for a more constructive positive rights approach so that developing countries and LDCs can implement clear exceptions which allow full access to educational and scientific information. Indeed, the statutory bundle within the preamble and Articles 7, 8, 13 and 40 of the TRIPS sets out general principles and objectives of international intellectual property law which is that rights must be balanced against national public policy objectives including indigenous societal and economic interests, including the promotion of innovation, education and the promotion of public interest, especially in the case of LDC countries which require maximum flexibility.[24]

Thus, the three-step test should be presumed to incorporate the spirit of Articles 7 and 8, TRIPS.[25] From this perspective, the three-step test is satisfied where the use in question fulfils a social, cultural, educational or other developmental benefit which outweighs the costs imposed by copyright provisions.[26] A 2002 study on the three-step test in relation to Australian educational defences also suggests that the three-step test, especially at the second stage, must consider

---

[22] WIPO Study on the Copyright Exceptions for the Benefit of Educational Activities for Asia and Australia (2009). SCCR/19/7, Geneva (26 October).

[23] Support for this is found in the Report of the Main Committee I at the Stockholm Conference, which referred to the possibility that while the making of a small number of photocopies without payment may be permitted for individual or scientific use, where a large number of copies are made for use in industrial undertakings, the payment of equitable remuneration may negate the unreasonable prejudice caused to the legitimate interests of the author, Records of the Intellectual Property Conference of Stockholm, 11 June–14 July, 1967, 1145–6.

[24] UNCTAD-ICTSD, *Resource Book on TRIPS and Development* (Cambridge University Press, 2005), Chapters 6.6 and 6.7; U. Suthersanen, 'The Future of Copyright Reform in Developing Countries: Teleological Interpretation, Localized Globalism and the "Public Interest" Rule', as part of the UNCTAD-ICTSD Dialogue on IPRs and Sustainable Development: Revising the Agenda in a New Context, 24–29 October 2005, Bellagio, Italy, available at www.iprsonline. org/unctadictsd/bellagio/Bellagio2005/Suthersanen_final.pdf.

[25] See Chapter 11.

[26] Article 3-1, Proposed Treaty on Access to Knowledge, promoted by the NGO Knowledge Ecology International, available at https://www.keionline.org/book/proposalfortreatyofaccesstoknowledgemay102005draft.

'non-economic normative' factors.[27] It must be determined whether the use in question is one that the copyright owner should control, or whether there is some other countervailing interest that would justify this not being so – such as educational exceptions in order to meet the educational and development goals of a nation. The report advocates a strong public interest ethos when applying the three-step test, as well as a teleological approach since the 'three-step test; is not a positive provision or right but emphasises the boundaries of authors' rights.

12.2.3 Fundamental rights to development and education

Most WTO countries are parties to the ICESCR and the Convention on the Rights of the Child, which codify the international right to education.[28] The human right to education 'epitomizes the indivisibility and interdependence of all human rights' and, as such, carries public interest and communitarian elements. Thus, free, compulsory primary education is not just for the individual but is also a societal concern which needs an educated citizenry.[29] Moreover, the UN General Comment No 13 recognises that education is an indispensable means of realising other human rights. It empowers the poor, women, and children from exploitative and hazardous labour, it protects the environment, and is a financial investment for states.[30] The right to education can also be considered as both a civil right and a political right, as it is also directed to the 'full development of the human personality and the sense of its dignity'.[31]

General Comment No 13 on the right to education states that part of the aim of the right to education is to oblige states to set up an adequate infrastructure to facilitate the proper functioning of educational institutions. Thus, the educational needs of individuals should be taken into account within the international IP framework, especially when considered within a development context. An interpretation which allows free use of copyright materials for educational purposes is supported by a number of national and international laws.

The main elements within the right to education (including those inherent in the rights of children) are: education shall be directed to the full development of the human personality and the sense of its dignity; compulsory, free primary education should be guaranteed; accessible secondary and higher education, especially by the progressive introduction of free education should

---

[27] S. Ricketson, *The Three-Step Test, Deemed Quantities, Libraries And Closed Exceptions – A Study of the Three-Step Test in Article 9(2) of the Berne Convention, Article 13 of the TRIPS Agreement and Article 10 of the WCT, with Particular Respect to its Application to the Quantitative Test in Subsection 40(3) of the Fair Dealing Provisions, Library and Educational Copying, the Library Provisions Generally and Proposals for an Open Fair Dealing Exception* (Centre for Copyright Studies Ltd, 2002).

[28] ICESCR, Arts 13–14 (based on UDHR, Art 26); Convention on the Rights of the Child 1989, Art 28.

[29] J. Morsink, *The Universal Declaration of Human Rights: Origins, Drafting and Intent* (Philadelphia, PA: University of Pennsylvania Press, 1999), 212–15, explaining that the drafting of Article 26, UDHR on education was influenced by the many delegates who emphasised the link between education and civic training.

[30] UN Committee on Economic, Social and Cultural Rights (CESCR), *General Comment No 13: The right to education (Art 13 of the Covenant)*, 8 December 1999, E/C.12/1999/10.

[31] Morsink, *supra* note 29, 212–15; General Comment No 13, ibid.

be ensured; and fundamental education shall be encouraged.[32] In implementing the rights to education (and development), factors to be considered include: (i) teaching materials; (ii) library and computer facilities; and (iii) information technology.[33]

Using the proposed three-step test approach in the above section, one could argue that mass copying of educational materials in developing countries and LDCs would not conflict with a normal exploitation of the work for several reasons. Developing countries, who are WTO members, should utilise the ambiguity of within the TRIPS Agreement (namely Art 13 as read with Arts 7 and 8) to carve out specific educational exemptions in their copyright laws. For such countries, there is no real benefit to be gained by looking at examples of educational exceptions within developed countries, which have a diverse range of developmental and socio-economic needs. This interpretation is also supported by other academics who have called for a more cultural-development sensitive interpretation of the three-step test under the various international copyright instruments, namely that:[34]

> [...] historic evidence, economic theory and the principle of self-determination suggest that individual states should have sufficient flexibility to shape copyright law to their own cultural, social and economic development needs. Copyright exceptions and limitations tailored to domestic needs provide the most important legal mechanism for the achievement of an appropriate, self-determined balance of interests at national level.

Educational institutions, students and scholars usually lack the financial means to purchase such material at the normal commercial rate. Neither do many developing nations have sophisticated CMO administrative and collection mechanisms to monitor mass usage. From the IP holder's perspective, there is no lost market opportunity in these instances of unauthorised use as there would be little practical exploitation of works within the country. Conversely, it may be argued that unfettered reprinting without control can affect normal exploitation in the future, especially in relation to direct contractual relationships with education ministries, or with specific university or research libraries. Finally, there are creative ways by which the 'non-prejudice' element in the three-step test can be interpreted so as to allow for free usage to most societal users, but with the cost transferred elsewhere. Issues that are of particular relevance when dealing with local educational needs, photocopying and international copyright law are:

• generous interpretation of limitations and exceptions, especially in relation to private use or educational or research acts, and whether free educational usage is allowed;

---

[32] General Comment No 13, ibid.

[33] UN Committee on Economic, Social and Cultural Rights (CESCR), *General Comment No 11: Plans of Action for Primary Education (Art 14 of the Covenant)*, 10 May 1999, E/1992/23.

[34] C. Geiger, R. Hilty, J. Griffiths and U. Suthersanen, 'Declaration: A Balanced Interpretation of The "Three-Step Test" in Copyright Law' (2010) 1 *JIPITEC* 119 para 1, an academic attempt to redress the perceived imbalance within the EU member states' jurisprudence where exceptions and limitations were being interpreted narrowly.

- levy schemes which are governed by user groups as well as copyright owners/managers and which have both economic and cultural goals, as well as investigating ways in which the monies can be re-directed back into supporting the indigenous authorial and publishing interests;
- active local stakeholders who routinely check and challenge blanket licensing schemes and other applications of the law in properly constituted local arenas or specialist courts dealing with licensing issues.

12.3 NATIONAL EDUCATIONAL EXCEPTIONS

Members of both international copyright and human rights agreements have implemented their obligations in different ways in order to enable teachers and educational institutions to allow access to copyright works within an educational setting. Depending on whether the national law originates from civil or common law or mixed bases, education-based provisions can be either specific (as in fair dealing exceptions under UK and other common law countries) or broad (as in the case of the fair use defence in US) or come under other guises (such as private use or quotations in Germany and France).[35]

12.3.1 Fair dealing, private study and research

The fair dealing defence is employed in most Commonwealth countries and over the decades, we have witnessed its modification to reflect the individual needs of a country. In more modern times, there has been a shift (especially in Australia, Canada, Singapore, Israel and India) towards a more liberal interpretation of the fair dealing defence. A brief explanation of the UK fair dealing concept is perhaps in order here. Unlike the concept of 'fair use' under the US copyright law, fair dealing is traditionally a circumscribed defence which is available only for certain purposes such as private study, non-commercial research, criticism, etc. First introduced under the 1911 Imperial Copyright Act, the British Parliament's intention was clearly to codify pre-existing case law which had accepted that certain types of substantial takings would be condoned on the grounds of 'fair quotation' or 'real and fair abridgement'.[36] 'Fair dealing' under UK copyright law is not defined within the statute and guidance must be sought solely from the courts and academic treatises. In the UK, most mass reprographic copying is considered to be beyond the fair dealing or educational

---

[35] For a comparative survey on different types of educational exceptions, see D. Seng, *WIPO Study on the Copyright Exceptions for the Benefit of Educational Activities for Asia and Australia*, SCCR/19/7, October 2009, available at http://www. wipo.int/meetings/en/doc_details.jsp?doc_id=130249; and D. Seng, *Updated Study and Additional Analysis of Study on Copyright Limitations and Exceptions for Educational Activities*, SCCR/35/5 REV. ORI, 2017.

[36] Copyright Act 1911, s 2; *Bradbury v. Hotten* LR 8 Ex 1 (1872); *Gyles v. Wilcox* 2 Atk 141 (1740); *Pro Sieben v. Carlton* [1999] FSR 610, 618, agreeing that there had been a general 'fair use' doctrine under pre-1911 Copyright Act. See also Chapter 4, section 4.8.

exceptions and thus libraries, universities and businesses must enter into voluntary blanket licences with the relevant collecting societies.[37]

Developing countries may find the Australian model more useful as to how to tailor flexibility into the educational provisions especially in relation to affordability. The law provides that fair dealing with a literary work (other than lecture notes) 'does not constitute an infringement of the copyright in the work if it is for the purpose of, or associated with, an approved course of study or research by an enrolled external student of an educational institution'. The Copyright Act, unlike its UK predecessor, has been reformed so as to provide a list of factors that should be taken into account when determining what constitutes 'fair dealing' for the purposes of research or study including, inter alia: (i) the purpose and character of the dealing; (ii) the nature of the work or adaptation; (iii) the possibility of obtaining the work or adaptation within a reasonable time at an ordinary commercial price; (iv) the effect of the dealing upon the potential market for, or value of, the work or adaptation; and (v) where only a part is reproduced, then the amount and substantiality of the part copied in relation to the whole work or adaptation.[38]

In the recent governmental review of Australian copyright law, a full review of the existing fair dealing exception was analysed, especially in relation to the technological challenges to the modes of teaching and research. A key recommendation was that the current exceptions within the law be replaced with a broader fair use exception – as deployed within US copyright law. In the discussion as to the merits of the fair use defence, one of the countervailing arguments was that such a broad exception would lead to the demise of the publishing industry as well as to the cessation of collecting societies. Much evidence was given of the Canadian experience, accompanied by accounts of major publishing houses cutting down on their operations. These were duly discounted by the Australian Law Commission, stating that the cost-benefit analysis was methodologically flawed, and that significant contextual differences existed between Canadian and Australian publishing industries and market demands.[39]

What is the Canadian experience? In order to meet its own educational needs, Canada amended its law and extended the fair dealing exception: 'Fair dealing for the purpose of research, private study, education, parody or satire does not infringe copyright.'[40] The Canadian changes have been controversial as it is feared that the switch to 'free educational copying' may have had a severe impact on the publishing industry within Canada. On the other hand, there is also disbelief that there is a correlation between the copyright reforms, and the business failure of some publishers

---

[37] UK Copyright Law, ss 29, 29(A) and 30 for fair dealing, and ss 32 *et seq.* for rather limited educational and library exceptions for educational institutions; Suthersanen, *supra* note 7, 585 (for UK position); *University of New South Wales v. Moorhouse* [1975] HCA 26 (for Australian position).

[38] Australian Copyright Law, ss 40(1A) and 40(2).

[39] Productivity Commission, *Intellectual Property Arrangements, Inquiry Report*, Commonwealth of Australia, 2016, Chapter 6 – 'Fair Use or Fair Dealing – What is Fair for Australia', 165–98.

[40] Canadian Copyright Law, ss 29–30.

in Canada.[41] According to some accounts, prior to the copyright changes in 2012, the Canadian educational books sector was already struggling due to a range of factors (other than copyright) including reduced spending on new curriculum by Canadian schools, increasing use of open education resources, the use of used textbooks, and the transition from traditional print books to digital products (which was said to be 'having a transformative effect on the business').[42]

12.3.2 Mass copying and institutional users

A thorny issue is whether teachers and educational institutions can avail themselves of the private study and research defence. The traditional view is that this defence should be limited to the person actually engaged in study or research and does not extend to the person or teacher or institution that facilitates these activities for others. Thus, copy shops or university libraries with photocopying facilities which enable such educational usage cannot avail themselves of this defence. This interpretation of the private study/research defence is now being challenged as being an outdated view of education and population demographics namely increasing student populations, increased reading materials, and online resources as compared to 30 years ago. A related issue is the phenomenon of course packs – excerpts of copyright materials copied on behalf of students and distributed to them.

Should universities pay a licence for such copying or should they be allowed to come within the private study/research exception? The WIPO studies on educational exceptions shows that national laws do restrict the liability of educational institutions from civil or criminal offences. Examples of exempted activities include the automatic or transient storage of copyright material on networks for teaching purposes (Australia and the US), and commercial-scale copyright infringement (Australia).[43] Other countries, such as the UK, prescribe strict limits to copying, subjecting institutions to voluntary licensing schemes with collecting societies. In the UK, for instance, the educational licensing scheme, as mandated under the copyright statute, is implemented by one collecting society which claims to represent the joint interests of all authors and publishers and grants a flat licence rate based on the number of full time educational students registered with the institution.[44]

---

[41] For the impact on the Canadian publishing industry, see PWC, Economic Impacts of the Canadian Educational Sector's Fair Dealing Guidelines, 2015; for a contrary view, see *Myth: Fair Use Decimated Educational Publishing in Canada*, Smartcopying — Australian National Copyright Unit on behalf of the Copyright Advisory Groups (Schools and TAFEs), April 2017.

[42] Productivity Commission, *supra* note 39, 180.

[43] Seng, 'Comparative Survey on Different Types of Educational Exceptions' 2009, *supra* note 35; and Seng, Updated Study and Additional Analysis, 2017, *supra* note 35.

[44] UK Copyright Law, s 36. The scheme is implemented by the Copyright Licensing Agency which set the rate at £7.37 (in 2018) per annum based on a complex calculation which takes into account university income and staff. For an example of a licence, see the CLA website https://www.cla.co.uk/higher-education-licence. In relation to course packs in the UK and Australia see: *Sillitoe and Ors v. McGraw-Hill Book Co (UK) Ltd*, [1983] FSR 545 (Ch D); *University of New South Wales v. Moorhouse and Anor*, [1976] RPC 151 (High Court, A'lia); and Suthersanen, *supra* note 7, 585–609, discussing collective

The new Canadian law introduces broader educational exceptions for institutions including: allowing institutions to reproduce works in order to display it; allowing institutions to reproduce, or communicate a work that is available on the internet, for education or training purposes; and allowing libraries to make copies of a work in alternate formats. The Canadian Supreme Court in *Alberta (Education) v. Canadian Copyright Licensing Agency (Access Copyright)* had to consider whether copies made at the teachers' initiative with instructions to students that they read the material were allowed for the purpose of 'research or private study'.[45] Access Copyright represents authors and publishers of printed literary and artistic works. It had proposed a tariff for the reproduction of its repertoire for use in elementary and secondary schools in all the provinces and territories other than Quebec. The Supreme Court held that these activities constituted fair dealing, by introducing new norms within copyright law and re-defining the notion of fair dealing within contemporary educational practices.

First, it approved the concept of 'user's right'. In doing so, the Court elevated the educational defence to a countervailing right – copyright holders can now be perceived to infringe the rights of individual and institutional users. This requires a shift in traditional copyright perspective since the Court must now consider competing and complementary rights and claims. As Vaver has explained: 'User rights are not just loopholes. Both owner rights and user rights should therefore be given the fair and balanced reading that befits remedial legislation.'[46] Secondly, the Court confirmed that the Canadian interpretation of the fair dealing exception differs markedly from the British approach – in light of the fact that fair dealing is a user's right, it must be given a 'large and liberal interpretation', and that 'research' is not limited to non-commercial or private contexts. Thirdly, and this bears some light on the *University of Delhi* decision we discuss below, one should not focus on the geography of classroom instruction when interpreting the concept of 'private study' – students do not necessarily learn in 'splendid isolation', but can be engaged in this with others, and not artificially separated from the teacher's instruction since teachers are there to facilitate the students' research and private study. 'The teacher/copier therefore shares a symbiotic purpose with the student/user who is engaging in research or private study. Instruction and research/ private study are, in the school context, tautological.'[47]

Finally, on the concept of mass copying of excerpts (and to recall the three-step test under the Berne and TRIPS instruments), the Court's view was that buying books for each student was not a realistic substitute as schools usually had original copies of the books. Moreover, mass copying of excerpts did not, in its view, affect the market demand for textbooks. Any fall in sales could be attributable to a number of factors including the longevity of text books, open access and online resources, etc.

---

management within the educational sector and course packs.

[45] *Alberta (Education) v. Canadian Copyright Licensing Agency (Access Copyright)* [2012] 2 SCR 345. *Cf, Canadian Copyright Licensing Agency v. York University*, 2017 FC 669; [2018] 2 FCR 43 (Federal Court, Canada), the decision was not about fair dealing but whether a university must pay royalties pursuant to an interim tariff set by the Copyright Tribunal; it is currently on appeal to the Canadian Supreme Court.

[46] D. Vaver, *Intellectual Property Law* (Irwin Law, 2011), 172.

[47] *Alberta (Education), supra* note 45, paras 22–23, 26–27.

In contrast to Canada, the educational exceptions within Indian copyright law still reflect its provenance in British copyright law. A recent Delhi High Court decision in 2016 has thrown a fresh light on how Indian courts are interpreting the educational defences. In *Oxford University Press et al. v. Rameshwari Photocopy Services and University of Delhi*,[48] the High Court had to determine whether university departments could authorise the creation and distribution of course packs containing photocopied excerpts from copyright-protected works. The Court, at first instance, held in favour of the defendants; the judgment was upheld on appeal to the Division Bench (though remanding the case back to trial on two issues). In summary, the two tribunals held that such course packs fell within the ambit of 'reproduction in the course of instruction' defence.[49] Three significant issues arise.

First, the Delhi court broadened the impact of the teaching exception, which derives from the ethos within Article 10(2), Berne Convention. The University could make multiple copies of copyrighted material for its students in the course of instruction as long as the photocopying itself constituted fair dealing; this was allowed since the photocopying of copyrighted books by individual students, acting separately, would be fair dealing (under a separate provision). Thus, it was immaterial whether the University carried out the photocopying through its employees or outsourced this work to a contractor (in this case the photocopy shop).

Secondly, course packs could not be considered as substitutes for the whole books; neither could the students be regarded as potential customers of the plaintiffs' books since it could not be expected that students would buy all the books. In this sense, the providers of the course packs (the copy shop and the university) could not be called competitors. Part of the rationale is surprising as the courts held that the educational exceptions did not impose any quantitative or qualitative restrictions when a work is being used for educational purposes. Thus, the copy shop could argue that entire textbooks were being photocopied by students/the shop for private study and research.

Finally, the meaning of education was contextualised within the Indian constitutional right of education, and modern teaching methods. It was pointed out that constitutionally, India is a socialist country and as such the appellate court held that education is the foundation on which a progressive and prosperous society can be built. As such, the court continued, the right to education warranted 'the promotion of equitable access to knowledge to all segments of the society, irrespective of their caste, creed and financial position'. Analogous to the Canadian court, the concept of education was defined to be more than 'a relationship in a classroom between one teacher and multiple students'. Thus, since neither the teacher nor the pupils are expected to purchase photocopiers and photocopy the literary work to be used during course of instruction in the class room:

---

[48] *The Chancellor, Masters & Scholars of the University of Oxford and Ors v. Rameshwari Photocopy Services and University of Delhi* (CS(OS) 2439/2012) 16 Sep 2016, Delhi High Court (single judge); 9 December 2016, Delhi High Court (division bench). An appeal was lodged with the Indian Supreme Court but was withdrawn in March 2017.

[49] Indian Copyright Law, s 52(1)(i), allowing the reproduction of any work by 'a teacher or pupil in the course of instruction'.

> Whether the teacher identifies the place and asks the man in question to photocopy the material and pay money for photocopying and then, while handing over the photocopied material to the pupils seek reimbursement or the teacher tells the pupils to get the work photocopied whether individually or collectively, would not matter.

What of the three-step test? The courts were clear. Nothing much turned on these tests within TRIPS Agreement and the Berne Convention as the contents are 'merely directory and have enough leeway for the signatory countries to enact the copyright law in their municipal jurisdiction concerning use of copyrighted works for purposes of dissemination of knowledge'. In other words, the Indian Court felt the international provisions were flexible enough to allow this wide interpretation. Similarly, the Court found case law and precedents from other common law jurisdictions to be of no relevance and of no persuasive value in the Indian context.

Countries which support stronger user rights in relation to educational and scholarly uses usually advocate adopting the US fair use provision *in toto* or at least the underlying ethos of guidelines contoured on the fair use provision. The statutory fair use exception allows any 'fair use of a copyrighted work'. There is an open list of such uses including reproduction for purposes such as 'teaching (including multiple copies for classroom use), scholarship, or research'. As this is an inclusive list, courts have readily allowed other non-listed uses as long as the use in question is 'fair' as determined with reference to the four statutory factors. Of especial importance is the first factor (whether the alleged use is of commercial nature or is for non-profit educational purposes) and the final factor (what is the effect of the alleged use upon the potential market for, or value of, the copyrighted work).[50] It is clear that non-commercial use, especially by educational institutions, will be given much more latitude in making use of copyrighted materials than commercial use of the same materials. And while the courts accept the non-profit educational nature of uses by universities or schools, they frown on '"non-transformative" use, verbatim copying' that served 'the same intrinsic purpose' for which the works were originally published.[51] In addition to this, there is a complex set of non-statutory guidelines as to whether multiple copying for the purposes of classroom teaching comes within the fair use defence.[52] On the other hand, a recent 2018 decision issued by the US 11th Circuit reveals that some courts frown on an overly formalistic and mathematical formula – instead, the four factors have to be evaluated qualitatively, not quantitatively, and should be considered holistically 'in light of the purposes of copyright'.[53]

---

[50] US Copyright Law, s 107; see also Chapter 4.8.

[51] *Princeton University Press v. Mich Document Servs, Inc*, 99 F 3d 1381 (6th Cir, 1996); *cf, Basic Books Inc. v. Kinko's Graphics Corp.* 758 F Supp. 1522 (SDNY 1991); *American Geophysical Union v. Texaco, Inc*, 60 F 3d 913 (2nd Cir, 1995); *National Association of Boards of Pharmacy v. Board of Regents of the University of Georgia*, 633 F 3d 1297 (11th Cir, 2011), holding that the copying of private board exams for a university review did not constitute fair use.

[52] US Copyright Office Guidelines, *Reproduction of Copyrighted Works by Educators and Librarians*, available at http://www.copyright.gov/circs/circ21.pdf.

[53] *Cambridge University Press, Oxford University Press, Inc., Sage Publications, Inc., v. J. L. Albert*, No 12-14676 (11th Cir, 2018).

12.3.3 Parallel imports

National laws usually accept that once a copyright (or any IP protected) work is sold, the initial purchaser may re-sell or otherwise distribute the work (as long as they do not infringe any of the rights). A second-hand market for used goods or lower priced goods is an essential element within a market-based economy especially in relation to lower-priced books or software. The problem arises when the second-hand/resale market is based on: (i) imported goods; and/or (ii) digital goods. From international and trans-national perspectives the issue of access and pricing of educational and cultural materials is exacerbated by the absence of an international exhaustion rule within the TRIPS Agreement, or within many countries' domestic legislation.[54]

There are some exceptions, most notably in Australia, New Zealand and Singapore,[55] and most recently in the US for used textbooks. The Australian Copyright Act allows commercial importation of legitimate copies of books in certain circumstances: for example, books which are not published in Australia within 30 days of their first publication overseas can be imported without the permission of the copyright owner in the literary work or published edition. However, it is lawful to parallel import computer programs, electronic books and musical items.[56] New Zealand has adopted the international exhaustion principle and any person can 'import' into New Zealand any object that was 'made by or with the consent of' the copyright owner.[57]

In the US, the first sale doctrine had always been applied nationally until 2013. In *Kirtsaeng v. Wiley*, the Supreme Court expressly applied the US 'first sale' doctrine to authorised foreign sales of US copyrighted works (sold anywhere in the world). In this landmark decision, the Supreme Court endorsed the policy of international exhaustion of copyright goods stating that in its opinion, a non-geographical interpretation of the 'first sale' doctrine was the right approach as it would not threaten ordinary scholarly, artistic, commercial, and consumer activities.[58] However, many of the laws and decisions in relation to international exhaustion may not have any relevance in the context of digital goods, including software and e-books (see Chapter 4.6.3).

---

[54] TRIPS Agreement, Art 6, confirming that the Agreement does not cover the issue of exhaustion. For the basic discussion on exhaustion of rights, see Chapter 4. Also see F.M. Abbott, 'Parallel Importation: Economic and Social Welfare Dimensions', a report for the Swiss Agency for Development and Cooperation – IISD, 2007, available at https://www.iisd.org/pdf/2007/parallel_importation.pdf; P. Mysoor, 'Exhaustion, Non-Exhaustion and Implied Licence' (2018) 49 *IIC* 656.

[55] Singapore Copyright Act 1987, ss 32, 40A, 116A, 261(C)(10), the general thrust is that importation of an article into Singapore is allowed if the making of the article is authorised by the copyright owner; exhaustion of the distribution right applies to all lawfully manufactured works sold anywhere in the world.

[56] Australian Copyright Law, ss 44A, 44E and 44F.

[57] New Zealand Copyright Act 1994, ss 5(A), 12(3)(b).

[58] *Kirtsaeng v. John Wiley & Sons, Inc*, 133 S Ct 1351 (2013) (United States); D. Tseng, 'Bypassed: The Kirtsaeng Decision's Underwhelming Impact on Exhaustion' (2015) 43(4) *AIPLA Q J* 559. See also discussion in Chapter 4.6.3.

12.4 DIGITISATION AND ORPHAN WORKS

Research and cultural heritage institutions involved in research, archival, data mining, preservation and access activities have complained that one of the greatest impediments to their digital activities involve 'orphan works' and/or 'out-of-commerce' works. This is due to the fact that the copyright status of works in heritage institutions (including printed literature, visual works, photographs, recordings, films and other ephemera which reflect humanity's culture and history), is unclear due to an inability to identify or locate the copyright owner. This has led to the fear that some of these works may not be available for public access due to the magnitude of research required to obtain copyright clearance of such works. An institution may persevere with its digitisation and access activities despite the lack of copyright clearance or licence arrangements, but then a correlated issue occurs – the copyright owners or their representatives and heirs may subsequently reappear and claim substantial damages or licensing fees for continued usage of the work. Indeed, the *Google Book Search* decision in the US demonstrates that failure of rights clearance for large-scale digitisation projects is difficult, and can lead to prolonged litigation.[59] On the other hand, there is a justified concern from authors that the notion of cultural rights, with the accompanying rhetoric as to the need to access all forms of intangible heritage, is being employed in order to make free and uncompensated use of copyright works. In particular, professional photographers are concerned as to the current digitisation practices of commercial institutions whereby their visual works are digitised with the identifying information (metadata) removed in order that the work can be presented as owned by an unauthorised seller.

12.4.1 EU law on orphan works, out-of-commerce works and text/data mining

The EU published its Directive on use of orphan works by cultural heritage institutions in 2012.[60] Several EU members have incorporated the Directive into their national laws, albeit in slightly varying ways. Italy and Ireland, for example, have introduced cultural exceptions in accordance with the Directive, while the UK has not only adopted the EU cultural and heritage exceptions but has also introduced in parallel a central licensing scheme. Legislative activity continues and the EU's recently adopted Directive on Copyright in the Digital Single Market now offers a licensing framework allowing cultural heritage institutions to digitally reproduce and disseminate their collections, including in-copyright/out-of-commerce works.[61]

---

[59] U. Suthersanen, 'Property and Culture: A Case Study on Orphan Works' (2017) XXII *Art, Antiquity and Law* 172–91.

[60] Directive 2012/28/EU of the European Parliament and of the Council of 25 Oct. 2012 on certain permitted uses of orphan works, OJ L299/5 (EU Orphan Works Directive). For a detailed commentary, see U. Suthersanen and M.M. Frabboni, 'The EU Directive on Orphan Works', in I. Stamatoudi and P. Torremans (eds), *EU Copyright Law* (Cheltenham: Edward Elgar Publishing, 2015), Chapter 13.

[61] *Decreto Legislativo*, 10 Nov. 2014, No 163, *tuazione della direttiva europea 2012/28/UE su taluni utilizzi consentiti di opere orfane* (14G00179) (GU Serie Generale n. 261 del 10-11-2014) (Italy); Certain Permitted Uses of Orphan Works Regulations 2014 (Ireland); Copyright and Rights in Performances (Licensing of Orphan Works) Regulations 2014

The 2012 EU Directive indicates one manner in which cultural heritage institutions digitise and allow access in a cross-border context. The Directive establishes the conditions under which the orphan work status can be declared throughout the EU region, and the limited cultural heritage exception permitting the use of orphan works. Only a limited class of beneficiaries are allowed to avail themselves of the exception, namely publicly accessible cultural heritage institutions, established within the EU, and with a public interest mission. It is presumed that the exception applies to both private and public cultural institutions which are publicly accessible, as long as activities are made in the pursuit of the organisation's public-interest mission namely: use for the purpose of indexing, cataloguing, preservation or restoration; or preservation, restoration and cultural and educational access to works and phonograms.

An orphan work is defined as a work, which is presumed to be a protected work because right holders of that work either cannot be identified or located. A work can only be classified as an orphan work after a potential user fulfils the criteria of diligent search and recordation.[62] The Directive applies to five types of orphan works: writings; films; sound recordings; broadcasts; and embedded protected works/subject matter. Intriguingly, artistic works especially stand-alone photographs and visual images are specifically excluded.[63] National laws are free to extend the exceptions to other types of cultural institutions as well as to embrace all types of orphan works. Once a work or phonogram is classified as being an orphan work, the beneficiary institutions can reproduce, i.e., digitalise the work, and make available such works.[64] The orphan works heritage exception sanctions the generation of revenues from the use of orphan works by cultural heritage institutions but only for the exclusive purpose of underwriting the expenses of digitisation and communication of the orphan works to the public.

In relation to out-of-commerce works, the 2019 Directive provides that cultural heritage institutions should be allowed to make available, for non-commercial purposes, out-of-commerce works that are permanently in their collections, as long as there is authorial attribution and the availability is made on non-commercial websites. Finally, the 2019 Directive also introduces mandatory exceptions allowing research organisations and cultural heritage institutions to reproduce and extract (but not distribute) a copyright work for the 'purposes of scientific research, text and data mining'.[65]

12.4.2 US fair use and Google

The 2006 US Copyright Office report recommended that legislation be introduced to allow good faith users of copyright works use of the works. This was based on three salient elements: potential

(United Kingdom); Art 8, Directive (EU/2019/790) on copyright and related rights in the Digital Single Market, OJ L 130/92.

[62] EU Orphan Works Directive, Arts 2 and 3.

[63] Ibid., Arts 1 and 10.

[64] EU InfoSoc Copyright Directive, Arts 2–4.

[65] EU Copyright in the Digital Single Market Directive, Arts 3–4, 6 and 8. The provisions also urge countries to adopt extended collective licensing as a means of concluding licences on behalf of authors and rights owners, though this has not been made a mandatory provision (Art 8(1)).

users must have, prior to the commencement of the infringement, performed a good faith, reasonably diligent search to locate the owner of the infringed copyright; throughout the course of
the infringement, provided attribution to the author and copyright owner of the work, if possible
and as appropriate under the circumstances; there would be a closed list of remedies that would
be available if the relevent author turns up and if the user proves that he conducted a reasonably
diligent search.[66] Despite several draft pieces of legislation, there has been no further action to push
the bills through.[67]

With the recent decision by the Court of Appeal on Google's mass-digitisation activities, it appears that fair use is the only sanctioned manner in the US to address the orphan works issue.[68]
Google had scanned more than 20 million books, by invitation from major libraries all over the
world, thus moving entire book collections from the analogue to the digital environment. The
works comprised both public domain and copyright works, with a vast majority of books being
non-fiction, out-of-commerce and probably orphan works. Participating libraries received digital
copies of the works, and Google created a digital corpus which enabled all sorts of searches including snippet views of copyright works, full text views of public domain books, text and data mining.
During the ten-year litigation, two separate solutions ensued. First, a settlement agreement was
concluded between Google and the publishing industry; secondly, the authors' group's suit against
Google was resolved in favour of the latter under the fair use doctrine.

The rationale for allowing Google's activities to come within the fair use defence was based on
the following factors, which may be useful for other jurisdictions which have recently adopted
the US 'fair use' approach, and are considering employing this.[69] First, the constitutional basis
of US copyright law directs that the 'ultimate, primary intended beneficiary is the public, whose
access to knowledge copyright seeks to advance by providing rewards for authorship'.[70] Secondly,
the Court's view was that the digitisation activities, coupled with the search function, constituted
transformative activities as they transformed the library's collection into a searchable data corpus.
Thirdly, the digitisation activities also augmented public knowledge by making available information about the plaintiffs' books without necessarily substituting the works, and prejudicing copyright (if any) in the works (original, or derivates of them).

---

[66] An amendment is recommended to s 514 – US Copyright Office Report 2006, 127; this continues to be the view of the
Copyright Office – see *Orphan Works and Mass Digitization: A Report of the Register of Copyrights in June 2015*, US Copyright
Office Report 2015, 3.

[67] Shawn Bentley Orphan Works Act of 2008, S. 2913, 110th Cong. (2008); the Orphan Works Act of 2008, H.R. 5889,
110th Cong. (2008); and the Orphan Works Act of 2006, H.R. 5439, 109th Cong. (2006).

[68] *Authors Guild v. Google Inc*, 804 F 3d 202 (2d Cir, 2015); *Authors Guild, Inc. v. HathiTrust*, 755 F 3d 87, 104 (2d Cir, 2014).

[69] Common law jurisdictions such as Israel and Singapore, which traditionally follow the British 'fair dealing' approach,
have recently amended their laws to allow courts to adopt the more liberal 'fair use' perspective – see, for example,
Singapore Copyright Act, s 35. The Australian Law Reform Commission has also recommended that its fair dealing
exception be replaced by the US fair use exception. (Australian Productivity Commission – Intellectual Property
Arrangements, draft report April 2016, p.16, available at http://www.pc.gov.au/inquiries/completed/intellectual-
property#report.

[70] *Authors Guild v. Google Inc*, 804 F 3d 202 (2d Cir, 2015), p. 12.

There are two noticeable elements in this decision. The first concerns the broad and generous interpretation of the fair use defence, extending to equate the digitisation-plus-search-function as a transformative activity. It is arguable that the act of digitisation is akin to translation, and that new digital platforms for viewing, searching and downloading such digital collections are modern-day versions of importers, book stores, retailers, etc. In other words, a new public has been introduced to a new derivative version of an existing work. And this leads to the second element of the *Google* decision namely the reinforced judicial policy emphasising that US copyright law is primarily intended for the public.

13
Health

The relationship between intellectual property and health is complex and constantly changes in response to numerous factors within and outside the law. These factors include legislative reform, court judgments, new business models, advances in science and technology, and new market conditions. As far as biomedicine goes, patentability issues have never been more complicated or challenging than they are today and the law appears to be unsettled, especially in the US. At international level, despite considerable diplomatic effort to improve matters, the challenge of how to promote innovation in health while enhancing public access to life-saving medicines remains not fully resolved and perhaps can never be as long as IP law is looked to as the solution to both promoting innovation and access.

This chapter starts by setting out a number of trends which provide a contextual basis for understanding how and why IP law is accommodating biomedical innovation, and the difficulties the law faces in doing so. The next part of the chapter explains the relationship between health and intellectual property, focusing mainly on the relevant international trade rules, the law in Europe and North America and some illustrative cases in different jurisdictions. It takes into account the five phenomena briefly introduced in the first part and shows their impacts on IPRs. The final section addresses the issue of access to medicines. This became especially controversial following the TRIPS Agreement and the public health situation in developing countries including the HIV/AIDS crisis, as well as ongoing concerns about diseases for which treatments do not exist because they mainly affect the poor and thus make it difficult for industry to makes profits out of selling treatments for them. However, in the past few years, due to the extremely high prices of certain valuable drugs that have recently been approved,[1] and in some cases old drugs too,[2] access to medicines has also attracted concern in the developed countries.

13.1 NEW TRENDS AFFECTING INTELLECTUAL PROPERTY AND HEALTH

To understand the dynamic nature of the relationships between health, innovation and the law it is necessary to take account of five major drivers of change. These drivers are not all new but their prominence has become more noticeable since the beginning of the modern health biotechnology era in the early 1980s, a time when the pharmaceutical industry was in the midst of a slump with fewer genuinely original drug products entering the market than in the 'Golden Age' of the 1960s and 70s. These are internationalisation, complexification, personalisation, digitalisation, and fragmentation. These all require explanation, as follows.

13.1.1 Internationalisation

By internationalisation, we mean a number of things. First, abilities to invest, innovate and purchase are spreading geographically. Emerging economies such as China and recently-developed ones like Singapore and South Korea are either producing health innovations of the kind they were not doing earlier, or are making large investments in the life sciences that will bear fruit sooner or later. This expansion in the geography of expertise and investment has entailed an increase in international research and commercial collaborations. Growing prosperity in these countries means also that the number of consumers of health products due to increased health spending and enhanced purchasing power has risen worldwide. Both phenomena have vastly increased the interest of pharmaceutical companies in the IP rules of other countries, especially those nations that are markets, or potential markets, for their products – or which are large producers and exporters of generic drugs such as India.

Second, the disease profiles of many developing countries are becoming more similar to those of the developed countries. This is not just because wealthier people anywhere in the world live

---

[1] For example, certain cancer treatments that are highly effective but for quite a limited number of patients, for example, the breast cancer drug Kadcyla.

[2] N.P. Tallapragada, 'Off-Patent Drugs at Brand-name Prices: A Puzzle for Policymakers' (2016) 3(1) *Journal of Law and the Biosciences* 238.

longer than the poor, and diseases that tend to affect the elderly most are broadly similar everywhere: non-communicable ones like cancer, cardio-vascular diseases, Alzheimer's, etc. It is also because there is a certain amount of uniformity in the lifestyles including diets of people having similar levels of income and purchasing power wherever they happen to live. As people get richer, for example, they tend to consume more meat products and processed foods. Quite a lot of these may be poor quality 'junk food'. This means diseases affecting people are also becoming more and more the same wherever they live. This prospect for industry of the global similarity of disease profiles and life expectancies with their attendant market and economies of scale opportunities appears to be quite new. You have to go back to before the end of the nineteenth century to return to such a situation. This was a time when populations in Western Europe and North America became much wealthier than in the rest of the world, and public health and hygiene had improved dramatically leading to a big fall in outbreaks of infectious disease that were continuing to decimate populations in other parts of the world. Admittedly, tropical disease research institutes were being set up in Europe then to find cures for diseases affecting people in the colonies but not in Europe, but these were mostly for the benefit of settlers and expatriates.

Of course we are talking about trends and there is no suggestion that even in the more successful developing countries, health problems, many of which are avoidable, do not continue to affect many people that even the least wealthy Europeans and North Americans need no longer fear. This explains current interest in the issue of neglected diseases. Moreover, Africa remains an exception to this generalisation about disease profiles, as do failing states and other war-torn countries elsewhere.

Admittedly, the adoption of unhealthy diets from other countries is not just due to prosperity, but also effective marketing and sheer convenience, cheapness and ubiquity. Hundreds of millions of people around the world can afford a regular cheeseburger. For example, Mexico is experiencing an explosion in diabetes incidences.[3] This has coincided with the increased consumption of fast food instead of more balanced and nutritious diets having fewer carbohydrates. Again, this is potentially quite advantageous for the pharmaceutical industry. Finally, as the industry increasingly looks to the world as a whole for potential consumers and faces local firms whose ability to copy can, in some countries at least, be quite sophisticated, it becomes ever more assertive about being able to avail itself of IP protection in every market it seeks to enter.

This leads us to the third aspect of internationalisation: the globalisation of IP rules relating to medicines. Since the mid-1990s, most countries have been held to a somewhat uniform set of intellectual property standards prescribed by the World Trade Organization's TRIPS Agreement. Previously, the countries of the world were pretty much free to provide intellectual property protection for medicines as they desired: a lot of protection, a little, or none. This is no longer the case. This has led to criticism that access to medicines, especially in the developing countries, has been hindered by these uniform standards which are largely transplanted from the developed countries into the developing ones albeit typically without the public health safeguards that balance out the otherwise strong protection.

---

[3] J.A. Rull et al., 'Epidemiology of Type 2 Diabetes in Mexico' (2005) 36(3) *Archives of Medical Research* 188.

13.1.2 Complexity

Complexity explains personalisation, digitalisation and fragmentation. It also has great implications for how businesses acquire and manage IPRs. A trend towards further complexity is evident in a number of ways, beyond the adage that the more one knows about something, the more one realises how much more there is out there that we do not or cannot know – true as that is. For one thing, understanding at the molecular level of specific malfunctions which lead to disease has increased dramatically, for example, in cancer. But this does not lead automatically to cures. Indeed, insights into disease causation are the start and not the end of a journey that may be long indeed. The likelihood is that it will engage the expertise of many individuals from numerous disciplinary fields not all of whom are likely to be working in the same laboratory, company or place of employment. There is still room for individual brilliance but teamwork (or better said teamswork because there may be many teams involved) is all. Innovation has always been primarily collective, even if certain individuals may stand out for making decisive contributions, but it is especially so in the life sciences of the present day.

One interesting aspect of our enhanced understanding of how cellular malfunctions lead to disease is that some disease categories are fragmenting so that out of what was once considered a single disease arise several or many diseases. And out of one patient population sharing the same disease and being given the same treatment there may become several patient populations being treated for different, albeit closely related, diseases; or even patient sub-populations forming a larger population all having the same diseases but who need to be given either a completely different treatment, or a different dose or formulation of the same one.

This latter observation leads to another form of complexification: the differences between people having the same disease in terms of how they respond to the same treatment. Human bodies are complex enough even before we look into individual human variation. Investigating the latter alone has cost vast amounts of money and generated staggering amounts of data out of which bioinformaticians and others strive to glean patterns, connections and insights that can contribute to better healthcare. But we have a long way to go. It is well-known that a powerful drug in a particular dosage can cure one person with minor or no side-effects, whereas the same dosage may not work on another person, cause harmful side-effects, or even endanger a patient's life. Being able to accurately predict how an individual will respond to a drug treatment and what the optimal mode of delivery should be for that person is very important, but it requires further research including the gathering of data big enough in volume and breadth of coverage to generate findings enabling precise and individualised treatment including the discovery of biomarkers. 'Personalised medicine':

> Refers to the tailoring of medical treatment to the individual characteristics of each patient; to classify individuals into subpopulations that differ in their susceptibility to a particular disease or their response to a specific treatment so that preventive or therapeutic interventions can then be concentrated on those who will benefit, sparing expense and side effects for those who will not.[4]

---

[4] President's Council of Advisors on Science and Technology, 'Priorities for Personalized Medicine', Executive Office

The word 'biomarker' is increasingly part of the lexicon of modern medical research including personalised medicine, denoting 'a broad subcategory of medical signs – that is, objective indications of medical state observed from outside the patient – which can be measured accurately and reproducibly'.[5] It is a somewhat broad term. Traditional physiological biomarkers include blood pressure and pulse rate, but nowadays the most valuable ones to discover (and patent) are molecular including proteins, metabolites and genes sequences. Why are biomarkers so useful medically especially in relation to complex diseases?

> Biomarkers and molecular individualized medicine are replacing the traditional 'one size fits all' medicine […] The essence of personalized oncology lies in the use of biomarkers […] Three different types of biomarkers are of particular importance: predictive, prognostic and early response […] Molecular diagnostics identify individual cancer patients who are more likely to respond positively to targeted chemotherapies. Molecular diagnostics include testing for genes, gene expression, proteins and metabolites.[6]

In this context it is worth noting that some 4,000 diseases are associated with single-gene defects. These include cystic fibrosis and sickle-cell disorder. Additionally, numerous health disorders have polygenic (involving more than one gene) and multifactorial causes in which genes, lifestyle and environment are involved. These include diabetes, heart disease, cancers and hypertension. Digitally recorded genetic and other molecular information acquired from large numbers of people, especially when combined with other information and information sources (lifestyle, demographic, medical history as found in electronic health records, etc.), can provide not only a massive volume of health-related data for analysis, but also a diversity in the kinds of information we can derive, from responsiveness to drugs, to likelihood of contracting a particular disease, and ways to prevent or reduce risk of certain diseases later in life. No doubt both volume and variety stand to increase tremendously in the coming years. Due to personalisation and to the sheer amount of molecular data being generated, modern day healthcare is becoming increasingly information intensive including at the personal level:

> The patient is an enormous repository of information that needs to be harvested as a partnership not only in clinical care but in discovery […] The ability to stratify the phenotypic expression of wellness and disease will ultimately lead to better validation of human therapeutic targets for drug discovery.[7]

Much of this data is of course collected, stored and analysed in digital form. The role of the drug is still quite central to a great deal of patient care. But prescribing a drug with a generalised instruction as to how much to take and when, except for minor ailments like colds, is becoming

---

of the President of the United States, 2008. Quoted in M. Kalia, 'Personalized Oncology: Recent Advances and Future Challenges' (2013) 62 *Metabolism* S11.

[5] K. Strimbu and J.A. Tavel, 'What are Biomarkers?' (2010) 5(6) *Current Opinion in HIV and AIDS* 463.

[6] Kalia, *supra* note 4.

[7] E. Elenco, L. Underwood and D. Zohar, 'Defining Digital Medicine' (2015) 33(5) *Nature Biotechnology* 460, 461.

insufficient. It is not just healthcare in the broad sense that is moving on to computer screens; medicine is becoming digital as much as it is chemical, especially when treatment concerns itself more and more with disease prediction, diagnosis, prognosis, and monitoring of sickness, health and treatment effects and side-effects, and of course with personalisation. Personalised medicine is frequently held to be a very promising development that could dramatically enhance the health of millions of people. However, doubts remain that the anticipated transformative effects of personalised medicine on healthcare will all come to pass.[8] Moreover, not all of this turn to big data is convenient for industry; for example, it might reveal links between a commercially successful drug and health risks for some people that would otherwise be very hard to detect. This could result in a shrinkage of the product's patient base, and even the withdrawal of the product.

A third area of complexification is in relation to the drug itself. Until quite recently drugs were almost by definition small molecule products. Historically, these were typically isolated plant metabolites or microbial products, or synthetic versions, perhaps with modifications, made in a lab. Others were synthetic without being modelled on ones found in nature. There were also animal products such as hormones. In recent decades there has been a big growth in biopharmaceuticals (or 'biologics') including therapeutic proteins like insulin, erythropoietin, and various monoclonal antibodies (MAbs). These now make up about one-quarter of global pharmaceutical sales. These cannot be synthesised and are produced in living organisms, initially bacteria, or cells including mammalian cells. This is because MAbs are very large complex chemicals and can only be made in eukaryotic cells, typically in those of Chinese hamster ovaries (CHO cells).[9] The processes used to make them are immensely challenging. CHO cells take a long time to create and prepare for production, and yields are quite low. To accurately and consistently mass-produce these large molecule products with a minimum of variability between batches, avoiding contamination, and without so-called post-translational modifications such as glycosylation, which can potentially drastically change the behaviour of the protein when it enters the body, is technically difficult and expensive. The manufacturing process itself is absolutely critical to what comes out at the end, and an originator company will certainly not disclose all of the details in a patent specification. As for making copies of such drugs, regulators struggled for a long time to find a way to approve generic versions which can never be considered to be exact reproductions as is possible with the active ingredients of small molecule drugs. So called biosimilars have now been approved in some countries.[10] Given the tremendous technical difficulties and enormous cost of manufacturing

---

[8] M.J. Joyner and N. Paneth, 'Seven Questions for Personalized Medicine' (2015) 314(10) *Journal of the American Medical Association* 999–1000.

[9] The first product to be manufactured this way was Genentech's plasminogen, Advase, in 1987. It has been suggested that microbial eukaryotes such as fungi are also suitable and may prove to be superior to CHO cells for some biologics in terms of production costs, expression yields, and quality. M. Emalfarb, 'The CHO's Over: An Inflexion Point' (2018) 45 *Medicine Maker* 20. Algae are also considered promising candidates – A. Dahl, 'Algal Boom' (2018) 40 *Medicine Maker* 20.

[10] The European Medicines Agency has been publishing its regularly updated biosimilars guidelines since 2005. The US was slow to start approving biosimilar, despite passage of the Biologics Price Competition and Innovation (BPCI) Act, 2010, the first biosimilar was not approved in that country until 2015 when the FDA allowed Sandoz's product Zarxio, which is similar to the reference product Neupogen. It is important to note that under the legislation 'similar' is not

biosimilars and of getting marketing approval,[11] there is quite a small number on the market thus far, although we must of course take into account that the first biologics only became available in the 1980s.[12] The substantial added time, expense and risk as compared to small molecule generics makes it enormously difficult for any firm other than a large generics or research-based business to enter this growing market.[13]

13.1.3 Fragmentation

The driver we leave to last in this opening section of the chapter is fragmentation. But this is not to understate its importance for intellectual property. Fragmentation follows from the point made earlier that the discovery and development of drugs and other health products such as vaccines and diagnostic tests increasingly require the expertise of numerous individual scientists and teams having quite diverse disciplinary backgrounds that are unlikely to be found under the same roof. Indeed, they may be spread across countries and continents and work in companies, universities, hospitals, government health research institutes, and health charities. Apart from these entities, organised patient groups are sometimes actively engaged in the search for new treatments as well. These are likely to have different missions, interests, and ways of getting their work funded. And increasingly, the private sector side contains not just the traditional giants ('Big Pharma') but highly specialised small firms, often spun out of universities who have useful services and possibly quite unique skills to offer, and perhaps a few highly valuable patents, but who have no products at all to sell. Building networks

---

the same as 'interchangeable', which requires further successful clinical studies. An interchangeable product may be substituted for the reference product even where the doctor prescribes the reference product.

[11] As compared to small molecule generics, proving equivalence with biosimilars is far more difficult.

> Developing a biopharmaceutical is incredibly challenging [...] The difficulty comes in ensuring that your biosimilar has the same protein and glycosylation profile as the originator drug, within specified limits. In this regard, the innovator company perhaps had the easy job – they made the drug and showed that it was safe and non-toxic.

P. Rudd, 'The Science of Sugar: Lessons Learned with Pauline Rudd' (2016) 22 *Medicine Maker* 52, 54. The possibility of developing enhanced versions ('biobetters') is one that the regulatory system does not encourage because of the likelihood that clinical trials would need to be undertaken prior to grant of marketing approval. Also, see R. Abbas, I.A. Jacobs, E.C. Li and D. Yin, 'Considerations in the Early Development of Biosimilar Products' (2015) 20(2) *Drug Discovery Today* 1; G.-B. Kresse, 'Biosimilars – Science, Status, and Strategic Perspective' (2009) 72 *European Journal of Pharmaceutics and Biopharmaceutics* 479.

[12] S. Smith Hughes, *Genentech: The Beginnings of Biotech* (Chicago University Press, 2011); N. Rasmussen, *Gene Jockeys: Life Science and the Rise of Biotech Enterprise* (Johns Hopkins University Press, 2014); W. Hoffman and L. Furcht, *The Biologist's Imagination: Innovation in the Biosciences* (Oxford University Press, 2014).

[13] 'Development of a biosimilar has been estimated to take 7–8 years and to cost between $100–250 million; in contrast, a small-molecule generic takes just 3–5 years and costs $1–4'. L. von Hertzen, 'Surveying the Biologic Patent Battleground' (2016) 22 *The Medicine Maker* 70. One proposal for accelerating and enhancing price-reducing competition is to require that the original biologic's cell-line be deposited as a condition for marketing approval. L. Diependaele, J. Cockbain and S. Sterckx, 'Similar or the Same? Why Biosimilars are not the Solution' (2018) 46(3) *Journal of Law, Medicine and Ethics* 776.

that satisfy all parties is no easy task. IPRs can help or get in the way, depending on who acquires them and how they are managed. The aggressive assertion of rights can be highly divisive and counter-productive in terms of stimulating innovation and ensuring that products are made available to all of those who need them and under fair terms and conditions. This in turn raises questions about the imperative to maximise taxpayer value (as opposed just to shareholder value) where much of the work is government supported, and the availability of public interest safeguards in patent law.

There is much talk in this context nowadays about 'open innovation'.[14] According to proponents of the concept, business sectors whose firms typically tried to do everything in-house, and were thus practicing 'closed innovation' are now collaborating with others, sharing each other's knowledge and materials in the hope that by widening participation in this way, the speed of innovation will go up. The life science industries appear to be embracing the concept. One must be cautious about the significance of this apparent turn to openness. First, to suggest that pharmaceutical innovation was closed in the past but is finally now opening up is inaccurate. There is no closed versus open dichotomy, at least in this industry. University scientists and drug companies have collaborated as far back as the nineteenth century, and at no time was this ever abnormal, although it has often been controversial. Furthermore, one must be careful not to equate the 'open' in open innovation with absence of intellectual property. There is no reduction in patent filing. Nonetheless, it is true that the industry is becoming more pro-active and strategic about research networking and knowledge management. Whether 'open innovation' is an accurate label for the various practices they are adopting in order to further such collaborating is a matter for debate.

The discussion so far in this chapter suggests that medical science innovation is multifaceted and diverse in terms of what is being done, who is doing it and where, and it is constantly evolving. As for patenting, the subject matter of what is nowadays being claimed is hugely challenging and not necessarily easy to accommodate within the traditional product, process, and use claim categories, nor to justify in view of the function of the patent system to promote invention in the public interest.

13.2 HEALTH INTELLECTUAL PROPERTY: LAW AND PRACTICE

The pharmaceutical industry discovers or copies, develops, makes and sells pharmaceutical products, primarily drugs and vaccines. A drug is a chemical, or a mixture, that reacts with the human body to cause a therapeutic effect. A modern drug typically works by binding to a protein such as an enzyme or receptor and inducing, modifying or disrupting chemical activity in human or foreign cells (in the case of infectious diseases). It may produce harmful side-effects unexpected even after years of testing. Nowadays, as mentioned, some pharmaceuticals are proteins (such as, insulin, monoclonal antibodies, etc.).

The industry is often considered as the one that is most dependent on the patent system. This is due to two main factors. The first concerns research and development. The costs are very high,

---

[14] H.W. Chesbrough, *Open Innovation: The New Imperative for Creating and Profiting from Technology* (Harvard Business School Press, 2003).

and while there is much debate about the average costs, getting new drugs to market is undeniably an expensive and risky business that few companies can afford. To make things worse there is much uncertainty, and lots of money is lost to failures: drugs that turn out after clinical trials not to be effective or safe enough to be approved or that get approved but do not make enough money to recoup the research, development and marketing costs. The second is that drugs can be copied by those with the requisite technical skill, equipment and resources. Upfront costs may be quite significant, but the marginal cost of making such copied drugs tends to be very low. This would enable copiers, absent a patent law, to sell their versions at low cost and still make a profit due to not having to pay the research and development costs. Whether our health would be better or worse without a patent system is a fascinating question that would be difficult to answer. What we can say with a degree of confidence is that the industry would be very different without a patent law, and it would probably be less innovative absent any alternative system to reward innovation such as funding schemes including those proposed to break the link between research and development costs and price.

But bear in mind that all innovations are not equal in quality or in terms of human welfare and the patent law does not discriminate: a new and useful coffee lid is inherently just as patentable as a new drug that saves thousands of lives and receives the same degree of monopoly protection, as is a new painkiller different chemically from aspirin but no more potent or effective. Obviously, industry patents what it thinks it can make money from. Patents offer little in the way of additional incentive to develop an important medicine that would benefit only a small number of very poor people. They will not create a market if the target users have no ability to pay. We need to think also about the types of innovation the patent system is, or is not, incentivising and whether the system serves the public interest as well as it should, while bearing in mind that the patent system can never be perfect even with a better balance between legal monopoly and public interest safeguards. We also need to come up with additional reward or research and development financing mechanisms outside the patent system that would not lead to monopoly pricing, a problem affecting not just the developing countries but the whole world. A number of proposals have been put forward including by James Love and Tim Hubbard,[15] Thomas Pogge and Aiden Hollis,[16] and these and others favouring systems that delink price from research and development costs.[17] These are all very worthy of closer investigations, especially delinkage.

---

[15] T. Hubbard and J. Love, 'A New Trade Framework for Global Healthcare R&D' (2004) 2(2) PLoS Biol. e52.

[16] A. Hollis and T. Pogge, 'The Health Impact Fund: Making New Medicines Accessible for All', Report for Incentives for Global Health, 2008. For a criticism of the HIF proposal, see H. Van den Belt and M. Korthals, 'The International Patent System and the Ethics of Global Justice', in S. Arapostathis and G. Dutfield (eds), Knowledge Management and Intellectual Property: Concepts, Actors and Practices from the Past to the Present, (Cheltenham: Edward Elgar Publishing, 2013), 235–51.

[17] C. Clift et al., 'Towards a New Global Business Model for Antibiotics: Delinking Revenues from Sales. Report from the Chatham House Working Group on New Antibiotic Business Models', Royal Institute of International Affairs, 2015; UNITAID, 'An Economic Perspective on Delinking the Cost of R&D from the Price of Medicines', Discussion paper prepared by James Love, WHO, 2016; United Nations Secretary-General's High Level Panel on Access to Medicines, 'Promoting Innovation and Access to Health Technologies', 2016.

13.2.1 Health in the TRIPS Agreement

The TRIPS Agreement makes only two references to health. The first of these is of special importance because it appears in the article on principles of the Agreement. Thus, Article 8.1 states that members may 'adopt measures necessary to protect public health and nutrition' provided that such measures are consistent with the Agreement. Some WTO members have sought to understate the legal power of this provision, as if principles expressed in a public international legal instrument are merely vague expressions of goodwill as opposed to binding obligations, rights or immunities that a treaty party must put into effect or may utilise taking into account other norms of international law such as the human right to health. This does not seem to be legally correct, at least if it precludes WTO members from the freedom to interpret the TRIPS Agreement in a flexible manner using this principle for interpretative guidance as well as related rules of international law, and in compliance with the Vienna Convention on the Law of Treaties (see Chapters 3 and 11).[18]

The other mention of the word health is in relation to patentable subject matter in Article 27.2, TRIPS that allows WTO members to prohibit the patenting of inventions whose commercial exploitation must be prevented 'to protect *ordre public* or morality, including to protect human, animal or plant life or health or to avoid serious prejudice to the environment'. The morality/*ordre public* exclusion clause, which was borrowed from the European Patent Convention, is discussed in Chapters 5 and 14.

However, TRIPS' implications for health may be greatest in provisions which do not mention the word. Above all, Article 27.1 states that 'patents shall be available for any inventions, whether products or processes, in all fields of technology, provided that they are new, involve an inventive step and are capable of industrial application'. This is quite a radical measure but it reflects the strong desire of the innovator branch of the pharmaceutical industry to use international trade law to constrain generic competition internationally. Up to the time the WTO was established drugs were unpatentable in numerous countries. Even in Europe, several countries had allowed drugs to be patented only a few years earlier. This measure required all WTO members, albeit with transition periods for developing and least-developed countries, to introduce patent protection for drugs. Article 31 lays out the conditions for use of a patent's subject matter without the holder's authorisation, otherwise known as compulsory licensing and government use. This is discussed in the next section.

Article 39 TRIPS concerns undisclosed information, whose meaning is somewhat broader than that of trade secrets. Paragraph 3 provides for the protection of test data in respect of pharmaceutical and agricultural chemical products that utilise new chemical entities. It must be protected against 'unfair commercial use'. Disclosure of such data is prohibited but may be allowed if necessary to protect the public or if legal protection measures against unfair commercial use are already in place. In justifying such provisions, Article 39.1 refers to Article 10*bis* of the Paris Convention, according to which 'any act of competition contrary to honest practices in industrial or commercial matters constitutes an act of unfair competition'.

---

[18] A. Slade, 'Articles 7 and 8 of the TRIPS Agreement: A Force for Convergence within the International IP System' (2011) 14(6) *Journal of World Intellectual Property* 413.

How countries may give effect to Article 39.3 did not immediately attract heated debate. This is because the vagueness of the TRIPS language appears to allow for broad interpretative freedom. Things changed with the emergence of bilateral and regional trade agreements having health-related IPRs provisions, accompanied by a greater understanding of the economic and social welfare stakes involved.[19] Typically these trade agreements require parties to introduce data exclusivity modelled on US or European standards which provide extended periods of exclusivity – typically at least five years – to the originator of the data during which drug regulators may not use the data to determine whether to approve the marketing of purportedly equivalent products.[20] The provision in TRIPS can be interpreted as not prohibiting regulators from doing this but merely as preventing generic producers from being able to acquire the data through dishonest commercial practices.[21] Needless to say, the US and the EU have been very keen to promote the former interpretation, and they have been quite successful in doing so despite the lack of any global consensus as to what is the correct or most socially optimal way to give effect to Article 39.3.[22]

The pharmaceutical industry, including both originator and generic producers, is also a heavy user of the trade mark system. However, patents merit the biggest coverage in any chapter purporting to explain intellectual property law in relation to health.

13.2.2 Patents and commercial biomedicine

What do pharmaceutical companies patent? Nowadays, it is increasingly simplistic if not erroneous to think merely in terms of product and methods of making claims. What types of product and process claims are we talking about? What about uses? Clearly there is much more to patenting than claiming the active ingredient of a drug and the means by which it is produced. We will go into the specifics, but before doing so one important matter needs to be discussed. Drugs often produce unexpected effects on patients. It might be presumed that all unanticipated side-effects are harmful. This is understandable when we consider that drugs are really poisons. As Paracelsus famously said half a millennium ago, 'all substances are poisons: there is nothing which is not a poison. The right dose differentiates a poison and a remedy'.[23] He is still right. However, medical scientists have long known that the opposite can also be the case: side-effects can be good. A treatment for disease x may turn out to be an excellent treatment for similar diseases y and z, or even for more distantly related (or unrelated) diseases d and h. Viagra is an excellent example of this but there are many others. This is why research continues to be done on old drugs, both

---

[19] O.H. Shaikh, *Access to Medicine Versus Test Data Exclusivity: Safeguarding Flexibilities Under International Law* (Springer Verlag, 2016), 2–3.

[20] UNCTAD-ICTSD, *Resource Book on TRIPS and Development* (Cambridge University Press, 2005), 531.

[21] Ibid.

[22] G.J. Michael, 'International Coercion and the Diffusion of Regulatory Data Protection' (2016) 19(1–2) *Journal of World Intellectual Property* 2.

[23] In the original German: '*Alle Ding sind Gift, und nichts ist ohne Gift; allein die dosis machts, dass ein Ding kein Gift sei.*' Philippus Aureolus Theophrastus Bombastus von Hohenheim (Paracelsus) (1538) *Die dritte Defension wegen des Schreibens der neuen Rezepte*, in *Septem Defensiones 1538*. Werke Bd. 2, Darmstadt, S. 510, 1965.

successful ones and failed ones, that is, natural or synthetic chemicals that were discovered, produced and tested but which failed to work well against drug targets known about at the time. As better knowledge of cell biology, genomics and proteomics increases the number of drug targets, there is a lot of interest in testing known substances against them in the hope of discovering new therapeutic applications. Nowadays this is referred to as drug repurposing.[24] Patent systems in many jurisdictions encourage such research by allowing claims on newly discovered medical uses of old chemical substances. We will look into how such claims are accepted below.

Another phenomenon driving drug repurposing is personalised or stratified medicine, which offers the possibility to save rejected chemicals found to have some therapeutic effects across the whole spectrum of individuals suffering from a particular disease but not enough to justify further development.[25] On the face of it, it seems counter-intuitive that personalised medicine is commercially attractive for industry. If we keep on splitting diseases and stratifying and personalising patients how can the industry make money? Until recently, the industry has made its biggest profits from blockbuster drugs that are prescribed to all (or most) patients having the disease or disorder for which the drug is intended. But if the disease is in fact several diseases and a drug works effectively only against one or two of these and not all sufferers can be given the treatment anyway, the size of the market in terms of the numbers taking the drug will be much smaller. That might suggest it would not be worth developing and selling the drug. In fact, the possibility still exists to make large profits, and the patent system can potentially offer some strong legal protection for reasons that will now be explained, starting with a discussion on the scope of what can be claimed.

For all the reasons given earlier, the pharmaceutical industry has seen a need – and been given the opportunity – to claim a wide diversity of subject matters in their attempts to protect their investments and secure legal monopoly protection with as much comprehensiveness as the law allows.

But before going further we need to consider the potentially negative consequences of a difficult dilemma that the industry faces concerning the timing of patent filings. As is well-known, once a promising discovery has been made, drug companies have a tremendous incentive to file a patent application as soon as possible. Companies may draft broad claims before a full set of data to support them has been obtained. The dangers of later findings of insufficient disclosure or obviousness are acute for all drugs, not least for the highly complex biologics. Recent litigation especially in the UK and validity decisions at the EPO have made manifest that such negative outcomes for patent owners are very much possible. The emerging 'plausibility doctrine' now requires the English courts and EPO boards in validity decisions to assess the credibility of the invention on the basis of the patent disclosure. In practical terms, we cannot expect the invention to be proven to work beyond any doubt. Subsequent marketing approval cannot be the test: seeking approval of a drug for this or that indication is a business decision not a purely scientific one. Neither would it be fair to demand clinical trial evidence.[26] However, there needs within reason to be a certain level of predictability and this must go beyond idle speculation. If the prediction is wrong, or if no

[24] G.M. Cragg et al., 'New Horizons for Old Drugs and Drug Leads' (2014) 77(3) *Journal of Natural Products* 703;

A. Mullard, 'Drug Repurposing Programmes Get Lift Off' (2012) 11 *Nature Reviews Drug Discovery* 1.

[25] M. Allison, 'Is Personalized Medicine Finally Arriving?' (2008) 26(5) *Nature Biotechnology* 509.

[26] *Regeneron Pharmaceuticals Inc. v. Bayer Pharma AG* [2013] EWCA Civ 93.

prediction could reasonably have been made on the basis of the specification, the patent is invalid for insufficiency or obviousness. There are good reasons why it would be unfair to apply hindsight using post-filing-date evidence without restraint. On the other hand, it is not unreasonable to include evidence beyond what was available on the priority date for the purpose of considering obviousness.[27] As regards sufficiency of disclosure in the case of vague claims to medical uses in a patent, later evidence cannot be used to support their plausibility.[28]

13.2.3 'Stretching' the novelty criterion

Determining whether a product is new or not for the purpose of granting or refusing a patent would appear to be a fairly straightforward calculation. But this is far from being the case with medicines. Apart from the fact that the concept of novelty in patent law is in large part a matter of description, specialised knowledge and public availability as opposed to whether the invention had no prior existence in any absolute sense, chemistry does present complications other types of invention do not necessarily share. A coffee lid with a useful slide to unlock mechanism aiding the retention of heat and reducing the risk of the drinker getting scalded while dashing to catch the train is novel if no such device on a coffee lid was known to exist before. The newness of a chemical composition is bound to be a lot less clear-cut and the patent system can apply novelty in a very strict way accommodating some variability or else it can be applied more narrowly. By being strict, the system might demand some additional novelty requirement so that a small or trivial variation is disqualified because it is essentially the same thing as the disclosed or prior art chemical it most closely relates to. This is done in India (see below). If narrow, the system will accommodate only very limited variability: similar but different is different. Take two substances A and B. There is some difference of significance between them notwithstanding that they vary by as little as one being merely purer than the other but otherwise identical, or as one being a racemic mixture comprising both left- and right-handed versions (enantiomers) of the molecule, and the other being one or other of the enantiomers. Either way, A and B can be patented as separate inventions in Europe and in the US. Accordingly, slightly different things are treated as being something else entirely if some new difference of therapeutic or other significance is disclosed (whether or not it is proven). Minor chemical modifications to existing medicaments such as enantiomers, combinations, and minor variants of existing products may well thus be deemed patentable.

Generally, the system has become relaxed about novelty with respect to pharmaceuticals and this of course suits the industry (albeit not the generics producers). Purified versions of existing substances can be patented on either side of the North Atlantic and in other jurisdictions too. There are old precedents for this in the US[29] and in the UK where purified insulin was patented in the 1920s. Selection inventions were discussed in Chapter 5. The door may also be open to the patenting of naturally-occurring drug metabolites which are basically 'made' by the human body (see below).

---

[27] *Generics [UK] Ltd t/a Mylan v. Yeda Research and Development Co Ltd and Anor* [2013] EWCA Civ 925.

[28] T 0609/02 (AP-1 complex/SALT INSTITUTE) of 27.10.2004.

[29] *Parke Davis and Co. v. H.K. Mulford and Co*, 189 Fed 95 (SDNY, 1911) affirmed, 196 Fed 496 (2nd Cir, 1912).

There is of course a difference between the active pharmaceutical ingredient (API) and the drug product in that the tablet (if that is the mode of delivery) contains a mixture of the API and other non-active chemicals called excipients which may perform certain functions such as protecting the API on its journey through the body, controlling its rate of absorption, or enabling more convenient modes of delivery. For example, it may be possible for the same API to be administered in liquid rather than solid form, or can be made to be chewable so it does not have to be swallowed whole. New dosage forms, such as a pill with a known API having a new coating offering some sort of advantage, genuinely therapeutic or otherwise, are patentable.

13.2.4 Interpreting excluded subject matter

European patent law is generally accommodating towards the pharmaceutical industry, arguably excessively so. The industry is highly organised and spends large sums of money on promoting its interests. Notwithstanding its power and influence, there are certain exclusions in terms of methods claims. As we shall see, though, these can largely be circumvented by claiming new or additional uses. There are no such statutory exceptions in the US, although medical practitioners cannot be sued for infringing a patent on a 'medical activity'.[30] EPC Article 53(c) excludes:

> methods for treatment of the human or animal body by surgery or therapy and diagnostic methods practised on the human or animal body; this provision shall not apply to products, in particular substances or compositions, for use in any of these methods.[31]

This is somewhat similar to the allowable exclusions of 'diagnostic, therapeutic and surgical methods for the treatment of humans or animals' in the TRIPS Agreement. The methods for treatments and diagnostic methods exclusions require some explanation in terms of their meaning, purpose and scope of application. Article 53(c)'s underlying policy rationale is to immunise physicians, surgeons and veterinarians from patent infringement suits concerning their adoption of methods.

---

[30] This is a quite limited immunity. Under US Patent Law, s 287 (c)(2)(A) 'the term "medical activity" means the performance of a medical or surgical procedure on a body, but shall not include (i) the use of a patented machine, manufacture, or composition of matter in violation of such patent'.

[31] As Tina Piper shows, the European medical methods exception reflects a compromise between the varied practices and negotiating positions of different countries in Europe which was possible because none 'allowed patents carte-blanche in that area'. Up to that time the UK's exception had evolved quite separately from the rest of Europe 'in dialogue with judges and courts' in Commonwealth countries, initially in Canada, which were especially influential in this regard. However, in time the latter country became more influenced by US law and heeded no longer the language of the Statute of Monopolies. In due course the remaining influential Commonwealth countries were primarily Australia and New Zealand. It is important to be aware that in the common law countries at least, the foundations of the exception are the norms and values of medical practitioners. T. Piper, 'A Common Law Prescription for a Medical Malaise', in C. Ng, L. Bently and G. D'Agostino (eds), *The Common Law of Intellectual Property: Essays in Honour of Professor David Vaver* (Hart, 2010), 158–9.

As such it is grounded in ethics and public health concerns.[32] This interpretation has been affirmed in a series of European Patent Office (EPO) cases.[33] However, the exclusion does not extend to drugs or equipment that may be under patent. As far as therapy goes, a line of EPO appeal board decisions has distinguished between methods intended to benefit the health of patients in a range of possible ways which fall within the exclusion, from treatments that are cosmetic in nature that do not. Cosmetic treatments are quite broad. EPO cases have found them to include methods or treatments relating to weight control, baldness and hair removal, snoring and contraception to name a few. Also falling outside the exclusion are treatments intended to kill humanely the recipient of the substance, for example, euthanasia treatments for pets.[34]

With respect to surgery, EPO cases over the years have been less consistent. But surgery is now deemed to constitute physical intervention on the body involving the application of professional medical skill and which entails substantial health risk to the subject person or animal.[35] Sterckx and Cockbain helpfully sum up the situation by suggesting that 'interventions such as massage, tattooing, tanning, shaving, ear-piercing, blood-drawing, and routine injecting or catheterisation will not classify as excluded methods of surgery', whereas 'bone-setting, castration, embryo implantation and cosmetic surgery involving anaesthetics seem likely to be included'.[36]

Diagnosis necessarily involves at least two steps including data gathering or comparison followed by the act of diagnosis itself. These are all primarily mental, thus non-technical, acts that are outside normal practice done on the body. But if diagnoses consist of 'methods for performing mental acts' and as such as inherently non-technical, they are not inventions anyway under EPC Article 52(2)(c). It follows that the exclusion is unnecessary. After all, why single out diagnostic methods for exclusion when the statutory requirements make them ineligible anyway? It is true that the Enlarged Board of Appeal decision in G-1/04 identified technical steps: those implying 'an interaction with the human or animal body, necessitating the presence of the latter'.[37] But this just seems like a questionable *ex post facto* justification for the existence of a redundant provision.

The European Patent Convention allows known chemicals to be patented for previously unknown uses in the abovementioned unpatentable methods set out in Article 53(c). Providing for

---

[32] S.J.R. Bostyn, 'Personalised Medicine, Medical Indication Patents and Patent Infringement: Emergency Treatment Required' (2016) 2 *IPQ* 151; S.J.R. Bostyn, 'Medical Treatment Methods, Medical Indication Claims and Patentability: A Quest into the Rationale of the Exclusion and Patentability in the Context of the Future of Personalised Medicine' (2016) 3 *IPQ* 203.

[33] Most notably, see G-5/83 Second medical indication/EISAI [1985], G-1/04 Diagnostic methods [2006], G-1/07 Treatment by surgery/MEDI-PHYSICS, [2011].

[34] T-866/01 Euthanasia compositions/MICHIGAN STATE UNIVERSITY, 2005.

[35] G-1/07 Treatment by surgery/MEDI-PHYSICS [2011].

[36] S. Sterckx and J. Cockbain, *Exclusions from Patentability: How far has the European Patent Office Eroded Boundaries?* (Cambridge: Cambridge University Press, 2012).

[37] G-1/04 Diagnostic methods [2006].

this (under Art 54(4))[38] is really a special purpose-bound exemption to the novelty provision which reflects the fact that much pharmaceutical discovery concerns extant substances, not just ones newly brought into existence by pharmaceutical chemists and designed with a specific application in mind. As we will see, this is not the only relaxation of the novelty criterion provided in the EPC in favour of the pharmaceutical industry.

13.2.5 New medical uses and other pharmaceutical-specific patent claims

The question arose of what to do about discoveries of new medical uses of substances that were already being used as medicines for something else; that is, second medical uses. Given the genuine possibility of drugs turning out to be useful for treating diseases other than the ones they were initially indicated for, the industry obviously had an interest in the patent system protecting second medical indications (NB: 'indication' in European patent law practice is more general in meaning and not confined to a specific disease or medical condition). Given that this is not product protection being sought, since of course there is no novelty there, the obstacle was the wording of Article 53(c). The 'solution' arrived at was devised by the Swiss Patent Office and became commonly known in consequence as the 'Swiss-type claim'. Accordingly, a second medical indication framed in this way as a process claim[39] could side-step the methods exclusions under Article 53(c) as long as the following claim language was adopted: 'Use of a substance or composition X for the manufacture of a medicament for therapeutic application Z.' The word 'manufacture' served the purpose of keeping the second use claim away from the ambit of the method of medical treatment exception. This explanatory formula for making claims was affirmed and construed broadly in a 1984 Enlarged Board of Appeal case: G-5/83 Second medical indication/EISAI. However, as from 29 January 2011, such claims are no longer accepted for new patent applications. This came after a decision of the Enlarged Board to end Swiss form claims on the grounds that they cast serious doubt – rather damningly when one stops to think about it – on whether they fulfil novelty and inventiveness requirements (see below).[40] Instead, a more straightforward claim is to be made: 'Product X for use in the treatment of Z.' This is a consequence of a clause added to the revised

---

[38] Art 54(4) states that the normal novelty requirements 'shall not exclude the patentability of any substance or composition, comprised in the state of the art, for use in a method referred to in Article 53(c), provided that its use for any such method is not comprised in the state of the art'.

[39] *Warner-Lambert v. Activis* [2015] EWCA Civ 556.

[40] G2/08 – Dosage regime/ABBOT RESPIRATORY:

Swiss-type claims could be (and have been) considered objectionable as regards the question as to whether they fulfil the patentability requirements due to the absence of any functional relationship of the features (belonging to therapy) conferring novelty and inventiveness, if any, of the claimed manufacturing process. Therefore, where the subject matter of a claim is rendered novel only by a new therapeutic use of a medicament, such claim may no longer have the format of a so called Swiss-type claim.

2000 version of the EPC which renders Swiss form claims unnecessary anyway. Article 54(5) now states that the novelty requirement, 'shall also not exclude the patentability of any substance or composition referred to in paragraph 4 for any specific use in any method referred to in Article 53(c), provided that such use is not comprised in the state of the art'.

This represents a shift from purpose-bound process claims to purpose-bound product claims,[41] which despite the absence of reference to manufacture is a strengthening of the patent right. That second and follow-on use claims may be under patent after the initial patent on the drug itself has expired gives rise to the following rather curious scenario: a generic version of a drug can enter the market, subject to regulatory approval, for the original indication. But if marketed for the second use, its preparation and sale would be patent infringing. This potentially raises difficulties for national health providers, physicians and pharmacists, especially in jurisdictions in which doctors are encouraged to write prescriptions using International Nonproprietary Names (i.e., generic names) and where indications may not necessarily be entered on the prescription note. It also means that generic drug-makers must be careful about the indications they mention on the label, making sure not to include ones that are under patent protection ('skinny labelling').[42] Given the undesirability of exposing physicians and pharmacists to patent infringement suits for just doing their jobs, and here one might reflect also on the purposes of the commonly provided 'pharmacy exemption' written into the Agreement on a Unified Patent Court,[43] whose coming into effect is imminent at the time of writing, this is serious cause for concern. Article 27 of this EU instrument on limitations to rights includes 'the extemporaneous preparation by a pharmacy, for individual cases, of a medicine in accordance with a medical prescription or acts concerning the medicine so prepared'. This is obviously not a blanket exemption for pharmacies but its inclusion in the law implies a preference for protecting them from the full weight of patent enforcement actions. It is because allowing medical indication patents entails infringement risks, not just for generic drug firms but also for clinicians and pharmacists, that Bostyn, who has considered a range of options,

---

[41] Case T 1780/12 *University of Texas Board of Regents/Cancer treatment* [2014] EPOR 28 at 16–24.

[42] This issue is central to a drawn out, complex and unresolved legal dispute between generic companies, principally Sandoz, and Pfizer concerning whether and to what extent Sandoz's generic version of Pfizer's Lyrica could be marketed for, prescribed and dispensed for certain medical uses disclosed in a patent in force after expiry of the initial patent granted on the compound itself. The dispute concerned not just the activities and obligations of Sandoz and other generic firms but also of pharmacies and the British National Health Service. Recent relevant decisions include *Warner-Lambert v. Sandoz and others* [2015] EWHC 3153 (Pat); *Warner-Lambert Company LLC v. Generics (UK) Ltd (t/a Mylan) & Ors* [2016] EWCA Civ 1006.

[43] There is no international harmonisation concerning the scope of exemptions for the benefit of pharmacies. Consequently, some countries have broader exemptions than those allowing only one-off preparations for patients with specific requirements. *See* World Intellectual Property Organization – Standing Committee on the Law of Patents (2013) Exceptions and limitation to patent rights: Extemporaneous preparation of medicines (SCP/20/5). Geneva: WIPO. What is permitted under international law in this respect is unclear. The Agreement on Trade-Related Aspects of Intellectual Property Rights (TRIPS) of the World Trade Organization is vague in this regard and the latter organisation has not been called upon so far to interpret the scope of allowable exceptions in this specific context.

has advocated a broad 'therapeutic freedom exception', a wide immunity from infringement actions.[44, 45]

Admittedly, there is little evidence that the pharmaceutical industry in Europe at least has much appetite for suing doctors or pharmacists. But pharmacists generally do not know what the medicine on a prescription is to be used for unless the patient is present to be asked and is happy to answer. One may question why they should be expected to. As mentioned, physicians may be expected to prescribe the cheaper generic version. Furthermore, they are normally permitted to prescribe medicines for known off-label uses and this is generally assumed to be in the public interest where the drugs have been properly tried and tested, and proven safe through extended periods of use.[46]

Whereas many second use claims are targeted towards diseases and other health problems that were not previously indicated, there are further types of claim that may be allowed in some jurisdictions where the disease is actually the same as before. This is where the earlier discussion on personalised medicine becomes particularly relevant. Following the EISAI decision, claims may be allowed on further uses and methods for optimised or personalised dosage regimes, that is, for a specific schedule of doses such as take one 200 mg. tablet every six hours. This rather generous interpretation of European patent law concerning second and further use claims was reaffirmed by the TBA in *Genentech/Method of Administration of IFG-1*. As with personalised medicine generally, there are potential advantages for industry here too: 'increasing the number of patients who respond well to drugs while decreasing those who experience adverse effects will facilitate drug approval and make it easier for payers to reimburse for the use of the drugs'.[47]

As an aside, it is important to differentiate between the terms 'formulation' when applied to a specific drug mixture in whatever type it is prepared for delivery, and a 'dosage form'. The latter tends to refer to the physical form of the drug. Dosage forms include tablets, capsules, injectable

---

[44] Bostyn, *supra* note 32, both works.

[45] Some jurisdictions do not allow second and further medical use patents at all. Thus, by virtue of the Common Regime on Industrial Property (Decision 486) Art 21, the Andean Community of Nations (Colombia, Ecuador, Peru and Bolivia) do not allow patenting of new uses of products or processes that have already been patented.

[46] This is a common practice that should be supported, albeit cautiously. According to the US-based Consumer Reports, 'One in five prescriptions in the U.S. is for a use not approved by the FDA. And most of those (about 75 percent) are for a use that lacks any evidence or rigorous studies to back it up' (Consumer Reports, 'Off-Label Drug Use', 2007. https://www.consumerreports.org/health/resources/pdf/best-buy-drugs/money-saving-guides/english/Off-Label-FINAL.pdf). Moreover, to say that off-label prescribing can often be a good thing should not be taken as an endorsement of its aggressive promotion by the industry as happens in the US even though off-label marketing has been illegal since 1962. According to the US-based NGO Public Citizen, 'The practice of illegal off-label promotion of pharmaceuticals has been responsible for the largest amount of financial penalties levied by the federal government over the past 20 years. This practice can be prosecuted as a criminal offense because of the potential for serious adverse health effects in patients from such activities.' S. Almashat, C. Preston and T. Waterman, 'Rapidly Increasing Criminal and Civil Monetary Penalties against the Pharmaceutical Industry: 1991 to 2010' (Public Citizen, 2010). http://www.citizen.org/hrg1924. Currently, and controversially, drug companies are lobbying the US Congress to relax the FDA ban on off-label marketing.

[47] T 1020/03, ECLI:EP:BA:2004:T102003.20041029. R.W. Peck, 'The Right Dose for Every Patient' (2016) 15 *Nature Reviews Drug Discovery* 145.

solutions, ointments or powders to give some examples. However, the term is also used to apply to the chemical composition of the drug. Thus, there is a certain overlap in the usage of the two terms, which can be a little confusing. As we will see below, new formulations such as different mixtures containing known APIs that might offer certain advantages to patients are patentable. Examples of such patient benefits include its enabling a more convenient dosage regimen (for example, a-one-a-day version of a drug previously to be taken every four hours), or a reduction in side-effects. Dosage forms presented as novel and unobvious routes of administration for known drugs can also be patented.[48]

In 2008, the British Court of Appeal made an important ruling on a medical product called Finasteride, which had first been patented in 1978 as a treatment for enlarged prostate.[49] A decade later the same company, Merck, filed a patent application on the same product but for its use to treat male baldness at a daily dosage of over 5 mg. using the Swiss form of claim. In 1996 a new patent relating to the same product was granted to Merck claiming its use 'for the preparation of a medicament for oral administration useful for the treatment of androgenic alopecia [male baldness] in a person and wherein the dosage amount is about 0.05 to 1.0 mg'. The Court, taking relevant EPO decisions into account reversed its earlier revocation, finding the new dosage regime to be novel and non-obvious. Regarding novelty, the Court stated that: 'a claim to a pill containing a 1mg dose of finasteride would be a claim to a new thing. No-one had made or proposed such a thing, so why should it not be novel?' It was considered non-obvious because there was deemed a low expectation of success. It is worthwhile mentioning here that dosage regimes arrived at through routine activities remain likely to be held obvious.[50] Indeed, as the Court in the present case sought to clarify:

> So holding is far from saying that in general just specifying a new dosage regime in a Swiss form claim can give rise to a valid patent. On the contrary, nearly always such dosage regimes will be obvious – it is standard practice to investigate appropriate dosage regimes. Only in an unusual case such as the present […] could specifying a dosage regime as part of the therapeutic use confer validity on an otherwise invalid claim.

Ironically, it was shortly after that the EPO decided in Decision No. G02/08 – Dosage regime/ ABBOT RESPIRATORY that use of Swiss-type claims should cease in light of the new language inserted into the EPC from 2000. This decision clarified two important points as follows:

1. Where it is already known to use a medicament to treat an illness, Article 54(5) EPC does not exclude that this medicament be patented for *use in a different treatment* by therapy of the *same illness*.
2. Such patenting is also not excluded where *a dosage regime is the only feature claimed* which is not comprised in the state of the art (emphasis added).

---

[48] H. Gupta, S. Kumar, S.K. Roy and R.S. Gaud, 'Patent Protection Strategies' (2010) 2(1) *Journal of Pharmacy and BioAllied Sciences* 2.

[49] *Actavis UK Ltd v. Merck & Co Inc* [2008] EWCA Civ 444.

[50] *Actavis Group PTC EHF & Anor v. Teva UK Ltd & Ors* [2017] EWCA Civ 1671.

Concerning personalised medicine and considering how far claims may be allowed for methods of use for something old, the following question arises: Is it possible to claim uses or methods relating to a patient population identified by a shared biomarker that forms part of a wider population of patients having the same disease and who may already have received the medicine?[51] Surely, if the drug has already been prescribed for that disease including to those members of the smaller population, there is no novelty. This is a tricky issue, but the EPO has allowed patents for uses targeted to clearly defined sub-populations. In T1399/04 (Combination therapy HCV/SCHERING), the TBA stated that prior public use is not necessarily novelty-destroying. Moreover, while defining a group of patients medically where there is overlap with a population already receiving the same drug for the same purpose would not normally lead to a patentable invention, there is a possibility that it can where the patent application discloses a scientifically distinguishable group. As stated by the Board in the above case:

> If the use of a compound was known in the treatment or diagnosis of a disease of a particular group of subjects, the treatment or diagnosis of the same disease with the same compound could nevertheless represent a novel therapeutic or diagnostic application, provided that it is carried out on a new group of subjects which is distinguished from the former by its *physiological or pathological* status.
> [...]
> According to the established case law of the Boards of appeal [...], the subject-matter [...] represents a new therapeutic application as the patient group concerned is distinguishable [...] by its *physiological and pathological* status.[52] (Original emphasis)

13.2.6 Gaming the system? The patenting of enantiomers and other variants

Often there is a degree of variability among a class of things that many would assume still to be identical to each other. Is a form or variant of a chemical the same thing as that chemical? Or is it something else entirely? What about drugs? While you ponder this last question, bear in mind that a pill is not just a package comprising multiple numbers of the specified active ingredient, but a collection of those plus various additional chemicals, formulated to enhance the effectiveness of the drug product after it has entered the body. Paradoxically, it is both a pure substance and a mixture.

Let us consider one potentially significant type of variability in the pharmaceutical context: stereoisomerism. Two or more compounds may consist of the same elements in the same atomic proportions but differ in shape. The basic chemical formula is the same but each variant may interact with the human body in different ways that give rise to different effects. Isomers that are

---

[51] S. Parker and B. Hall, 'Patenting Personalized Medicines in the UK, Europe and USA' (2014) 3(2) *Pharmaceutical Patent Analyst* 163–9.

[52] T 1399/04 (Combination therapy HCV/SCHERING), ECLI:EP:BA:2006:T139904.20061025. For detailed discussion, see Bostyn, 'Medical Treatment Methods', *supra* note 32.

mirror images of each other are called enantiomers. A racemate is a chemical that has two forms, each a mirror image of the other. Racemic mixtures tend to comprise both in equal measure, and many pharmaceutical products are such mixtures. Technically speaking, a racemate is a molecule of a certain type: it is chiral, meaning it comes in two opposite forms: left-handed and right-handed. Whether they are in the left-handed half of the mixture or in the right-handed one they do not differ in their atomic constituents. In terms of their relationship to the mixture and to their counterpart in the other half of the combination, they are referred to in chemistry-speak as enantiomers. Each may also be referred to as an optical isomer. It is possible that both enantiomers have the same therapeutic effect. But there may also be huge and crucial differences in the medical impacts of a different enantiomer. To make matters more complicated, it is possible for the human body to convert a supposedly safe and effective enantiomer taken as a drug into a potentially harmful racemic mixture in the body. In recent decades, separating enantiomers has become easier. Needless to say, the ability to carry out such a separation can provide genuine benefits for patients. It is much easier, as of course it should be, to acquire regulatory approval for an enantiomer than for a genuinely new chemical entity. Moreover, enantiomers are patentable. This might all appear to be reasonable, but the possibilities for 'gaming' the regulatory and patent systems are very much present. Chiral switching, that is, moving from the racemic mixture to an enantiomer, and filing a patent on the latter, is frequently attempted as the original patent covering the racemic mixture progresses through its 20-year life cycle.

Stereoisomerism is not the only type of variability that can be managed for commercial advantage. Prodrugs are chemically inactive drugs that are converted in the human body into the active ingredient by the action of enzymes. There are numerous reasons why prodrug forms can provide benefits, such as by enhancing in-body transportation or reducing toxicity effects. However, the actual metabolised product which causes the therapeutic effect can itself lead to an improved patient experience if delivered in that form instead. For example, the antihistamine prodrug terfenadine, marketed as Seldane, has cardio-toxic effects on some people. The metabolite, fexofenadine, subsequently marketed as Allegra (among various other names), is not. Metabolites of previously patented prodrugs can be patented too, as were both these two products. However, the situation is far from certain for companies. In the UK, the House of Lords revoked the patent on fexofenadine as the earlier patent on terfenadine had rendered it no longer novel even though the metabolite product had not been explicitly disclosed in the earlier patent.[53] But this did not necessarily make it impossible to patent a metabolite given the facts of the case were specific to the patents at issue. Indeed, in a 2003 US Court of Appeals for the Federal Circuit case, Judge Rader found a metabolite to be inherently anticipated (that is, not novel), but he went on to clarify that 'With proper claiming, patent protection is available for metabolites of known drugs.'[54] He suggested different ways to evade anticipation including claiming an isolated and purified form of the metabolite or on a method of administering it to a patient.

Correa provides a useful summary of patenting targets chosen by companies to extend their monopolies on drugs. These include polymorphs (crystalline forms of the active compound);

---

[53] *Merrell Dow Pharmaceuticals Inc and Anor v. HN Norton & Co Ltd* [1995] UKHL 14.

[54] *Schering v. Geneva Pharmaceutical*, 339 F 3d 1373 (FCCA, 2003).

pharmaceutical forms (i.e., new ways of administering the active compound); selective inventions (elements selected from a group that were not specifically named in earlier patents claiming the group); analogy processes; combinations of known products; optical isomers; active metabolites; prodrugs (inactive compounds that produce active metabolites when introduced into the body); new salts of known substances; variants of existing manufacturing processes; and new uses for old products.[55]

Follow-on patents of these kinds that claim meaningful distinctions between similar things that in other contexts might be regarded as practically identical may promise benefits for patients. For example, whereas one patented minor molecular modification to a drug may make no difference to the average patient, another could lead to a much improved therapeutic effect on at least some patients. The former type would appear to be commercially valueless. If so, why file patents on it?

Notwithstanding possible benefits, patenting strategy here is clearly aimed to extend the market exclusivity of an existing drug or to support marketing aimed at switching patients to a supposedly upgraded version of a company's existing product. This is why they are controversial. Such incremental inventions may be regarded as examples of gaming the system by acquiring extended or new patent monopolies that are not justified by the minor level of inventive contribution or the possibly negligible added benefit to the public. Such practices are commonly referred to as secondary patenting or 'evergreening'.[56] The industry, of course, sees them as perfectly justifiable. For critics, they reflect a flaw in the patent system, one with serious implications for access to medicines, and for the promotion of innovation. If you can get 20 years' added monopoly for a modest change that may not even be an improvement relating to a product in which you already enjoy a dominant market position, why invest in more expensive and risky radical innovation?

The phenomenon of tertiary patenting has recently emerged, albeit as yet without attracting much attention. Here, the patent covered 'product' is not a new chemical, whether radically new or a cosmetically modified version of an old one; nor is it even a chemical, at least not by itself. Rather, what is patented is a drug delivery device to be used in combination with an existing drug.[57] Such devices include items such as self-injector pens for drugs like insulin and epinephrine. Given that these can themselves be evergreened by means of patenting incremental variations that may or may not provide enhanced therapeutic value, tertiary patenting seems bound to attract controversy.

Even when the end of the monopoly on the existing branded drug can no longer be delayed any further, with good marketing it may be possible to shift patients from an about to become off-patent drug on to a new version marketed under a different name that is fundamentally the same thing and thus hardly better therapeutically if at all. If the original drug was successful and profitable while the patent was valid, such product switching could well generate a lot of money. Some have alleged that this tactic was used by AstraZeneca. When its highly successful anti-ulcer drug omeprazole (sold as Losec, or Prilosec) was coming to the end of its patent life, and attempts

---

[55] C.M. Correa, *Trends in Drug Patenting: Case Studies* (Corregidor, 2001), 11–12.

[56] T. Amin and A.S. Kesselheim, 'Secondary Patenting of Branded Pharmaceuticals: A Case Study of How Patents on Two HIV Drugs could be extended for Decades' (2012) 31(10) *Health Affairs* 2286–94.

[57] R.F. Beall and A.S. Kesselheim, 'Tertiary Patenting on Drug-Device Combination Products in the United States' (2018) 36(2) *Nature Biotechnology* 142–5.

to evergreen its monopoly were thwarted, the company sought to switch users to esomeprazole, branded as Nexium, a product that was both chemically and therapeutically virtually identical to Losec, but was ten times more expensive than the former drug. They did this by deploying aggressive marketing tactics claiming that it was both newer and better. Admittedly, the fact that it comprises optically pure salts of omeprazole enabled it to pass the novelty test in the key jurisdictions. But novelty in this context is of course a legal fiction. Like more than half of the drugs currently on the market, the active ingredient of Losec is a racemic mixture: a 50-50 mix of molecules that are mirror images of each other. Nexium is the so-called (S) enantiomer of omeprazole, the one that is therapeutically active. Putting it another way, esomeprazole is one of two optically pure salts of omeprazole. Therefore esomeprazole was part of the contents of omeprazole. In other words, it was contained in the API of Losec.

This effort cost hundreds of millions dollars in marketing, but it was worth it. 'About 40 percent of Prilosec users made the switch to Nexium earning the drug over $3 billion in 2003 and almost $5 billion in 2004.'[58, 59] So was Nexium any better than Losec to which it is chemically very closely related? It appears that the improvement was modest to say the least.[60] Apart from needing less of it to have the same therapeutic effect by dint of the fact that the other enantiomer is inactive, both Losec and Nexium are prodrugs. As we saw, prodrugs are those which are converted by the human body into the substance which is the real active ingredient. Both Losec and Nexium are converted into the same compound, sulfenic acid, which only has a single-handed form: it is achiral, not chiral. Therefore, whether omeprazole or esomeprazole are taken, an optically and pharmacologically identical API is formed *in vivo* which goes about its business in a way that does not depend on which of the two products it is derived from.

The courts are not the place to provide a definitive answer to a scientific question, but in July 2015, the Canadian Federal Court of Appeal provided a response of sorts. The Court upheld a Federal Court decision invalidating AstraZeneca's Nexium patent. The reason was not for lack of novelty or for obviousness, but the absence of utility. As the Court put it: 'while the patent promised that its compounds provide improved pharmacokinetic and metabolic properties which will give an improved therapeutic profile, such as a lower degree of interindividual variation, this promise was neither demonstrated nor soundly predicted at the time the patent was filed'.[61] This ruling came towards the end of the patent life so AstraZeneca had had plenty of time to enjoy the benefits of its rather questionable marketing practices and its ownership of a patent in that country. In the event, AstraZeneca appealed, and in June 2017 the Supreme Court found in favour of the company.[62]

---

[58] S. Manners, *Super Pills: The Prescription Drugs We Love to Take* (Raincoast Books, 2006) 46.

[59] In Europe, the company sought also to delay generic competition with Losec by means that the European Commission found in June 2005 to be an abuse of its dominant position. AstraZeneca was fined €60 million.

[60] M. Angell, *The Truth about the Drug Companies: How They Deceive Us and What to Do about It* (Random House, 2004) 79; M. Goozner, *The $800 Million Pill: The Truth behind the Cost of New Drugs* (University of California Press, 2004) 222; J. Law, *Big Pharma: How the World's Biggest Drug Companies Control Illness* (Constable, 2006), 76–8.

[61] *AstraZeneca Canada v. Apotex* 2015 FCA 158.

[62] *AstraZeneca v. Apotex* 2017 SCC 36 (see also Chapter 5).

Whereas rigorous application of the novelty and inventive step criteria by patent offices and court decision may prevent the most egregious attempts to unfairly extend patent monopolies, India's patent law actually has an anti-evergreening provision. Accordingly, Article 3(d) of the Patents (Amendment) Act, 2005 states as follows:

The following are not inventions within the meaning of this Act, [...]

(d) the mere discovery of a new form of a known substance which does not result in the enhancement of the known efficacy of that substance or the mere discovery of any new property or new use for a known substance or of the mere use of a known process, machine or apparatus unless such known process results in a new product or employs at least one new reactant.

Explanation. – For the purposes of this clause, salts, esters, ethers, polymorphs, metabolites, pure form, particle size, isomers, mixtures of isomers, complexes, combinations and other derivatives of known substance shall be considered to be the same substance, unless they differ significantly in properties with regard to efficacy.

This measure was the subject of a highly publicised Supreme Court case which decided on the patentability of a new chemical form of the anti-cancer drug Glivec and found it not to be, interpreting 'efficacy' for a medicine of necessity to mean 'therapeutic efficacy'. Novartis failed to prove that the new form had an enhanced and significantly different efficacy as compared to the earlier version of Glivec.[63]

Anti-evergreening measures have been adopted elsewhere. Indonesia revised its patent law in July 2016 along the lines of India's Article 3(d), ruling out patents for discoveries of new uses of existing or known products and new forms showing no increased efficacy. In Brazil, an agency set up by the health ministry (ANVISA) scrutinises pharmaceutical patents explicitly to reduce secondary patent grants. However, a recent empirical study suggests that India's and Brazil's anti-evergreening approaches have had less impact in terms of filtering out the grant of secondary patents than many hoped for. However, the reasons are not entirely clear.[64]

13.2.7 Patents, research and competition

There are two other important issues. One relates to the patent incentive to invent such as it really exists, the other concerns competition. The first is part of a wider debate about whether the availability of 20-year legal monopolies for incremental inventions is a good thing if we would prefer to

---

[63] *Novartis v. Union of India*, Civil Appeal No 2706-2716 of 2013 before the Supreme Court of India (2013). For commentaries on the case, see P.R. Thikkavarapu, 'The Indian Supreme Court's Judgment in the Case of Glivec® – The Uncertain Future of Pharmaceutical Patents in India' (2014) 3(2) *Pharmaceutical Patent Analyst* 117–19; S. Thambisetty, 'Novartis v. Union of India and the Person Skilled in the Art: A Missed Opportunity', (2014) 4(1) *Queen Mary Journal of Intellectual Property* 79.

[64] B.N. Sampat and K. Shadlen, 'TRIPS Implementation and Secondary Pharmaceutical Patenting in Brazil and India' (2015) 50(2) *Studies in Comparative International Development* 228.

see breakthrough inventions that entail high risk and greater investment. It may be unfair to place all of the blame for the industry's conservatism on the patent system but clearly it does not seem to be helping. According to a recent article:

> The human genome encodes more than 500 protein kinases, of which hundreds have been shown to have genetic links with human diseases. Yet around 65% of the 20,000 kinase papers published in 2009 focused on the 50 proteins that were the 'hottest' in the early 1990s. Similarly, 75% of the research activity on nuclear hormone receptors in 2009 focused on the 6 receptors – out of the 48 encoded in the genome – that were most studied in the mid 1990s.[65]

As regards natural products we have a similar situation and this is reflected in the patent system:

> [...] human innovative activity involving biodiversity in the patent system focuses on approximately 4% of taxonomically described species and between 0.8–1% of predicted global species [...] We conclude that the narrow focus of human innovative activity and ownership of genetic resources is unlikely to be in the long term interest of humanity.[66]

With respect to competition, generic companies are able to supply the drug only for some but not all indications. This makes it harder to challenge the market power of the first entrant. If one believes in full patent rights for new medical uses that is fair enough. If one is more sceptical that this lengthy term of protection is justified for such minor discoveries, it follows that the public may not be getting the full benefits it should from a truly competitive market in medicines. In addition, and this may be speculation on our part, aggressive assertion of patent rights could well be having a chilling effect on generic market entry.[67]

13.2.8 US law

Generally speaking, if it is patentable in the US, it is likely to be patentable in Europe and vice versa. However there are some differences in terms of eligible subject matter and in legal reasoning. It would be fair to say that the situation in the US regarding eligibility is confusing and in a state of flux. The Supreme Court has missed a number of opportunities to provide legal clarity. One particularly interesting example is the 2012 *Mayo v. Prometheus* decision of the Supreme Court[68]

---

[65] A.M. Edwards et al., 'Too Many Roads Not Taken' (2011) 470 *Nature* 163–5.

[66] P. Oldham, S. Hall and O. Forero, 'Biological Diversity in the Patent System' (2013) 8(11) *PLOS 1* e78737.

[67] In this context it is important to note that generic drugs are a huge saving: according to a study sponsored by the generics industry itself, $227 in 2015 for the US and €100 billion in 2014 for the EU. Generic Pharmaceutical Association, '2016 Generic Drug Savings and Access in the United States Report', 2016. Available at http://www.gphaonline.org/media/generic-drug-savings-2016/index.html; IMS Institute for Healthcare Informatics, 'The Role of Generic Medicines in Sustaining Healthcare Systems: A European Perspective, 2015. Available at http://www.imshealth.com/files/web/IMSH%20Institute/Healthcare%20Briefs/IIHI_Generics_Healthcare_Brief.pdf.

[68] *Mayo Collaborative Services v. Prometheus Laboratories, Inc* 566 US (2012).

which again concerned personalised medicine. The two patents at issue involved use of thiopurine drugs for treating auto-immune diseases. They claimed methods to calibrate dosage of known drugs for an individual patient to achieve optimal therapeutic efficacy. This was done by measuring the amount of a drug metabolite present in the patient such that the dosage could be adjusted accordingly. This is important because different patients metabolise the drug at different rates. Thus at a given dosage, one patient may have a relatively large amount of the metabolite in the body which if too high may cause harmful side-effects. Another patient may produce so little of the metabolite from the dosage administered as to be therapeutically ineffective. So clearly the disclosed methods offered a therapeutic advantage for patients. But did that make them patentable?

The USPTO had found the patents to comprise eligible subject matter on the grounds that administering the drug providing the metabolite was a transformative step that made the whole process patent-eligible. The Court of Appeals for the Federal Circuit reversed a lower court judgment and found the patents to claim eligible subject matter in which physical 'transformation', a word for which European patent law and jurisprudence has little use, was present in the first two steps of the process. This rendered as insignificant the third and last step being deemed a 'mental step': taken as a whole, the methods were patentable.

The Supreme Court reversed this, stating its view that the patents described a general method to apply a law of nature, with administration of the drug adding nothing inventive to the state of the art. While it seems reasonable to conclude that there was nothing especially inventive about the patents, arguably all inventions apply natural laws to something practically useful – assuming we accept that 'law of nature' has any clear meaning. To be fair, the Court did accept this point, but it still found that transforming a law of nature into a patentable invention requires more than merely applying the law, and the patents were thus held to claim ineligible subject matter by failing to achieve this.

One does not wish to discourage research and investment in personalised medicine by foreclosing opportunities for companies to make profits. However, given how few granted patents are revoked in court, one can only speculate as to how many similarly questionable patents were granted and reached full term that should not have been. The scale of negative social welfare impacts arising from such mistakenly granted (as far as today's jurisprudence is concerned) and unchallenged legal monopolies is potentially very large. Something to add here is that the Court did reaffirm the purpose of the three exclusions, which was that they be left freely available so as to encourage future discovery the incentive to invent function being an essential function of the patent system. That at least seems perfectly reasonable.

Another aspect of personalisation is the preparation of medicines comprising certain active ingredients for specific patients. Using the patented ingredient to make a medicinal product is an infringing activity. In about 40 countries there is an express pharmacy exception, as was briefly mentioned earlier in this chapter. For example, in the UK, an act that would otherwise infringe, is permitted if 'it consists of the extemporaneous preparation in a pharmacy of a medicine for an individual in accordance with a prescription given by a registered medical or dental practitioner or consists of dealing with a medicine so prepared'.[69]

---

[69] UK Patents Act, s 60; WIPO Document SPC/20/5 9 October 2013).

Another defence to infringement that is probably better known, is the so-called Bolar exemption (or Bolar provision as it is sometimes called). This originates in the US Hatch-Waxman Act referred to above. For the research-based firms, the Act allowed patent term extensions of up to five years to compensate for the restriction on the effective protection term because of the time needed to acquire the FDA's marketing approval. There was of course some justification for this. It was taking increasingly long periods of time for the FDA to approve new chemical entities for sale, and this was reducing the effective period of market exclusivity. As for the generic firms, the Act meant that they would only need to file a so-called Abbreviated New Drug Application (ANDA) with the FDA, rather than go through extensive clinical trials to demonstrate the safety and efficacy of their version of the soon to go off-patent drug. This meant that approval could take as little as three months. Second, the legislation incorporated the Bolar exemption, which meant that certain acts performed before the expiry date of the patent that would normally infringe it were allowed as long as they were confined to those actions necessary to secure FDA approval, and not those intended to prepare the generic drug for commercialisation including stockpiling the product. The Bolar exemption was named after a court case involving Hoffman LaRoche and a generic producer called Bolar. Since a World Trade Organization dispute settlement panel upheld Canada's Bolar (or 'regulatory review') provision in 2000[70] but not its rule allowing also the manufacture and storage of the medicine with intention to sell, it has now been incorporated into the patent laws of a growing number of countries including the EU.

13.3   ACCESS TO MEDICINES

13.3.1 Neglected diseases, high prices and developing countries

The relationship between intellectual property and public health has attracted controversy in both the developed and the developing worlds. However, the debate has, for understandable reasons, been most heated in areas like Africa where millions of people suffer and die from diseases for which medicines exist that could vastly improve and prolong their lives. As a recent report put it:

> Many of the diseases and health conditions that account for a large part of the disease burden in low- and middle-income countries are far less common in high-income countries. These burdens are primarily associated with infectious diseases, reproductive health, and childhood illnesses. Just eight diseases and conditions account for 29 percent of all deaths in low- and middle-income countries: TB, HIV/AIDS, diarrheal diseases, vaccine-preventable diseases of childhood, malaria, respiratory infections, maternal conditions, and neonatal deaths. Approximately 17.6 million people in low- and middle-income countries die each year from communicable diseases and maternal and neonatal conditions. Both the occurrence of and the death rates from such diseases and conditions are far lower in all high-income countries.[71]

---

[70] *Canada – Patent Protection of Pharmaceutical Products. Report of the Panel* (WT/DS114/R). WTO, 17 March 2000.

[71] D.T. Jamison et al., 'Cost-effective Strategies for the Excess Burden of Disease in Developing Countries', in D.T. Jamison

High-profile pandemics like HIV/AIDS understandably attract considerable attention. Millions of people have died of this terrible disease – 2.6 million in 2003 and 2.8 million in 2005, of which Sub-Saharan Africa contributed 1.9 million and 2.0 million respectively.[72] But as the above quote makes clear there are a whole host of diseases that have particularly devastating impacts on the poor.

The obvious reason why treatment access is such a problem is poverty. People do not have the money to buy the drugs, and governments, even those that are not corrupt or otherwise woefully dys-functional, lack the resources and infrastructure to get them to those who need them but cannot af-ford them. The pharmaceutical industry certainly prefers to blame poverty and poor governance, and rejects arguments that patent rights allow them to set high prices that keep them out of the reach of the poor.[73] But one should be sceptical of such defences, which are both insufficient and misleading.

High drug prices are not of course the only factor limiting patients' access to them. Access even to very cheap drugs tends to be inadequate too. Poor people often live far away from clinics and hospitals. Also, many countries are short of medical practitioners trained to prescribe drugs to patients in the appropriate combinations and dosages. Nonetheless, high prices obviously have a profound impact on the ability of cash-strapped governments and other health-care-providing organisations to deliver drugs to the poor. High prices are also increasingly afflicting rich-country markets too such as treatments for complex diseases targeted at relatively small patient popula-tions. National pharmaceutical markets are often highly regulated, and companies are not always free to set prices entirely as they wish. Patent monopolies place the companies holding them in a strong bargaining position for as long as they can keep out the generic competition which po-tentially could drive prices downwards towards the marginal cost of making the drug in question.

The pharmaceutical industry is frequently criticised in relation to its research priorities. Spe-cifically, critics point out that the industry invests heavily in developing treatments for relatively trivial ailments rather than life-threatening ones, drugs for chronic health problems that do not cure patients but that need to be taken continually for many years, and ones that address the diet-related health concerns of the 'worried well' in affluent societies but not those of the un-der-nourished.[74] Relatively little is spent on diseases that disproportionately affect the poor, such as malaria and tuberculosis, and public and non-profit sector research efforts are insufficient to make up for the lack of interest in neglected diseases.[75] Thus, while 95 per cent of active TB cases

---

et al. (eds), *Priorities in Health* (World Bank and Oxford University Press, 2006), 59.

[72] Joint United Nations Programme on HIV/AIDS (UNAIDS), *2006 Report on the Global AIDS Epidemic*, Geneva, 2006, 13.

[73] Concerning access, patents are not the issue but the overwhelming poverty of individuals, absence of state healthcare financing, lack of medical personnel, transport and distribution infrastructure plus supply chain charges which can make affordable originator or generic products unaffordable. In many countries, medicines are unaffordable from whatever source, price or patent status.

Statement by Trevor Jones, former Director-General of the Association of the British Pharmaceutical Industry, as published in the annex to the World Health Organization report: 'Public Health, Innovation and Intellectual Property Rights. Report of the Commission on Intellectual Property Rights, Innovation and Public Health', 2006.

[74] A. Weintraub, 'Are Pharmas Addicted to Lifestyle Drugs?' *BusinessWeek*, 15 June 2007; D. Gilbert, T. Walley and D. New, 'Lifestyle Medicines' (2000) 321 *British Medical Journal* 1341–4.

[75] *Médicins Sans Frontières* (MSF) and Drugs for Neglected Diseases (DND) Working Group, 'Fatal Imbalance: The Crisis

occur in developing countries, only three new drugs for the disease were developed between 1967 and 2019.[76] And the World Health Organization has estimated that only 4.3 per cent of pharmaceutical research and development expenditure is aimed at those health problems mainly concerning low- and middle-income countries.[77]

In addition, many of the 'new' products that come on the market are variants of, or slight improvements upon, existing rather than radically novel drugs.[78] A further criticism of the industry is that it is guilty of so-called 'disease mongering', defined by Moynihan and Henry as 'the selling of sickness that widens the boundaries of illness and grows the markets for those who sell and deliver treatments'.[79] In an economic sense, prioritising research in these ways is perfectly rational, whether or not it is entirely admirable.

It is rather difficult to say whether patents are directly responsible for this lack of interest in addressing the needs of the poor. With or without patents, the pursuit of profit and shareholder value is in any case bound to encourage pharmaceutical research to be aimed at areas where the most money can be made. But this does not let patents completely off the hook. One could argue that if patents are meant to serve the public interest then they should do more to encourage research where public needs are greatest.

But let us say no more about this particular issue, important as it is. The most heated attacks on the industry at the international level concern the lack of access to existing life-saving medicines for the poor in developing countries, and this issue and its solutions are the focus of this chapter insofar as intellectual property is treated as part of the problem. This debate was triggered by the HIV/AIDS crisis, and coincided with the research-based pharmaceutical industry's success in securing changes to international rules on intellectual property by means of the TRIPS Agreement that were intended to eliminate or delay price-lowering competition from generic producers.[80] It did not take long for individuals and NGOs to link the two, that is, lack of treatment access and intellectual property rules.

---

in Research and Development for Drugs for Neglected Diseases', MSF and DND Working Group, 2001.

[76] For most of that period there were none at all. J. Orbinski, 'Health, Equity, and Trade: A Failure in Global Governance', in G.P. Sampson (ed.), *The Role of the World Trade Organization in Global Governance* (United Nations University, 2001), 230–31; A. Maxmen, 'Treatment for Extreme Drug-Resistant Tuberculosis Wins US Government Approval' (2019) *Nature* 14 August, https://www.nature.com/articles/d41586-019-02464-0.

[77] WHO, 'Investing in Health Research and Development: Report of the Ad Hoc Committee on Health Research Relating to Future Intervention Options' (WHO, 1996).

[78] For two critical perspectives on this issue and the industry more generally, M. Angell, *The Truth about the Drug Companies: How They Deceive Us and What to Do about It* (New York: Random House, 2004); M. Goozner, *The $800 Million Pill: The Truth Behind the Cost of New Drugs* (Berkeley and Los Angeles: University of California Press, 2004).

[79] L. Payer, *Disease-Mongers: How Doctors, Drug Companies, and Insurers Are Making You Feel Sick* (New York: John Wiley, 1992); R. Moynihan and D. Henry, 'The Fight against Disease Mongering: Generating Knowledge for Action' (2006) 3(4) *PLoS Medicine*; R. Moynihan and A. Cassels, *Selling Sickness: How the World's Biggest Pharmaceutical Companies are Turning us all into Patients* (Vancouver: Greystone Books, 2005).

[80] S.K. Sell, *Private Power, Public Law: The Globalization of Intellectual Property Rights* (Cambridge: Cambridge University Press, 2003).

The extent to which patents affect the prices of drugs varies and it is not enough to say that drugs will always be expensive where they are patented and cheap where they are not. Nonetheless, to the extent that patents restrict competition they are likely to have the effect of keeping prices artificially high, and also of making it more difficult for countries to respond speedily to health crises where drugs do exist but cannot be accessed either because they are expensive or because they are not sufficiently available in that particular market.

The advantage of high prices for industry in poor country markets is not self-evident. However it may be very rational economically in that the wealthy sick will be willing to pay whatever the drug costs, while pricing the drug at levels the poor could afford would not generate as much overall revenue. This is because the rich would be paying so much less than they could be made to pay and many poor people could still not pay for it even at a lowered price. There is another possible reason why patent-holding companies are reluctant to drop drug prices in developing countries to marginal cost or just above it. Trebilcock and Howse suggest that drug companies have a:

> Strategic desire [...] not to reveal, by such pricing, just how low their marginal costs actually were; this information could be used by large purchasers of medicines – governments or private health insurers – to bargain down the price of medicines in rich, developed countries. Hence, drug companies have been prepared in some instances to give away medicines to poor countries, rather than price them at marginal cost – and have presented this behaviour as 'charitable'.[81]

Of course, giving away drugs to the poor is to be welcomed whether or not the motivations are altruistic, but of course generic providers cannot compete with free products.

Research-based pharmaceutical companies and associations representing them have been highly effective in recruiting some governments to support their international commercial interests.[82] The US government in particular has been very willing to offer political support for the IP interests of pharmaceutical companies. Indeed, as we saw earlier in this book, the TRIPS Agreement was in large part a consequence of aggressive lobbying of the US government by a grouping of corporations[83] that were intent on eliminating copyright piracy, the unauthorised use of trade marks, and unwelcome competition from generic drug firms able to take advantage of patent regimes excluding drugs from protection.[84]

The US, in particular, has openly expressed its displeasure when developing country governments have brought in measures to prioritise public health in ways that limit the full enjoyment of the IPRs of US businesses, such as through compulsory licensing and parallel importation, or even where they just indicated they were seriously considering doing so. This is extraordinary. For

---

[81] M.J. Trebilcock and R. Howse, *The Regulation of International Trade* (3rd ed., Abingdon: Routledge, 2005), 430.

[82] This is particularly well evidenced by the annual Special 301 Reports of the Office of the United States Trade Representative.

[83] P. Drahos, 'Global Property Rights in Information: The Story of TRIPS at the GATT' (1995) 13(1) *Prometheus* 6; Sell, *supra* note 80.

[84] G. Dutfield, '"To Copy is to Steal": TRIPS, (Un)free Trade Agreements and the New Intellectual Property Fundamentalism' (2006) *Journal of Information Law and Technology* 1.

one thing, governments have human rights obligations to put the lives of their citizens before the commercial interests of foreign companies. The basis for this view is the existence of Article 12 of the International Covenant on Economic, Social and Cultural Rights,[85] which states that:

> The States Parties to the present Covenant recognize the right of everyone to the enjoyment of the highest attainable standard of physical and mental health. The steps to be taken by the States Parties to the present Covenant to achieve the full realization of this right shall include those necessary for:
> (a) the provision for the reduction of the stillbirth-rate and of infant mortality and for the healthy development of the child;
> (b) the improvement of all aspects of environmental and industrial hygiene;
> (c) the prevention, treatment and control of epidemic, endemic, occupational and other diseases;
> (d) the creation of conditions which would assure to all medical service and medical attention in the event of sickness.

Furthermore, as we saw in Chapter 5, public interest safeguards go back to the very beginnings of patent law so such practices are entirely consistent with five centuries of intellectual property regulating. These particular measures are also consistent with present international law.

One might also add that expressions of outrage in this context are hypocritical given the behaviour of the US government in the Cipro case. In 2001, mail infected with anthrax spores killed a number of unfortunate individuals. Consequently, the government decided to stockpile vast quantities of Bayer's ciprofloxacin (Cipro), which it considered to be the most effective drug for anthrax. Tommy Thompson, then Secretary of Health and Human Services, threatened Bayer that if they did not halve the price he would simply acquire the drug from other sources. At one stage he even raised the possibility of asking Congress to pass legislation exempting the government from compensating Bayer for ignoring its patent.[86] Thompson successfully negotiated a large discount. Since then, the US government has been pressuring developing country governments not to issue compulsory licences to generic drug producers.

Correa provides more evidence to suggest that the condemnation of developing country governments' threatening of compulsory licensing is an instance of what one might call 'selective indignation':

> In the case of the acquisition of shares of Rugby-Darby Group Companies by Dow Chemical Co, the Federal Trade Commission required Dow to license formulations, patents, trade

---

[85] It should be noted that the access to essential medicines issue implicates several other international human rights standards: the right to life, the right to the benefits of scientific progress, the rights to education, to work, and to an adequate standard of living. See UN Millennium Project Task Force on HIV/AIDS, Malaria, TB, and Access to Essential Medicines, Working Group on Access to Essential Medicines, *Prescription for Healthy Development: Increasing Access to Medicines* (London: Earthscan, 2005), 33–4.

[86] K. Bradsher, 'Bayer Agrees to Charge Government a Lower Price for Anthrax Medicine', *New York Times*, 25 October 2001.

secrets, technology, know-how, specifications, processes, quality control data, the Drug Master File, and all information relating to the FDA approvals to potential entrants into the dicyclomine market.[87]

It should be emphasised that the FTC's decision had nothing to do with saving lives but about competition policy. In addition, one finds that the use of compulsory licensing by developing countries to safeguard public health gets referred to, misleadingly by critics and journalists, as 'breaking patents', as if the patents are being revoked or ignored, as Thompson had suggested might be done in the Cipro case. Brazil is frequently condemned for being a tough negotiator with drug companies in demanding that prices be drastically reduced and for threatening to grant compulsory licences if they are not. Such licensed patents of course remain in force and can still be enforced against other infringing parties. In addition, the owners are legally entitled to compensation.

Developing countries have found themselves being attacked merely for interpreting TRIPS in ways that differed from those of powerful firms and governments yet are nonetheless legal. South Africa came under extremely heavy pressure both diplomatically and in the courts when it passed amendments to its Medicine and Related Substances Control Act concerning, among other matters, parallel importation and compulsory licensing. The US government repeatedly demanded that the law be repealed, and in 1998, the Pharmaceutical Manufacturers Association of South Africa and 39 pharmaceutical corporations initiated legal proceedings against the national government to have the legislation overturned. In early 2001, the case was dropped in the face of severe national and international condemnation that only the companies involved appeared not to have expected, and probably in the realisation that they would have lost anyway.[88]

It is certainly true that not all important medicines are patented in countries where they are needed. This raises the question of why cannot local firms or governmental public health institutions make them. Recently, there has been much discussion on this issue, particularly in Africa. The main obstacles to this are technical and financial. First, while quite a few firms and other institutions in that continent have the manufacturing facilities and the expertise to produce dosage units of acceptable quality, a very small number is able to manufacture the active pharmaceutical ingredients, which have to be sourced and purchased from overseas. Moreover, the most capable drug-makers tend to be concentrated in a small number of countries. Second, production costs can be quite prohibitive. In order to achieve economies of scale and make reasonable profits to plough back into research, development and production, it is necessary to be able to supply quite a large market. But start-up funding is scarce. Second, vital as the contribution of Indian firms is in supplying the pharmaceutical needs of many non-producing developing countries at relatively affordable prices, this role is not an unmixed blessing. African firms struggle to compete for price due to their higher costs.

---

[87] C.M. Correa, 'Protecting Test Data for Pharmaceutical and Agrochemical Products under Free Trade Agreements', in P. Roffe, G. Tansey and D. Vivas-Eugui, *Negotiating Health: Intellectual Property and Access to Medicines* (London: Earthscan, 2006), 81, 91.

[88] According to a key World Bank publication of the time, 'while it may be a heavy dose of regulation, South Africa's law is probably consistent with TRIPS', The World Bank, *Global Economic Prospects and the Developing Countries 2002: Making Trade Work for the World's Poor* (World Bank, 2001), 138.

13.3.2 Not just patents: other rights and IP-regulatory interactions

With respect to intellectual property, it is not just patents that may be an obstacle to access. Other IPRs can have an effect. Perhaps the most important is the emerging data exclusivity right. New drugs in the industrialised countries must undergo extensive clinical trials and other tests to demonstrate efficacy and safety. Data arising from these trials and tests must be submitted to a government regulatory office before marketing of drugs can be approved. Some countries, especially developing countries, may not require such data but merely approve a drug on the basis that it has been approved by a reliable authority such as the US's Food and Drug Administration (FDA).

Amassing the data can be hugely expensive in both time and money. Since patents on new therapeutic substances have to be filed at the drug discovery phase prior to the development period, by the time the product reaches the market the patent may well have less than half of its 20-year term left to run. And once patents on drugs expire in Europe and the US, it does not usually take long for much cheaper generic versions to enter those markets.[89]

In the US and Europe, the law promotes the early entry of generic competitors by requiring firms only to demonstrate that their version of the soon to go off-patent drug is a safe and effective equivalent rather than to repeat the clinical trials performed earlier. To have to do so would not only entail unnecessary expense, but would also constitute unethical behaviour towards those patients involved in these additional trials who are given placebos. In practice, then, authorisation to market the drug is given on the basis of proof of equivalence and by reference to the clinical trial data submitted by the maker of the original drug (see Chapter 5).

Developing countries are being pressured to emulate the developed countries by implementing Article 39.3 in their national laws in the form of a limited period of data exclusivity. Frequently data exclusivity provisions crop up in bilateral and regional free trade agreements where the US is one of the parties. In some cases, they are bound to become a barrier to the market entry of generic drugs.

Consider two free trade agreements, the 2004 US-Chile FTA and the 2005 US-Dominican Republic-Central America FTA (US-DR-CAFTA). The US-Chile FTA provides that generic companies are prohibited from marketing a new chemical entity-based drug on the basis of undisclosed clinical trial data submitted to the government as a condition of its approval. This prohibition is for at least five years after the approval date. Conceivably, this could hold up the marketing of some generic drugs until some years after the expiry of any patent on the drug.

The US-DR-CAFTA differs somewhat, for example, in recognising that some countries may approve a new drug on the basis of its prior approval in another country (for instance, the US) without the company having to submit clinical trial data in those countries too. But as with the US-Chile FTA, the prohibition on marketing the generic version is for at least five years from the date of approval of the original pharmaceutical product.

Such a provision applies even in cases where a generic firm is seeking to enter the national market before the original manufacturer, who may not be genuinely interested in supplying this

---

[89] But having made this point, drug companies can be very creative and aggressive in using legal means to prevent generic producers from entering the market even when the patents protecting the drug have expired. See G. Dutfield, *Intellectual Property Rights and the Life Science Industries: A Twentieth Century History* (Aldershot: Ashgate, 2003), 109–11.

particular market. Clearly, these requirements have the potential to stall the introduction of generics in cases where the patent has already expired or where there was no patent in the first place, and are not balanced by any language affirming the right of countries to respond to public health crises as they see fit.[90] Not only that, but data exclusivity requirements are bound to make it harder for governments to grant compulsory licences. Indeed, this is almost certainly one of the reasons for having these requirements in FTAs.

These provisions in FTAs, which have formed templates for subsequent free trade agreements are testament to the influence of the pharmaceutical industry in Washington and Brussels. But by insisting on respect for their patent and rights throughout the world in such an aggressive manner, the research-based pharmaceutical industry has paid a heavy price. While it was busy asserting its economic interests, others were able to portray the industry as ruthless, over-remunerated and uncaring.

Something else that developing countries are encouraged to adopt is so-called patent-linkage. According to one international survey of this form of pharmaceutical regulation, 'generic entry is controlled increasingly through an emerging form of global intellectual property law referred to as "linkage regulations".[91] What are they? According to the authors, 'Linkage regulations tie generic drug availability to existing drug patents by connecting approval to the resolution of patent validity or infringement.' The authors also note that 'The linkage regime is in the process of rapidly spreading worldwide through international free trade agreements.' Accordingly, the drug regulators' marketing approval of a generic drug requires that the active ingredient not be under patent. This denies the opportunity for a generic competitor willing to accept the risk of litigation from entering a market. It might be the case that the competitor believes the patent will not stand up in court. At least a few of the many patents granted every year will have been awarded in error or with excessively broad claims, denial of the opportunity to have them tested in a court of law is perhaps unfortunate.

In Europe, patent linkage is forbidden. However, the US is somewhat different. Under the Drug Price Competition and Patent Term Restoration Act of 1984 (the Hatch-Waxman Act), a generic company can get approval to enter a market occupied solely by a patented product but this is subject to its making a formal declaration to the Food and Drug Administration that the originator's patent 'is invalid or will not be infringed by the manufacture, use, or sale' of their drug. This still leaves it open for the patent holders to challenge the generic company applying for approval. Alternatively, the two firms can settle out of court. So-called reverse payment settlements (or 'pay-for-delay' as they are sometimes called), which are largely a US phenomenon, refer to financial incentives being paid to – rather than by – would-be infringers in exchange for agreement by the latter not to enter the market. Such settlements would appear not to be in the public interest if patients and public health institutions and services are in this way potentially being denied the benefits of price-lowering competition on the basis of patents or patent claims whose validity may not stand up in court. But one may defend them on the grounds that they are a legitimate means of managing

---

[90] For more detailed explanations of the data protection-related problems with US-DR-CAFTA and other FTAs, see F. Abbott, 'The Doha Declaration on the TRIPS Agreement and Public Health and the Contradictory Trend in Bilateral and Regional Free Trade Agreements', Occasional Paper No 14, Geneva: Quaker United Nations Office, 2004.

[91] R.A. Bouchard et al., 'Structure-Function Analysis of Global Pharmaceutical Linkage Regulations' (2011) 12(2) Minnesota Journal of Law, Science & Technology 391.

IP and that parties are entitled to a measure of freedom to enter into contractual relations concerning private property. In a 2013 Supreme Court case,[92] it was ruled that such settlements are not immune from antitrust legislation and the attention of the Federal Trade Commission even where the monopoly powers of the patent holder are no greater than are provided by the exclusionary rights of a valid patent. However, they are not presumptively unlawful either. It really depends on whether the settlement in question has anticompetitive effects or not, and this requires an analysis of each agreement. The Court opted not to provide a detailed structure for such an analysis.[93] In Europe, the European Commission is opposed to reverse payment settlements on the basis of breach of EU antitrust rules.[94] In September 2016, the General Court of the Court of Justice of the European Union found that Lundbeck had illegally colluded with four generics firms enabling the company to prevent price-reducing competition, breaching Article 101 of the Treaty on the Functioning of the European Union.[95] However, it remains to be seen how national courts might view them.[96] In India, Bayer's effort to restrain the drug controller from approving a generic version of its drug Nexavar failed in the Supreme Court after the Delhi High Court's earlier dismissal of Bayer's petition which was partly on the basis of there being no intent by parliament that India should establish a linkage system. Therefore, the court held, it would be incorrect to read such meaning into the relevant statutory law.[97, 98]

13.3.3 Giving TRIPS a (healthy) human face

TRIPS Article 31 sets out a list of conditions on unauthorised use by the government, or by government-approved third parties, of a patent's subject matter. Normally, before using the invention, the proposed user is required, under clause (b), to make 'efforts to obtain authorization from the right holder on reasonable commercial terms and conditions'. Such efforts should not have 'been successful within a reasonable period of time'. However, and this is extremely important in the present context, 'this requirement may be waived by a Member in the case of a national emergency or other circumstances of extreme urgency or in cases of public non-commercial use'. For reasons that will become clear, it is important to note, as clause (f) states, that 'any such use shall be

---

[92] *FTC v. Actavis, Inc,* 570 US (2013).

[93] B.M. Miller, 'Antitrust Analysis after *Actavis*: Applying the Rule of Reason to Reverse Payments' (2015) 15(3) *Wake Forest Journal of Business and Intellectual Property* 382.

[94] For a critical commentary on the European Commission's more assertive approach, see J. Straus, 'Can Antitrust Adequately Assess Patent Settlement Agreements Disconnected from Patent Law Relevant Facts? The Servier Case – Its Public Perception and its Underlying Facts' (2016) 38(9) *EIPR* 533.

[95] Case T-472/13 *Lundbeck v. European Commission.*

[96] For discussion, see V.K. Unni, 'India's Tryst with Pharma Patent Settlements Whether a Turbulent Decade of Litigations would Give Way to Meaningful Compromises?' (2015) 6(2) *WIPO Journal* 165–77.

[97] *Bayer* MANU/DE/0316/2010.

[98] For a discussion on the relationship between intellectual property and competition law in the health context, see H. Yu, *Achieving Proof of Concept in Drug Discovery and Development: The Role of Competition Law in Collaborations between Public Research Organizations and Industry* (Cheltenham: Edward Elgar Publishing, 2016).

authorized predominantly for the supply of the domestic market of the Member authorizing such use'. However, as clause (k) states in part, all of these conditions may be set aside 'where such use is permitted to remedy a practice determined after judicial or administrative process to be anti-competitive. The need to correct anti-competitive practices may be taken into account in determining the amount of remuneration in such cases.' This allows for the possibility of fast-tracking compulsory licensing procedures as long as use of the patent made by the owning company can be deemed anti-competitive.[99] According to clause (h), 'the right holder shall be paid adequate remuneration in the circumstances of each case, taking into account the economic value of the authorization'.

It must be said that compulsory licensing, while a potentially useful mechanism to enhance access, is not a panacea.[100] In cases where prior authorisation from the patent owner is required (as is normally the case), negotiations can be complicated and take a long time to conclude. Second, the patent specification may not provide sufficient information to enable copying of the drug. In fact, with some drugs, the most efficient manufacturing process is protected by a separate patent, which may even be owned by a different company, or it may involve know-how that is protected under trade secrecy law. Third, many countries may lack chemists who can do the copying, and licensees may not necessarily be able profitably to sell the drug at a much lower price than that of the patent-holding firm. Fourth, data exclusivity provisions may render a compulsory licence worthless if a licence to copy the invention is not accompanied by freedom to use the data so that approval can be given for the generic drug to be made available to the public. This may be one of the reasons why data exclusivity provisions crop up so often in FTAs.

However, the very possibility of compulsory licensing tends to strengthen the bargaining position of governments, even if it is rarely used. It has worked for Brazil in its negotiations with companies to lower the prices of anti-AIDS drugs and also for the US when in 2001 it requested Bayer to lower the price of Cipro, considered to be the best treatment for anthrax.

In 2001, the Doha Ministerial Conference of the WTO adopted the Declaration on the TRIPS Agreement and Public Health, incorporating very similar language to that proposed initially by the developing countries. The Declaration consists of seven paragraphs. The Declaration allows least-developed countries to delay implementation of patent protection for pharmaceutical products and legal protection of undisclosed test data submitted as a condition of approving the marketing of pharmaceuticals until 1 January 2016. In November 2015, the Council for TRIPS agreed to extend this implementation deadline to 1 January 2033.[101] Perhaps the most important paragraph is the fifth, which clarifies the freedoms all WTO members have with respect to compulsory licensing, their determination of what constitutes a national emergency or other circumstances of

---

[99] Curiously this clause is rarely discussed in debates on access to medicines. The reason may be that many developing countries have deficient competition regulations.

[100] F.M. Scherer and J. Watal, 'The Economics of TRIPS Option for Access to Medicines', in B. Granville (ed.), *The Economics of Essential Medicines* (London: Royal Institute of International Affairs, 2002), 32–56, 37–8.

[101] Separate WTO decisions provide for LDC extensions regarding TRIPS as a whole. In November 2005, the TRIPS Council extended the deadline for LDCs to fully implement TRIPS from the original 2006 (as provided under Article 66.1) to 1 July 2013. A further extension has since then been agreed allowing LDCs to delay full implementation until 1 July 2021.

extreme urgency, and exhaustion of rights. Thus, the Declaration reaffirms the right to use to the full the provisions in TRIPS allowing each member 'to grant compulsory licenses and the freedom to determine the grounds upon which such licenses are granted'. The Declaration explicitly mentions that public health crises 'relating to HIV/AIDS, tuberculosis, malaria and other epidemics, can represent a national emergency or other circumstances of extreme urgency'. Moreover, WTO members are free to establish their own regime for exhaustion of IPRs. This is important because it means that, if national laws indicate that patent rights over drugs are exhausted by their first legitimate sale anywhere in the world, countries can then import drugs legally purchased in countries where they are sold at a lower price.[102] Understandably, such freedom is anathema to the industry. The persistence of parallel importation freedom helps to explain why companies are so reluctant to be open about the prices they charge for the same drugs in different countries.

One matter the Declaration left unresolved concerns the predicament of countries that cannot manufacture drugs themselves. Since TRIPS stipulates under Article 31(f) that unauthorised use of a patent shall be, as we mentioned, 'predominantly for the supply of the domestic market', awarding a licence to an overseas manufacturer would conflict with TRIPS since the use would be to supply a foreign market. This is an important issue because many poor countries lack the capacity to manufacture life-saving drugs such as HIV/AIDS treatments, and would therefore need to import them from countries like India, an important international supplier of relatively cheap generic drugs. To make the situation even more difficult, India was required by TRIPS to introduce product patents on drugs from 1 January 2005 and subsequently complied.[103] Normally patents prevent not just the unauthorised sale of protected products but also their manufacture. Therefore, even if a poor country granted a compulsory licence to a generic firm in India or in any other foreign country, if the drug were protected by a patent in the generic firm's country too, the licensee would not actually be able to make the drug unless the government of India also granted a compulsory licence, something that it would not be allowed to do on account of Article 31(f).

Paragraph Six of the Declaration recognised that 'WTO Members with insufficient or no manufacturing capacities in the pharmaceutical sector could face difficulties in making effective use of compulsory licensing under the TRIPS Agreement', and instructed the TRIPS Council 'to find an expeditious solution to this problem and to report to the General Council before the end of 2002'. No solution was reached within this deadline, and it was only in August 2003 that one was agreed, the 30 August Decision.[104]

The most important part of the 30 August Decision is Paragraph 2, which provides the terms under which a WTO member may export a pharmaceutical product under a compulsory licence to a country with no or insufficient manufacturing capacity on the basis of a waiver of the condition

---

[102] This is known as 'international exhaustion'. It may be contrasted with 'national exhaustion' according to which rights are exhausted only in the case of first sale in that country. With national exhaustion regimes, parallel importation is not permitted.

[103] J. Sundaram, 'India's Trade-Related Aspects of Intellectual Property Rights Compliant Pharmaceutical Patent Laws: What Lessons for India and Other Developing Countries?' (2014) 23(1) *Information & Communications Technology Law*.

[104] WTO, 'Implementation of Paragraph 6 of the Doha Declaration on the TRIPS Agreement and Public Health: Decision of 30 August 2003' [Document WT/L/540].

in Article 31(f). These terms are fairly detailed in part because the pharmaceutical industry was concerned that drugs manufactured under the waiver might be diverted to other markets.

'Eligible importing Members' of the WTO who may take advantage of the system are all least-developed countries or any other country that notifies the TRIPS Council of its intention to do so. According to the Decision, an eligible exporter's normal obligations under Article 31(f) may be waived in order for a domestic producer to manufacture and export the requested pharmaceutical to an eligible importer under the grant by itself of a compulsory licence. For this to be permitted, the importing country must make a notification to the TRIPS Council that:[105]

(i) specifies the names and expected quantities of the product(s) needed;
(ii) confirms that the eligible importing Member in question, other than a least-developed country Member, has established that it has insufficient or no manufacturing capacities in the pharmaceutical sector for the product(s) in question [...]; and
(iii) confirms that, where a pharmaceutical product is patented in its territory, it has granted or intends to grant a compulsory licence in accordance with Article 31 of the TRIPS Agreement and the provisions of this Decision.

The exporter is required to notify the TRIPS Council and provide full details of the compulsory licence, which is required to contain certain conditions. In practice, this at least should not be particularly onerous.

Patent holders whose inventions are subject to a compulsory licence are normally entitled to remuneration. On this issue, Paragraph 3 places the obligation to remunerate the owner on the exporter who in calculating the amount must take 'into account the economic value to the importing Member of the use that has been authorized in the exporting Member'. As for the compulsory license granted for the same products by the importer, the obligation to remunerate is waived, leaving this requirement to the exporter.

All of this requires, of course, the existence of a generic company both willing and able to make the drug to supply this particular market. Since generic companies are just as much in the business of making a profit as the research-based ones, it is not self-evident that such a company will always be found. One important consideration here is the size of the market and the possibility of economies of scale. Since 23 developed countries stated in a footnote to the Decision that they would not use the system as eligible importers, one may reasonably wonder whether there is sufficient incentive for many generic firms to produce a pharmaceutical to supply only one or a few developing countries with low populations. However, the Decision recognises this may be a problem, since in the case of a developing or LDC importer being a party to a regional trade agreement at least half of whose members are LDCs, the pharmaceutical can be exported to those other party countries, albeit without prejudice to the territorial nature of the patent rights.[106] It is mentioned in the Decision that regional patent systems are a good thing in this respect since a compulsory licence would have effect in all countries in which the regional patent is valid.

---

[105] Paragraph 2(a).

[106] Paragraph 6(i).

On 6 December 2005, a more permanent solution was found when the WTO members agreed to amend TRIPS by adopting a Protocol that supplements TRIPS with the insertion of an Article 31*bis* and an annex, which follow very closely the text of the earlier Decision.[107] In July 2007, Rwanda informed the WTO of its intention to import some anti-AIDS medicines from Canada. Strictly speaking, as an LDC, Rwanda was not required to do this. In its submission to the TRIPS Council,[108] the Rwandan government indicated its desire to import '260,000 packs of TriAvir, a fixed-dose combination of Zidovudine, Lamivudine and Nevirapine manufactured in Canada by Apotex, Inc'. As a combination of drugs, Apotex needed to agree terms with two companies to make TriAvir, Boehringer Ingelheim and GlaxoSmithKline.

13.3.4 Will the amendment make a difference?

For the Amendment to be fully incorporated into TRIPS it needed to be approved by two-thirds of the WTO membership. In January 2017 it achieved sufficient approval, including by the US, the EU, Switzerland, India and China, and is therefore now in force. However, developing countries have been slow to come forward to take advantage of the Amendment. The Rwanda-Apotex arrangement did make the drugs available, but Apotex reportedly found the process to be highly inconvenient and commercially unviable, and this remains the only instance of the system (such as it is) ever being used. This suggests that cross-boundary compulsory licensing procedures may still be too complex. It may also be the case that generic firms outside India, which has only quite recently introduced a product patent regime, may not be very interested in the rigmarole of negotiating with both domestic patent-owning firms and foreign governments and in such a public way. As for developing country governments, since the notification must be made it is very possible that many of them fear trade retaliation, particularly from the US, which is so hostile to 'breaking patents' when it is done abroad.

Scepticism about this 'solution' is warranted for two reasons. The first is the low uptake so far. It would be useful to investigate the reasons for this. The second is that while the Amendment reflects a genuine attempt, albeit an imperfect one, to improve access, the intellectual property chapters of recent Free Trade Agreements seem to reflect a deliberate attempt to undermine anything that the international community can achieve multilaterally.

---

[107] WTO, 'Amendment of the TRIPS Agreement: Decision of 6 December 2005' [Document WT/L/641].

[108] WTO, 'Notification under Paragraph 2(A) of the Decision of 30 August 2003 on the Implementation of Paragraph 6 of the Doha Declaration on the TRIPS Agreement and Public Health', 2007 [Document IP/N/9/RWA/1].

14
New biologies

14.1 LIFE IN A TEST-TUBE

The assumption that inventions are essentially mechanical devices and that patents are therefore intended to protect clever gadgets is commonplace. New mousetraps? Yes, of course. Mice? Surely not. But this has never been accurate, true as it is that the patenting of living things and the constituent molecular parts of life forms was not at all common until well beyond the middle of the twentieth century. In principle, creative results of applied biological work are no less suitable for the patent system than chemistry, to which biology is closely related. Chemical substances have been patentable for a very long time despite their raising certain difficulties (see Chapter 5). And yet, biology and biotechnology present a whole host of distinct challenges for the patent system. Perhaps most fundamental of them all: does it even make sense to treat all of such 'inventions' (or discoveries?) as human artefacts in the first place? Clearly, nothing is human-made if that means being constructed atom-by-atom. But that is not the point being made here. As fine chemistry led over the course of many decades to molecular biology, the fundamental question of where the line can be drawn between a discovered thing found in nature but identified in a laboratory and a human-invented object, also made in a lab, became no easier to answer. Indeed, as we will see, how the US and Europe deal with patentability in this area has actually diverged in recent years due to differences in framing and dealing with basic patentability questions.

From a scientific perspective, the question of whether inventions in this general field are really human-made notwithstanding the undeniable ingenuity and economic commitment invested in coming up with them cannot be avoided. Methods are one thing,[1] products are another, especially whole life forms which however well 'engineered' remain things very far removed from more traditional human creations like lightbulbs, vacuum cleaners, and aeroplanes. And yet this matter tends to get subsumed within the standard deontological and consequentialist justifications for patents which have nothing at all to do with science, and thus get overlooked.

Is there a scientific logic behind patenting in this field? Many if not most patent attorneys would see little point in addressing the question. If it meets the criteria, is not excluded subject matter, and offends no patent examiner or judge, it goes in. Why wouldn't it? Let scientists, philosophers and whoever else may be interested discuss it if they wish. This is an academic book and we feel entitled, if not obligated, to address such queries as best we can. We can do a lot worse than turning first to two distinguished scientists who, inadvertently or otherwise, happened to frame their science according to language patent attorneys are familiar with: John Cornforth and Jacques Loeb.

Over two decades ago, the Australian Nobel Prizewinning chemist Sir John Cornforth eloquently demystified the art of synthesis in a published lecture.[2] He suggested a modern definition of synthesis as 'the intentional construction of molecules by means of chemical reactions'. What synthesis does not mean, he said, is 'making new compositions of matter'. Perhaps purposely, but possibly accidentally, he was using a term in American patent law, 'composition of matter' being mentioned in the statute as a type of invention. As he put it:

> It happens that Nature and especially living Nature has exhibited to the chemist a very large variety of molecules. They are there, they are not new; but if we can make them from something else we say that we have synthesized them. And sometimes we proudly call our synthesis a total synthesis. Briefly, we are then claiming that, if we were given adequate supplies of all the chemical elements composing our compound, we could make a specimen of the compound totally derived from the matter supplied. In practice, nobody ever executes a total synthesis and few of the raw materials used have in fact been made from their elements.

Cornforth went on to point out that 'synthesis of compounds from elements is not peculiar to human beings', and that 'the rejection of competition, or even help, from other organisms in the execution of chemical synthesis is another nineteenth-century legacy'. He is of course not being disrespectful towards his fellow synthetic chemists or belittling their achievements. But it is as

---

[1] This is not to say that methods claims are uncontroversial or simple, whether in the fields of software and digital technology, healthcare, or of plant sciences.

[2] J.W. Cornforth, 'The Trouble with Synthesis' (1993) 46 *Australian Journal of Chemistry* 157–70. All quotes below are from this paper.

well to be aware that chemical synthesis is a creative mimicry of nature – perhaps as artistic as it is scientific – which arguably gives nature far less credit than it deserves and humans rather too much. Nonetheless, patents, as we will see, are embedded in the world of commerce more than of science (or for that matter art) and such subtleties are likely to get lost in translation. In fact, they have to for much of life science patenting to be viable.

What about life itself? Let us turn to a great scientist of an earlier era. Jacques Loeb, a US-based German scientist of the late nineteenth and early twentieth centuries, was the subject of one of the most startling headlines in the history of newspapers, announcing his successful experiment in developing a sea urchin from an unfertilised egg and thereby inventing animal cloning:[3]

Creation of Life. Startling Discovery of Prof. Loeb. Lower Animals Produced by Chemical Means. Process May Apply to Human Species. Immaculate Conception Explained.[4]

A pioneer in both genetic engineering and synthetic biology, as they would much later be called, Loeb inadvertently used what would become European patent law language in defining the ambitions of his scientific approach. This was in 1903: 'We cannot allow any barrier to stand in the path of our complete control and thereby understanding of the life phenomena. I believe that anyone will reach the same view who considers the control of natural phenomena as the essential problem of scientific research.'[5] This chimes with a recent statement made by the European Patent Office Enlarged Board of Appeal, which incidentally – and highly conveniently – favours quite an expansive view of the concept of invention:

Human intervention, to bring about a result by using the forces of nature, pertains to the core of what an invention is understood to be. Like national laws, the EPC does not define the term 'invention' but the definition that was given many years ago in the 'Red Dove' ('Rote Taube') decision of the German Federal Court of Justice [...] set a standard which still holds good today and can be said to be in conformity with the concept of 'invention' within the meaning of the EPC.

In that decision [...] the [...] Court [...] defined the term 'invention' as requiring a technical teaching. The term technical teaching was characterised as 'a teaching to methodically utilize controllable natural forces to achieve a causal, perceivable result'.[6, 7]

---

[3] P. Ball, *Unnatural: The Heretical Idea of Making People* (London: Bodley Head, 2011), 138. He managed also to clone a frog but unfortunately Loeb let it die due to his failure to realise the implications of frogs being amphibians: he let it drown.

[4] This was in an 1899 issue of the *Boston Herald*, and is quoted in Ball, ibid., 137.

[5] Quote in P.J. Pauly, *Controlling Life: Jacques Loeb and the Engineering Ideal in Biology* (New York: Oxford University Press, 1987), at 114.

[6] G1/08 (Tomatoes/STATE OF ISRAEL). Decision of the Enlarged Board of Appeal of 9 December 2010.

[7] The definition of 'invention' under Japanese statutory law is not dissimilar: 'highly advanced creation of technical ideas utilizing law of nature'. Quoted in M.D. Janis, 'Patenting Plants: A Comparative Synthesis, in R.L. Okediji and M.A. Bagley (eds), *Patent Law in Global Perspective* (Oxford: Oxford University Press, 2014), 217.

Let us ponder what the two scientists were saying here and search for some meaning that may or may not have been intended but which is capable of having legal repercussions. In doing so we must first understand that 'invention' can be used to refer both to a creative thought process leading to a result, and to the result itself. Cornforth does not state a point of view about the patent system and neither does Loeb. But one is left with some intriguing thoughts. A chemical newly made in the lab is certainly a composition of matter (how can anything made of atoms not be?). But how might it not be novel? Here things are less clear. If Cornforth is alluding to the 'things' made in the lab, he would be suggesting that the things, that is, the synthetic chemicals, lack the novelty to be patentable, at least insofar as nature has anticipated these chemicals by having made them already. But arguably he is saying something a little different: that there is nothing novel in what the scientist does, because there is nothing in chemical synthesis that is novel. And if there is nothing novel about what she does, there is nothing novel either about the result. This is because it is a matter of making molecules, albeit in a different way from what happens in nature, and with a continuing reliance on natural products and processes to do most of the work. In other words, the scientist is doing nothing creative but is relying on nature's bits and pieces and the natural forces that transform these parts into a whole. Where this leaves the patentability of synthetic chemicals that are not copies of, or closely derived from, naturally-occurring ones, is less than clear. Perhaps these could be new compositions of matter, but one can read Cornforth both to accept and to deny this possibility.

The law has in fact been grappling with this question since the late-nineteenth century and the US and Europe continue to have a different view on this. In the well-known *Funk Bros. Seed Co. v. Kalo Inoculant* case, Justice Frankfurter, in his concurring opinion stated that:

> It only confuses the issue [...] to introduce such terms as 'the work of nature' and the 'laws of nature'. For these are vague and malleable terms infected with too much ambiguity and equivocation. Everything that happens may be deemed 'the work of nature', and any patentable composite exemplifies in its properties 'the laws of nature'. Arguments drawn from such terms for ascertaining patentability could fairly be employed to challenge almost any patent.[8]

In much of the European continent, the inherent patentability of chemicals was confirmed only quite recently. While public interest considerations and industry demands were often behind the prohibition, it is possible that more conceptual grounds were sometimes applied such as those proffered by the turn of the twentieth century German legal philosopher, Josef Köhler. Köhler denied chemicals could be inventions:

> On the basis of the theoretical possibility that one day these synthetically produced chemicals might also be found in nature. He further argued that the tendency of chemical substances to combine with each other reflects an inherent, natural disposition, so that man's

---

[8] *Funk Bros Seed Co. v. Kalo Inoculant Co.* (1948) 333 US 127.

contribution consists not so much in the creation of a new compound as in the removal of the obstacles that block its formation.[9]

The fact that Germany did not allow patent claims on chemicals until the late 1960s, almost a century after infant industry protectionist and anti-monopoly arguments against such patenting had ceased to be credible, suggests these arguments would have been convenient and thus may have been influential. It also implies that in much of continental Europe, the chemicals-to-microbes-to-plants-to-animals analogical shifts may have more shaky foundations than some might suppose, an issue we will return to later in the book. However, there does not appear any likelihood of reverting to the ban on chemicals era. Patenting of chemical products is so much embedded in the ways that companies do business that it is difficult to imagine a reversal.

Returning to Loeb, the very close similarity between his statement made in 1903, and the definition of invention in the 1969 German *Red Dove* case cited with approval by the European Patent Office in 2010, might just be a coincidence signifying little of substance. But directing nature and natural forces for practical ends is arguably what all inventing involves. The question remaining is that of how much human intervention in natural forces is required, and in what form, to convert a natural product into an artificial one. Bear in mind here that 'human intervention' has to be physical and not purely mental though this is not an entirely clear-cut issue as they may not be entirely separable.

This might all seem rather unimportant if not esoteric. In fact this discussion raises an interesting issue. Is the patent system inherently receptive towards scientific achievements in the biological sciences having therapeutic or commercial application? In other words, is the patent system bound to become ever more inclusive so as to accommodate the expanding scientific 'frontier'? In reality, logic, language and legal reasoning make nothing inevitable. As we will see, history reveals no guaranteed alignment between the scope of patentable subject matter and what commercially-oriented scientists do in biology and in the medical sciences for which they or their employees would like to acquire intellectual property protection. Recent case law in the US makes this very evident.

14.2 ANTECEDENTS

Historically, the expansion of patentable subject matter has been driven by advances in scientific knowledge harnessed to improved technical means to generate products that could make money for their developers. The relationships between science, technology, business and capitalism are much debated but this much at least is beyond dispute. For new biologies, as we call them in this chapter, the precedent was chemistry. In 1828, Friedrich Wöhler synthesised, albeit partially and by accident, a naturally-occurring chemical produced previously only in animal bodies: urea. He boasted, incontinently one might say, that 'I can no longer, so to speak, hold

---

[9] H. van den Belt, 'Philosophy of Biotechnology', in A. Meijers (ed.), *Philosophy of Technology and Engineering Sciences* (Elsevier, 2009).

my chemical water and must tell you that I can make urea without needing a kidney, whether of man or dog; the ammonium salt of cyanic acid is urea.'[10] Antoine Lavoisier (1743–94), a major figure in the history of science, showed that living processes are chemical processes. From that time, the chemical basis of living things and biological processes became ever more apparent. It became evident that life is made of the same stuff that non-life is made of, nothing more nothing less. In other words, organisms were made of bits of non-life, as were the products made in living cells: proteins, hormones, metabolites, and so on. Justus Liebig may have been the first to realise, following his friend Wöhler's breakthrough that these bits could be made artificially in a laboratory.[11]

In the early-nineteenth century, French chemists learned how to extract alkaloids from plants.[12] Among the most important were morphine and codeine from opium, and quinine from Cinchona cordifolia. This made them industrial products. Once chemical substances could be identified and characterised according to a universally accepted nomenclature, eventually some fundamental questions about the patentability of newly-described chemicals 'found' in nature were bound to arise. Was the process of extraction a kind of remaking? If so, was doing so tantamount to creating a new thing, an artefact as opposed to a product of nature? What about synthesis, whereby a chemist using natural starting materials made something in the laboratory that was not known to exist in that or any other form in nature? What if the same means were employed not to make something original, but an imitation of a natural product different only in being artificial? As we will see, these questions have yet to be definitively answered.

From the 1850s, advances in fine chemistry led to the possibility of making microscopic substances in the laboratory which were either novel in the sense of being different from anything known to exist, or that were copies of natural products, and then making enough to put them in a container with a fancy label. At the same time, in Britain, France and the US which allowed chemical products to be patented, patents were filed on isolated natural products, new lab-made synthetic ones, and synthetic molecules that were copies of ones found in nature. Among the first of the latter were dyes such as alizarin and indigo which had hitherto been extracted from plants, but which could then be made through industrial processes obviating the need to acquire them from the natural sources. Inevitably, concerns about novelty and inherent patentability arose.

Britain, where patents were registered without substantive examination until the early-twentieth century, was quite relaxed about what got patented. Synthetic alizarin was patented twice,

---

[10] G.K. Hunter, *Vital Forces: The Discovery of the Molecular Basis of Life* (London and San Diego: Academic Press, 2000), 56–9. For discussion on the sometimes overstated significance of Wöhler's achievement, see also B. Bensaude-Vincent and I. Stengers, *A History of Chemistry* (Cambridge: Harvard University Press, 1996), 145–6; J.H. Brooke, 'Wöhler's Urea and the Vital Force – A Verdict from the Chemists' (1968) 15 *Ambix* 84–114; G.J. Goodfield, *The Growth of Scientific Physiology: Physiological Method and the Mechanist-Vitalist Controversy Illustrated by the Problems of Respiration and Animal Heat* (Hutchinson, 1960); D. McKie, 'Wöhler's Synthetic Urea and the Rejection of Vitalism: A Chemical Legend' (1944) 153 *Nature* 609.

[11] Hunter, ibid., 57–8.

[12] A. Burgen, 'François Magendie and the New Science of Drugs' (1996) 4 *European Review* 165–72.

granted on consecutive days in 1869.[13] There was never a dispute as to eligibility or novelty. The US was different. The US Supreme Court held synthetic alizarin not to be novel for being a copy of an old and previously isolated natural product with known chemical formula. According to the Court:

> The article produced by the process described was the alizarine of madder, having the chemical formula C14H8O4. It was an old article. While a new process for producing it was patentable, the product itself could not be patented, even though it was a product made artificially for the first time, in contradistinction to being eliminated from the madder root. Calling it artificial alizarine did not make it a new composition of matter, and patentable as such, by reason of its having been prepared artificially, for the first time, from anthracine, if it was set forth as alizarine, a well-known substance.[14]

What about isolated natural products? Hormones are a major part of the story here. According to the historian of science Nicolas Rasmussen, 'in the first half of the twentieth century, hormones took pride of place as life's master molecules, and the endocrinologist took precedence over the geneticist as the scientist offering the means to control life […]'.[15] The hormones era from around 1900 to the 1960s was a period of intensifying pharmaceutical industry internationalisation and competition within and across national boundaries. Hormones, which include steroids, are chemical messengers produced by living organisms including humans. They form a wide range of products from anti-inflammatories to contraceptives, and of course insulin. As soon as hormones were found to have commercial potential industry faced the challenge of how to mass-produce them. This was obviously a scientific matter, but it was also a business issue and an intellectual property one. Both production pathways of extraction and hormone synthesis turned out to be equally capable of resulting in patentable subject matter. This was so even when said matter was based on a substance produced by an organism or else was a laboratory-produced copy of one. This set a historic precedent for the patenting of 'natural' things like antibiotics, genes, cells, microbes, plants and animals. Thus the patenting of hormones helped allow us to conceive of biotechnological products as patentable inventions.

Adrenaline was one of the first commercial hormones. Around the turn of the last century, John Jacob Abel at Johns Hopkins University in the US produced a relatively pure form of a glandular product he called epinephrin.[16] This substance is produced in humans and animals. A few

---

[13] Patent number 1936 was filed on 25 June 1869 by Caro, Graebe and Liebermann. On the following day patent number 1948 was filed by Perkin. Both were granted. The former invention was the subject at issue in the US *Cochrane v. Badische* case (see below). It seems odd that the same subject matter could be claimed in two separate patents filed by completely different inventors. In fact, this is not so unusual as it might seem. For example, much more recently the US granted several patents all claiming the human gene coding for the CCR5 receptor that is implicated in HIV infection (M.W. Jackson, *The Genealogy of a Gene: Patents, HIV/AIDS, and Race* (Cambridge: MIT Press, 2015), 35–8.

[14] *Cochrane v. Badische*, 111 US 293–1884.

[15] N. Rasmussen, 'Steroids in Arms: Science, Government, Industry, and the Hormones of the Adrenal Cortex in the United States, 1930–1950' (2002) 46 *Medical History* 299–324.

[16] R.P. Rubin, 'A Brief History of Great Discoveries in Pharmacology: In Celebration of the Centennial Anniversary of the

years later, Jokichi Takamine, a US-based Japanese scientist, came up with an extract of sufficient purity to display some of the effects of the hormone as it functioned in the mammalian body. He filed two patents in 1903 and 1904 for a glandular extractive product claiming purified forms of adrenaline, as it was also called,[17] and for this compound in a solution with salt and a preservative.[18] Takamine licensed the patents to Parke Davis & Co. Around this time, a number of adrenaline-based products were sold in the US and Germany, but Parke Davis's trademarked Adrenalin products became market leaders on account of their relative purity, safety and efficacy.

As with alizarin, in Britain Takamine's adrenaline inventions covering the preparations themselves were patented without challenge or controversy. In the US, Takamine's two patents were the subject of a 1911 court case in which Parke Davis successfully sued H.K. Mulford & Co for infringement. The litigants were primarily concerned about priority and not really about subject matter including the issue of whether isolating or purifying a natural product made something that was new. According to precedent it did not. Accordingly, the court established that the novelty of such extracts was not necessarily destroyed by the prior existence of less pure extracts if the difference was of kind rather than of degree.[19] Regarding the first of the two patents, Judge Learned Hand, who later became a very famous jurist in the US, held that:

> Takamine was the first to make it available for any use by removing it from the other gland-tissue in which it was found, and, while it is of course possible logically to call this a purification of the principle, it became for every practical purpose a new thing commercially and therapeutically.[20, 21]

However, the judge went further than this – and much further than he needed to do to settle the case. He denied that there was any rule to prevent the patentability even of natural products merely extracted from living things if to do this made them 'available' for the first time. Thus patentability may be extended to an otherwise unchanged naturally occurring substance, as long as the active principle in its original surroundings is not also claimed: 'But, even if it were merely an extracted product without change, there is no rule that such products are not patentable.' By saying this, he misunderstood legal precedents that sought to impose strict novelty requirements in respect of natural products. Nonetheless, despite this ruling coming from a district court, this statement has had enduring legal influence in the US affecting judgments regarding patentability of types of invention that could reasonably be considered more natural than artificial.[22]

Founding of the American Society of Pharmacology and Experimental Therapeutics' (2007) 59 *Pharmacological Reviews* 289–359, 292.

[17] US Patent no 730,176 ('Glandular extractive product'), issued on June 2 1903.

[18] US Patent no 753,177 ('Glandular extractive compound'), issued on February 23 1904.

[19] Takamine had originally claimed the natural substance itself but this was refused by the examiner.

[20] *Parke Davis and Co v. H.K. Mulford and Co*, 189 Fed 95 (SDNY, 1911) affirmed, 196 Fed 496 (2nd Cir, 1912).

[21] Since Parke Davis registered 'Adrenalin' as a trade mark in the US, the natural substance is referred to as epinephrine in that country, and this is becoming international practice.

[22] For a detailed analysis of the case and its implications see J.M. Harkness, 'Dicta on Adrenalin(e): Myriad Problems

In the early 1920s, US, UK and Canadian patents were filed by the University of Toronto for isolated and purified insulin and the extractive process was granted and assigned to the University of Toronto. In none of these three jurisdictions was there any particular controversy about the patentability of insulin per se, although public sector and university patenting was often criticised at the time for being unethical. Over the course of the century, as scientific interest in the sex hormones increased, private investment and patenting activity followed. By the 1950s, after 30 years of patenting activity in the field of sex hormones leading to the first contraceptive pills, considerable change had taken place in their status from crude glandular extracts to industrial products and this was reflected in the patent system. As French historian of science Jean-Paul Gaudillière explains:

> Steroids had become drugs manufactured by industry in (relatively) large quantities, and were now biochemical substances defined in terms of structure and metabolism rather than anatomical origins and mode of action. In other words, the sex hormones had become biotechnological 'goods'. The management of intellectual property played a critical role in these processes of industrialization and molecularization, because it helped align sex hormones with chemicals and chemically constructed therapeutic agents.[23]

What about other types of natural product? Two early pharmaceutical breakthroughs that turned out to be patentable despite their being new types of subject were vitamin B12 and the antibiotic streptomycin. In December 1947, scientists at Merck isolated a naturally occurring substance called cyanocobalamin. This substance, christened vitamin B12 by the scientists who had isolated it, was protected by two US patents issued in 1951 and 1955. Although the product claims of the latter patent were invalidated by a district court in 1957, they were reinstated on appeal. Both patents were the subject of another court case in 1967. The court upheld the first patent entirely.[24] Although five of the 12 claims in the second patent were invalidated, the principle that a 'composition of matter' consisting of a purified form of a natural product could be patented subject to passing the tests of non-obviousness and utility was not called into question.

In 1948, Merck was granted a US patent for crystalline salts of the antibiotic, streptomycin, and for a process for preparing them. Streptomycin, the second antibiotic to come onto the market after penicillin and the first drug to be effective against tuberculosis, was discovered by scientists at Rutgers University in the US. The streptomycin patent was in itself an important development, reaffirming post-*Parke Davis* that the new antibiotics were patentable despite being 'products of nature'.

Today, we are living with the legacy of the hormones' era. As stated earlier, once hormones emerged as products, patent granting offices and courts were generally quite favourably disposed

---

with Learned Hand's Product-of-Nature Pronouncements in Parke-Davis v. Mulford' (2011) 93(4) *Journal of the Patent and Trademark Office Society* 363–99.

[23] J.-P. Gaudillière, 'Professional or Industrial Order? Patents, Biological Drugs, and Pharmaceutical Capitalism in Early Twentieth Century Germany' (2008) 24(2) *History and Technology* 10–733, 126.

[24] *Merck and Co, Inc v. Chase Chemical Company et al.* (1967) USPQ 155, 152.

towards hormone-related patent claims. Of course, not all countries allowed chemicals and medicines to be patented for much of the last century. Even Britain, from 1919 till 1949, barred the patenting of substances 'produced by chemical processes or intended for food or medicine' though product protection was available for substances 'prepared or produced by the special methods or processes of manufacture described and claimed or by their obvious chemical equivalents'. But for those jurisdictions that did, and for those that do today, hormones were inherently patentable whether as synthetic chemicals[25] or as preparations extracted from body tissue or fluid. On the basis of similar rationales, genes, microbes, plants and animals are now patentable too.

Let us consider the language of the 1998 European Union Directive on the Legal Protection of Biotechnological Inventions in relation to synthesised and isolated chemicals that are copies of, or are themselves, natural products. There is no reason to suppose that the drafters had read the *Cochrane* or *Parke Davis* cases, disapproving of the former judgment and approving the latter. After all, why would they have bothered to read these ancient cases from the US? And yet, upon reading certain provisions of the Directive, one can be forgiven for wondering whether they had. Thus Recital (20) of the Directive states in part:

> [...] an invention based on an element isolated from the human body or otherwise produced by means of a technical process, which is susceptible of industrial application, is not excluded from patentability, even where the structure of that element is identical to that of a natural element, given that the rights conferred by the patent do not extend to the human body and its elements in their natural environment.

Reference is made to the human body rather than, as in *Cochrane*, to a produced 'element' that is identical to a natural element existing in a plant. Nonetheless, the issue of whether a synthetic or isolated chemical can be patented despite its being identical to a naturally occurring substance is again answered but this time affirmatively.

Turning to the question of whether a substance isolated from the human body or other life form can form the basis of an invention capable of passing the novelty test, Article 3.2 states that 'biological material which is isolated from its natural environment or produced by means of a technical process may be the subject of an invention even if it previously occurred in nature.' No doubt Learned Hand would approve. Article 5.2 follows this up linking this general principle specifically to gene sequences and the human body: 'an element isolated from the human body or otherwise produced by means of a technical process, including the sequence or partial sequence of a gene, may constitute a patentable invention, even if the structure of that element is identical to that of a natural element'.

Given that the main patent jurisdictions have accepted an invention's possessing life as being without legal significance,[26] it becomes far easier to conceive of a human modified bacterium as an invention whether as a chemical composition or a manufactured entity, or both. Once done, a

---

[25] The *Cochrane v. Badische* ruling arguably qualifies this generalisation with respect to the US.

[26] See, for example, *Diamond v. Chakrabarty*, 447 US 303 (1980).

2002 Canadian Supreme Court decision notwithstanding,[27] it becomes very hard logically or scientifically to defend the refusal to extend patent scope to plants and animals. The higher-lower life form distinction makes little sense given, for example, the strong argument favouring the view that human beings have far more in common biologically with humble yeasts than the latter do with their fellow microbial but very distant cousins, the bacteria. Despite this influence on the present, the hormones' era has been largely overlooked by legal scholars.

14.3 PATENTING LIFE IN THE BIOTECHNOLOGY ERA

14.3.1 From microbes to plants to animals

Biotechnology: patents and the emergence of a new industry

Biotechnology is an old word but its modern use coincides with the invention of recombinant DNA in the 1970s, attributed to Stanley Cohen at Stanford University and Herbert Boyer at University of California at San Francisco. The technique, which enables foreign genes to be inserted into micro-organisms and passed on to others through cell division, was patented by Stanford and licensed widely, earning over $200 million in royalties between 1975 and 1997, when the patent expired.[28] This was despite reasonable claims as to whether the invention was genuinely novel even with the 12-month grace period under US patent law.[29] A few years later, the era of commercial biotechnology got underway. This was largely due to its wide dissemination, but was probably not unrelated either to the fact that, following *Diamond v. Chakrabarty* (see below), inventions in this new field were definitely patentable making this emergent sector attractive for investors.[30] Until the modern biotechnology era began in the US in the 1970s, of the four million US patents issued since 1790, only 70 had protected 'mixtures or compounds that included micro-organisms in unmodified form'.[31] Only Pasteur's anomalous yeast culture product patent granted in 1873 exclusively covered living organisms. The 'product of nature' doctrine adopted by the courts and the

---

[27] *Harvard College v. Canada (Commissioner of Patents)* 2002 SCC 76.

[28] M. McKelvey, *Evolutionary Innovations: The Business of Biotechnology* (Oxford: Oxford University Press, 1996), p. xix. The initial patent application was filed in 1974, but was overridden by subsequent applications. The definitive patent (number 4,237,224) was filed in 1979 and awarded in 1980 following the Supreme Court decision in *Diamond v. Chakrabarty*. The title of the patent was 'Process for producing biologically functional molecular chimeras'.

[29] H. Holzapfel and J.D. Sarnoff, 'A Cross-Atlantic Dialog on Experimental Use and Research Tools' (2008) 48(2) *IDEA* 122–223, 127.

[30] For a discussion on the full commercial significance of the patent, see S.S. Hughes, 'Making Dollars out of DNA: The First Major Patent in Biotechnology and the Commercialization of Molecular Biology, 1974–1980' (2001) 92(3) *ISIS* 541–75, 571–2.

[31] D.J. Kevles, 'Ananda Chakrabarty Wins a Patent: Biotechnology, Law, and Society, 1972–1980' (1994) 25(1) *Historical Studies in the Physical and Biological Sciences* 111–35, 111.

granting office had since the 1880s apparently precluded the patenting of any further life forms and products taken unchanged from the natural world.

Genentech was the first company started up to exploit the new biotechnological applications coming out of the universities. It was founded in 1976 and was responsible for the first biotechnology-based health product to reach the market, which was genetically engineered human insulin, in 1982. It was developed by Genentech in collaboration with Eli Lilly. During the 1980s Genentech followed up insulin with two more genetically engineered human proteins sold as pharmaceutical products. These were human growth hormone, which was approved in 1985 and marketed as Protropin, and tissue plasminogen activator (tPA), a 'clot-buster' drug for heart attack patients approved in 1987 and sold as Activase. Amgen followed in Genentech's footsteps two years later with Epogen (erythropoietin), a hormone used to treat anaemia caused by kidney failure. Healthy kidneys produce erythopoietin to promote oxygen-carrying red blood cell formation.[32]

Key to the success of biotechnology company initial public offerings (IPOs) was the possession of patents protecting important technologies and promising products in the making. The *Diamond v. Chakrabarty* decision provided a tremendous fillip in this respect. In that 1980 decision, the Supreme Court ruled by a narrow majority that a man-made oil-eating bacterium produced by Anand Chakrabarty, an employee of General Electric, could be classed as a 'composition of matter' or a 'manufacture', and therefore be treated as a patentable invention. According to the majority opinion, the US legislature (that is, Congress) 'recognized that the relevant distinction was not between living and inanimate things, but between products of nature, whether living or not, and human-made inventions'.

Initially, the Patent and Trademark Office rejected the claims directed to the bacterium itself on the grounds that it was a product of nature. On appeal, the patent rejection was overturned. This was consistent with an earlier decision of the Court of Customs and Patent Appeals at which Judge Rich had made the following statement when delivering the majority opinion:[33] 'we think the fact that micro-organisms, as distinguished from chemical compounds, are alive is a distinction without legal significance'. He also opined that micro-organisms 'are much more akin to inanimate chemical compositions such as reactants, reagents, and catalysts than they are to horses and honeybees or raspberries and roses'. And so, when the same court ruled jointly on the patentability of the Chakrabarty micro-organism and a similar patent application by Bergy that was assigned to Upjohn, Rich applied the same logic, finding in favour of Chakrabarty's application. Ground-breaking as this case may have been in the US, the fact is that Europe was hardly a follower. Five years earlier, the German Federal Supreme Court had affirmed the patentability of micro-organisms. Chakrabarty's invention was quietly patented in the UK.

There is no question that this 'life as chemistry' conceptualisation is a powerful one. Indeed, it is now implicitly recognised by other patent offices, including the European Patent Office.[34] By

---

[32] M.G. Sargent, *Biomedicine and the Human Condition: Challenges, Risks, and Rewards* (New York: Cambridge University Press, 2003), 256.

[33] *In re Bergy – Application of Malcolm E. Bergy*, 1977, SPQ, 195, 344, 346.

[34] 'DNA is Not "Life", but a Chemical Substance which Carries Genetic Information', *Howard Florey/Relaxin*, EPOR 1995, 541, 551.

treating micro-organisms as natural chemical substances into which a useful new characteristic has been introduced and thereby rendered unnatural, they are assumed to be patentable in accordance with long-established practice with respect to chemical products that allows a natural chemical to be the basis for an invention as long as the version claimed differs by being more purer, modified chemically, or by being mixed with something else that results in a different effect.

What about other types of living thing? Animals had never been patented. Patents claiming plants were granted in the decades either side of the Second World War, but this was rare. After the war, some European countries for a brief period allowed plants to be patented. But between the adoption of the UPOV Convention in 1961 and the advent of the new biotechnologies, plants were clearly excluded in Europe for the obvious reasons that there was a *sui generis* intellectual property system for plant varieties, and that possibilities to transform plants through new gene technologies did not exist (see Chapter 9).

Despite some recent reversals, the US has tended to be the boldest jurisdiction for subject-matter expansiveness. In a 1985 patent appeals case, the Patent and Trademark Office affirmed the patentability of plants, seeds and plant tissue cultures. By 1988 over 40 patents on crop plants had already been issued. In 1987, the PTO Board produced another ground-breaking ruling (in *ex parte Allen*) concerning a patent application on oysters. Although the patent was rejected, the ruling established that multicellular organisms were patentable. A year later the first ever animal patent was granted for 'a transgenic nonhuman mammal' containing an activated oncogene sequence. The patent is commonly referred to as the oncomouse patent, since it describes a mouse into which a gene has been introduced which induces increased susceptibility to cancer (see below).

Biotech patenting in Europe

During the 1980s and 90s, Europe tended to follow these trends, albeit with some important differences. In 1988 the European Patent Office granted the first patent on a plant. The European oncomouse patent, about which much more will be said below, was also granted after initially being rejected. In the late 1980s, the European Commission decided to draft a directive on the legal protection of biotechnological inventions. The European Commission was motivated by concerns about the legal uncertainties which, it was felt, could be prejudicial to the future of biotechnology in Europe, and fears that some European countries might respond to mounting controversy by banning patents on living organisms and genes. However, it was only in 1998 that the Directive on the Legal Protection of Biotechnological Inventions was finally adopted.

The situation in Europe with respect to the patenting of plant-related inventions has been plagued by legal uncertainties, due to the difficult wording of European patent legislation in the face of rapidly changing scientific and business possibilities, concerns about the moral implications of the new biotechnologies, and the ambivalence about biotechnological innovation among citizens and some of the governments.

The 1973 European Patent Convention (EPC) states in Article 53(b) that patents shall not be granted in respect of 'plant or animal varieties or essentially biological processes for the production of plants or animals'. This did not settle matters completely (see below).

According to Article 3(2) of the Directive on the Legal Protection of Biotechnological Inventions, 'biological material which is isolated from its natural environment or produced by means of a technical process may be the subject of an invention even if it previously occurred in nature'. As with the Convention, animal and plant varieties and essentially biological processes for the production of plants and animals are excepted (for more discussion on the meaning and scope of this – see below).[35] Article 2.2 clarifies that 'a process for the production of plants or animals is essentially biological if it consists entirely of natural phenomena such as crossing or selection'. This definition has been accepted by the EPO. In recent years, though, it has proved to be a complex issue. This is hardly surprising when we consider that classical plant breeding nowadays is often assisted by biotechnological methods. Where the production of a new plant stems from a method comprising a mix of both, at what point does the whole process cease to be essentially biological? We will look at this specific matter below.

Aside from patenting a human being, the most radical subject matter for a patent would appear to be an animal. Let us now turn to the first animal patent, the oncomouse. One of the reasons why the oncomouse case is interesting is that patent-granting offices and courts in three important jurisdictions have been called on to assess the patentability of the oncomouse but have failed to come up with the same conclusions. This not only raises the question of how far patent law should go but also how far the harmonisation of patent standards in biotechnology can go.

The oncomouse patents

The oncomouse patent saga begins in June 1985, when Harvard University filed a patent application for 'transgenic non-human mammals', naming as inventors Philip Leder and Timothy A. Stewart. The patent was granted in April 1988. The primary claim covers the following:

> A transgenic non-human mammal all of whose germ cells and somatic cells contain a recombinant activated oncogene sequence introduced into said mammal, or an ancestor of said animal, at an embryonic stage.

Three things are interesting here. The first is the obvious fact that a living organism is being claimed as an invention. The second is that the patent describes the successful introduction of oncogenes into mice and yet it claims not only mice but all transgenic non-human mammals transformed through the same process. The third is that the scope of the patent includes not just animals with activated oncogenes, of which an increasing number are being discovered, but also their ancestors into which the oncogenes were initially introduced by the inventors. In other words, the patent owners have rights to all future generations of mice that inherit the oncogenes up to the expiry date of the patent.

The first interesting feature, that for the first time, an animal has been claimed as a patentable invention, raises the question of whether this is consistent with well-established patent doctrines. While no US courts were called on to answer this question, the decision of the Supreme Court in *Diamond v. Chakrabarty* suggests that the Court may have answered in the affirmative. Indeed, the ruling in *ex parte Allen*, mentioned above, relied in part on the *Chakrabarty* decision (as for that matter did the Court in *J.E.M. Ag Supply v. Pioneer* – see below).

---

[35] In Canada the equivalent phrase is 'essentially natural biological purposes.' *Re Application No 079,973* (1979) 54 CPR (2d) 124 (Pat. App. Bd. & Commissioner of Patents).

As for the second feature of the US oncomouse patent, this appears to claim too much, since for all anybody knew, the use of the technique to transform other animals may prove to be far more difficult and may require unobvious modifications to the technique. This is a problem of excessive patent breadth that is not limited to the life sciences, but is nonetheless very important and will be considered further below.

Turning to the third feature, this situation is clearly problematic. One of the ways in which the patent system seeks to balance the interests of owners and the public is through the concept of exhaustion of rights (or the first sale doctrine in the US). Once a patent-protected product is sold by the owner or the licensee, his or her rights over that product are usually exhausted, unless there is a contract of sale imposing conditions on buyers. When it comes to patents on life forms, the rights are not exhausted when the 'product' is sold but extend to the progeny whether or not the progeny is directly 'manufactured' by the 'inventors'. In this sense, we are making a concession to the patent owner in order to make the patent monopoly meaningful. It is not necessarily wrong to do this. After all, the public may benefit from the use of transgenic animals for such purposes as medical research (as with the oncomouse) or so-called pharming (the use of transgenic animals as producers of therapeutic proteins for human health).

As far as patentability goes, the oncomouse was treated quite differently in the US, Canada and Europe. Let us now turn to Canada, where the Supreme Court was called on to decide as to its eligibility and considered that matter at far greater depth than did the US Supreme Court in *Diamond v. Chakrabarty* the scientific and technical character of the claimed invention. Despite similar statutory language, namely the terms 'manufacture' and 'composition of matter',[36] the Court came up with a very different interpretation than its US counterpart.

Upon examination, the Canadian Patent Office allowed the process claims but rejected the product claims. This was overturned on appeal. The case made its way to the Supreme Court, which in 2002 ruled that the terms 'manufacture' and 'composition of manufacture' in the Patent Act were insufficiently broad to encompass higher life forms within their scope. In doing so, and in contrast to its US counterpart (but perhaps consistently with Judge Rich), the Canadian Supreme Court: (i) rejected the applicability of the above two terms to higher life forms: and (ii) drew a distinction between higher life forms, which were not patentable, and lower life forms, which were. Accordingly, the Court took 'manufacture' 'to denote a non-living mechanistic product or process, not a higher life form'. It denied that the body of a mouse could be considered as a 'composition'. Furthermore, '"matter" captures only one aspect of a higher life form, generally regarded as possessing qualities and characteristics that transcend the particular genetic material of which it is composed'. Setting aside the Federal Court of Appeals' ruling in 2000 that the oncomouse is a composition of matter, the Supreme Court was drawn to conclude that:

> Since patenting higher life forms would involve a radical departure from the traditional patent regime, and since the patentability of such life forms is a highly contentious matter that

---

[36] *Harvard College v. Canada* (Commissioner of Patents) 2002 SCC 76. In the US Patent Law, 'invention' is defined as 'any new and useful art, process, machine, manufacture or composition of matter, or any new and useful improvement in any art, process, machine, manufacture or composition of matter'.

raises a number of extremely complex issues, clear and unequivocal legislation is required for higher life forms to be patentable. The current Act does not clearly indicate that higher life forms are patentable.

With respect to the distinction between higher and lower life forms, the Canadian Supreme Court had the following to say:

> If the line between lower and higher life forms is indefensible and arbitrary, so too is the line between human beings and other higher life forms. It is now accepted in Canada that lower life forms are patentable but this does not necessarily lead to the conclusion that higher life forms are patentable, at least in part for the reasons that it is easier to conceptualize a lower life form as a 'composition of matter' or 'manufacture' than it is to conceptualize a higher life form in these terms.
>
> Patentable micro-organisms are formed in such large numbers that any measurable quantity will possess uniform properties and characteristics. The same cannot be said for plants and animals. It is far easier to analogize a micro-organism to a chemical compound or another inanimate object than it is to analogize an animal to an inanimate object. Moreover, several important features possessed by animals distinguish them from both micro-organisms and plants and remove them even further from being considered a 'composition of matter' or a 'manufacture'. Given the complexity of the issues involved, it is not the task of the Court to situate the line between higher and lower life forms. Also, the specific exception for plants and animals in trade agreements demonstrates that a distinction between higher and lower life forms is widely accepted as valid.

In all probability, like the Court, most people would consider it somewhat easier to think of a lower life form in these terms than a plant or an animal. Nonetheless, contrary to the US Supreme Court, we would suggest that the fact of micro-organisms being alive and chemical compounds not is significant. This is not only because members of the public are likely to have difficulties in conceptualising living things as inventions, but because they can reproduce out of the control of the patent owners. Normally, as indicated earlier, once a patent-protected product is sold by the owner or the licensee, his or her rights over that product are usually exhausted. So allowing patent claims to cover organisms not directly 'manufactured' by the inventors or by anybody else who could be identified as a patent infringer is a generous concession that may or may not be in the public interest.

The dissenting judges had the following response to the point of whether a human-transformed higher life form is any less a composition of matter than a lower life form:

> The oncomouse is patentable subject matter. The extraordinary scientific achievement of altering every single cell in the body of an animal which does not in this altered form exist in nature, by human modification of the genetic material of which it is composed, is an inventive 'composition of matter' within the meaning of s. 2 of the Patent Act.

Justice Binnie, speaking for the minority went on to point out that to find a fertilised, genetically altered oncomouse egg to be patentable, as the majority did, but not the resulting mouse growing from that egg, was unsupported by the statute.

In doing so, the minority confronts us with a vital question: if the transformation of a single-cell organism constitutes an invention, why should a collection of transformed cells forming a multi-cellular organism be treated any differently? To answer this question it would be important, among other factors, to take account of the extent to which current processes to genetically transform micro-organisms are more predictable and controllable than those to transform multicellular organisms.

Politically, what is interesting to note here is that industry used to find the distinction drawn in the Supreme Court decision between higher and lower life forms to be convenient but does not any more. An amicus on behalf of the Pharmaceutical Manufacturers Association before the US Supreme Court as it deliberated on the Chakrabarty microbe was intent on challenging efforts by others to raise 'slippery-slope' concerns. Falsely, as subsequent events would prove, it dismissed the possibility that the issue of patenting higher life forms could be settled without congressional action. In consistency with Judge Rich's statement in *Bergy*, the amicus expressed that 'if a line must be drawn, it may easily be drawn between the mindless, soulless micro-organism involved in Chakrabarty (as well as Bergy) and higher forms of life'.

As for Europe, from an early time all life forms were not equal as far as patentability went, and that applied also to methods of producing or utilising them. To some extent at least, this is what industry wanted. The 1963 Strasbourg Convention on the Unification of Certain Points of Substantive Law on Patents for Invention, from which the relevant parts of the European Patent Convention and TRIPS borrowed language, stated that 'parties were not required to grant patents in respect of […] (b) plant or animal varieties or essentially biological processes for the production of plants or animals; this provision does not apply to microbiological processes and the products thereof '.

Thus, the decision was taken to keep plant and animal breeding outside the patent system. The terms 'essentially biological' replaced 'purely biological' from an earlier version of the text. The Council's Committee of Experts on Patents, that was responsible for drafting the Strasbourg Convention, changed the wording to broaden the exclusionary language to embrace such 'essentially biological' processes as varietal selection and hybridisation methods even if 'technical' devices were utilised to carry out the breeding processes.[37] The singling out of microbiological processes and products was made at the suggestion of AIPPI, which pointed out that micro-organisms were commonly used in well-established industrial activities such as brewing alcoholic beverages and baking bread.[38] Note that TRIPS follows Strasbourg by making the exclusions optional whereas the EPC makes them mandatory. Why the shift from optional to mandatory? Taking UPOV, a legal regime of clear European provenance, into account was clearly a factor, but the overriding reason

---

[37] S. Sterckx and J. Cockbain, *Exclusions from Patentability: How far has the European Patent Office Eroded Boundaries?* (Cambridge University Press, 2012), 35–6.

[38] S.A. Bent, R.L. Schwaab, D.G. Conlin and D.D. Jeffery, *Intellectual Property Rights in Biotechnology Worldwide* (Basingstoke: Macmillan, 1987), 66–7, 66.

is that whereas the EPC was 'fuelled by a desire of the EEC States to create a common patent code', Strasbourg reflected more an intent 'not to attempt to unify legal aspects of law affected by public interest issues'.[39]

As far as animal patenting goes, the story begins, as in the US, with the oncomouse. The European one, though, is long reaching a final conclusion only in 2004. During prosecution of the patent application, the Examining Division objected to the broad scope of the product claims, which extended to 'transgenic non-human eukaryotic animals' despite, as with the US patent, only disclosing the insertion of the oncogenes in mice. In response, the applicants narrowed the claims to 'non-human mammalian animals'.

Nonetheless, while the Canadian Patent Office rejected the product claims alone, the European Patent Office in July 1989 rejected the patent entirely on two grounds. The first was that in claiming animals that were new on the basis of the introduction of oncogenes, the patent was to all intents and purposes claiming animal 'varieties'. According to Article 53(b) of the European Patent Convention (EPC), animal varieties are not patentable.

The second was insufficiency of disclosure, which was not satisfied by the narrowed-down product claims. According to Article 83 of the EPC, 'the European patent application must disclose the invention in a manner sufficiently clear and complete for it to be carried out by a person skilled in the art'. The Examining Division's reasons for rejecting the patent on the grounds of insufficient disclosure were as follows:

> The claims as they presently stand refer to non-human mammalian animals, i.e. not only to mice or more generally to rodents but to any kind of mammals such as anthropoid apes or elephants, all of which have a highly different number of genes and differently developed immune systems.

The Examining Division added that:

> Mr Philip Leder, one of the inventors of the present case, declared [...] before the United States Patent and Trademark Office how surprising it was to obtain positive results on the mouse and reasons are given why he thought that he might have failed. This clearly shows that the success with the transgenic mouse cannot be reasonably extrapolated to all mammals.[40]

On appeal, the Technical Board of Appeal (TBA) decided in October 1990 that animals per se were not excluded from patentability under Article 53(b) EPC. It followed that since claims to genetically modified animals, mammals or any other taxonomic groups higher than that of species were not animal varieties, the oncomouse patent could not therefore be rejected on such grounds. In addition, the TBA pointed out that animals produced by microbiological processes would not fall under the exception anyway. It therefore requested that the Examining Division reconsider its

---

[39] J. Pila, 'Article 53(b) EPC: A Challenge to the *Novartis* Theory of European Patent History' (2009) 72(3) *Modern Law Review* 436–62, 441.

[40] Decision of the Examining Division dated 14 July 1989, 12 OJEPO (1989), 451–61.

interpretation. The TBA also denied that the disclosure was insufficient. Furthermore, in light of the many objections to the patent from animal welfare, religious and environmental organisations on the basis of Article 53(a) of the EPC, according to which patents 'in respect of inventions the publication or exploitation of which would be contrary to ordre public or morality'[41] would not be granted, the TBA came up with a so-called balancing test which it requested the EPO Examining Division to apply. According to the test, the examiners were required by the TBA to conduct 'a careful weighing up of the suffering of animals and possible risks to the environment on the one hand, and the invention's usefulness to mankind on the other'.[42] In October 1992, the grant of European Patent 169,672 was formally announced.

But the story did not end there. Further oppositions to the patent were filed during the 1990s and led in 2001 to the EPO's Opposition Division's response of restricting the product-related scope of the patent from 'non-human mammalian animals' to 'transgenic rodents'. In 2003, an interlocutory decision of the EPO's Opposition Division held the patent to be valid on the basis of the reduced scope but also affirmed that EPC rule 23d(d),[43] which requires that patents not be granted for 'processes for modifying the genetic identity of animals which are likely to cause them suffering without any substantial medical benefit to man or animal, and also animals resulting from such processes', is applicable for drawing the appropriate scope of a patent such as the oncomouse one.

In July 2004, the TBA was again required to assess the validity of the patent. The TBA's application of both the balancing test it had formulated in 1990 and rule 23d(d) resulted in a finding that the patent was valid but only on the basis of claims confined to 'transgenic mouse',[44] thereby vindicating the Examining Division's objections 15 years earlier to the patent's over-broad scope!

The differing treatment of the oncomouse patents in these three jurisdictions suggests that without a clear understanding of why we have patent systems in the first place and what they are meant to achieve, it may not be easy to argue conclusively that patenting life departs from the basic tenets of patent law and should not therefore be allowed. However, one clear point of divergence from conventional patent norms is that since living things have a tendency to reproduce by themselves, or at least with willing partners, in granting patents on life forms we are being very generous to the owners when we allow them to claim ancestors and progeny. But in our view, to know whether this is right or wrong we need to consider what we, that is to say, the public, gets out of the bargain so simply expressed by Lord Mansfield over 200 years ago (see Chapter 5).

14.3.2 Agricultural biotechnology

Biotechnology has applications in a whole range of fields of science, technology, and economic activity. It has a very big impact in agriculture. It was not long after the technique of recombinant DNA was invented that the possibility of transforming plants through the introduction of 'foreign'

---

[41] In 2000, the contracting states agree to strike out the words 'publication or' from the Convention text, and this and other amendments agreed at the time have now entered into force.

[42] Decision of Technical Board of Appeal 3.3.2 dated 3 October 1990. T 19/90 – 3.3.2 OJEPO 13, 476–91, 1990.

[43] This is the updated version of the TBA's balancing test (see ibid.).

[44] T 0315/03 – 3.3.8.

genes became evident to plant scientists. Perhaps the most important technique relies on the use of Agrobacterium tumifaciens, a common plant-infecting bacterium, to insert genes into plants thereby modifying these plants with new traits, such as pest and herbicide resistance. This technology was complex enough to be covered by more than one patent. Other molecular biological methods have been developed to improve plants with greater precision and speed than classical plant breeding methods alone, and by enabling the exploitation of a radically expanded genetic resource-input base. Valuable traits can be characterised, inserted and expressed more easily than ever before. For proponents, this makes biotechnology more accurate and rapid, although critics claim that these advantages can, to some extent at least, be challenged on scientific grounds. Moreover, they enable the possibility of incorporating traits not just from the same species of plant or from a wild or semi-domesticated relative, but from a virtually limitless array of life forms including bacteria. The resource base is thus no longer just earlier varieties of the same or related species, but life in its broadest sense. Even viruses, which arguably lie on the 'wrong' side of the life/non-life divide, have their uses as genomic reservoirs and gene transfer vectors.[45]

None of this replaces classical plant breeding based on crossing and selection. It is still needed. Once you have genetically modified a crop you still need to breed varieties that farmers want to grow under conditions varying from place to place and farm to farm. This is evident from the fact that many plant variety protection certificates in the US, where genetically modified (GM) crops are of course widely cultivated, are held by companies like Monsanto. For example, soybean variety A1026742, was granted PVP certification in April 2013. Provided in the documentation submitted to the Plant Variety Protection Office is a notification that the 'technology' in the plant is covered under nine patents. Those patents claim the transformation techniques, the added genetic elements, and the plant and plant parts containing them. The variety itself is also the subject of a separate patent application. That is quite a weighty bundle of rights around a single plant variety. Molecular biology including genomics can assist breeders in ways enabling them to accelerate their work but without eliminating the need for the classical techniques they have always employed. Moreover, in some areas of crop breeding, conventional methods continue to obtain better results than GM such as in developing efficient plants able to thrive in nutrient-poor soils.[46]

Patents, ownership and genetically-modified plants: the United States

By the end of 2001, there were more than 1,800 US patents with claims to plants, seeds, or plant parts or tissues.[47] Nonetheless, the 1985 decision did not permanently settle the question of whether or not plants are patentable (see below). In December 2001, the Supreme Court finally confirmed the legality of patents on plants. The opportunity to do so arose because lawyers representing a company called J.E.M. Ag Supply, which was being sued by Pioneer Hi-Bred for patent infringement, requested the court to determine whether plant-related patents are invalid because

---

[45] T.M. Wilson, 'Plant Viruses: A Tool-Box for Genetic Engineering and Crop Protection' (1989) 10(6) *Bioessays* 179–86; A.R. Mushegian and R.J. Shepherd, 'Genetic Elements of Plant Viruses as Tools for Genetic Engineering' (1995) 59(4) *Microbiological Reviews* 548–78.

[46] N. Gilbert, 'The Race to Create Super-crops' (2016) 533 *Nature* 308–10.

[47] *J.E.M. Ag Supply, Inc v. Pioneer Hi-Bred Int'l, Inc*, 534 US 124 (2001).

of the existence of two intellectual property laws designed specifically to protect plants: the 1930 Plant Patent Act and the 1970 Plant Variety Protection Act (the legislation for implementing the UPOV Convention nationally – see Chapter 9). By a six–two majority, the Supreme Court rejected J.E.M. Ag Supply's argument and upheld Pioneer's patents.[48]

It is of course no secret that agricultural biotechnology especially genetic modification involving the incorporation into plant genomes of foreign DNA is a hugely controversial issue (see also Chapter 9). GM seeds provide numerous benefits for many farmers. But that is not the whole story. For one thing, there is no certainty that the gains are sustainable in the longer term. For another, these crops come at a huge cost and not just in the monetary sense. The steady erosion of farmer autonomy under the iron grip of a small number of large monopolistic corporations using, at least in Monsanto's case, the full panoply of contract law, intellectual property protection and corporate-friendly regulation in Canada and the US (albeit still not in Europe) is changing the practice of agricultural production in far-reaching and ways that alarms many people.

In North America, buying Monsanto's seed is a bit like buying software with the main exception being that whereas Microsoft has no legal right to routinely inspect all of its customers' homes, Monsanto is authorised by contract to carry out such checks on any seed buyers' farm. You can use it but you'd better not copy it after the initial multiplication of the first harvest. In a sense, farmers are not really buying anything at all since their possession of the seed they purchase is incomplete. All they have are certain limited usage rights. Accordingly, saving harvested seeds to plant on the farm, a practice going back to the earliest days of agriculture, is simply not tolerated. Seeds found on one's farm containing Monsanto's patented genes are Monsanto's not the farmer's, regardless of how the seed containing them got there. Monsanto has been able effectively to separate ownership from legal liability.

In North America, regulatory authorities, patent offices and courts seem invariably to make decisions that favour the business model of Monsanto, which also happens to be highly litigious. Through IPRs, the law of contract, and court judgments, Monsanto wields a great deal of power over farmers. But to many critics, it is power without responsibility, ownership without liability.

Are genetically modified crops and foods good or bad? The debate continues to be highly polarised between those who see GM as being something to be unreservedly welcomed and those for whom GM is to be condemned and opposed. In recent years both sides have accused advocates of the other of needless deaths: allegations of suicides of GM cotton farmers in India said to be caused by debt and crop failures on the one side; on the other, of starvation due to the refusal by African governments 'brainwashed' by Greenpeace and their ilk to accept emergency GM seed and food aid, and opposition to vitamin A-enhanced GM rice varieties thus denied to millions of dangerously malnourished children. GM provides no long-term mastery over nature, whose vagaries defy all such technological fixes after a few years, just as antibiotics, miracle cures as they may be when first introduced, need in time to be replaced as obsolescence sets in. So with GM. Bugs will become resistant to the toxin expressed by the Bt gene engineered into crops; the glyphosate-resistance of Roundup Ready crops will spread to the weeds as has reportedly happened to over 20 weed species in the US. Their adoption limits choice and enables companies like Monsanto to control farmers' livelihoods.

---

[48] Ibid.

Many farmers do like GM seeds and have gained from them financially and through reduced labour. These are by no means only large-scale industrial agriculturalists. Those who are most opposed to GM might as well accept this. On the other hand, to be sceptical about GM is not to be inherently anti-science, deluded, sinister or otherwise self-serving, but to be able to see behind the hype that these technologies are not innocent apolitical inputs into existing modes of production. Instead, they are used to drive profit-making business strategies based on deploying the full weight of the law to disadvantage the buyers to the greatest extent the 'market' (such as it is) can bear while maintaining them as repeat customers. Users may well adopt them willingly and some will consider the price in terms of money and loss of freedom to be worth paying. But the inexorable disenfranchisement may not be worth it at all in the long term as choice is effectively eliminated and the technological treadmill becomes inescapable wherever it may lead.

Farmers adopt GM with all the drawbacks of dealing with Monsanto perfectly rationally, as have farmers in numerous other countries. It is understandable that many feel compelled to so as to stay competitive with those who adopted GM seeds before them. But once done, shifting back to conventional crops is a great deal more difficult. Commonly, one or two companies are completely dominant. In Mississippi, Monsanto is more or less a monopolist in GM seed ownership, and provision through its licensed dealers, and is close to being one in Saskatchewan. There and elsewhere, public sector breeding has been drastically cut back, and there is very little else available on the market that is competitive in yields.[49] Besides, Monsanto has over the years bought up so many independent seed companies that virtually all the good-quality varieties available are GM and under Monsanto's ownership.

A full discussion on the rights and freedoms of farmers in the context of private sector agricultural biological innovation and the increasing role of IPRs in the seed and agro-chemicals markets falls beyond the scope of this book. However, two high-profile patent cases in North America, both having Monsanto as a party, merit discussion in this context.

In 2013, the US Supreme Court by a unanimous decision upheld Monsanto's claims that a farmer named Vernon Bowman had infringed two patents claiming aspects and embodiments of its Roundup Ready technology including seed.[50] Bowman had been acquiring and planting Monsanto beans perfectly legally over several years. However, he also separately acquired Monsanto beans from a grain elevator for a late-season planting. Grain elevators are facilities that farmers typically sell much of their seed to. His motivation for doing so was that late-season plantings are more risky in terms of yields, therefore his preference was to evade the normal premium pricing for authorised Monsanto beans which are patented and whose use is subject to the company's usual stipulations. Since Monsanto is a virtual monopolist in the vicinity, it was obvious that the commodity beans acquired from the grain elevator would almost entirely be Roundup Ready. Bowman retained seed and replanted it for the following year's late season planting and continued this practice in subsequent years.

He justified his actions with the defence that without Monsanto's licensing terms being applicable, Bowman's freedom to do what he wished with the purchased seed extended to harvested seed

---

[49] G. Pechlaner, *Corporate Crops: Biotechnology, Agriculture, and the Struggle for Control* (Austin: University of Texas Press, 2012).

[50] *Bowman v. Monsanto Co* 569 US 278 (2013).

from plants grown from it. The rights of patent owners are exhausted upon first sale. It followed, the argument ran, that farmers have full freedom to do as they wish with plant material descended from legally acquired seed, and patent owners have no rights to interfere with this. From Bowman's perspective he had therefore done nothing wrong. The seed was legally purchased and this was not in dispute. He had planted the beans so acquired as farmers do. Nature does the rest and that is no longer any of Monsanto's business.

The Court would have none of it. It dismissed Bowman's 'blame-the-bean defence': that beans have the capacity independent of humans to germinate and develop new plants, therefore he did not make the bean-yielding plants from the beans he planted. The Court acknowledged that he had the right to consume or resell the acquired seed. What he could not do with it was to use it to make more seed. Why? Because in doing so he was 'making' the invention and doing so without the authorisation of the patent holder. Two questions arise. First, is planting equivalent to making? Second, if it is, why is this making an infringement? According to the dictionary planting is making and for the Supreme Court this was good enough. It was infringing because it denied Monsanto a benefit that the patent system is supposed to provide to inventors. Justice Kagan of the Court had this to say about the legal implications:

> Bowman was not a passive observer of his soybeans' multiplication; or put another way, the seeds he purchased (miraculous though they might be in other respects) did not spontaneously create eight successive soybean crops. [...] Bowman planted Monsanto's patented soybeans solely to make and market replicas of them, thus depriving the company of the reward patent law provides for the sale of each article. Patent exhaustion provides no haven for that conduct.

One angle of the case that attracted wider attention was the self-replicating nature of the invented object. Seed when it lands, or is placed, in the ground under suitable conditions 'makes' multiple copies of itself and each of those copies will in turn make even more. This is a fact of biology. However, on the farm there is a certain artificiality to what goes on. Farmers will seek to optimise those 'suitable conditions' by, for example, removing competing plants, tilling the soil, watering, and applying chemicals to protect them. They also plant the seeds in locations they deem to be appropriate. Farmers intervene in nature in such ways, but nature undeniably 'rules'. Be that as it may, Bowman's actions were 'making' according to *Webster's Third New International Dictionary*[51] even if they did not amount to manufacturing as the word is commonly understood. The Court consulted the dictionary to support a decision founded on conventional reward and incentive-to-innovate justifications for patents. Suffice it to say that the authors of this book are not alone in questioning whether such a calculation of fairness and public interest in the patent system should hang on an obscure extension of the meaning of 'make', or on assumptions as to how we balance the economic interests of farmers, biotechnology companies and the general public vis-à-vis the patent system.[52]

---

[51] Also the *Shorter Oxford English Dictionary*.

[52] R.H. Stern, 'Bowman v. Monsanto: Exhaustion versus Making' (2014) *EIPR* 255–61; B. Charnley, 'Cui bono? Gauging the Successes of Publicly-Funded Plant Breeding in Retrospect', in C. Lawson and B. Charnley (eds), *Intellectual Property and Genetically Modified Organisms* (Cheltenham: Edward Elgar Publishing, 2015), 7–26.

As for the issue of self-replicating inventions, which are not confined to biology, the Court, prudently this time, refused to draw any general conclusions.

Another well-known case, albeit from another jurisdiction, that appears to expand the scope of infringing behaviour in rather controversial ways is the Canada Supreme Court's decision in *Schmeiser*.[53] We discuss it here because the relevant statutory language in that country is very similar to that of the US.[54] The facts of this case are as follows. Monsanto's patent concerning Roundup Ready canola covered genes, plant cells, and expression and transformation vectors but not the plants themselves. By the time the dispute reached the Supreme Court, following the oncomouse decision, plants per se, being higher life forms, were not patentable anyway. In 1996 Percy Schmeiser, a farmer in Saskatchewan province, planted canola seed on a 370-acre field, and replanted some of the harvested seed. He sprayed a small three-acre strip of land by the road with Roundup and 60 per cent of the canola present survived. He harvested the seeds and set them aside for storage. Monsanto checked by the roadside boundaries of his lands and found the plants there to be Roundup Ready and subsequently warned him. Schmeiser went ahead anyway and after getting the saved seed cleaned he planted it on several fields covering 1,000 acres in total area. In 1998, Schmeiser was found to have at least 95 per cent of his harvest to be Roundup Ready. This was despite the fact that he had never purchased Monsanto's glyphosate-resistant seed. Indeed, there was no conclusive explanation for its appearance on his farm. As to its abundance, this is a difficult matter. The Court did not discount the possibility of its derivation from seed harvested the year before from that small patch of roadside land, though the trial judge had been sceptical to say the least. As mentioned, he had sprayed that area with Roundup, so the survival of these canola specimens obviously proved they were Roundup Ready, and he stored these seeds rather than sold them.

Had Schmeiser made the invention? The Court was not persuaded that he had made the claimed genes, cells or vectors. In other words, by planting and cultivating seed he had not made these things contained in the resultant plants. What about use? On the basis of dictionary definitions and established principles of statutory interpretation, the majority concluded that he had. In the present context, and following a line of case law, 'use' of an invention was taken to mean utilisation with a view to production or advantage, and infringement is established where commercial activity involves use of a thing of which the patented part is a component. By a purposive construction of claims, the Court surmised, a person skilled in the art would have interpreted what was claimed in the patent to include use of those plants that were regenerated from the patented cells. There is no need to prove use of the isolated elements. Consequently, the Court held that there was infringement.

But had Schmeiser interfered with Monsanto's enjoyment of its legal monopoly, or actually taken advantage of the genetically modified characteristics of the seed for which Monsanto was responsible? Schmeiser's motives and actions are somewhat opaque. He denied that he had used Roundup herbicide. If we accept his testimony, surely he did not use Monsanto's invention because

---

[53] *Monsanto Canada Inc v. Schmeiser* [2004] 1 SCR 902, 2004 SCC 34.

[54] For an overview of how Canada deals with patenting in biotechnology, see M. Perry, 'From Pasteur to Monsanto: Approaches to Patenting Life in Canada', in Y. Gendreau (ed.), *An Emerging Intellectual Property Paradigm: Perspectives from Canada* (Cheltenham: Edward Elgar Publishing, 2008), 67–80.

without applying Roundup it was not performing its function of protecting plants from glyphosate herbicide. And if the seeds he planted were no more useful to him than the closest non-GM alternatives, it is hard to see how his actions had much impact upon Monsanto's enjoyment of its patent monopoly. The Court faced this issue head on defending its finding on the basis that the properties of Roundup Ready had 'stand-by or insurance utility', that is, that the option was there to spray with glyphosate in case of future necessity even if the farmer was choosing ordinarily not to do so.

As for remedies, respondents wanted an account of profits rather than damages. On this matter, the Court took the view that no profits were made from the invention itself. Schmeiser earned no more than he would have done had he grown non-GM canola.

One issue that has generally been overlooked in a debate that has tended to be highly polarised between those who favour GM technologies and their opponents, is that of generic market entry and the market effects of regulation. In contrast, the role of regulation in encouraging (or discouraging) generic competition in pharmaceuticals has attracted a great deal more attention. In fact, regulation can potentially extend the market power of agricultural biotech firms well beyond the life of patents on their products. Thus, Monsanto's patents protecting the technology in Roundup Ready (RR1) crop species have now mostly expired. The company has in recent years introduced the next generation of separately patented Roundup Ready crops (Roundup Ready 2 Yield, or RR2Y). Thus Monsanto cannot sue dealers and farmers for using, making and selling generic first-generation (i.e., RR1) glyphosate-resistant seeds and plants. Neither can Monsanto stop competing firms from incorporating the technology into less commonly cultivated crop species, including so-called 'orphan' crops, taking advantage of its public domain status. However, in several countries regulatory approvals must be periodically renewed. This applies, for example, to Europe, China, Japan and South Korea. The process of securing approval can be complex, expensive and time-consuming and must be done separately for each crop species. There is no harmony of national rules on this matter. In some cases traits will be 'stacked' meaning the species will incorporate a number of traits, not just one, increasing the complexity of regulating on a species-by-species basis. It is not hard to see that this situation potentially presents severe entry barrier problems. Nowhere is there counterpart legislation to the US Hatch-Waxman Act which balances regulatory data exclusivity with provisions to encourage early generic market entry. The absence of agbiogenerics is not surprising given the relative novelty of GM crops as compared to pharmaceuticals. However, at some point this problem will need to be resolved.[55]

Patents on plants in Europe

Europe has a difficulty that the US does not have. This is that since the early 1960s, European countries took the decision to keep out of the patent system conventional plant breeding, both the methods of crossing and selection and the plant varieties so developed. Legally, this was perfectly straightforward until the arrival of genetic transformation technologies. With genetic engineering,

---

[55] G. Graff and D. Zilberman, 'How the IP-Regulatory Complex Affects Incentives to Develop Socially Beneficial Products from Agricultural Genomics', in E. Marden, R.N. Godfrey and R. Manion (eds), *The Intellectual Property-Regulatory Complex: Overcoming Barriers to Innovation in Agricultural Genomics* (Vancouver: UBC Press, 2016), 68–101; D.J. Jefferson, G.D. Graff, C.L. Chi-Ham and A.B. Bennett, 'The Emergence of Agbiogenerics' (2015) 33(8) *Nature Biotechnology* 819–23.

the plants so transformed, not being explicitly excluded, were deemed to be inherently patentable, at first. In 1988 the European Patent Office (EPO) began to grant patents on plants.

But at some point this was bound to lead to problems given the exclusion of plant varieties in favour of national UPOV-compliant PVP systems. The line of demarcation between plants and plant varieties is a source of difficulty not least because plant variety protection and patents are not natural bedfellows. In 1995, the EPO Technical Board of Appeal in *Greenpeace v. Plant Genetic Systems* ruled on an appeal against the upholding of a plant-related patent and determined that a claim for plant cells contained in a plant was unpatentable for not being capable of excluding plant varieties from its scope, and also that 'plant cells as such cannot be considered to fall under the definition of plant or of plant variety'.[56] This implied that transgenic plants per se were unpatentable because of the plant variety exclusion. Consequently, for the next four years, the EPO stopped accepting claims on plants per se. However, in December 1999, the EPO Enlarged Board of Appeal decided that, while 'plant varieties containing genes introduced into an ancestral plant by recombinant gene technology are excluded from patentability', 'a claim wherein specific plant varieties are not individually claimed is not excluded from patentability under Article 53(b), EPC even though it may embrace plant varieties'.[57]

Let us briefly return to the essentially biological processes exclusion. It is an odd turn of phrase really and raises questions again about where to place the natural/artificial boundary and whether the law is consistent or logical about it. It is implicitly accepted for the sake of convenience that classical plant breeding is so beholden to underlying biological phenomena that what breeders do is biological. But what if the plant production process comprises steps other than 'mere' crossing and selection, that is to say is a mix of biological and non-biological elements? And what if the process works for any plant variety than one or a few named ones, that is, that plants are claimed at a higher taxonomic level than the variety?

The answer to the first question is 'it depends'. It matters whether the technical interventions enable or assist the crossing and selecting activities, or whether the interventions introduce or modify a genomic trait. The latter process, overcoming concerns about unrepeatability, and lack of inventiveness including technical character, will escape the exclusion.[58]

As regards the second question, in 2015 the Enlarged Board of Appeal ruled that plants or plant material are not excluded merely because the method of producing them was essentially biological, including when it is the only method available on the filing date. Moreover, in the circumstances of the case, product-by-process claims were permissible even when the process is an essentially biological one. Legally one might concede that this is (somewhat) logical. Scientifically, though, this is being utterly inconsistent in that it immediately shifts the line between nature and human intervention so that what in another context is purely natural is now artificial.[59] Moreover, it appears not to match what the drafters of the EU Directive intended. In 2016, the European Commission

---

[56] *Greenpeace v. Plant Genetic Systems NV* [1995] OJEPO 545.

[57] EPO Decision G 01/98 Transgenic Plant/NOVARTIS II.

[58] G-2/07 Broccoli/PLANT BIOSCIENCE II. For a more complete discussion, see Sterckx and Cockbain, *supra* note 37, 183–92. This line of argument was affirmed subsequently in T0915/10 (Soybean event/MONSANTO).

[59] G2/12 Tomatoes/STATE OF ISRAEL-MINISTRY OF AGRICULTURE II; G2/13 Broccoli/PLANT BIOSCIENCE.

issued a note expressing the view that no human, plant or animal products (varieties or otherwise) are patentable if obtained through essentially biological processes that involve no non-biological, including microbiological, steps.[60] In June 2017, the Administrative Council of the EPO decided to take this Commission Notice into account and amend the regulations accordingly.[61] However, in December 2018, in case T1063/18, the Technical Board of Appeal rejected the amendment to the regulation thereby asserting its independence from the European Union. At this time of writing we cannot be sure this is the end of the matter.

One final question: is a patent claiming a DNA sequence (among other things) incorporated into a plant infringed by the existence of that DNA in an industrial product derived from that plant? The Court of Justice of the European Union had to decide this question following Monsanto's action to restrain the importation and circulation throughout Europe of soybean meal, a product made from soybeans or soybean hulls that is typically used as animal feed.[62] The source of the meal was Argentina where Roundup Ready soybean has no patent protection.[63]

The key legal provision at issue was Article 9 of the European Directive on the Legal Protection of Biotechnological Inventions, which states that 'The protection conferred by a patent on a product containing or consisting of genetic information shall extend to all material, [...], in which the product is incorporated and in which the genetic information is contained and performs its function.' It is obvious that soybean meal contains DNA. However, it is an inert part of what composes the meal. It is not doing anything. Accordingly it is not performing the function disclosed in the patent. Therefore, the existence of the DNA alone is not infringing the patent. In the words of the Court, no patent protection can be conferred:

In which the patented product is contained in the soy meal, where it does not perform the function for which it is patented, but did perform that function previously in the soy plant, of which the meal is a processed product, or would possibly again be able to perform that function after it had been extracted from the soy meal and inserted into the cell of a living organism.

Moreover, the Court opined that nothing in the TRIPS Agreement affected this interpretation of Article 9 of the Directive.

---

[60] European Commission, 'Commission Notice on Certain Articles of Directive 98/44/EC of the European Parliament and of the Council of 6 July 1998 on the Legal Protection of Biotechnological Inventions'.

[61] In accordance with the Law No 2016-1087 of August 8, 2016 *pour la reconquête de la biodiversité, de la nature et des paysages* (Law for the Recovery of Biodiversity, Nature and Landscape), the French Intellectual Property Code now states that '[P]roducts exclusively obtained by the essentially biological processes [...], including the elements constituting these products and the genetic information they contain' shall not be patentable. The amended rules are now consistent also with the patent laws of Germany, Italy and the Netherlands.

[62] Case C-428/08 *Monsanto v. Cefetra*.

[63] For a comprehensive background to the *Cefetra* case and excellent analysis of the case itself, see S. Hubicki, '"The Story of a Love Spurned": Monsanto in the United Republic of Soy', in C. Lawson and B. Charnley (eds), *Intellectual Property and Genetically Modified Organisms* (Cheltenham: Edward Elgar Publishing, 2015), 27–80.

Patents and livestock

Compared to plants, the connection between intellectual property and the breeding of animals attracts very little attention. It never really has. There is a good reason for this: historically breed society membership and the use of pedigrees afforded animal breeders with at least some of the benefits that IPRs provide today for plant breeders. Breed societies existed even in pre-Mendelian days, perhaps the best known being the Dishley Society founded in Leicestershire, England in the late-eighteenth century although there were others on the European continent.[64] The famous eighteenth-century Leicestershire animal breeder Robert Bakewell made a fortune from renting his rams and bulls. In a sense, his animals were not just physical property but also *de facto* intellectual property *avant la lettre*. He owned not just his breeding stock but also their family trees.[65] This suggests that 'owning life' through patent monopolies is hardly a radical shift but a logical development of existing attitudes concerning the relationship between humans and nature, and towards doing business. It is worthwhile also to mention that Bakewell's refusal to disclose the lineage of his animals is similar to the practice today of hybrid seed companies of protecting the parent lines of their plants as trade secrets.

There are many breed societies in existence today. For example, currently 42 cattle breed societies dealing in pedigree animals are recognised by the UK government, 34 sheep breed societies, five pig breed societies, and one goat breed society. Recognition is voluntary so others exist too. Not all have active breeding programmes, though, and some may be more concerned with preservation than with improvement. The societies maintain herd and flock books and, like the Kennel Club with dogs, issue pedigree certificates. There is an operational market in livestock semen, ova and embryos, and pure-bred individuals for mating purposes. This trade has never been dependent on IPRs. Consequently, the animal varieties exclusion in European patent law has been quite uncontroversial.

Of course, biotechnology has changed the situation somewhat and there is plenty of patenting activity nowadays in (for Europe: non-essentially biological) animal improvement methods and technologies as there is with plants. A recent global study on patenting in the field of animal genetic resources for food and agriculture identified six areas of patenting activity as follows: (i) artificial insemination, sex selection and control of oestrus; (ii) marker-assisted breeding; (iii) transgenic animals; (iv) animal cloning; (v) xenotransplantation; and (vi) animal models.[66]

One especially high-profile technique developed in the last few decades is animal cloning based on nuclear transfer; that is to say the insertion of an adult cell nucleus into an egg cell that has had its nucleus removed. In 1996, the now world-famous sheep called Dolly was cloned by Ian Wilmut and Keith Campbell at Roslin Institute in Scotland from a cell taken from a mature sheep's udder. It was not the first cloned animal but the first to be cloned from an adult mammal.[67] The methods were

---

[64] R.J. Wood and V. Orel, *Genetic Prehistory in Selective Breeding: A Prelude to Mendel* (Oxford: Oxford University Press, 2001), 84–5.

[65] H. Ritvo, 'Possessing Mother Nature: Genetic Capital in Eighteenth Century Britain', in J. Brewer and S. Staves (eds), *Early Modern Conceptions of Property* (London: Routledge, 1996), 413–26.

[66] P. Oldham, S. Hall and C. Barnes, *Patent Landscape Report on Animal Genetic Resources. A Patent Landscape Report Prepared for the World Intellectual Property Organization* (WIPO, 2014), 9.

[67] See I. Wilmut, K. Campbell and C. Tudge, *The Second Creation: The Age of Biological Control by the Scientists Who Cloned*

patented in a number of countries and the animals produced were claimed too. In Europe nothing in the language of the EPC or the Directive precluded this. However, in the US the situation was somewhat different. The USPTO rejected claims in the Roslin Institute's patent application directed to the products of the technology. One of the key rejected claims was for: 'A live-born clone of a pre-existing, nonembryonic, donor mammal, wherein the mammal is selected from cattle, sheep, pigs, and goats.' Taking into account a body of case law demonstrating the unpatentability of laws of nature, natural phenomena and abstract ideas, and unreflexively assuming the coherence of these concepts, the Court rejected the claims. In the words of Judge Dyk, paraphrasing from *Diamond v. Chakrabarty*, 'Dolly herself is an exact genetic replica of another sheep and does not possess "markedly different characteristics from any [farm animals] found in nature." [...] Dolly's genetic identity to her donor parent renders her unpatentable.' As he pointed out, Roslin created or altered neither the genetic information nor the structure in the making of its clones; rather, these were preserved.[68]

A brief comparison with Europe is in order here. In Europe it matters how something is produced, whereas in the US it matters more what is produced. Thus in Europe, a cloned animal produced through technical (that is, non-essentially biological) means is patentable notwithstanding its essential genotypical identical-ness with an existing animal. In the US, this is not good enough. It must be different. It is the marked difference that makes the product the inventor's handiwork and not that of nature. It does not matter how it was invented (though new methods claims are likely to be patentable). As we will see below, the same cross-Atlantic difference applies to DNA.

It remains here to note that in common with plant genetic resources, similar concerns have been raised about the erosion of animal biodiversity[69] and the general failure to appreciate 'traditional' agriculturalists, in this case the livestock-keeping communities' vital role in creating and conserving breeds and safeguarding the genetic diversity that they embody. However, whereas farmers' rights[70] is now a recognised legal concept, albeit a vague one, there is no counterpart right for pastoralists although one has been proposed.[71] IPRs are not directly implicated except insofar as the 'standard models' promoted by Europe and the US provide no incentives for innovations that would counter the tendency towards the uniformity of minor differences based on the 'recycling' of a relatively narrow resource base.[72]

Dolly (London: Headline, 2000).

[68] *In re Roslin Institute (Edinburgh), No 2013-1407* (Fed Cir, May 8, 2014).

[69] FAO Commission on Genetic Resources for Food and Agriculture, *The State of the World's Animal Genetic Resources for Food and Agriculture* (Rome: FAO, 2007).

[70] Art 9 of the FAO International Treaty on Genetic Resources for Food and Agriculture concerns farmers' rights, a term coined by Cary Fowler in the 1980s while he was working for a Canadian NGO called Rural Advancement Foundation International (now ETC Group).

[71] J. Santilli, *Agrobiodiversity and the Law: Regulating Genetic Resources, Food Security and Cultural Diversity* (Abingdon: Earthscan, 2012), 240–56; I.U. Köhler-Rollefson, E. Mathias, H. Singh, P. Vivekanandan and J. Wanyama, 'Livestock Keepers' Rights: The State of Discussion' (2010) 47 *Animal Genetic Resources* 119–23.

[72] For a much broader discussion on the relationship between intellectual property rights and innovation in agriculture, largely from a US perspective, see M.S. Clancy and G. Moschini, 'Intellectual Property Rights and the Ascent of Proprietary Innovation in Agriculture' (2017) 9 *Annual Review of Resource Economics* 53–74.

14.4 PATENTING THE HUMAN: GENES, DNA SEQUENCES AND STEM CELLS

14.4.1 DNA as patentable subject matter

The ease with which DNA claims slipped into patent claims belies the subsequent controversies about such 'things' being patented. DNA sequences started being claimed in the early 1980s. By the end of the century this number had increased enormously. Nobody doubts that DNA is a chemical. As molecules go it is enormous and complex in structure. It can be broken up along its length into an almost infinite number of smaller pieces of varying sizes. It can also be pulled across-ways into two separate strands like an unzipped zipper. Sections of DNA can be assembled artificially in a lab. Among the three billion nucleotide bases on each strand are those which form genes. As such, these bases are essential in molecular processes leading to the production of proteins specified according to the order and identity of the nucleotide bases involved. DNA has four such bases: adenine ('A'), cytosine ('C'), guanine ('G'), and tyrosine ('T').

In brief, the coding regions of each gene specify one or more proteins for the cell to synthesise. Proteins comprise an ordered assembly of amino acids of which there are 20 in all. Each of these protein building blocks is added according to a three-part combination of the four nucleotide bases which for DNA are A, C, G and T, and for RNA – which is chemically similar to DNA but much more active in this three billion year-old manufacturing process – are A, C, G and U (for uracil). These three-base long DNA and RNA parts are called codons. If bases can be analogised to letters, codons are the words and as such are the smallest units of meaning in this whole process. Simple arithmetic shows that 64 types of codon are possible: AAA, AAC, ACA, CAA […] and so on. One codon signals the start of the process. This is AUG in eukaryotic cells, which codes for an amino acid called methionine, always the first 'brick' in the under-construction protein. Large proteins may contain vast numbers of amino acids. Others, of which there are three, serve to terminate the process: UAA, UAG and UGA.

Scientists have been working to identify all of the 20–25,000 or so genes and match them with their associated proteins, that is, the ones 'expressed' by each of the genes. Note here that more than one type of protein can be expressed by a gene. Human and animal bodies have more proteins than genes. For a number of reasons, this endeavour is of huge importance for human health and therapeutics. In brief, mutations, in which 'misplaced' bases affect protein production, can have harmful effects that could prove fatal. Some mutations are inherited, others arise due to the attritional effects of a life well (or badly) lived, or to such insults as exposure to lethal toxins like radioactive material. Unsurprisingly they tend to accumulate as one ages, hence the increased risks of cancer as one gets older. Some diseases are caused by single gene defects. Others are directly associated with more than one defective gene. Many diseases are linked to a combination of genetic and environmental factors. Susceptibilities and risk factors identifiable in the human genome are worth knowing about – especially if you can do something in advance to reduce them through lifestyle changes among other possible actions. This is why it is important to understand the human genome in all its variability. Human genetic diversity is narrow compared to most other animals. We are a young species and there has not been sufficient time for isolated human populations to evolve separately. But individual and group variations exist and identifying and analysing those sequences associated with sickness and health can be very useful, for example, in developing diagnostic and predictive testing services, and in designing better tailored treatment regimes. In addition, linking genes to specific proteins is essential for the production of human protein drugs, such as insulin and monoclonal antibodies in cloned microbes and cultured cells such as Chinese hamster ovary cells.

Is DNA just a chemical? Surely this cannot be correct. Humans 'share' genes with every single living thing from bacteria to beetles and beavers. Most of our genome is identical to that of chimpanzees and gorillas. Individually, our differences are minuscule. And yet the role of DNA in heredity, our individual destiny and in our sense of identity – as persons, and members of family and humankind – already makes human DNA patenting a sensitive issue to many even before we get into debates on access and supply of DNA-based diagnostic tests subject to patent monopolies.[73] For many of those taking issue with the notion that DNA is like any other chemical for the purposes of intellectual property law, it is an emotive issue. Here 'Playing God' types of objection come to the fore as do ones proffered by opponents of unbridled capitalism and other social critics concerned that commodification of life has no apparent limits. Wherever one stands on the matter, DNA undeniably has unusual properties. The main feature about DNA making it unique is that it has a dual nature being both a physical object and containing, or even itself being, information. Accordingly it fits neatly within a wider perspective on life: that life itself is an information system. The idea that biological molecules and molecular processes can be defined in informational terms is hardly new. When Ernest Starling coined the word 'hormones' in 1905, he immediately referred to them as 'chemical messengers'.[74] But life-as-information technology goes back to the post-World War Two era, a time when biology became especially susceptible to information and computer science analogies, metaphors and definitions. In the mid-1950s, physicist George Gamow conceptualised the cell as 'a storehouse of information' and also as 'a self-activating transmitter which passes on very precise messages that direct the construction of identical new cells'.[75] According to

---

[73] S. Ghosh, *Identity, Invention, and the Culture of Personalized Medicine Patenting* (New York: Cambridge University Press, 2012).

[74] E.S. Starling, 'The Croonian Lectures on the Chemical Correlation of the Functions of the Body. Lecture I' (1905) 4275 *The Lancet* 339–41, 340.

[75] G. Gamow, 'Information Transfer in the Living Cell' (1955) 193 *Scientific American* 70–78, 70; quoted in L.E. Kay, *Who Wrote the Book of Life? A History of the Genetic Code* (Stanford: Stanford University Press, 2000), 154. Arguably, this conception originates with physicist Erwin Schrödinger, whose 1944 book, *What Is Life?* was extremely influential: E. Schrödinger, *What Is Life?* (Cambridge: Cambridge University Press, 1944). The elevation of the notion that DNA initiates an irreversible flow of information to a fact of life can be attributed to Francis Crick. His Central Dogma posits that:

Once 'information' has passed into protein it cannot get out again. In more detail, the transfer of information from nucleic acid to nucleic acid, or from nucleic acid to protein may be possible, but transfer from protein to protein, or from protein to nucleic acid is impossible. Information means here the precise determination of sequence, either of bases in the nucleic acid or of amino acid residues in the protein.

a historical account of molecular biology by Michel Morange, information terminology was hard-wired into the discipline's language from its inception:

> Molecular biology is a result of the encounter between genetics and biochemistry, two branches of biology that developed at the beginning of the twentieth century […] Strictly speaking, molecular biology is not a new discipline, but rather a new way of looking at organisms as reservoirs and transmitters of information.[76]

The life-as-information idea has obvious contemporary appeal, given the digital nature of so many modern technologies, including those used by molecular biologists (as in the field of bioinformatics), and, of course, the apparent similarity between raw DNA sequence data and computer code. Indeed, there is growing interest in the possibility of using synthetic DNA to store vast amounts of digital data. There are several reasons among which are the following: first, it is getting ever cheaper and easier to synthesise novel DNA sequences to order and to 'read' it afterwards in order to extract the data; second, DNA is extremely dense – one could call it an example of natural nanotechnology. This has enabled scientists at Harvard University to story about 700 terabytes of date in a gram of DNA;[77] third, in normal conditions the DNA molecule can maintain its form for vast periods of time without deterioration.

Scientists are thus encouraged to assume that information technology provides the best means for us to understand how life 'works'. Indeed, it hardly seems a stretch to regard molecular biology as a branch of information science with the enormous amount of genetic sequence data now available to be processed and analysed. From this, many are inclined to take the next step, which is to understand cells and organisms as highly sophisticated information-processing systems which are capable of being harnessed, reconstructed and improved for our benefit. According to one account, 'an organism's physiology and behaviour are dictated largely by its genes. And those genes are merely repositories of information written in a surprisingly similar manner to the one that computer scientists have devised for the storage and transmission of other information'.[78]

Terms like 'genetic code', 'translation', 'transcription' and 'messenger RNA' are well established. A review of the current popular science literature reveals a highly imaginative but sometimes confused use and mixing of the same largely IT-related analogies, metaphors and definitions. Frequently one comes across terms like 'programmers', 'software' and 'hardware'. Are such writers using them metaphorically, analogously or as definitions? One sometimes wonders if writers are sure themselves. Such language is popular in journalism too, hence the title of a 2007 *Newsweek* feature on synthetic biology: Life 2.0.[79] Tom Knight of MIT's Artificial Intelligence Laboratory reveals some of the current ambitions in synthetic biology in saying that 'the genetic code is 3.6

The Central Dogma has not gone unchallenged. See R. Olby, *Francis Crick: Hunter of Life's Secrets* (Cold Spring Harbor Laboratory Press, 2010), 308–13.

[76] M. Morange, *A History of Molecular Biology* (Cambridge: Harvard University Press, 1998), 1–2 (emphasis added).

[77] G.M. Church, Y. Gao and S. Kosuri, 'Next-Generation Digital Information Storage in DNA' (2012) 337 *Science* 1628.

[78] 'Drowning in Data', *The Economist* 26 June 1999, 97–8.

[79] L. Silver, 'Life 2.0', *Newsweek*, 4 June 2007, 41–5.

billion years old. It's time for a rewrite';[80] as if life is just a set of coded instructions for 'packages' of chemicals to maintain themselves and self-replicate.

Thus humans become authors of life; or so the analogies imply. Is making synthetic life akin to writing a novel, poem or play in which case perhaps copyright should apply rather than patents?[81] A software program is a literary work for the purposes of copyright law. So, some might argue, why shouldn't a synthetic life form, or at least its genome, be one too?

A decision handed down by the Delhi High Court addressed this question. The dispute concerned alleged infringement of rights over seeds. The claimant alleged that in 'manufacturing, selling and offering for sale, genotypically identical seeds', the defendant's activities amounted 'to a copyright infringement of the unique sequencing information of the hybrid seeds'.[82] The basis for the claim to originality of the 'work' lay in the hybridisation process, 'the sequences being the result of skill and labour involved in decoding and recording it'. In supporting this view, the claimant relied on Laddie, Prescott and Vitoria's classic text *The Modern Law of Copyright and Designs* (2nd ed.). This volume had come to the conclusion that 'a scientific record consisting of a series of letters or other characters symbolising the sequential structure of DNA, proteins and similar constructs found in molecular biology'[83] may be protectable under the skill, labour and judgement test of originality. (Whether and how DNA sequence data may constitute an author's own intellectual creation may of course be another matter entirely.) However, the Court, adopting a higher originality standard than mere sweat of the brow, opined that there can be no independent creation in what it considered the discovery of facts. A naturally occurring sequence when recorded in some way may be a literary work as is computer code. But it cannot be an original literary work. Moreover, citing the US 'merger doctrine', the software code analogy fails because with DNA sequence data the idea and the expression unavoidably merge: the two are inseparable and only one way to express the idea is possible anyway.

One of the key problems some critics have identified with all this information talk, especially in the context of genetics, is the woolliness and inconsistency in how some scientists use words like 'information' and (genetic) 'code', and a tendency to over-rely on their explicatory power.[84] There are those who talk of information about DNA in relation to growth, development, regeneration, reproduction, disease, resistance to disease and general cell functioning, of which vast

---

[80] Quoted, ibid., 44.

[81] For a discussion on the possible application of copyright law to synthetic biology, see A.W. Torrance, 'Synthesizing Law for Synthetic Biology' (2010) 11(2) *Minnesota Journal of Law, Science and Technology* 629–65, 640.

[82] *Emergent Genetics India Pvt Ltd v. Shailendra Shivam And Ors* on 2 August 2011, Delhi High Court.

[83] H. Laddie, P. Prescott and M. Vitoria, *The Modern Law of Copyright and Designs* (2nd ed., London: Butterworths, 1995), 859.

[84] P.E. Griffiths, 'Genetic Information: A Metaphor in Search of a Theory' (2001) 68 *Philosophy of Science* 394–412. According to one especially critical commentator: 'there is no clear, technical notion of "information" in molecular biology. It is little more than a metaphor that masquerades as a theoretical concept and [...] leads to a misleading picture of possible explanations in molecular biology': S. Sarkar, 'Biological Information: A Sceptical Look at some Central Dogmas of Molecular Biology', in S. Sarkar (ed.), *The Philosophy and History of Molecular Biology: New Perspectives* (Dordrecht: Kluwer Academic Publishers, 1996), 187–232, 187, quoted in Griffiths, 'Genetic Information', 395.

amounts are being generated and await definitive interpretation. Understood this way, of course, the information one wishes to acquire cannot be acquired simply by looking at the data, that is, the sequence of bases.

Scientists may alternatively think of 'DNA information', by which they refer to the arrangement of the 'letters' of the so-called genetic 'code', which is frequently presented in the form of sequences of As, Cs, Gs and Ts. Here 'information' refers to what might more accurately be called 'raw data'. As with the former use of 'information', though, the complex chemistry of the DNA molecule is deemed to be rather less interesting than the possibility of information being presentable in an easily readable form.

The former approach (i.e., 'information about DNA') is surely the correct use of the word 'information' and a more accurate vision of the limits to what DNA sequence data can really tell us by itself. For the scientists, DNA sequence data does contain information, but it is not in itself information. This is why we have bioinformatics, whose purpose is to apply information science and digital technology to interpret this data. In so doing, bioinformatics generates information that is intelligible, usable and sharable (albeit potentially proprietary). If not for the scientist then, for whom DNA sequences are data and not information, are cells able to treat them as information? This is worth considering because if we accept for a moment that cells are a category of computational information processing system, it may appear plausible to regard genetic sequences as complete information for that cell's immediate application.

But that does not stand up to critical examination either. Genetic sequences are mere data, and partial data at that, that the cell's organisational faculties need actively to extract meaning from and thus find useful in a far less complete and direct manner. Biology is not information technology, and there is no programmer – only natural selection. As Paul Griffiths, a firm critic of information talk in biology explains, just as planets do not 'compute their orbits around the sun' but just blindly go round elliptically according to the laws of physics, cells cannot 'compute' in any kind of intentional way.[85] Furthermore, complicated as genomes are, their informational value is limited. They simply cannot explain everything about such phenomena as growth and development. While a direct relationship can clearly be made between a codon (as we saw above, a three-base sequence) and a specific amino acid, that is about as far as one can go in treating DNA sequences as pure information, and even then that tells the cell little about what protein to assemble and how to do it properly so it folds in the right way. There is in fact some considerable conceptual distance between a lengthy sequence of base pairs and a correctly folded protein; even more between those base letters and a whole functional cell or organism. The sheer complexity, subtlety, context-dependence and informational-incompleteness of DNA requires us to cast a sceptical eye on the view that genes may be treated as instructional texts using four letters and 64 words comprising all the necessary information for the cell or organism to use. It may be reasonable to say that cellular machinery 'reads off' the DNA 'code', but this does not make the genome an instruction manual for the cell. It is far more complicated than that. It would be completely incorrect to treat DNA sequences as a how-to guide with instructions for making proteins as if they are a recipe, car repair manual, or flat-pack furniture assembly leaflet.

---

[85] Griffiths, ibid.

That is quite enough philosophy of biology for a law text. Suffice it to say that DNA is a chemical but it is so much more than just a chemical whether one goes by its social standing or applies more technical criteria. DNA is not just a thing but a hybrid. But the nature of this hybridity and the question of why it matters in terms of law are a little unclear because we seem unable fully to agree on what exactly information has to do with DNA, genes, and life in general, other than, well, quite a lot obviously. Nonetheless to regard DNA as having a dual chemical-informational nature is certainly a lot more helpful than treating it as stuff and nothing but stuff whose scientific investigation and commercial exploitation requires one first to have a physical sample in one's test tube. Gleaning knowledge and extracting commercial value does not always require direct contact with a single DNA molecule. Vast amounts of sequence data are stored on computers and all the advantages of big data in other fields of human endeavour including science and business are available here too.

If this discussion is useful at all it is because it helps us to understand that DNA is a chemical but of a very special kind. As we will see, there is a danger of the conceptual differences leading to practical difficulties. Patent law must do more than treat DNA exactly as if it is any other type of chemical, but the question is how should it? We will look first into the different types of DNA product claims in patents. After this we will consider some of the practical concerns that have arisen. Then we will see how different jurisdictions have dealt with patentability of 'new' subject matter and determined the appropriate scope of protection.

There are three types of DNA claim: (i) isolated pieces of genomic DNA (gDNA) cut out of the bigger DNA molecule extracted from living cells; (ii) synthetic DNA the order of whose sequences are unchanged; (iii) synthetic DNA the order of whose sequences differ from the equivalent section of gDNA by the exclusion of inactive bases. This product is called complementary DNA, or cDNA for short.

In response to arguments that full product patent protection of DNA sequences is undesirable, France and Germany have opted, in the case of human sequences, for so-called 'purpose-bound protection' according to which DNA can only be claimed in respect of a specified use. Let us suppose there is a gene that codes for proteins A, B and C. The company that finds the gene discovers only that it codes for A and patents it on that basis. In the UK and the US, that company can control use of the gene for any application or function subsequently discovered while the patent remains in force. But in Germany and France, another company that discovers the gene's role in producing proteins B and C can independently patent the gene in relation to those functions (but only those functions). It appears that this limitation to full product patent rights was a response at least in part to popular concerns in Europe (including the European Parliament) about the behaviour of one company, Myriad Genetics (see below).

So what is the appropriate position to adopt: full product protection or purpose-bound protection? The only honest answer is the underwhelming one of 'it's difficult to say for sure'. Nonetheless, the purpose-bound approach makes much sense whether or not it makes much difference in actual practice.

One can argue on sound scientific grounds that treating genes as patentable inventions on the basis of a single disclosed function or discovery such as that it codes for a particular protein, or that it is associated with a disease, is a rather generous interpretation of the 'inventor's' relatively modest addition to the state of the art. This is not to say that such discoveries are necessarily easy or inexpensive to attain and undeserving of any reward. The point is that there may well be much more to be discovered about the gene of both scientific and commercial interest, and such future discoveries may well be a whole lot more important.

It is worth noting here that the US patent system has until recently been rather permissive in terms of applying the non-obviousness and utility criteria with the result that inventions patented in the US were too obvious to be patentable in Europe. Indeed, a recent study in *Science* found that of 74 US human gene patents examined by researchers, 73 per cent of them contained one or more claims considered to be 'problematic'.[86] However, the situation has been corrected to some extent (see below).

This is not just academic. Gene patenting can be a life or death issue.[87] Patents on genes linked to particular diseases tend to claim a range of applications including diagnostic tests, and owners can be quite aggressive in enforcing their rights even though the validity of such patents is often considered to be questionable. Even non-commercial entities like public sector hospitals may be the target of companies demanding royalties. It was recently reported, for example, that 'after the gene for the iron overload condition haemochromatosis was patented, 30 per cent of labs surveyed stopped testing for the disease-causing gene variant, or developing such tests'.[88]

However, just as it is difficult to prove that extending the coverage of the patent system to cover DNA sequences as protectable subject matter guarantees there will be more investment in public health-improving research and development than there would be otherwise, proving the opposite is just as difficult. In addition to the example just given, the well-publicised patenting by Myriad Genetics relating to and covering two genes (BRCA1 and BRCA2) linked to a certain proportion of breast cancer cases and the aggressive assertion of these patents by the company lend plausibility to the view that DNA patenting is bad for public health research (see below).[89] Human Genome Sciences' patenting of the CCR5 receptor gene that was subsequently discovered by other scientists to have a link to HIV infection raises serious doubts about the wisdom of allowing genes to be patented when very little is known about them.[90] Nonetheless, the use of a limited number of examples such as these does not prove beyond doubt that DNA patenting

---

[86] J. Paradise, L. Andrews and T. Holbrook, 'Patents on Human Genes: An Analysis of Scope and Claims' (2005) 307 *Science* 1566–7.

[87] See D. Montgomery, 'Human Gene Patent Plan Could Hit Tests to Cure Fatal Diseases', *The Scotsman*, 24 April 2001, 5; G. Anand, 'HIV Patent Holder is Slowing Spread of Fast AIDS Test', *Wall Street Journal Europe*, 20 December 2001, 1, 11.

[88] K. Kleiner, 'Bad for your Health: Are Gene Patents Stopping Patients Getting the Latest Tests?' *New Scientist* 23 March 2002, 6.

[89] See P. Aldhous, 'Patent Battle Could Hold up Tests for Cancer Gene' (1996) 149 *New Scientist* 8; P. Brown and K. Kleiner, 'Patent Row Splits Breast Cancer Researchers' (1994) 143 *New Scientist* 4; K. Ernhofer, 'Who Really Owns Your Genes?' *Christian Science Monitor* 27 February 2003; J. Henley, 'Cancer Unit Fights US Gene Patent' *The Guardian* 8 September 2001; S. Krimsky, *Science in the Private Interest: Has the Lure of Profits Corrupted Biomedical Research?* (Lanham: Rowman & Littlefield, 2003), 67–8; J. Meek, 'US Firm May Double Cost of UK Cancer Checks' *The Guardian* 17 January 2000.

[90] M.W. Jackson, *supra* note 13; see also Nuffield Council on Bioethics, 'The Ethics of Patenting DNA: A Discussion Paper' (London: Nuffield Council on Bioethics, 2002), 39–42.

is necessarily per se a bad thing. But while empirical studies have been published that find little evidence to support the view that there would be more and better public health-oriented research without DNA patenting,[91] one should not rely too much on such findings. It is very difficult to estimate the size of the 'chilling effect' of patents on such research, which anecdotal evidence suggests may be substantial. Furthermore, reliable empirical evidence exists to support the claim that the aggressive assertion of DNA patent rights is unduly restricting the availability of diagnostic tests for patients in hospitals and other public service institutions.[92] This is sometimes the case even when testing by others does not require access to information disclosed in a patent.[93]

Of course concerns about DNA patenting are not confined to their effects on research. To the extent that patents are legal monopolies that can in some cases create market monopolies, they are bound to affect the prices of health products protected by patents including in developing countries. While the relationship between DNA patents and the prices of drugs, vaccines, diagnostic kits and other health products in the developed and developing worlds is often a complex one, to the extent that patents restrict competition it seems implausible, as is sometimes claimed, that patents can have no effect on prices.

The question is what to do? One could simply exclude DNA sequences from patentability. But would this necessarily be good for innovation or for society? In such a case, business would likely resort to copyright or trade secrecy. Since legal and technological measures provided under current copyright and trade secrecy laws lock up information much more securely than under patent law, the cure could become more harmful than the disease.

The Myriad patent cases

Myriad Genetics is a company known as much for its aggressive assertion of its gene patents as for the genetic testing services it provides. The company's IP acquisition and management activities form an essential part of any account of the evolution of patent law in the field of molecular biology, especially genetics. This is because the controversies motivated litigation and legal reforms that in a few cases actually affected the scope of patent protection in the field of genomics. As we saw, that some European countries opted for purpose bound patent protection appears to be a response of sorts to concerns arising from Myriad's aggressive patent acquisition and assertion practices. Myriad's patents have been litigated in a few countries, but we will focus just on those few cases which have resulted in changes to the scope of protectable subject matter: the recent US Supreme Court and Australian High Court cases. But first, we present some background.

Human gene patenting and the assertion of patent rights have proved to be intensely controversial. Patents on genes linked to particular diseases tend to claim a range of applications including

---

[91] National Academies of Science, Board on Science, Technology, and Economic Policy (STEP), and Committee on Science, Technology, and Law (STL), *Reaping the Benefits of Genomic and Proteomic Research: Intellectual Property Rights, Innovation, and Public Health*, Washington, DC: NAS, 2005; M.J. Howlett and A.F. Christie, 'An Analysis of the Approach of the European, Japanese and United States Patent Offices to Patenting Partial DNA Sequences (ESTs)', University of Melbourne Faculty of Law Legal Studies Research Paper No 82, 2004.

[92] J.F. Merz, A.G. Kriss, D.G. Leonard and M.K. Cho, 'Diagnostic Testing Fails the Test' (2002) 415(6872) *Nature* 577–9.

[93] Meek, *supra* note 89.

diagnostic and predictive tests. Some patent owners have been quite determined in enforcing their rights, including in one instance against patients that had collaborated in the discovery of the gene resulting in a lawsuit.[94] Often the validity of such patents is considered to be extremely questionable.

Perhaps the best-known case with the most far-reaching implications concerns the patenting activity of the aforementioned Myriad Genetics relating to and covering two large genes (BRCA1 and BRCA2) linked to a certain proportion of breast cancer cases. The discoveries of the genes were not made by Myriad alone – far from it. Mary-Claire King of University of California, Berkeley showed in 1990 that both breast and ovarian cancer could run in families, and that a variant of a gene located somewhere on chromosome 17, given the name BRCA1, substantially increased a woman's susceptibility to both cancers.[95] BRCA1 codes for a protein that is 'critical for DNA repair and transcription regulation; when the gene is inactivated through mutation and the protein is altered, it leads to abnormal cellular gene expression'.[96] In April 1995, King filed a US patent assigned to the Regents of the University of California on 'genetic markers for breast, ovarian, and prostatic cancer', which was granted in April 1997.[97] However, two companies, Myriad Genetics and OncorMed, patented the sequenced gene.[98] In Myriad's case it was actually a collective effort involving scientists from the University of Utah, the National Institutes of Health (NIH) and McGill University. Myriad filed its BRCA1-related US patents on 7 June 1995.[99] These claimed the whole gene sequence plus some harmful mutations.[100] OncorMed's first US patent on BRCA1 sequences was filed a few months later, on 12 February 1996.[101] The sequences claimed were very similar to those of Myriad.

Subsequently, another variant gene linked to breast cancer incidence, dubbed BRCA2, was also patented by Myriad even though the claimed invention drew heavily on publicly available sequence data and a considerable amount of public sector research. It is probably more accurate, and certainly fairer, to say that BRCA2 was discovered by an international team led by Mike Stratton at the Institute of Cancer Research (ICR), which had determined that the gene was located somewhere on chromosome 13. According to Stratton, on 23 November 1995, the Sanger Centre

---

[94] L. Andrews and D. Nelkin, *Body Bazaar: The Market for Human Tissue in the Biotechnology Age* (New York: Crown Publishers, 2001).

[95] J.M. Hall et al., 'Linkage of Early-Onset Familial Breast Cancer to Chromosome 17q21' (1990) 250 *Science* 1684–89.

[96] B. Williams-Jones, 'History of a Gene Patent: Tracing the Development and Application of Commercial BRCA Testing' (2002) 10 *Health Law Journal* 123–46, 127.

[97] US Patent no 5,622,829 ('Genetic markers for breast, ovarian, and prostatic cancer'), issued on 22 April 1997.

[98] Patents on BRCA1 were granted to Myriad at the USPTO in 1999 and the EPO in 2001.

[99] US Patent no 5,707,999 ('Linked breast and ovarian cancer susceptibility gene'), issued on 20 January 1998; and US Patent no 5,710,001 ('17q-linked breast and ovarian cancer susceptibility gene'), issued on 20 January 1998. In each case ownership of the patents was shared, with Canada's Centre de Recherche du Chul and Japan's Cancer Institute ('999), with the University of Utah and the US government ('001).

[100] Williams-Jones, *supra* note 96, 131.

[101] US Patent no 5,654,155 ('Consensus sequence of the human BRCA1 gene'), issued on 5 August 1997. This was superseded exactly one year later by the filing of Patent no 5,750,400 ('Coding sequences of the human BRCA1 gene'), issued on 12 May 1998.

in Cambridge and Washington University's Genome Sequencing Center jointly released onto the internet a sequence of 900,000 nucleotide bases containing the gene. Their intention in doing this was to accelerate the identification of the gene's precise location but without favouring any of the research groups involved in the race. The Cancer Research Campaign (CRC) filed two UK patents, the first on the very same day that the sequence was released on the internet in the same month, the second on 21 December. The applications claimed a 1,000 base pair stretch of cDNA but not the whole sequence of the gene. The idea of doing so was controversial but it was meant as a public-spirited gesture. In this case it was done to try and prevent Myriad from controlling both genes and also to ensure the test would be widely available on the National Health Service and that it would be marketed and carried out in an ethical manner respectful towards patients. It achieved this by licensing the patent to OncorMed with very strict pro-public health stipulations.[102]

On December 22, the ICR-led consortium publicly announced the sequencing of BRCA2, that they had filed the above UK patents, and that an article would be coming out the following day in *Nature*.[103] However, Myriad, who had downloaded the internet data, and drawing on automated sequencing technological capacity that the public consortium could not match, had very quickly sequenced the whole gene. Myriad made its own announcement on the same day and filed an initial US patent application one day before the second and most important of the UK patent applications.[104] As with BRCA1, it subsequently filed patents on BRCA2 elsewhere including at the European Patent Office.

Myriad, which was spun off the University of Utah and was receiving some funding from Eli Lilly and the NIH, was determined to assert its priority and monopolise diagnostic testing services in the US for hereditary breast and ovarian cancer. It was successful on both counts. But the company's behaviour not only made it hugely unpopular, but also brought gene patenting itself into disrepute.

By 1996, four institutions in the US offered commercial testing services: Myriad, OncorMed, the Genetics and IVF Institute, and the University of Pennsylvania's Genetics Diagnostics Laboratory. These were all a bit different in terms of how they did the testing, the specific sequences being tested for, and the types of people they tested. Myriad claimed that its test called 'BRACAnalysis' was the so-called 'gold standard', but none of them was perfect, and Myriad's was very expensive, in part because it was done in-house at the company's headquarters in Salt Lake City. The company came to an arrangement with OncorMed, which had licensed King's and the CRC's patents, according to which Myriad took over the latter firm's patents. It then used its patent rights to have all of its rival testing programmes closed down. Having cornered the US market it sought aggressively to do the same thing in Canada and Europe. In Europe the only legal obstacle was the ICR patent and the fact that its aggressive commercial practices were running into opposition at various

---

[102] Notes from a presentation delivered by Professor Mike Stratton ('Patenting of Genes – A Case Study of BRCA2') at St Catherine's College, University of Oxford, 1 June 2000. On file with authors. See S. Parthasarathy, 'Comparing Genetic Testing for Breast Cancer in the USA and the UK' (2005) 35(1) *Social Studies of Science* 5–40; Williams-Jones, *supra* note 96, 137.

[103] R. Wooster et al., 'Identification of the Breast Cancer Susceptibility Gene BRCA2' (1995) 378 *Nature* 789–92.

[104] US Patent no 5,837,492 ('Chromosome 13-linked breast cancer susceptibility gene'), issued on 17 November 1998. The patent was jointly filed with Endo Recherche, HSC Research and Development and University of Pennsylvania.

levels, from patient groups who believed Myriad was taking improper advantage of women's anxiety about their health,[105] to professional medical associations, genetics laboratories and other public health organisations and parliamentarians, who were in varying degrees shocked by the sheer ruthlessness of Myriad and were questioning the wisdom of allowing genes to be patented at all. The outrage was perhaps greatest in those countries, like the UK, Canada and France, which have largely state-provided healthcare systems with fairly tight budgets. In Europe, the French *Institut Curie*, whose own research in this area cast doubts as to the quality of Myriad's test, organised a campaign to have the company's European patents revoked. The Institut and its partners in this effort relied primarily on classic patentability grounds rather than resorting to moral arguments, and this strategy proved to be successful with Myriad's patents either being invalidated or having their claims drastically reduced.[106]

The Myriad patents in the US were challenged in court by public interest groups and patients, initially successfully. The lower court threw out all of Myriad's 15 patent claims in seven patents relating to BRCA1 and BRCA2 on isolated DNA, cDNA, and methods of comparing and analysing.[107] On appeal, the court's decision regarding the product claims to isolated DNA and cDNA were reversed. After some toing and froing between the Court of Appeals for the Federal Circuit and the Supreme Court, the latter made its final decision in 2013.[108] In answer to the question of whether human genes are patentable, Judge Thomas speaking for the Court declared that isolated DNA is ineligible under section 101 of the Patent Act. However, cDNA was eligible subject to fulfilment of the criteria. Interestingly, the Court took a utilitarian approach. Citing *Prometheus* (see also Chapters 5 and 13), the Court stated that in deciding what is naturally occurring, a law of nature, or a product of nature, one must take into account the purpose of patent law – as if patent law itself must form the source by which practical meanings for these difficult concepts are to be sought. That makes sense as long as the malleability of such terminology, as Justice Frankfurter recognised decades before, is kept within some reasonable limits. Accordingly, the Court argued, the inventive capacity of people should not be restrained by patenting what should be freely available to all. Finding the location of

---

[105] In the United States, where its patents are still valid [when the cited work was published in 2008], Myriad has launched wide-ranging direct mailing shots to women, urging them to ask their doctors for a diagnostic test. This sort of scaremongering plays on patients' understandable confusion about the effect of the genes: although the vast majority of women with the BRCA1 gene will develop breast cancer, most breast cancers are not caused by the gene. So urging women to undergo an expensive genetic test for the sake of peace of mind raises both false alarm and false hope: false alarm because the gene is comparatively rare, false hope because even if you test negative for the gene, you can still develop breast cancer.

See D. Dickenson, *Body Shopping: The Economy Fuelled by Flesh and Blood* (Oxford: Oneworld, 2008), 92.

[106] For details of the challenges to Myriad's European patents relating to BRCA1 and 2, as well as a pending counter-challenge by Myriad to CRC's main BRCA2 patent, see M. Rimmer, *Intellectual Property and Biotechnology: Biological Inventions* (Cheltenham: Edward Elgar Publishing, 2008), 190–200. For a very fair and objective presentation and commentary on the Myriad BRCA controversy, see E.R. Gold and J. Carbone, 'Myriad: In the Eye of the Policy Storm', Montreal: The Innovation Partnership and McGill University Centre for Intellectual Property Policy, 2008.

[107] *Association for Molecular Pathology v. U.S. Patent and Trademark Office* (SDNY, 2010).

[108] *AMP v. USPTO* (569 US 2013).

something already in existence is not patent-eligible under section 101 however extensive the effort entailed. As for the nature of the DNA disclosed and claimed in the patents, the Court noted that it was not DNA as chemistry but as information. Therefore breaking chemical bonds to isolate DNA is not significant because the information is not altered by doing so. Claiming a separated fragment of code that is part of a much longer code, none of which you have written yourself, is not inventive and would be harmful for innovation. Oddly, when it came to cDNA the fact of its being a chemical synthesised in the laboratory seems to make it a new thing. Clearly it is not new as information since the messenger RNA leaving the nucleus would only differ from it by the substitution of a U for a T but it was at least 'made' by human effort and this makes it a new artefact: it is 'an exons-only molecule, that is not naturally occurring'. As expressed by Thomas:

> [The petitioners] argue that cDNA is not patent eligible because '[t]he nucleotide sequence of cDNA is dictated by nature, not by the lab technician.' [...] That may be so, but the lab technician unquestionably creates something new when cDNA is made. cDNA retains the naturally occurring exons of DNA, but it is distinct from the DNA from which it was derived. As a result, cDNA is not a 'product of nature' and is patent eligible under § 101 [...].

What the Court did not consider was the patent status of synthetic single-strand DNA primers?[109] These are not isolated but are, like cDNA made in the lab. So they are human artefacts, not natural products. However, unlike cDNA the sequences are identical to the naturally-occurring ones. The Court of Appeals faced this question a year later and, treating such claims as chemical rather than informational, considered them to be patent ineligible:

> [N]either naturally occurring compositions of matter, nor synthetically created compositions that are structurally identical to the naturally occurring compositions, are patent eligible [...] A DNA structure with a function similar to that found in nature can only be patent eligible as a composition of matter if it has a unique structure, different from anything found in nature [...] Primers do not have such a different structure and are patent ineligible. Primers necessarily contain the identical sequence of the BRCA sequence directly opposite to the strand to which they are designed to bind. They are structurally identical to the ends of DNA strands found in nature.[110]

Since the case, in the US, the availability of BRCA1 and 2 test options has reportedly improved while prices have fallen.[111] Nonetheless, the decision has highlighted the fact that Myriad (and other

---

[109] 'Probes' and 'primers' are commonly used terms in genomics. A very useful explanation of the terms and of their uses in the laboratory is provided in University of Utah Research Foundation *et al* v. Ambry Genetics, (*D. Utah* 2014). The case is interesting in itself, representing a failure effort by Myriad to get a preliminary injunction to stop a company selling BRCA tests after the Supreme Court judgment.

[110] *In re BRCA1 – and BRCA2 – Based Heredity Cancer Test Patent Litigation* (Fed Cir, 2014).

[111] E. Clain et al., 'Availability and Payer Coverage of BRCA1/2 Tests and Gene Panels' (2015) 33(9) *Nature Biotechnology* 900–902.

patent owners) have been enjoying legal monopolies they should not have been given, and this has had negative social impacts in terms of people being deprived of access to the test. Moreover, Myriad used its monopoly position to generate vast amounts of data acquired through its testing service which it has been refusing to disclose since 2004. It has been argued that it now has a moral obligation to freely disclose it.[112]

In a detailed newspaper article published in Canada, Abraham, Gold and Castle critiqued the role of patents in the field of human genetics that the US decision might have gone some way towards mitigating, albeit not yet in that country.[113] These authors point out that most gene patents focus on single gene defects linked to disease. Often, they fail to take into account other genes, and the wider complexities involved in disease development. Thus patents tend to be awarded on the basis of discovery of a single gene. However, the real innovation lies not in discovery but 'interpretation of errors – mutations – in those genes and the analysis of their interaction with other genes […] gene testing today involves innovation in data interpretation, competition between ways of analyzing the data and constant questioning and review of results'. Despite this, the patent system allows owners to restrict access to data. This is because, as the above authors asserted:

> Firms holding gene patents are motivated to keep data to themselves and […] not share their insights into the impact of particular errors on disease development. Unlocking those patents will enable new generation of firms that compete not on the basis of exclusive rights, but on the accuracy of their methods of analysis, their service to patients and doctors and the reliability and reproducibility of their results.

They conclude that 'patents on these methods, rather than on genes themselves, will spur innovation as competing groups will try to outdo each other, provided that they all have access to same basic data'.

Thankfully, the US may be part of a trend to roll back patent rights in this area to promote genuine innovation. Courts from Australia to Turkey (an EPO member) have followed the example of the US in excluding isolated DNA from patentability. In Australia's case, Myriad was one of the parties in the litigation. Previously, courts in Australia in deciding on relevant inventions were guided by the 1959 *NRDC* case which was not about natural products per se but that considered the patentability of certain weed control measures in light of the language of the English Statute of Monopolies.[114] It is worth discussing this case in some detail before moving onto the Myriad litigation. Previously, the patent examiner had rejected the weed control method claims on the basis of being 'not directed to any manner of manufacture in that they are claims to the mere use of

---

[112] J.M. Conley, R. Cook-Deegan and G. Lázaro-Muñoz, 'Myriad after *Myriad*: The Proprietary Data Dilemma' (2014) 15(4) *North Carolina Journal of Law and Technology* 597–637. For further discussion on the implications of the Myriad decision, see S. Levy, 'Our Shared Code: The Myriad Decision and the Future of Genetic Research' (2013) 121(8) *Environmental Health Perspectives* 250–53.

[113] S. Abraham, D. Castle and R. Gold, 'How a Gene-Patent Test Cases will Help both Patients and Inventors', *Global and Mail*, 4 November 2014.

[114] *National Research Development Corporation v. Commissioner of Patents* [1959] HCA 67; (1959) CLR 252.

known substances – which use also does not result in any vendible product'. The Court dismissed the value of seeking to draw a distinction between invention and discovery:

> The truth is that the distinction between discovery and invention is not precise enough to be other than misleading in this area of discussion. There may indeed be a discovery without invention – either because the discovery is of some piece of abstract information without any suggestion of a practical application of it to a useful end, or because its application lies outside the realm of 'manufacture'. But where a person finds out that a useful result may be produced by doing something which has not been done by that procedure before, his claim for a patent is not validly answered by telling him that although there was ingenuity in his discovery that the materials used in the process would produce the useful result no ingenuity was involved in showing how the discovery, once it had been made, might be applied. The fallacy lies in dividing up the process that he puts forward as his invention. It is the whole process that must be considered.[115]

The Court affirmed the view that to be inherently patentable in line with a reasonable understanding of the statutory language there much be a product, and it must be a 'vendible product'. As such, to be patentable the claimed invention, whether a product, use or method, must 'consist[s] in an artificially created state of affairs', and it must be of economic significance, hence vendible. In 2014, the Federal Court of Australia cited this case favourably in support of an expansive interpretation of inherent patentability finding isolated DNA claims to be patentable.[116] However, the High Court of Australia reversed this decision finding unanimously all three isolated DNA claims in Myriad's just-previously expired Australian patent to be invalid.[117] It is worth noting that in doing so it took much more of an informational view of DNA than did the Federal Court, and it also took public policy matters into account in making its decision. According to three of the judges in their joint opinion:

> Despite the formulation of the claimed invention as a class of product, its substance is information embodied in arrangements of nucleotides. The information is not 'made' by human action. It is discerned. That feature of the claims raises a question about how they fit within the concept of a 'manner of manufacture'. As appears from s 6 of the Statute of Monopolies, an invention is something which involves 'making'. It must reside in something. It may be a product. It may be a process. It may be an outcome which can be characterised, in the language of NRDC, as an 'artificially created state of affairs'. Whatever it is, it must be something brought about by human action.[118]

As for public policy and the purposes of the patent system:

---

[115] Ibid., para 8.

[116] *D'Arcy v. Myriad Genetics Inc* [2014] FCAFC 115.

[117] *D'Arcy v. Myriad Genetics Inc* [2015] HCA 35.

[118] Ibid., para 6.

There is a real risk that the chilling effect of the claims, on the use of any isolation process in relation to the BRCA1 gene, would lead to the creation of an exorbitant and unwarranted de facto monopoly on all methods of isolating nucleic acids containing the sequences coding for the BRCA1 protein. The infringement of the formal monopoly would not be ascertainable until the mutations and polymorphisms were detected. Such a result would be at odds with the purposes of the patent system.[119]

In early 2016, the Specialised Court of Istanbul for Intellectual and Industrial Property Rights invalidated a claim in a patent to an isolated human DNA sequence relating to an inherited condition called Familial Mediterranean fever (FMF). Genetic probes for identifying normal and mutated versions of the gene and primers for DNA amplification, though, were held patentable.[120]

14.4.2 Stem cell patenting

Humans possess about 200 different kinds of cell. Since all except red blood cells contain in their nuclei each person's entire genome without variation, it follows that the kind they are depends on which genes are activated and which are 'switched off'. All cells in the body are descended from undifferentiated cells that first appear in the fertilised egg once cell division has started. These are stem cells, so called because it is from them that all other cell types branch out. When a fertilised human egg (zygote) starts to divide, each cell has the potential to develop into an entire human being with placenta. This cellular capability, of totipotency, exists for the first three divisions. Once eight cells have become 16 this potential diminishes somewhat. These then pluripotent cells can develop into all cell types but no placenta or umbilical cord can form. This means that developing into a fully-fledged individual human from the separate growth of a single cell is no longer possible but in all respects these cells can be converted into any somatic human cell. This makes them scientifically useful, and medically too for such purposes as regenerative treatments, drug testing and for basic research into human development, both normal and abnormal. After five days, the zygote has graduated to a blastocyst which looks under a microscope rather like an open clam, the 'shell' being the outer cell mass, and the 'fish' the inner cell mass. By that time the latter is a rich source of pluripotent cells that can be cultured in a laboratory. Although scientific definitions of 'embryo' vary to some extent, zygotes, blastocysts and morulas (those in the stage between the two) are all generally considered to be embryos in different states of development.[121] So, by most definitions a blastocyst is an embryo but it has not yet implanted in the womb, and neither are the cells differentiated. Differentiation takes place from about 14 days, from when splitting into twins becomes impossible, and it takes longer still for the embryo to have any consciousness or feeling. Of course, despite their genetic similarities, twins

---

[119] Ibid., para 8.

[120] 'Turkish Intellectual Property Court Rules on the Patentability of Genes and Other Nucleic Acid Sequences', *The National Law Review* 23 March 2016. See more at: http://www.natlawreview.com/article/turkish-intellectual-property-court-rules-patentability-genes-and-other-nucleic-acid?utm_content=buffer34000&utm_medium=social&utm_source=twitter.com&utm_campaign=buffer#sthash.tbObLmcV.dpuf.

[121] J.K. Findlay et al., 'Human Embryo: A Biological Definition' (2007) 22(4) *Human Reproduction* 905–11.

are completely different people. It follows from this obvious fact, and the total absence of a brain and nervous system, that the early-stage embryo is not yet a human being and arguably is not one for some time afterwards. Worldwide, 14 days tends to serve as the limit beyond which research becomes illegal. However, following reports of scientists keeping embryos alive in vitro for almost that length of time, some have argued for a reconsideration with a view to possibly extending the allowed term so as to learn more about human development.[122]

It is important to understand that 'Embryonic Stem Cells' (ES cells) are in vitro cell cultures (cell lines) from a single source – they are derived from embryos rather than being embryonic cells themselves. Accordingly, they are not cells existing in blastocysts but laboratory 'products' kept in artificial conditions to keep on dividing without differentiating for as long as possible so that cells can continue to be 'harvested' over time for experimentation and use. They are of course descended from the original cells obtained from the inner cell mass of a blastocyst but they are not the same ones due to the continuous process of division and subdivision. The embryo itself is destroyed in the process of extraction. What is controversial about all this is not just that embryos are destroyed but that they are being used at all for purposes that may be of medical benefit to patients but at the expense of foreclosing the potential that the destroyed embryo had to develop into one (or more) people. It is others who will derive any advantage from their use. While it is possible to snip out a single cell from an early-stage embryo for examination without affecting its integrity, this is not yet a viable approach to producing an ES cell line.

Health benefits in terms of regenerative medicine and other fields of healthcare are largely for the future. However, some treatments have been used with success. Thus, the *New Scientist* reported on 25 May 2013 as follows:

> A man blinded by the degeneration of his retinal cells has had his sight restored in one eye after receiving a stem cell treatment. Human embryonic stem cells were turned into retinal pigment epithelial cells and then transplanted into his retina, as part of a trial by Advanced Cell Technology in Marlborough, Massachusetts.

Different countries adopt a range of positions on how far they support and the ways they regulate the development and use of ES cells. The European Commission funds stem cell research but it must be legal in the country where it is to be done. It is in fact illegal in Poland and Lithuania. Where legal it must also use leftover embryos from IVF. These would ultimately be destroyed anyway. Currently, the UK, Belgium and Sweden allow creation of new embryos for research, whereas in Germany to do so is a criminal offence. Much research takes place in the US where the first methods of deriving stem cell lines from human embryos were invented. However, the 1996 Dickey-Wicker Amendment bans federal funding for 'research in which a human embryo or embryos are destroyed'. Government-funded research must use existing cell lines. Accordingly, the National Institutes of Health Guidelines for Human Stem Cell Research, 2009, permits funding as long as research 'utilizes cells from lines: (1) created by in vitro fertilization for reproductive purposes, (2) no longer needed for that purpose, and (3) voluntarily donated by the individuals who owned them'.

---

[122] I. Hyun, A. Wilkerson and J. Johnston, 'Embryology Policy: Revisit the 14-day Rule' (2016) 533 *Nature* 169–71.

What about elsewhere? It is fair to say that many people are perfectly relaxed about the use of blastocysts to generate stem cell lines – atheists, agnostics and believers in a deity alike. Science and religion have never stood entirely apart and it remains the case that religious doctrine, in the West going as far back as Aquinas if not earlier, influences views on the ethical limits of scientific practice and even what people believe to be the scientific truth. This is very apparent when we look at the range of views concerning this particular field of biomedical endeavour. For example:

> Although the use of human ES cells is opposed by the Roman Catholic Church and some Protestant denominations, it is generally supported by the Jewish community and accepted in many Muslim countries. There is no consensus on when human embryonic life begins, but the majority of Muslim scholars consider it to start 40–120 days after conception and therefore hold the view that a fertilized egg up to 5 days old has no soul – it is not 'human life' but 'biological life'.[123]

There are adult stem cells too. For example, haematopoietic stem cells in our bone marrow can differentiate into the various blood cells but not into other types of cell. These have been used medically for some time now for patients with certain bone marrow and immune system disorders that can be treated by the transplantation of these cells. But adult stem cells are a lot less versatile, forming at most a limited number of related cell types. For scientists, the property of pluripotency is what the philosopher's stone was to alchemists – something that converts the most basic and universal units of human life into precious cellular gold and silver.

The science is moving rapidly and it gets harder to speak of inevitabilities and impossibilities. Scientists mostly in Japan have found out how to reprogram adult cells into pluripotent stem cells. These are known as Induced Pluripotent Stem cells (iPS cells). Compared to ES cells, use of these has both advantages and disadvantages. Because they may be derived from the cells of a patient-donor they may counter the problem of 'foreign' cell rejection and enhance personalised health care. They also do not require destruction of embryos, which may allay some of the ethical concerns. On the other hand, they may be less stable and effective than ES cells. There are also possible dangers in the use of retroviruses to deliver the genetic factors that induce the pluripotency, with the possibility of causing tumours. Other methods are in development and research is ongoing to find the safest and most effective one.[124] A new safer method was announced in January 2014 but was subsequently retracted. The first patient trials using cells derived from two patients receiving treatment took place in Japan in 2014, but they were discontinued a year later. Despite this lack of practical outcomes to date, there has been an immense amount of patent activity. In 2014 it was reported in a survey of patent filings that globally there are 650 patent families on iPS cell production technologies, and over 1,300 relating to cell differentiation methods.[125] The US is the source of more than half of these inventions, with Japan coming a very distant second.

---

[123] R. Dajani, 'Jordan's Stem-Cell Law Can Guide the Middle East' (2014) 510 *Nature* 189.

[124] T.M. Schlaeger et al., 'A Comparison of Non-Integrating Reprogramming Methods' (2015) 33(1) *Nature Biotechnology* 58–65.

[125] M. Roberts et al., 'The Global Intellectual Property Landscape of Induced Pluripotent Stem Cell Technologies' (2014) 32(8) *Nature Biotechnology* 742–8.

There has also been some success in deriving stem cells from cloned human embryos, which may possibly resolve some ethical concerns too. In 2014, scientific teams in South Korea and US used the 'Dolly technique' to derive ES cells lines from skin cells donated by two men,[126] and to transform ES cells into insulin-producing cells using cells donated by a diabetic woman.[127] Of course, the fact that the embryos' genomes are identical to the adult donors' still makes them embryos no more nor less than if they were not cloned. Moreover, the enucleated eggs still had to come from somewhere.

With respect to patents, the US treats stem cell-related inventions no differently from other types with the restriction under Section 33 of the America Invents Act, 2011 that 'no patent may issue on a claim directed to or encompassing a human organism'. Indeed, Brüstle's invention, which will be discussed below, was patented there as it was in Japan, Australia and Israel.

In Europe the situation is completely different.[128] The sources of law concerning the morality of biotechnological inventions are the European Patent Convention (see Chapter 5) and its internal rules, and the EU Directive discussed above. We need to say more about the latter instrument here.

Recital (16) states in part that 'patent law must be applied so as to respect the fundamental principles safeguarding the dignity and integrity of the person'. This would appear to be inapplicable to stem-cell related inventions given that blastocysts are not yet persons having any dignity or integrity to safeguard. As we will see below, things are not as simple as that.

Article 6, which has been incorporated almost verbatim into the Implementing Regulations of the EPC (Rule 28), states as follows:

1. Inventions shall be considered unpatentable where their commercial exploitation would be contrary to *ordre public* or morality; however, exploitation shall not be deemed to be so contrary merely because it is prohibited by law or regulation.
2. On the basis of paragraph 1, the following, in particular, shall be considered unpatentable:
   (a) processes for cloning human beings;
   (b) processes for modifying the germ line genetic identity of human beings;
   (c) uses of human embryos for industrial or commercial purposes;
   (d) processes for modifying the genetic identity of animals which are likely to cause them suffering without any substantial medical benefit to man or animal, and also animals resulting from such processes.

It should first be noted that (a) to (c) are quite definite, absolute even. Commercially exploiting these processes and uses, which patents are assumed to promote or facilitate, is immoral or contrary to *ordre public*. Therefore there can be no patents on them. Whether there are societal benefits

---

[126] Y.G. Chung et al., 'Human Somatic Cell Nuclear Transfer Using Adult Cells', *Cell Stem Cell*, April 2014.

[127] Yamada et al., 'Human Oocytes Reprogram Adult Somatic Nuclei of a Type 1 Diabetic to Diploid Pluripotent Stem Cells' *Nature*, April 2014.

[128] For a detailed comparative study on treatment of stem cell-related patents in the US, Europe and China, see L. Jiang, *Regulating Human Embryonic Stem Cell in China: A Comparative Study on Human Embryonic Stem Cell's Patentability and Morality in U.S. and E.U.* (Singapore: Springer, 2016).

and how substantial they may be are not considerations to be applied. There are sound reasons to ban patents on (a) and (b) given that human reproductive cloning and germ line modification are illegal in most countries, as they should be. Such practices are unethical, highly risky, and raise profound concerns regarding whether or not we wish to live in a society in which babies can be designed and 'created' to order. Interested readers are referred to Aldous Huxley's dystopian novel *Brave New World*, an ever-increasing number of science fiction novels and movies, as well as some weighty bioethical writings expressing a diverse range of opinions as to the ability of humankind to use such technologies wisely if we are to use them at all. But what about (c) and (d)? (d) differs from the others in being utilitarian. It is also somewhat vague in practice given the lack of guidance regarding the level of medical benefits needed to attain substantiality, besides which they may be no more than future possibilities as opposed to present-day certainties. What is it that is immoral here for which denying a patent is the right response? What really is the point of these exclusions? Is it that nobody should commercially exploit such inventions as if we are to leave the research to governments, public universities, and public domain-oriented scientists with no commercial agenda? Or is it that gaining legal monopolies over these processes and uses with monetary gain in mind is itself immoral? There is nothing in the text to say unequivocally that the inventions in themselves are immoral, just the base motives of those who might wish to patent them to make money. The present authors are sceptical about exclusion (c) on grounds of moral consistency – unless one holds that such research should not be conducted anyway and are unsure that patent examiners should be burdened with utilitarian judgements embodied by exclusion (d).

In the 1990s, James Thomson of University of Wisconsin succeeded in isolating primate including human embryonic cells and generating sustainable purified cell lines. Subsequently, three US patents – all titled 'Primate embryonic stem cells' – were granted with Wisconsin Alumni Research Foundation as assignee: 5,843,780, 6,200,806 and 7,029,913. These patents have attracted controversy, including about their broad scope and the rather restrictive licensing practices employed by WARF especially in the early years.[129] But they have never been successfully challenged. The first patent has expired but the latter two remain in force. One could perhaps see this as a case of evergreening through secondary (and tertiary) patenting, but we will leave it to others to assess the extent to which the '806 and '913 patents disclose substantial technological advances over the '780 invention. WARF's experience of effective patent management goes back to the early-twentieth century.[130]

In Europe things turned out very differently. When law, moral philosophy and bioethics meet in the same forum, religious dogma shouts to get a word in, and somehow a decision must be made, unimpeachable logic is probably too much to hope for. The welfare of future sick people standing to benefit from the research was not to be a concern, but that of the embryo whose actual or potential personhood made dignity relevant considerations in its treatment. Accordingly, WARF's efforts to patent Thomson's work ended in failure. In 2008, the EPO Enlarged Board of Appeal handed down a decision concerning WARF's patent application rejecting it on the basis of the immorality/

---

[129] J.M. Golden, 'WARF's Stem Cell Patents and Tensions Between Public and Private Sector Approaches to Research' (2010) 38(2) *Journal of Law, Medicine and Ethics* 314–31.

[130] G. Dutfield, *Intellectual Property Rights and the Life Science Industries, Past, Present and Future* (Singapore: World Scientific, 2009), 135.

contrary to *ordre public* exclusion and more specifically the language of Rule 28(c) incorporating the text of Article 6.2(c) of the EU Directive.[131] It was irrelevant that the method involving the embryo destruction was not claimed in the patent. At first glance, the decision appears entirely straightforward: 'Since [...] the only teaching of how to perform the invention to make human embryonic stem cell cultures is the use (involving their destruction) of human embryos, this invention falls under the prohibition of Rule 28(c) (formerly 23d(c)) EPC.'

Obviously there was an underlying industrial purpose to this necessarily embryo-destroying invention. Industrial application is a basic criterion and one wonders why anybody would file a patent on something lacking this capability. As for commercial purpose, one wonders why anybody files a patent if there is no commercial purpose behind the invention. It is perhaps noteworthy here that WARF had been actively licensing its patents in the US for a few years by this time. But, of course, the exception applied specifically not to purposes of the invention as a whole but to the embryo use. Destruction of something to extract useful parts is without a doubt a use of it so to escape the exception that part of the invention's performance would have to have not been for industrial or commercial purposes. Up to this point, the EBA's reasoning appears perfectly sound given the text of the exclusion and the original intent of the framers.

The EBA might have just let those facts speak for themselves and kept its decision as short as possible. But it did not do that, declaring that patenting the invention was not the source of the immorality, but the invention itself. That was perhaps implicit but by stating it expressly, it raised legitimate concerns about overreaching, that is, going well beyond the bounds of what a patent-granting organisation should have to take into account when deciding to grant or not. This is what the EBA went on to say:

> [...] it is not the fact of the patenting itself that is considered to be against ordre public or morality, but it is the performing of the invention, which includes a step (the use involving its destruction of a human embryo) that has to be considered to contravene those concepts.[132]

If so, why is a patent-granting organisation the one to decide and why should its views carry any weight or have legal implications of any kind? As we saw, several European governments had already deemed the legality of practicing the invented techniques to be in the public interest. In this field, inventions are original bio-scientific achievements with potential for practical use. But in most countries non-IP regulations exist setting limits as to what scientists can do in their labs. What is the purpose of a patent office telling us that what they achieved is immoral when they are perfectly legal?

To its credit the Enlarged Board clarified that the decision was not a blanket prohibition on patenting in the stem cell field:

> [...] this decision is not concerned with the patentability in general of inventions relating to human stem cells or human stem cell cultures. It holds unpatentable inventions concerning

---

[131] *Wisconsin Alumni Research Foundation (WARF)*. EPO, Decision of the Enlarged Board of Appeal of 25 November 2008, G 0002/06.

[132] Ibid., para 29.

products (here human stem cell cultures) which can only be obtained by the use involving their destruction of human embryos.[133]

What if the invention starts and ends with the transformation of stem cells in laboratory cultures and their use in therapy, and not their isolation and derivation from embryos? Wouldn't the invention also be morally tainted in the sense that at some point in time there would have had to be actual use of embryos in order to produce the stem cell line? And if so, wouldn't this invention also fall under the exception? These questions were answered by the Court of Justice of the European Union in the Brüstle case.[134] Brüstle's German patent was one concerning 'isolated and purified neural precursor cells, processes for their production from embryonic stem cells and the use of neural precursor cells for the treatment of neural defects'. Whereas Thomson's inventions teach how to produce lines of undifferentiated stem cells, this invention takes matters much further, providing a means to differentiate those cells into ones with genuine applications in regenerative medicine, specifically treatment of neural defects. On its face, this appears to be a great leap forward towards actual therapy. To class this invention as immoral is troubling to say the least. The Court did not dispute that:

> In order to remedy such neural defects, it is necessary to transplant immature precursor cells, still capable of developing. In essence, that type of cell exists only during the brain's development phase. The use of cerebral tissue from human embryos raises significant ethical questions and means that it is not possible to meet the need for the precursor cells which are required to provide publicly available cell treatment.[135]

So the claimed invention resolves a serious ethical difficulty: that the only other potential source of the cells would be far more developed human embryos. And yet the Court, again, would have none of such considerations. His invention was still immoral:

> Article 6(2)(c) of the Directive excludes an invention from patentability where the technical teaching which is the subject-matter of the patent application requires the prior destruction of human embryos or their use as base material, whatever the stage at which that takes place and even if the description of the technical teaching claimed does not refer to the use of human embryos.[136]

Further:

> [...] an invention must be regarded as unpatentable, even if the claims of the patent do not concern the use of human embryos, where the implementation of the invention requires the

---

[133] Ibid., para 35.

[134] Case C-34/10 *Oliver Brüstle v. Greenpeace eV*, judgment of 18 October 2011.

[135] Ibid., para 17.

[136] Ibid., para 52.

destruction of human embryos [...] The fact that destruction may occur at a stage long before the implementation of the invention, as in the case of the production of embryonic stem cells from a lineage of stem cells the mere reproduction of which implied the destruction of human embryos is, in that regard, irrelevant.[137]

Again, as long as embryos' destruction whenever it took place is indispensable to practicing the invention, there can be no patent, an approach that the EPO followed in a later decision of the TBA.[138] The CJEU overreached and to a greater extent than the EBA. But in doing so it shifted focus also to the patent and patent rights, not just to the invention. Whereas the EBA sought to claim that it is the invention that is immoral not the patent, for the CJEU the patent and the rights attached are 'connected with acts of an industrial or commercial nature' whether or not the invention is. In a sense, then, filing the patent application is an admission of 'guilt' – that the purposes of the research, including the use of the embryos, are industrial or commercial.

The Court took an extremely broad interpretation of 'embryo', bizarrely including unfertilised human eggs. It took the view that a broad and uniform definition was necessary not just to uphold human dignity but for the sake of the internal market. However, the Court left it up to national courts to decide whether a pluripotent stem cell isolated from an embryo at the blastocyst stage is itself a 'human embryo'. In the present case, following this CJEU ruling the German Federal Supreme Court correctly concluded in the negative.[139]

It did not take long for the Court to correct the first error following a referral from the UK. Unfertilised human eggs can be engineered to begin cell division but the fact remains that these are incapable of developing beyond the blastocyst stage. Such embryos are called parthenotes. In 2013, Henry Carr QC, in *International Stem Cell Corporation v. Comptroller General of Patents*, referred the following question to the CJEU:

> Are unfertilised human ova whose division and further development have been stimulated by parthenogenesis, and which, in contrast to fertilised ova, contain only pluripotent cells and are incapable of developing into human beings, included in the term 'human embryos' [...].

In 2014, the CJEU clarified as follows:

> An organism which is incapable of developing into a human being does not constitute a human embryo within the meaning of the Biotech Directive.
>
> Accordingly, uses of such an organism for industrial or commercial purposes may, as a rule, be patented.[140]

---

[137] Ibid., para 49.

[138] T 2221/10 (Culturing stem cells/TECHNION), ECLI:EP:BA:2014:T222110.20140204.

[139] Case X ZR 58/07, 2012.

[140] *International Stem Cell Corporation v Comptroller General of Patents* [2013] EWHC 807; Case C-364/13, ECLI:EU:C:2014:2451.

15

Genetic resources, traditional knowledge and traditional cultural expressions

This chapter concerns legal responses to three related issues that have gained massive international attention in recent decades. None is necessarily, even less exclusively, related to intellectual property law. But they have become so by way of a number of international instruments and the determination of a large number of (mostly developing) countries, that they are IP law-related:[1]

(i) *Intellectual property and unequal exchange, and the lack of benefit sharing* – The first issue has roots in the commonly-shared concern that developing countries rich in biological diversity fail, despite having sovereign jurisdiction over their natural resources, to capture significant benefits from the commercial exploitation of products developed using them, and that this can be remedied by legal and regulatory frameworks. The link with intellectual property law is two-fold: (i) that patents in their conventional form are regarded as part of the problem, their monopolistic effects being just one reason for this; and (ii) that they can be turned into a (partial) solution through a requirement known as disclosure of origin (see below).

(ii) *Ethnocentricity in intellectual property law* – The second is that certain forms of knowledge about nature are not capable of being legally protected as intellectual property for being 'traditional' (whatever that means) but are still commercially useful. This a complex matter that does not lend itself to simple analysis. Suffice it to say that many hold it to be self-evidently true. It follows that either traditional knowledge (TK) be made legally protectable through a special *sui generis* regime based perhaps, but not necessarily, on variations of existing norms, or that steps be taken to prevent others from incorporating it into property-right claims made

---

[1] For a detailed discussion on these issues, G. Dutfield, 'A Critical Analysis of the Debate on Traditional Knowledge, Drug Discovery and Drug-based Biopiracy' (2011) 33(4) *EIPR* 237.

to secure exclusive (and uncompensated) commercial exploitation. The former is generally referred to as positive protection, while the second approach is defensive protection. Regarding the latter, disclosure of origin has again been suggested as one way to achieve this goal as are the making available to patent granting offices enhanced access to TK prior art such as is presented in academic journals on topics like anthropology, ethnopharmacology and ethnobiology, and searchable databases such as India's Traditional Knowledge Digital Library (TKDL).[2] In this case the origin that must be disclosed to the patent granting authorities is not just that of genetic resources relevant to the invention but also of traditional knowledge.

(iii) *Lack of adequate and appropriate protection for cultural works and expressions that are considered as 'traditional'* – The third issue concerns the lack of legal protection for cultural expressions, again due to their being 'traditional' with all that word implies for authorship, ownership, term of protection, public interest and relatedness to intellectual property law, especially copyright. Trade marks and designs are also implicated.

In this chapter, to quite a large extent we blend the three issues because they cannot easily be treated completely separately.

15.1 INTERNATIONAL INSTRUMENTS AND FORUMS ASSOCIATED WITH GENETIC RESOURCES AND TRADITIONAL KNOWLEDGE

Since the early 1980s, international debates on the erosion of genetic resources, biodiversity loss, and the protection of TK have implicated IPRs, mostly patents. But what do patents have to do with genetic resources, biodiversity TK? A number of factors triggered these debates, including the following.

1. The extension of patent law to cover life forms, starting with micro-organisms and then stretching even further to embrace plants and animals. This gave rise to strong opposition from some quarters on moral and other grounds.
2. The perceived threat from patents and plant variety rights to the supposedly time-honoured norm of free international exchange of plant genetic resources for food and agriculture.
3. The perceived injustice felt by many that while developing countries were allowing others to take and use their genetic wealth for free, corporations in the rich world could acquire monopoly protection and sell back 'improved' resources at heavily marked up prices thanks

---

[2] The much-heralded TKDL is a searchable database of published information on India's traditional health systems such as Ayurveda intended to enhance prior art searches. There is in fact little evidence so far that it has had much effect in enhancing the quality of patents in those jurisdictions whose granting offices have access to the TKDL, or in halting biopiracy, sufficient to justify the not inconsiderable expense of producing it. T.P. Reddy and S. Chandrashekaran, *Create, Copy, Disrupt: India's Intellectual Property Dilemmas* (New Delhi: Oxford University Press, 2017), 271–5.

      to IPRs in the form of patent or plant variety protection (or both). Different views on this
      and factor two above sparked off the so-called 'seed wars'.[3]

4.   Concerns about the loss of genetic, biological and cultural diversity,[4] and a new appreciation
      during a period of biodiversity loss of indigenous peoples as being the original environmen-
      talists and traditional cultures deemed to be 'authentic'.

5.   The GATT Uruguay Round, which introduced intellectual property norms into the international
      trade regulatory system for the first time and provoked a backlash. It should be added here that
      the Uruguay Round was just one, albeit perhaps the most important) expression of an increas-
      ingly committed pro-IP stance among governments of Europe, North America and Japan.

International law has been highly responsive, with such agreements as the 1992 CBD and its 2010
Nagoya Protocol on Access to Genetic Resources and the Fair and Equitable Sharing of the Bene-
fits Arising from their Utilization ('Nagoya Protocol'), the 1983 FAO International Undertaking on
Plant Genetic Resources, which was superseded by the 2001 International Treaty on Plant Genetic
Resources for Food and Agriculture (see also Chapter 9), and the 2007 United Nations Declaration
on the Rights of Indigenous Peoples (see also Chapter 11). In addition, since 2001 the WIPO Intergovernmental Committee in Intellectual Property, Genetic Resources, Traditional Knowledge and
Folklore (the 'IGC') has deliberated on the above three issues with a possible view to one or more
legally-binding instruments. The World Trade Organization has also served as a negotiating forum
on the same subject matter.

15.2 THE CONVENTION ON BIOLOGICAL DIVERSITY AND THE NAGOYA PROTOCOL

The CBD was opened for signature at the 1992 Earth Summit in Rio de Janeiro. Agreeing a text acceptable to governments of the biodiversity-poor industrialised world and of the biodiversity-rich developing countries turned into an unexpectedly long, difficult and contentious process. Some developing
countries complained that it was unfair for developed country governments to expect them to protect
their forests and forgo the economic benefits from selling timber or converting them to other uses.
These countries argued vociferously that a *quid pro quo* for biodiversity preservation was fair and necessary. Realising the potential economic value of their biodiversity wealth, and needing to improve
their scientific, technological and financial capacities to exploit it, their position was that they had
the right to set conditions on those seeking their resources, including the fair and equitable sharing of
benefits such as the transfer of technology. Needless to say, perhaps, developed countries and transnational corporations wanted as few restrictions as possible on access to biological resources.

---

[3] K. Aoki, *Seed Wars: Controversies and Cases on Plant Genetic Resources and Intellectual Property* (Carolina Academic Press,
2008); J. Kloppenburg and D.L. Kleinman, 'Seed Wars: Common Heritage, Private Property, and Political Strategy' (1987)
95 *Socialist Review* 7–41.

[4] There are of course massive political differences as to the causes, but further discussion on this falls outside the scope of
the book.

The CBD has three main objectives, which are:

(i) the conservation of biological diversity; (ii) the sustainable use of its components; and (iii) the fair and equitable sharing of the benefits arising out of the utilisation of genetic resources, including by appropriate access to genetic resources and by appropriate transfer of relevant technologies, taking into account all rights over those resources and to technologies, and by appropriate funding.

None of these objectives appear at first glance to have a great deal to do with intellectual property. In fact, all three of them do, especially (i) and (iii).

Article 8 of the CBD concerns in situ conservation. In paragraph (j), three obligations are placed on Contracting Parties:

(i) respect, preserve and maintain knowledge, innovations and practices of indigenous and local communities embodying traditional lifestyles relevant for the conservation and sustainable use of biological diversity;
(ii) promote the wider application with the approval and involvement of the holders of such knowledge, innovations and practices; and
(iii) encourage the equitable sharing of the benefits arising from the utilisation of such knowledge, innovations and practices.

Article 15 on access to genetic resources assigns to national governments the authority to determine such access, which is subject to the prior informed consent of the provider country and the fair and equitable sharing of benefits. Presumably, the expectation here is that the exercise of such authority will enable countries to capture more of the benefits from industrial use of their genetic resources while conserving and sustainably utilising biodiversity.

Intellectual property is only explicitly referred to in the CBD in the context of technology transfer, which is supposed to be one of the main kinds of benefit for provider countries to receive. Article 16 on access to and transfer of technology requires parties to the Convention to undertake to provide and/or facilitate access and transfer of technologies to other parties under fair and most favourable terms. The only technology referred to is biotechnology, but Article 16 is concerned with any technologies 'that are relevant to the conservation and sustainable use of biological diversity or make use of genetic resources and do not cause significant damage to the environment'. Paragraph 16.5 requires the parties to cooperate to ensure that patents and other IP rights 'are supportive of and do not run counter to' the CBD's objectives. This reflects the profound disagreement during the negotiations between those who believed that IP rights and the (then forthcoming) TRIPS Agreement conflict with the CBD's objectives and others that saw no contradiction.

In 2010, contracting parties to the Convention adopted the Nagoya Protocol and it is fair to say that the Protocol has been welcomed by many advocates of the rights of indigenous peoples. For our purposes the most significant articles are 7 and 12, which deal with TK and associated genetic resources, and 10 and 11 on global benefit-sharing and transboundary issues respectively. Article 7 explicitly extends the right of prior informed consent in the context of access from governments to indigenous and local communities:

> In accordance with domestic law, each Party shall take measures, as appropriate, with the aim of ensuring that traditional knowledge associated with genetic resources that is held by indigenous and local communities is accessed with the prior and informed consent or approval and involvement of these indigenous and local communities, and that mutually agreed terms have been established.

Article 12 states in its first paragraph that:

> In implementing their obligations under this Protocol, Parties shall in accordance with domestic law take into consideration indigenous and local communities' customary laws, community protocols and procedures, as applicable, with respect to traditional knowledge associated with genetic resources.

There is a major lacuna which the Protocol does at least acknowledge even if it offers no solution for the time being though it may at least helpfully divert the gaze of policy-making and biodiplomacy from bilateralism towards multilateralism. Article 10 requires parties to:

> Consider the need for and modalities of a global multilateral benefit sharing mechanism to address the fair and equitable sharing of benefits derived from the utilization of genetic resources and traditional knowledge associated with genetic resources that occur in transboundary situations or for which it is not possible to grant or obtain prior informed consent.

Two questions arise. First, how much of the existing stock of genetic resources and TK associated with them does occur in transboundary situations? Second, under what circumstances might their use occur without the grant or acquisition of prior informed consent being possible? While it is difficult to say what proportion of genetic resources and TK is cross-boundary, the overall extent of transboundaryness is likely to be very high. Political boundaries are artificial and many ethnic groups' territories straddle borders. The chances are that this situation is frequently going to complicate negotiating between users and providers and thereby increase transaction costs to a potentially prohibitive scale. Another potential negative outcome is that the existence of other countries with overlapping resources and knowledge endowments will undermine providers' bargaining power. Article 10 acknowledges that the Protocol cannot yet resolve this, at least until a workable multilateral mechanism is in place to deal with this specific issue assuming that such a mechanism is politically or practically attainable.

In Article 11, the Nagoya Protocol itself urges cooperation rather than competition where the same genetic resources and TK straddle national boundaries. Where blocs of neighbouring countries adopt common access and benefit sharing regulations, as does the Andean Community,[5] this

---

[5] This is by virtue of Andean Community Decision 391: common system on access to genetic resources.

appears to be a workable approach. However, in most cases individual countries will have their own rules. Accordingly, opportunities to cooperate meaningfully are in most cases rather limited. For countries that welcome users on the basis of mutually agreed terms of access and benefit sharing, competitiveness is bound to creep in. Like the rest of us, companies respond to carrots as well as sticks. In the market economy, frequently multiple suppliers exist for identical but similar goods yet some are better at attracting customers than others despite starting off with similar endowments. Companies do not want to waste time and money rummaging around blindly. They want direction. If there are lots of capable and easily contactable people and institutions in one country, such as taxonomists and other plant scientists, knowledgeable indigenous peoples and good universities, who can direct them to what might be valuable, but fewer of them in another, that might influence their choice where to go even if such useful partners insist that rigorous access and benefit sharing rules be properly observed. In such situations, companies prefer legal and regulatory certainty. Scientific capacity building is key here. This is so whether we are talking of university-trained scientists or indigenous people with sophisticated knowledge about local resources and ecosystems.

Turning to the second question, that of what circumstances would make granting or obtaining prior informed consent impossible, one influential legal guide to the Protocol has this to say:

> [...] it would not be possible to obtain PIC for the utilization of genetic resources obtained from a country that has decided not to establish access requirements. Another possible instance would be in cases in which there is utilization of genetic resources from ex-situ collections with no information on country or countries of origin. Although ex-situ collections, such as gene banks and other repositories of biological or genetic material, increasingly maintain information about where and when a sample was collected, such information does not always allow identification of the country of origin of the genetic material utilized or the pertinent PIC to be obtained. In these circumstances, a global multilateral benefit-sharing mechanism would nevertheless allow discharge of benefit-sharing requirements.[6]

The authors also observe that:

> An international instrument does not apply retroactively – that is, it cannot be binding to acts that took place before or situations that ceased to exist prior to its entry into force. Nevertheless, new benefits arising from prior or ongoing uses could be considered as new situations for benefit-sharing requirements – though access requirements would not apply retroactively. A global multilateral benefit-sharing mechanism could potentially cover these cases.[7]

What are we to make of this? First, genetic resources and TK that are in general circulation may no longer have traceable origins or else have known origins that may go back a long time, possibly centuries. The sources of the genetic resources and the knowledge may be completely different.

---

[6] T. Greiber et al., *An Explanatory Guide to the Nagoya Protocol on Access and Benefit* (IUCN, 2012) 129.

[7] Ibid.

A good example is the rosy periwinkle (*Catharanthus roseus*), the source of the valuable anti-cancer vinca alkaloids, Vincristine and Vinblastine, which entered the market in the 1960s and have generated very large revenues for Eli Lilly over the decades. The plant originally comes from Madagascar but now grows throughout the tropics and has grown in the Caribbean long enough to be considered as a native plant there, among other places.[8] This frequently used to be presented as the classic biopiracy case with Madagascar and its people the unfortunate victims.[9] In fact, it is many years since the company relied on Madagascar for supplies of the plant, and most now come from plantations in Texas. The Eli Lilly researchers who discovered and patented[10] Vincristine and its anti-cancer properties decided to study the plant when a literature search uncovered its use by rural populations in the Philippines. Those at the University of Western Ontario who discovered and patented[11] Vinblastine received plant samples from Jamaica that were considered worth testing, again, because people used the plant for therapeutic purposes there. In both countries the plant was used by rural communities not to treat cancer but diabetes.[12] Neither of the research teams made any secret in their publications of the fact that they were inspired by TK. On the other hand, only the University of Western Ontario team was reliant upon both overseas sources of plant material and unpublished ethnobotanical information when it began research on the periwinkle. Since then two further vinca compounds have come on the market: GlaxoSmithKline's Vinorelbine and Eli Lilly's Vindesine.

The rosy periwinkle case exemplifies the fact that portraying pharmaceutical development as a linear process taking place over a relatively short period is grossly inaccurate with many if not most drugs.[13] It also suggests that in many cases a prior informed consent requirement is not practicable or applicable. Madagascar has no compelling legal or moral claims to a share of the billions of dollars generated since these drugs came on to the market half a century ago and at no point did a bioprospecting trip to that country ever need to be undertaken. The information on the use of the rosy periwinkle was already in the public domain, and while this should not in itself make benefit sharing inapplicable, it would require a very strict legal regime of broad geographical scope for prior informed consent to be mandatory in such circumstances. There was no necessity at any point for the scientists to have visited the Philippines once the proverbial cat was out of the bag and the plant grew in various other countries anyway. It was only with Vinblastine that ethnobiological

---

[8] H.A. Curry, 'Naturalising the Exotic and Exoticising the Naturalised: Horticulture, Natural History and the Rosy Periwinkle' (2012) 18(3) *Environment and History* 343–65.

[9] R. Stone, 'The Biodiversity Treaty: Pandora's Box or Fair Treaty?' (1992) 256 *Science* 1624.

[10] US Patent no 3,205,220 (issued September 7, 1965) ('Leursidine and Leurocristine and their production').

[11] US Patent no 3,097,137 (issued July 9, 1963) ('Vincaleukoblastine'). The patent was assigned by the inventors, Beer, Cutts and Noble, to Canadian Patents and Development Ltd, who made a deal with Eli Lilly allowing the latter company to commercially exploit the invention.

[12] As expressed by three medical researchers at the University of Western Ontario, 'the disease of cancer was certainly far from our thoughts when we learned of a tea made from the leaves of a West Indian shrub that was supposedly useful in the control of diabetes mellitus'. R.L. Noble, C.T. Beer and J.H. Cutts, 'Role of Chance Observation in Chemotherapy: Vinca Rosea' (1958) 76 *Annals of the New York Academy of Sciences* 882–94, 882.

[13] Dutfield, *supra* note 1.

information and plant samples were directly acquired from local people. In that case prior informed consent and benefit sharing might have benefited the local healers and their communities.

The third CBD objective, which has been reduced – at least terminologically speaking – to access and benefit sharing (ABS for short), has justified the design and adoption of a considerable and still growing number of national and regional laws and policies regulating bioprospecting by foreign researchers from the Andean Community of Nations to Brazil, India and the Philippines. It is widely acknowledged that these have been pretty unsuccessful in generating commercial and non-commercial benefits for sharing. The CBD has rightly been criticised for its furtherance of the bilateral contractual arrangements that these implementing laws and policies tend to promote, as opposed to multilateralism.[14] The ability of individual biodiversity rich but biotechnologically backward countries to capture the benefits of their stocks of genetic resources is weak for a number of reasons. First, genetic resources tend not to be endemic. Species have no citizenship and require no visa – they do not confine their movements and distributions to political boundaries. Second, species' genomes are not discrete. For example, some genes in the human genome can be found in life-forms as different as bacteria; and much 'human' DNA has viral origins. Third, the ability to amass, store, combine, compare and analyse genetic and other molecular information from different sources is more important in value capture than just happening to possess within one's national boundaries a large number of plant or animal species. Accidents of biogeography are actually (and increasingly) quite irrelevant. Besides, much of the world's genetic diversity having industrial value is found in microbes whose global ubiquity does not map on to what are generally recognised as the most megadiverse areas, which tend to be in or near the tropics and within the national boundaries or territorial waters of one or more nation states. Finally, many valuable resources are small molecules such as plant metabolites that do not contain 'functional units of heredity'[15] (i.e., genes) and are therefore not genetic resources in the strict sense.[16]

Another source of the policy dysfunction may be the aforementioned contraction of the third objective of the CBD to ABS which overlooks the fact that access is one of the benefits to be shared, along with technology transfer and funding. The ABS concept strongly implies that shared benefits are the 'payment' for access and that this simple quid-pro-quo schema works at all levels from indigenous communities, to countries, and to regions. The fact is that commercially-oriented

---

[14] M. Ruiz Muller, *Genetic Resources as Natural Information: Implications for the Convention on Biological Diversity and Nagoya Protocol* (Abingdon: Routledge, 2015).

[15] See CBD, Art 2 definitions of 'genetic material' and 'genetic resources'.

[16] It has been argued that 'genetic resources' under the Nagoya Protocol, and hence all of its ABS provision can be interpreted as embracing biochemical derivatives such as proteins and metabolites. It is certainly arguable though one would like to have seen this expressed much more explicitly in the text. C. Chiarolla, 'Genetic Resources', in E. Morgera and K. Kulovesi (eds), *Research Handbook on International Law and Natural Resources* (Cheltenham: Edward Elgar Publishing, 2016). It has also been suggested that 'derivative' can be interpreted as embracing information derived from genetic material, as Brazil and the Andean Community have done through their implementing legislation. For a review of the very important debate on the scope and legal implications of 'derivative', see J.H. Reichman, P.F. Uhlir and T. Dedeurwaerdere, *Governing Digitally Integrated Genetic Resources, Data, and Literature* (New York: Cambridge University Press, 2016), 146–9.

research, development, production and marketing using genetic resources often does not require access at all in the physical sense. Much information has been published, and a great deal of biological material is already in wide circulation. This is the problem with treating access as a bargaining tool rather than as an intrinsically positive element of what could be a broad array of non-monetary and monetary benefits.

This book is about intellectual property law. Accordingly, we confine the discussion to how the CBD has affected IP whether directly, via other international institutions or agreement, or through implementing national or regional laws. The main impact so far is two-fold. The first is to introduce disclosure of origin into patent law. The second has been to create a *sui generis* right in TK. Of the two, disclosure has been far more successful.

15.3 DISCLOSURE OF ORIGIN

The idea that biopiracy[17] would be reduced by requiring inventors to disclose the geographical origin of genetic resources forming, or being used in the attainment of, an invention for which a patent is filed, has a history going almost as far back as the CBD itself. Although the Nagoya Protocol does not refer to it, the Conference of the Parties to the CBD has over several of its biannual meetings debated it with many parties supporting it as a mandatory requirement. Similarly many WIPO member states attending the numerous meetings of the IGC would like to see a legal instrument providing for it. WTO members have gone so far as to propose its inclusions as an amendment to TRIPS.

At the fourth meeting of the WTO Ministerial Conference which took place in Doha in November 2001, a Ministerial Declaration was adopted according to which the WTO member states instructed 'the Council for TRIPS [...] to examine, inter alia, the relationship between the TRIPS Agreement and the CBD, the protection of traditional knowledge and folklore'.

As a contribution to this examination, Brazil, China, Cuba, Dominican Republic, Ecuador, India, Pakistan, Thailand, Venezuela, Zambia and Zimbabwe jointly submitted a paper to the Council for TRIPS in June 2002.[18] The paper, noting the relevant provisions of the Bonn Guidelines, proposed that TRIPS be amended to provide that WTO member states must require:

> that an applicant for a patent relating to biological materials or to traditional knowledge shall provide, as a condition to acquiring patent rights: (i) disclosure of the source and country of origin of the biological resource and of the traditional knowledge used in the invention;

---

[17] Biopiracy is: '(i) the theft, misappropriation of, or unfair free-riding on, genetic resources and/or traditional knowledge through the patent system; and (ii) the unauthorized and uncompensated collection for commercial ends of genetic resources and/or traditional knowledge'. G. Dutfield, 'What is Biopiracy?', in M. Bellot-Rojas and S. Bernier (eds), *International Expert Workshop on Access to Genetic Resources and Benefit Sharing: Record of Discussion*, Cuernavaca, Mexico, 24–27 October, 2004 (Mexico City: CONABIO/Environment Canada, 2005), 89–92.

[18] WTO, 'The Relationship between the TRIPS Agreement and the Convention on Biological Diversity and the Protection of Traditional Knowledge', 2003. [Document No IP/C/W/356].

(ii) evidence of prior informed consent through approval of authorities under the relevant national regimes; and (iii) evidence of fair and equitable benefit sharing under the national regime of the country of origin.

Several follow-up proposals have been tabled.[19] The most recent of these, in May 2006 was submitted by Brazil, Pakistan, Peru, Thailand and Tanzania.[20] Annexed to this document is text that would form an additional section of TRIPS, namely Article 29bis ('Disclosure of Origin of Biological Resources and/or Associated Traditional Knowledge'). The most substantial part is paragraph 2, which states as follows:

Where the subject matter of a patent application concerns, is derived from or developed with biological resources and/or associated traditional knowledge, members shall require applicants to disclose the country providing the resources and/or associated traditional knowledge, from whom in the providing country they were obtained, and, as known after reasonable inquiry, the country of origin. members shall also require that applicants provide information including evidence of compliance with the applicable legal requirements in the providing country for prior informed consent for access and fair and equitable benefit-sharing arising from the commercial or other utilization of such resources and/or associated traditional knowledge.

A modest amendment aimed at improving access to medicines (see Chapter 13) involved a considerable amount of effort and the odds are probably against such a revision for the time being also being adopted despite the considerable developing country support behind it. However, this is not to suggest that disclosure of origin need not be discussed at the WTO. Indeed, the TRIPS Council has a clear mandate to do so, and compared to positive TK protection, the measure is fairly uncomplicated.

A lot of countries have introduced such a measure either directly in their patent laws or indirectly through ABS laws. These mainly comprise developing countries although a few European countries have also adopted disclosure of origin, in some countries only genetic resources but in other jurisdictions TK must be disclosed too. Accordingly, disclosure of origin is an emerging norm in IP law whose adoption was largely not driven by the major economies. This may reflect a new trend, mentioned earlier in this book, that sees developing countries shifting from being mere policy-takers to developing original IP policies that suit their own perceived best interests. As yet though, disclosure of origin requirements are not harmonised and the approaches used by countries and regional organisations including China, Egypt, India, Norway and the Andean

---

[19] These are summarised and listed in WTO, 'The Relationship between the TRIPS Agreement and the Convention on Biological Diversity: Summary of Issues Raised and Points Made. Note by the Secretariat. Revision', 2006 [Document IP/C/W/368/Rev.1].

[20] 'Doha Work Programme – the Outstanding Implementation Issue on the Relationship between the TRIPS Agreement and the Convention on Biological Diversity. Communication from Brazil, India, Pakistan, Peru, Thailand and Tanzania', 2006 [Document WT/GC/W/564].

Community are quite varied. The US has always been vigorously opposed to disclosure of origin and to all efforts to achieve international harmonisation of the requirement.[21]

15.4 THE FAILURE (SO FAR) OF *SUI GENERIS* PROTECTION

International efforts to come up with positive protection legal norms have been unsuccessful. The TK-related aspects of what we might call the 'bilateral ABS+plus IP' model as embodied by the CBD and the Nagoya Protocol have taken us as far to an international framework as any other initiative. Indeed, the WIPO IGC's work has sought to be consistent as possible with the Nagoya provisions. Despite this apparent progress, there are four main reasons why one must be doubtful that we are on the way to a workable solution.

First, inherent in much of the international debate and the national and regional schemes adopted is a basic conceptual mistake that would make a correct assignment of rights in a clearly defined 'piece' of intangible property in the form of TK somewhat quixotic. The beliefs that TK is (i) clearly identifiable, pure, unadulterated and all the better for that; and (ii) mostly solely attributable to a specific group or country are persistent but largely false. This matters a great deal. For one thing, specific groups claiming sole benefit allocations may be claiming an exclusive right to which others may be equally, or even more, entitled. Furthermore, treating tradition and modern (or scientific) as binary opposites blinds one to mutual interdependence and hybridisation which raises moral questions of their own that few people seem willing to address, including the fundamental issue of who if anybody has a moral debt, if any, to whom as knowledge and associated biological material move around the world and get absorbed into different systems of knowledge and technology. In fact, free exchange of knowledge and material has been common in human history and has done much good for givers, recipients and humankind generally. It has also done harm to some and that needs to be acknowledged too. Those who currently self-identify as indigenous peoples have been among those most victimised. Apart from free exchange, there has of course been control, priority and attribution as well as secrecy too.[22] These are just as much a part of human social interaction and probably for about as long.

---

[21] There is a profusion of literature on disclosure of origin, for example, M. Chouchena-Rojas, M. Ruiz Muller, D. Vivas and S. Winkler (eds), *Disclosure Requirements: Ensuring Mutual Supportiveness between the WTO TRIPS Agreement and the CBD* (Gland, Cambridge and Geneva: IUCN and ICTSD, 2005); A.L. Hoare and R.G. Tarasofsky, 'Asking and Telling: Can "Disclosure of Origin" Requirements in Patent Applications Make a Difference?' (2007) 10(2) *Journal of World Intellectual Property* 149–69; UNCTAD, 'The Convention on Biological Diversity and the Nagoya Protocol: Intellectual Property Implications. A Handbook on the Interface between Global Access and Benefit Sharing Rules and Intellectual Property' (Geneva: UNCTAD); WIPO, 'Technical Study on Disclosure Requirements in Patent Systems Related to Genetic Resources and Traditional Knowledge (WIPO, 2004).

[22] On Europe since the ancient Greeks, see P.O. Long, *Openness, Secrecy, Authorship: Technical Arts and the Culture of Knowledge from Antiquity to the Renaissance* (Baltimore: Johns Hopkins University Press, 2001).

Assuming that it is possible to come up with a clear and meaningful definition of traditional knowledge, or else an illustrative list of manifestations of TK to be included, we would still have to decide how broadly or narrowly should the term be applied. A number of countries seem to favour legal norms that would apply to pretty much anything that might be regarded as traditional, no matter how tenuous or commonly known about. The problem is that broad understandings of TK could have unduly negative impacts on the public domain that benefits all people. This is a contentious point and will therefore be discussed further below so as to avoid misunderstanding. Suffice it to say here that the public domain is worthy of our support but public domain evangelism may unduly curtail the rights and cultural norms of indigenous peoples.[23]

Third, embedding TK protection in ABS regulations reduces a broad range of possible exchange norms to a single one, that of top down bureaucratic frameworks which vest strong regulatory powers in governments but that also permit conditional private contracting. CBD-inspired access and benefit sharing frameworks tend to imply that mediating between the different interests of providers and users can only be done through the oversight of state bureaucracy and the more the better. None of this is to deny that misappropriation of genetic resources and TK happens, that state action may be necessary in some form or another, nor that there is anything wrong with the principle that commercial users should share benefits with original providers of biological material and local and indigenous knowledge and that exchanges should be based on mutually agreed terms and prior informed consent. Indeed, we are wholly supportive of the latter principle. But regulation needs to be grounded on a much higher degree of realism and be based on the cautious encouragement of fully consensual partnerships under norms that are appropriate both for providers and users. Between free exchange at one end and secrecy enforced by threats of violence at the other is a broad spectrum of possibilities which fall mostly outside what is envisaged in the CBD and Nagoya.

The desire to protect TK from aggressive, inappropriate and unwanted modernity is entirely understandable, and is a sentiment that the Nagoya Protocol seeks to give legal expression to. Accordingly, countering the otherwise inevitable TK erosion is to be done by valorising it, creating a market for knowledge transactions so that access is exchanged for benefits. What else could be done? Eliminating all exchange of knowledge and materials is not the only alternative. It would almost certainly not work anyway. Knowledge is inherently 'leaky', plants get around pretty easily, and duplicates of both are likely to exist elsewhere. In comparison ABS regulation allowing conditional access seems at first blush to be perfectly reasonable and sensible.

To the extent that Nagoya provides for enhanced negotiating powers for indigenous peoples and local communities, this is of course welcome. However, indigenous peoples inhabiting their own territorial spaces and elsewhere and rural communities are not companies having suitable governance structures and business nous sufficient to negotiate business deals. Corporations engage in impersonal knowledge transactions because IPRs make doing this possible, and such exchanges work for them because IPRs are the common currency that they all use and understand and which fits into their business models and the governing commercial law legal frameworks.

---

[23] Tulalip Tribes of Washington, 'Statement by the Tulalip Tribes of Washington on Folklore, Indigenous Knowledge, and the Public Domain, July 9, 2003, WIPO Intergovernmental Committee on Intellectual Property and Genetic Resources, Traditional Knowledge and Folklore, Fifth Session, 5–17 July 2003'.

There are many who accept this point but assume that top-down regulatory regimes on the lines of the CBD and Nagoya remain the least-worst answer. Unfortunately, national and regional ABS regimes have generally done little to generate officially sanctioned bioprospecting arrangements. If ABS regimes are supposed to be promoting fair deal-making, they are not succeeding.[24] To the extent they encourage anything much, they tend to assume impersonal transactions based on conventional business practices albeit with the aim that these be 'fair and equitable' to be the normal mode of exchange. Experience strongly suggests that after 20 years of trying these have done far less to encourage fair exchange – or any exchange for that matter – than we expected. There are certainly strong arguments favouring the need to have governments play the role of correcting the power disparities when these are so extreme. However, a consequence of government paternalism, expansive understandings of TK, and the North-South slant on the TK debate is typically a downplaying of the independent claims of specific national subpopulations. As a result, some governments seem inclined to treat TK as national property, akin perhaps to mineral resources, with little consideration as to whether certain minority or indigenous groups may have perfectly legitimate claims to ownership or at least to claim independent benefits from inalienable usage rights which in turn may have several plausible legal bases. But whether property claims are made by corporation or by state it is still biopiracy. This is a somewhat controversial position and one must admit that it is likely to be uncommon for national ownership of TK explicitly to be provided in a country's statutory law. However, implicit in much of the rhetoric and even some of the practices of national governments is the assumption that TK existing in a country belongs to that country and that the government on that basis has the moral authority to pursue claims as if it had a property interest. When a government agency initiates a legal challenge against a wrongly granted patent claiming common knowledge of that country, as the Indian government did when it successfully opposed a US patent on the use of turmeric in wound healing, what lies behind an apparently straightforward legal request that the patent be revoked for lack of novelty is effectively an effort to enforce a right over the 'biopirated' knowledge. If this were not so, why would it take the trouble of challenging the patent (which in this case had no economic value but was heavily laden with symbolism)? Another example: if a government sets up a competent authority to collect benefits from use of TK that cannot be traced to a specific indigenous group and which is common knowledge, is this not tantamount to *de facto* nationalisation of common knowledge whose distribution may not even be confined to that country anyway?[25]

A fourth problem is that the current approaches to TK protection are concerned primarily with the exchange values of genetic resources and TK as if the importance is purely for their industrial

---

[24] The small number of transactions struck through national and regional ABS regulatory frameworks since the late 1990s may be contrasted by the vastly higher quantity achieved by the FA International Treaty on Plant Genetic Resources for Food and Agriculture whose multilateral system of facilitated access has proved to be highly successful, least in terms of the number of transactions made, and beneficial to all state parties.

[25] Iraq's Draft Law on the Protection and Exchange of Genetic Resources for Food and Agriculture states that information related to plant genetic resources is owned by the state, and the clear implication is that this includes TK. N.M. Khalaf, 'Green Economy in the Arab Region: Regulating Agricultural Biodiversity and Plant Related Innovation in Egypt and Iraq' (PhD thesis, Bangor University, UK, 2016).

potential. This downplays their intrinsic and local (commercial and non-economic) values which are in fact much more significant especially for indigenous peoples for whom knowledge is an essential aspect of the cultural identity that binds them together and ensures their well-being. It also tends to push them towards acceptance of legal instruments and property rules that businesses have much more experience of using. Again, terminology and rhetoric do not help. By treating TK as a unified, discrete counter-modern stock of useful knowledge, it gets reduced to an array of 'raw' inputs for life science corporations, which is then regulated accordingly. In doing so, we devalue it, essentially reducing it to a random compilation of leads, hints, hopes, errors, deceptions and cul-de-sacs from which the useful needs to be separated from the supposedly useless. The rhetoric might suggest it is something more worthy and significant than that but close inspection of how TK gets inputted into commercially oriented scientific research reveals that TK has those diverse and generally rather limited qualities in that particular context. Anyway, the persisting hopes that TK has genuine value in that setting leads regulators and policy-makers to focus their attention on the instrumental value of TK to others, and away from the holders themselves within their own communities and among others with which they socialise and otherwise interact. This has negative practical implications, and the approaches being considered internationally in their current form will not help, especially as these aforementioned leads, hints and hopes will not in most cases be reducible to traceable and enforceable single legal claims justified by having made a tangible contribution to a commercial product.[26] Meanwhile, the land and other rights of indigenous groups within the borders of countries whose representatives in Geneva clamour for international protection of TK continue often to be denied.

Traditional knowledge continues to be the operative term and that is the way it is. The question arises of how broadly or narrowly should the regime define TK so as to protect whatever is to be protected with as much effectiveness as possible? Clearly breadth can be excessive. Where does TK end if anything done to or with turmeric (or some other product deemed to be a national heritage) by non-Indians is deemed to be misappropriation? An excessively broad meaning will unreasonably lock up vast amounts of publicly available knowledge which no identifiable group of people or nation could make any credible claim to, and whose circulation can no longer realistically be controlled anyway.

Let us consider the celebrated example of neem. A general presumption behind many of the attacks on neem-related patents in Europe and the US was that India was a victim on the basis that: (a) neem is an Indian tree; (b) the knowledge being 'stolen' is Indian; and (c) that neem-related patents are essentially theft of India's biocultural heritage. There are several problems with this.

---

[26] Albeit expressed rather differently, a similar argument is made by Angerer. K. Angerer, 'Frog Tales – On Poison Dart Frogs, Epibatidine, and the Sharing of Biodiversity' (2011) 24(3) *Innovation: The European Journal of Social Science Research* 353–6. Related to this difficulty is the issue of potentially extensive distance in material and cognitive terms between biological material and associated TK, the invention claimed in a patent, and a final product. Should benefit-sharing obligations be calibrated so as to be in proportion to distance according to some kind of measurement? Accordingly the shorter the distance the greater would be the benefits. Similarly: P.S. Harrison, 'Distal Horizons: An Investigation of the Justifiable Downstream Limits to the Positive Protection of Traditional Knowledge Associated with Genetic Resources within Drug Discovery' (PhD thesis, University of York, UK, 2015); M.W. Tvedt, V. Eijsink, I.H. Steen, R. Strand and G.K. Rosendal, 'The Missing Link in ABS: The Relationship between Resources and Product' (2016) 46(3–4) *Environmental Policy and Law* 227–37.

First, research suggests the species is native to a broad area, probably large enough to span Afghanistan and Myanmar. Second, the relevant 'traditional knowledge' is mostly very commonly known and is most unlikely to be bounded by the artificial frontiers of modern India. The way that farmers in South Asia use neem tree seeds to protect their crops really is public domain information. Consequently compensation is due to nobody. Third, the tacit assertion that all neem-related patents are biopiracy with India as victim is tantamount to the assertion of reach-through claims over all global neem-related innovations. This is hard to justify legally, morally or on policy grounds. There is no compelling argument for saying it belongs to the farmers of this generation or to the government of India, none of whom actually came up with the idea of using neem this way. In any case, India, as with all countries, is not biologically or intellectually self-sufficient.

Likewise, neither James Watson nor the families of Francis Crick or Rosalind Franklin or the UK government has any right to claim benefits from those depicting DNA as a double helix or taking advantage of this discovered fact of nature to make money. They did not have such an entitlement at the time of the discovery and do not two generations later. It is hard to find a moral case for the government of India or of any other country to claim that any knowledge that ever came from their country that people and businesses elsewhere found commercially useful should be compensated for even when it gets hybridised, altered or otherwise transformed. The custodianship argument, that generations 'invest' in the responsibility of caring for resources and associated knowledge for future generations and should have rights on that basis, cannot take us very far in this particular context (although it might in others). It really is too widespread for that. In recent years, complaints about neem patenting have largely died down, but they have not disappeared completely.

A narrower meaning, on the other hand, might exclude much of what many countries would like to have protected. Even so, this would get us far closer to a workable approach. What if one confined the legal regime to the knowledge, innovations and practices of 'indigenous peoples' as defined internationally under the 1989 International Labour Organization Convention 169 Concerning Indigenous and Tribal Peoples in Independent Countries? This approach could be justified in at least two ways.[27] First, these are often culturally quite distinct groups of people. Consequently for such people an item of traditional knowledge may be more attributable unequivocally to such people. In some parts of the world, their knowledge and 'traditionality' are relatively unadulterated by mainstream knowledge systems and technologies. Second, they may have functioning customary norms governing access and use of certain knowledge and resources they possess.[28] This is very important: what is deemed to be public domain in the IP sense should not automatically be considered to be freely open for others to appropriate because rights and duties over knowledge even after its circulation may be a matter for customary law. Why should we not take into account their own laws? In principle we must, though how this might be done requires further consideration.

---

[27] According to Art 1(b) of ILO Convention 169:

> Peoples in independent countries who are regarded as indigenous on account of their descent from the populations which inhabited the country, or a geographical region to which the country belongs, the time of conquest or colonisation or the establishment of present state boundaries and who, irrespective of their legal status, retain some or all of their own social, economic, cultural and political institutions.

[28] B. Tobin, *Indigenous Peoples, Customary Law and Human Rights: Why Living Law Matters* (Abingdon: Routledge, 2014).

There is a real dilemma here, though. By adopting this approach, much of what some countries regard as being TK would be excluded from protection, perhaps unfairly. Just because they may not be the originators of some valuable knowledge it does not necessarily follow that communities have no rights over it or deserve no compensation. We would still need to discuss this, but an international instrument should not have to deal with this. Also, we would still need to have a conversation about the innovations of this generation including those of individuals in communities that, in the words of the CBD, embody traditional lifestyles broadly construed? As for indigenous peoples their levels of acculturation vary widely. Should we ignore this or does it raise difficulties we would have to face up to? What about those who no longer live in such communities, and not necessarily by choice? Should their knowledge, innovations and practices be protected? After all these years important questions remain.

Another reasonable and very basic concern that the approach suggested here cannot fully satisfy is that even with 'indigenous peoples' so defined, attributing knowledge to one group and one group alone can still be controversial. To name one example, the use and knowledge of hoodia as a thirst and appetite suppressant is almost universally attributed to the San people of Southern Africa. However, recent research suggests the situation is not entirely clear. While the San may well be the original discoverers, many of them did not consume it, while various non-San and mixed populations have used it in recent centuries, and some of them cultivated it too.[29]

Yet another dilemma arises. On the one hand, as explained above, a legal regime for TK that focuses on culturally distinct indigenous communities appears to be the most realistic approach. However, for such people biopiracy is simply not the biggest problem that they face. Land rights and other economic, social and cultural rights may be far more important. Is there a point to seeking to protect their knowledge when their absence of legal title may be causing them much more harm? There is a point to parallel campaigns to promote the various rights that are crucial to their welfare. However, progress on land rights is probably an essential condition for a knowledge protection regime, or regime complex linking together two or more agreements, to work. In this sense, the more holistic approach to indigenous peoples' rights offered by the 2007 United Nations Declaration on the Rights of Indigenous Peoples is more appropriate. Politically, confining the application of the regime in this way is a lot less interesting for governments who may lose interest in negotiating a legal instrument because other than a few indigenous groups who would benefit, the national economy perhaps does not stand to gain in any substantial sense.

15.5 TRADITIONAL CULTURAL EXPRESSIONS

Folklore, which nowadays tends to be termed 'traditional cultural expressions' (TCEs), predates TK as a subject for discussion at the international level, going back to the 1970s. UNESCO and WIPO were

---

[29] E.C. Kamau, 'Common Pools of Traditional Knowledge and Related Genetic Resources: A Case Study of San-Hoodia, in E.C. Kamau and G. Winter (eds), *Common Pools of Genetic Resources: Equity and Innovation in International Biodiversity Law* (Abingdon: Routledge, 2013), 40–54; A.D. Osseo-Asare, *Bitter Roots: The Search for Healing Plants in Africa* (Chicago and London: University of Chicago Press, 2014).

the two institutions where discussions on folklore protection took place, and continue to provide forums for negotiating legal norms. UNESCO's involvement is of course due to its interest in culture. This is very evident in UNESCO's definition provided in the Recommendations on the Safeguarding of Traditional Culture and Folklore, which were adopted by the organisation's members in 1989:

> Folklore (or traditional and popular culture) is the totality of tradition-based creations of a cultural community, expressed by a group of individuals and recognised as reflecting its cultural and social identity; its standards and values are transmitted orally, by imitation or by other means. Its forms are, among others, language, literature, music, dance, games, mythology, rituals, customs, handicrafts, architecture and other arts.

Folklore/TCEs thus understood are tradition based, collectively held, and are orally transmitted. In traditional societies, TCEs are not historical manifestations, but, as UNESCO recognises, are living and evolving, handed down from generation to generation orally rather than in fixed form, and are essential elements of cultural identity among many ethnic groups and in many countries.

The economic value of TCEs is substantial and far easier to assess than with TK. It is also much easier to demonstrate its national importance as a provider of employment and generator of financial gain. According to Fowler, 'artisan handicrafts represent an estimated US$30 billion world market. In addition, handicraft production and sales represent a substantial percentage of gross domestic product (GDP) for some countries'.[30] However, continued production and further development of traditional handicrafts and artworks are threatened sometimes by the disappearance of traditional skills. Another serious problem is copying and mass production by outsiders, who thereby deprive artisans of a source of income.

From an IPR perspective separating traditional knowledge and traditional cultural expressions is highly convenient. TK lends itself to consideration of industrial property especially patents (though trade marks, geographical indications and trade secrecy are also relevant). As for traditional cultural expressions, those which are tangible works of craftsmanship can also be covered under trade mark law, perhaps by collective or certification marks or product labelling schemes, or by the use of geographical indications. Intangible expressions, fixed or otherwise, would be literary or artistic works as defined under copyright law. Indeed, TCEs seem more compatible with conventional IP legal norms than does TK with patent law.

Indeed, copyright infringement can be a major problem for creators, makers, users and performers of traditional cultural expressions. Even where copyright legislation is in place, collection and distribution of royalties among the key parties (i.e., composers, performers, publishers and the recording companies) is difficult without an efficient, transparent and fully accountable collective management structure that seeks primarily to benefit local musicians rather than international ones.[31] Indeed, while a weak copyright system may on balance benefit some nations by decreasing the rate of imported IP goods in certain areas such as software and educational products, such a

---

[30] B.J. Fowler, 'Preventing Counterfeit Craft Designs', in J.M. Finger and P. Schuler (eds), *Poor People's Knowledge: Promoting Intellectual Property in Developing Countries* (Washington, DC: World Bank, 2004), 113–31.

[31] UNCTAD-ICTSD, *Intellectual Property Rights: Implications for Development* (Geneva: UNCTAD and ICTSD, 2003).

policy may also undermine those industries which a developing nation may wish to nurture. The local music industries in Mali and South Africa have complained that they suffer heavily from losses and damages due to copyright infringement.[32]

But there are also conceptual difficulties. A major one is that this kind of fragmentation by which the productions of 'exotic' cultures can be placed neatly, for the purposes of engaging fruitfully with the rest of the world, into our commerce-driven legal categories pays no heed to a diversity of quite radically different world-views and cultural and spiritual values. A number of court cases in Australia concerning Aboriginal artworks demonstrate that copyright can easily subsist in such visual expressions. However, copyright law was shown to have severe limitations in two spheres: (i) the highly limited extent to which normal legal remedies can accommodate cultural harm caused by unauthorised and culturally inappropriate reproduction and commercialisation; and (ii) the complex, very strong and highly spiritual bonds linking place, image, guardianship and ownership which copyright law cannot possibly accommodate.[33]

15.6 IS 'TRADITION' THE PROBLEM?

Since the 1990s the biopiracy discourse has tended to treat traditional and modern[34] as binary opposites. Not explicitly perhaps, because 'traditional knowledge' is rarely given a definition, but certainly implicitly. Proponents of this tendency, which remains the conventional wisdom, are probably largely unaware that such an opposition between tradition and modernity is a fundamental assumption of post-Second World War modernisation theory which has largely been discredited.[35] At its crudest, modernisation theory saw social progress and economic development as the necessary transformation of traditional societies into modern ones. The more tradition you have the more modernisation you need; the less tradition the better. That should immediately be cause for reflection: that the term has tended to be used negatively as something outmoded and undesirable and, one might add here, unowned.

---

[32] Business Day (Johannesburg), 21 November 2002; *Daily News* (Harare), 14 May 2003.

[33] *Yumbulul v. Reserve Bank of Australia* (1991) 21 IPR 48; *Milpurrurru & Ors v. Indofurn Pty Ltd & Ors* (1995) AIPC 91–116; *John Bulun Bulun & Anor v. R & T Textiles Pty Ltd* [1998] 1082 FCA.

[34] Or similar (in usage) words like western or scientific.

[35] A number of mostly US-based social scientists in the post-war era identified fundamental social and cultural differences between traditional and modern societies and assigned to each a set of descriptive terms that were in opposition to each other. Accordingly, as they saw it, social and cultural evolution could be best understood in terms of progress that would entail the replacement of terms applicable to traditional societies such as 'community', 'patron-client relationship', 'routine', and 'solidarity', with their modern polar opposite counterparts: 'individual', 'bureaucratic relationships', 'innovation' and 'competition' respectively. Since evidence of progress essentially entailed the latter terms applying rather than the former ones, there was little accommodation for hybridity including its positive aspects for both societies. Ironically, like the Marxism that modernisation theory sought to counter, both approaches were susceptible to somewhat deterministic evolutionary stages notions. See J.-P. Olivier de Sardan, *Anthropology of Development: Understanding Contemporary Social Change* (London and New York: Zed Books, 2005), 46–8.

It is true that tradition in some sense has recently gained a certain prestige that one might have thought could never be recovered. Unfortunately, those who admire tradition and those who think it is doomed and for good reason tend to agree on one thing, which is incorrect. This is that tradition and modernity are opposite, pure and unadulterated by each other. This is old thinking but in that area of international law which concerns us in this chapter, it goes back to the negotiations on the CBD. It persists to this day. Thus the use, borrowing, appropriation, misappropriation, or whatever name one chooses to call the inclusion of information, knowledge, methods and materials from one system of knowledge and practice into another different system is seen as being unidirectional. As tradition wanes and modern waxes, the latter takes bits of tradition, used in the form of informational leads or raw materials, and gives nothing back in return. Modern appears no less modern for doing this because there is a translation and repackaging which generally strips tradition of its origins and cultural and spiritual entanglements. Accordingly, modernity is parasitic on tradition. An understanding of global power disparities reinforces such a perspective. It follows that the way to respond is to create a market for knowledge transactions so that access is exchanged for monetary or non-monetary forms to even things up. Enter the Nagoya Protocol.

However, systems of knowledge tend to be hybrids because they are generally open, and they tend to have two-way 'valves': knowledge and materials go both out and in. So might there be advantages in no longer defining tradition as the polar opposite of modernity and instead seeing the two as actually related to each other and capable of interacting positively? Perhaps to some extent they already do. That might sound counter-intuitive. But if it happens to be true then we should go with it and follow it to its logical conclusions.

It might be advantageous not to put too much faith in IP law, or for that matter contracts and top-down government regulations. If it is valuable and culturally enriching but will disappear without legal protection, then it deserves urgent protection. But IP rights are meant to protect or promote commercial interest in something. They are not useful as a means to block commercial circulation of goods. That is not their purpose. They insert knowledge, innovations and cultural works into trade. With the arguable exception of authors' moral rights they do not remove them. Instead, the rules and principles of the weaker party should apply in the first instance. The weaker party is not the corporation, nor is it the government but the indigenous peoples. That is a matter of fairness but it is also the only practical basis for mutually advantageous relationships. We cannot wish away the patent system, nor inappropriate heavy-handed access and benefit-sharing rules which might just deliver very occasional windfalls not all of which will filter down to the local level anyway. Instead, we need to strengthen the role of customary law as a third source of regulatory norms that facilitates rather than stops two-way exchange but in ways that are culturally compatible with indigenous peoples' values that further their interests.[36] Either that, or to develop 'hybrid approaches that interweave elements of western law and local, traditional rules for the circulation of knowledge'.[37] How to do this effectively is of course a big challenge.

---

[36] R. Coombe, 'The Recognition of Indigenous Peoples' and Community Traditional Knowledge in International Law' (2001) 14 *St. Thomas Law Review* 275–85.

[37] M.F. Brown, 'Heritage Trouble: Recent Work on the Protection of Intangible Cultural Property' (2005) 12 *International Journal of Cultural Property* 40–61.

16
Networked technologies and intellectual property

> Judges have no specialized technical ability to answer questions about present or future technological feasibility or commercial viability where technology professionals, engineers, and venture capitalists themselves may radically disagree and where answers may differ depending upon whether one focuses upon the time of product development or the time of distribution.
>
> Justice *Stephen Breyer*[1]

This final chapter looks at how digital (and networked) technologies affect IP laws and policies, especially from a contemporary historical perspective. The US jurist Paul Goldstein postulated that: 'Copyright was technology's child from the start. There was no need for copyright before the

---

[1] *Metro-Goldwyn-Mayer Studios, Inc and ors* 125 S Ct 2764 (US S Ct, 2005).

printing press.' Thus, in his view, copyright is the obvious legal mechanism when mass production leads to mass consumption.[2] Nevertheless, one should also appreciate that the birth of the printing technology was not the sole cause of mass production and consumption – such changes were concomitant with the establishment of new merchant cities throughout Europe and the expansion of a new middle class, which saw the secularisation of the arts, including literature and music. This, in turn, ushered in the consumer and the entrepreneurial bookseller (stationer) or music publisher, and yes – all these changes wrought new legal rules in relation to literary and artistic property.

Problems do not arise from any single revolutionary invention but are rather due to the convergence of different technological developments: networked computers, digital file compression, increased computing power, the semiconductor chip leading to personal computing (not to mention affordable PCs), increased telephony coverage and, most important, higher communication speed. With the advent of smartphones, powerful search engines and dedicated online contents services, these issues have exponentially expanded to include concerns about cross-border portability, profit-sharing between creators and platforms, and user-generated rights. This is a repetitive cycle as we note below when we briefly consider the impact of reprography and tape recording on the ease and cost of copying and distribution.[3] Despite the opportunities offered by these new technological breakthroughs, we still witness legislative confusion as to how rules should be moulded especially in relation to the scope of protection and the acceptable allowances for the downloading and sharing of digital goods.

16.1 STAKEHOLDERS' PERSPECTIVES

Technologies including reprographic, digital and compression technologies are often branded as disrupters of established patterns of production, distribution and consumption of goods. And are usually accompanied by cries for a broader copyright regime. Nevertheless, it is also accepted that digital and networked technologies have opened fresh revenue streams through licensing and exploitation ventures. The worldwide acceptance of e-commerce enables the global branding of goods, which were hitherto geographically limited to national markets. Societal beneficence is also evident through greater access to digital goods not only via the internet, but through augmented reality applications, and virtual reality environments. In terms of jurisprudential maturity, each new technological breakthrough has encouraged new justifications and perspectives especially within copyright law such as the need for new categories of rights, or for private copying levies or for removing or expanding free usage of works for certain purposes (such as text/data mining or parody), or the need to look elsewhere to solve problems such as competition law, unfair

---

[2] P. Goldstein, *Copyright's Highway: From Gutenberg to the Celestial Jukebox* (Stanford: Stanford University Press, 2003), 21.

[3] Also see, W.W. Fisher III, *Promises to Keep: Technology, Law and the Future of Entertainment* (Stanford: Stanford University Press, 2004) 18–37; U. Suthersanen, 'Technology, Time and Market Forces', in M. Pugatch (ed.), *The Intellectual Property Debate: Perspectives from Law, Economics and Political Economy* (Cheltenham: Edward Elgar Publishing, 2006); and S. Ranjek, *American Popular Music and Its Business: The First Four Hundred Years. Volume 1: The Beginning to 1790* (Oxford: Oxford University Press, 1988), 37–8.

competition/tort law, and even trading standards regulation. These legal tactics do not preclude other market-based tools to control piracy such as pricing wars to ward off the imitator. All these various schemes may seem outmoded – the more modern versions of smartphones have scanning technology enabled within them, and the modern digital photocopier machines are equipped with the ability to copy, digitise and share digital files over the internet.

16.1.1 Panics and risks

Politically and legally, the technology incursions have caused so much consternation that copyright reform has become a public concern as witnessed by the passage leading to the 2019 EU Copyright Directive. Past reforms within international, US, and EU copyright laws and policies have focused on widening the scope of copyright protection, without necessarily contemplating the corresponding safeguards for technological innovation. Technological protection measures and digital rights management – two regulatory tools which control access to and reproduction by placing 'digital locks' on works – are now core concepts within international copyright law. However, these measures do not solve anything unless the corollary areas of concern are also tackled: these include freedoms, transparency, privacy, fair pricing and accessibility. It may well be true that we will need new legislation to expand IP laws in the impending post-digital era. Whether or not that is the case, policy-makers do need to consider how we structure a competitive *and* socially responsible framework for the multiple activities which rely on the digital and network technologies – whether it is through IP, competition, civil wrongs/tort or contract laws. Many of the risks technology poses to the enforcement of IPRs can also be viewed as opportunities for the IPR owner, the consumer and society as we see in the next section.

The risks for IP owners can be reduced to two concerns: (i) *perfect copies* – all protected content in the networked environment is in a digital form, and each new generation of software and hardware technology makes it easier to make perfect mass copies of such works; and (ii) *distribution* – the distribution of digital works undermines the ability of creators and rights owners to derive profits from their works which may in some circumstances lead to the stifling of creativity as the rewards and incentives for producing works disappear. However, conversely, IP owners can count several blessings. First, with price diminution, digital technology has led to the reduction of most transaction costs involved in printing, manufacturing and distributing creative goods. This in turn has quelled the average consumer's enthusiasm in developed countries for photocopying whole books as opposed to purchasing either physical or e-books lawfully (at least for reasonably priced fictional books as opposed to expensive educational texts). The same holds true with respect to other creative industries. Retail stores like Amazon, on demand services like Netflix or Spotify, or gaming platforms like Steam offer highly competitive pricing packages which have halted, at least in some demographic sectors, the taping, sharing or downloading of music, films, and video games. Secondly, these new formats and means of access have created new income sources. Existing works have become re-contextualised as a music album first released in the LP format is re-formatted into the CD format, then into an MP3 format, and then re-introduced to a new generation of users via a streaming service while both the millennial and older generations have turned back in a rather surreal fashion to LPs again. Moreover, the increased storage/distribution capacity on media and broadband has allowed the creative industries to persuade consumers to purchase the 'uncut' or 'director's cut' versions of previously viewed films on DVD or via streaming platforms.

16.1.2 Societal and cultural perspectives

From the consumer's perspective, a similar list of balancing factors offer themselves. First, consumers benefit from the lower costs of products as books, music, videos, etc. can be created, published and distributed in electronic digital formats directly from the creator and/or the producer to the consumer. Middlemen or retailers could, eventually, be eliminated. Secondly, there can be a wider geographical distribution of products as consumer demands force the creative industries into instituting a more demand-based distribution network which simultaneously dampens search and consumer transaction costs of global consumer goods. Thirdly, with the advent of digital libraries, knowledge accessibility is enhanced as out-of-commerce works are made accessible.

From a societal perspective, technology can undoubtedly enhance cultural diversity, preservation and distribution. In the field of music and film production, for example, technology has displaced yesterday's norm where global production and distribution was controlled by a small group of producers and distributors, catering and dictating to a narrow range of consumer/market demands. Digital film and music, coupled with streaming technologies now allow esoteric and niche works to be independently produced and made available via paid-for subscription platforms. Moreover, far from being marginal actors within the global entertainment market, new technologies have enabled technology-based corporations such as Netflix and Amazon to embark on new activities within the entertainment sphere.[4]

A similar scenario is unrolling in the area of cultural heritage. One of the techniques employed by libraries, archives, museums and other memory institutions since the 1980s to increase access to and appreciation of our cultural heritage collections is the use of digital technology (for example, from the use of multimedia terminals in the 1980s to the use of tablets and smartphone applications in the current era). Part of this trend also involves the digitisation of analogue-based collections for the purposes of preservation of heritage for current and future generations – including remarkable digitisation projects involving the mapping of human medical history, fossils, and indigenous artefacts and ways of lives.[5] Emerging collaborative experiences also show that the creation and exploitation of these digital collections can allow increased public access especially when immersive technologies (such as virtual reality – VR and augmented reality – AR) are harnessed to create interactive experiences for the public. Take for example, the use of the iBeacon

---

[4] Netflix, for example, has, since 2013, begun to stream and produce original television and film content, some of which have won multiple accolades including Academy Awards – making it the first technology company to win an Oscar. For an account of the controversy, see B. Raftery, '3 Lessons Netflix Could Learn From *Roma's* Rickety Rollout' *Wired* 18.12.2018, http://www.wired.com.

[5] These activities are well discussed and displayed in the various institutional websites including those of the Natural History Museum (UK). A remarkable project is the Peoples' Palace Projects (with the British Tate and Horniman galleries), which involved the digitisation of a people, their customs and the village – https://www.vi-mm.eu/2018/12/23/peoples-palace-goes-on-virtual-reality-journey-to-amazons-xingu-people-with-horniman-museum-installation/.

by the New York Metropolitan Museum to give museum visitors an augmented reality experience via special tablets. Another example of using VR technology is the non-profit Google Cultural Institute's active collaboration with more than 50 natural history museums.[6] A more controversial application of technology is when digital misappropriations of museum or cultural objects occur without institutional or community permissions, especially when such digital files are then used to re-create (via 3-D printing or VR/AR technologies) the original objects.[7]

16.2 FROM PRINTING TO DIGITAL LIBRARIES

16.2.1 Controlling reprography

Prior to the mass introduction of reprographic technology, publishers and authors had generally tolerated unauthorised hand transcriptions of written works despite these being clear acts of infringement. This was largely due to the cost and sheer inconvenience of enforcing the rights, and also to the relative lack of economic harm arising from an activity that took place mostly in libraries rather than in bookshops. Even when photocopy technology became available, publishers were at first quite unconcerned about library copying. Indeed, the US National Association of Book Publishers entered into a Gentlemen's Agreement with the American Council of Learned Societies and the US Social Science Research Council, whereby duplication 'for profit or as a substitute for purchase of a protected work was forbidden, but single photocopies in lieu of loan or in place of manual transcription and solely for the purpose of research were explicitly recognised as fair use'.[8]

With the introduction of low-cost photocopying machines into libraries, offices and schools, it was no longer feasible to condone such blatant copying of books, especially with the possibility of libraries creating competing markets. In the US, for example, the photocopying technology had by the 1970s enabled enough libraries to become secondary producers of IP-protected goods and to deflect the initial consumer purchase from the copyright owner. The Supreme Court decision in *Williams & Wilkins Co v. United States*[9] represented a landmark decision in this area where the publishers sued the National Library of Medicine, claiming that the mass reproduction and distribution of their medical journals constituted infringements of the copyright in the journals. The Court held that this amounted to fair use – one factor taken into consideration was the fact that

[6] M. Terras, 'Cultural Heritage Information: Artefacts and Digitisation Technologies', in G. Chowdhury and I. Ruthven (eds), *Cultural Heritage Information: Access and Management* (Facet, 2016); M. Katz, 'Augmented Reality is Transforming Museums' *Wired*, 23.4.2018, www.wired.com; M. Bawaya, 'Virtual Archaeologists Recreate Parts of Ancient Worlds' (2010) 327(5962) *Science* 140–41.

[7] U. Suthersanen, 'Property and Culture: A Case Study on Orphan Works' (2017) XXII *Art, Antiquity and Law* 172.

[8] R. Adelstein and S. Peretz, 'The Competition of Technologies in Markets for Ideas: Copyright and Fair Use in Evolutionary Perspective' (1985) 5 *International Review of Law and Economics* 209.

[9] 487 F 2d 1345 (Court of Claims) (affirmed 420 US 376 (S Ct, 1975)). Also see S. Breyer, 'The Uneasy Case for Copyright: A Study in Copyright for Books, Photocopies and Computer Programs' (1970) 84 *Harvard Law Review* 281.

such copying had been accepted since the Gentlemen's Agreement (see above). The Court refused to accept the proposition that where there is a marked increase in volume, a use that was hitherto accepted as 'fair use' changed to 'unfair use'.[10]

The reprography problem was dealt with in alternative ways in most countries.[11] Some courts and laws condoned reprographic copying as an act of fair use without compensation; other countries condoned certain amounts of reprographic copying as an act of fair dealing for private study or research,[12] or for educational purposes, subject to licensing or levy schemes.[13] The latter (known as private copying levy) has been included as one of the limitations that EU member states may provide for under the EU Copyright in the Information Society Directive. The provisions allow for copying that is 'private and for ends that are neither directly nor indirectly commercial', on the condition that rightholders must receive 'fair compensation'.[14] The implication is that levies are to be imposed on the copying, scanning and recording equipment. The CJEU has been very prolific providing clarifications on what constitutes minimal harm in relation to private copying and compensation.[15]

16.2.2 Digital libraries

Technology has undoubtedly changed the nature and role of libraries. The current wave of changes from digitisation to online contents provision has democratised scholarship on a global scale. Technologies also allow libraries with a public interest mandate to repurpose the 'library' from a physical repository of books, films, sound recordings, and pictures to easily accessible and interactive environments. For libraries and archives, digitisation of their collections can alleviate the financial pressures they face due to government and charitable support. Google's own (admittedly generous) estimation is that its digitisation venture would make millions of otherwise unavailable works for institutional subscriptions and consumer purchases; while the British Film Institute estimates that digitisation of its orphan film works might generate an additional annual gross

---

[10] The subject of educational copying has not been fully resolved in the US – see Chapter 12.3.2.

[11] For a historical review on the position taken in other countries during this period, see G. Kolle, 'Reprography and Copyright Law: A Comparative Law Study concerning the Role of Copyright Law' (1975) 6 *IIC* 382.

[12] As in the UK, for instance. A new private copying exception was introduced in 2014 in order to allow digital private copying; the law was quashed after a judicial review which noted that the proposed law's possible incompatability with EU law due to the absence of a compensatory mechanism – *BASCA v. The Secretary of State for Business, Innovation and Skills* [2015] EWHC 1723 (Admin).

[13] Chapter 12.3.

[14] EU Copyright in the Information Society Directive, Art 5(2)(b), together with Art 5(3)(a) allowing reproduction for non-commercial teaching and scientific research. See H. Wijminga, et al., *International Survey on Private Copying: Law & Practice 2016* (WIPO/Stichting de Thuiskopie), available at the WIPO website.

[15] Including: Case C-463/12 *Copydan Båndkopi*; Case C-462/09 *Stichting de Thuiskopie*; Case C-435/12 *ACI Adam*; Case C-572/13 *Hewlett Packard Belgium SPRL v. Reprobel SCRL*; Case C-467/08 *Padawan*; Case C-457-11 *VG Wort*; Case C:2011-397 *Luksan*; Case C-521/11 *Amazon.com International Sales*; Case C-572/14 *Austro-Mechana*.

income for itself of more than £500,000.[16] Some libraries, such as the British Library, Bibliothèque Nationale de France, and the Library of Congress have also embraced new roles as business advisory centres and commercial publishers of their works.[17] Well-known digital library projects (such as the Google Books Library Project, the Europeana, HathiTrust and Project Gutenberg) aim to digitise millions of volumes of books. The Google venture, for instance, involves working in partnership with several libraries worldwide including those in Harvard, Oxford, Ghent, and Stanford universities, as well as several national libraries.[18]

Digital and electronic libraries are predicted to become 'a universal archive that will contain not only all books and articles but all documents anywhere – the basis for a total history of the human race'.[19] The relevant entry in Wikipedia, itself a phenomenon of the digital age, sets out the advantages of digital libraries: trans-boundary, multiple and easy access to a vast amount of resources comprising printed materials, images, sound and film recordings; reduced costs of maintenance (though this can be offset through the costs of software and digitisation equipment); enhanced text and data mining possibilities; multiple preservation and conservation without any degradation in quality; networking as digital libraries can provide a seamlessly integrated and shared resource.

The ultimate aim is to increase access to information – not just to works currently in circulation, but more importantly to those out-of-commerce works, orphan works and out-of-copyright works. The concern is that the lack of modern copyright rules may create a serious hindrance to mass digitisation of collections, which, in turn, is obstructing greater public and scholarly access and use of cultural assets, including data and text mining activities. The EU Copyright in the Digital Single Market Directive has introduced mandatory provisions in relation to the last.[20]

Can digitisation only work in relation to out of copyright works? Can in-copyright but out-of-commerce works be digitised? Should we have a general exception for digitisation activities? Some of these issues have been discussed in other chapters especially with respect to the litigation between rights holders and Google, and the new EU laws in respect of orphan works, cultural heritage and out-of-commerce works.[21] Here we return to a more basic concern, namely, should we instinctively protect everything that is within an institutional collection, including scraps of paper, random letters and pamphlets, historical or family photographs? What sort of behaviour do we wish to control under the copyright rubric?

---

[16] *Orphan Works and Mass Digitization: A Report of the Register of Copyrights* (US Copyright Office Report, 2015), 14; P. Samuelson, 'Google Book Search and the Future of Books in Cyberspace' (2009) 94 *Minn. L. Rev.* 1308, 1324 *et seq*. For the UK situation, see I. Hargreaves, *Digital Opportunities: A Review of Intellectual Property and Growth* (Intellectual Property Office, 2011), 39. Also see *The Hargreaves Review of Intellectual Property: Where Next?* (Business, Innovation and Skills Committee, 2012), available at www.parliament.uk.

[17] N. Canty, 'Libraries as Publishers: Turning the Page?' (2012) 23(1) *Alexandria* 55.

[18] https://www.google.com/googlebooks/library/index.html. The works are also accessible via HathiTrust – https://www.hathitrust.org/partnership.

[19] A. Grafton, 'Future Reading: Digitization and its Discontents' *The New Yorker*, 5 November, 2007.

[20] EU Copyright in the Digital Single Market Directive, Art 4.

[21] See Chapter 12.

A final conundrum is that if licensing is the way forward for third parties, who owns these digital collections? Copyright may vest in an individual printed work residing within the library's collection, where the ownership of copyright in the work may be readily identified, or where the work is classified as an orphan work. Upon digitisation, the institution may also assert property rights in the physical work itself, and in the subsequent digitised work. The Getty Museum, for example, has coined 'digital surrogate' as a classification term for the digitised images of works of art that are in the Getty's collection. Should libraries, museums and archives claim 'digital surrogate' property rights in the digitised versions of the artefact or book or painting? The British Museum, for instance, clearly exercises surrogate copyright in digital images of public domain works – see, for example, the Museum's assertion of copyright in relation to the digital image of Michelangelo's Studies for a Virgin and Child.[22]

16.3   CAPTURING IMAGES AND SOUNDS

16.3.1 Mechanical creations

Eighteenth- and nineteenth-century music industries generated income through the control of the sale of music sheets and subscription concerts. This economic picture changed considerably as several technological inventions arrived including the domestic piano as well as the Aeolian machine (or pianola). Early US and English decisions were of the view that the unauthorised pianola rolls did not infringe copyright in sheet music; the US Supreme Court went further to indicate that this approach would also extend to other mechanical reproductions including musical boxes, gramophone records or to mechanical pipe organs.[23] Calls for wider protection were duly made especially in relation to the increased sales of pirated music and to the unauthorised 'mechanically produced music'.[24]

The nineteenth century saw further innovative leaps in the field of mechanical sciences which profoundly affected the existing world of imagery and sound: Talbot's calotype process, the Daguerre photographic inventions, Scott's phonoautograph, Edison's phonograph process, Berliner's gramophone, and of course, the Lumière brothers' film recording techniques. The birth of the photograph, the sound recording and the film as 'new' intangible products led to a re-evaluation of the copyright system as conceived in the nineteenth century. On the one hand, we have the pirates in this historical context, namely, the sound recording and film producers who had to rely on authored contents; on the other hand, one sees the authors and publishers of original contents

---

[22] See https://www.bmimages.com/results.asp?image=00018195001&imagex=6&searchnum=0003. For usage of the term surrogate intellectual property rights and cultural heritage institutional policies, see http://displayatyourownrisk.org/digital-surrogates/.

[23] *Boosey v. Whight* [1899] 1 Ch 836 (H Ct); [1900] 1 Ch 122 (CA-UK); *White-Smith Music Publishing Co v. Apollo Co* (1908) 209 US 1. See M. Rimmer, 'The Pianola Roll: A Precursor to Kazaa' (2004) 7(5) *Internet Law Bulletin* 103.

[24] V. Bonham-Carter, *Authors by Profession, Vol. 1* (The Society of Authors and Bodley Head, 1978), 214–15.

pressurising for an expansion in copyright law in order to control such derivative uses, and to ensure benefit-sharing arrangements. As with today's dilemma with digital surrogates (discussed above), the new query at the turn of the nineteenth century was whether such derivative techno-logical manifestations of existing works were worthy of separate protection. Were films, photo-graphs and films creatively authored works?

The early legal reactions were from the French and US jurisdictions. The French courts' initial reaction was that such objects could not to be viewed as paintings. The authored work was 'imbued with something of the human soul', whereas a photograph was a completely soulless machine-pro-duced work. A marked change in legal attitudes came with the commercialisation of photographs and the appearance of a new stakeholder – the professional photographer. With the discovery of an 'author' in this mechanical operation, courts also discovered that creativity could be imbued in photographs. A photographer had to choose the angle, lighting, order and framework and by this process his production was more than a mere reproduction, but a genuine creative work.[25] In the famous 1884 case concerning the unauthorised reproductions of the photograph of Oscar Wilde, the US Supreme Court agreed that the portrait photograph deserved copyright protection, analogizing photography with authors' 'writings'. Moreover, it was clear that the photograph was densely imbued with the author's 'original mental conception'.[26] This sort of reasoning was further extrapolated to other technologies; films, for instance, were initially thought of as soulless, finan-cially-dictated productions but were consequently re-labelled as creative authored-works.[27]

By the 1960s, the international framework which had only comprised mainly traditional au-thors' rights was adjusted. First, authors' rights were expanded to include the exclusive right to au-thorise use of works in both sound recordings and films, while recognising cinematographic works explicitly. Secondly, a parallel international legal framework comprising the rights of performers, phonogram producers and broadcasters (and in many national laws, film producers).[28]

16.3.2 The *Sony* defence – VCRs and MP3s

The *Sony* defence remains important as the US courts are called upon to continuously draw the red lines around technologies, which undermine the IPR holder's control. The defence is that, once it is proven that a product is *capable* of substantial non-infringing uses, the remaining issue is whether the defendants have reasonable knowledge of infringing activities but fail to act on that knowledge to prevent infringement. Indeed, without such considerations, lawful purchasers of copyright works or services would not now be able to shift, for the sake of convenience and portability, their lawful

---

[25] B. Edelman, *Ownership of the Image* (Routledge & Kegan Paul, 1979), 44–7; J. Gaines, *Contested Culture: The Image, the Voice, the Law* (The University of North Carolina Press, 1991), 46.

[26] *Burrow-Giles v. Sarony* (111 US 53, 1884); *cf, Baumann v. Fussell* (1978) RPC 485, UK Court of Appeal declining to hold infringement of a photograph, noting that a photographer cannot be said to 'control' two fighting birds, and as such there are no protectable elements within a photograph in relation to the positioning of the birds.

[27] Edelman, *supra* note 25, 44–67; *Edison v. Lubin* 122 F 240 1903 (3rd Cir, 1903), US courts recognising a celluloid sheet (which represented 4,500 moving pictures) as a 'photograph', and thus a copyright work.

[28] Chapter 4.2.3.

purchases from one place-time-medium dimension (such as scheduled TV programming, CDs, or DVDs) to another place-time-medium dimension (such as an MP3 player, an iPod, or a TiVo). As we see below, the *Sony* defence has also been evoked in relation to the file sharing technologies.

In the landmark US Supreme Court decision *Sony Corp v. Universal Studios, Inc*,[29] the issue was whether Sony had committed copyright infringement through its sale of its Betamax home video-tape recorders. These (now obsolete) machines were hugely popular on a worldwide basis during the 1980s as they allowed consumers to record their television broadcasts on blank videocassettes for later viewing (euphemistically called 'time-shifting'). The recording industry brought suit arguing that the use of Sony recorders by private individuals in their homes for their own private use constituted copyright infringement of the works; the further claim was that Sony, as the manufacturer and retailer of the recorders and the blank cassette tapes, was liable as a contributory infringer. The Supreme Court refused to hold the manufacturer and retailers of video tape recorders liable for contributory infringement despite evidence that such machines could be and were used to infringe plaintiffs' copyright-protected television shows. The Supreme Court stated that if liability is to be found, it must be shown that Sony had 'sold equipment with constructive knowledge of the fact that their customers may use that equipment to make unauthorized copies of copyrighted material'.[30] And although Sony may have had general knowledge that its machines would be used for unauthorised copying, and although it had advertised the machine for just such a purpose, this was insufficient. The Court was of the express opinion that such generalised knowledge was insufficient to impose liability for vicarious or contributory infringement. Moreover, the Court noted that the equipment was also capable of substantial non-infringing uses (such as copying non-copyright works).[31]

Similar issues arose with the development of the MP3 compression technology in the mid-90s, and its revolutionary effects on music file sharing. Music files were previously in WAV file format – they were large, utilised hard drive space on a computer, and made the transmission of a single song over the internet a long and cumbersome task. MP3 technology allowed digital encoding of music files, thus enabling quick transfers over the internet, without any great degradation of quality.[32] In *Recording Industry Association of America, Inc v. Diamond Multimedia Systems Inc*[33] at issue was the liability of a user of a portable, hand-held playing device (RioPlayer) which was capable of receiving, storing, and re-playing MP3 files which had been transferred from a CD to the device, via the hard drive of a personal computer. The Court held that this could not constitute infringing

---

[29] 464 US 417 (S Ct, 1984). For an interesting analysis of this decision, see Fisher, *supra* note 3, 70–75.

[30] Ibid., 439.

[31] Ibid., 434–42; a similar stance was adopted in the UK decision of *C.B.S. Inc v. Ames Records & Tapes Ltd* [1982] Ch 91 and *C.B.S. Songs Ltd v. Amstrad Consumer Electronics plc* [1988] AC 1013. In the latter case, the House of Lords held that a manufacturer may have conferred on the purchaser the power to copy 'but did not grant or purport to grant the right to copy'.

[32] MP3 is the abbreviated term for MPEG 1 Audio Layer 3. A summary of the technology is given in *RIAA v. Diamond Multimedia Systems Inc*, 180 F 3d 1072 (9th Cir, 1999), at 1073; and also in A. Berschadsky, 'RIAA v. Napster: A Window into the Future of Copyright Law in the Internet Age' (2000) 18 J. Marshall J. Computer & Info. L. 755, 758. As of 2017, all the salient patents on the MP3 technology expired, and it is now available on free/open source projects.

[33] 29 F Supp 2d 624 (CD Cal, 1998), 180 F 3d 1072 (9th Cir, 1999).

activities – the device merely made copies in order to render portable, or 'space-shift' those MP3 files that already resided on a user's CD or hard drive. Placing reliance on the *Sony* decision, the court opined that such copying of files was paradigmatic non-commercial personal use which was entirely consistent with the purposes of the copyright law.[34]

16.3.3 Remote (cloud) digital recorders

The latest technological advancement in this area is represented by remote recorders, which are now at the centre of IP disputes globally.[35] These services allow users to record television programmes remotely on the service platform and subsequently watch them from any device. In *VCAST Ltd v. RTI SpA*, the CJEU was requested to give a preliminary ruling on whether it was an infringement to make available television broadcasts to the users of the cloud recording system. The user would select a programme and a time slot, the system would then pick up the television signal using its own antennas, and the selected programme would be recorded and stored in the cloud data storage space indicated by the user. The whole procedure entails making a copy of the broadcast available to the customer online.[36] The CJEU concluded that the (re)transmission made by these services constituted communication to a new and different public – this new communication requires a separate authorisation, and a remote recording service falls outside the private copying exception under the EU law.[37]

In the US, the question was addressed in several decisions before the final resolution of the issue in *Aereo*. Appellate courts in the First and Second Circuits limited the applicability of the 'right of public performance' to scenarios where the streaming originated from a single 'master file'[38] (thus applying Cablevision). Other appellate courts rejected this approach and instead interpreted the 'right of public performance' as covering scenarios where the streaming to multiple users originated from multiple files.[39] The Supreme Court held in *Aereo*[40] that the public performance right encompasses the transmission of copyright works to the public through individual transmissions

---

[34] Ibid., at 1079.

[35] US – *American Broadcasting Cos, Inc v. Aereo, Inc* 573 US__(S Ct, 2014); *Cartoon Network, LP v. CSC Holdings, Inc*, 536 F 3d 121 (2d Cir, 2008); *Australia – National Rugby League Investments Pty Ltd v. Singtel Optus Pty Ltd*, [2012] FCAFC 5; [2012] FCA 34 (*Singtel No. 2*).

[36] Case C-265/16, *VCAST Ltd v. RTI SpA*, ECLI:EU:C:2017:913.

[37] EU Copyright in the Information Society Directive 2001/29, Art 5(2)(b).

[38] *Hearst Stations Inc v. Aereo, Inc*, 977 F Supp. 2d 32, 38–39 (D Mass, 2013); *Am. Broad. Cos. v. Aereo, Inc*, 874 F Supp 2d 373, 388 (SDNY, 2012) – applying *Twentieth Century Fox Film Corp v. Cablevision Sys. Corp*, 478 F Supp 2d 607, 622–3 (SDNY, 2007); *Cartoon Network LP v. CSC Holdings, Inc*, 536 F 3d 121, 134 (2d Cir, 2008); *WNET v. Aereo, Inc* 712 F 3d 676, 686–94 (2d Cir, 2013). For a similar situation in Australia, see *National Rugby League Investments Pty Ltd v. Singtel Optus Pty Ltd* [2012] FCAFC 59; *Singtel Optus Pty Ltd v. National Rugby League Investments Pty Ltd [No. 2]* [2012] FCA 34 [105].

[39] *Cmty. Television of Utah, LLC v. Aereo, Inc*, 997 F Supp. 2d 1191, 1200 (D Utah, 2014); *Fox Television Stations, Inc v. FilmOn X LLC*, 966 F Supp 2d 30, 48 (DDC, 2013); *Fox Television Stations, Inc v. Barry Diller Content Sys*, 915 F Supp 2d 1138, 1144 (CD Cal, 2012).

[40] *American Broadcasting Cos v. Aereo, Inc* 874 F Supp 2d 373 (SDNY, 2012).

made by the remote recording service. In this case, Aereo had performed within the meaning of the right, and had done it 'publicly', notwithstanding that the transmissions were to individual subscribers from their personal copies. The Court concluded that Aereo's technique in using dedicated copies did not render Aereo's commercial objective any different from that of cable companies; neither did it significantly alter the viewing experience of Aereo's subscribers.

16.4 FILE SHARING TECHNOLOGIES

File sharing, digital and Internet-related technologies only started to challenge the IPRs' regime when several other technological factors converged. First, the arrival of the affordable personal computer with the invention of the integrated circuit chip explains the increased global consumption of digital computing. Secondly, the internet had exploded exponentially since its birth within the US Defense Department's ARPANET, especially with the invention of the World Wide Web, the electronic mail framework, and the eventual privatisation and commercialisation of the internet in the 1990s. And finally, all this would have been to no avail without sophisticated technological support and infrastructure including wireless hot spots, internet cafes, extensive cable telephony, accessible and affordable broadband, compression software technology coupled with increasing storage capabilities including cloud computing. We now live in a technology and internet friendly society, in a world of DVD and Blu-ray players, iPods and MP3 players, smartphones, webcasts, interactive streaming, and designer-made virtual avatars.[41] The digital age has added several more technological milestones and services – Mp3.com, Usenet, Napster, Grokster, Kazaa, Bittorrent, Newzbin, Megaupload, the PirateBay, Popcorn Time and Kodi. As the argument goes, the copyright industries argue that all these technologies have undermined the basic rules of the creative industries' production, distribution and enforcement models, multiplying the numbers of potentially infringing actors and activities, and stressing the copyright system in a way and intensity previously unknown.[42]

16.4.1 Authorisation and inducement – newsgroup and P2P systems

The first file sharing technology worth mentioning, as it pre-dates the World Wide Web and is still active, is 'Usenet' or 'newsgroups'. These are interest groups that share information using a system similar to a bulletin board. Users may post their own messages and read messages posted by others. To obtain access to the Usenet, users must gain access through a commercial Usenet provider or an internet service provider. Messages posted to Usenet are commonly known as 'articles' and posted on bulletin boards: the 'newsgroups', are often named and organised according to a specific topic or subject matter they relate to. Other users can then review the headers or titles of the messages

---

[41] For the historical account, see Fisher, *supra* note 3, 13–18; and T.J. Misa, *Leonardo to the Internet: Technology and Culture from the Renaissance to the Present* (Johns Hopkins University Press, 2004), 213, 252.

[42] Digital Millenium Copyright Act 1988 (DMCA).

available by selecting a newsgroup and download messages that are of interest. Although Usenet was designed to transfer only text files, this system became ideal for sharing all other types of content by simply converting the digital file in order to appear as a text message. The message can then be distributed through the newsgroup, downloaded, reassembled and converted (decoded) back into the original file type.

Newsgroups became the centre of attraction with the 2010 *Newzbin* decision by the UK High Court. The court held that the operator of a Usenet indexing website was liable for infringement of copyright in the claimants' films as it authorised the copying of the claimants' films, it had communicated the claimants' films to the public, and it had procured and engaged with its premium members in a common design to copy the claimants' films.[43]

The next technology subjected to copyright litigation is peer-to-peer (P2P) systems. These usually lack dedicated, centralised infrastructures but depend on the voluntary participation of peers to contribute resources out of which the infrastructure is constructed. The key element in a P2P network is the software, which provides a method of indexing all the files so that users may access and download them. The genesis of the file sharing litigation was in 1999 when several sound recording companies claimed that Napster's P2P file-sharing technology should be stopped under copyright law. Napster's attempt to use the *Sony* defence (discussed above) was rejected as the primary issue, from the court's perspective, was whether the file sharing phenomenon caused market harm to the property owner. Although the file sharing program was capable of non-infringing uses, the program had unacceptably harmed the sound recording industry's market, especially in relation to sales within college markets. The courts were unimpressed with a report alleging that P2P file sharing stimulated more music sales than it displaced. Instead, it emphasised that Napster could not deprive the copyright holder of the right to develop alternative markets for the works and that having 'digital downloads available for free on the Napster system necessarily harms the copyright holders' attempts to charge for the same downloads'.[44]

Important factors in considering the P2P technology are that the servers do not create, copy, store or make available any of the sound, text or image files on its servers (whether transient or otherwise). Neither are the contents of the files routed or transmitted through the P2P network or servers. The contents of all files are held at all times on the users' computers. In these circumstances, how could Napster be held liable for enabling multiple infringing acts by its users? Nevertheless, Napster was held to have committed vicarious and contributory liability under US copyright law as it had both actual and constructive knowledge that its users were illegally exchanging copyrighted music. Thus, regardless of Napster's non-infringing uses, the evidentiary record was that Napster knew or had reason to know of its users' infringement of plaintiffs' copyrights, and had the means to block access to the system by suppliers of the infringing material. It is difficult to discern, from a reading of the *Sony* decision whether this approach is correct – as far as the Supreme Court

---

[43] *Twentieth Century Fox Film Corp v. Newzbin Ltd* [2010] EWHC 608 (Ch). For the US position, see *Arista Records LLC v. Usenet.com Inc* 633 F Supp 2d 124 (SDNY, 2009).

[44] *A&M Records Inc v. Napster Inc*, 114 F Supp 2d 896 (ND Cal, 2000); 239 F 3d 1004 (9th Cir, 2001), at 1017. See R. Garofalo, 'From Music Publishing to MP3: Music and Industry in the Twentieth Century', *American Music*, (Fall, 1999); Suthersanen, *supra* note 3.

in the *Sony* case was concerned, the fact of potential non-infringing uses led directly back to the activities of the users which, in turn, led to the Court's declaration that 'time-shifting' activities constitute fair use. In the *Napster* decision however, the appellate court proceeded from a reverse direction: having held all activities of users as being non-fair uses of a copyright work, the fact of the capability of the system for potential non-infringing uses did not sit well in its rationale for contributory infringement.

The Napster technology was replaced by faster P2P technologies and the US Supreme Court had, once again, to resolve the interface between copyright rules and technological disruption in the *Grokster* decision. The manufacturers and distributors of two P2P software applications, Grokster and Morpheus, were sued by a consortium comprising major film and sound recording companies.[45] The district and appellate courts had held for the P2P manufacturers stating that no control was possible under the decentralised, Gnutella-type network or the quasi-decentralised, supernode Kazaa-type network since no central index is maintained. Thus, even if the defendants 'closed their doors and deactivated all computers within their control, users of their products could continue sharing files with little or no interruption'.[46] On appeal to the Supreme Court, the majority opinion was that the *Sony* defence had been misapplied and that the defendants were liable for secondary infringements. In doing this, the court transplanted the common law rule of inducement of infringement into US copyright law:

> [O]ne who distributes a device with the object of promoting its use to infringe copyright, as shown by clear expression or other affirmative steps taken to foster infringement, is liable for the resulting acts of infringement by third parties [...] Accordingly, just as *Sony* did not find intentional inducement despite the knowledge of the VCR manufacturer that its device could be used to infringe, mere knowledge of infringing potential or of actual infringing uses would not be enough here to subject a distributor to liability [...] The inducement rule, instead, premises liability on purposeful, culpable expression and conduct, and thus does nothing to compromise legitimate commerce or discourage innovation having a lawful promise (citations omitted).[47]

The reasoning of the Supreme Court as to the technological capabilities of software platforms to 'control' user activities is prescient especially when one examines the approach of current EU legislators in relation to the EU Directive on Copyright in the Digital Single Market, to monitor

---

[45] *Metro-Goldwyn-Mayer Studios, Inc et al. v. Grokster, Ltd, Streamcast Networks Inc et al.* 259 F Supp 2d 1029 (CD Cal, 2003), at 1041; 380 F 3d 1154 (CA, 2004); 125 S Ct 2764 (S Ct, 2005).

[46] *Metro-Goldwyn-Mayer Studios, Inc* 259 F Supp 2d 1029 (CD Cal, 2003), at 1041.

[47] It is worth reading Justice Breyer's intriguing concurring opinion whereby he appears to have painstakingly proven that, had it not been for the inducement issue, the facts relating to this decision were indeed very similar to the *Sony* facts. Breyer also emphasised the significant future market for non-infringing uses of Grokster-type peer-to-peer software, citing Robert Merges' work in 'A New Dynamism in the Public Domain' (2004) 71 *University of Chicago Law Review* 183 – *Metro-Goldwyn-Mayer Studios, Inc and ors* 125 S Ct 2764 (S Ct, 2005), at 2789–91.

and prevent unauthorised streaming of copyright contents.[48] Not only was the majority opinion in *Grokster* persuaded that advertising and internal emails could be tantamount to inducing acts, but it was convinced that the P2P networks could have filtered out copyright works and blocked 'anyone from continuing to use its software to share copyrighted files'.[49]

The Australian Federal Court reached similar conclusions in relation to P2P technology. Under the Australian Copyright Act, copyright will be infringed where a third party 'sanctions, approves, or countenances' acts of infringement by others.[50] In determining whether authorisation has occurred, the courts must consider several mandatory factors including the party's power to prevent infringement, the relationship existing between the party and the infringer, and whether the reasonable steps taken by the party to prevent or avoid infringement (including compliance with any relevant codes of practice).[51] In the *Sharman* decision, the Federal Court ruled that Sharman could have adopted technical measures (through keyword filtering or gold file flood filtering) to 'control users' copyright infringing activities'.[52] Mindful of the need to find an appropriate balance 'so as to protect the applicants' copyright interests (as far as possible) but without unnecessarily intruding on others' freedom of speech and communication', the Court provided that the continuation of the system would not be regarded as a violation if the software was modified to implement filtering technology to a standard agreed between the parties or approved by the court.

These decisions confirmed that third-party liability theories (whether under vicarious, contributory or authorisation clauses) were flexible enough to prohibit the distribution of decentralised software technologies on the grounds of its capacity to be used by purchasers to infringe copyright despite the technologies' inherent non-infringing uses. Largely unexplored, however, were the uncertainties as to the encroachment on user rights, and the need for technological development. Of course, file sharing and related technologies inevitably expanded.

---

[48] EU Copyright in the Digital Single Market Directive, Arts 17–22.

[49] *Metro-Goldwyn-Mayer Studios, Inc and ors,* 125 S Ct 2764 (S Ct, 2005), 2772–9. Similar advertising activities in the *Sony* decision were deemed acceptable as there was:

> No evidence that Sony had expressed an object of bringing about taping in violation of copyright or had taken active steps to increase its profits from unlawful taping. Although Sony's advertisements urged consumers to buy the VCR to 'record favourite shows' or 'build a library' of recorded programs, neither of these uses was necessarily infringing.

Moreover, the *Grokster* court emphasised that the *Sony* staple article rule is applicable only if there is no evidence of intent and actions directed to promoting or inducing infringement.

[50] *University of NSW v. Moorhouse* [1975] HCA 26.

[51] Australian Copyright Act 1968, s 101(1A).

[52] *Universal Music Australia Pty Ltd v. Sharman License Holdings Ltd* (2005) 65 IPR 289, 387. Note a further P2P decision where the Federal Court confirmed the extra-territorial reach of the authorisation clause should a nexus be found between Australia and infringing activities taking place outside Australian territory – *Cooper v. Universal Music Australia Pty Ltd* [2006] FCAFC 187). For a comparative analysis of the 'authorisation' clause under Australian, Canadian, British and Singaporean laws, see S.C. Lim and W.B. Chik, 'Revisiting Authorisation Liability in Copyright Law' (2012) 24 *Singapore Academy of Law Journal* 698.

16.4.2 BitTorrent protocol and *The PirateBay*

The unique network architecture of the BitTorrent file sharing protocol enables the dissemination and download of immense amounts of data, thus making it a global internet standard. Files are not transferred from a single source or as a single file but are broken into segments that can be distributed to an unlimited number of users whose computers act as servers. The technology involves a user ('seeder') who downloads a torrent client which is used to create a '.torrent file' that, in turn, acts as a magnetic link to the data/work which is to be shared and disseminated ('swarm') over the internet. The BitTorrent client facilitates users' connecting to other users (or in BitTorrent terminology, seeders swarming a particular file will be connected to 'leechers') with the .torrent file/ magnetic link instructing the BitTorrent client as to the location of the segments of the file – which then can be downloaded separately, and then reassembled by the client.[53] File transfer is facilitated by BitTorrent tracker websites that provide searching of files and coordinate the file distribution.

The potentially infringing nature of the torrent file/magnetic link is contested since the file does not include any copy of the copyright work being shared.[54] Moreover, as the BitTorrent protocol does not offer facilities to search files across the internet, users need to find the .torrent files, usually from the numerous tracker websites that host them. Thus, cases involving BitTorrent technology have targeted such websites and employed various liability theories in order to gauge the legality of their activities (such as hosting, indexing, and linking to .torrent files). Decisions focusing on liabilities for primary infringements, such as making available and authorisation, are limited. In the *Mininova* decision, a Dutch court found Mininova (one of the largest BitTorrent index sites in the world at the time) liable for enabling, inducing and benefiting from the uploading activities of its users; however, it held that the site was not liable for directly infringing activities such as communicating or making available such works. Similar conclusions have been made by Australian and British courts.[55] Since these decisions, hundreds of Torrent indexing sites have been either shut down or blocked by court orders or raids,[56]

---

[53] While downloading, every leecher automatically 'reseeds' the file and becomes an additional source. Moreover, each segment of the file can be downloaded from different seeders as the BitTorrent client will connect to as many seeders as available to download several segments simultaneously, and in a random order.

[54] G. Dimita, 'Six Characters in Search of Infringement: Potential Liability for Creating, Downloading, and Disseminating .torrent files' (2012) 7(6) *JIPLP* 466.

[55] *Brein v. Mininova B.V.*, District Court of Utrecht, Case No 250077/HA ZA 08-1124 (26 August 2009); also see *Cooper v. Universal Music Australia Pty Ltd* [2006] FCAFC 187 (Australian Federal Court); *Dramatico Entertainment Ltd & others v. British Sky Broadcasting Ltd and others* [2012] EWHC 268 (Ch) (UK High Court).

[56] For instance: in 2004, Supernova was discontinued under the threat of litigation; LokiTorrent shortly followed, and the website was changed to display a message intended to intimidate users: 'You can click but you can't hide'; in 2005, the Federal Bureau of Investigations in the US shut down elitetorrents.org; in 2009, the Italian Supreme Court issued an order requiring ISPs to block access to the PirateBay website as part of a preventative seizure in criminal proceedings (*Bergamo Public Prosecutor's Officer v. Kolmisappi* (Italian Supreme Court, 29 September 2009)); in 2010, the Swedish Court of Appeal ordered ISPs to block access to a tracker associated with the PirateBay (*Columbia Pictures Industries Inc v. Portlane AB* (Swedish Court of Appeal, 4 May 2010)).

including the infamous 'PirateBay' website. The website has been the subject of numerous cases and court orders in multiple jurisdictions, although the decision which commands attention is *BREIN/Ziggo*.[57]

Before delving into the decision, it should be noted that the situation in relation to service providers operating within the EU is covered to some extent under the E-Commerce Directive which provides certain safe harbour exemptions for ISPs and platforms which are considered to be passive conduits of information (the 'mere conduit' exception).[58] In *BREIN/Ziggo*,[59] the claim against The PirateBay website was analysed by the CJEU in relation to its activities, namely, making available and managing a sharing platform which indexes metadata relating to protected works, thereby facilitating P2P file sharing among users of the BitTorrent protocol. It was acknowledged that defendants were intermediaries in that it did not upload or download the materials (as this is done by the seeders and leechers). On the other hand, it was noted that The PirateBay did not only serve the role of a search engine for online content within the BitTorrent protocol, but that it also offered an index classifying the works under different categories, based on the type of works, their genre and their popularity, with the operators checking and deleting as appropriate. The CJEU held that it had infringed the right of communication to the public since it had intervened with full knowledge of the consequences of their conduct. The Court held that, as a rule, any act by which a user, with full knowledge of the relevant facts, provides its clients with access to protected works is liable to constitute an 'act of communication'. The PirateBay could not be a mere conduit since it had played the essential role of indexing and cataloguing works.[60]

Thus, with the *BREIN/Ziggo* ruling, the CJEU has made P2P operators liable for primary copyright infringement despite them not hosting contents themselves, and this is done by branding the act of 'knowingly sharing infringing content online' as an act of communication to the public. The ruling is in line with the approach in the EU Copyright in the Digital Single Market Directive where online platforms are being made to monitor infringing activities.[61] However, is this the correct approach? A plausible critique is set forth by Cordell and Potts who argue that with this approach, 'the CJEU appears to be saying that knowingly managing facilities, which play an essential role

---

[57] For instance, to name a few: *Ftd BV v. Eyeworks Film & TV Drama BV*, The Hague District Court, 366481/KG ZA 10-639, 2 June 2010; *Dramatico Entertainment Ltd & others v. British Sky Broadcasting Ltd & others* [2012] EWHC 268 (Ch); *IFPI Danmark v. DMT2 A/S*, Frederiksberg Court, 29 October 2008; *Sonofon A/S v. IFPI*, High Court of Eastern Denmark, 26 November 2008; *Telenor v. IFPI*, Danish Supreme Court, 27 May 2010; *Bergamo Public Prosecutor's Officer v. Kolmisappi*, Italian Supreme Court, 29 September 2009; *Columbia Pictures Industries Inc v. Portlane AB*, Swedish Court of Appeal, 4 May 2010; *Stichting Bescherming Rechten Entertainment Industrie Nederland (BREIN) v. Ziggo BV*, District Court of the Hague, 11 January 2012.

[58] The defence applies when the provider does not initiate a transmission, or when the provider does not select or modify the information within a transmission, E-Commerce Directive, 2000/31/EC, Art 12.

[59] C-610/15, *Stichting Brein v. Ziggo BV*, EU:C: 2017: 456; [2017] ECDR 19.

[60] Ibid., para 50.

[61] EU Copyright in the Digital Single Market Directive, Arts 17 and 19.

in allowing users to share unauthorised content, is a communication to the public. This appears much closer to accessory liability than strict copyright infringement'.[62]

Is the CJEU compensating for the gap in secondary liability within EU copyright law? The answer is in the affirmative especially when contrasted with national cases (such as in Sweden and UK) where courts have managed to find other legal bases for granting blocking injunctions, without recourse to expanding or contorting the right of communication to the public.[63] As a commissioned report to the European Parliament confirms:

> For the (secondary) liability of other persons, until now different national secondary liability concepts apply, which may lead to different results from member state to member state. This is unsatisfactory against the background of European harmonisation; in particular, this does not create a level playing field, for example, for damage claims for right holders in the EU. But there is a development from CJEU case law to harmonise secondary liability within the primary liability rules of EU law in the series of judgments GS Media/Sanoma, Filmspeler and BREIN/Ziggo.[64]

---

[62] N. Cordell and B. Potts, 'Communication to the Public or Accessory Liability? Is the CJEU using Communication to the Public to Harmonise Accessory Liability across the EU?' (2018) 40 *EIPR* 289, 293, authors critically note that the CJEU in *BREIN/Ziggo* has invented new law.

[63] Of some import is the Swedish *PirateBay* decision (Stockholm District Court, Verdict B 13301-06, 17 April 2009; an unofficial translation is available at www.ifpi.org). The defendants were found guilty of secondary liability for copyright infringement, as well as criminal liability for hosting a file sharing site that provided a catalogue of .torrent files and a tracker. A crucial argument by the defendants – that the website was covered under the 'mere conduit' safe harbour – was rejected. The Court concluded that PirateBay's users infringed copyright law, and that it had facilitated the execution of these primary infringing activities, regardless of any knowledge concerning the infringements. The defendants' negligence to take action prevented them from benefiting from the 'mere conduit' protection – discussed in relation to the *BREIN/Ziggo* decision in the main text. Moreover, the court held that the defendants' guilt under criminal law was strengthened by the commercial and organised nature of their activities.

In the UK case relating to the request for an injunction to block The PirateBay, the High Court held that the latter was liable as a joint tortfeasor, or for authorising the infringement of its users (authorisation as discussed above) – *Dramatico Entertainment Ltd & others v. British Sky Broadcasting Ltd and others*, [2012] EWHC 268 (Ch). Also of note is the UK decision in *Twentieth Century Fox Film Corporation and Ors v. Sky UK Ltd and Ors* [2015] EWHC 1082 (Ch) which dealt with another BitTorrent-powered technology namely 'Popcorn Time', a cross-platform and movie streaming application which uses the BitTorrent protocol to obtain film and TV content from a number of host and indexing websites. A key difference is that popcorn time runs on the user's computer and shows the catalogued and indexed connections to the sources of the copies – this information is not provided by the website from which the application is downloaded. The Court, while finding the provider liable for authorisation and joint-tortfeasance, held that Popcorn Time did not infringe the right of communication to the public.

[64] Jan Bernd Nordemann, *Liability of Online Service Providers for Copyrighted Content – Regulatory Action Needed?*, commissioned for the European Parliament Policy Department A (Economic and Scientific Policy), IP/A/IMCO/2017-08, January 2018, 24.

16.5 REGULATING SOCIETY AND INTERNET

It is tempting to view the litigation discussed above as acting as disincentives to the creation of new technologies and business models. File sharers indulge in infringing activities by making available, downloading and generally trafficking in unauthorised digital versions of music, films and texts. Should the law then punish the producers and enablers of the technology? Is there a balance to be achieved between compensation to creators and the public purpose?[65]

Two 2018 reports appear to suggest that the file sharing phenomenon is far from dead. Notwithstanding the years of battering from continuous litigation, blocking injunctions, and competition from new and lawful streaming platforms (such as Netflix and Amazon Prime), there is still an appetite for BitTorrent-based file sharing. The first study on global internet trends notes that BitTorrent is the number 1 file sharing protocol in Europe and Asia-Pacific (and number 2 in the Americas) for upstream bandwidth consumption.[66] The second study on file sharing activities confirms that file sharing has a negative effect on legitimate music sales; but the report also points out that the negative effects were economically modest, and impacted top-tier artists the most. Conversely, file sharing activities helped mid-tier artists.[67] Older studies also indicate the importance of sharing activities in achieving societal and public policy aims. Take, for example, Benkler's study of large-scale sharing activities, which led him to conclude that sharing enables market models through which excess capacity of private goods could be cleared.[68] He pointed out, for example, that many users take part in file sharing for social reasons as well as for personal gains.[69]

16.5.1 Alternative compensation models: levies or licensing?

What regulatory and legal approaches should be adopted to deal with the sheer complexity of issues arising from file sharing? One solution would be to accept that file sharing will continue, and materials will be distributed unlawfully across the internet. In such cases, the only means of control would be to extract the value of the copyright work through levies, private copying or blanket licensing schemes. The last, for example, is the *modus operandus* for use of materials within universities, libraries, and commercial organisations. Another approach may be to place a tax levy on all devices and equipment, which enable individual users to commit mass infringing activities. The rationale

---

[65] N. Scharf, 'Napster's Long Shadow: Copyright and Peer-to-Peer Technology' (2011) 6(11) *JIPLP* 806.

[66] Sandvine, *The Global Internet Phenomena Report*, October 2018, available at www.sandvine.com.

[67] J. Lee, 'Purchase, Pirate, Publicize: Private-Network Music Sharing and Market Album Sales,' Working Paper 1354, Economics Department, Queen's University, 2018, assessing a data set of 250,000 albums and 4.8 million downloads on one popular BitTorrent tracker.

[68] Y. Benkler, 'Sharing Nicely: On Shareable Goods and the Emergence of Sharing as a Modality of Economic Production' (2004) 114 *Yale Law Journal* 273, 281. Note also his discussion of the open source phenomenon in Y. Benkler, 'Coase's Penguin, or, Linux and the Nature of the Firm' (2002) 112 *Yale Law Journal* 369, 398.

[69] Such as the SETI@home project, 5.3 million users from 226 countries allow their idle computers to be used for analysis of radio astronomy signals as part of the search for extraterrestrial intelligence – https://setiathome.berkeley.edu and the Genome@home projects, dedicated to modelling new artificial genes that can create artificial proteins.

of a copying levy is based on placing the fault on the secondary or accessory infringer, that is, the manufacturer, supplier, or importer of the copying or disseminating device including photocopying machines, tape recorders, file sharing software, scanners, cloud recorders, and even the computer.

It is proposed that perhaps the most feasible proposal to address the continuous problem of on-line infringement is via a collection of pre-existing tools: (i) the collective management of the right of making available; with a (ii) blanket licensing regime to cover basic or commonplace repertoires of protected content; and supplemented with a (iii) levy or remuneration system to address the harm caused by infringements of the reproduction right. These proposals have come in a number of different forms and names: alternative compensation system, content or kultur flat-rate, licence global, artistic freedom voucher, non-commercial use levy, and sharing licence.[70]

Early proponents of the levy system as a solution were Netanel and Ku.[71] Other suggestions were to modify existing collective licensing schemes – to either extend it to all file sharing activities, or to subject the making available right to mandatory collective management; or to employ the Scandinavian extended collective licensing scheme.[72] Another alternative offered is the administrative compensation system which Fisher suggested could replace copyright law with a voluntary licence and a 'tax'.[73] Lessig proposed a similar solution as an interim solution although his view was that the file sharing phenomenon should be addressed by compulsory licensing – a mechanism utilised in cable retransmission with the fee being set by the governments striking the right balance.[74] Litman suggested that copyright owners should either choose to 'share' or to 'hoard': the former entails a compensation via a blanket licence fee or a levy, while the latter would result in works being exclusively exploited online via sales.[75] The list goes on and one can trace the various proposals advanced by academics, industry experts, consumer and user organisations, collecting societies and political parties on the 'sharing licence library'.[76]

---

[70] Dimita suggests that a 'positive' remuneration right be introduced for authors and copyright owners, centrally and collectively administered, which would compress and specify the condition under which the communication to the public and the reproduction rights might be exercised. See G. Dimita, 'Copyright and Shared Networking Technologies' (Ph.D thesis: 2010), available at https://qmro.qmul.ac.uk.

[71] N.W. Netanel, 'Impose a Non-Commercial Use Levy to Allow Free P2P File Sharing' (2003) 17 JOLT 1, advocating compensation to rights holders through a levy placed on products and services which benefited from the file-sharing activities; R.S.R. Ku, 'The Creative Destruction of Copyright: Napster and the New Economics of Digital Technology' (2002) 69 University of Chicago L. Rev. 263, 311–15; R.S.R. Ku, 'Consumers and Creative Destruction: Fair Use Beyond Market Failure' (2003) 18 BTLJ 539, 566, suggesting a levy on internet service subscriptions.

[72] D. Gervais, 'The Price of Social Norms: Towards a Licensing Regime for File-sharing' (2005) 12 JIPL 39; L. Guibault et al., The Future of Levies in a Digital Environment: Final Report (Institute for Information Law, 2003), 26–7; P. Aigrain, Internet & Création-Comment reconnaître des echanges sur l'internet en finançant la creation? (Inlibroveritas, 2008); NEXA, Remunerating Creativity, Freeing Knowledge: File Sharing and Extended Collective Licenses (Nexa, 2009), available at nexa. polito.it/licenzecollettive.

[73] Fisher, supra note 3.

[74] L. Lessig, Free Culture: How Big Media uses Technology and the Law to Lock Down Culture and Control Creativity (Penguin Press, 2004), 254–5, 300–304.

[75] J. Litman, 'Sharing and Stealing' (2004) 27(1) Hastings Communications & Entertainment L.J. 1.

[76] Available at https://www.vgrass.de/.

It appears that the mixture of alternative remuneration systems may be well-received by consumers as they are willing to experiment with alternative modes of access and compensation. Moreover, such alternative modes may ameliorate the worst aspects of the traditional copyright model, especially in relation to the concentration of market power and licensing fees (through collecting societies).[77]

16.5.2 Digital rights management[78]

Should licensing or levy systems be adopted, collecting societies or rights management organisations are essential practical and economic actors. Alongside these mechanisms, international copyright law has also sought to help IP owners by prioritising rights management. The two 1996 WIPO Internet Treaties introduced a new regulatory landscape for the governance of copyright and related rights, especially in the digital and internet context. The Treaties envisage IP owners locking up digital versions of works by employing technological protection measures (TPMs).[79] The provisions require contracting states to provide adequate legal protection and effective remedies against the circumvention of the effective TPMs that copyright owners use *in connection* with the exercise of their rights and that restrict acts, which they have not authorised and are not permitted by law. A key query is whether these new WIPO provisions are tantamount to a new 'right of access'? Can these technological measures prevent access to those who have a legitimate right to use a technologically protected work? Can this 'right' be abused by digitally locking up non-copyright works especially compilations or databases of public domain materials?[80]

Since copyright has traditionally never granted rights of access to an author or rights holder, the concern is that TPMs can, if unchecked, overprotect works by denying user rights under private copying, fair use or fair dealing defences. Thus, TPMs may not only prevent copying or downloading of copyright works, but they can also prevent access to works, which are excepted under general copyright principles. The TPM provisions, as implemented in some countries, can also be used to prevent a lawful purchaser from copying any part of the digital product even where the lawful purchaser of the physical product wishes to copy insubstantial parts of the work (which is a non-infringing act under copyright law), or where the user has a valid defence for copying parts of the work (for example, educational or library or archival usage).

Finally, TPMs can be used by rights holders to allow a lawful purchaser of the digital product to access (and maybe to copy) the product but to limit the number of times this may be done. There

---

[77] J.P. Quintais, *Copyright in an Age of Access: Alternatives to Copyright Enforcement* (Kluwer Law International, 2017).

[78] The OECD Working Party on the Information Economy describes DRM as three key procedures: (a) the encryption of content to keep it unavailable to unauthorised users; (b) the establishment of a licence system for controlling who can access the content and what can be done with it in specific circumstances; and (c) the authentication of the identity of the user, a required step for accessing the different usage rights awarded by the licence, DSTI/ICCP/IE(2004)12/FINAL, June 8, 2005.

[79] WCT, Art 11 and WPPT, Art 18; for a historical account, see M. Ficsor, *The Law of Copyright and the Internet* (Oxford University Press, 2002), Chapter 11.

[80] G. Dutfield and U. Suthersanen, 'The Innovation Dilemma: Intellectual Property and the Historical Legacy of Cumulative Creativity' (2004) *IPQ* 379, 399, for examples of TPMs employed by copyright owners, and how they may obstruct the exercise of such legitimate rights.

are a variety of permutations, which allow the rights holders to wield the TPMs as a Damocles sword over traditional copyright principles. The question then is: should we be allowing provisions on TPMs to override traditional copyright defences? This relegation of copyright principles to the second division is already being accepted by courts in some jurisdictions, though it is being surprisingly pushed back in others.[81]

In the US, the federal copyright law protects digital rights management under its Digital Millennium Copyright Act (DMCA) 1998 and, more importantly, it has a specific mandatory provision in section 1201(f) for reverse engineering for the purpose of interoperability between software components – these are similar to the EU's Computer Program Directive.[82] Moreover, courts appear to be somewhat cautious in allowing the DMCA to create monopolies by tying in protected works to manufactured goods.[83]

The Canadian law on TPMs was established in 2012 and has been interpreted by the Federal Court in the *Nintendo* decision.[84] Here, the Federal Court found that TPMs for Nintendo's gaming systems had been circumvented and awarded massive statutory damages for each circumvention. In doing so, the Court adopted a wide interpretation to the TPM provision while restricting the TPM exceptions. Thus, it rejected the argument that users should play 'homebrew' games, which although designed for Nintendo consoles are not owned by Nintendo.

Within the EU context, Article 6(4) of the copyright in the Information Society Directive sets out TPM rules, which work together to create an internal balance. The Directive provides for a right to fair compensation to IP owners for reprographic reproduction, private copying, and for reproduction of broadcast programmes by certain public institutions; the term 'fair compensation' is a thinly veiled reference to the private copying levy schemes which operate in most European civil law systems.[85]

In *Nintendo PC Box Srl*,[86] Nintendo's gaming consoles used encrypted code to prevent not only use of illegally copied Nintendo videogames, but also to prevent non-Nintendo multimedia content from being used on the consoles. Thus, the DRM system was preventing users using non-Nintendo games or multimedia content that they had lawfully purchased. The CJEU stressed that the legal protection only covers the TPMs intended to prevent or eliminate certain acts for which authorisation from the copyright holder is required. The court also added that the legal protection must

---

[81] For the US approach, see *Lexmark International v. Static Control Components Inc*, 387 F 3d 522 (2004), holding that the *Lexmark* court ruled that circumventing a printer's scheme to prevent the use of third-party toner cartridges did not violate the US copyright law.

[82] EU Software Directive 2009/24/EC, Art 6.

[83] See *Chamberlain Group, Inc v. Skylink Technologies, Inc* 381 F 3d 1178 (Fed Cir, 2004); *Lexmark Int'l, Inc v. Static Control Components, Inc* 387 F 3d 522 (6th Cir, 2004); cf *Davidson & Associates v. Jung* 422 F 3d 630 (8th Cir, 2005) (*Blizzard v. BnetD*).

[84] *Nintendo of America Inc v. Jeramie Douglas King and Go Cyber Shopping*, 2017 FC 246 (Canadian Federal Court).

[85] EU InfoSoc Directive, Arts 5(2)(a), (b), (e); 6–7; also see Recital 7, EU Directive on Copyright in the Digital Single Market, Recital 7 affirming the non-applicability of TPMs in relation to the newly introduced exceptions on teaching, text/data mining and out-of-commerce works.

[86] Case C-355/12 *Nintendo v. PC Box Sol* [2013] ECDR 16; M. Favale, 'A Wii too stretched? The ECJ extends to game consoles the protection of DRM-on tough conditions' (2015) 37 *EIPR* 101, 104; A. Chinn, 'How has Technology Affected the Copyright Framework? A Focus on Digital Rights Management and Peer-to-Peer Technology' (2016) 22(2) *CTLR* 44.

consider proportionality, and must not prohibit devices or activities that have a commercially significant purpose or use other than to circumvent the TPMS for unlawful purposes. In other words, the EU approach was that if a right is not being infringed, then there appeared to be no logical reason as to why devices that circumvented the game, for legitimate reasons, would be unlawful.

A related concern is that TPMs can be employed to stop the progress of technology by allowing rights holders to sue manufacturers and suppliers of decryption and decoding hardware and software tools. Are there adequate checks and balances to ensure that encryption and other related technological research and study is not stifled? This issue arose in France in relation to the effect of TPMs on the private copying exception. In 2006, the French Supreme Court in the *Mulholland Drive* case held that copyright owners can assert their TPMs against users. In doing so it reversed the Court of Appeals' ruling that TPMs unduly restricted the private copying exception under French copyright law. However, according to the Supreme Court, private copying was not an absolute right for consumers, only an exception to an author's rights – an exception, which, as all exceptions under French law, should be strictly construed.[87] The problem of TPMs has proved so difficult that the French legislature has tackled it by providing for the establishment of the 'Authority for the Regulations of Technical Measures' with the objective of ensuring the interoperability of all DRM systems and allowing private copies.[88] The attempt to regulate and limit (and even neutralise) DRMs caused a furore and led to an unexpected statement by Steve Jobs, the Apple CEO:

> Imagine a world where every online store sells DRM-free music encoded in open licensable formats. In such a world, any player can play music purchased from any store, and any store can sell music which is playable on all players. This is clearly the best alternative for consumers, and Apple would embrace it in a heartbeat […] Every iPod ever made will play this DRM-free music. Though the big four music companies require that all their music sold online be protected with DRMs, these same music companies continue to sell billions of CDs a year which contain completely unprotected music […] Much of the concern over DRM systems has arisen in European countries. Perhaps those unhappy with the current situation should redirect their energies towards persuading the music companies to sell their music DRM-free.[89]

Since 2009, the largest recording companies have released DRM-free music to Apple's iTunes music store, with Apple offering variable pricing.[90]

---

[87] Cass. 1re civ., 28 févr. 2006, no 05-15.824 et no 05-16.002, Sté Studio canal SA et Sté Universal Pictures vidéo France c/M; more intriguing was the French Supreme Court's application of the 'three-step' test under Art 5(5), InfoSoc Directive – see W. Maxwell and J. Massaloux, 'French Copyright Law Reform: French Supreme Court Upholds Legality of DVD Anti-Copy Measures' (2006) 17(5) *Ent. LR* 145.

[88] Decree No 2007-510 of 4 April, 2007. See N. Jondet, 'La France v. Apple: Who's the Dadvsi in DRMs?' (2006) 3(4) *SCRIPTed: A Journal of Law, Technology and Society* 473; D. Sobel, 'A Bite out of Apple? iTunes, Interoperability, and France's Dadvsi Law' (2007) 22(1) *Berkeley Technology Law Journal* 267.

[89] S. Jobs, 'Thoughts on Music', now available on http://macdailynews.com/2007/02/06/apple_ceo_steve_jobs_posts_rare_open_letter_thoughts_on_music/.

[90] A. Edgecliffe-Johnson, 'Apple brings in Variable Pricing on iTunes', *Financial Times*, 6 January 2009.

16.5.3 Interoperability and global standards

With the *Microsoft*[91] decision, the company was ordered for the first time in its history to change its business strategy and practice. The European Commission held Microsoft liable for illegally tying its Windows Media Player (WMP) application with its operating system. As Ayres and Nalebuff suggest, firms employ tactics to dominate and control the complementary downstream market. In their view, Microsoft bundled products and then used IPRs to deny licences of access to such products to prevent secondary markets becoming 'entry point(s)' into Microsoft's operating system software. Media players could, the authors asserted, morph into operating systems for mobile phones, TV set-top boxes, and handheld devices.[92]

The practice of bundling reflected the wider concern about Microsoft using its IPRs to prevent interoperability. By using its IPRs and by refusing licences on its protocols, Microsoft intended to ensure that when digital media was to be delivered to other platforms beyond the PC, there would not be effective competition in the player market since all content would be in Microsoft's propriety WMP format.

A further reason for exercising caution in allowing firms to employ IPRs to control the downstream market is that the extension can be used to develop a *de facto* standard. Standard-setting takes place when investors agree to invest in a particular technology as the *de facto* standard in the marketplace. The International Organization for Standardization (ISO) defines a formal standard as 'a document, established by consensus that provides rules, guidelines or characteristics for activities or their results'.[93] The existence of standards makes it possible to develop compatible or interoperable products by competing firms. In particular, the global ICT sector requires compatible and harmonised standards to be fully effective, especially in relation to the internet, telecommunications, computer hardware, and software. Moreover, due to the interrelated nature of these technologies, and the ways in which they interact, new innovation within the different ICT sectors requires a number of different components which may be covered by different patents. If one firm in the market dominates through the creation of a *de facto* standard, or alternatively secures a patent, which covers key aspects of the preferred standard, it can exert substantial leverage and even threaten to block the standard setting process. As Lemley notes:

---

[91] The Windows Media Player (WMP) used to be pre-installed on over 90 per cent of all Windows machines, with the result that media streams were encoded in the WMP format. This reflected not just platforms on computers but also the DRM controls on the downstream markets, i.e., mobile phones or television. See European Commission Decision 2007/53/EC, 24 May 2004, OJ 2007 L 32, p. 23; affirmed in Case T-201/04, *Microsoft Corp v. Commission of the European Communities*, CFI, 17 September 2007; ECLI:EU:T:2007:289. See I. Ayres and B. Nalebuff, 'Going Soft on Microsoft? The EU's Antitrust Case and Remedy' (2005) 2(2) *The Economists' Voice*, retrieved 2 April 2019, from doi:10.2202/1553-3832.1045; P. Samuelson, 'Are Patents on Interfaces Impeding Interoperability?' (2009) 93 *Minnesota L. Rev.* 1943. P. Magnani and M. Montagnani, 'Digital Rights Management Systems and Competition: What Developments within the Much-Debated Interface Between Intellectual Property and Competition Law?' (2008) 39(1) *IIC* 83; T. Hoehn, 'Interoperability Remedies, FRAND Licensing and Innovation: A Review of Recent Case Law' (2013) 34(2) *ECLR* 101.

[92] Ayres and Nalebuff, ibid.

[93] See www.iso.org/home.html.

Therein lies the basic problem. In the pharmaceutical industry or the medical device field or the traditional mechanical field, you might have a patent on your invention or maybe you have had to combine a couple of different patents. In IT, you regularly have to combine 50, 100, even 1,000, or – as Intel lawyers, themselves, say with respect to their own core micro-processor – 10,000 different patent rights together into one product. You've got to clear all those rights or do something about them in order to get your product to market.[94]

How then should we balance the legitimate rights of IP owners to receive reasonable compensation against the interests of those seeking harmonisation by implementing international standards? Lemley sets out ten different legal and business tactics that can be adopted by standard setting organisations in order to soften the impact of IP owners in this area, including revising the law on injunctions and damages. Tellingly, none of his remedies include enlisting the help of antitrust law.[95]

Within the international arena, there are no clear rules governing the area of IPRs and standards. The WTO is not a standard setting organisation. Nevertheless, the WTO Agreement on Technical Barriers to Trade (TBT) recognises that Members have the right to adopt technical regulations to achieve legitimate objectives, protection of human health and environmental safety. To this end, the TBT Agreement encourages the use of existing international standards as a basis for national technical regulations.[96] Currently, the TBT Agreement is silent on the issue of IPRs in relation to international standard setting and trade restrictions; similarly the WTO–TRIPS Agreement does not address standards issues. One recommendation is that IPRs should be integrated into the TBT Agreement framework. This recommendation has become especially relevant in light of the trade dispute between China and the US, which arose as a result of China's 2003 policy in relation to proprietary encryption standard for wireless communications – the WLAN Authentication and Privacy Infrastructure (WAPI). When China approved the WAPI standard, in 2003, and decreed that all wireless devices imported into China would need to incorporate this technology, the objection was raised that China's policy was detrimental to existing international standards. Of course, China's response was that the mandatory adoption of international standards was detrimental in terms of cost and innovation for developing countries, especially in relation to IPRs, which stand as obstacles to trade. Since 2015, the issue of patents and standards has been one of the agenda items discussed by the US-China Joint Commission on Commerce and Trade.[97]

---

[94] M. Lemley, 'Ten Things to Do About Patent Holdup of Standards (And One Not to)' (2007) 48 *Boston College Law Review* 149, 150–51.

[95] Ibid.

[96] The TBT Agreement, Art 2. See also WTO, 'Decision of the TBT Committee on Principles for the Development of International Standards, Guides and Recommendations with Relation to Articles 2, 5 and Annex 3 of the TBT Agreement' (13 November 2000) G/TBT/9, paras 17–25, and annex 4.

[97] X. Wu, 'Interplay between Patents and Standards in the Information and Communication Technology (ICT) Sector and its Relevance to the Implementation of the WTO Agreements', WTO Working Paper ERSD-2017-08, April 2017; UNCTAD, 'Trade in ICT Goods and the 2015 Expansion of the WTO Information Technology Agreement', TN/UNCTAD/ICT4D/05, December 2015.

Index